FRONTIER FAREWELL

NEW EDITION

FRONTIER FAREWELL

The 1870s and the End of the Old West

GARRETT WILSON

with a new foreword by Candace Savage

University of Regina Press

Printed and bound in Canada at Friesens. The text of this book is printed on 100% post-consumer recycled paper with earth-friendly vegetable-based inks.

COVER AND TEXT DESIGN: Duncan Campbell, University of Regina Press
INDEXER: Patricia Furdek
COVER IMAGE: Tiffany Craigo
BACK COVER IMAGE: Sergeant Kay's Royal Engineers Survey Camp on North Antler Creek, 1873. *Library and Archives Canada C73303*

Library and Archives Canada Cataloguing in Publication
Wilson, Garrett, 1932-, author
    Frontier farewell : the 1870s and the end of the Old West / Garrett Wilson ; with a new introduction by Candace Savage.—New edition.

Reprint with new introduction. Originally published: Regina : University of Regina, Canadian Plains Research Center, 2007.
Includes bibliographical references and index.
Issued in print and electronic formats.
ISBN 978-0-88977-361-5 (pbk.).—ISBN 978-0-88977-363-9 (pdf).—ISBN 978-0-88977-362-2 (html)

    1. Northwest, Canadian—History--1870-1905. 2. West (U.S.)—History—1860-1890. 3. Great Plains—History—19th century. I. Savage, Candace, 1949-, writer of introduction II. Title.

FC3217.W45 2014   978'.02   C2014-906063-7   C2014-906064-5

10   9   8   7   6   5   4   3   2   1

University of Regina Press, University of Regina
Regina, Saskatchewan, Canada, S4S 0A2
tel: (306) 585-4758   fax: (306) 585-4699
web: www.uofrpress.ca
U OF R PRESS

The University of Regina Press acknowledges the support of the Creative Industry Growth and Sustainability program, made possible through funding provided to the Saskatchewan Arts Board by the Government of Saskatchewan through the Ministry of Parks, Culture, and Sport. We also acknowledge the financial support of the Government of Canada through the Canada Book Fund and the support of the Canada Council for the Arts for our publishing program.

For Lesley,
Taralyne
& Kevin

CONTENTS

Foreword to the 2014 Edition

T HEY SAY, "DON'T JUDGE A BOOK BY ITS COVER," AND HERE is a case in point. There is so much more on offer in Garrett Wilson's *Frontier Farewell* than first meets the eye. The account you are about to read is warm and engaging, but under that charming exterior, it is made of tougher stuff. This is a book that packs a punch.

In these pages, Regina lawyer and author Garrett Wilson chronicles the final, tortured phase of the buffalo ecosystem on the North American plains. If there were a Richter-style ranking for ecological and humanitarian disasters, that cataclysmic transition would be off the scale. An entire world was lost in the space of a generation: 30,000,000 buffalo gone. The impact of that upheaval can be measured by the ton, as the weight of baled hides and bleached bone hauled away by the trainload in the late nineteenth century. It can be estimated by the thousands of buffalo-dependent people who were lost to disease and malnutrition during the Great Hunger. Even today, the aftermath of the trauma can be sensed in the stories of survivors of residential schools and other racist sequellae. Although the buffalo prairie has vanished, never to be experienced again, the aftershocks from its destruction are still being felt. In a very real way, the end of the Old West marked the birth of the present.

What Garrett Wilson offers us in these pages is a kind of creation story. This, he tells us, is how the two great transcontinental nations of North America—*a mare usque ad mare,* from sea to shining sea—came into being. It's a story we think we know. First came the explorers, Radisson and Groseilliers, Lewis and Clark: we learned this in grade five. The fur traders were next and then, a while later, there was that little mix-up when John Wayne had to ride to the rescue and put the tribesmen in their place. Finally, when all the fuss was over, along came grandma in her poke bonnet, perched on the seat of a covered wagon, rolling in to take possession of an untouched, "virgin" land.

Wilson plays to our expectations by opening his origin story with a character we think we've seen before. Glass in hand, a weathered old-timer rises from his place at dinner, proposes a toast to the vanished days of the Wild West—falters—and subsides into a boozy heap under the table. We recognize him at once: he's the dopey sidekick from a thousand TV westerns. But Wilson wastes no time in anchoring this anecdote in time and place. Turns out that the old codger was a real flesh-and-blood person and a friend of Wilson's own father. That's how close the lost world of the Old West really is, just a generation or two beyond our grasp. As an early recruit to the North-West Mounted Police, James H. (Jimmy) Thomson had witnessed the turmoil of the 1870s at first hand. His wife, Alice—born Iha Wastewin, Good Laughing Woman— was Lakota, and her family had been among the thousands of refugees who fled north from the wrath of the United States military after the Battle of the Little Big Horn. The Lakota had come to Canada in the late 1870s looking for humanitarian aid and peace. The truth about what they received instead is one of the chapters that makes this book both important and incendiary.

As American historian Bernard Devoto once noted, "No frontier is marked between the Western landscape and a country of fable." It is this metaphorical final frontier—the borderland between what we'd like to believe and what we can know for sure—that Garrett Wilson sets out to explore and map as fully as possible. Always, he is looking for stories, small events that he can set into the frame of his main narrative to enliven his telling with vitality and surprise. (What fun, for instance, to learn that an engraved lead plate placed out in the middle of nowhere by a French grandee in 1742, claiming the plains for France, was uncovered 170 years later by a fourteen-year-old named Charlotte Johnson.) But even deeper than Wilson's love of stories is his passion for evidence. Garrett Wilson brings to this work a fierce, forensic intelligence and a determination to leave no book unopened, no archive unsearched, no document unread, if it might help him understand how the old order of the West was shattered so that a new one could be put in its place. What he has discovered is revealed in these pages without fear or favour. Although we cannot change what happened, we can open ourselves to the truth. The stories we tell about the past can change the future.

Candace Savage, April 2014

Foreword to the 2007 Edition

THIS BOOK TELLS THE STORY OF THE CANADIAN WEST FROM THE first explorers in the 18th century to the year the Sioux chief, Sitting Bull, surrendered to the Americans and the Blackfoot chief, Crowfoot, led his starving people back to Canada, both in 1881, and which Garrett Wilson designates as "the end of the Old West." The story of these early days of the settlement of the Canadian West is here in its entirety—treaties and agreements, disagreements and controversies, ignoble motives and noble ones, along with dates, short biographies of the famous and the not-so-famous, births and deaths, letters, reports, speeches and anecdotes, and all the details in between. Wilson has pursued not just the familiar narrative, but wherever written histories have faltered, he has sought information, no matter how buried or obscure, and filled in the gaps, so that the reader cannot fail to be surprised at and also riveted by this original and fascinating, richer and more complete version of our history. The story he has so carefully documented here is not merely the story of Europeans, nor of the First Nations people, but of how their lives and their needs and desires worked together and against each other at each turn in Western history, ending, tragically and shamefully with the impoverishment and dispossession of the first people of the West, even as the European settlement was made possible and would soon burgeon and prosper.

Gracefully written, fully and meticulously researched, and above all, original in its presentation of a history we thought we knew, this book will illuminate the viewpoint of both professional historians and lay-readers alike. It is an invaluable, as well as unique, addition to the literature of the West.

Sharon Butala, July 2007

Preface

"**B**UFFALO!**"**
The old horseman struggled to his feet and boldly began his toast with glass held high, his weather-worn visage conspicuous in the room full of young men.

Then "BUFFALO," this time more quietly. Then, after a long pause, *"buffalo,"* almost in a whisper.

With that, the toastmaker slid under the table and was heard from no more. The glass, still clutched in the gnarled fingers of his outstretched hand, was the last feature to disappear from the view of the other guests, some startled, some bemused.

The host of the gathering, Inspector Richards, the Officer Commanding the Royal North-West Mounted Police[1] detachment at Wood Mountain, Saskatchewan, was offended at the breach of decorum. Rising, he was about to take action when another member of the Force alertly spoke into his ear. "Sir. His service number was 387." That number told the OC that his over-refreshed guest had been one of the very early members of the Force, enlisting not long after its formation in 1873.

The OC nodded in understanding, resumed his seat, and the incident passed. The toastmaker slept quietly and undisturbed beneath the table.

That was my father's introduction to Jimmy Thomson.

It was New Year's, 1913, in the mess hall of the Wood Mountain post in those historic hills just 40 km (25 mi) north of the United States boundary. The previous season the railway had entered the region and the community of Limerick had been established 48 km (30 mi) to the north. In welcome, the Officer Commanding had invited a few businessmen from the new village to join the detachment's mess dinner. Late 1912 was an open winter with little snow and my father was one of an intrepid carload of bachelor pioneers who responded eagerly and negotiated their way down the Old Pole Trail, the line that in 1887 carried the telegraph from Moose Jaw to the Wood Mountain post and then became a settlers' road.

As a boy in the 1940s, I often accompanied my Irish immigrant father on his travels as a financial and insurance agent through what he lovingly called "The South Country," that area of Saskatchewan lying between the Canadian Pacific Railway mainline and the American border. This was the world "Irish Charlie" had chosen for his life after several early years in North Dakota, Manitoba, mid-Saskatchewan and a homestead north of Saskatoon. Our trips frequently took us through Wood Mountain—two Wood Mountains, in fact. There was the village that grew where it had been placed by the railway that arrived in 1928, and the "Old Post," the tiny settlement 6.5 km (4 mi) further south, on the north slope of the uplands where the North-West Mounted Police had maintained a detachment after their 1874 incursion into what was then the North-West Territories.

The Old Post was a magical place. There were trees, then rare on the plains. And a creek, spring fed, with water flowing all summer. And a ford across that creek. Where the tires actually slopped through gravel and water and the current quickly filled in the ruts and carried away the small curtains of mud, turning it all clean and clear again in a moment. To a boy born and raised in the dustbowl, the sparkling water of that ford was a fascination.

But just further south were two features that seldom failed to provoke the story-teller in my father, the site (then barren) of the old NWMP quarters[2] and, high on a hill, a gravesite.

That 1913 New Year's dinner had been long, with many toasts. It was well on towards the end of the evening when Jimmy Thomson, a local rancher, stood to present his toast to the buffalo that once had sheltered in the coulees of the Wood Mountain uplands.

Jimmy Thomson's adobe-chinked log home was just a few hundred metres south of the site of the Old Post. During his travels in those early years, Irish Charlie would often overnight on the floor of the Thomson living room; hotels arrived only after 1928 with the new town of Wood Mountain. When he took his discharge from the NWMP, Jimmy married a Native girl, Mary Thomson, a Lakota, one of the few American Sioux who fled to Canada after Little Big Horn in 1876 and never did return. Her people were finally granted a reserve at Wood Mountain in 1910. A quiet, gentle woman, it was Mary's custom to withdraw from the presence of visiting whites.

After that inauspicious meeting in 1913, my father became a good friend of the Thomsons, and so it was that when Jimmy died in March 1923, Mary Thomson sought his help to provide a funeral in the way of the white people. A preacher was located and transported down to the Old Post and a service conducted in the room where Irish Charlie had so often spread his bedroll. To honour Jimmy's wish that he be buried on the hill overlooking his home, his pallbearers struggled up the steep slope to the crest over which the dawn had for so many years slipped down to awaken the old pioneer.

But it was done, and there Jimmy rests today, looking down upon both his home and the now-restored Old Post, beneath a headstone that reads:

> 387 EX-CORPORAL
> JAMES H. THOMPSON
> N. W. M. P.
> 3RD MARCH, 1923
> AGE 68

The "P" in Thompson was an error incurred when the Royal Canadian Mounted Police erected the headstone years after Jimmy's death. Beside Jimmy lies his wife whose much more modest marker records her name, "MARY THOMSON," and only her birth date: 1864. She was a girl of 12 at the Little Big Horn. Other members of the family lie nearby.

The Thomson house continues in use. For a few years it did service as a Red Cross hospital, and then reverted to a residence and is still the home of local ranchers.

James Harkin Thomson had been an Easterner. He joined the North-West Mounted Police in Ottawa and was promptly sent out west with a troop of other recruits up the Missouri River via the steamboat *Red Cloud*. He took his oath of service on the dock when they arrived at Fort Benton, Montana Territory, on June 9, 1879, and then moved 160 miles north to Fort Walsh, 175 miles due west of the Wood Mountain post. Jimmy made corporal in April 1883, but left the Force when his term of service expired in July 1884 and was discharged at the new headquarters in Regina. Jimmy had the idea of promoting a Wild West show but quickly gave up that notion and, in August 1884, applied for a land grant. He received a Police Bounty Land Warrant and established a small horse ranch next to the Wood Mountain Post. And he married.

Jimmy's Lakota wife, Iha Wastewin, or Good Laughing Woman, became Alice Mary Thomson. They raised a family of 11 children, all of whom were given both Lakota and English names and taught the Lakota traditions and language. Mary, an excellent horsewoman, raised and tamed the Thomson stock. Their home became the centre of the community, serving as post office and school.

Jimmy Thomson never quite left the Wood Mountain NWMP Post. When the telegraph line arrived in 1887, he was appointed a special constable and served the detachment as operator. When the telephone came, Jimmy ran the exchange. Fluent in Native dialects, he was the Post interpreter, and also its guide, scout, horse wrangler, carpenter and caretaker. Acting as caretaker during a temporary closing of the Post, over a severe cold spell Jimmy gave shelter in the NWMP stables to a passing horse trader and his herd and was embarrassed when it was later learned that the trader was a thief and his horses stolen.

Jimmy Thomson was with the NWMP when one of their major concerns was the presence in Canada of those several thousand Sioux seeking refuge from the American army after the near-destruction of the 7th Cavalry Regiment under General Custer at Little Big Horn, in June 1876. During the five years Sitting Bull and his people remained in Canada, they were involved with the Wood Mountain Post more than any other detachment. NWMP officers from Wood Mountain were present in July 1881, when Sitting Bull finally crossed back over the border and surrendered.

During his visits at the Thomson home, my father listened to many stories from those historic times, first-hand accounts from a participant. Naturally, as we drove together through the countryside where many of those dramatic events had played out, those stories were relayed to me, stories of Sitting Bull, of buffalo, of the North-West Mounted Police, of the early Métis settlers, and of Jean-Louis Légaré, the local trader who had assisted Sitting Bull in his return to the United States.

I heard none of this in my Limerick school rooms just 48 km (30 mi) north. In fact, I doubt that my teachers were even aware of the drama that had unfolded in our neighbourhood, and so recently, at least in usual historical terms.

Some years ago I came across an extraordinary statement in the 1879 Annual Report of the then Indian Commissioner, Edgar Dewdney. There had been a prairie fire in that fall of 1879, Dewdney said, that raged all the way from Wood Mountain to the Rocky Mountains. Wildfires on the plains were common events, and often they ran for many miles, but a fire of this magnitude was unheard of. More remarkable, this fire had not been caused by accident, or by lightning, the usual case, but had been deliberately set. Even that was not unknown, but this fire had been started at not just one location but at a number of pre-determined sites along the 49th Parallel, the border between the North-West Territories and the United States. Dewdney speculated that the motive behind the fire was to destroy the grass—the grazing—so as to deter the buffalo herds from migrating into Canada from Montana Territory. That in turn would deprive the Indians north of the border of their food source.

Why starve the Indians in Canada? Well, a large group of those Indians were the American Sioux who had fled across the border after the defeat of Lieutenant Colonel George Armstrong Custer at Little Big Horn. Sitting Bull, their famous leader, was prominent among the Sioux who had taken refuge in Canada. The American Army was patrolling just below the border, waiting to take the Sioux into custody and corral them on reserves.

But who would stoop to mass starvation as a tactic, even in those harsh times?

That was a question that drew me ever-deeper into the history of that period. The answer was elusive, but in my search I found that the 1870s, the first decade of the prairies in Canada, was a fascinating time and that much of its story had never been told. Immediately following their transfer from the Hudson's Bay Company to the Dominion of Canada, the Canadian plains and their helpless occupants were swept by winds of change, relentless and incredibly swift. In little more than 10 short years, the vast prairies were converted from a great commons that was home to all, to a neatly surveyed system of land titles designed for the individual ownership of thousands of immigrant homesteaders.

These pages carry the story of those tumultuous times, with as much attention to the injustices, misery and suffering inflicted upon the first inhabitants of the West as my research would support. If it is true that history is written by the victors, it was totally true in the case of the western plains in the 1800s, for the uprooted and displaced peoples of those plains had no written language with which to record their agonies. The Sioux were the victors at Little Big Horn, but they were portrayed as the villains by those who first wrote the history of that tragic event. Not until more than 100 years later did the real truth begin to emerge and finally expose why the American Army attacked a peaceful village of Plains Indians, and that it did so unlawfully and without provocation.

After 1870 the western frontier faded away, and with it the entire way of life of the Plains Indians, for centuries totally dependent upon the buffalo. As the vast herds were slaughtered, the peoples of the prairies faced sudden starvation and misery. Their only hope of survival was the mercy of new nation states centred in faraway Ottawa and Washington, mercy that came only at a price—the surrender of their homelands.

This is an account of the agony of those times.

Garrett Wilson
Regina, Saskatchewan
July 2007

Acknowledgments

MY FRIEND DR. GEORGE BAXTER ADVISES FROM EXPERI-
ence that one should never choose as a subject for a thesis
a topic that one finds particularly interesting—one becomes
so engrossed in the research that it becomes difficult to put it
aside and turn to the writing. Same problem with this book. I found that delving into the history of the Great Plains quickly became an addictive pleasure,
so much so that this project consumed many more years than first planned.

Adding to my pleasure on the research trail were the unique facilities and
accommodating personnel of the many repositories of the history of the West,
several of which are worth a visit even without research as an excuse. Particular mention must go to the National Archives of Canada, Ottawa; Minnesota
Historical Society, St. Paul; State Historical Society of North Dakota, Bismarck; Montana Historical Society, Helena; Manitoba Archives, Winnipeg;
Saskatchewan Archives, Regina; Alberta Archives, Edmonton; and the Glenbow Museum, Calgary. Sharon Maier of the barely rescued Prairie History
Room at the Regina Public Library was very generous with her assistance.

Much, perhaps most, of the extensive research behind these pages was carried out by Rob Nestor, to whom I am deeply indebted. Rob, then the Librar-
ian at the First Nations University of Canada, Regina campus, and a lecturer at
both the University of Regina and the First Nations University of Canada, not
only served up marvelous research, but also provided sound interpretation
and editorial advice. He deserves a great deal of credit for the final product.

A few of the usual suspects lurk in the background. Aydon Charlton and
Dave Margoshes once again have given me valuable literary criticism and

direction. Henrica van Lieburg once more contributed vital translations. Marian Hebb, of Toronto, has for more than twenty years provided sound legal and editorial guidance. Bill Armstrong again assisted, this time with archival research. Much gratitude goes to sister, Sheila McMullan, for reading and critiquing early drafts and for non-flagging encouragement.

Joann Decorby Blaise kindly arranged for me to review the correspondence of her distinguished ancestor, Father Jules Decorby, OMI, who ministered to the people of the Canadian prairies from 1867 to 1913. Professor Bill Waiser of Saskatoon generously found time to review the manuscript and share his expertise. Paul Taylor, an original Saskatchewanite and former British Columbia Deputy Minister of Finance, supplied detail on the current state of the 1870 Ottawa/BC Pacific rail agreement. Finally, my sincere appreciation goes to Brian Mlazgar and his staff at Canadian Plains Research Center whose professionalism transformed a rough manuscript into a polished work.

The reception of the first edition of *Frontier Farewell* has been very gratifying, receiving extremely positive reviews and personal accolades. And it sold so well that it fell out of print.

Canadian Plains Research Center Press is now the University of Regina Press, with Bruce Walsh as director and publisher. I am more than appreciative that Bruce and his staff have given *Frontier Farewell* a second life with this new, updated edition, which also includes a fine new map that provides important context for the events and places in the book.

A Note on Terminology

LTHOUGH THE WORD INDIAN AS APPLIED TO THE ABORIG-
inal inhabitants of North America has fallen somewhat into disfa-
vour, so that some writers now prefer Amerindian, I have chosen
to continue the more common usage, if only for simplicity. Plains
Indian is employed somewhat casually to describe all the horse-mounted buffalo-hunting tribes who ranged the Great Plains.

Because it originated as a pejorative, and also because it is seen as too
embracing, the word Sioux also carries disapproval, Dakota being the more
acceptable term. There are three main linguistic divisions, Dakota, Nakota
and Lakota, spoken, respectively, by groups known as the Santee, Yankton and
Teton, each group in turn consisting of numerous individual bands or tribes.
The Tetons, the most westerly, alone divided into seven councils. Crazy Horse,
for example, was of the Oglala and Sitting Bull was of the Hunkpapa. Again,
for simplicity, Sioux has been employed to refer to all.

Similarly, the term Blackfoot is used collectively to refer to not only the
Blackfoot people proper, but also those of the Blackfoot Confederacy, which
included the Blood, the Sarcee, and the Peigan.

As well, Ojibwa and Saulteaux refer to one common people. And no
attempt has been made to distinguish between the Plains Cree, Woodland
Cree or Swampy Cree.

In the early years of the Red River Settlement, the terms Half-Breed
and Métis carried separate definitions. Half-Breed designated mixed-blood
descendants of Indian and Scottish or English parentage, while Métis referred

to those of French descent. Métis is now the accepted term for all and is the term employed in the Constitution Act, 1982.

Prior to 1870, "North-Western Territory" referred to the area outside Rupert's Land but still administered by the Hudson's Bay Company, mostly consisting of the lands that drained into the Arctic Ocean rather than Hudson Bay. After the 1870 transfer of both regions to Canada, they became (minus the new province of Manitoba) "The North-West Territory," a name that has since evolved into the "Northwest Territories."

MAP OF THE OLD WEST (*Selected Locations and Geographical Features*)

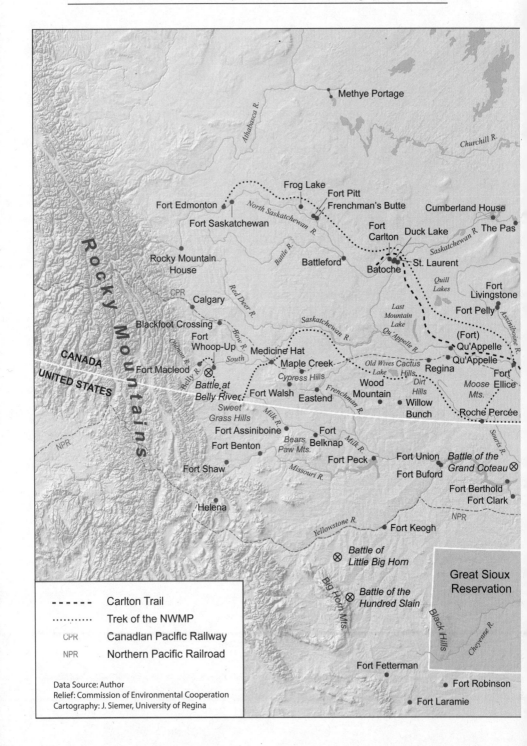

Methye Portage

Athabasca R.

Churchill R.

Frog Lake
Fort Pitt
Fort Edmonton
Frenchman's Butte
Cumberland House

Fort Saskatchewan
North Saskatchewan R.
Fort
Carlton
Duck Lake
The Pas
Saskatchewan R.

Rocky Mountain
House
Battle R.
Battleford
Batoche
St. Laurent

*Quill
Lakes*
Fort
Livingstone

CPR
Calgary
Red Deer R.
Saskatchewan R.
*Last
Mountain
Lake*
Fort Pelly

Blackfoot Crossing
Bow R.
Qu'Appelle R.
(Fort)
Qu'Appelle
Assiniboine R.

CANADA
Fort
Whoop-Up
Medicine Hat
Maple Creek
*Old Wives Cactus
Lake Hills*
Regina
Qu'Appelle
Fort
Ellice

UNITED STATES
Fort Macleod
Oldman R.
South
Cypress Hills
Wood
Mountain
*Dirt
Hills*
*Moose
Mts.*

Belly R.
Battle at
Belly River
Fort Walsh
Eastend
Frenchman R.
Willow
Bunch
Roche Percée

*Sweet
Grass Hills*
Milk R.
Fort Assiniboine
Fort
Belknap
Souris R.

NPR
Fort Benton
*Bears
Paw Mts.*
Milk R.
Fort Peck
Fort Union
*Battle of the
Grand Coteau*

Fort Shaw
Missouri R.
Fort Buford

Fort Berthold
Fort Clark

Helena
NPR

Yellowstone R.
Fort Keogh

Battle of
Little Big Horn
Great Sioux
Reservation

Big Horn Mts.
Battle of the
Hundred Slain
Black Hills
Cheyenne R.

Rocky Mountains

– – – – –		Carlton Trail
· · · · · · · · ·		Trek of the NWMP
CPR		Canadian Pacific Railway
NPR		Northern Pacific Railroad

Fort Fetterman
Fort Robinson
Fort Laramie

Data Source: Author
Relief: Commission of Environmental Cooperation
Cartography: J. Siemer, University of Regina

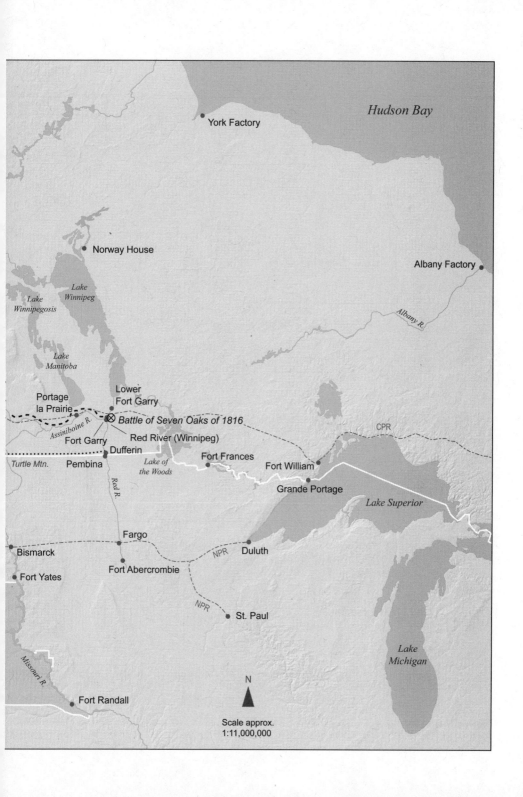

Hudson Bay

York Factory

Albany Factory

Norway House

Albany R.

Lake
Winnipeg

Lake
Winnipegosis

Lake
Manitoba

Lower
Fort Garry

Portage
la Prairie

CPR

Assiniboine R.

⊗ Battle of Seven Oaks of 1816

Fort Garry

Red River (Winnipeg)

Dufferin

Fort Frances

Fort William

Turtle Mtn.

Pembina

Lake of
the Woods

Grande Portage

Red R.

Lake Superior

Fargo

Bismarck

NPR

Duluth

Fort Abercrombie

Fort Yates

NPR

St. Paul

Lake
Michigan

Missouri R.

Fort Randall

N

Scale approx.
1:11,000,000

CHAPTER 1

Between the Rivers

C HARLOTTE JOHNSON WAS CERTAIN THERE WAS SOME-
thing unusual and important about the piece of metal sticking out
of the ground on the path to her family's home. Six years earlier,
in 1907, when her attorney father, Julius Johnson, had built their
house on the upper level of a hill near Pierre, South Dakota, the spot where
the metal now protruded had been covered by a large stone cairn. The neighbourhood boys appropriated the stones to build a fort and, as the Johnson
foot-traffic wore down the path, the upper edge of the metal object appeared.
The Johnsons found it a handy boot-scraper.

 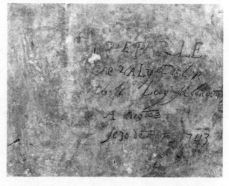

The La Vérendrye plate, discovered by Charlotte Johnson. The front of the plate (left), translated into
English, reads: "Year 26 of the reign of Louis xv. For the king, most illustrious lord. By the Marquis de
Beauharnois, 1741. Placed by Pierre Gaultier de La Vérendrye." The back of the plate (right), translated into
English, reads: "Placed by the Chevalier de la Vérendrye, witnesses Louis-Joseph, La Londette and A. Miotte,
the 30th of March 1743." *Courtesy of the Vérendrye Museum, Pierre, South Dakota.*

By 1913 enough of the object was above ground to allow Charlotte to see that there were printed letters and an interesting figure on one side, and writing scratched into the other. It was a flat piece of metal buried vertically in the ground.[1]

Charlotte was right. In February 1913, when the object was pulled from the ground, it was found to be a lead plate, about 18 cm high, 20 cm wide and .3 cm thick (7 in × 8 in × .125 in). Cast in Quebec, the plate had been carried more than 4,800 km (3,000 mi) to the interior of the continent by the French explorer, Pierre Gaultier de Varennes, Sieur de La Vérendrye, and his sons. The senior La Vérendrye held the monopoly of the fur trade in the North West but was more interested in searching for a route to the Western Sea. *Père et fils* had explored much of the North-West and had established several fur-trading posts on the Red and Assiniboine Rivers.

In April 1742, two La Vérendrye sons, the Chevalier, Louis-Joseph, and François, with two French companions, set out from Fort La Reine on the Assiniboine River determined to cross the continent and reach the Western Sea. They crossed the Missouri River near today's Sanish, North Dakota, and travelled as far as the vicinity of the Black Hills and the Big Horn Mountains before turning back. On their return journey they forded the Missouri River near Pierre. There, on March 30, 1743, on a scenic overlook, they deposited the lead plate, claiming the region for France.

The cast lettering on the face of the plate, in Latin, read: *"Year 26 of the reign of Louis* XV. *For the king, most illustrious lord. By the Marquis de Beauharnois, 1741. Placed by Pierre Gaultier de La Vérendrye."* Obviously, the senior La Vérendrye had intended to deposit the plate himself two years earlier. Above the lettering was a *fleur de lis*, the interesting figure that had caught the eye of Charlotte Johnson. The back of the plate carried a correction, in French, carved into the lead by knifepoint: *"Placed by the Chevalier de la Vérendrye, witnesses Louis-Joseph, La Londette and A. Miotte, the 30th of March 1743."*

Over the plate the explorers piled a large protective cairn of stones. There, their unique claim on behalf of the King of France would remain for 170 years until unearthed by the curiosity of a 14-year-old American schoolgirl.

The lead plate is now displayed in the Vérendrye Museum at Pierre, South Dakota. The Vérendrye National Monument near Sanish, North Dakota, marks the site where the Vérendryes camped in 1742 upon first reaching the Missouri.

LIKELY THE VÉRENDRYES WERE unaware that their claim to the Missouri River on behalf of France was redundant. As a tributary of the Mississippi

River, the Missouri was included in the vast territory of Louisiana claimed for France 61 years earlier, in April 1682, by René-Robert Cavalier, the Sieur de la Salle, exploring out of Quebec. La Salle travelled the full length of the river and then claimed all of the lands drained by the Mississippi and its river system on behalf of Louis xiv, the reigning king of France, and named the territory "Louisiane" or "Land of Louis." La Salle's claim took in all the territory from the Appalachian Mountains to the Rocky Mountains and stretched from the Great Lakes to the Gulf of Mexico. Even if they were aware of the Louisiana claim, the Vérendryes had no way of knowing that the great river they had discovered was merely a tributary, albeit the longest, of a greater river further downstream.

La Salle and La Vérendrye were claiming lands under a doctrine of international law known as the Right of Discovery, which recognized that discovery of an unappropriated and uninhabited territory, *terra nullius*, gave title or ownership to the discoverer. The fact that North America was inhabited by millions of Native residents was disregarded. To make the point that this might have been inappropriate, in 1992 a Chippewa chief stepped off a trans-Atlantic jet at Rome and claimed Italy by Right of Discovery, disregarding the Italian inhabitants just as Columbus had disregarded the American Indians 500 years earlier.

La Salle, like the Vérendryes, had been hoping to find a river that would lead to the Western Sea, the Pacific, and provide a route to the Orient. La Salle's Mississippi, unfortunately, flowed south, but the Vérendryes' Missouri still held promise; it rose somewhere to the west and might possibly provide a connection to the Pacific. It would be another 160 years before that western source was explored.

The mighty Missouri was the first of two noble rivers of the Great Plains discovered by the Vérendryes. The Saskatchewan was the second.

In 1749, the Chevalier paddled from Lake Winnipeg up the Saskatchewan River to The Pas and perhaps as far as The Forks, where the North and South branches divide. Tragically, that was the year of the elder La Vérendrye's death and the end of the family's explorations. But the remarkable journeys of the Vérendryes remain as the opening chapters in the recorded history of both the Missouri and the Saskatchewan, the two rivers that figured most prominently in the chronicles of the great North-West.

To be sure, in 1691, nearly 60 years before the Chevalier de La Vérendrye, the Saskatchewan River had been first visited by Henry Kelsey, an employee of the Hudson's Bay Company. Kelsey, sent to investigate the inland region that sent its furs to the Company's posts on Hudson Bay, crossed the Saskatchewan and journeyed on to the plains. But it was the French who first really explored both the Saskatchewan and the Missouri.

In 1673, 70 years before the Chevalier de La Vérendrye planted his plate, two other French explorers out of Quebec, the travelling priests Jacques Marquette and Louis Joliet, had met the Missouri. Serenely floating down the Mississippi near present-day St. Louis, they suddenly found their canoes overtaken by a boiling, yellow, muddy torrent full of wildly tossing logs and debris. The terrified travellers had encountered the mouth of the Missouri, a savage river before it was tamed by dams and channels.[2]

THE MISSOURI AND THE Saskatchewan rivers, and the lands that lie between them, hold a unique connection to the history of the Great Plains.

The Great Plains of North America is a magnificent swath of original prairie roughly 650 km (400 mi) wide lying on the east of the Rocky Mountains and stretching 4,000 km (2,500 mi) through the interior of the continent from Mexico into western Canada. This North American grassland ranks with the pampas of South America, the steppes of Eastern Europe, and the savanna of Africa as one of the world's four great grasslands. It encompasses almost all of Kansas, Nebraska, North and South Dakota, most of Montana and Oklahoma, as well as good parts of Texas, Colorado, Wyoming and New Mexico. In Canada the Plains cover most of southern Alberta and Saskatchewan and a fair slice across the southwest corner of Manitoba—all of the western prairie. This huge, treeless expanse, the last region of both the United States and Canada to succumb to settlement, became known simply as "The West."

Once the floor, or bed, of a great inland ocean, the Great Plains emerged from the waters during a period of continental uplift about 70 million years ago. A more momentous uplift along the western flank of the new plains produced the Rocky Mountains. Rivers rising in the Rockies flowed eastward, depositing sediment over the vast flatlands. Later, as more uplift occurred, those rivers trenched the plains with deep valleys as they carried their silt away to new depositories. The Saskatchewan and the Missouri are two of the rivers that dissect the Great Plains, and perhaps the greatest of them.

The Saskatchewan system lies like a huge east-pointing "Y" over the Canadian West. The North Saskatchewan, one arm of the "Y," rises in the Columbia icefield of the Rocky Mountains and runs eastward 1,287 km (800 mi) to its meeting with the other arm, the South Saskatchewan, at The Forks, 50 km (31 mi) east of Prince Albert, Saskatchewan. It marks the northern reach of the Great Plains, the boundary roughly following the river's course across Alberta.

The South Saskatchewan begins with the meeting of the Oldman (Belly) and Bow Rivers 70 km (43 mi) west of Medicine Hat and courses 1,939 km (1,205 mi), mostly through Saskatchewan, to its meeting at The Forks. The two rivers, now joined, run another 1,392 km (865 mi) before dropping into Lake Winnipeg. Altogether, the Saskatchewan system provided over 4,618 km (2,870 mi) of river highway to the early explorers of the West.

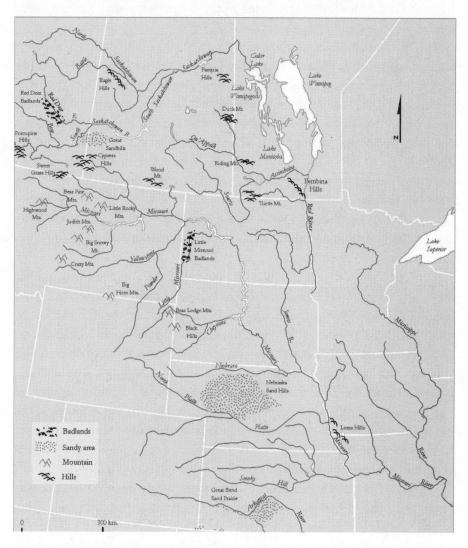

The "Land Between the Rivers." *Map by Diane Perrick, GIS Information Services, CPRC*

As it flows through the western half of Saskatchewan, the South Saskatchewan River roughly coincides with the northern boundary of the Great Plains. When the river, heading to The Forks, abruptly turns north at the Elbow, it leaves this boundary marking to the Qu'Appelle River, once an overflow extension of the South Saskatchewan. The Qu'Appelle serves as the Great Plains boundary as it flows east into Manitoba where it meets the Assiniboine. There the boundary line is continued as the Assiniboine angles across Manitoba to join the Red River at Winnipeg.

The Missouri River officially originates at Three Forks, Montana, about 75 km (47 mi) south of Helena, where the Gallatin, Madison and Jefferson Rivers meet and combine. From there the new river angles north and east until it reaches a point roughly due south of the Alberta/Saskatchewan boundary, where it too makes its way easterly across the Great Plains, following a line roughly parallel to the South Saskatchewan and Qu'Appelle, some 320 km (200 mi) to the south. The Missouri remains on an easterly course until it reaches a point below the Saskatchewan/Manitoba border where it drops sharply southward to meet the Mississippi at St. Louis. Its course ends 4,097 km (2,546 mi)[3] later, just above St. Louis, Missouri, where it joins the Mississippi. With its tributaries, the Missouri drains one-sixth of the North American continent.

Between these two great rivers, the Saskatchewan and the Missouri, lies the most northerly section of the Great Plains, a wedge comprising a good tenth of the huge North American grassland. It was the last of the prairie to be invaded by European-style civilization. Although both the Saskatchewan and the Missouri were early rivers of discovery, their water-borne explorers stuck to their canoes and boats and seldom ventured far afoot. On the plains between these rivers the fierce horse-mounted, buffalo-hunting dwellers of the plains were finally vanquished by modern weaponry. Here, too, died the last of the millions of those buffalo which had once grazed over the grasslands. As the entire Great Plains were "The West," the portion between the Saskatchewan and the Missouri was "The Last Best West."

The two rivers are swift. These northern plains slope steeply eastward away from the Rocky Mountains; dropping approximately 1.5 m (5 ft) every 1.5 km (1 mi). The South Saskatchewan descends from 721 m (2,365 ft) above sea level at Medicine Hat to 501 m (1,643 ft) at Saskatoon. The North Saskatchewan flows through Edmonton at 668 m (2,192 ft) and at Prince Albert is down to 428 m (1,404 ft). Lake Winnipeg, the terminus of the Saskatchewan River, is 218 m (714 ft) above sea level. The Cree aptly called the Saskatchewan *kis-is-ski-tche-wan*, meaning *the river that flows rapidly*.

The Missouri begins its career at Three Forks at the considerable elevation of 1,200 m (3,937 ft) but meets the Mississippi at only 163 m (535 ft). Named after an Indian tribe that once lived along its banks, the Missouri earned the sobriquet "Big Muddy" from the tremendous load of silt it carries. It was also dubbed "Old Misery" by rivermen frustrated by the challenges they faced on the capricious and dangerous river.

At high water, in spring and again in June with mountain snow melt, both rivers were often treacherous torrents, currents sweeping wildly with logs and branches from trees torn out of eroding banks. As the river levels dropped, sandbars appeared and disappeared with a suddenness to astonish and confuse a traveller. One day's relatively safe water might easily be somewhere else entirely by the next morning. At low water, from August until freeze-up, navigable channels became scarce and difficult to locate.

TRICKY AND DANGEROUS THEY were, but the Saskatchewan and Missouri attracted the early explorers hunting the Holy Grail of a passage to the Pacific Ocean. Fur traders, gold seekers, and adventurers found the rivers to be their wilderness highways and well placed for their needs.

One difference in the characteristics of the two rivers caused a huge divergence in their history. The snags, deadheads and floating debris of the Missouri were lethal to the delicate birchbark canoe. Worst were the sawyers, trees trapped by their branches beneath the surface, leaving the hidden trunk swinging up and down in the current ready to disembowel or capsize even large vessels. The light, portable canoes that crossed Canada were not suitable for the Missouri. The heavy and cumbersome dugout canoe, or *pirogue*, made by hollowing out huge tree trunks, was first used on the Upper Missouri; later came heavy boats such as the keelboat or mackinaw, the latter really a floating lumber yard, a huge raft built of heavy planking, equipped with oars but really suitable for downstream travel only. The keelboats were powered upstream with oars, by poling, by sails when conditions were right, or by lining, sending men (or sometimes oxen) forward on the banks or in the shallows hauling the craft behind with heavy ropes. To reach the Upper Missouri, its first explorers, Lewis and Clark, used a 16.8-m (55-ft) keelboat that carried a cargo of twelve tons plus the 29 men that made up their Corps of Discovery. The keelboat carried them as far as the Mandan/Hidatsa villages, about 65 km (40 mi) downriver from today's Garrison Dam, where the Corps spent the winter of 1804–05. The keelboat turned back to St. Louis in the spring and the expedition carried on in sturdy dugout canoes, two larger models of which they called *pirogues*.[4]

But the Missouri was not fully conquered until the steamboats arrived, reaching Fort Benton, the head of navigation, in the 1860s.

The Saskatchewan, although no millpond, was benign in comparison to the Missouri and easily suited to the *canot du nord* that carried the fur traders from Montreal and their cargoes west of Lake Superior. Steamboats conquered the Saskatchewan also, reaching as far inland as Fort Edmonton and Medicine Hat. These huge vessels, as much as 45 m (150 ft) long, driven by great stern-mounted paddlewheels and capable of carrying more than 150 tons of cargo, displaced the canoes and York boats of the Hudson's Bay Company until they, in turn, were put out of business by the railways in the 1880s.

In February 1764, Pierre Laclede, a French fur trader from New Orleans, established a trading post at a site on the west bank of the Mississippi River, just 29 km (18 mi) downstream from its juncture with the Missouri. Believing that he was in Louisiana, Laclede named his new location St. Louis after King Louis IX, who had reigned 500 years earlier and was the only king of France to become a saint. The founder correctly prophesied that his St. Louis would grow into a major centre; it became the distribution and clearance centre for almost all the huge volume of commerce that moved in and out of the West along the great highway of the Missouri River. The fur trade was the first industry on the Missouri and Laclede had chosen well; from his selected focal point traders fanned out along the several waterways and St. Louis prospered. Twenty-five years later it was a minor metropolis with a population of more than 1,000. But in 1774 St. Louis had just come under Spanish administration. And the territory just across the Mississippi River was now British. The old Louisiana was no more.

When Laclede returned to New Orleans he learned the disturbing news that had just reached the settlement; Louisiana no longer belonged to France. Two years earlier, in November 1762, Louis XV, the reigning king, had transferred all of Louisiana lying west of the Mississippi to Spain. It was part of a package that saw France, in defeat at the end of the Seven Years War (1756–63), surrender all its holdings in North America. King Louis considered the loss of unprofitable Louisiana as almost a happy circumstance, but not so New France, the valuable colony along the St. Lawrence River that now belonged to the hated British.

The fall of New France sent shock waves rippling west and south along the trading routes developed by the fur merchants of Montreal, who had capitalized upon the trailblazing of La Salle and the Vérendryes. A string of posts stretched through the Great Lakes, the Illinois region and down the Mississippi River. As early as 1715 a "Voyagers Road" was established connecting

Green Bay on Lake Michigan with the Mississippi River at the juncture with the Missouri.[5] More posts were established west of the Great Lakes along Lake Winnipegosis, the Red and Assiniboine Rivers and into the Saskatchewan River system. A temporary post built by The Chevalier at the Forks of the North and South Saskatchewan Rivers in 1748 became the more permanent Fort St. Louis in 1753. Fort Paskoyac near present-day The Pas was occupied in 1754 with an outpost, Fort à la Corne, further west. Some historians contend that as early as 1751 penetration extended to within sight of the Rocky Mountains where a temporary post, Fort La Jonquière, was located near Calgary.[6] This extensive trading network produced a huge volume of furs; by the 1690s beaver pelts flowed into New France at a rate four times larger than could be consumed by the market in France.[7]

Not for the first time had the monarchs of Europe disposed of vast tracts of North America like pieces on a great chessboard, without any reference or notice to the inhabitants, and with litle, if any, knowledge of the true nature and potential of the asset. Almost a century earlier, in 1670, Charles II of England, assuming to himself the right to do so, had granted the Hudson's Bay Company a trading monopoly over a huge region in what became Canada, an action later attacked as presumptuous and invalid. The future would see more such transfers, two of them again involving Louisiana, and as before there would be no notice to—or consideration of—the inhabitants.

With the conquest of New France, all this was lost to the French traders in Montreal. They were out of business, their supply lines to France cut off. But the canoe routes remained, as did the trading connections in fur country. And the voyageurs who manned the canoes awaited employment. Opportunity beckoned to men of ability, vision, courage and capital.

More than 30 alert entrepreneurs[8] stepped into the breach, including several canny Scots. New contracts for the supply of trade goods were negotiated with manufacturers in England. After only a brief interruption the well-stocked canoes headed again into the *pays d'en haut*. There the traders found the Indians anxious to trade for the European goods upon which they had come to depend. Fur once more flowed into Montreal.

By 1774 the value of the fur trade was such that the new merchant class in Montreal and Quebec had influence in London, enough influence to secure the enactment of protective legislation. The Quebec Act, designed to cut off bothersome French and Spanish competition from New Orleans and, of course, the new posts at St. Louis, grandly extended the boundaries of Quebec all the way to the Mississippi River. The great portion of Louisiana lying east of the Mississippi that Britain had won from the French was incorporated, so that west of Pennsylvania the Ohio River became the southern limit of Quebec down to its juncture with the Mississippi at today's city of Cairo, Illinois. The merchant princes of Montreal and Quebec controlled operations over a huge region in the interior of North America, from Newfoundland to the Rocky Mountains and south to within approximately 1,600 km (1,000 mi) of the Gulf of Mexico. Four years later they would reach the Arctic Ocean. Their operations west of the Great Lakes were, strictly speaking, within the 1670 grant to the Hudson's Bay Company, but the new traders ignored that restriction, as had their French predecessors. But trouble was about to break out on that front. The patience of the Hudson's Bay Company was wearing thin.

English entrepreneurs had been inspired to enter the Canadian fur trade by a pair of disaffected French promoters, Sieur Medard Chouart Des Groseilliers and Pierre-Esprit Radisson, who had conceived the concept of Hudson Bay as a route to the interior that would be far more economical than the St. Lawrence River. Unhappy with French officialdom, the two took their proposal to London. The result was the Hudson's Bay Company,[9] chartered by King Charles II of England in May 1670, by the grant of a monopoly over

> the sole Trade and Commerce ... of all those seas, streights [sic] and bays, rivers, lakes, creeks, and sounds ... within the streights commonly called Hudson's Streights together with all the lands, countries and teritories [sic] upon the coasts and confines of the seas, streights, bays, lakes, rivers, creeks and sounds aforesaid. ..

Neither Charles nor his grantees had any concept of the magnitude of his grant, 3.9 million km^2 (1.5 million mi^2) stretching from Labrador to the Rocky Mountains on the west and reaching from the Barren Lands through the Great Plains almost to the Missouri River:

> On a modern map the Company received those portions of the Provinces of Ontario and Quebec north of the Laurentian watershed and west of the Labrador boundary, the whole of Manitoba, most of Saskatchewan, the southern half of Alberta, and a large portion of the North West Territories.[10]

In total, 43% of today's Canada was turned over to the Company. The grant also covered a good portion of what is now Minnesota and North Dakota drained by the north-flowing Red River and its tributaries.

The Company set up shop at the mouths of several rivers emptying into Hudson Bay and James Bay. Within a few years it was operating posts at Fort Nelson, later York Factory, at the mouth of the Nelson River, at Albany Factory, on the Albany River, at Moose Factory, on the Moose River, and at Rupert's House, on the Rupert River. Indians from the interior travelled up the rivers to trade, exchanging fur pelts for goods of European manufacture.

For more than a century after receiving its charter, the Hudson's Bay Company remained comfortably within its outposts on the Bay while the Indians brought their furs to its forts. Then came the competition. Operating from posts along the North Saskatchewan River the Montreal traders intercepted so much of this fur almost at its source that in 1772 the Company sent a young employee at Fort York, Matthew Cocking, inland to investigate. Cocking canoed up the North Saskatchewan, wintered with the Blackfoot on the plains, then returned to Fort York with unpleasant news; traders from Montreal had established numerous posts in the interior and were capturing much of the fur supply from the Indians who naturally preferred to trade closer to home. Unable to enforce its monopoly franchise, the Company responded to this threat by directing its seasoned explorer, Samuel Hearne, to establish a trading post on the North Saskatchewan River. In 1774 Hearne chose a strategic location and built Cumberland House, now the oldest continually occupied community in Saskatchewan.[11]

With the construction of Cumberland House the Hudson's Bay Company accepted the challenge of the Montreal traders and the competition grew fierce, even vicious, as posts sprang up along the North Saskatchewan River, each leapfrogging the other in a determined effort to gain advantage. Even among the Montrealers rivalry became so costly and dangerous that several prominent traders joined in partnership under the title North West Company. Partners came and went, but the North West Company continued and for 40 years was the single most forceful opponent of the Hudson's Bay Company. North West personnel (called Nor'Westers) opened up much new territory, exploring as far as the Arctic and the Pacific Oceans. In 1778 Peter Pond worked up the Churchill River into the Athabasca region, returning overloaded with beaver pelts more luxurious than any before seen. The next year Alexander Mackenzie, searching for the Pacific, followed the great river that bears his name to the Arctic Ocean. In 1793, in a 7.5-m (25-ft) foot canoe specially designed and built for lightness,[12] Mackenzie tried again for the Pacific.

This time he succeeded, although he travelled overland part of the way after caching the canoe. On July 22, 1793, Mackenzie reached the Pacific Ocean at Dean Channel, 460 km (285 mi) north of Vancouver, the first European to cross the North American continent.

The Hudson's Bay Company followed into the Athabasca region, ignoring the fact that these waters drained to the Arctic, not Hudson Bay, and were not included in its charter. Neither was the Missouri River, but by 1787 both firms were trading with the Mandans on the Missouri.[13] Even they had been preceded as early as 1704 by two *coureurs de bois*, independent traders out of New France who traded on the Missouri for at least two years.[14]

SO IT WAS THAT when Merriwether Lewis, William Clark and their Corps of Discovery arrived at the Mandan and Hidatsa villages near today's Bismarck in the fall of 1804 and settled in for the winter, they entertained traders from both the Hudson's Bay Company and the North West Company who were well known in the communities.[15] A former North West Company trader, turned independent, a French Canadian by the name of Toussaint Charbonneau, was living among the Hidatsas. When Lewis and Clark learned that Charbonneau had two wives who came from the Shoshone, or Snake, bands at the headwaters of the Missouri in the Rocky Mountains, they quickly signed the trader to join their expedition, on condition he bring along one of his Shoshone wives.[16] Charbonneau chose Sacagawea, only 15 and pregnant, but destined to enter American history when her family connections contributed mightily to the survival and success of the Corps of Discovery.

After Lewis and Clark pushed off from the Mandan and Hidatsa villages in the spring of 1805, headed for the Pacific, they saw no more white men until their return. Yet, just a few hundred kilometres north as many as 2,000 Europeans were engaged in the fur trade along the Saskatchewan and Athabasca Rivers.[17] And Alexander Mackenzie had blazed the trail to the Pacific 12 years earlier.

After Lewis and Clark returned to St. Louis in late September 1806, completing a difficult but successful journey to the Pacific Ocean and back, fur traders were emboldened to follow their track into the Upper Missouri. One of the Corps of Discovery crew members took his discharge at Mandan, then turned right around and, with two partners, immediately went back up the Missouri to trap fur. The next season an expedition organized by Manuel Lisa, a Spaniard out of St. Louis, poled and paddled a keelboat 1,930 km (1,200 mi) up the Missouri and Yellowstone Rivers as far as the Bighorn River where they established Fort Raymond.[18]

Fur traders on the Upper Missouri met far more resistance from the resident Indians than had been experienced by the French and Scots on the Saskatchewan and other northerly rivers. The Blackfoot were brutally antagonistic, attacking almost every party entering their territory. Blackfoot hostility to white men was attributed partly to a fatal encounter with a party under Merriwether Lewis in the summer of 1806 and partly to their concern that the new traders would equip their traditional enemies with firearms, removing the advantage the Blackfoot had enjoyed since securing muskets from Hudson's Bay Company and North West Company traders farther north. Also, the newcomers were trappers as well as traders. Taking the view that the Indians were not sufficiently industrious, the men out of St. Louis hunted beaver themselves and a new species was born, the "Mountain Man," often an employee trapper, but usually an independent operator. The Blackfoot severely resented the mountain men taking their beaver.

Whatever the reason, every year some 40 to 50 white men lost their lives in Blackfoot country, even after 1832 when Fort McKenzie was successfully established near today's Fort Benton.[19] In his Reminiscences, *Thirty-Six Years in the Rockies, 1864–1900*, Robert Vaughn, an early Montana resident, provides a grisly tolling of the deaths of more than 121 pioneers, most listed by name, all at the hands of Indians between the years 1863 and 1877.[20]

There were still no boundaries on the Great Plains in the years immediately following Lewis and Clark's exploration and both the Hudson's Bay Company and the North West Company entered the region west of the Missouri River. In 1808 Finnan McDonald, a Nor'Wester, built Kootenai Post on the north side of the Kootenai River opposite today's town of Libby, Montana. The next year David Thompson established the North West Company on the Clark Fork River near today's Thompson Falls, a post that continued in operation for 40 years although it changed location three times and became known as Flathead Post.[21]

Fittingly, the Upper Missouri and the Saskatchewan boasted the two grandest of all the fur-trading establishments in the interior, Fort Union and Fort Edmonton. In spite of their names, neither were military facilities, but were the flagship posts of two of the greatest fur-trading empires in North America.

Fort Union, located in 1828 on the north bank of the Missouri about 8 km (5 mi) upstream from the mouth of the Yellowstone River, was built by the American Fur Company, organized in 1808 by John Jacob Astor, who dominated the American fur trade for more than a quarter of a century. Well deserving of the title "fort," it was designed and constructed for defence. A 6-m (20-ft) high palisade of upright cottonwood logs protected a 22 m² (240 ft²) interior containing storerooms and living quarters. On the corners were 9-m (30-ft) stone bastions equipped with cannon and swivel guns. The Fort, a self-sufficient community that numbered 100 during its heyday, was complete with dairy, henhouse, coopers, blacksmith, gunsmith, stables—everything necessary to provide civilized comfort out on the lonely plains. Fort Union was built to capture the beaver trade, and it did, but before long buffalo robes supplanted beaver and during the 1850s as many as 150,000 robes passed through the trading gate each year.

The officer in charge of the American fur forts was called the *bourgeois*, testimony to the early French influence on the industry. As befitting his station, each *bourgeois* strove to achieve a lifestyle as luxurious as possible, often with results that were startling in such primitive regions. Fort Union was famous for the sumptuous accommodation of the *bourgeois'* 25-m (80-ft) long living quarters and the epicurean menu in his dining hall, but it could not compare with the aristocratic grandeur found at Rowand's Folly at Fort Edmonton.

The Hudson's Bay Company built the first Fort Edmonton in 1795 and the last and most magnificent in 1832 under the direction of Chief Factor John Rowand, a larger-than-life Irishman who spent more than 50 years in the fur trade in the country of the Saskatchewan. For his quarters Rowand constructed a three-storey log house with a gallery running its full length on the second floor and complete with a gentlemen's mess hall and a ballroom. In addition to Rowand's personal rooms, the building contained offices, bedrooms, steward's room, armoury, storerooms and cellars. Its windows, hundreds of them, were fitted with glass panes, a rare luxury at a time when parchment was the standard material. Little wonder that such a structure in the Saskatchewan wilderness of 1832 was dubbed "Rowand's Folly."[22]

In addition to the great house, the stockade contained a large number of cabins for residents and visitors, stables, warehouses, a blacksmithy, carpentry and boatbuilding shops and the like, and even a church. The victualling of the huge establishment that was Fort Edmonton was a herculean task. Father Peter John De Smet, an American Jesuit missionary who overwintered with Rowand in 1845–46, recorded that "the ice-house contained 30,000 whitefish, each weighing four pounds, and 500 buffaloes, the ordinary amount of the winter provisions."[23]

Rowand could, and frequently did, set a magnificent table in the wilds of the West. While his personal piper played from the gallery above, the Chief Factor's guests dined upon turnips, potatoes and bread, all rare delicacies on the Saskatchewan, as well as buffalo hump, unborn buffalo calf, buffalo tongue, white fish, beaver tail, moose nose and roast goose.

CHAPTER 2

The "Medicine Line"

I N 1783 ANOTHER GEOPOLITICAL REORDERING OF THE INTERIOR of North America took place in Europe, directed by plenipotentiaries who had but little knowledge of the effect their decisions would have on the actual landscape and the inhabitants thereof. The American War of Independence was settled by a treaty between Great Britain and the United States executed at Paris, France on September 3, 1783. Great Britain acknowledged its former 13 colonies along the Atlantic seaboard to be "free, sovereign and independent states." That made it necessary to draw a boundary line between the new nation and what was left of British North America. The treaty makers agreed upon a border between Canada and the United States down the St. Lawrence River and through the Great Lakes as far as Lake of the Woods, but there they ran into trouble. From what became known as the North-West Angle of the Lake of the Woods they tried to extend the boundary line "on a due west course to the river Mississippi." A quick look at a map discloses that the Mississippi does not reach far enough north to meet such a line; it actually commences at Lake Itasca, in Minnesota, several kilometres south of the intended boundary from Lake of the Woods.

The Mississippi River was declared to be the western boundary of the United States, but there was a huge gap between that western boundary and the northern boundary that stopped at Lake of the Woods because it had nowhere to go. The northern Great Plains were left much in a state of limbo. Spain held the remnant of Louisiana west of the Mississippi while the Hudson's Bay Company held Rupert's Land to the north. The Missouri River drainage was the northern limit of Louisiana and the Saskatchewan River system was the effective southern limit of Rupert's Land on the prairie, but what about the territory between the two rivers? The Native inhabitants were familiar with the country, of course, and so were any number of fur traders, but none of these were called upon by officialdom in Washington and London, where very little was known about the region.

The matter of a boundary line west of Lake of the Woods was not resolved until 1818, 25 years after the Treaty of Paris. On October 20, 1818, in London, the United States and Great Britain decided upon the 49th Parallel as the western border from Lake of the Woods to the Stony Mountains (as the Rocky Mountains were then called). Although not the first time the 49th had been proposed in boundary discussions,[1] its final selection appears to have been made almost capriciously, since the negotiators did not know whether it lay north or south of the dead-ended border at Lake of the Woods. They directed that a line be drawn from the North-West Angle

> due North or South as the Case may be, until the said Line shall intersect the said Parallel of North Latitude, and from the Point of such Intersection due West along and with the said Parallel shall be the Line of Demarcation between the Territories of the United States, and those of His Britannic Majesty, and that the said Line shall form the Northern Boundary of the Territories of the United States, and the Southern Boundary of the Territories of His Britannic Majesty, from the Lake of the Woods to the Stony Mountains.[2]

That settled the issue for the Great Plains. The Rocky Mountains and the Pacific Coast could wait another day.[3]

To the American and British negotiators in London in 1818, the 49th Parallel running across their maps of the northern Great Plains surely presented a neat and simple solution. There were no natural geographic features on the prairies between Red River and the Rocky Mountains to utilize as a border, no river, no lake, no mountain range or continental divide and certainly no coastline. Nor, so far at least as the plenipotentiaries were concerned, were there any inhabitants with traditions and cultures to be taken into account. Artificial or not, the 49th Parallel would serve admirably as a border.[4]

As it turned out, the 49th Parallel lay approximately 40 km (25 mi) south of the North-West Angle, but for more than half a century that mattered almost not at all. It was not until 1873, 55 years later, that surveyors arrived on the scene to mark out the boundary. To London and Washington, the western border remained "so little frequented and so little worth" that no physical marking of its placement was considered necessary.[5] As late as 1859, the Colonial Secretary in London referred to the North West Territory as "barbarous and immeasurable." That would be only ten years before arrangements were concluded to transfer the "barbarous" territory to Canada.

No one in the West paid any attention to the fact of an ethereal boundary line running somewhere across the plains, "the imagined glyph of two distant officialdoms."[6] Even after the 49th Parallel was surveyed, the now-marked border continued to receive scant attention from the residents of the western plains, a condition that persisted for many years.

Well before the selection of the 49th Parallel as a boundary line, the inhabitants and the travellers of the grasslands had been aware that somewhere on the unbroken plains one country ended and another began, but exactly where was of little concern. Many of the Plains Indians had chosen sides during the War of 1812, most supporting the British against the Americans. Several chiefs of bands whose territory lay south of the 49th had been presented with medals bearing the likeness of King George III and had been promised sanctuary if ever needed. Farther east at Rainy Lake in 1822, the Ojibway became concerned when David Thompson was surveying the border from Lake Superior to Lake of the Woods. They understood and were content when Thompson explained that all he was doing was "measuring how far north fell the 'shadow' of the United States and how far south extended 'the shadow of their great father, King George.'"[7]

After the 49th Parallel, or a reasonable approximation thereof, was marked out on the grasslands during the summers of 1873 and 1874, its incongruity became apparent. It stretched across the west "as disturbing as a hair in butter,"[8] as Wallace Stegner and his family found it even 40 years later when they lived along the border. The Montana historian, Joseph Kinsey Howard, was severely critical of the 49th: "Artificial," "absurd," "did not make sense and doesn't yet" (1952):

> The forty-ninth parallel, cutting east to west through the heart of the basin and the plain, was a conceit of congressmen, not of ecologists. It could not arrest the movement of men and ideas any more effectively than it could that of the buffalo herds.[9]

The 49th sliced away a portion of Louisiana that lay where the Milk and Frenchmen Rivers drain out of the north, and a larger portion of Rupert's Land that lay to its south along the north-flowing Red River. It cut across many of the fur trade routes as well as the incipient but swelling buffalo hunt of the Red River Métis. It divided the traditional lands of many of the Plains Indians, from the Ojibway on the east, through the Assiniboine and Gros Ventre, to the Blackfoot on the west. The Plains Indians promptly dubbed the new border "The Medicine Line," in tribute to the magical properties that accorded status and sanctuary to those who crossed.

As a border, the 49th Parallel came with many undesirable features that did not become apparent until much later, partly for the reason that for more than 50 years it was merely a political abstract. Also, it ran neatly between the Missouri and Saskatchewan River systems, *terra incognito* for almost as long.

The Lewis and Clark Corps of Discovery was the first serious exploration of the northern Great Plains.[10] Some 50 years later other scientific expeditions began to probe the west and one penetrated the region between the Missouri and the Saskatchewan Rivers. In 1853, Isaac I. Stevens, the newly appointed Governor of Washington Territory, on his way to his new command, headed a party that travelled overland from St. Paul to Puget Sound searching for a route for a Pacific railway near the 47th and 49th Parallels. Stevens was accompanied by a full complement of scientific observers, including a naturalist, a topographer, astronomical and magnetic analysts, a meteorologist, a geologist and an artist. Stevens concluded that a railway through the region was entirely practicable and 20 years later the Northern Pacific Railway roughly followed Stevens' route.

The trail blazed by Governor Stevens came into use 10 years later, during the American Civil War. On June 16, 1862, the Northern Overland Expedition, under the command of Captain James L. Fisk, and accompanied by 125 hopeful emigrants, left St. Paul headed for Fort Benton. The Expedition successfully avoided the feared Sioux and Blackfoot and in early September made it through to Fort Benton and then went on to the mining camps near today's Helena. Fisk, with some of the emigrants, continued over the mountains to Walla Walla. An experienced and disciplined leader, Fisk took other expeditions over the route in subsequent years.

The Americans were getting to know their country between the Missouri River and the 49th Parallel. But, in Canada, the area between the border and the Saskatchewan/Qu'Appelle Rivers was pretty much unknown territory except to the Aboriginal inhabitants, the fur traders and the Métis buffalo hunters out of Red River. The only maps of the Canadian interior that existed were those created by the fur trade, and its personnel travelled almost exclusively by water. It was, in the words of North West Company surveyor David Thompson, "an obscure part of the world."[11]

Thompson's superb map of the North West Territory, finally completed in 1814, "Embraces the Region lying between 45 and 60 degrees North Latitude and 84 and 124 degrees west Longitude comprising the Surveys and Discoveries of 20 years."[12] Measuring 200 cm × 315 cm (6'9" × 10'4"), it contains more detail of the North American West than anything that preceded it. Yet the region between the Missouri and the Saskatchewan Rivers is shown as totally void, the largest empty sector anywhere on the massive display.

More than 40 years later scientific expeditions began to explore the Canadian plains to assess its agricultural potential. Upper Canada was eyeing the West as a region of free land that could continue to attract the immigrants that fuelled its economic engines. The explorations were thorough and professional, but they, too, stayed close to the waterways and avoided the unknown and difficult country next to the 49th Parallel. They were also disappointing to the boosters of Canadian expansion to the West.

In 1857 Captain John Palliser brought a British-financed enterprise to the Canadian West. Accompanied by a geologist-naturalist, magnetic and astronomical observers and a botanist, he spent three seasons travelling the prairies and the mountains but, except for two side trips, one to Roche Percée, and one to the Cypress Hills, he avoided the lands south of the rivers. Palliser had spent most of the year 1847–48 hunting and touring in the American West, much of that time on the Upper Missouri where he made one or two forays overland north of the river. Perhaps that earlier experience contributed to the pessimistic assessment of much of the Canadian West he reported 10 years later.

Palliser advised that a huge portion of the grasslands, his famous triangle, were "arid plains" unsuitable for settlement. The base of his triangle lay along the 49th Parallel and ran from Turtle Mountain to the Sweet Grass Hills and extended north as far as today's Lloydminster. Palliser had not approached the 49th Parallel and accepted the then-current belief that at least the lower portion of his triangle was merely an extension of the Great American Desert.

In 1857 and 1858, Professor H.Y. Hind of Trinity College, Toronto, surveyed the country from Red River to the elbow of the South Saskatchewan River on behalf of the Canadian government, but he, too, did not enter the southern region. However, that did not deter him from agreeing with Palliser that it, and more, was "not, in its present condition, fitted for the permanent habitation of civilized man."[13]

The Palliser and Hind reports contained little encouragement for the boosters of expansionism, but were particularly negative about the borderlands:

Captain John Palliser (1817–1887). Saskatchewan Archives Board *R-A 4962-1*

Henry Youle Hind (1823–1908). Saskatchewan Archives Board *R-A 4896*

Whole areas including the upper Qu'Appelle Valley, the South Saskatchewan, and the prairies between them and the border thus became identified with the enormous wasteland which for more than a generation had been accepted as the heritage of the United States.[14]

Hind did, however, provide some good tidings to the expansionists of Upper Canada. He identified what he called the "fertile belt," a wide swath of good, arable land commencing where the Red River crossed the 49th Parallel and sweeping northwest along the North Saskatchewan River to the Rocky Mountains.

Having accepted the premise of the Great American Desert, it was natural for Palliser and Hind to stay clear of that portion believed to extend north of the 49th Parallel. The lands between the Missouri and the Saskatchewan/Qu'Appelle Rivers were described on the maps of the time as the northern reach of the Desert, arid, tough country with no advantages and little, if any, potential. It was an uninviting region, the last on the list of any explorer searching out fertile lands suitable for settlement. As recently as 1872 the Surveyor General estimated that the portion of the Great American Desert extending into Canada was 129,500 km² (50,000 mi²) in extent, or 12,950,400 ha (32,000,000 acres) "unavailable for cultivation."[15] Palliser had included only some 42,000 km² (16,000 mi²) in his triangle.

The descriptions of the day were not entirely inaccurate. The region contains some very inhospitable lands, what the Métis called *Les mal à Terre*, the Bad Lands, on both sides of the 49th Parallel—in Montana, also known as The Big Dry. These are large areas of clay with soil too thin to support enough grass to satisfy either grazing buffalo or cattle and eroded into strange formations called "buttes" and "hoodoos."

On January 12, 1888, a deadly blizzard blew from the North-West Territories southeast into Dakota Territory, Minnesota and Nebraska. The day had begun with unseasonably fine weather, a mid-winter thaw, but the racing cold front yanked the thermometer down 10°C (18°F) in just three minutes. In a few hours the temperature had dropped to -40° with a gale-force wind that dealt quick death to the unlucky and unprepared. By the next morning, Friday, January 13, some 500 settlers lay dead on the bitter, drifted prairie. So many of those who perished were children, caught on their way home from their country schools, that the tragedy became known as "The Children's Blizzard."[1]

NOTE

1.   David Laskin, *The Children's Blizzard* (New York: Harper Collins, 2004).

Hundreds of kilometres inland from the ocean's moderating influence, and behind the barrier of the Rocky Mountains, these northern plains offer another discouraging feature—one of the most extreme climates in the world. Only central Russia has a climate of similar severity. Winters can be despairingly long and bitter; six full months of frost and snow is not rare and temperatures frequently average -25°C or -30°C (-32°F to -35°F) for a full month. Lows of minus -40°C (-40°F) are common. Blizzards howl across the landscape with such ferocity as to suck the breath from one's lungs and obliterate all visibility. Exposed flesh freezes in minutes and life-threatening conditions can arrive with astonishing speed. In January, 1916, at Browning, Montana, "the mercury dropped from forty-four above to fifty-six below—100 degrees—in twenty-four hours."[16] The early settlers paid dearly, often with their lives, in learning how suddenly, and with what ferocity, a blizzard could strike.

Summer, particularly the months of July and August, provides the other extreme—heat reaching into the 30°C (86°F) range, occasionally as high as 40°C to 45°C (104°F to 113°F) has been recorded, accompanied by winds that sear like a blast from a furnace. Plant life withers in such conditions, especially so in the low-precipitation regions of the short-grass prairies where annual rainfall averages only 300 mm (12"). Thunderstorms on the open plains are awe-inspiring and fearsome events, thunder crashing like cannon bursts as lightning splits the sky, all accompanied by torrential rain and often hail that sometimes reaches life-threatening dimensions. Flash floods caused by the rain and hail could be dangerous. Rainfall of 375 mm (14.8") in an eight-hour period has been recorded.[17] The Red River Métis buffalo hunters, experienced as they were in selecting camp sites, sometimes found themselves dangerously close to drowning on the open prairie. Even worse are the tornadoes, funnel clouds spawned by thunderstorms that can rearrange the landscape in mere seconds.

Travellers and early settlers on the Great Plains suffered insects that transcended the merely annoying. Mosquitoes in immense, ravenous swarms rendered existence almost intolerable and sleep impossible. Horses were near-maddened by the whining mass clustered about their heads and eyes where the wipe of the rider's hand came away full of blood and crushed pests. Early waterfowl hunters at Red River found the clouds of mosquitoes so dense as to obscure their aim, making it difficult to see the flights of ducks they targeted.

Accounts of the ravages of attacking hordes of grasshoppers on the Great Plains in the 1870s seem unbelievable until it is understood that the insects were a different species than the more benign variety encountered today. The Rocky Mountain Grasshopper, really a locust, was an engine of destruction, a creature that would easily fit into science fiction. Windborne, they would arrive in swarms that darkened the sun and devastate an entire landscape. Almost nothing was immune to their attacks. Rangeland and crops were reduced to barren soil, trees were stripped of leaves. Then the creatures would devour saddles, laundry, tent canvas, whatever was available. Settlers who protected their gardens with blankets lost blankets first and gardens second. Axe handles and fence posts were attacked. When a swarm finally departed it left the ground as black as if recently tilled. Farmers complained that the insects "ate everything except the mortgage."

In flight they filled the sky to dimensions that defy belief. "In 1875, the species formed the largest locust swarm in the history of humankind, nearly 3,000 kilometres long and 180 kilometres wide."[18] This horde flew over Nebraska from July 20–30 and would cover more than 80% of Saskatchewan. "The swarm must have contained at least 12.5 trillion insects with a total weight of 27.5 million tons."[19] Yet, the Rocky Mountain Grasshopper was extinct 25 years later; the last specimen was seen in 1902. The pest became victim, it is believed, of the settlers whose lives it plagued. The tilling of the land destroyed the insects' breeding grounds.

Somehow, in spite of such a bleak and formidable environment, the Great Plains had supported millions of roving buffalo, a fact overlooked by Palliser and others. The arid prairies were covered by grasses, grasses that were not only drought-resistant but remarkably nutritious.

Subsequent history has debunked Palliser; most of his triangle has proven to be very productive and today supports bountiful agricultural enterprises. Hind's "fertile belt" became meaningless and lost as settlers poured into the West and established farms and communities where he had predicted there could be no "permanent habitation of civilized man."

As with every respectable desert, there were several oases between the Missouri and the Saskatchewan/Qu'Appelle Rivers, wooded uplands with abundant water and luxuriant grasses, havens well known to the nomadic Indians and Métis. Almost all lie close to, or even astride, the 49th Parallel; Turtle Mountain, Moose Mountain, Wood Mountain, Little Rocky Mountains, Cypress Hills, Bears Paw Mountains, Sweet Grass Hills. Wood Mountain and the Cypress Hills, the latter the highest terrain between the Rocky Mountains and Labrador, were not quite engulfed by the last glacier and possess unique flora. In the last half of the decade of the 1870s, three of these places of refuge, the Cypress Hills, the Bear's Paw Mountains, and Wood Mountain, unheard of until then, became famous throughout North America.

The country between the Missouri and the Saskatchewan/Qu'Appelle Rivers was not uninhabited. From earliest times its buffalo had attracted several tribes of Native Indians that contested for occupation and hunting rights. On the Canadian side could be found Saulteaux/Ojibway to the east, then Assiniboine, Plains Cree, Gros Ventre, and the Blackfoot Confederacy (consisting of the Blackfoot, Peigan, Blood and Sarcee). After the 1862 uprising in Minnesota, a number of refugee Sioux moved into the region. In the mid-1800s, Métis from Red River following the retreating buffalo herds began to overwinter and then settle more or less permanently in the sheltered coulees of the uplands and along the Milk River. The competition between these jostling neighbours was frequently fatal.

As they became better known in Europe, the western plains drew a growing number of tourist adventurers, hunters mostly, but, like their predecessors, these travellers also tended to avoid the inhospitable region. The reports of the few who did venture south of the Saskatchewan/Qu'Appelle Rivers pretty much confirmed the country's unpleasant reputation. Dr. John Rae, better known as an Arctic explorer, in 1861 guided two members of Britain's aristocracy through the southern prairies as far as Old Wives Lakes, which he presumptuously re-named after his charges as Lake Johnstone and Chaplin

Lake. Rae described the country south of today's Regina as "a dry, parched and barren country."[20]

In 1872, Lieutenant Colonel Patrick Robertson-Ross, Adjutant General of the Canadian Militia, travelled into the western plains and on his return reported on the need for a police force or militia to provide some law and order to the Territories. He also reported on the existence of Fort Whoop-Up, an American whiskey fort north of the border that was preying on the Blackfoot Indians. Unfortunately, Robertson-Ross incorrectly reported the site of Whoop-Up to be at the junction of the Bow and Belly Rivers, an egregious error that two years later caused confusion and hardship. The North-West Mounted Police (NWMP), sent into the West to put Fort Whoop-Up out of business, followed Robertson-Ross's directions but were unable to locate the illegal establishment. After retaining a guide, the NWMP found Whoop-Up where it had been all along, at the junction of the Belly and St. Mary's Rivers, about 95 km (60 mi) further west from where Robertson-Ross had placed it.

This lack of accurate and reliable information about the terrain south of the well-travelled South Saskatchewan/Qu'Appelle route proved extremely costly to the NWMP. Its famous 1874 expedition into the West came perilously close to total failure and annihilation. As it was, the recruits and their mounts suffered bitterly and dozens of horses died of starvation and exposure.

In 1873, the year before the NWMP entered the West, surveyors began the huge task of laying out and marking the Canada/United States border, the 49th Parallel, which lies roughly midway between the Missouri and the South Saskatchewan/Qu'Appelle Rivers. The coming of the huge survey parties, followed by the troops of the NWMP, ended the obscurity of the region.

And just in time. For just two years after the arrival of the NWMP, several thousand American Sioux Indians, seeking sanctuary after defeating the United States Army at Little Bighorn, began to cross the newly surveyed border. As they settled in, from Wood Mountain to the Cypress Hills, they presented a huge international diplomatic predicament and drew the attention of the powers in Ottawa, Washington and London, as well as the newspapers across North America. Suddenly, the remote area of the Canadian West that had been virtually unknown five years earlier became the scene of an intense historical drama.

CHAPTER 3

The Era of Expansion

A LEXANDER MACKENZIE'S EPIC CROSSING TO THE PACIFIC in 1793 caused consternation in Washington and was primarily responsible for the Lewis and Clark expedition 10 years later. His account of his journeys was published in London in 1801 under the ponderous title *Voyages from Montreal, on the river St. Lawrence, through the continent of North America, to the Frozen and Pacific oceans; in the years 1789 and 1793; with a preliminary account of the rise, progress, and present state of the fur trade of that country.* The next year a second edition was published in New York and Philadelphia and that summer a copy was eagerly read by President Thomas Jefferson at Monticello, his mountaintop home in Virginia.[1]

Jefferson, the third president of the United States, was an unusually learned man, knowledgeable in such diverse disciplines as botany, astronomy, celestial navigation, mineralization and ethnology, with a particular interest in the geography of North America.[2] Included in the latter was an intense curiosity about the unknown territory beyond the Mississippi River, the northwest region of the Missouri River. In earlier years Jefferson had organized several expeditions intended to explore the Missouri, but all had failed, usually for lack of sufficient funding and planning.

Mackenzie's account of his crossing to the Pacific stirred Jefferson to a fever. The words *"Alexander Mackenzie, from Canada, by land, the twenty-second of July, one thousand seven hundred and ninety-three,"* written by the Canadian fur trader upon a rock in Dean Channel, goaded like fire. Like many others of the time, Jefferson was afflicted with Northwest Passage disease. He believed that a practical water route to the Pacific existed, obstructed only by an easily crossed mountain range, likely not more than 915 m (3,000 ft) in height, certainly no more of a barrier than the Blue Ridge Mountains of Virginia. Jefferson saw in Mackenzie's feat a challenge to American national honour.

Even more worrisome was a commercial concept Mackenzie laid out in his book, a concept of global reach. The Canadian trader envisioned a compact involving his North West Company, the Hudson's Bay Company, and the East India Company that would import trade goods to the interior via the economical Hudson Bay route and permit the marketing in China of furs exported from the Pacific coast. Jefferson quickly saw that such an arrangement would lead to control of almost all of the North American fur trade and easily extend to fish and other commodities. It was time for action.

Over the winter of 1802–03 Jefferson determined to send a properly financed and prepared expedition up the Missouri to the Pacific. To command it, he appointed Merriwether Lewis, an army officer with experience on the frontier and, since the spring of 1801, the president's personal secretary. It was an imposing responsibility for a man just 29 years of age, but Jefferson had full confidence in Lewis. After all, he was the same age Mackenzie had been when he led his expedition to the Pacific.

Jefferson planned to assign a dozen soldiers to Lewis' command. That created their first major problem. The Missouri River was in Louisiana, Spanish territory, and the proposed mission was clearly military in nature. Jefferson first sought permission, claiming that he was interested only in acquiring knowledge of the geography, but Spain was not taken in and refused. Undeterred, Jefferson carried on with his plans. He knew that Spain had, in 1800, secretly agreed to return Louisiana to France and was maintaining only nominal control of the territory. There was no Spanish administrative or military presence north of St. Louis and any authority could be easily avoided. In January 1803, the president sent to Congress a clandestine request for funding. It was approved. The expedition was a go.

Then, in the spring of 1803, events cascaded with electric speed and within a matter of weeks the somewhat astonished United States found that it had acquired Louisiana Territory and more than doubled its size.

Whether owned by Spain or France, New Orleans, at the mouth of the Mississippi River, was a foreign port and the United States chafed at restrictions on its use of the facility. The Mississippi carried three eighths of America's exports and control of New Orleans had become essential.

When France openly acknowledged its ownership of Louisiana, Jefferson instructed his minister in Paris to negotiate the purchase of the port, with authority to take the price as high as 50 million francs ($9,375,000). Napoleon's minister refused to sell New Orleans alone but countered with the suggestion that America take all of Louisiana, including the port settlement. It was an offer the United States could not refuse and the deal was quickly done at the price of 80 million francs ($15 million). The United States now owned the entire Louisiana Territory west of the Mississippi River, as well as New Orleans. That took care of any diplomatic impediment to the Missouri River expedition.

It was a huge transaction, covering the wide belt of land extending from New Orleans northwest up the Mississippi and taking in the entire Missouri River and its watershed west to the Continental Divide. In fact, the Louisiana Territory reached so far beyond the known frontier that the French representative grandly asserted that the northern boundary "is lost in the vast wilderness in which there is no European settlement and in which it seems that even the necessity for boundaries is unknown."[3] When those boundaries were settled, the Louisiana Purchase added up to 2,140,000 km^2 (827,000 mi^2), more than the previous total land mass of the United States. It provided the real estate for part or all of 13 states. Almost all of the present state of Montana was included. Jefferson made a very good deal. The $15 million purchase price worked out to about 4¢ an acre and could easily have been covered by the production of almost any one of the many gold mines discovered in Montana alone.

On May 9, 1804, the formal transfer of Upper Louisiana[4] took place at St. Louis, attended by Merriwether Lewis as official witness. By then Lewis had enlisted William Clark as his co-captain and the expedition, in camp nearby on the Mississippi, was in the final stages of preparation. It officially got underway five days later, on May 14, 1804.

The website of the Library of Congress in Washington claims that "The Louisiana Purchase is considered the greatest real estate deal in history."[5] Wrong. The greatest deal was yet to come and would take place in Canada.

The Louisiana Purchase was another rearrangement of the political landscape in the interior of North America, carried out by plenipotentiaries in Europe without any reference to, or consideration of, the residents of the affected territory. The 1803 transaction took in a huge swath of the Great Plains, a region inhabited by several tribes of horse-mounted, buffalo-hunting Indians whose culture was just reaching its zenith. These real owners of the West were not even aware that two modern states, supposedly enjoying a more advanced civilization, had bought and sold their prairie homeland. It would come to pass that only one more generation of these proud and fierce inhabitants would enjoy undisturbed occupation of that homeland before they would be forced into desperate but futile defence against the onrush of that encroaching civilization.

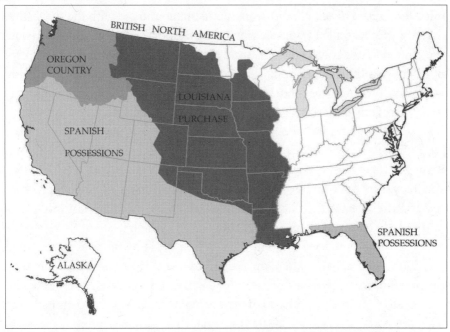

The westward expansion of the United States, 1803–1867. *Map by Diane Perrick, GIS Information Services, CPRC.*

The United States was in an acquisitive mood during the 19th century. After the Louisiana Purchase came Florida (1819: 155,000 km^2/60,000 mi^2), Texas (1845: 1,000,000 km^2/390,000 mi^2), Oregon (1846: 740,000 km^2/ 285,000 mi^2), and, in 1848, another 1,370,000 km^2 (529,000 mi^2) were taken by force from Mexico.[6]

Then, on March 30, 1867, the United States put its signature to a treaty providing for another huge acquisition—the ceding of Russian North America, today known as Alaska. The treaty, if ratified by the United States Senate, would add another 1,518,690 km^2 (586,412 mi^2) of territory at a price of $7,200,000, only about 2¢ per acre this time. The Russians regarded their territory at the northwestern tip of North America as an economic wasteland and were pleased to be rid of it. Many Americans had the same view of the sub-arctic lands and thought the proposed cost to be foolhardy. Senate ratification was doubtful, but more forward thinking prevailed and the treaty was passed on April 9, 1867.

With Alaska in its bag, the United States thought it had neatly bracketed the great northwest lying above its border with British North America and that the huge territory of Rupert's Land under the control of the Hudson's Bay Company would be forced into the Union. Thus would be fulfilled the great American dream of a continental empire stretching from the Atlantic to the

Pacific and even north to the Arctic Ocean. The remaining British possessions in North America, Upper and Lower Canada, New Brunswick and Nova Scotia, soon to be melded into the Dominion of Canada, would be forced by economic and political expediency to join the American republic. Prince Edward Island, the hold-out province, and Newfoundland could be picked up when convenient.

The American aspiration was expressed in the House of Representatives in July 1867, by Congressman Ignatius Donnelly of Minnesota:

> With our great nation on the south of this region, and our new acquisition of Alaska resting upon its northern boundary, British dominion will be inevitably pressed out of western British America. It will disappear between the upper and the nether mill-stones. These jaws of the nation will swallow it up.[7]

But competing nation-builders in Ottawa had similar ambitions towards those western lands. In 1869, the deal-makers of the two-year-old Dominion of Canada stepped in with a contract to annex those vast land holdings known as Rupert's Land. It would be by far the largest of the three great real estate deals of the 19th century, or of all time.

THE DESIRABILITY OF THOSE western lands lying north of the unsurveyed 49th Parallel was more widely accepted in Minnesota than in Canada. Certainly that was so in the years immediately following the end of the American Civil War in 1865, when immigrants flooded into the state—Germans, Swedes, Norwegians, "rushing towards the Red River Valley."[8] In Canada, doubt remained about the suitability of Rupert's Land for settlement.

Until the mid-1850s, the public image of the territory west of Lake of the Woods was of a country fit only for the fur trade, the rock, trees and water of the north shading south into the extension of the Great American Desert. Only Indians could live in such a land, or would want to. Besides, the western territory was nearly inaccessible, separated from Upper Canada by hundreds of kilometres of Great Lakes and the rock, forest and swamp of the Canadian Shield. Access was possible only in summer by the *voyageur* canoe route through the lakes, or via Hudson Bay. The tiny community on the Red River that had survived since Lord Selkirk's settlement in 1811 was regarded as an anomaly, a small agricultural oasis in an otherwise barren estate.

Minnesotans knew better. Only the still-unsurveyed 49th Parallel lay between them and the British lands and they knew how fertile was the valley of the Red River that flowed north along their western border to Fort Garry. Further, the natural and growing transportation route ran from St. Paul to Fort Garry, a route that by 1866 was already carrying $2 million worth of goods.[9]

The artificiality of the 49th Parallel as an international boundary was particularly evident where it lay south of the Red River Settlement. It was almost totally ignored in the activities of the region. Twice a year the huge Métis buffalo hunt trekked south into American territory without a thought given to the crossing of the border. In June and September, men, women and children, entire travelling communities, hundreds strong with more hundreds of horses, driving crude, high-wheeled carts drawn by oxen or horses, moved over the invisible boundary in search of the retreating herds of plains bison.

Those carts also searched out routes stretching the more than 650 km (400 mi) between Fort Garry and St. Paul, trails that carried a swelling trade as the hunters and trappers of Red River transported their furs and buffalo robes to the Minnesota markets and exchanged them for goods of every description, enjoying almost total immunity from customs or other border niceties.

In the view of an American historian of the region:

> As a boundary, the 49th parallel is entirely man-made and will never really divide the Northern Great Plains, for it is a region at once geographically and historically united. Certainly from 1821 to 1869–70 . . . a unity was most evident; the history of the British Northwest was inextricably bound up with that of the American Northwest.[10]

JAMES WICKES TAYLOR, A St. Paul lawyer, was a strong and persistent booster of American annexation of the lands running from Red River through the valley of the Saskatchewan, so much so that he became known as "Saskatchewan" Taylor. He predicted the region would support a population of 6–8 million and never really gave up his dream even long years after the Canadian Confederation reached across the western plains to the Pacific. In 1866 Taylor presented to the House of Representatives a report describing the region in glowing terms, a country with unlimited agricultural potential:

> For the production of wheat, barley, rye, oats, peas, potatoes, vegetables, grass—whatever is grown in Minnesota, except maize—the region in question will be unsurpassed by any other area of similar extent on the continent.[11]

Based upon Taylor's report, a bill was introduced to Congress calling for the annexation of the British territory on the other side of the 49th Parallel. The proposal died and received only lukewarm American editorial support, but it awakened those in Canada who favoured expansion into Rupert's Land. If the United States coveted the western prairies, perhaps they were of some value.

Both Palliser and Hind had given some encouragement to the expansionist movement. Their reports of the "fertile belt" running westerly from Red River to the Rocky Mountains, between the Great American Desert to the south and the rugged and rocky fur country to the north, identified a considerable region with potential for agricultural settlement. And, in the United States at least, the Desert was being exposed as mostly myth, even though this was partially achieved by what today would be called "junk science."

The descriptor "desert" had been applied to the Great Plains as early as 1540 by the Spanish explorer Francisco Coronado,[12] but it had been confirmed by the reports of two men who explored the American West in the early 1800s— Zebulon Pike in 1806, and Stephen Long in 1820. The existence of the desert became a matter of firm public belief corroborated by two obvious characteristics of the region: it supported no trees, other than in watered valleys, and it was arid—precipitation west of the 100th Meridian was much lower than in the east.

In the 1860s American settlers began to penetrate the Great Plains, supported by an unusually humid weather pattern. Scientists drew a correlation between the two events and concluded that activities such as plowing the land and planting trees caused an increase in rainfall. Thus was born the theory that "rain follows the plow," which must rank among the great misery-making inducements of all time. Seized upon by land companies and railways, it led hundreds of thousands of eager and naïve homestead seekers to settle upon land that could never support them, but could, and did, destroy their spirits as they persevered against hostile and unyielding elements.

The myth of the Great American Desert was weakening, but it did not follow that a 65-ha (160-acre) farm—the size contemplated by the free homestead program—was suitable for the Great Plains as it was in the more humid regions in the east. There was no western desert in the popular image of barren and shifting sand dunes, but there was a very much lower precipitation record and 65 ha (160 acres) on the Great Plains were utterly incapable of supporting a family; a great deal of human misery was endured before this fact became generally accepted. Successful dryland farming required large land holdings tilled by massive machines.

To the proponents of the expansion of Canada into the great North-West, farming was farming—small holdings intensely cultivated by industrious yeomen and their families. That was the proven style from Prince Edward Island to the Great Lakes and the style that, it was assumed, would also prevail on the western prairie. It provided high-density occupation of the land; the North-West would be where "millions yet unborn may dwell in peace and prosperity."[13] Those millions would also need to be supplied with everything from clothing to farm implements. The wheels of commerce in Upper Canada would grind out stupendous profits.

No one bothered to seriously search for factors that might limit the agricultural potential of the North-West; the phrase "due diligence" had not yet come into common usage. Trial and error would serve, as it always had, and such minor risk as existed would be met by the migrants who would take up the new lands.

It was a time for optimism only. The eloquent Father of Confederation, D'Arcy McGee, spoke for many when he declared in 1868 that "the future of the Dominion depends on our early occupation of the rich prairie land."[14]

There was a good deal more than "rich prairie land" in the acquisition proposed by the Canadian government. The Hudson's Bay Company holdings encompassed an amazing 3,625,000 km^2 (1,400,000 mi^2), even though Rupert's Land was limited to the country that drained into Hudson Bay. But Methye Portage, north of La Loche, in present-day northwest Saskatchewan, divides the Hudson Bay and Arctic Ocean drainage systems. West of Methye, the waters of the Clearwater, Peace, Athabasca, Slave and Mackenzie Rivers run to the Arctic. Although the Hudson's Bay Company had been trading fur out of this region for many years, it was not part of its original charter. London wished to add this territory, then called the North-Western Territory, to the Rupert's Land transfer, another 2,100,000 km^2 (810,000 mi^2). This inclusion would cover what became northern Saskatchewan, the north half of Alberta, and much of the new North-West Territories.

The possible annexation of the great western lands had been contemplated by the Fathers of Confederation. When the provinces of New Brunswick, Nova Scotia, Upper Canada (Ontario) and Lower Canada (Quebec) cobbled themselves together in the political compact they entitled "The Dominion of Canada" (having discarded "Kingdom" and "Viceroyalty" as too monarchist and likely to offend the powerful republic with which they would share North America),[15] they kept an eye on the need to acquire and expand into the North-West.[16] The British North America Act of the British Parliament, which brought Canada into existence on July 1, 1867, contained a special provision for the entry of "Rupert's Land and the North-Western Territory, or either or them, into the union," as well as Newfoundland, Prince Edward

Island and British Columbia.[17] John A. Macdonald, the first prime minister of the new Dominion of Canada, included western expansion in his party's platform during the country's first election in August 1867:

> If the United States desires to outflank us on the West, we must accept this situation, and lay our hand on British Columbia and the Pacific Ocean... "From the Atlantic to the Pacific" must be the cry in British North America as much as it ever has been in the United States.[18]

Macdonald then included the acquisition of the North-West in the legislative program announced in his government's first Speech from the Throne on November 7, 1867. Debate on the issue opened just a month later. The resolutions were approved, although not without opposition, and an Address to the Queen from the Senate and the House of Commons was forwarded to London requesting transfer of Rupert's Land and the North-western Territory. The Address clearly identified the objectives of the new government of Canada for the western lands:

> the colonization of the fertile lands of the Saskatchewan, the Assiniboine, and the Red River districts; the development of the mineral wealth which abounds in the region of the North-west; and the extension of commercial intercourse through the British possessions in America from the Atlantic to the Pacific...

The term "colonization" would rankle among the residents of those "fertile lands" for years to come.

IT WAS FIRST NECESSARY to clear away the 1670 Charter granting Rupert's Land to the Hudson's Bay Company. The validity of that Charter had been questioned for years and Canada would have preferred a legal challenge to the Company's claim to the huge territory. But London declined that option and determined to buy out the Company's rights rather than litigate them.

Negotiations in London produced acceptable terms. The Hudson's Bay Company would surrender its Charter in return for £300,000 ($1,460,000 then equivalent), the right to retain more than 18,200 ha (45,000 acres) around its 120 trading posts, and the further right to claim over the next 50 years up to one twentieth of the fertile lands. This last item would amount to 2,830,000 ha (7,000,000 acres),[19] a tremendous value to the old company.[20] The use of the purchased assets as part of the price of acquiring them was an early example of the leveraged buyout[21] that became a common technique in corporate acquisitions a century later. It was also to be the first, but not the last, occasion on which the assets of the new West would be utilized by the government in Ottawa in its building of the nation.[22]

Rupert's Land. *Map by Diane Perrick, GIS Information Services, CPRC*

The deal went forward, but not without a hiccup. Intended to close in 1869, it closed instead in 1870. But it closed, and Canada acquired the largest territory ever transferred from one nation state to another in a non-hostile situation. Speaking during the debate on ratification of the terms of transfer, Senator Jonathon McCully of Nova Scotia declared:

> There was no precedent could be found in history for the transfer of so large a tract of territory by a Legislative Act, or by any cession made by one country to another.[23]

With the purchase of Rupert's Land and the North-Western Territory, Canada leapfrogged the United States and became the largest state on the North American continent, in terms of geography. The deal included all the fertile acres,[24] being those bounded by the 49th Parallel and the North Saskatchewan River, the Rocky Mountains and Lake Winnipeg and Lake of the Woods. That was almost all of the arable land in what would become the provinces of Manitoba, Saskatchewan and Alberta.[25] The huge annexation meant that Canada, too, was becoming a nation.

This one transaction now covered a total of 5,725,000 km^2 (2,210,000 mi^2), or 62,500,000 ha (1,414,400,000 acres), approaching three times the size of the Louisiana Purchase, and more than all the American acquisitions other than the territory seized by force from Mexico. While the United States had doubled its landmass with the Louisiana Purchase in 1803, Canada increased its size fivefold when it acquired Rupert's Land and the North-Western Territory in 1870.

Only three years after its own creation, Canada transformed itself "from a federation of equal provinces each . . . vested with the control of its own lands, into a veritable empire in its own right, with a domain of public lands five times the area of the original Dominion, under direct federal administration."[26] The West would begin a new life as a colony of Canada.

With the deal came the seeds of future strife. The Rupert's Land annexation transformed the political ownership of the vast North-Western Territory and, as with the earlier North American territory transfers, the deal-makers failed to consult with the Territory's inhabitants; their allegiance was presumed to go with the land. In 1870 that presumption would be costly.

With the terms settled, Macdonald and his government set about to take possession of their new acquisition. Legislation to provide for the provisional government of the North-Western Territory was enacted in June 1869. It provided for a lieutenant-governor and a council of up to 15 members. The date for the takeover (and the payment of the £300,000) was fixed for December 1, 1869. William McDougall, Minister of Public Works in Macdonald's cabinet, was designated to be the lieutenant governor. He would never take office.

With the acquisition of Rupert's Land nearly concluded, Macdonald turned his attention to the inclusion of British Columbia in Confederation, the real purpose behind the acquisition of the prairies. While the annexation was in process, he had been preparing the groundwork, nurturing the notion of Confederation among the English colonists on Vancouver Island and mainland British Columbia. The future was a hot topic of debate in the Pacific colonies as they suffered economic depression after the passing of the gold rush.

BRITISH COLUMBIA HAD PRETTY well concluded that it could not make a go of it alone and that joining either the United States or Canada had become inevitable. The two colonies of Vancouver Island and British Columbia had merged on November 19, 1866, but their union had not improved their nearly desperate financial situation. After the Alaska Purchase in 1867, British Columbia found itself sandwiched north and south by United States territory; an American destiny seemed almost inescapable. In fact, a number of residents organized a petition addressed to President Ulysses S. Grant in Washington requesting annexation by the United States.[27] Then, in 1869, the Canadian alternative received powerful support when, with the Rupert's Land issue settled, the new Liberal government of Prime Minister William Gladstone in London decided that it was in the interest of the Empire that all of British North America should be unified as the Dominion of Canada. Although many of the English colonists felt betrayed by their Mother Country, political sentiment began to move towards Confederation. At least with Canada they would still be in the British Empire.

British Columbians are sometimes thought to march to a different political drum. Certainly, there is some early evidence to support that belief. In March 1870, during debate on the terms of union with Canada, the British Columbia legislature decided it would be a good idea if Alaska could be included. One member thought the state of Maine would also fit well into the new Canada. So the motion, introduced by Amor de Cosmos, was amended and adopted, "that Canada purchase the territory of Alaska and the State of Maine."[28] No explanation was provided as to why it was thought the United States might be willing to part with Alaska, or Maine, even as Washington was still scheming to annex British Columbia itself as well as the western plains.

Amor De Cosmos (1825–1897) is one of the more colourful figures in Canadian history. A Nova Scotian by birth, William Smith moved to California during the Gold Rush in 1853. There, he set up a photography studio, and prospered taking pictures of the miners and their operations. The following year he petitioned the California State Assembly to change his name to "Amor De Cosmos," which he claimed (inaccurately) translated as "Lover of the Universe." He moved to Vancouver Island in 1858, and embarked upon a career as a journalist. After British Columbia entered Confederation in 1871, he became one of the first six Members of Parliament elected from the new province. He later served as the province's second premier, 1872–1874. In 1895 he was declared to be of "unsound mind," and died two years later.

On May 10, 1870, a three-man delegation left Victoria for Ottawa carrying British Columbia's proposed terms of Confederation. Dr. J.S. Helmcken, J.W. Trutch and Dr. R.W.W. Carrall travelled down the coast to the rival city of San Francisco, the western terminus of the Union Pacific Railway, completed just the year before, in 1869. As they journeyed eastward on North America's first transcontinental railroad, the Canadians little realized that they would be bringing home to British Columbia another great ocean-to-ocean rail connection.

Negotiations in Ottawa commenced on June 3, 1870. Macdonald had been taken seriously ill and the file was handled by Sir George-Étienne Cartier. The British Columbians were astonished when Ottawa's proposal not only met their demands, but exceeded them.

Both sides knew that the new province would require an overland transportation connection to Canada. British Columbia's modest suggestion of a coach road from Fort Garry and railway construction to commence in three years was quickly trumped by Ottawa's proposal of rail construction to commence in two years and to be completed in ten.

The generosity of the federal offer guaranteed its acceptance by the British Columbia legislature, but came near dooming it in Parliament where the Liberal, and some Conservative, members felt it was fiscal folly to underwrite the cost of building a railway through the uncharted Rocky Mountains.

British Columbia's contribution to the huge construction cost would be the grant of a 32.5-km (20-mi) belt on each side of the right-of-way. In return, Ottawa would pay the province an annual annuity of $100,000 in perpetuity (still dutifully paid in 2007).

The requirement that British Columbia provide a 65-km (40-mi) belt of land was dictated by Ottawa's conviction that "the Pacific Railway must be built by means of the land through which it had to pass." Not all the land the railway passed through was of equal value, the Rocky Mountains being valueless, at least for agricultural purposes. Consequently, very little of the British Columbia corridor was dedicated to the cost of the project and was eventually returned to the province. The deficiency was made up from the "fertile acres" on the prairies.

With the acquisition of British Columbia came approximately 30,000 members of at least 18 Indian bands.[29] Since none of the new province's lands were required for the railway, it was not thought necessary to deal with the matter of Aboriginal title, a decision that would later prove to be of incalculable cost.

IT WAS MUCH DIFFERENT in the North-West Territories. There all the lands through which the railway to the Pacific must pass were occupied by Indian bands. On the prairies the route sliced through the "fertile acres," valuable land that would be required to finance the project and to entice the settlers who would support the railway when it was built. A great deal of land was needed and Macdonald was prepared. Except for a special provision made for the Métis residents of Red River, Ottawa had retained ownership of all the lands in the North-West Territories, as needed for the "purposes of the Dominion." One large impediment stood in the way—the matter of the Indian title to the western plains.

The North-West Territories that were created after the Rupert's Land and North-Western Territory transfer to Canada was a vast area that extended from the Great Lakes to the Rocky Mountains, from the 49th Parallel into the Arctic Ocean and included the Arctic islands, and as far east as the Labrador Coast. On these lands lived thousands of Aboriginal peoples who held some undefined title or claim of ownership to those lands.

Whether by Right of Discovery or Conquest, the British Crown claimed original ownership of Rupert's Land and the North-West Territory, subject to such rights as had been granted to the Hudson's Bay Company by the 1670 Charter. The Crown also recognized that the Aboriginal residents held an undefined claim or title to the lands they traditionally occupied.

The Hudson's Bay Company's claim had been extinguished by agreement prior to the transfer to Canada. But, at the time of the transfer, London had made it plain that Canada received ownership of Rupert's Land and the North-Western Territory subject to whatever rights or title were properly held by the Aboriginal residents.

By Royal Proclamation of 1763, Great Britain had decreed that all surrenders of Indian lands must be negotiated by proper representatives of the Crown and reduced to writing—a treaty document. During the course of the next century, a number of treaties were signed with Indian bands in Upper and Lower Canada, the last and most westerly being the Manitoulin Island Treaty of November 3, 1862, negotiated by William McDougall, then Superintendent-General of Indian Affairs, the same William McDougall who would run afoul of Louis Riel at Pembina seven years later.

No Indian treaties had been negotiated in Canada since Confederation, and none west of Manitoulin Island, in Lake Huron. The Saulteaux/ Ojibway, the Cree, the Assiniboine and the Blackfoot Confederacy retained their title to the lands they occupied between Rainy River and the Rocky Mountains. Any railway to the Pacific would have to cross those lands.

Sir John A. Macdonald set about developing a process to negotiate clearance of the Aboriginal title to the western plains.

CHAPTER 4

Confederation Comes West

O N A COLD, BLUSTERY DAY IN LATE OCTOBER 1869, TWO
members of the government of John A. Macdonald met south
of Georgetown,[1] on the border of Dakota Territory and Minnesota, 240 km (150 mi) below the as-yet-unsurveyed Canadian–
American boundary. One was northbound and the other southbound, but
both were travelling the well-worn cart trail that wended more than 640 km
(400 mi) over the open prairie between Fort Garry, in Rupert's Land, and
St. Cloud, the terminus of the St. Paul and Pacific Railroad. The two statesmen stopped and conversed, leaning against a howling nor'wester, while their
horses snorted and stamped, their drivers checked harness and rigs, and their
companions stretched stiffened limbs and then quickly grew impatient to
continue their unpleasant journey. Although there was much of importance
to discuss, the bitter gale sweeping over the plains forced the two politicians
to quickly resume their travel. Little, in fact, passed between them, but what
was said, or not said and perhaps should have been, during that brief encounter, became the subject of a bitter debate that raged back home in Canada for
the next five years.

The business of both ministers had to do with the pending acquisition of
Rupert's Land. The largest real estate transaction in history was due to close
on December 1, 1869, less than six weeks in the future. The purchaser, the
two-year-old nation of Canada, lay on the other side of the Great Lakes, several hundred kilometres east of this unlikely meeting place on the American
plains, and had no easy access to its new territory. The old fur-trade routes
through the Great Lakes and Hudson Bay were not only slow and difficult but

were now closed for the season. Winter was about to descend. The American route was not only faster and easier, it was at this time of year the only practicable way to reach Red River from Canada.

The southbound traveller on that October day was The Honourable Joseph Howe, Member of Parliament from Hants, Nova Scotia, President of the Privy Council and soon to be Secretary of State for the Provinces in the Conservative government of Prime Minister John A. Macdonald. Howe was returning from what had been, considering the transportation of the day, a flying trip to Fort Garry, where he had made an assessment of the readiness of the community to join Confederation. Just recently appointed, Joseph Howe would be the minister responsible for the new North-West Territories.

The northbound traveller was The Honourable William McDougall, Member of Parliament for Lanark North, Ontario, and Minister of Public Works in John A. Macdonald's cabinet, but now designated to serve as the first Lieutenant-Governor of the North-West Territories when the transfer of Rupert's Land to the Dominion of Canada was formally consummated. McDougall was not travelling lightly. His entourage included several members of the provisional government planned for the Territories as well as family members. A train of more than 60 wagons and carts stretched impressively along the trail behind. Although the government he would lead was a provisional one only, the Lieutenant-Governor designate intended to reside and rule in Fort Garry for some time. But, as well as baggage and household furnishings, the transport carried 350 modern breechloading rifles and 30,000 rounds of ammunition, a late addition and a precaution in the event of resistance to the transfer of power to the Canadian government.

FORT GARRY, THE LARGE stone fortification of the Hudson's Bay Company at The Forks of the Red and the Assiniboine Rivers, the beginning village of Winnipeg a mile to the north, the long-established settlement of Point Douglas in between, and the French-speaking community of St. Boniface across the Red River together made up the centre of what was the Red River Settlement in 1869. From its well-chosen location, the Fort dominated the most important intersection of the western routes of the fur trade. Winnipeg was then a primitive collection of some 50 ramshackle buildings, most of log construction, with "grog shops as the principal feature of the place."[2] Settlement had evolved as parishes—individual communities—nearly 20 of which lay along the rivers; on the Assiniboine, the Catholic parish of St. François Xavier was 30 km (18 mi) west and Portage La Prairie some 70 km (45 mi) further.

Habitation also stretched down the Red River where the Protestant parish of St. Andrew included Lower Fort Garry, 30 km (18 mi) north of the Forks.

Scattered among the various settlements were about 12,000 residents, almost all of whom (92%) had been born in the North-West. French Métis totalled 5,757; English "half-breeds" (as English-speaking individuals of mixed blood were then known) were 4,083; and 1,565 were white.[3] It was not an insignificant body of citizens. By way of contrast, in 1870 Ottawa's population was about 20,000, and Victoria's was just 4,200.

Several thousand more Métis lived hundreds of kilometres west of Red River, out on the plains where they had followed the receding buffalo herds. *Hivernants*, they had trekked west from Red River, overwintered and established temporary communities in the valleys of the Qu'Appelle and Saskatchewan Rivers, and the coulees of the Wood Mountain uplands and Cypress Hills. Some of these settlements became permanent, like the longer-established Métis communities on the North Saskatchewan River in what 35 years later became Alberta.

The great grassland between Red River and the Rocky Mountains was the homeland of several Indian tribes: the Cree, the Assiniboine, the Gros Ventre, and the Blackfoot Confederacy. Also living on the northern plains were a number of Lakota Sioux, fugitives from the American Army after a bloody uprising in Minnesota in 1862. To the north, reaching into the great islands of the Arctic Ocean, and northeast to the Labrador Coast, all included in the new North West Territories, were Chipewyan, Dene, Inuit and more Cree. Many thousands of Aboriginal inhabitants were about to become residents of Canada. None were consulted, or advised of the pending transfer of their homelands and most knew nothing of the event. But a few on the prairies, closer to Red River, heard something of the transaction and raised questions.

The Red River system of land allocation had been imported from early settlements in Quebec, as well as New Brunswick where it could be found along the Miramichi River. River lots that provided only narrow frontages, usually about 60 m (200 ft) but extended 3.22 km (2 mi) back, allowed the settlers both water access and livestock pasture. A form of land registry was maintained by the Hudson's Bay Company but many lots were occupied by squatters who claimed ownership. The Métis feared that annexation with Canada would mean the loss of their land holdings. It was a sensitive issue. In 1861 the Hudson's Bay Company attempted to levy a fee against all lands in the settlement, threatening to enforce collection by selling the lots of those who failed to pay. Resistance was so fierce that the Company backed down but the attempt had not been forgotten. In 1869 the residents of Red River were alarmed to hear that the Hudson's Bay Company was selling all its lands; how that might affect their holdings was unknown. When surveyors from Ottawa arrived in the vicinity in the fall of 1869 and set about creating a new and strange pattern of land ownership, the Métis, not unreasonably, believed their fears were justified.

Sketch of Winnipeg, 1869. The "Canada" flag is flying over Schultz's store. *Archives of Manitoba N5398*

Fort Garry and Winnipeg might not have been much to look at in 1870, but together they formed the metropolis of the entire West. Fort Garry was the western headquarters of the mighty Hudson's Bay Company and the seat of the Governor and Council of the District of Assiniboia, the only government that existed between the Great Lakes and British Columbia. All the economic currents of Rupert's Land, and beyond, ran through this primitive community. The fur trade, the buffalo hunt, the remnants of the agricultural pioneering of the Selkirk Settlers, the import/export routes, by water to Fort York and latterly by land to St. Paul, all began and ended at the junction of the Red and Assiniboine Rivers. A discerning eye could detect that, before many years, Winnipeg would achieve its destiny as wholesaler to the vast, burgeoning West.

WHEN JOSEPH HOWE ARRIVED at Fort Garry in the first week of October 1869, he was the first federal cabinet minister to set foot upon what soon became Western Canada. He spent nine days in and about the settlement checking out local conditions and attitudes. In the manner of a long line of emissaries from Ottawa who would follow him, he had interviewed a few prominent residents, avoided some whose views were deemed to be suspect, and in turn been avoided by others. That these others held aspirations and intentions that ran directly contrary to his government's plans was, Howe would later claim, entirely unknown to him.

Howe was satisfied with his observations at Fort Garry and was on his way back to Ottawa to personally report his conclusions and advice to the Prime Minister. He had already sent Macdonald an account of his observations in a letter written at Fort Garry on October 16:

> I have been here a week, and shall leave for home in three or four days. I shall probably meet McDougall on the way, and will give him the benefit of my observations. For many reasons, my visit here has been opportune and useful. Any amount of absurd rumours were afloat when I came, and a good deal of strong prejudice had been excited. Some fools wanted to get up addresses, and have me speak at a public meeting. This I declined, but by frank and courteous explanations to leading men, who largely represent the resident population, I have cleared the air a good deal, and I have done my best to give McDougall a fair start. All will now depend on his tact, temper, and discretion.[4]

McDougall would claim that, out on the Minnesota prairie, Howe voiced little warning about difficulties that might lie ahead:

> He [Howe] stated that the people of Red River settlement were well disposed towards the Canadian Government, but from some circumstances, of which he would advise me by letter from Fort Abercrombie, the feelings of a certain section of the population had been excited, and that delicate handling would be necessary to allay them.[5]

Fort Abercrombie, a United States army post on the west bank of the Red River, lay just ahead of their meeting place and was likely where Howe intended to put up for the night. McDougall later told the House of Commons that Howe spoke only of the soil and the climate: "The former was excellent, but the latter was execrable. He [Howe] had not felt warm for three weeks."[6] The departing Nova Scotian had made it very plain that he did not envy McDougall his appointment to the North-West Territories.

As the two Canadian ministers separated, both must have believed that they were on the verge of great and exciting personal achievement. After all, as McDougall described it, they were engaged upon the acquisition—by *purchase*—and the political reorganization of a territory estimated to cover an area of 3,557,000 km² (2,210,000 mi²)—not an everyday occurrence. Indeed, it was a transaction without precedent in ancient or modern times. It should have brought glory to the two statesmen but instead it would blight both their futures. Each would find that their careers had peaked at the moment of their intersection on the Minnesota plains and their value to Prime Minister John A. Macdonald would soon end.

McDougall and his entourage carried on northward as far as Pembina, which he found to be a very rude frontier settlement. There, in the Custom House on October 31, 1869, McDougall met a delegation of Red River Métis who for three or four days had been awaiting the arrival of the new Lieutenant-Governor. They presented McDougall with the following edict, written in French:

> Dated at St. Norbert, Red River,
> this 21st day of October, 1869,
>
> Sir,
> The National Committee of the Métis of Red River orders William McDougall not to enter the Territory of the North West without special permission of the above-mentioned committee.
>
> By order of the President, John Bruce.
> Louis Riel, Secretary.[7]

It was useless for McDougall to sputter and protest. He was stymied. The designated Lieutenant-Governor of the North-West Territories, and through him the government of Canada, were thus denied entry to their intended domain and formally advised that their proposed takeover of the vast Rupert's Land did not meet with the approval of at least some of its new citizens. And, in a few more days they would learn that the dissidents were increasingly determined and aggressive.

On the same day that William McDougall in Pembina received his bleak news, Joseph Howe was ensconced in St. Paul, having arrived on October 30, twelve days out of Fort Garry. He had not written from Fort Abercrombie, but now Howe addressed a short letter to his plenipotentiary on the frontier:

> I was sorry not to have had an hour's chat with you, but what I had
> to say lies so obviously on the surface that your own judgment will

guide you correctly, even if it be unsaid. I found a great deal of misapprehension and prejudice afloat, and did my best to dissipate it.[8]

If Howe was warning McDougall not to expect a cheering populace and brass bands when he arrived at Fort Garry, this was very old news indeed by the time his letter made its way back up the trail to Pembina. McDougall had somewhat ignored the edict handed to him and taken quarters at the Hudson's Bay Company post just north of the border. But on November 2 he had been ordered out of Rupert's Land by armed Métis insurgents and early the next morning, before they had breakfasted, the Canadian party was forced to comply. Humiliatingly escorted across the unmarked border, they were unhappily camped on American territory, bereft of any decent accommodation.

McDougall's position was hardly the "fair start" Howe's letter to Macdonald had promised. And the intended Lieutenant-Governor might well wonder, as he later did, what "leading men, who largely represent the resident population," Howe had met with in Fort Garry.

None of the "leading men" interviewed by Howe represented the Métis population of Red River. Although he attempted to meet with Louis Riel and was refused,[9] there is no evidence that he connected with any other leader or representative of that portion of the population which was most concerned that their pending annexation to Canada might disregard the rights they had so recently won.

In fact, Red River contained several "leading men" who felt very strongly that the Macdonald government was seriously misjudging the temper of the residents and that a colossal blunder was in the making. William McTavish, the senior Hudson's Bay Company official in Fort Garry, and also the Governor of The Council of Assiniboia, a form of local government established by the Company, thought the Canadian government "would not find it child's play to rule the North-West. It had in the past been no easy place to govern, and under new rulers he thought the difficulties would increase."[10] Because he had been in the country 40 years and Governor for 15, McTavish not unnaturally thought his views should carry some weight. He had tried to impart them to the government when he had been in Ottawa earlier in the year, but had been ignored. Although the Governor was ill at the time, he was in Fort Garry during Howe's visit attending to his duties and the two did meet.

The Anglican Archbishop of Rupert's Land, Robert Machray, was so concerned that trouble was in the offing that he had written the Colonial Secretary in London warning that there was "imminent risk any day of some outbreak leading to the utter prostration of law and order."[11] Machray recommended that military units be sent to Red River.

Alexander Taché, Archbishop of St. Boniface, was equally convinced that Red River was approaching crisis because of the Métis fears of the coming new order. The eminent cleric was so concerned that, during the summer of 1869, on his way to Rome to attend an Ecumenical Council, he made a side trip to Ottawa "to inform the authorities of the position of affairs and the discontent which existed: 'I endeavoured to cause it to be understood that serious trouble would arise, but I did not succeed."[12] Taché spoke to Sir George-Étienne Cartier, Prime Minister Macdonald's Quebec lieutenant, but was told that "he knew it all a great deal better than I did, and did not want any information."[13] Taché was treated so rudely by Cartier that the man of God found himself incapable of further conversation with the politician. The Bishop was in Rome when Joseph Howe visited Fort Garry, but Father Jean-Marie-Joseph Lestanc, left in charge of the diocese, shared the Bishop's fears.

How was it possible for Joseph Howe to carry out his inquiries in Fort Garry during October 1869 without learning of such strong views held by such prominent citizens? We know that Howe and Lestanc did meet.[14] The priest certainly told the cabinet minister the unpleasant truth about the probable consequences of his government's intentions. Howe told the House of Commons that he spoke with both Machray and McTavish.[15] Both of those very concerned men would have seized such an opportunity to speak frankly of the tinder box that was Red River at that time.

Macdonald's minister in Fort Garry in October 1869 could not have escaped awareness of the most newsworthy event of the month in that community, one that was full of portent for him and the Canadian government.

The famous incident that is popularly regarded as being the ignition point of the Red River Rebellion occurred just 4 km (2.5 mi) out of Fort Garry on October 11, five days before Howe wrote his self-congratulatory letter to Macdonald. A band of some 18 French Métis, headed by Louis Riel, stepped upon the survey chain and stopped the work of a party of surveyors commissioned by the government of Canada. Riel told the surveyors to leave the country on the south side of the Assiniboine River. His reason? The Métis claimed ownership of those lands and they would not allow it to be surveyed by the Canadian government.

The next day, October 12, the survey crew chief, militia colonel John Stoughton Dennis, registered complaint in Fort Garry with the magistrate, Dr. William Cowan. Cowan and his fellow magistrate, Roger Goulet, promptly summoned Louis Riel to appear before them. Riel attended but firmly claimed "that the Canadian Government had no right to make surveys in the Territory without the express permission of the people of the settlement."[16]

Cowan then passed the problem up to Governor McTavish, and once more Louis Riel was called on the mat. And again the Métis leader was defiant: "Riel still persisted that injustice was being done by the Canadian Government, and utterly refused to withdraw from the position he and those under him had taken."[17] At this, the officials threw up their hands and Cowan turned to Father Lestanc. Cowan felt sanguine that since Lestanc was temporarily in charge of the diocese, he could, if so disposed, put a stop to the trouble at once. Lestanc, however, declined to pull the Canadian government's chestnuts from the fire. What followed became history.

These confrontations took place on October 12, 1869, in Fort Garry. The story that Riel and the local Métis had faced down the federal surveyors, the magistrates and the governor would have run through the little community like quicksilver. It could not have failed to come to the attention of Joseph Howe; he did not leave Fort Garry until six days later. It is beyond belief that the responsible minister and the only representative of the Canadian government there present would not have grasped some part of the significance of Riel's challenge of Ottawa's authority.

Through Reverend Lestanc, Howe had requested a meeting with Louis Riel before writing his letter to the Prime Minister.[18] Why did Howe want to meet Louis Riel? The 25-year-old Riel was not one of the "leading men" of Fort Garry. He had achieved some notoriety from his interference with the federal survey party and his defiance of Magistrate Cowan and Governor McTavish, but the prominence that would come to him as leader of the Métis resistance was still in the future. The conclusion seems inescapable that Howe knew much more about the storm about to descend upon Red River than he confessed to either Macdonald or McDougall.

For the young Métis to rudely reject the invitation of a federal cabinet minister was highly unusual and a serious affront. It was also a strong signal to Howe that something both unnatural and unpleasant was afoot in Red River.

Why did Howe think only "fools" would have him "speak at a public meeting"? The people of the settlement surely needed some explanation of what the new form of government would mean to them. A "clearing of the air" was obviously wanted. Why not provide it? This was how Donald A. Smith, emissary appointed by Macdonald, won over the residents three months later. By then the situation was desperate. Riel and his Métis had seized Fort Garry and established a provisional government. Smith, sent by Macdonald to investigate the cause of such serious discontent and to placate the population, addressed two open-air mass meetings, on successive days, in -30°C (-20°F) weather. More than a thousand turned out each day, listened carefully and accepted Smith's assurances that Canada's intentions were honourable.

Donald Smith's first biographer, Beckles Willson, was severely critical of Joseph Howe's failure to speak to the residents of Red River:

> Howe ... at least might have addressed himself directly to the mal-
> contents, to the settlers and pioneers and the ignorant half breeds. He
> might surely have uttered a word of explanation and conciliation to
> the people about to come under the rule of his Government; he might
> indignantly have repudiated the current suggestion that the inhabi-
> tants were being "bought and sold like so many cattle"; he might have
> declared the benevolent intentions of Canada and appeased the set-
> tlers by a promise of generous treatment in the matter of lands. Howe
> was an orator, and at the thunder of his eloquence the whole agitation
> might have died quietly away.[19]

Back in Parliament some months later, McDougall charged that Howe had contributed to the unrest in Red River. On February 21, 1870, Howe offered the House an unusual explanation. On his journey from St. Cloud to Red River in September, his party had reached Fort Abercrombie about October 1. There, he "heard these rumours and reports that Governor McDougall would not be allowed to enter the country. These were common in the bar-rooms and on the streets ... I believe it to be due to every one that the fact of meeting these rumours 315 miles [507 km] from Fort Garry should be known."[20] Yet, Howe said, he and his party met no obstruction on their journey to Red River "but were met everywhere with the utmost courtesy and rough hos-pitality."[21] And, Howe continued, "when I left Winnipeg there was not the slightest murmur which would lead me to believe that any armed opposition would be presented."[22]

Howe had expressed very different sentiments in a letter he wrote to a friend almost the very day he separated from McDougall out on the trail:

> My visit to Red River has utterly cured me of any lingering hope I may
> have had of a peaceable transfer. The only thing we can do now is to
> minimize the extent of the mischief. Trouble is bound to come either
> before or after, and if it were not for Mr. McDougall and the extent to
> which we have pledged ourselves, I would say let us keep our hands
> out of this Manitoba business into which we have been hurried and

which promises to jeopardise our Government and the interests of Confederation. It will be hard to pull out now, but if we see a chance of it we must do it. This country is not necessary to us, and at this stage it will only be a drag upon our energies and resources.[23]

That letter is dated October 23, 1869. Howe was five days on the trail out of Fort Garry. He reached St. Paul on October 30, seven days later. The letter might well have been written from Fort Abercrombie on the evening of the very day Howe and McDougall spoke out on the prairie. Howe did know that trouble awaited McDougall and gave him no warning.

JOSEPH HOWE WAS AN unfortunate choice as ambassador to the settlers of Red River, who were apprehensive that their rights would be lost in the proposed takeover by Canada. Howe had once held similar concerns as a leader of the anti-Confederation movement in Nova Scotia. Only a little more than a year earlier he had been in London unsuccessfully pleading with the British government to repeal the Union. He had then accepted the finality of Confederation and joined Macdonald's cabinet, but his background made him vulnerable to the charge that he advised the westerners that they might improve the terms of the deal by following the Nova Scotia example of protest.[24] And that charge was levelled by McDougall and his supporters.

Perhaps the 65-year-old Howe was not physically up to his task. In those days a cabinet appointment required the new minister to return to his constituency and be re-elected in a by-election, and Howe had encountered a vigorous contest back in Hants. Although too ill to participate in most of the campaign, the veteran was successful. When he won, on April 23, 1869, he "was too ill to be present to thank his supporters."[25] When he spoke in the House of Commons on May 13, Hansard noted that he "was rather indistinctly heard, his voice being apparently still weak in consequence of his recent illness." Heavy rains had made travel difficult in September 1869, and Howe and his party spent 22 days making their way up the trail to Fort Garry. Alexander Begg, a Fort Garry resident and a defender of Howe, acknowledged that "fatigued by his hard trip over the plains, and not being in good health at the time, Mr. Howe kept a good deal in his quarters at the hotel."[26]

The hotel was Emmerling's, and its Dutch George's Saloon was one of the two rude establishments in the village where the resident American annexationists gathered nightly. The United States consulate was quartered in the hotel. The place was a hotbed of anti-Canadian gossip and intrigue. Joseph Howe, no teetotaller, could not have escaped hearing much of the seditious discourse that filled the tiny bar. He knew that his government's plans were in jeopardy. Why did he fail to warn McDougall, and the Prime Minister? Only because McDougall so mishandled the situation before him as to bring a storm of censure down upon his own head did Joseph Howe escape a full measure of condemnation for so completely misreading, or failing to report, the real state of affairs in Red River.

At the time of his involvement in the North-West, Joseph Howe's health was leaving him. He had less than four years to live. Macdonald moved him out of his cabinet and appointed him Lieutenant-Governor of Nova Scotia on May 6, 1873. Howe served less than a month; he died on June 1, 1873.

AT PEMBINA, DAKOTA TERRITORY, in November 1869, William McDougall seethed in frustration. On the morning of November 3, he and his party had been mortified by their forced march back into the United States. The accommodation in the frontier settlement was not to McDougall's liking, and little wonder. There were only two houses and they were occupied by the postmaster and the customs officer. "All the others, four or five in number, are mere huts, and offered very poor accommodation for their present occupants."[27] The tents that had served on the trail would not suffice with winter threatening. McDougall finally rented a small farmhouse about a mile out of Pembina and ordered the construction of a larger building, which, of course, took some time. Settled in, he began to plan his course of action. He would be forced to rely upon his own judgement. There was no telegraph to Fort Garry. McDougall had to wait a week for instructions from Ottawa in response to his report of the fix he was in.

It was a humiliating situation. McDougall, 57, was a lawyer, a publisher, an editor, and a writer. First elected to the Legislative Assembly of the Province of Canada in 1858, he had been a delegate to the Charlottetown, Quebec and London conferences that brought about Confederation. Since at least 1857 he had been an advocate of the annexation of Rupert's Land and he and George-Étienne Cartier had formed the delegation to London in 1868 that negotiated the terms of transfer. On July 1, 1867, McDougall, a Liberal, had been included in Canada's first cabinet, a Liberal-Conservative coalition headed by Macdonald.

Later, with hindsight, it was easy to see that McDougall also had not been the best choice for what turned out to be a very difficult assignment.

Physically prominent, he was tall, erect, heavily-built, with a dark mane of hair and a luxuriant moustaché, but possessed of a tendency to be authoritative and demanding, traits that did not stand him in good stead on the frontier. As Minister of Public Works, McDougall had overridden good advice and ordered the surveyors into Red River, the surveyors whose work had been frustrated by Louis Riel.

In spite of Cartier's rude rebuff of Bishop Taché, stating that "he knew it all," the truth was that the Canadian government knew next to nothing about the huge western territory it was acquiring. Macdonald was frank in admitting this: "We are in utter darkness as to the state of affairs there; what the wants and wishes of the people are—or, in fact, how the affairs are carried on at all."[28]

For this very reason, Macdonald had prepared a provisional form of government for the new territory, one to fill the gap from takeover until Parliament could better consider what was needed, whatever that might be: "I am as ignorant as possible of the future mode of administering the affairs of that country."[29]

Macdonald's Act for the Temporary Government of Rupert's Land appeared to be a reasonable approach. The problem was that there had been no consultation with anyone at Red River and no effort whatsoever was made to explain the government's good intentions to the inhabitants. There was not only no marketing plan but, as if there was no need, there was no marketing whatsoever of the provisional plan among those intended to be governed. The patronizing assumption by the powers in Ottawa that they best knew what policies would serve the interests of the West was resented by the unconsulted residents of that West.

On the surface, Macdonald's *pro tem* approach to the design of the most suitable form of government for the western territories appeared reasonable and high-minded. In truth, however, the far-seeing politician fully intended that the expected tide of immigration would overwhelm the "wild people" of the settlement and transform it into a little Ontario, white, Protestant and tractable. "In another year, the present residents will be altogether swamped by the influx of strangers who will go in with the idea of becoming industrious and peaceable settlers,"[30] he explained to an Ontario Member of Parliament.

That letter was written on October 14, 1869. Three days earlier Louis Riel and his Métis had shut down the federal survey. Macdonald and his government were not only out of touch with public opinion in the West, they were unaware that their plans were being overtaken by events.

The total lack of accurate information about the provisional government William McDougall was bringing to Red River created a great opportunity for those who wished to derail the Canadian plan.

UNIMPRESSED BY MCDOUGALL'S EARLIER accomplishments in Canada, a number of Americans delighted in his discomfiture. The activists in Minnesota and Dakota Territory who coveted the vast territory to the north for their own burgeoning nation saw in the Canadians' troubles an opening for their cause.

The most prominent and determined of those American annexationists was Alexander Ramsey, a Minnesota Republican who, from 1849 to 1881, held office as Territorial Governor, State Governor, United States Senator and Secretary of War in the cabinet of President Rutherford Hayes. Before his appointment as Minnesota Territorial Governor in 1849, Ramsey, a lawyer, had served two terms as Congressman from Pennsylvania and knew his way around Washington. He had visited Red River in the fall of 1851 and promptly fell in love with the potential of the region. "It was like giving Commodore Perry a peek at Japan," one historian put it. During almost all of his public life thereafter Ramsey never deviated from his dream of wrapping "Western British America" in the American flag.

Ramsey meant business. On December 9, 1867, he introduced in the United States Senate a resolution calling for Canada and Great Britain to cede to America a huge slice of the continent. Ramsey had his eye on everything west of a line stretching roughly from Lake of the Woods north to the Boothia Peninsula in the Arctic all the way to the Pacific Ocean. That would effectively cement Montana Territory and Minnesota up against Alaska. For this the United States would buy out the interest of the Hudson's Bay Company for $6 million and assume $2 million of the public debt of British Columbia. Ramsey's resolution was only five days after William McDougall placed before the House of Commons in Ottawa the government's resolution initiating the transfer of Rupert's Land to Canada.[31]

The Senator from Minnesota was unable to mobilize much support from his colleagues on any of the several occasions he attempted to enlist them to his mission, but he did not confine his campaign to Washington. And he did not serve alone. Ramsey enlisted James Wickes "Saskatchewan" Taylor, who shared, even exceeded, Ramsey's passion. As early as 1861, Taylor had promoted the use of troops to seize "Fort Garry and the immediate district thence extending along the valley of the Saskatchewan to the Rocky Mountains."[32] He thought "1,000 hardy Minnesotans, aided by the French, American and half-breed population" could do the job in a couple of months.[33] Ramsey and Taylor made an effective partnership. In 1867 Ramsey sent Taylor into Red River as a special agent for the United States.

Another Ramsey confederate was Oscar Malmros. The Minnesota Senator succeeded in having an American consulate established in Red River and Malmros was appointed to head the mission. In August 1869, while William McDougall was preparing to lead his provisional government into Red River, Malmros set up the American Consulate in Emmerling's Hotel in Winnipeg. Ramsey now had established two listening posts at the centre. He would soon do even better.[34]

In spite of his lack of success in the Senate, Ramsey knew he was not the only statesman in Washington with an eye on the great North-West. In fact, the United States made no secret of its desire to wrap its border around Rupert's Land, or all of Canada for that matter. In June 1869, Hamilton Fish, President Ulysses S. Grant's Secretary of State, proposed to the British ambassador in Washington that Great Britain should cede all of Canada to the United States as reparation for damages to American shipping during the Civil War by vessels built in British shipyards.[35]

Fish kept himself fully informed on the situation in Red River but as the problems of the Canadian government deepened he took an unusual step to ensure that his information was even more timely and accurate. On December 30, 1869, he appointed "Saskatchewan" Taylor as a secret agent on the ground in Fort Garry to investigate and report full details of the revolt as well as all aspects of the territory and its inhabitants. Taylor's two-year-old commission as an agent for the United States at Red River was thus elevated to a special mandate with instructions to remain under cover: "All your proceedings under this commission are to be strictly confidential, and under no circumstances will you allow them to be made public. This injunction includes the fact of your appointment."[36]

The information that flowed out of Red River to Washington was timely and valuable. Malmros claimed to have found among the inhabitants a strong distaste for union with Canada.[37] He also thought that money would win the day for American annexation and suggested that $100,000 would do the trick.[38] "Saskatchewan" Taylor thought $25,000 might be enough.[39]

Money was available, and in much larger sums than $100,000. Bishop Taché reported that American interests had offered Riel and his colleagues more than $4 million, plus arms and men, to bring Red River over to the United States.[40] If an inducement so huge was in fact proposed, it was surely kept very quiet, or perhaps not taken seriously, for that was wealth beyond imagination in the Red River settlements of 1869–70. When Donald Smith arrived, he was able to undermine much of Riel's support by the judicious application here and there of bribes totalling the far more modest sum of $2,000. Yet, corroboration of the existence of the offer Taché described, although not necessarily of the amount, came years later from the Archbishop of St. Paul.[41] And, 20 years after the events, Donald Smith learned that Minnesotans had been ready "to place a very large sum of money at the disposal of Mr. Riel and his friends, upwards of half a million dollars, with a view to having the country annexed to the United States."[42]

Malmros and Taylor, once inserted into Red River, were valuable assets to Washington. But already on the ground, at Pembina and with a connection into the Red River Métis community, was a far more valuable agent, a colourful frontier pioneer, one Enos Stutsman.

Stutsman would be a remarkable character in today's easier times, but on the rough fringe of civilization he was truly extraordinary. Born without legs, using short crutches for locomotion, he was an attorney, a politician, a land speculator, a journalist, a member of the Dakota Territorial Legislature, a master of intrigue and a *bon vivant*. His biographer describes him as "a man of limitless energy, charm and ambition . . . great spirit and courage."[43] A contemporary description by one of his countrymen is more fitting to the evil genius McDougall came to believe the Pembina attorney to be:

> He is a sharp and scheming Yankee; smooth and captivating in conversation; genteel and temperate in habits; daring in deeds; ambitious of fame, and susceptible of mischief . . . in activity, pluck and acuteness he stands head and shoulders with the shrewdest of men.[44]

Stutsman had come to Pembina, the only port of entry in Dakota Territory, in 1866 on his appointment as a special customs investigator. Three years later, when McDougall arrived, the little attorney was practising law, living with the postmaster and scheming to see Rupert's Land annexed to the United States. There were other Americans who were conspiring to see the great territory of Rupert's Land fall into the United States, but no one was closer to the centre of the action in Red River than Enos Stutsman.

Stutsman was well acquainted with the Red River settlements. Just the previous year, in the courts at Fort Garry, he had successfully defended a Portage La Prairie settler on a charge of manslaughter. A year later that case brought him a new client—Louis Riel.

Enos Stutsman (no date). *Courtesy of the Elwyn B. Robinson Department of Special Collections, Chester Fritz Library, University of North Dakota OGL 1243-93*

It is not known just when Louis Riel and the Pembina lawyer first came together, but Stutsman seems to have been present at early organizing meetings of the dissident Métis group in August and September 1869.[45] Certainly, he was deeply involved in the Métis planning by the time McDougall arrived at Pembina and was handed the famous ultimatum. On November 2, when the band under arms ordered McDougall out of the country, they first consulted with their lawyer, then proceeded to McDougall's quarters, and then reported back to Stutsman.[46]

Stutsman wielded a sharp pen and used it to exacerbate McDougall's discomfort. This letter in the St. Paul *Daily Press* describing the plight of the Lieutenant-Governor designate in Pembina is attributed to him:

A king without a kingdom is said to be poorer than a peasant. And I can assure you that a live Governor, with a full complement of officials, and menials from Attorney-General down to cooks and scullions, without one poor foot of territory, is a spectacle sufficiently sad to move the hardest heart.[47]

Louis Riel had great need of a lawyer during the fall of 1869. He was embarked upon a desperate course of action that required every atom of legal justification that could be brought to bear. Born into and raised in a Red River Métis family, Riel had been advantaged by almost seven years of classical and religious education in a Montreal seminary that he suddenly abandoned in the spring of 1865, a decision perhaps provoked by the death of his father. At loose ends, the young Riel attempted a legal career and was briefly employed in the office of a prominent Montreal lawyer. There he likely learned just enough to appreciate the value of legal advice, particularly when embarked upon such a perilous mission as the overthrow of established authority.

ON NOVEMBER 2, THE day the Métis ordered McDougall out of Rupert's Land, they seized Fort Garry, the Hudson's Bay Company fortress that commanded "the geographical and strategical centre of the Red River settlement."[48] Riel then proceeded to organize a convention of the residents of Red River, a first step in his plan to create a Provisional Government for the territory that could, with some claim to legitimacy, negotiate with the government of Canada for better terms of admission. During this time, Stutsman, as well as several other American annexationists, was "admitted to the secret councils of Riel."[49] Most galling to McDougall, stalled at Pembina, was the fact that, on the authority of Louis Riel, Stutsman was issuing passes through the Métis barricades to those wishing to enter Red River. The passes were addressed "To The Commanding Officer of the Patriot Army."[50]

McDougall was in a fix, but he should not have been entirely surprised. He later claimed that the notion of proceeding early with a survey had come from Prime Minister Macdonald, and that he, McDougall, had objected, knowing it to be an unpopular and dangerous course and had succeeded in having the size of the survey greatly reduced.[51] Colonel J.S. Dennis and his survey crews had been sent to Red River in July and immediately upon arrival encountered serious opposition. In August, Dennis twice wrote back to Ottawa advising against continuing with the survey. McDougall was not in Ottawa when the warnings were received, but he surely had been aware of them on September 22 when he submitted to cabinet a recommendation to adopt a system of township survey that had been proposed by Dennis. The proposal was adopted. On October 4, after McDougall had departed for Fort Garry, his department wrote Dennis, authorizing him to "proceed with the surveys on the plan proposed."[52] That letter could not have reached Red River by October 11 when Louis Riel stepped into the picture.

But McDougall had encountered more recent warnings. According to Joseph Kinsey Howard, a Riel biographer,[53] McDougall had been told at St. Cloud that trouble awaited him. John H. O'Donnell, a medical doctor also en route to Fort Garry, had met James J. Hill of St. Paul, a man soon to be well known to Canada as a member of the Canadian Pacific Railway syndicate. Hill told O'Donnell that McDougall would never see Fort Garry and the doctor relayed that information to the Lieutenant-Governor designate. McDougall shrugged off the news. He shrugged again when, two days up the trail, O'Donnell received the same prophesy from two travellers just out from Fort Garry. By then McDougall was so committed to his mission as to be well beyond the point of no return.

Nomenclature for the areas which comprised parts of British North America, and later Canada, can be confusing and inconsistent. However, generally speaking, the "North-Western Territory" refers to those areas in the northwest which were not part of Rupert's Land, but were still administered by the Hudson's Bay Company. The "North-West Territories" refers to the vast expanse of British North America which was not given provicial status after the transfer of the Hudson's Bay Company lands to Canada in 1869–1870. The spelling of the region's name was modernized as time went by, and since Saskatchewan and Alberta became provinces in 1905, it has generally been known as the "Northwest Territories."

During November 1869, while McDougall fumed impotently at Pembina, 100 km (60 mi) north a determined struggle was under way for the minds and hearts of the 12,000 residents of Red River. Almost all of the French Métis were with Louis Riel, as were most of the English-speaking "half-breeds"—a third of the settlement—but they were more circumspect. Of the 1,500 whites, those from Ontario strongly favoured union with Canada. Hudson's Bay Company personnel, unhappy to learn they were not to be included in the distribution of the sale proceeds of Rupert's Land, were not disposed to be helpful to the transaction. The Quebec clergy, unconvinced that the interests of their people would be well served by Canada, were sympathetic to the Métis.

The Indians were a wild card, particularly the Sioux. Although they had been living peacefully since they escaped Minnesota in 1862, they had not lost their fearsome reputation. Would they take advantage of the situation and turn to murder and plunder?

The settlement was ripe for intrigue, and there was plenty on hand. As he consolidated his political position, Riel more and more became the key. Would he lead his people into Canada, after dictating better terms of admission? Or would he succumb to the blandishments of the Americans? Or, would he attempt an independent state? American supporters openly advocated independence as a first step to joining the United States.[54]

At Pembina, McDougall's mind was fixed on December 1, 1869, which was fast approaching. That was the date established for the formal transfer of Rupert's Land to the Dominion of Canada—or at least it had been when he left Ottawa and he had received no notification of any change in those plans. That date was also when his appointment as Lieutenant-Governor of the North-West Territories took effect.

Or did it? The commission, dated September 29, 1869, which McDougall received in Ottawa before he headed west, stated that he was appointed "on, from, and after the day to be named by us for the admission of Rupert's Land

... into ... Canada."[55] That meant that there could be two significant dates, the date of the actual transfer of the real estate, and the later date "named for the admission" of that real estate into Canada by Imperial Order in Council. Thus, the appointment would not take effect until both dates had arrived. McDougall, a lawyer, was aware of the second date condition but allowed himself to ignore its significance.

McDougall convinced himself that when December 1 came, and Rupert's Land was transferred to Canada—while he, the legitimate government, remained sequestered out of the country, in Pembina, in the United States—the North-West Territories would fall into anarchy. Worse, the vacuum thus created would enable the Riel insurrectionists to claim a mantle of legality and assume the government of the settlement.

That logic led McDougall to a bizarre series of actions that not only doomed his personal future but jeopardized the intended annexation of the great territory to the Dominion of Canada.

CHAPTER 5

The Crisis in Red River

THE PRISONER OF PEMBINA WAS KEEPING IN TOUCH WITH the Canadian faction in Red River who were working against Louis Riel. They easily convinced McDougall, who desperately wanted to believe them, that on a word from him the settlement would rise in protest and put down the insurrectionists for whom, they claimed, there was little real support.

On that fateful December 1, McDougall, betting that the transfer and Order in Council would proceed as planned, took two stupendous rolls of the dice, with calamitous consequences. First, he drafted and issued a proclamation in the Queen's name announcing that Rupert's Land was now part of Canada and that he was the designated representative of the new government. Then he commissioned the survey chief, Colonel J.S. Dennis, to raise and arm a force to put down the insurrection. Dennis took the proclamation into Red River, had it printed up and distributed while he attempted to muster enough men to face down Riel's several hundred armed Métis.

After dark on December 1, McDougall and a small party crossed the border back into the disputed territory where he read his proclamation into the teeth of a blizzard before retreating back to Pembina. His bizarre behaviour provoked the poison pen of Enos Stutsman:

> On the 1st instant, at the hour of 10 p.m., while the mercury indicated 20 below zero, and Old Boreas was on a bender, seven lonely pedestrians, fully armed and equipped, might have been (and were) seen stemming the blast, and, as best they could, shaping their course in

the direction of the oak post marking the international boundary—their brows contracted with firm resolve to do or die.

The intrepid little band consisted of Governor McDougall and his entire official staff. His Excellency was armed with the Queen's proclamation, the Dominion flag, and two pointer dogs. The fat Attorney-General felt quite secure with an old-fashioned Colt, that had not been discharged for fifteen years, while the Collector of Customs (of a more practical turn of mind), thinking that the aforesaid Boreas would prove the most formidable enemy he should encounter very wisely armed himself with a well charged flask of "forty rod"—hence, while the other members of the party were shivering like frightened puppies—the festive Collector felt as comfortable as could be expected.

On nearing the boundary a skirmish line was advanced—to reconnoitre—and finding all save the firmament, clear, a charge was sounded, and, on double-quick, the brave little band dashed across the line into much coveted territory; whereupon the Dominion flag was unfurled, and, in defiance of the blinding storm and the inky darkness, Mr. McDougall, in the name of that government, assumed formal possession of the great Northwest Territory. After which the entire command, elated with victory, returned in triumph to their quarters on Uncle Sam's side of the international boundary.

And *thus* was accomplished the conquest of the Northwest Territory."[1]

ON THE EVENING OF December 1, while this comedy was being played out on the bitter western plains, Prime Minister Macdonald was with his family in their Ottawa home, warm and comfortable by his fireside, reading a Trollope novel, serene in the knowledge that he had solved the problem presented by Louis Riel and the Métis simply by delaying the transfer of Rupert's Land.[2] The insurrection, Macdonald believed, did not amount to much and, if left alone, would whimper to an end. It was important only not to fall into the trap of providing Riel with confrontation.

But there was one niggling worry at the back of Macdonald's mind—McDougall. The Prime Minister feared that McDougall "will not go the right way about settling matters."[3] It was a good worry.

The luckless William McDougall, nominated as the first Lieutenant-Governor of the North-West Territories, was prevented by Louis Riel from entering the Red River Settlement in November 1870. *Archives of Manitoba N12586*

McDougall's preposterous gamble failed utterly. As he soon learned, Macdonald had arranged to delay the transfer of Rupert's Land until he could be assured of quiet possession. Thus, there was no significance to December 1 and McDougall's actions, questionable as they were, had been deprived of any shred of legitimacy. All he had accomplished, as Macdonald pointed out, was to extinguish the last vestige of Hudson's Bay Company rule and legitimize Riel's actions in forming a provisional government. And the few Canadian recruits who had rallied to Colonel Dennis found themselves imprisoned in Fort Garry under the command of Louis Riel.

The situation in Red River was now deteriorating daily and the planned acquisition of Rupert's Land was in real jeopardy. Well-intentioned or not, the Canadian government had sowed with nescience and arrogance and now reaped failure and humiliation. The only real settlement in the North-West Territories was under the firm control of a band of insurrectionists whom Macdonald and his cabinet had considered to be wild and illiterate nomadic hunters barely above the savage state. Their revolt could spread across the Western Plains. And the Americans, who Macdonald knew had long coveted his western extension, would now attempt to capitalize upon his plight.

Canadian concern for the American interest in the North-West Territory had been publicly expressed as early as 1857. A Canadian submission to the British parliamentary committee, inquiring into the condition of the Territory under the administration of the Hudson's Bay Company, worried about securing the region "against the sudden and unauthorized influx of immigration from the United States" or even "violent seizure or irregular settlement."[4]

Although Macdonald was alert to the danger, at least for the time being he was unable to do much to protect against what he described as the "Yankee wire-pullers, who are to some extent influencing and directing the movement from St. Paul."[5] That was an accurate assessment.

Enos Stutsman was certainly one of the "Yankee wire-pullers," although operating from Pembina, not St. Paul. Early in November, after McDougall had been evicted, he recognized just how propitious conditions at Red River were and wrote directly to President Ulysses S. Grant:

> I should be deficient in my duty both as an official and as an American citizen if I did not solemnly call your attention to the situation as it exists in this part of the Continent of North America and the opportunity it offers for instant and decisive action on the part of the Government of the United States. At this moment this country is properly without any government, and a large number of its inhabitants—the majority, I believe,—are favorably disposed to its annexation by the United States.[6]

American sympathizers of the rough-and-ready type common to the frontier gathered at drinking establishments with names worthy of dime novels, "Dutch George's" and "O'Lones Red Saloon" in Winnipeg, the "Robbers Roost," "Dead Layout" and "The Ragged Edge" in Pembina. They spotted opportunity when Riel suppressed the *Nor'Wester*, a paper published by the Canadian faction. Plans were hatched and *The New Nation* appeared, with Enos Stutsman's financial backing, an American editor and an undisguised pro-annexation policy. Riel issued a "List of Rights" demanded by the people of Red River. It had been prepared by Stutsman and had "a distinctly American flavor."[7] The List contained 14 items, five of which the attorney had announced earlier to the St. Paul newspaper. Then Riel followed up with a proclamation of his own, a "Declaration of the People of Rupert's Land and the Northwest" in which he announced the establishment of his provisional government. It immediately became known as "Riel's Declaration of Independence."[8]

The air was thick with proclamations. Even the Hudson's Bay Company issued one. From Ottawa came one in the name of the Queen. Dated December 6, it stated that "certain misguided persons in Her Settlements on the Red River, have banded themselves together to oppose with force" and "Her Majesty . . . believes those men, who have thus illegally joined together, have done so from some misrepresentation."[9] Amnesty was promised if everyone would peaceably disperse and return to their homes.

That was too naïve a solution for the crisis in the West. More would be needed. But in Ottawa, Prime Minister Macdonald and Joseph Howe struggled against a lack of up-to-date information from Red River. Reports from McDougall were a good five days in transit, and he was still in Pembina. The eminently advisable decision to delay the takeover of the territory having been made, it was far from clear what should be done to quell the disturbance at Fort Garry.

LIST OF RIGHTS

1. That the people have the right to elect their own Legislature.

2. That the Legislature have the power to pass all laws local to the Territory over the veto of the Executive by a two-thirds vote.

3. That no act of the Dominion Parliament (local to the Territory) be binding on the people until sanctioned by the Legislature of the Territory.

4. That all Sheriffs, Magistrates, Constables, School Commissioners, etc., be elected by the people.

5. A free Homestead and pre-emption Land Law.

6. That a portion of the public lands be appropriated to the benefit of Schools, the building of Bridges, Roads and Public Buildirgs.

7. That it be guaranteed to connect Winnipeg by Rail with the nearest line of Railroad, within a term of five years ; the land grant to be subject to the Local Legislature.

8. That for the term of four years all Military, Civil, and Municipal expenses be paid out of the Dominion funds.

9. That the Military be composed of the inhabitants now existing in the Territory.

10. That the English and French languages be common in the Legislature and Courts, and that all Public Documents and Acts of the Legislature be published in both languages.

11. That the Judge of the Supreme Court speak the English and French languages.

12. That Treaties be concluded and ratified between the Dominion Government and the several tribes of Indians in the Territory to ensure peace on the frontier.

13. That we have a fair and full representation in the Canadian Parliament.

14. That all privileges, customs and usages existing at the time of the transfer be respected.

All the above articles have been severally discussed and adopted by the French and English Representatives without a dissenting voice, as the conditions upon which the people of Rupert's Land enter into Confederation.

The French Representatives then proposed in order to secure the above rights, that a Delegation be appointed and sent to Pembina to see Mr. Macdougall and ask him if he could guarantee these rights by virtue of his commission ; and if he could do so, that then the French people would join to a man to escort Mr. Macdougall into his Government seat. But on the contrary, if Mr. Macdougall could not guarantee such rights, that the Delegates request him to remain where he is, or return 'till the right be guaranteed by Act of the Canadian Parliament.

The English Representatives refused to appoint Delegates to go to Pembina to consult with Mr. Macdougall, stating, they had no authority to do so from their constituents, upon which the Council was dissolved.

The meeting at which the above resolutions were adopted was held at Fort Garry, on Wednesday, Dec. 1, 1869. Winnipeg, December 4th, 1869.

The resolutions in the "List of Rights" were adopted at Fort Garry on December 1, 1869. *Archives of Manitoba N5402*

What was clear was the enormity of McDougall's blunder. At the end of December, Macdonald expressed his exasperation in a letter to a confidant:

> McDougall has made a most inglorious fiasco . . . he has ingeniously contrived to humiliate himself and Canada, to arouse the hopes and pretensions of the insurgents, and to leave them in undisputed possession until next spring.[10]

That much was clear. Until its water routes opened up, Canada could not move a military force into the West except through the United States, and that was out of the question. So long as Washington hoped, and expected, that the insurrection at Red River would result in the Territory falling into its hands, it would never permit such a transit.

By late January Macdonald was convinced that the Americans were doing more than merely observing the situation at Fort Garry:

> It is quite evident to me . . . that the United States Government are resolved to do all they can, short of war, to get possession of the western territory and we must take immediate and vigorous steps to counteract them.[11]

But, in the grip of winter, Macdonald was literally frozen out of Red River. He could only send more emissaries to the settlement, and he did—goodwill ambassadors in the persons of the Very Reverend Jean-Baptiste Thibault and Colonel Charles de Salaberry, both of whom were well-known and respected in the settlement. Both were instructed only to persuade the local inhabitants of the merits and good intentions of Ottawa's plans. Thibault and de Salaberry arrived at Pembina on Christmas Eve.

In the meantime, Macdonald met Donald A. Smith, the senior officer of the Hudson's Bay Company in Canada. Much impressed, the Prime Minister decided to send Smith out to Fort Garry and to give him some real authority. He appointed Smith as a Special Commissioner to inquire into and report upon the troubles at Red River, and to propound once more the merits of Ottawa's policy. But Smith was also charged with finding a way through the impasse and, in doing so, to use his own judgement. Because Macdonald admittedly knew so little of the true state of affairs in the West, he was unable to provide much direction. The license thus awarded would return to Macdonald results he would find nearly unpalatable.

Perhaps the most useful tool the Prime Minister provided to his new agent was the suggestion that he employ bribery as a method of weaning away Riel's support. Macdonald might not have known much about the men of the West, but he was confident that they would possess the universal frailty of mankind. They could be had.

CHAPTER 6

The Birth of Manitoba

ONCE AGAIN THE FROZEN PLAINS OF MINNESOTA WITnessed a meeting of Canadian statesmen on the trail between Fort Garry and St. Paul. This one took place on December 21, 1869, about two o'clock in the afternoon of a very wintery day. While the encounter two months earlier had been south of Georgetown, this one was just north. Both parties were travelling by horse-drawn sleighs with canvas covers to provide some protection against the bitter cold.

Heading south in full retreat was the party of William McDougall, the intended viceroy of Rupert's Land, defeated and dejected. Following the failure of his proclamation, McDougall had swallowed the last of his pride and written Louis Riel directly, seeking a meeting "without the knowledge or privity of certain American citizens here who pretend to be *en rapport* with you."[1] The letter also threatened the imposition of military rule. But when Riel ignored him, McDougall knew he was finished. He packed up and headed home. Whether or not he knew at that time, his future was very bleak.

Heading north were two men whose careers were very much in the ascendancy, Donald A. Smith and Dr. Charles Tupper. Smith was on the mission assigned to him by the Prime Minister. Tupper was on a private mission. His daughter was married to Captain Donald Cameron, a member of McDougall's party, and still in Pembina. Tupper was determined to rescue her from the wild frontier.

Both the northbound men later served as Canadian High Commissioner in London, England. Smith rose to become the Lord Strathcona we see in the famous photograph driving the last spike of the Canadian Pacific Railway at

Craigellachie, British Columbia, in 1885. Tupper, already a parliamentarian, was, like Joseph Howe who preceded him up this trail, a Nova Scotian. But Tupper, premier from 1864 to 1867, defeated Howe, took their province into the Union and became a Father of Confederation. In 1896, Tupper, by then knighted, would succeed to the office of prime minister, albeit very briefly, the last of the Conservative prime ministers before the 15-year reign of Sir Wilfrid Laurier.

On that bitter December day it was the turn of William McDougall to lean into the eternal wind of the plains and provide a report on the situation he had left behind him. Standing beside the trail, knee-deep in snow, the vanquished Lieutenant-Governor was understandably not fully gracious to his northbound countrymen. He was even less so when he learned that Smith was a senior officer of the Hudson's Bay Company which, McDougall believed, had done so little to assist him in the transfer of power to Canada. When Smith presented McDougall with instructions from Joseph Howe, and requested that he "consult and cooperate with that gentleman [Smith] in order that, if possible, some peaceful solution may be found of the difficulties which obstruct your entrance to the new territory,"[2] McDougall had had enough. He bowed to Smith and carried on to St. Paul, a hot bath, clean clothes, a decent meal and a warm bed.

ALTHOUGH HE MIGHT HAVE misplayed the cards he had been dealt, McDougall and his colleagues had been through an ordeal. A.N. Richards, who was to have been Attorney General in McDougall's government in Red River, told Dr. Tupper that day on the trail, perhaps exaggerating only slightly, that he had not had his clothes off for two months and lived in hourly peril of losing his life.[3]

When McDougall arrived in St. Paul, and was at last free from the influence of Enos Stutsman, the Canadian revealed the extent to which he had become obsessed with the diminutive attorney. Displaying judgment not much improved since his wrong-headed conduct on December 1, McDougall spoke to the press and blamed pretty much the entire Red River Rebellion on Stutsman:

> From first to last, Col. Stutsman, claiming to be an American, has been the head and front of the rebellion. He is Riel's advisor and plans every move that Riel makes. It was Stutsman who counselled the Governor's capture and the seizing of Fort Garry. It was Stutsman who wrote the declaration of independence which was issued, and who vises every document that is put forward in Bruce's or Riel's name, and it was Stutsman who set on foot the many glaring falsehoods calculated to arouse and inflame the passions of the French half-breeds engaged in the rebellion.[4]

When McDougall returned to Canada, "very chop-fallen and sulky," as Macdonald described him, he was equally intemperate when he blamed the Fort Garry fiasco on Joseph Howe.

The armament McDougall had carried into the West became a problem. Concerned that the rifles and ammunition might fall into rebel hands, Ottawa requested Washington to move them to Fort Abercrombie and the United States Army complied.[5]

Donald Smith turned out to be Macdonald's saviour. He was a man of intelligence, tact and courage who was the match of Louis Riel in the manipulation of public opinion in Red River. Although he encountered a substantial sentiment in favour of annexation to the United States, and was kept under virtual house arrest in Fort Garry, Smith was able to get his message, and his money, out to the influential men of the community.

Smith's arrival at Fort Garry in the evening of December 27, 1869, was none too soon to place a spoke in the wheels of the American annexation movement which had been gaining strength and prestige. Two weeks later, on January 12, the American flag was raised over Emmerling's Hotel in Winnipeg and "Bob O'Lones Saloon resounded with the jubilant noise of Americans drinking toasts to annexation."[6]

But Smith's work soon produced results. Riel's support weakened. When Smith was able to speak over Riel's head to the large assemblies on January 19 and 20, he achieved real progress in selling the merits of Canada's position. The meeting determined to elect 20 delegates from each of the French and English-speaking communities, who would meet in convention "to decide what would be best for the welfare of the country."

The convention met, agreed to negotiate with the Canadian government, settled upon another "List of Rights" as their bargaining position, and chose three delegates to travel to Ottawa.

On January 26, the American flag over Emmerling's Hotel came down. It did not fly again in Red River.[7]

All was proceeding smoothly until mid-February when the Canadian faction decided to accelerate matters by taking up arms against the Riel forces. Although open conflict was avoided, some prisoners were taken by Riel's men and the atmosphere of peace dissipated. Riel, who to this point had displayed admirable surefootedness, then, in the words of his pre-eminent biographer, "committed the greatest blunder of his career,"[8] and "set his foot upon the path which led not to glory but to the gibbet."[9]

Sketch of the execution of Thomas Scott, by R.P. Meade. *Archives of Manitoba N5953*

On March 4, 1870, by the order of Louis Riel, head of the Provisional Government of Red River, Thomas Scott, an Ontarian and an Orangeman, arrested and tried on a charge of "insubordination," was executed by firing squad. Riel brushed off the fervent entreaties of Donald Smith, Reverend Lestanc, and the Protestant leader, George Young, and insisted that the execution be carried out. That decision would haunt Riel to his own grave. Prime Minister John A. Macdonald's ultimate reaction to Scott's death in turn brought consequences that reverberated down through the decades to the present.

While Donald Smith was burrowing into the pro-American sentiment at Red River, the activists in the United States continued their campaign. In January, Senator Ramsey of Minnesota met with President Ulysses S. Grant and Secretary of State Hamilton Fish about the situation in Red River. On February 1, Ramsey introduced another resolution in the United States Senate; this one, while calling only for American mediation in the Canadian troubles, was clearly a front for the annexation movement.[10] Also that month, Fish had the United States ambassador in London interrogate the Deputy-Governor of the Hudson's Bay Company on the attitudes of the Company's employees respecting the political future of Rupert's Land.[11] As the summer of 1870 approached, and the Canadian government was on the verge of a solution to its problem in Red River, the State Department in Washington still confidently believed that not only Rupert's Land, but British Columbia as well, could yet be snared.[12] In fact, a petition had come in from British Columbia requesting annexation by the United States.[13]

American public opinion was firmly behind the Red River settlers who were seen to be patriots in a situation similar to that of the Thirteen Colonies who had successfully thrown off the yoke of British rule in their own War of Independence. Louis Riel was even compared to George Washington.[14] But the administration of President Grant declined to make any overt moves to assist the Métis rebels, even declining to send into Red River the funds that Malmros and "Saskatchewan" Taylor recommended. Any such action was thought to be unnecessary; the insurrection would succeed without any direct intervention by Washington that would offend the British lion. The Macdonald government in Ottawa, separated from Fort Garry by hundreds of miles of inhospitable terrain, was considered to be incapable of putting down the rebellion. "In short, the consensus was that Canada was clearly unable to enforce its power and authority on the prairies. The Dominion was believed powerless to act against the settlers at Red River."[15] It was not a shallow assessment of the Canadian problem.

IN OTTAWA, WHEN PARLIAMENT convened in February, William McDougall, no longer a cabinet minister but still the Member for Lanark North, furiously attacked Joseph Howe, blaming him for the uprising in Red River and the failure of his mission as Lieutenant-Governor of the North-West Territories. Then appeared two of the most remarkable documents in Canada's political history.

The first was a 69-page pamphlet entitled *Red River Insurrection—Hon. Wm. McDougall's Conduct Reviewed*. Dated 1870, it was printed by John Lovell, a mainstream Montreal publisher of the day, but was otherwise anonymous. But it could not have been compiled without the complicity of Joseph Howe. The pamphlet examined poor McDougall's actions throughout the entire sorry episode, commencing with his department's survey instructions in July 1869, and concluding with references to documentary evidence dated as late as May 1870.

McDougall retaliated in kind. He published eight open letters to Howe, then collected them in a pamphlet almost equal in length to Howe's. Sixty-eight pages in all, it was printed by Hunter, Rose & Co., a prominent Toronto publishing house, and bore the turgid title *The Red River Rebellion, Eight Letters to Hon. Joseph Howe, Secretary of State for the Provinces, etc., In Reply to an Official Pamphlet*. McDougall made no pretense at anonymity. His pamphlet stated: "By Hon. Wm. Macdougall [*sic*] C.B., Late Minister of Public Works, and Commissioned to be Lieutenant-Governor of Rupert's Land and the North-West Territories."

Both pieces were high-class political invective, with McDougall's perhaps the most vicious. Canadians were treated to the spectacle of two Members of Parliament, who had both been ministers in the same cabinet (and one still was a minister), abusing each other publicly and in print. Prime Minister Macdonald had already found that McDougall had served out his usefulness. Small wonder that he soon reached the same conclusion about Joseph Howe.

Louis Riel (middle row, third from left) and Council in 1870 (photo by J. Penrose). *Archives of Manitoba N5396*

Macdonald overlooked very little in his campaign to neutralize the Riel-led Métis insurrection in Red River. He knew that Georges-Étienne Cartier, the leader of his Quebec wing, had seriously snubbed Archbishop Taché the previous summer. No matter. Taché was needed to calm the troubled waters in Red River where his stature made him invaluable. But Taché was in Rome attending the Vatican Council. No matter. Call him back. And they did. Ottawa could reach Rome by telegraph, but not Red River.

And Taché came. He swallowed his resentment at the treatment accorded him by Cartier and returned to Canada where he placed himself at the service of Macdonald's government. The Bishop reached Ottawa in early February 1870 and sat down with the duly apologetic Cartier and other members of the administration. The amnesty that had been included in the proclamation of December 6 was updated and renewed. Armed with this, Taché set out for the West.

Once again Ottawa suffered from lack of information and understanding as to the true state of affairs in Red River. The situation was much more desperate than Macdonald and Cartier even supposed. They had not contemplated that there might be loss of life, particularly in the manner of the death of Thomas Scott.

Archbishop Alexandre Taché, c. 1890 (photo by Bennetto & Co.). *Archives of Manitoba N3959*

Bishop Taché reached Red River on March 9, 1870, five days after Riel's execution of Scott. The entire community anticipated the arrival of the highly regarded cleric. The delegates chosen to negotiate in Ottawa had delayed their departure in case Taché brought news that would affect their mission.

Taché found the citizens of Red River to be calm—surprisingly so—following Scott's execution. While brushing aside all pleas for mercy, Riel had explained that the execution was necessary to gain Ottawa's respect. Ottawa did not yet know of the event, but the stratagem, if that is what it was, had created the desired effect in the western settlement. It was as if no one dared to provoke the Métis leader.

Macdonald now had four agents on the ground in Red River: Thibault, de Salaberry, Smith and Taché. (Tupper had returned, with strong criticism of Donald Smith whom he judged to be cowardly. That assessment turned out to be very wrong.) Unknown to the prime minister, three of his agents had gone over to Riel, or at least accepted that his demands had some merit, and the fourth (de Salaberry) was ineffective. Thibault and Taché in particular were in sympathy with the Métis fears of losing their way of life to a Protestant invasion from Ontario. Smith, very much a realist, quickly understood that Canada would have to grant major concessions if Rupert's Land was to peacefully join the new nation. His assurances that the delegates from Red River would be well received in Ottawa went far beyond his instructions from Macdonald.

A peaceful resolution of the Red River problem was the only one open to Macdonald. He was working on the military option, but that meant assistance from Great Britain, and London insisted upon a political settlement with the disaffected westerners. An all-Canadian force was impractical and might well invite intervention from the United States. It was essential that the British demonstrate to Washington that they maintained a strong interest in their North American territories. Troops would be sent to Red River, but not to conquer, merely to restore order and establish federal authority.

The three delegates, or "commissioners," chosen by the convention headed east on March 23 and 24. They were Abbé Ritchot, a priest from St. Norbert, "Judge" John Black, a Hudson's Bay Company employee who was the Recorder at Red River, and Alfred Scott, a bartender from O'Lone's Red Saloon. They carried with them the list of "terms and conditions" that had been agreed upon by the convention as the basis for negotiations with Ottawa, with some additions that had been privately tailored by Riel. Without the knowledge of the convention, Red River was now demanding provincial status and a separate school system, the last item contributed by Bishop Taché.

Ontario became a hotbed of agitation fomented by several self-styled "refugees" from Red River, who provided colourful and distorted descriptions of events there—in particular, the "murder" of Thomas Scott. Demonstrations were organized and resolutions adopted demanding suppression of the revolt. Vengeance was called for. The public debate deteriorated as religious and racial lines were drawn; it flowed into Quebec. The battle became Orange Protestant Ontario versus French-Canadian Catholic Quebec with Louis Riel as the centrepiece. Sir John A. Macdonald had a new tiger by the tail. It would concentrate his attention for the rest of his career and create divisions that plague Canada still.

Negotiations got off to a troublesome start when the commissioners reached Ottawa. Angry citizens had initiated a private prosecution that succeeded in having Ritchot and Alfred Scott arrested for the murder of Thomas Scott. Macdonald was embarrassed but could do little more than retain counsel for the two accused. The charges were cleared away for lack of evidence, but Abbé Ritchot was not amused.

Macdonald, an old pro, had expected to have an easy time of it with the Red River delegates who, after all, were on their first political mission. When he thought the delegation would be headed by Riel himself, Macdonald gloated, "If we once get him here, he is a gone coon."[16]

But Abbé Ritchot was no pushover. Labelled a "fanatic" by some, he had been the early inspiration and brains behind Riel. A trusted advisor of the Métis, he was determined to win some protection for his people against the tide of immigration that he knew would follow when Rupert's Land became Canada West. The other two commissioners, Alfred Scott (who "preferred the bar at the Russell Hotel to the negotiation table"[17]), and Judge Black, were quite willing to defer to Ritchot's leadership.

Ritchot spent 75 hours in hard-nosed bargaining with Macdonald, Cartier and Joseph Howe, and came away with almost all his (and Riel's) demands. Provincial status was won, even though the size, at not quite 36,250 km^2

(14,000 mi^2), with a population of fewer than 15,000, might have been Lilliputian, as the Opposition described it when the Manitoba Act came before the House of Commons. Macdonald was forced to concede a province, but ensured that it was as small as he could manage.

Washington kept its eye on the Ottawa negotiations. "Saskatchewan" Taylor followed the Red River delegates to the capital, stayed in close communication with them, and relayed progress reports to Hamilton Fish. Taylor's sources were so impeccable that his almost daily bulletins to Washington are today considered to be the most reliable and accurate account of the bargaining between the westerners and Macdonald's government.[18] He erred only on the side of optimism; not until summer did the United States fully concede that Canada had won the coveted western territory. Even then Taylor continued in his quest. There might be other methods of bringing the Canadian prairies into the American fold. If the western economy could be drawn south, its territory would naturally follow.

The United States might well have realized its ambition to secure Rupert's Land. It had succeeded in annexing Oregon, even though that territory had been first occupied by British and Canadian traders. But the writ of the Hudson's Bay Company, even though headquartered in London, ran strong through Rupert's Land. And Canada was the accidental beneficiary of three events that together paralysed Minnesota, the prime and natural mover into the British North-West: the financial panic of 1857; the American Civil War of 1860–65 that bled away her young and adventuresome men; and the Sioux Uprising of 1862 that rolled back her frontiers.[19] By the luck of historical timing, when Prime Minister Macdonald made his move to incorporate Rupert's Land in his nation building, his American opposition was so crippled as to be almost unable to prevent him.

Canada benefited from two other factors that impeded the American desire for the North-Western Territory. Washington, and the American public, believed that Ottawa was so blocked by geography from its western region that it could not maintain effective control. Rupert's Land would naturally fall into the United States and little or no direct intercession would be required.[20] And, still recovering from the ravages of the Civil War, the United States was in no position to provoke a serious confrontation with Great Britain, no matter how great the temptation.

With its provincial status, Red River had won four Members of Parliament, two Senators, separate schools, official equality of the French and English languages, and suitable financial guarantees. In lieu of provincial control over lands, 566,580 ha (1,400,000 acres) were to be set aside for the Métis and their children. As well, all their existing titles or squatters' rights would be recognized.

Back in Red River, the bargain was ratified by the Provisional Government which registered its "consent to enter into Confederation on the terms entered into with our delegates."

But Macdonald came away with what he wanted, and needed. The immense fertile lands stretching from Red River to the Rockies remained under Ottawa's ownership. The new province failed to gain control even over its tiny realty. As Macdonald explained to Parliament, Ottawa required the western lands to obtain repayment of the $1,460,000 purchase price and to carry out its program of expansion to the Pacific. The New West would be expected to pay its way in Canada.

There was also the matter of a general amnesty to those involved in the insurrection. That had been delivered by Bishop Taché in March. Abbé Ritchot was satisfied that he had confirmed it in Ottawa. The Provisional Government's consent was based on the understanding that such an amnesty was in effect. But the extension of that amnesty to Louis Riel would be the subject of controversy for years to come.

THE TRANSFER OF RUPERT'S Land and the North-Western Territory to Canada now went forward. The official and effective date became July 15, 1870.

The military expedition departed for Red River under the command of Colonel G.J. Wolseley. Hamilton Fish got in one last lick by denying the support vessels passage through the canal at Sault Ste Marie. The order was lifted when London protested, pointing out that no military supplies were involved, and reminding Fish that the United States had enjoyed free passage of armed cutters through the Welland Canal.

On August 24, 1870, Wolseley and his troops arrived at Fort Garry to find it open and abandoned. Louis Riel had waited in the Fort until that very morning, expecting to hand it over to Wolseley, but, upon hearing reports that his life was in danger, the Métis leader fled. It was the right decision. The Provisional Government evaporated and its leader sought refuge in the United States. The promised amnesty did not materialize in spite of Taché's best efforts and Riel was a fugitive. But he would return to the North-West Territories and bedevil Macdonald.

The arrival of the troops turned Red River into turmoil. Disappointed at finding no defence to overcome, and freed from the weeks of deprivation on the trail from Ontario, discipline disappeared and they descended, as soldiers sometimes do, to drunkenness and debauchery. Worse, the militia element—volunteers from Ontario who had accompanied the British regulars—also turned to vengeance on the Métis. In this they were joined by some of the civilian population whose bigotry had been suppressed during the period of control by Riel and the Provisional Government. There were threats, bullying, beatings and even death. A period of serious discontent settled upon the little colony and worsened as the expected immigrants from Ontario arrived. The French-speaking Catholic Métis understandably wondered what had been achieved by the Rebellion.

Perhaps the improvements were hard to see through the brutality and oppression suffered by the Métis, but the Manitoba Act had vastly bettered the position in Canada of the Red River settlements that occupied the 36,250 km² (14,000 mi²) of the new province. But what about the other 5,687,208 km² (2,196,000 mi²)? After all, the total territory transferred to Canada on July 15 was 5,723,458 km² (2,210,000 mi²).

The North-West Territories entered Canada in 1870 on the same terms as had been intended in 1869. The Temporary Government Act was dusted off and re-enacted and applied to that huge region that extended from Portage la Prairie[21] to the Rocky Mountains and from the yet unsurveyed 49th parallel to the Arctic Ocean, and east of Red River as well. The former Rupert's Land that became the North-West Territories extended from Red River to Lake Superior and then across what is today northern Ontario and Quebec to the Labrador border.

Except for later extensions of the borders of Manitoba, no further provincial status would be granted to the North-West Territories until the formation of the provinces of Alberta and Saskatchewan in 1905. Ottawa retained control over the resources of the West until 1930.

Ottawa's 1870 legislation contained one new element: the Lieutenant-Governor of Manitoba would also be the Lieutenant-Governor of the North-West Territories. That would not be William McDougall. The Honourable Adams G. Archibald, of Nova Scotia, arrived at Fort Garry on September 2 to take up his new offices. He would prove to be a fitting selection.

In the fall of 1870, "Saskatchewan" Taylor again appeared on the scene at Red River, but now he was no longer undercover. The United States had not given up on the North-West Territories. A new, more subtle approach had been developed, based on the widely held belief that it would be prohibitively expensive to construct an all-Canadian railway through the terrain north of Lake Superior. If Canada could be persuaded to accept as its rail connection to Manitoba the American lines already in use, perhaps the Northern Pacific Railroad then being built could be sold as a joint route to the Pacific. Or, at least, the Northern Pacific might be constructed so close to the border that it would, with feeder lines, drain away so much economic activity of the Canadian West that the hearts and minds of the inhabitants, and then their political allegiance, would soon follow. It was the Golden Age of railways and the belief that whosoever controlled the trackage and the rolling stock would rule the world was not far in advance of reality.

Taylor was appointed United States Consul at Winnipeg on September 14, 1870. He arrived at his new post on November 12 and promptly established an excellent relationship with Lieutenant-Governor Archibald, whom he found to be remarkably in sympathy with the American railway concept. A highly competent, determined man, Taylor continued his work at Winnipeg until his death in 1893.

The conflict at Fort Garry and Winnipeg in 1869–70, since mis-named the "Red River Rebellion," or the "First Riel Rebellion," passed into history. But more and more it is looked back upon as the first skirmish in the continuing struggle of the prairie West against its real or perceived political and economic subjugation by "the East." The disaffection of western residents (and voters) with the domination of central Canada, now known as "Western Alienation," can be dated back to the Red River protest against the presumptuous agenda of Prime Minister John A. Macdonald and his government. Perhaps Louis Riel was merely the first prairie politician, and one more conventional than some of the many who followed him, such as "Bible Bill" Aberhart of Alberta.[22] More than any other region of Canada, prairie grievances have spawned new political movements—the Progressives, the United Farmers, the Co-operative Commonwealth Federation (CCF/NDP), Social Credit, Reform/Alliance. Perhaps this was inevitable "since the system that Sir John A. Macdonald and the early Canadian governments sought to impose on the prairies was an Ontario imperialism masquerading as federalism, aimed at making use of the land in ways most favourable to central Canadian interests."[23]

In any event, dissension in the West, first heralded by Louis Riel, has not yet been stilled.

CHAPTER 7

Twin Scourges: Smallpox and War

A S THE DECADE OF THE 1870S OPENED, PRIME MINISTER SIR
John A. Macdonald and his government were so fully engaged by
the tumultuous events at Red River that they were oblivious to
conditions and events even further out in the new hinterland.

But west of Fort Garry the great plains of the new nation seethed with life—
and death. A great deal of death. On the prairies that stretched from the Red
River to the Rocky Mountains the new decade opened onto a period of strife,
tumult and excitement, and a revolution of its own. A storm of change—cultural, economic, demographic and ecological—would sweep over the western grasslands, more change by far in just 10 years than in the previous 10,000.

Strife, of course, was no stranger to the plains. The Cree and Blackfoot,
Ojibway, Gros Ventre, Assiniboine and Sioux (as the Dakota, Nakota and
Lakota nations were then collectively known)—all the Aboriginal residents—
could not remember a time when they had not been in conflict, usually over
territorial dominance.

But in 1870 a new form of conflict was introduced to the northern plains,
warfare initiated by a modern military invading and uprooting the Aboriginal
peoples residing upon those lands. More savage and deadly by far than inter-
tribal battle, this conflict had been raging for years in the American territories,
but now it was moving closer to Canada. The effects would sweep over the
border into the Canadian plains and occupy much of the attention of the new
wardens of the West in Ottawa.

On January 23, 1870, on the Marias River, near present-day Shelby, Montana, about 65 km (40 mi) south of the as-yet-unmarked southern boundary

of Canada's new western estate, units of the United States Army came upon a sleeping village of Peigan. The military expedition consisted of six companies of troops commanded by Major Eugene M. Baker who held instructions to strike a band of Peigan, under the leadership of Mountain Chief, suspected of attacking white settlers. Baker had with him two guides, Joe Kipp and Joe Cobell.

The village Baker and his troops came upon belonged not to Mountain Chief but to Chief Heavy Runner, a band so peaceful and friendly that they carried a safe-conduct certificate. The camp had been struck by smallpox and many of the Peigan were confined to their lodges, suffering horribly. Joe Kipp immediately recognized the camp as Heavy Runner's but Major Baker angrily ignored his warning. Baker, a notorious drunk and intoxicated on this morning, was so determined to attack that he put Kipp under armed guard and threat of death if he made any attempt to warn the sleeping village.

The troops surrounded the camp and opened fire. Heavy Runner ran frantically towards the soldiers waving his safe-conduct papers but was shot dead in his tracks. The encampment and its occupants were almost totally destroyed: 173 Peigan were killed, 120 men and 53 women and children. Another 140 women and children were taken prisoner.[1] The prisoners were later "released unharmed" but, suffering from smallpox and without adequate clothing or food, many died walking the 145 km (90 mi) to Fort Benton through the bitter January weather.

The event, soon dubbed the Baker Massacre, set off conflicting emotional reactions. The killing was generally applauded by Montana residents but condemned by Easterners. The Army proclaimed the attack "a complete success" and smothered the official reports. Even so, the *Chicago Tribune* reported that some government spokesmen regarded the Massacre as "the most disgraceful butchery in the annals of our dealings with the Indian."[2]

Mountain Chief and his band, the intended victims, and many other Peigan, were quick to depart Montana Territory for safety and sanctuary well north of the border, a move that would have serious consequences before the year was over.

The only casualty among Major Baker's troops was a Canadian. Walton McKay, a 24-year-old private, was shot from his horse by a young Peigan as the troopers mopped up the village.[3]

The American method of managing their Aboriginal inhabitants was coming into full view of Canada when its green governors were just beginning to think about a policy to deal with their own Indian population on the western plains. Because of the difficulties at Red River over the winter of 1869–70, it was well on into the year 1870 when Ottawa was finally able to establish its presence in the North-West Territories.

Lieutenant-Governor Adams Archibald arrived at Fort Garry in early September 1870, just a month behind the military expedition that ensured he would be able to properly assume his official responsibilities. Immediately he was confronted by an emergency that required instant action, if, indeed, there was any effective action that could be taken.

While the earlier events at Red River consumed all attention, an epidemic of smallpox had been raging throughout the plains west to the Rocky Mountains and was now working its way down the valley of the Saskatchewan River towards the settlements. The community was full of dread. Both by legend and fact the lethal reputation of the disease was well known.

Archibald's authority as Lieutenant-Governor was yet not clear; he did not even possess a copy of the Temporary Government Act under which he was appointed. He could not act alone and he had no Council because no members had yet been appointed. In any event, there was little effective defence Archibald could mount. The Hudson's Bay Company, just recently back in possession of Fort Garry after its seizure by Riel's Provisional Government, had only a limited supply of vaccination serum.

Smallpox had ravaged the continent since it had been carried to North America by the European "discoverers," and the western plains had not escaped. The Native population had little or no immunity to the disease and their death rate had been devastating. Smallpox arrived in the western hemisphere after 1492 with Columbus and those who followed him. Extreme mortality was immediate. When Columbus landed, Hispaniola (the island now occupied by the Dominican Republic and Haiti) held a population now estimated as high as 8 million. By 1535, little more than 40 years later, that population had been reduced to zero.[4] In 1520 the disease reached Mexico with the Spanish invaders. There it required less than a century to cut a people of 20 million down to a remnant of just 1.6 million.[5] The pandemic continued, decimating the inhabitants of Central America and the Andes. The empires of the Aztecs and the Incas were destroyed, leaving an open field to the Spanish Conquistadores. In the words of geographer William Denevan, it was "the greatest demographic disaster in the history of the world."[6]

Disease raced among the Native inhabitants of North America so far ahead of its European carriers that little is known about the devastation that had been worked long before the arrival of witnesses and recorded observations.

Today anthropologists challenge the traditional view that the continent north of the Rio Grande was mostly empty territory prior to European arrival, containing at most only a sparse Aboriginal population. Estimates of the pre-1492 numbers of Native residents now range from a low of 7 million to a high of 18 million. North America was not a virgin land; it was empty only because it had been rendered so by imported disease:

> Europeans did not find a wilderness here; rather, however involuntarily, they made one . . . The so-called settlement of America was a *re*settlement, a reoccupation of a land made waste by the diseases and demoralization introduced by the newcomers.[7]

One of the earliest European invaders was the Spaniard Hernando de Soto who landed in Florida in 1539. For four years he led an expedition through the southern states and into the Mississippi valley where he encountered a large number of settlements; some were small cities complete with moats and earthen battlements. But 150 years later, when the next European visitor, the Sieur de la Salle, paddled down the Mississippi headed for New Orleans he found not one native village for 320 km (200 mi). Where 50 settlements existed at the time of de Soto's travels, only 10 remained when La Salle arrived, and some of these were inhabited by recent arrivals.[8]

Some of the early epidemics were continent-wide. An onslaught of smallpox occurred in 1752 and "finally spread to the western Indians and attacked many tribes over the entire continent."[9] Much more is known about the three last pandemics that struck the great plains and northern Canada, the first in 1780–82, the second in 1837, and the third in 1869–70, the one that gave concern to Lieutenant-Governor Archibald.

The 1780–82 plague "raged over the upper Missouri, the Saskatchewan and Columbia River and Great Slave Lake region, paralysing the fur trade for two years."[10] When the disease invaded, it raced across the West:

> Smallpox appears to have spread most rapidly in the grassland area, as might be expected considering the greater mobility of these tribes by that date. Having been first picked up by the Sioux, it was transmitted by them to the trading villages along the upper Missouri River. From these centres it quickly diffused in all directions. In the Canadian prairies, it was first reported in the South Saskatchewan River area near the Red Deer River in the month of October. By November it extended to the forks of the Saskatchewan, then continued spreading to the north and east. In December it broke out in the Cumberland

Lake region and by the end of January it erupted in The Pas area of Manitoba.[11]

The epidemic of 1780–82 had first broken out near Boston in 1774, during the American War of Independence, according to historian Elizabeth Fenn, who gives us a collection of observations on the impact of the disease in the western interior of Canada:

> The North West Company trader John Macdonnell believed that the outbreak carried off three-fourths of the natives near Portage La Prairie. He also stated that thanks to "wars with their neighbours, the small Pox of 1780/81 and other misfortunes," the Cree population had dropped by two-thirds. The Peigans told David Thompson that the epidemic "swept away more than half of us." Of the Atsina, or Gros Ventre who inhabited the Saskatchewan River country, Alexander Henry said simply, "The Small Pox carried off the major portion of them." In the same region, the sick Indians encountered by Mitchell Oman in the autumn of 1781 "allowed that far more than one half had died." Oman himself was more precise: "From the number of tents which remained it appeared that about three fifths had perished." Farther north among the Chipewyans, Samuel Hearne pushed the estimates still higher, suggesting that smallpox had "carried off nine-tenths of them." Tomison likewise informed Cocking at York Factory "that of the several Tribes of Assinnee Poet (Assiniboine) Pegogomew and others bordering on Saskachiwan River he really believed not one in fifty have survived." Umfreville, who may well have overheard Tomison's statement, echoed his estimate: "It was computed that scarce one in fifty survived it." Of the plains Indians, he guessed "that at least one half of the inhabitants were swept off."[12]

Fenn thinks that some of those estimates might be exaggerated, but admits that "in the few instances in which actual numbers or ratios exist, small glimpses reveal a loss of life that was indeed staggering."[13] She then quotes William Tomison, the Hudson's Bay Company factor at Cumberland House, on the Saskatchewan River: "We have buried Upwards of 30 for Which Number there is only two recovered." Fenn points out that this reflects "a case fatality rate exceeding 93 percent."[14]

Tomison turned his post into a hospital but still lost his Indian trappers. "My Debtors are all Dead," he mourned in 1782, and sent men to collect the beaver robes from the Cree tents that had been emptied by death.[15] Tomison was a hard and unloved man. He was running a trading post and beaver was beaver. Another trader, farther north, described "the Indians lying dead about the Barren Grounds like Rotten Sheep, their Tents left standing and the Wild Beasts devouring them."[16] Edwin Thompson Denig, an observant trader at Fort Union, was told by Assiniboine elders that they lost about 300 lodges of their people during the 1780–82 onslaught; they called it their "greatest first misfortune."[17]

David Thompson, who spent the winter of 1787–88 with the Peigan near the foothills, was told of how the calamity struck that tribe after they raided a camp of Snakes. It was a death camp: "There was no one to fight with but the dead and the dying, each a mass of corruption." The Peigan plundered the lodges, but with their loot carried away the dreaded disease, an adversity beyond their experience. "We had no belief that one man could give it to another, any more than a wounded man could give his wound to another. One third of us died, but in some of the other camps there were tents in which every one died."[18]

Although the mortality of the 1780–82 epidemic was "staggering," equal, or perhaps even greater death struck the Indian population between the Missouri and the Saskatchewan with the two later epidemics.

In 1837 the paddle-wheel steamer, the *St. Peter*, set out from St. Louis on its annual trip up the Missouri River to provision the trading posts and collect another season's yield of furs and robes. One of the *St. Peter*'s passengers was Major Joshua Pilcher, the United States Indian Agent at St. Louis. Others were Jacob Halsey and his wife. Halsey was on his way to assume command of Fort Union, the trading post at the mouth of the Yellowstone River.[19]

On June 19 and 20, the *St. Peter* stopped at Fort Clark, on the west bank of the Missouri, about 95 km (60 mi) north of present-day Bismarck. Fort Clark served a community of Mandan Indians, a sedentary tribe whose earth-lodge homes were a powder keg to the smallpox spark.

Three weeks after the *St. Peter* had departed upriver, the first Mandan died—smallpox had been unwittingly delivered along with the year's supplies. Six months later the village of 1,600 had been reduced to fewer than 100, some accounts (including Pilcher) say as few as 30. No matter. The Mandan, believed to have numbered 15,000 a century earlier,[20] now ceased to exist as a recognized society. The few survivors were taken in by other tribes, the Minnetare and Arikara.[21]

Before the *St. Peter* reached Fort Union, its next port of call, Captain Bernard Pratte, Jr., knew he had death aboard. Jacob Halsey, and then his wife, came down with the disease shortly after leaving Fort Clark. Halsey survived, his wife did not. Quarantining Halsey on arrival at Fort Union was unsuccessful; the garrison was soon infected. And in spite of the best efforts of Halsey and his men, the Assiniboine, who were accustomed to trading at the fort, made contact and the disease was loosed again.[22] But, unlike the Mandan, the Assiniboine were riders of the plains and as they fled in terror they carried death with them across the prairies and into their ancestral homeland, much of which lay in today's provinces of Saskatchewan and Manitoba. Yet their scattering was their best hope. Some achieved isolation and escaped. Although not destroyed as the Mandan were, the Assiniboine never recovered their prominence as a tribe. Dispirited, their faith in their gods destroyed, many abandoned their traditional homelands and trekked hundreds of kilometres westward, to the foothills of the Rocky Mountains. There they commenced life anew and became known as the Stoney.

Fort Union was then the head of steamboat navigation on the Missouri. Shallow-draft keelboats serviced the trading posts farther upstream. The keelboat from Fort McKenzie, on the Marias River, a tributary of the Missouri, had been waiting at Fort Union for the *St. Peter*. The crew attempted to escape the disease by loading quickly and heading back upriver. No luck. The boatmen pulled ashore and sent word on to Fort McKenzie that some of their crew were infected. The commander at the fort, Alexander Culbertson, properly directed the keelboat to stay put. But Culbertson had a larger problem. Five hundred lodges of Blackfoot were camped outside his fort waiting to commence summer trading. Culbertson made a valiant effort to explain to the assembled Blackfoot the terrible danger they faced by exposure to the disease.

The Blackfoot would have none of it. They lacked any understanding of smallpox, and to them the concept sounded suspicious, a white man's swindle in the making. They had come to trade and the Blackfoot demanded that the trade goods be produced, or they would go down river and get them. Culbertson capitulated, but only after delivering a stern warning of the risk if trading went ahead.

The determined Blackfoot ignored the warning and were not deterred even when two members of the keelboat crew died horribly. But they did trade quickly and hasten their departure. None of the Blackfoot appeared ill when they left and Culbertson hoped for the best as he and almost his entire garrison came down with the disease.

But in the fall, Culbertson, now recovered, faced a new dilemma. He was running a trading post and all summer not one Indian customer had appeared.

He went out into the Blackfoot country. At Three Forks, the beginning of the Missouri River, he found his explanation; a large village without sound:

> Presently they smelled the stench and then "hundreds of decaying forms of human beings, horses, and dogs lay scattered everywhere among the lodges." (The animals had been killed either sacrificially or in the frenzy of the deathlust.) They found two old women alive, too weak to travel with those who had fled, crawling demented among the corpses. And out from the village, on the prairie, on toward the mountains, every so often the rotting body of a Blackfoot who had died as he fled from his angered gods.[23]

Thus the epidemic, which had first entered the plains through the Assiniboine on the east, now attacked via the Blackfoot on the west. Few records exist of the extent of mortality on the Canadian side of the unmarked border, but there is little reason to think it any less than on the American side where more observers were present. Denig stated that the mortality of the Assiniboine at Fort Union was almost 90% and that those who fled onto the plains suffered equally.[24] The Assiniboines never recovered. Sixteen years later, in July 1853, Governor Isaac Stevens, heading an expedition investigating a route for a Pacific railway, encountered a band of Assiniboines not far from the old Fort Union site. Stevens counted 150 lodges and estimated there were 10 residents in each. The Assiniboines were in a bad way. They had plenty of buffalo meat but, Stevens recorded, "All had the look of poverty ... filthy and miserable." In a large council tipi, Stevens met with the chiefs and headmen where a spokesman pleaded:

> My father, you see us now as we are. We are poor; we have but few blankets and little clothing ... As the white man advances, our means of life grow less. We will soon have to seek protection in our poverty from the Great Father, who can so well provide it.[25]

Joshua Pilcher, the Indian Agent passenger on the *St. Peter*, had as his superior William Clark, the famous co-captain of the Lewis and Clark expedition of 1803–06, then serving as the Superintendent of Indian Affairs at St. Louis. On February 27, 1838 (which turned out to be the last year of Clark's life), Pilcher reported to Clark on the conditions on the Upper Missouri:

It appears that the effects of the Small pox among most of the Indian tribes of the Upper Missouri Surpass all former Scourges, and that the county through which it has pass'd is litterally depopulated & converted into one *great grave yard*. The Mandans, consisting of 1600 Souls, had been reduced by the 1st of October last, to thirty one persons—The *Gros Ventres* or Minetaries a tribe about One thousand strong, took the disease a month later than their Neibours the Mandans,—One half had perished, and the disease was still raging—they no doubt Shared the Same fate of the Mandans—The Riccaras who had recently joined the last named tribe, and number about three thousand—Most of them were out on a hunting excurtion when the disease broke out among the Mandans—and consequently received it sometime later—one half of *them* had fallen, and the disease was raging with unabated fury, not more than one out of fifty recovering from it, and most of those that survived, subsequently committed Suicide, dispairing I suppose at the loss of friends and the changes wrought by the disease in their persons; Some by shooting others by Stabing & some by throwing themselves from the high precipices along the Missouri. The great band of Assineboins, Say ten thousand (10,000) Strong, and the Crees numbering about three thousand, have been almost annihalated and notwithstanding all the precautions used by the gentlemen engaged in the trade of that region to prevent it, the disease had reached the Blackfeet of the Rocky Mountains—a band of 1000 lodges had been swept off and the disease was rapidly spreading among the different bands of that great tribe—numbering *I think* about 10,000 Souls.[26]

Historian Bernard deVoto, quoting the Commissioner of Indian Affairs, reports that, of the six Missouri River tribes principally affected—the Mandan, Arikara, Minnetare, Sioux, Assiniboine, and Blackfoot—at least 17,200 died. Of this, deVoto says, "It may be: this is as good an estimate as any other and no estimate could be even moderately accurate."[27] On the Canadian plains, it is likely that not more than half of the nomadic population survived.

There were islands of survival. The farsighted directors of the Hudson's Bay Company in London had sent supplies of cowpox vaccine, the recently discovered wonder drug that gave immunity to smallpox, to their trading posts for use among Company employees and neighbouring Indians. The Company was not being entirely altruistic; its business required a population of fur-trapping and trading Indians.

THE SCOURGE OF SMALLPOX

The Europeans had an inherent resistance to many of their diseases, due to centuries of exposure. Some historians think that immunity was lost to the Aboriginals of North America when their progenitors first entered the continent over the Bering Strait land bridge. Their population was then so sparse that the Arctic environment acted like a disinfection chamber and cleansed them of many diseases. This theory is discredited by recent archeological discoveries that evidence human residence in North America long before the Berengian Walk.[1] But Jared Diamond renders both theories irrelevant by his convincing argument that many of the so-called "crowd diseases" such as smallpox, cholera, measles, scarlet fever, influenza and typhus originated from domestic livestock.[2] Thus, Eurasians with a long history of association with domesticated animals had developed some immunity to their diseases. The unfortunate residents of North America, with no domesticated animals other than the ubiquitous dog, developed no similar immunity.

The introduction of disease to a non-immune and susceptible population is called a "virgin-soil" implantation. North America was virgin-soil to a host of often fatal diseases. Cholera, measles, malaria and influenza were killers almost equal to smallpox.

Known as a "crowd disease," smallpox best wreaks its havoc among dense and stable populations. In the Mandan and Hidatsa villages, its mortality rate came close to 100%. But out on the western plains, the disease cut through the scattered tribes like a scythe of death, and then was gone. In the first situation, there were few survivors, but they would have achieved immunity. In the second, the death rate was lower, but so was the level of immunity:

> the population density on the Plains was never great enough in the eighteenth and nineteenth centuries to maintain smallpox endemically. Consequently, every 30 to 50 years it reappeared in epidemic form to a new and susceptible generation that lacked any immunity to the disease.[3]

Smallpox incubates in its victims for approximately two weeks before making its presence known with muscular pain and high fever followed by a skin rash that develops into pus-filled pimples or pox sores. These lesions may run together, causing the skin to slip away and creating hideous wounds with exposed raw muscle and even bone. Death occurs when the infection reaches the lungs, heart or brain. Survivors carried permanent scars from the lesions; the descriptive phrase "pockmarked" entered the North American vocabulary.

For a description of those symptoms in real terms we have Father Albert Lacombe, who in 1870 administered to his stricken flock at the mission St. Paul des Cris on the North Saskatchewan River between Fort Edmonton and Fort Pitt:

> The patient is at first very feverish; the skin becomes red and covered with pimples, these blotches in a few days form scabs filled with infectious matter. Then the flesh begins to decompose and falls off in fragments. Worms swim in the parts most affected. Inflamation of the throat impedes all passage for meat or drink. While enduring the torments of this cruel agony the sufferer ceases to breathe.[4]

Today, thanks to universal vaccination, smallpox has been eradicated. The United Nations World Health Organization declared the world smallpox free in May 1980. It was believed that only two laboratory stocks of the virus remained, one in the United States and one in Russia, and it was intended that these be destroyed, ridding the world of the disease permanently and forever. But, since September 11, 2001, there is serious concern that stocks of the virus could be in the hands of other states and that the disease could be employed as a weapon of biological warfare. New strains of the virus, developed in laboratories, now have a mortality rate as high as 90%.

Even today there is no cure for smallpox, only the long-discontinued vaccination program of prevention. And passing from person to person, the disease is so contagious as to be virtually unstoppable once let loose. In 1970, in Germany, a quarantined patient opened his hospital window a few centimetres to smoke a cigarette. Within days he had infected 17 other people, including several nurses who had never been in the same room with him. "Scientists later discovered that the smallpox virus emerging from a patient's breath can creep out of a window and up the walls of a building, then back in another window, and infect people two floors above."[5]

When smallpox was eradicated, the program of vaccination was discontinued. Even following vaccination immunization survives only several years. The result is that entire populations, regardless of racial origin, are now "virgin soil" and as hopelessly vulnerable to the disease as were the Native Americans. Post 9/11 fears of bioterrorist smallpox attacks have prompted several nations to mount new immunization programs. Israel has set about vaccinating its entire population. The United States will first immunize one million soldiers and health care workers and then make the vaccine available to the public on a voluntary basis. Canada has vaccinated several hundred high-risk, front-line military and health care workers and has stockpiled 30 million doses of vaccine in case of an outbreak, enough for the entire population.

Even so, one or two terrorists with aerosol cans of smallpox could ignite an epidemic. Scenarios of bioterrorist attack among modern high-density cities predict stupendous mortality such as to cripple and terrify entire nations.

This is how it was when smallpox first struck the inhabitants of North America. As James Wilson describes it:

> The impact of this disaster on Indian life is hard to imagine. The death rate far exceeded anything that modern Western nations have experienced: the First World War, for instance, which is often seen as the apotheosis of mass destruction, killed around 2 per cent of the British population over a four-year period. Many Native American communities lost 75 per cent or more of their members within just a few weeks, the kind of losses predicted for a nuclear holocaust and certainly greater than those suffered at Hiroshima. The survivors, inevitably, were shocked, grief-stricken and bewildered . . . The virtual elimination of whole lineages . . . disrupted the complex web of kinship and authority that held communities together and drastically altered the relative positions of different nations.

Perhaps most vitally of all, European disease undermined the Native-Americans' confidence in themselves and their view of the world. The failure of the shamans to contain and cure smallpox and bubonic plague was the failure of an entire system of belief: the rituals, ceremonies, checks and balances were no longer working, and the whole universe seemed to be spinning terrifyingly out of control.[6]

NOTES

1. Elaine Dewar, *Bones* (Toronto: Random House, 2001).
2. Jared Diamond, *Guns, Germs, and Steel: The Fates of Human Societies* (New York: W.W. Norton & Company, 1999), 195–214.
3. Jody F. Decker, "Tracing Historical Diffusion Patterns: The Case of the 1780–82 Smallpox Epidemic Among the Indians of Western Canada," *Native Studies Review* 4, nos. 1–2 (1998).
4. James G. MacGregor, *Father Lacombe* (Edmonton: Hurtig, 1975), 204.
5. Richard Preston, *The Demon in the Freezer: A True Story* (New York: Random House, 2002), as quoted by Helen Epstein in "Bugs Without Borders," *New York Review of Books* (January 16, 2003): 20.
6. James Wilson, *The Earth Shall Weep: A History of Native America* (New York: Grove Press, 1998), 76–77.

Not all of the trading posts received the vaccine, not all of those that did made good use of it, and not all of the vaccine retained its effectiveness. Fort Pelly on the Assiniboine River was in the command of William Todd, medically trained and familiar with vaccination. Todd not only vaccinated the Indians who came to his post, he succeeded in convincing them of its value and instructing them in its use so that they could carry the program back to their bands. As a result, most of the Cree in Todd's district escaped the disease.[28]

The Plains Indians recovered, although never to their original strength, and some less successfully than others. Dr. John Maclean states that in 1858 the plague came again to the Qu'Appelle Cree "and the tribe was nearly wiped out."[29]

The Great Plains smallpox epidemic of 1837, with all its horror, suffering and death, was merely a prologue to the invasion of the disease that came a generation later, in 1869 and on into 1870. Again the Indian population between the Missouri and the Saskatchewan succumbed and died in horrific numbers.

In 1869, as in 1837, smallpox swept up the Missouri River, through the American trading posts and into the lodges of the helpless tribes. This time there were no Assiniboines to carry the disease north into Canada and the plague came to the valleys of the Saskatchewan and the Qu'Appelle only from the west. Late in the season, while Louis Riel and his Métis contested for control

of Red River, the plague raced first into the camps of the Peigan. The following spring, while Abbé Ritchot and John A. Macdonald bargained over the
future of Red River, the disease seized the Blood, then the Blackfoot, Stoney
and Sarcee. The Cree were next. By September of 1870, when Lieutenant-Governor Archibald arrived in Fort Garry, the stink of death hung in the air over
the entire Saskatchewan valley.

This time there were observers on the Canadian plains who have left
enough accounts of the progress of the insidious disease to provide a picture
of its horror. One of Father Lacombe's fellow Oblates, Father Fourmond, was
out on the plains with a travelling camp of Métis, hunting buffalo. The group
contracted the disease from a meeting with some Blackfoot, and Father Fourmond found himself ministering to the dying:

> I spent all my time tending to the sick in our sixty tents. I cannot
> describe the revolting stench. When the disease was in the dessi-
> cation stage, the victims were masses of putrefaction so that it was
> impossible to see in them the resemblance of a human being—And
> still, beneath that hideous exterior there was a soul, created to the
> likeness of God, a soul to save![30]

The victims suffered unspeakable agony while those who were spared
endured almost equal torments of fear and revulsion. The best advice the
more immune white population could give the Indians was, if disease struck,
they should break up their large camps and scatter across the plains. The tribes
were reluctant to follow this advice, until it was too late. Then, wrote Father
Lacombe:

> This dreadful epidemic has taken all compassion from the hearts of
> the Indians. These lepers of a new kind are removed at a distance
> from the others and sheltered with branches. There they witness the
> decomposition and putrefaction of their bodies several days before
> death.[31]

Lieutenant William Butler, out in "The Great Lone Land" on a journey of
exploration and inquiry into the extent of the smallpox epidemic, noted the
same reaction:

> By streams and lakes, willow copses, and upon bare hill-sides, often
> shelterless from the fierce rays of the summer sun and exposed to the

rains and dews of night, the poor plague-stricken wretches lay down to die—no assistance of any kind, for the ties of family were quickly loosened, and mothers abandoned their helpless children upon the wayside, fleeing onward to some fancied place of safety.[32]

Father Lacombe's faith was deeply tested as he was called upon to serve the dead as well as the living:

The hideous corpse must be buried, a grave must be dug and the body carried to the burial ground. All this devolves to me and I am alone with Indians disheartened and terrified to such a degree that they hardly dare approach even their own relations. God alone knows, what I have had to endure merely to prevent these mortal remains being devoured by dogs.[33]

Perhaps because the Hudson's Bay Company itself was facing an uncertain future at the time, in 1870 there was little smallpox vaccine at its trading posts along the North Saskatchewan River. Much of the vaccine at Edmonton and St. Albert had been procured from traders at Fort Benton, in Montana Territory, and "was of a spurious description."[34] The wonderful experience of William Todd at Fort Pelly in 1837 had not resulted in the precautionary requirement of an ample store of the protective medicine at all the Company posts.

At Prince Albert, the Reverend James Nisbet, struggling to develop a Presbyterian mission, did have some vaccine on hand. He vaccinated 150 of his followers and lost none. The following year, the missionary dolefully reported a lack of gratitude among his flock: "very few seem to have been much impressed by the remarkable deliverance wrought for them last year."[35] But farther up the North Saskatchewan River, the residents of Fort Pitt were grateful to Reverend Nisbet. There John Sinclair had secured serum by drawing lymph from a Saulteaux Indian who had been vaccinated at Prince Albert, with the result that only three persons within the fort were infected.[36]

Lieutenant Butler had been provisioned with vaccine for his expedition up the North Saskatchewan River in 1870, but he discovered when he reached the country where it was needed that his medicines had been lost to careless packing and consequent freezing.[37]

Isaac Cowie, Hudson's Bay Company factor at Fort Qu'Appelle, was the son of a Scottish doctor and had himself attended two semesters of medical courses at Edinburgh University. Familiar with the technique, he too secured some lymph from a recently vaccinated visitor, created his own serum and shared it with the Cree in his district. Cowie claimed his success was such that "among the Qu'Appelle and Touchwood Indians not one single case of smallpox was ever heard of among them."[38]

The reports of the impact of the epidemic again come from the trading posts, all situated along the rivers of the West, the Missouri, the Saskatchewan, the Qu'Appelle, the Assiniboine. No word came from the great expanse of country between the Missouri and the Saskatchewan/ Qu'Appelle valley, from such refuges as the Moose Mountains, Wood Mountain, the Cypress Hills, the Sweet Grass Hills, the Bears Paw Mountains. The Métis buffalo hunters, the *hivernants*, had taken to wintering at Wood Mountain and the Cypress Hills. The White Eagle band of Santee Sioux from Minnesota customarily camped between the Souris River and Wood Mountain. How severely did the smallpox strike the residents of this lonely region?

THE PANDEMICS OF 1837 and 1870 both perpetuated the story of "The Infected Blanket," an early-day urban legend that convicted villainous whites of deliberately transmitting smallpox to the Native populations by gifts of blankets permeated with the germs of the disease. The story loses credibility, not because of any shortage of eager villains, or opportunity, but because of the number of times it appears throughout more than a century of North American history, and the fact that no one then knew how the disease was communicated. Similarly, latter day historians have castigated the American Fur Company for callously continuing the voyage of the disease-carrying *St. Peter* up the Missouri River in 1837.[39]

DeVoto gives an entirely satisfactory response to both the infected blanket legend and the criticism of the *St. Peter*:

> In 1837 the germ theory and the concept of immunization did not exist ... No one knew how smallpox was communicated. If the best physicians of America had been aboard the *St. Peter*, they would have done exactly what the Company's agents did; they would have instructed the uninfected to avoid miasmas, to eat no foods that were held to alter the proportion of mythical bodily attributes, and on the first symptoms of any illness whatever to take strong physics and various magical substances.[40]

That explains the continued voyage of the *St. Peter*. It also answers the nonsense of the infected blanket legend. For, "if no one knew how smallpox was communicated," how would the notion of transmission by a so-called infected blanket arise? And what delivery system would be employed for the infected blanket? What protection would there be for the transporter of the blanket? And why a blanket? (It was always a blanket.) Why not utilize the corpse (or part thereof) of a victim? Or, for more certain penetration, why not contaminated firewater (*sans* alcohol, if thought necessary to avoid antiseptic effect, if that much knowledge then existed)?

The blanket legend, somewhat burnished, was used to fix blame for the 1869–70 epidemic, and given credence by at least one writer:

> The smallpox plague of 1869 which so ravaged the Blackfoot Confederacy was caused by the malevolence of a single white man. An American trader named Evans and his partner had trouble with the Blackfoot in 1868, the partner being slain and all their horses stolen. Evans made his way back to St. Louis, where he swore revenge. Purchasing several bales of blankets infected with smallpox, he set them out on the banks of the Missouri in Indian country, and the plague swept through the tribes like wildfire. The Blackfoot tribe alone lost nearly 1400 men, women and children in five months—truly, a life for a life, with a vengeance.[41]

No explanation is provided as to how one would order up, on the St. Louis or any market, bales of infected blankets, or how such a supposedly dangerous cargo could be handled and transported in safety to all but the intended victims. The steamboat journey from St. Louis to Fort Benton required at least eight weeks of slow, monotonous, upstream travel.

Butler found along the Saskatchewan the general belief that smallpox had been deliberately "communicated to the Blackfeet tribes by Missouri traders."[42]

Whether deliberately transmitted or not, the Indians knew that smallpox had been brought to them by the white intruders. Frequently the suffering Natives thought that the apparent immunity of the whites was due to a magic potion they refused to share. In 1837, Fort Clark was virtually under siege as the dying Mandan attempted vengeance. Four Bears, or Mah-to-toh-pa, a powerful Mandan chief who had long been a supporter of the whites, recanted that view and on his deathbed called for retribution against "those dogs, the whites. Rise all together and not leave one of them alive."[43]

Howard describes the Blackfoot desperately trying to turn their suffering back on the whites secure behind their palisades:

Soon convinced that the wind could carry the pestilence, its demented victims dragged the bodies of their dead to the windward side of the white men's forts and stacked them there.[44]

Father Lacombe reported no animosity toward the members of his missions, perhaps because Fathers Leduc and Bourgine at St. Albert were stricken. But the father and son Methodist missionaries, George and John McDougall at Whitefish Lake and Victoria, came under siege by the angry Blackfoot even though the family lost three children to the disease. When John Macoun visited the two missions in 1872, "only the chimneys of the houses remained standing. Their occupants were either dead or scattered to the four winds."[45]

The suffering Indians must finally have made a desperate guess as to how their terrible affliction was transmitted. Dr. John Maclean reports in his work on John McDougall:

Ignorance, famine and bereavement aroused the passions of the red men against everyone at the missions and fur-trading posts. Determined on revenge, they began to pillage, murder and spread the disease wherever it was possible to do so. The Blackfeet came north, stealing horses and cattle. The Crees threw garments from corpses into the gardens, spat on the floors, besmeared door handles and picked the diseased scales from their bodies, leaving them in places where white people would come in contact with them.[46]

Butler observed similar conduct at Fort Pitt, but noted "they appear to have endeavoured to convey the infection into the fort, in the belief that by doing so they would cease to suffer from it themselves."[47]

Yet, in 1870, it was considered by officialdom that blankets and the like could carry the disease. In April of that year, the U.S. War Department issued a ban prohibiting the shipment of infected buffalo robes. Interpreted to apply to all products originating in areas where smallpox had raged, the order froze in place almost all of the robe and fur collection of the previous winter that was gathering at Fort Benton for transport down the Missouri.[48]

At Fort Garry, Lieutenant-Governor Archibald responded quickly to the rising fear in the settlement. Ignoring legal niceties, in October he appointed a three-man Council that passed legislation to meet the smallpox menace. It mattered not that it was later discovered that Archibald had no power to appoint the members of his Council and that his legislation was *ultra vires*. It served its purpose.[49]

The ordinance enacted by "The Lieutenant-Governor and Council of Rupert's Land and the North-West Territories" on October 22 was put into immediate effect. It declared that "Smallpox of a very malignant type is now extensively prevailing in the Valley of the Saskatchewan" and provided that "The following articles shall be considered as capable of carrying infection— that is to say: Furs, Buffalo Robes and Hides, Tents, Skins, Clothing, Blankets, and Peltries of all descriptions." None of the items enumerated "shall be permitted to pass eastward of the south branch of the Saskatchewan River."[50]

Any of the proscribed materials found in between were presumed to have crossed the Saskatchewan and were subject to seizure. Travellers arriving in Manitoba from the West were to be quarantined for 10 days and until they had secured a certificate of health.

Perhaps the action taken in the spring by the American government prompted the similar proscription at Fort Garry, but the War Department order had been lifted by September 1870, and robes and furs were again moving down the Missouri River.[51]

Lieutenant-Governor Archibald also initiated a more proactive defence. He sent a supply of vaccine, with careful instructions for its use, to the trading forts up the North Saskatchewan. Looking for someone who could ensure delivery so late in the season, he found his perfect candidate in Lieutenant William F. Butler, an Irish-born officer of the 69th Foot of the British Imperial Army. Butler, who arrived in Fort Garry that summer loosely attached to Colonel Wolseley's command, had shown unusual initiative and competence. Archibald directed his man to deliver the vaccine, but also undertake an intelligence-gathering mission into the heart of the new territory, perform a census of the Indian population, and generally make observations and recommendations as to conditions on the frontier. Although the vaccine delivery failed, through no fault of Butler's, his journey paid remarkable dividends; his articulate and clear-sighted account was of huge value to the administrations in Fort Garry and Ottawa.

Butler made a remarkable winter trip; he left Fort Garry on October 15, 1870, reached Rocky Mountain House in the first week of December, and returned to Fort Garry on February 20, 1871. In his words, "The journey from first to last occupied 119 days and embraced a distance of about 2,700 miles [4,345 km]." Not bad for a greenhorn. He expanded his journal into a book published in 1873; *The Great Lone Land* is fascinating reading even today.

THE EPIDEMIC OF 1869–70 struck hard and viciously, but also swiftly. It was gone almost as quickly as it had come. The death and devastation it brought, however, did not put an end to ancient tribal animosities; hostilities were interrupted only and soon resumed.

In October 1870, while Lieutenant-Governor Archibald was framing legislation to prevent the smallpox from reaching Red River, an epic battle between a Cree raiding party and an encampment of Peigan and Blood of the Blackfoot Confederacy broke out at the junction of the Oldman (then the Belly) and St. Mary's Rivers, southwest of Lethbridge. Many western histories describe conflict between the Plains Indians almost as sport, contests of skill and endurance, but little blood and death. Not so with the Cree and the Blackfoot. Since the arrival of the Cree on the western plains, the two nations had maintained an almost constant war footing, punctuated by the occasional peace treaty, often solicited when one of them needed time to recover strength and then violated at the first opportunity. In March 1866, at Red Ochre Hills, on the South Saskatchewan River, the Blackfoot suffered a crushing defeat at the hands of the Cree. Unaware of the presence of a huge Cree encampment, a large Blackfoot raiding party was slaughtered. Isaac Cowie reports that the Blackfoot losses were "no less than six hundred" and that five years later he personally viewed "for miles . . . a trail of bleached bones of the Blackfeet who had fallen, in the panic-stricken retreat, to the fury of the pursuing Crees."[52]

In the spring of 1869, the Blackfoot had employed an offer of truce and the pipe of peace to murder the Cree chief, Maskepetoon (Broken Arm), his son and a party of followers. The enraged Cree immediately set upon a campaign of revenge.[53]

So determined were the vengeful Cree that they were not deterred by either pestilence or death. In April 1870, a war party of 17 stormed a Blackfoot camp and suffered the same fate as Thompson's Peigan 90 years earlier. The lodges held only death, and that death rode with the Cree as they carried scalps and plunder back to their people. Thus came the epidemic that raced down the valley of the Saskatchewan bringing misery and death to the missions of Father Lacombe and his colleagues. Only two of the 17 Cree raiders survived, and they were terribly disfigured.[54]

Incredibly, hostilities were only temporarily put aside because of the smallpox epidemic. William Butler discovered that one of the Blackfoot tribes continued raiding even during the sickness: "at the period when the smallpox was most destructive among them they still continued to carry on their horse-stealing raids against the Crees and half-breeds."[55]

By the fall of 1870, the Cree were recovered and ready. Thinking they held a numerical advantage over the disease-weakened Blackfoot, a large Cree war party headed west. It was an unusually large war party, 600 to 800 warriors under the great chiefs Big Bear, Piapot, Little Mountain and Little Pine. They carried both muskets and their traditional bows and arrows. This was vengeance on a huge scale. There are a number of accounts of the great conflict. One of the participants, the mixed-blood Jerry Potts, fought with the Peigan. In 1885, 15 years after the battle, Charles Conybeare arrived and set up a law practice. A native of England, Conybeare had taken his legal training in Winnipeg and then moved further west to Lethbridge where he was the first lawyer in town. An acquaintance of Jerry Potts, Conybeare provided this version of the encounter:

> My information as to the battle was actually given to me by Jerry Potts and I stood with him in the Sikotoka coulee, which was where he and his band were during the fight, which he called the *mokiwan*, being the Indian name for Belly. According to the story as he told it to me, the Southern Indians engaged were the Peigans, who are now on the reserve between Macleod and Pincher, and the Bloods and some of the South Peigans who happened to be in this country. Apparently there were no Blackfeet in it, unless there were some stragglers who were intermixed with the Bloods. Some of the Peigans appear to have been camped on the bench lands above the Junction with the St. Mary's and the river then called the Belly; this would be in the southern portion of Twp. 8-22. The Belly River from its junction with the St. Mary's to Lethbridge runs in the form of a "V"—the angle of the "V" being to the East. A body of Crees fell upon two lodges of the Peigans and massacred all of the occupants, except one boy who made a getaway and carried the news to the other Peigan lodges which were in the vicinity. They appeared to have rallied together, and the call was sent to the Bloods who lay further to the West, presumably scattered on what is now known as the Blood Reserve. (Where the South Peigans were I do not know.)

> Jerry Potts did not have really good command of English. He was a very poor interpreter. A witness would make quite a little speech and all Jerry interpreted would be "He says he did," or "He says he didn't." At all events Jerry was not in the first stages of the fight, which took place in the forenoon. The numbers of the Peigans and Bloods kept steadily increasing and the Crees retreated before them north and east to the other arm of the "V" when they were forced down the river bank. It was just before they reached the bank of the river across from Lethbridge

that Jerry Potts and the band he was with got into action. They tried to head off the Crees before they got into the coulees but evidently did not succeed in this so they followed down flinging themselves into what he called the Sikotoka coulee, which was just above the old Sharon mine and the next coulee below that which the Crees were going down, and enfiladed the Crees as they came down the coulee. Some other Indians, Bloods I think, were in the next coulee above, so that the Crees were between two fires. Meanwhile a party of the Bloods following a coulee higher up went right down to and across the river at Old Ford, which we used to use when driving to Macleod, and when the body on this side pushed the Crees and they were endeavouring to make their retreat good across the river, they found the Bloods all ready to receive them on the other side. There appears to have been a running fight of the Cree survivors all the way from the Ford to where the high level bridge now stands, where Jerry claimed the last of the Crees were killed. At that time [evidently when Potts gave the writer the narrative] this site was occupied by Elliot Galt's house which was removed to make room for one of the piers of the bridge.

From Jerry's account, it seemed to me that it may have been a fight in the beginning, but it very quickly developed into a massacre as the Bloods and Peigans evidently outnumbered the Crees, and the trapped Crees were merely trying to make a get-away. It was evidently a small marauding band of Crees that had come down horse-stealing and they got into a wasp's nest and got wiped out.[56]

Potts made an oft-quoted statement to another interviewer: "You could fire with your eyes shut and would be sure to kill a Cree."[57] Jerry Potts, of course, was the frontiersman who later achieved fame as the scout and guide enlisted by the North-West Mounted Police when they arrived on the plains in 1874.

Conybeare was mistaken about the attackers being "a small marauding band of Crees." It was a major invading force that encountered two unexpected difficulties. The "South Peigans who happened to be in this country" were the band of Mountain Chief and other refugees who fled the United States after the slaughter on the Marias River the previous January. Apparently the Cree reconnaissance had failed to identify the presence of this additional number of enemy.

But the real "wasp's nest" the Cree ran into were the Henry and Sharp's rifles possessed by the defenders. Lever-action carbines with 15-shot magazines, these modern weapons could throw lead as fast as the shooter could work the action. The Peigan particularly, accustomed to trading in the Missouri country, were well supplied with the newer weapons. The American traders were quite willing to sell the rifles, army surplus from the American Civil War. The Hudson's Bay Company, however, would not sell repeating rifles to the Indians. Thus, the Cree, with their outmoded muskets and bows, were overwhelmed by the superior firepower. Almost impossible to reload on the run, the muzzleloaders were next to useless in a running firefight, which much of this battle was. Even in a set piece engagement, they were no match for the modern rifles.

The battle commenced before dawn on October 25, 1870, and went on all day:

> The river valley was filled with dust and smoke, the air resounded with the report of rifles and the deafening war cries of the Blackfeet, while thick and fast came the death yells of the Crees.

> The slaughter did not end at the river. The Blackfeet followed the Crees across, and being joined by a large contingent of their brethern, who had crossed higher up, the butchery went on, and at one spot where the Crees made a sort of stand, about fifty of them were killed.[58]

At sunset the Peigan and Blood withdrew and the remaining Cree were allowed to escape on foot.

Because so many Cree were killed in the river and carried off by the currents, the number of their fatalities has only been estimated, but is placed at between 200 and 300. About 40 Blackfoot were killed and 50 wounded.[59] This loss, and the Blackfoot loss at Red Ochre Hills, are among the largest body counts ever in Indian warfare, where casualties usually were modest by comparison to European battles. Life was precious to the tribes. Recruitment to replenish gaps in the warrior ranks was not available; replacements could come only from the next generation.

The Battle at the Belly River is generally considered to have been "the last great inter-tribal battle to be fought in North America."[60] Certainly it was the last one of its size, but four years later surveyors running the boundary along the 49th Parallel came upon the desiccated corpses of 20 Crow Indians killed by the Peigan the previous season. The brutal scene was evidence that peace had not by 1873 become a permanent condition on the plains. And even seven years later, well after the North-West Mounted Police brought law and order to the West, tribal clashes still occasionally turned fatal.

Dead Crow Indians, c. 1874. Thomas Millman, physician to the North American Boundary Commission, kept a diary of his experiences while in the West. On July 31, 1874, he wrote, "we met with Boswell & Dawson & the photographers. They were getting the photo of some dead Indians. They appear to be Crow Indians killed last winter by the Pegans [sic]. About 20 altogether were riddled with bullet holes & every one scalped. Most of them had their shirts & every one had a gash in their side. Bodies were shrivelled up but skin pretty sound." *Library and Archives Canada / Thomas Millman fonds PA-074646*

One remarkable feature of the bloody combat at the Belly was the size of the engagement after the terrible loss of tribal numbers on both sides to the smallpox epidemic.

The epic battle passed entirely unnoticed by the new governors of the West, both at Fort Garry and in Ottawa. They had no lines of communication into their new territory. Even Butler, who visited Edmonton House and Rocky Mountain House in December, six weeks after the fight, picked up no hint of the event. Word did not come in to Chief Factor William Christie at Edmonton until early January 1871. Sometime that winter the news reached Isaac Cowie at Fort Qu'Appelle, who found he had lost a number of his customers:

> About twenty of the slain had book debts at Touchwood Hills, which I had to write off to profit and loss with the explanation "Killed by Blackfeet."[61]

Two and one half years after the Battle of Belly River, in May 1873, a much smaller skirmish, a drunken encounter between a group of hard-case wolfers (mostly, but not all, American) and a band of Assiniboine, took place in the

Cypress Hills. Although it produced only 22 fatalities, a fraction of those at Belly River, that shootout hit the headlines. Known ever since as The Cypress Hills Massacre, the Sunday afternoon firefight created a demand that law and order be imposed on the West and expedited the formation of the North-West Mounted Police.

THE SMALLPOX EPIDEMIC OF 1870 stopped short of the Red River Settlement. The villages on the Assiniboine and Red Rivers were spared. Vaccination in the community helped. So did Isaac Cowie's efforts on the Qu'Appelle, by creating a buffer zone through which the plague did not pass. Also, the illegal quarantine imposed by Lieutenant-Governor Archibald and his Council contributed to the safety of their people.

How many of all the Indians of the northern plains were lost to the pandemic of 1869–70? As with the earlier plagues, only rough estimates are available. Father Lacombe tallied 300 dead out of the 700 Métis and Indians at his mission,[62] a mortality rate exceeding 40%. Chief Factor Christie at Fort Edmonton thought the disease had "swept away one-third of the population of the Saskatchewan district."[63] He also thought that one-half of the Indians of the Alberta district had been lost. John McDougall endured the epidemic at his mission at Victoria. Forty years later he wrote, "From the best information we could obtain it was reasonable to estimate that fully half of the native tribes perished during the season of 1870 through the ravages of smallpox."[64]

Statistics prepared on the American side give some idea of the extent of the depopulation of the nomad tribes there over a period of almost a century[65] (see facing page). The Assiniboine and the Blackfoot on the Canadian plains must have suffered losses as extreme as those farther south. How hard were the Ojibway and the Cree hit? Who is to say?

But the losses were brutal. Out on the plains entire villages perished, those stricken later scattering in terror only to die themselves in some lonely bluff. The corpses were devoured by the camps' dogs who in turn fell prey to the ever-vigilant coyotes and wolves. The horses wandered away. Only the lodges remained, flapping and tattered in the ceaseless wind, skeletons on sentry duty, until they too toppled, one by one.

In the summer of 1878, a survey party discovered the tragic evidence of just such a disaster north of Sounding Lake. An entire camp of some 300 Assiniboine had perished, leaving only their scattered bones to witness the calamity that had befallen them.[66]

DEPOPULATION OF NOMAD TRIBES (AMERICAN STASTICS)

NOMAD	1780	1877	PERCENT REDUCTION
Assiniboine	10,000	1,719	83%
Atsina	3,000	600	80%
Comanche	7,000	1,695	76%
Blackfeet	15,000	4,560	69%
Kiowa and Kiowa-Apache	2,300	1,433	38%
Crow	4,000	3,300	18%
Sioux (Teton)	20,000	18,106	9%
Cheyenne	3,500	3,236	8%
Arapaho	3,000	2,964	1%

THE NATIVE INHABITANTS OF the northern plains were still present, but in numbers greatly reduced by the unceasing waves of death that had swept over them. Probably not since the faraway landing of Columbus nearly 400 years earlier had there been so few original residents of the flatlands between the Missouri and the Saskatchewan/Qu'Appelle Rivers.

Pestilence had handed a boon to the government of Prime Minister John A. Macdonald. There were now many fewer members of the Plains Indian bands residing on the grasslands between Red River and the Rocky Mountains, the lands needed for the Pacific railway.

As the *annus horribilis* that had been 1870 in the New West drew to a close, the westerlies continued to sigh across the savannah stretching from the valley of the Saskatchewan and the Qu'Appelle to the Missouri and beyond. But the great grassland was now strangely empty and quiet. Its people had all but vanished. However, the emptiness would be for a time only. Others would soon fill the void.

CHAPTER 8

The Métis

MORE THAN 400 PADDLES STROKING IN UNISON FLASHED IN the moonlight as the two great canoe brigades raced each other through the choppy waters. The men pulling those paddles were silent, grimly fixed on maintaining the tempo, now increased to 55 strokes a minute from their usual day-long routine of 40. That rate might increase yet again, they knew, and surely would if the other brigade stepped up first.

The mockery that had been thrown across the water between the two squadrons had long since ceased—and for good reason. The race had been underway for more than 15 hours now and there was no spare energy for insult. Only the occasional barb now was tossed by the few non-paddlers, the pilots who commanded small groupings of canoes, from four to six. The *bourgeois*, the men who held overall command of the brigades, did not engage in the scorn, but the race would run until they gave the word.

The taunts and insults had begun almost as soon as the large brigades of North canoes lined out in formation along the eastern shore of Lake Winnipeg, separated according to their destinations, and headed north to Grand Rapids where the Saskatchewan River tumbled into the lake. As usual, the gauntlet had been thrown by the more seasoned and select members of the Athabasca brigade, who were headed up through the Churchill River, over Methye Portage and down the Athabasca River to Fort Chipewyan on Lake Athabasca. The men of the Saskatchewan River brigade, on their way to provision the fur-trading posts as far west as Rocky Mountain House, were quick to accept the challenge, and the race was on. This year more than 80 canoes participated. In later years as many as 100 *canots du nord* were required to provision the outlying trading posts. Almost all were crewed by six paddlers; some by four.

This contest between the two outbound brigades had become an annual tradition, eagerly anticipated and much discussed over later campfires and winter layovers. Reputations and honour were at stake, and no participant would be a slacker.

Lake Winnipeg is large and likely the most dangerous lake in Canada for small craft. More than 450 km (280 mi) long, it is shallow, easily whipped into waves, 2-m (6-ft) foaming combers deadly to the canoes when they could find no place of refuge. And much of the shoreline is hostile, with high, cliff-like banks that provide few safe landing sites. When conditions were right, the brigades ran night and day to clear the dangerous waters. Tonight the lake was almost a mill-pond and the *bourgeois* would let the race run until they reached security.

To the racers, the calm of the lake was a relief after the wild water of the Winnipeg River the canoes had just descended. The men driving the paddles, accustomed to brutal industry and terrifying danger, were no strangers to disabling injury and death. Whitewater rapids, terrifying chutes and seemingly unavoidable boulders and rock faces were daily routine, but the Winnipeg was truly fearsome:

> It was unquestionably the grandest and most beautiful river the Montreal Northmen saw on their whole journey from Lake Superior to Lake Athabasca. Running through tortured rock and dropping fast, it was a river of spectacular rapids and falls.[1]

"Canoe Manned by Voyageurs Passing a Waterfall, 1869" (by Frances Anne Hopkins). *Library and Archives Canada / Frances Anne Hopkins fonds C-002771*

In later years of the fur trade when the sturdy York boat, powered by oar and sail, replaced the more fragile canoe, Lake Winnipeg in a storm was still a dreadful experience. One trader described crossing under sail at 3:00 a.m. when they were struck by a sudden gale. The crew, drenched by the great waves, stripped to the waist and bailed furiously:

> We had little food or rest for three days. Our lives, the cargo were in peril. From the mouth of the Red to Berens River, a distance of a hundred and fifty miles [240 km], we never went ashore. We made a record trip of three hundred miles [480 km] to Norway House in three days.[1]

NOTE
1. Dennis F. Johnson, *York Boats of the Hudson's Bay Company* (Calgary: Fifth House, 2006), 65.

Over its 225 km (140 mi) it dropped a full 100 m (328 ft) and presented 26 carrying places, or portages. One of those portages avoided a whirlpool that one near-fatal day had swallowed a 7-m (23-ft) canoe and two unfortunate *voyageurs*. Miraculously, the river regurgitated the paddlers, much the worse for wear, but, to the amazement of their colleagues, still alive. The canoe was shredded. Fatalities often occurred on their 3,200-km (2,000-mi) annual journey and when they did there was little time for grief. In the manner today seen along many North American highways, a simple cross was placed on the riverbank to commemorate the loss, and the place of burial if the river had given up the dead, and the brigade moved on. Beside just one of the many boiling rapids of the Winnipeg River 14 crosses silently mourned.

Sixty strokes a minute. Which canoes first increased the pace would be a subject of later debate. But the paddles now churned through the water every second. And the race ground on, hour after grueling hour. To maintain energy, the paddlers chewed strips of pemmican, sliced and stuffed in their mouths by the pilots, guides, or steersmen—whoever was not pulling a paddle or could be spared for the task. But never a pause for comfort or relief.

The Athabasca brigade held two advantages over the Saskatchewan paddlers. To enable their canoes to make the 6,400-km (4,000-mi) round trip from Grand Portage at Lake Superior up to Lake Athabasca and back before ice clogged the rivers, they carried one-quarter less cargo. And the Athabasca crews were specially select and seasoned. But the Saskatchewan brigade determinedly stayed in contention.

Twenty-five hours. The brigades had cleared the Winnipeg River and entered the lake in the early morning. The race had run all day, all through the night, and now it was morning again. And still the paddles flashed in unison to the killing pace. And then . . .

Sixty-five strokes a minute. Minds now floated as total exhaustion neared. But stubborn pride maintained the tempo.

Thirty hours. No winner was yet clear, but the two brigades began to lose their formation. The separation between the canoes grew and some straggled.

Then it was over. The *bourgeois* signaled the end of the race, the men slumped over their shipped paddles, then pulled wearily into shore. A keg of rum was opened, the last until the end of the journey. A quick dinner of rice and pemmican and the paddlers curled up among the rocks and slept like death.

It had been a great race and would live in the retelling for years. Not quite a record, but very respectable. Forty hours of non-stop paddling up Lake Winnipeg was the longest of the yearly events.[2]

THE MEN OF THE "GREAT RACE"

The men with the strength and stamina to endure such contests were, pound for pound, the toughest ever to enter the Canadian and American West. They were the *voyageurs*, almost exclusively French Canadians recruited in Quebec. It was their muscle that drove the two great transportation systems of the Canadian fur trade. First to reach the inland waters was the North West Company, directed out of Montreal but stretching more than 5,000 km (3,000 mi) to the sub-Arctic and the Rocky Mountains. The Hudson's Bay Company followed in 1774, forced by the competition from its posts on the Bay. Before long the fur trade touched both the Arctic and Pacific Oceans. For more than 50 years in the late 1700s and early 1800s, the indomitable voyageurs plied the interior waterways of North America.

They were the progenitors of a new race. Not the sole progenitors, but, in their relationships with the women of the resident Natives, they were the main contributors to the development of a unique and distinct people—the Métis. Accurately described as "Children of the Fur Trade," the Métis were brought into being by the men of the fur trade in their unions with the Cree and Ojibway women. Their historical season was brief, but the *voyageurs* were the largest group of players on the river routes of Western Canada during the wild and primitive years of the quest for fur.

Some of the *voyageurs* themselves were of shared European and Indian ancestry. The official policy of New France had so encouraged marriage with the resident Natives that by the early 1700s a sizable mixed-blood population had come into being. Also among the paddlers could be counted a number of Iroquois, also from Quebec, many of whom remained in the West making a further contribution to the mixed ancestry of the Métis.

THE ORIGIN OF THE MÉTIS

It was both natural and inevitable that so many European men, months and years and thousands of kilometres removed from their womenfolk at home, would seek and find liaison with women of the Native tribes with whom they came into contact. Both the Hudson's Bay and North West Companies learned that a "country marriage" between their traders and a woman of a prominent Indian family could create an alliance to be relied upon to produce a stable fur-producing clientele. And the Cree and Saulteaux/Ojibway families were pleased to have an inside track with the providers of the highly desired European trade goods. The progeny of these liaisons, and those of the *coureurs de bois* and the *voyageurs*, were scattered all along the Great Lakes canoe routes and next to the trading posts of the North-West.

By the middle or late 1700s, the issue of these unions began to lose identification with either parental race and instead to appear as a distinct Aboriginal people. The European parentage was French, Scots and English, with French predominating. Native ancestry was almost exclusively Cree or Saulteaux/Ojibway, with Cree wives heavily favoured. Described variously as *les bois brûlés* (because of their dark complexion), "half-breeds," "country born," "half-caste," "mixed bloods" or "Métis," they fell into two basic categories, English-speaking Protestants and French-speaking Catholics. Over time, "half-breed" came to apply to the English-speaking and "Métis" to the French-speaking.[1] Later still, "half-breed" acquired a derogatory connotation and "Métis" became the acceptable term for all regardless of ancestry. "Métis" was sanctified by its adoption in The Constitution Act of 1982.

NOTE

1. John Foster, "The Métis: The People and the Term," in A.S. Lussier (ed.), *Louis Riel and the Métis* (Winnipeg: Pemmican Publications, 1983).

LACHINE, WEST OF MONTREAL, lay at the head of the great rapids of the St. Lawrence River and was the natural point of embarkation for the great canoe brigades loaded with trade goods for the inland fur posts. Each spring during the heyday of the North West Company, the warehouses and wharves of Lachine seethed with the energy and excitement of another expedition into the *pays d'en haut*, or *le pays sauvage*, the wilderness, or Indian country, west of Lake Superior. And the busy taverns served as the hiring-halls. There gathered hardy and experienced *engagés* of previous years, as well as callow youths seeking adventure and fortune.

Lachine. The very name spoke of adventure. It had first been the residence of the Sieur de La Salle, the claimant of Louisiana. The locals, deriding La

Salle's ambition to discover a route to the Orient, had dubbed his estate "La Chine" (China) and the name evolved into Lachine.

John Jacob Astor of New York, building an American fur-trade empire, knew the value of the Canadian boatmen. Declaring that one *voyageur* was equal to any three Americans, in May 1810 Astor sent his agents to Lachine to recruit two 14-man crews, one for a cross-continental journey to Fort Astoria, his Pacific Fur Company post on the Columbia River, the other to make the trip by sea around Cape Horn. Astor's men were swarmed with prospects and easily filled their quotas. A few clerks were also signed up— to five-year contracts at £80 per year. One of the clerks hired, an immigrant Scots school teacher looking for a better future, was Alexander Ross, who 15 years later found himself at Fort Garry. Today he is known as The Historian of Red River.[3]

THE DEMAND FOR FURS was fueled, then as now, by fashion. There was a market for most furs, such as fox, otter, mink and marten, but a tree-eating rodent was particularly sought after. The under-hair of the beaver made excellent felt for the hats then in high favour with the European upper-classes.

During the early years of the trade, the felt makers lacked a suitable technique to remove the outer, or guard, hair of the beaver. Thus there was a premium demand for *castor gras*, a specially conditioned beaver hide. The Indians used beaver skins for clothing and sleeping robes. After a year or so of the fur rubbing against the user's skin, the guard hairs would slip away and the pelts became soft and pliable from the natural oils of the human epidermis. Thus, for years the gentry of Europe unknowingly paraded in headgear made from the cast-off clothing of North American Aboriginals.

The beaver pelt became such an integral element of the fur trade that it evolved into a unit of currency known as the "made beaver," or MB. Other pelts and trade goods were priced according to their relative value in made beaver. Since the value assigned to made beaver was fixed and not subject to market fluctuations, one beaver skin might be worth several made beaver. Trade tokens in made beaver denominations were issued by the Hudson's Bay Company, the inventor of the accounting device.[4]

The mark-up on trade goods in the hands of the Native middlemen was often considerable; a musket acquired at York Factory for 14MB resold on the plains for 50 MB.[5] During the years of the French regime in Canada, the fur trade was subjected to strict license and regulation. Rejecting officialdom, many free spirits ventured west as independent traders. These were the romantic *coureurs de bois*, men who dared the wilderness, the *pays d'en haut*, and who learned to survive and prosper among the resident Indians. From the very early days of the fur trade the Hurons had served as middlemen, but in 1650 the Huron nation collapsed. Weakened by epidemics of smallpox, it was unable to further resist the continued attacks of its traditional enemy, the Iroquois. The survivors dispersed, joining other tribes. The sudden disappearance of the Huron middlemen from the fur-trade delivery system created an opportunity that the *coureurs de bois* were quick to fill. Hundreds of young Quebec men, French, Catholic and virile, moved onto the fur trade-routes along the Great Lakes. Only the quick learners survived.

The *coureurs de bois* discovered that to succeed in the wilderness a wife was not a luxury but a necessity; she was a teacher of woodcraft, a help-mate, a guide, an interpreter, sometimes a protector from, and certainly an introduction to, the resident Indians. A liaison with the local tribes provided not only security but an edge in obtaining their trade. And so the *coureurs de bois* took wives, informal marriages according to the custom of the land. The children of these unions were the forerunners of the Métis people.

Some of the *coureurs de bois* returned to Quebec in retirement, leaving any wilderness family behind, but often they remained in the West. Mixed-blood communities soon developed and the Great Lakes Métis people came into being. Sault Ste. Marie traces back to 1615 when French Jesuits established a mission. French traders followed and a Métis settlement grew. By 1812 the population had reached 1,000, but as the region became trapped out many moved west to the Red River area.

The Scots and English employees of the Hudson's Bay Company had even greater need for support services to maintain themselves and their trading posts. Once-yearly supply from England left the forts on the Bay so dependent upon the resident Cree for firewood, hunting, snowshoes, toboggans, moccasins and the like that permanent encampments grew next to the posts. Far away in pre-Victorian England, head office decreed that there would be zero fraternization, but in the lonely wilderness nature prevailed and liaisons developed between Company personnel and women of these "Home Guard" Cree. The Company stiffly held to its unrealistic policy for many years but eventually was pleased to discover that the mixed-blood progeny resulting from disregard of its edict made outstanding employees, "useful hands," in their employer's terminology. Woodcraft skills learned from their mothers blended with some rudimentary schooling supplied by their fathers, and often a second language, enabled these children of the fur trade to work at almost all levels of the industry. For nearly half a century the river systems of Canada witnessed vicious rivalry between the two forces, the Hudson's

Bay Company and the Montreal traders who evolved into the North West Company. The Hudson's Bay Company enjoyed an initial advantage in the proximity of its supply depot at York Factory that permitted return trips to the interior in one season. The Nor'Westers faced stupendous logistical problems supporting trading operations that reached more than 5,000 km (3,000 mi) inland from Montreal, a distance that could not be covered in a single season, much less a round trip. Their solution was to divide their transport system into two stages, one eastern and one northwestern, broken at Grand Portage west of Lake Superior.

The Montreal traders adopted Indian technology, the Algonkian birchbark canoe, and modified it for their heavy, long-distance transport. Two models were utilized: one 11 m (36 ft) in length, 2 m (6 ft) across, was able to carry three tons of cargo as well as crew; another 7.5 m (25 ft) long with a 1.2-m (4-ft) beam carried a ton and a half. The larger canoes, *canots de maître*, ran through the Great Lakes, the smaller, *canots du nord*, were used for transport through the smaller waterways west of Lake Superior.

In July each year, the two divisions would rendezvous at the North West Company's great staging and meeting depot at Grand Portage. More than 1,200 men would gather to eat, drink and converse but also to sort and repack their cargoes and exchange the eastbound furs for the westbound trade goods. Then the great canoes would head out, the *canots du maître* back to Montreal and the smaller *canots du nord* to the trading posts deep in the interior. When it was discovered that the border of the new United States placed Grand Portage in American territory, the great depot was closed in 1802. The next year Fort William was constructed on a new all-Canadian canoe route.

Birchbark canoes are fragile; they lasted only one or two seasons of the punishing travel. The steady demand created a secondary industry of canoe manufacture, centred at Trois-Rivières.

These vessels were manned by the new occupation of *voyageur*. From dawn to dusk, occasionally from dawn to dawn, from spring break-up to fall freeze-up, they paddled the huge, cargo-laden canoes thousands of kilometres into the Canadian wilderness, and then back again, carrying equally heavy loads of fur. Forty strokes a minute, or sometimes 45, hour after hour, with only brief stops for breakfast and nooning, and the periodic pauses for a pipe when the paddles were shipped and they could light up the blessed tobacco. Each canoe carried a sail and on the odd occasion when the wind and water were right the men could happily lean back and relax.

The scores of portages that lay along the trade routes were dreaded relief from the routine of paddling. By his contract, each *voyageur* was required to carry eight 40 kg (90-lb) packs; there was a small bonus for extras. These were small men, 162–165 cm (5'4" to 5'5"), 72 kg (160 lb) was the optimum weight. Larger and heavier men took up too much room and displaced too much cargo. Two packs, or 82 kg (180 lb), was the usual portage load and that was generally more than the weight of the man beneath, but sometimes three packs were slung from the tumpline across the *voyageur's* forehead as he leaned into the rough trail.

The portages were seldom short or easy going. The Grand Portage between Lake Superior and Lake of the Woods was 14.5 km (9 mi) long and rose in many places more than 215 m (700 ft). Methye Portage, leading from the head of the Churchill River into the Athabasca system, was 20 km (12 mi) long. Little wonder that the *voyageur* was used up and retired by his 30s.

Provisioning the hard-driving *voyageurs* raised another logistical problem. Their incredible labour required a huge intake of calories. Covering the distances of the lengthy trade routes permitted no time for hunting or fishing. The solution was pemmican: dried, powdered buffalo meat mixed with fat (and berries when available) secured first from the Plains Indians and later from the Métis buffalo hunters. Pemmican was the first concentrated, nearly unperishable travel food, and in its preparation and supply another industry was born. When the Hudson's Bay Company turned to the same source to feed its rivermen, the demand made a significant impact upon the supposedly inexhaustible herds of buffalo on the plains.

For nearly 50 years, until 1821, the Hudson's Bay Company and the Nor'Westers competed fiercely for the furs of Western Canada. Taking the trade to its source, each sought to establish itself ahead of the other until hundreds of trading posts dotted the landscape from the Great Lakes to Lake Athabasca and from Hudson Bay to the Rocky Mountains. The North West Company alone was operating 102 posts in 1805 with 1,610 male employees, accompanied by 450 women and 600 children.[6]

By 1821 the unceasing rivalry between the Hudson's Bay Company and the North West Company had so weakened both enterprises that they were forced to accept merger. The two became one, continuing as the Hudson's Bay Company. One immediate result was a surplus of personnel. Rationalization decreed that the canoe route from Montreal be discontinued in favour of the more economical connection to Hudson Bay. Trading posts were closed in the search for efficiency and profit.

"Voyageurs and Raftsmen on the Ottawa about 1818," oil on canvas, 1930–31, by Charles William Jefferys (1869–1951). The pack being carried by the voyageur on the left is typical of those transported during portages. *Library and Archives Canada / Credit: Charles W. Jefferys C-005946*

The reorganized Company encouraged those uprooted by the new order to move to Red River, the settlement founded in 1811 by Lord Selkirk as a new home for evicted Scottish crofters, forced from their Highland homes by the conversion to sheep grazing. The tiny colony had survived natural calamity and the enmity of the North West Company, which resented the colony's presence athwart its canoe routes. Very shortly after the merger, some 1,300 French and English/Scottish Métis migrated to the parishes stretched along the Red and Assiniboine Rivers. More would follow in later years.

During the years of conflict between the two fur-trading giants, Métis residents of Red River had sided with the North West Company. Métis resentment at Hudson's Bay Company restrictions on buffalo hunting and the trade in pemmican flared into a confrontation on June 19, 1816, with armed settlers led by Governor Robert Semple. A firefight broke out, and Semple and 20 settlers were killed. One Métis also died. Known as the Battle of Seven Oaks, the incident is an early milestone in the Métis claim to nationhood, the first armed defence of their rights.

MANY OF THE MÉTIS who congregated at Red River after 1821 came from scattered trading posts throughout the West. Now members of a greatly enlarged community, they adopted a new lifestyle. Their small river lots permitted modest cultivation, yielding little more than subsistence produce, pasturing enough for a small horse herd, and freedom to partake in the twice yearly buffalo hunt, the signature activity of Red River for 50 years.

Until 1820 the buffalo had ranged within reach of individual hunters riding from the settlement, but in later years the herds had retreated so far out on the plains that group hunting became essential, if only to provide protection from the Sioux who strongly objected to the invasion of their hunting grounds. The Red River hunters went forth twice each season. The spring/summer hunt began in June and remained out on the plains until early August, leaving very little turnaround time before the fall hunt that moved out just a month later, in early September, returning in late October or perhaps November, if winter held off.

If the Sioux were displeased with these invasions of their territory, they had good reason. The hunt grew in size until it became the equivalent of an army regiment, complete with quartermaster and supply units, moving in formation across the prairies. It systematically butchered the buffalo in numbers that caused serious distress to the plains Indians whose very lives were totally dependent upon the animals.

The Red River buffalo hunt as an organized affair grew quickly after 1820. As the Company's drive for economy and rationalization continued, more former employees descended upon the settlement in search of a new livelihood. The buffalo hunt beckoned. The fur trade's demand for pemmican remained strong and the ostensible purpose of the hunt was the taking of meat for pemmican as well as personal consumption. Also, trekking over the open prairies with friends and relatives and running buffalo on fast horses was huge fun. And a successful hunt held the promise of quick profit. The two annual journeys out onto the plains drew the high-spirited Métis away from the more secure but stodgy vocation of tending crops and livestock at the Red River settlement, although many attempted to fit a small agricultural operation around the timing of the hunts, seeding tiny plots before June and harvesting and haying before the September departure.

The technique of the Red River hunt was simple, but the execution called for discipline, skill and daring. Entire families, equipped with carts, oxen, horses and tools, swarmed across the plains in search of the great herds of buffalo. When outriding scouts reported the presence of a herd, the hunters mounted their fastest buffalo-runners and rode slowly and as close as possible to their prey. On command from the captain of the hunt, and only then, they charged, overtook the fleeing beasts and raced through them, firing their flintlock muskets point-blank at their chosen animals. When the dust and the smoke cleared, often more than 1,000 dead buffalo littered the prairies. Then up came the waiting women and children with the carts and the butchering began.

The Métis became extremely adept at rapid fire with their smooth-bore muskets. Several lead balls were carried in the mouth and powder was loose in a pocket. Reloading was simply tossing a handful of powder down the barrel, spitting in a ball, tapping the butt of the musket on knee or saddle to tighten the charge, then quickly firing into the nearest buffalo. One unlucky hunter's rate of fire caused his barrel to heat to the point that it ignited the powder just as he placed his mouth over the muzzle to spit in a ball. He survived the impact and the fall from his horse but the discharge so severely burned his throat that he could take neither food nor water and died very unpleasantly.[7]

The definitive account of the Red River buffalo hunt comes from the writings of Alexander Ross, the young dominie (schoolmaster) who signed on with John Jacob Astor at Lachine in 1810. Ross served at Astoria, the fur post Astor's Pacific Fur Company operated on the Columbia River. When the North West Company acquired Astoria in 1813, Ross was assigned to their post on the Snake River and resumed his connection to Canada. In 1825 he moved to Red River with his wife, a member of the Okanagan tribe, and their children. The mixed-blood family fitted easily into the community and became prominent in its affairs.

Ross accompanied the spring hunt in 1840 and provided a detailed description in his book, *The Red River Settlement*, published in 1856, the year of his death. The assembly of carts, Métis and accompanying animals that year was huge, perhaps the largest that ever trekked out of Red River. Ross tells us that the first hunt in 1820 consisted of 540 carts. Five years later 680 carts went out. In 1830 the number rose to 820 and in 1835 to 970. But in 1840 a grand assembly of 1,210 carts with 400 hunters and 1,230 family members began gathering on June 15. Ross even counted the dogs: 542 "camp followers" (as Ross called them) slunk among the carts. We are not given the number of horses and oxen but it must have been at least 2,000 with over 1,200 draft animals plus 400 hunters, each with at least two horses for riding and buffalo running. When the carts were circled for the night with tents and animals within, Ross thought the entire camp might have been the largest of its kind in the world, and he was very likely correct. Travelling with the great caravan, on their first great hunt, was a young Métis family, Isadore and Louise Dumont, with their daughter, 5-year-old Pelagie, and three sons: Isadore, 4, Gabriel, 3, and Joseph, just 1. The Métis had learned that a form of government was essential to the successful operation of their hunting caravans. Thus, the first order of business before setting forth on the plains was the election of officers to govern and the adoption of laws for them to enforce. Ten captains, including a chief, or president, were chosen. Each captain was provided 10 soldiers under his command. Ten guides were also selected. (Ross observed that "people in a rude state of society, unable to read or write, are generally partial to the number ten.")

The rules adopted by the 1840 expedition were recorded by Ross. They became more or less standard but each hunt debated and established its own laws:

1. No buffalo to be run on the Sabbath-day.
2. No party to fork off, lag behind, or go before, without permission.
3. No person or party to run buffalo before the general order.
4. Every captain with his men, in turn, to patrol the camp, and keep guard.
5. For the first trespass against these laws, the offender to have his saddle and bridle cut up.
6. For the second offence, the coat to be taken off the offender's back, and be cut up.
7. For the third offence, the offender to be flogged.
8. Any person convicted of theft, even to the value of a sinew, to be brought to the middle of the camp, and the crier to call out his or her name three times, adding the word "Thief," at each time.[8]

The 1840 hunt ran smoothly and was successful. Ross describes only minor breaches of discipline, and none that affected the killing of buffalo, but it was not always so. The success or failure of each season's caravan was directly dependent upon the degree of discipline and coordination achieved. Father George Belcourt, who accompanied the fall hunt in 1845, stated that the summer hunt that year had been "pitiful, for after having suffered the rigors of a long march under a burning sun, all the men returned with but a quarter of their accustomed loads. This was due more to a lack of unity among them than to the scarcity of game."[9]

A Red River cart, the "birchbark canoe of the prairies." Note the shaganappi wrapped around the rim of the cart's wheel. *Saskatchewan Archives Board R-A3278*

THE RED RIVER CART

The wholesale or commercial hunting of buffalo, especially when the herds could be found only at ever-greater distances from Red River, required transportation, some sort of wheeled conveyance, so the Métis invented one. It became their trademark—the Red River Cart.

It began as the simplest form of vehicle, two wheels on a single axle supporting a box, but soon evolved into a masterpiece of ingenuity nearly perfect for western conditions and terrain. The first models, built about 1800, were crude; the wheels were merely rounded slabs sliced from large tree trunks. Twenty-five years of adaptation produced spoked wheels almost 2 m (6 ft) in height to discourage tipping and were broad-rimmed and dished to prevent sinking too deeply into soft ground. Such a cart could carry 360–450 kg (800–1,000 lb) over very uneven ground and could be floated across rivers by removing the wheels and placing them under the box for buoyancy. The entire affair was constructed of wood, simplifying repairs on the trail, although shaganappi—wet rawhide that dried to the consistency of iron—was often employed, both in original construction and in repair. It was best used as a rim for the wooden tires.

The oak trees that grew in the valley of the Assiniboine River provided perfect material for the carts and a cart-building industry developed. Prices were in the $5 to $10 range in the 1860s. The Hudson's Bay Company, quick to adapt, began to supply several of its western posts overland by cart train and maintained a standing order for as many carts as were available. Competition was keen as Red River cart transport became the order of the day.[1]

Because grease collected dust and grit that caused the whole assembly to seize, the wooden axle was allowed to turn against the dry wooden hub. This produced an unearthly screeching likened to a banshee's lament. When several hundred carts were in concert, as they often were, the din was unforgettable. Many of the music-loving Métis must have been rendered at least partially tone deaf after years of exposure to the racket of the carts. Another result of the greaseless travel was the loss of axles due to wearing. No matter. Spares were carried, and extras could be secured from the nearest tree.

The Red River cart was usually drawn by an ox unless more speed was desired, when a horse would be placed between the shafts. Usually one driver would control several carts, up to half a dozen tied in tandem.

The Red River Cart was the birchbark canoe of the prairies, a conveyance uniquely designed for its environment. With its advent, the entire western plains opened up to the Métis. It became practical for families to over-winter on the prairie after the fall buffalo hunt, in locations remote from the trading posts along the river systems. The wooded coulees of the Saskatchewan, Qu'Appelle and Milk Rivers and the uplands of Cypress Hills and Wood Mountain provided shelter and timber for housing. In this way the *hivernant* settlements gradually developed, many of them evolving into communities of today.

NOTE

1. Gerhard J. Ens, *Homeland to Hinterland* (Toronto: University of Toronto Press, 1996), 89.

DURING THE YEARS OF competition with the North West Company, the Hudson's Bay Company was at a disadvantage in the matter of canoes, lacking both raw material for construction and skilled paddlers to handle the tricky vessels. Few birch trees grew in the vicinity of Hudson Bay and the men the Company imported knew nothing of the art of canoeing.

But the men from the Orkney Islands knew boats, and boats were sturdier than canoes and could carry far more cargo. They were, however, much heavier than birchbark canoes, a major handicap at the many portages. Out of the Company's experiments with design and construction evolved the York Boat, propelled by oar or by sail, durable and with great cargo capacity. The largest were "over thirteen metres [40 ft] in length with a beam of three metres [10 ft] and propelled by eight oars. When loaded to capacity, with about one hundred pieces of freight, the combined weight of cargo and crew amounted to roughly 5,500 kilograms [12,000 lb]."[10]

The birchbark canoe, elegant but fragile and inefficient, passed into history as the York boats, with twice or three times the carrying capacity, took over the trade routes. After the 1821 merger and the abandonment of the canoe routes from Montreal through Fort William, the York boat almost totally replaced the canoe. The occupation of *voyageur* was no more.

A new occupation was born, that of "tripman." The York boats required crew. The Orkneymen could not man all the York boats that came into service. To cover all the routes more than 200 were needed, powered by the muscle of over 1,200 men.[11] The Métis of Red River supplied much of this manpower.

The new line of work was even more gruelling than that of *voyageur*. Trip-men pulling the 4.5-m (15-ft) oars reminded observers of galley slaves. The portages were brutal. All the usual freight still had to be carried across, but in addition there was now the great boat instead of a light canoe. The empty weight of the 13-m (42-ft) York boat was one ton. Even when portages were cleared and equipped with log rollers, manhandling such a heavy and ungainly craft was cruel and dangerous work where a slip often meant serious injury, or even death.

To the Métis at Red River, the Hudson's Bay Company was their economic master no matter what livelihood they chose. The tripmen were employed by the Company, usually on a two- or four-month contract for specific routes. All furs and the produce of the buffalo hunt, pemmican, dried meat or robes, could be sold only to the Company. The same with any meagre cereal grain they were able to harvest from their tiny river lots. Whatever basic food-stuffs, such as sugar, tea, salt, flour, and any clothing or utensils that the Métis required to maintain their modest lifestyle, could be purchased only from the Company, the sole importer to the territory. Resentment directed at the Company was the natural result of such a monopoly.

The hides of buffalo taken in the early winter months, cured and tanned with the hair in place, made excellent robes. Used for coats and blankets, they had a modest trade value, but in the late 1830s the price of buffalo robes escalated when a new market developed in eastern Canada and the United States. The Métis were quick to take advantage of the opportunity and increasingly they moved from Red River to the wintering settlements to be closer to the herds. The hunting and skinning of buffalo in winter, and the scraping, curing and tanning of the hides was a labour-intensive activity that fully engaged all members of the Métis families in their rude communities on the plains.

Living out on the plains required at least one annual trip back to Fort Garry, usually in the spring, to market the produce of the hunt and to purchase supplies. A network of trails evolved across the western grasslands, well-marked by the ruts of the great wheels of the heavily laden Red River carts.

Replica of a York Boat afloat on the Bigstone River at Cumberland House in August 1993. *Photo courtesy of Sid Robinson, La Ronge, Saskatchewan*

Initially the Hudson's Bay Company had little interest in buffalo robes as they were bulky and difficult to transport on the river route to York Factory. The American market, however, would take all the robes the Métis could produce and, in defiance of the Company's monopoly, buffalo robes were smuggled south out of Red River. Relations between the Red River Métis and the Hudson's Bay Company worsened after 1844 when Norman Kittson, Quebec-born but now American, set up a trading post at Pembina, only 95 km (60 mi) south of Fort Garry. Kittson attracted an increasing supply of robes and furs.

In 1846, the English Métis at Red River worked up a submission to London complaining of their treatment by the Company. The French-speaking Métis joined in and, with the assistance and encouragement of one of their great supporters, the local parish priest Father George-Antoine Bellecourt, prepared a petition demanding free trade and a political voice. With 977 signatures affixed, the dissidents carried their petitions to London where they enlisted the assistance of one of their own, Alexander Isbister, born at Cumberland House to a Hudson's Bay Company employee and his Métis wife. The 25-year-old Isbister, only five years out of Canada and very sympathetic, agreed to present their grievances to the government. He attached his own covering letter in support and forwarded the submissions to the Colonial Secretary on February 17, 1847.

It was to no avail. The Company's defence prevailed. On January 23, 1849, Isbister was advised by the Colonial Office that "no oppression alleged by you to have been suffered by the inhabitants of the territory over which the powers of the Hudson's Bay Company extend" had been made out. Case closed.

The case was not closed in Red River. Over the winter of 1848–49 the Métis dissatisfaction with the Company intensified. Much of the credit for the unity of purpose that sprouted and took root among the Métis at Red River must be given to the officials of the Hudson's Bay Company, who missed few opportunities to aggravate dissent in the settlement. Early in 1849 the Company arrested and charged four Métis, Guillaume Sayer and three others, with trading in furs, contrary to its monopoly. Sayer, a trapper, had sold his furs to Norman Kittson at Pembina. The four came to trial on May 17.

A courthouse surrounded by several hundred armed men, all friends and supporters of the accused, and all determined that they should receive no punishment, is not conducive to the even-handed administration of justice. Worse when the presiding jurist was widely regarded in the community as the toady of the prosecution.

On the morning set for the Sayer trial, the Métis of Red River thronged to the Fort Garry courthouse. Alexander Ross watched from his front door, and then strolled over for a better look. He counted 377 firearms and a considerable number of more primitive weapons. The crowd was very excited and Ross feared that some small incident might "set these inflammable elements in a blaze."[12]

When the Recorder of the Court, Adam Thom, arrived, opened court and called for the accused to appear, the Métis at first refused to surrender them. The demonstrators sent in a "complaint" demanding that "all prosecutions against individuals for trading in furs be suspended."[13]

A compromise was worked out. Sayer and the other three accused were allowed to bring into the courtroom 12 supporters who left their guns at the door where 20 more stood guard, fully armed. It was uncomfortable, but proceedings got under way.

Literally under the gun as the court was, it is no surprise that the trial was a clumsy pretense. Sayer's case was called first. He admitted having purchased some furs from a Native and a verdict of guilty was entered. Then Sayer claimed that he had been given permission to trade. Recorder Thom, seeing a way out of his dilemma, used this as a pretext to discharge the accused without penalty. The prosecution, the Company, acquiesced. All four accused left the courtroom in triumph. Although the Métis right to trade in defiance of the Company's monopoly had not been raised or even mentioned in the court proceedings, other than in the "Complaint," someone called out: *"Le commerce est libre! Le commerce est libre! Vive la liberté!"* The excited mob took up the cry and it was heard all through the settlement.

It was the effective end of the Hudson's Bay Company trade monopoly. Instead of moving north to York Factory and on to London, more and more of the produce of Rupert's Land bypassed Fort Garry and was carted south to St. Paul. Another occupation was born—the freighter. By 1858, 800 Red River carts creaked down the 650-km (400-mi) trail; 20 years after the Sayer trial, in 1869, 2,500 fully laden carts delivered their cargo at St. Paul.

The Métis of Red River, by unified and determined action, had successfully challenged the authority of the powerful Hudson's Bay Company. It was another step, a giant step, on the road to nationhood.

One of the Métis leaders who had much to do with organizing the demonstration at the Sayer trial, and one of several who signed the "Complaint" was Louis Riel, a prominent member of the Red River community. Riel's son and namesake, only four and a half years old on May 17, 1849, would become more famous at another great disturbance at Fort Garry 20 years later.

OVER THE 50-YEAR SPAN of its history, the Red River buffalo hunt came to characterize the development of the Métis nation. The success of the hunt required organization, discipline and teamwork, attributes not common among the free-wheeling and independent-minded Métis people. By disciplining themselves to the common purpose of killing buffalo they developed the cohesion that took them to nationhood. When they applied the lessons of the hunt in advancing their political aspirations in Red River in 1869 and 1870, and again at Batoche in 1885, they certified their status as a true nation. Because their communities were scattered over the western plains, their claim to a defined territory, the common hallmark of a nation, was a bit nebulous, but no more so than with other Aboriginal peoples of North America. The Métis land question remains troublesome to this day.

CHAPTER 9

The Battle of the Grand Coteau[1]

OUNG GABRIEL DUMONT, LYING PRONE IN A SHALLOW, hastily dug pit, peered through an opening between two heavy sacks. The sacks were part of the primitive but effective defensive position he held on the sun-baked prairie that in a later century would come to be known as a "fox-hole." Stretched out in this posture he was protected from direct line-of-fire but he had to be careful not to expose himself when reloading his musket. That process required him to roll over and raise himself somewhat while inserting powder and ball, tamping the charge and spreading powder into the flash-pan by striking the musket's butt against the floor of his pit. Gabriel remained alert, vigilant to ensure that no sniper crept close enough to take him unawares. Destined in later years to become the most famous of all the Métis plainsmen, this day was the baptism of fire for Gabriel Dumont.

It was quiet out front. But the young defender did not relax. Just over the brow of the next hill was a huge army of Yankton Sioux—more than 2,000, McGillis had reported this morning when he galloped wildly back into camp. And McGillis should know. He had spent the night among the Sioux as their prisoner before breaking away and outrunning his pursuers. "They told me they will take our camp and kill us all," he announced breathlessly.

When the entire Sioux army arrayed itself before them, no one among the encampment of Métis buffalo hunters out of Red River doubted McGillis' estimate. Never had any of them seen such numbers of warriors. Painted and in full regalia, mounted on their war ponies, armed with bows, lances and guns, all glistening in the brilliant July sunshine, they were a terrifying spectacle.

The Sioux had been expected, of course, but not in such numbers. Scouts of the Red River hunters had spotted them the previous evening. Jean-Baptiste Falcon, the party leader, gave five of his men a telescope and sent them forward to investigate. Foolishly, the five had brazenly ridden towards the Sioux encampment and soon found themselves surrounded. Two managed to break away and escape but the other three, McGillis, James Whiteford and Baptiste Malaterre, spent the night as prisoners.

The usual two parties trekked out of Red River for the hunt in June 1851, only moderately concerned by the Sioux menace. Gabriel Dumont's family was with the Saint François-Xavier band, from White Horse Plains, on the Assiniboine River 32 km (20 mi) west of Fort Garry. This was a small party, only 200 carts, 67 hunters, and an uncounted number of women and children. The second party, combining hunters from Saint Boniface and Pembina, was much larger, 1,100 carts, 318 hunters, 1,300 persons in all.

The two groups rendezvoused on June 19, not only to conduct the usual formalities of electing the commanders and fixing the rules of the hunt, but to coordinate their routes. For maximum security it was agreed that they would move in parallel but maintain a separation of approximately 30–50 km (20–30 mi) so as not to interfere with each other's hunt. They would remain in communication and come to each other's assistance in the event of a Sioux attack.

Gabriel felt a friendly hand grasp his ankle. Jean-Baptiste Falcon was encouraging his defenders, slipping from pit to pit during a lull in the action. They had been stretched out in the blazing July sun for more than four hours without food or water. Gabriel was fortunate. The sacks protecting him were full of dried buffalo meat. He worked a piece loose and chewed it gratefully. In later years, when telling of this battle, Gabriel would joke that he "ate his ramparts."

The two parties had worked their way west and south, deeper into Sioux territory. The Saint Boniface/Pembina group, following the southern route, had two minor encounters with Sioux, but were easily able to fend them off. The incidents were duly reported to the Saint François-Xavier party on a parallel course to the north.

In keeping with the tradition that the buffalo hunt be accompanied by a priest, each party enjoyed the company of a missionary. With the Saint François-Xavier band was Reverend Louis François Lafleche, later to be Bishop of Trois-Rivières, and after whom the town of Lafleche, Saskatchewan is named. The larger group was joined by a recent arrival in the West, Father Albert Lacombe, on his first buffalo hunt. Later locating in what became the province of Alberta, Father Lacombe became the best-loved and most widely known cleric in all of Western Canada.

The Coteau, sometimes called "The Dirt Hills," is "knob and kettle topography," a jumble of small, rolling, sometimes rugged hills intermixed with catch-basins, or pot holes and small sloughs. Detritus from glacial action, a recessional moraine deposited more than 10,000 years ago by the receding Wisconsin Glacier when it stalled in place for a few thousand years, it ranges in a narrow irregular band north-westerly from just above the Nebraska border, near Mitchell, South Dakota almost 900 km (560 mi) to the valley of the Saskatchewan, ending about 100 km (60 mi) south of Battleford. Encompassing almost 67,000 km² (26,000 mi²) in all, the Missouri Coteau is the second of the three steppes by which the plains rise westward from the Red River to the foothills of the Rockies.

On Saturday, July 12, the main party reached the Missouri (or Grand) Coteau, the height of land dividing the drainage of the Missouri and Assiniboine Rivers. Father Lacombe noted that his band was in the vicinity of a prominent landmark of the Coteau, the *maison du chien*, or Dog's House, better known today as Dogden Butte.

Dogden Butte lies on the eastern escarpment of the Missouri Coteau, ll km (7 mi) southwest of the present community of Butte, North Dakota. With an elevation of 698 m (2,291 ft), it is an imposing standout among the lesser hills surrounding it and this is particularly so when viewed from the east, the direction from which the Red River hunters came. Father Lacombe observed that it could be plainly seen from "three leagues eastward." (Today the crest of Dogden Butte is marked by a mast and antenna of the radio network of the North Dakota Highway Patrol.) The parallel courses of the two bands of hunters would place the Saint François-Xavier party 30–50 km (20–30 mi) northwest of Dogden Butte, approximately 16 km (10 mi) south of Minot, North Dakota.

On that Saturday Father Lacombe's party finally sighted a large herd of buffalo. Since it was their first, the priest provided dispensation from one of the cardinal rules of the hunt—no buffalo to be run on the Sabbath—and the next day the hunters pressed forward in pursuit of the herd.

On that same Saturday, the hunters under Jean-Baptiste Falcon sighted not buffalo, but Sioux. After the capture of their five scouts, the White Horse Plains party went into defensive action. As they did every night, they circled their carts, wheel to wheel, with the shafts in the air. But now extra measures were taken. Poles carried for the drying of meat were thrust between the spokes to prevent the separation of the carts. Cargo, harness and baggage was piled under the carts to complete the bulwark and trenches were dug to protect the women and children. The horses and oxen, buffalo runners and draft animals, were placed inside the barricade.

Much of this was innovative in plains warfare of the day. But the most innovative and effective feature of the defensive preparations of the Métis was the digging of pits in a perimeter outside the circled carts. From this protective outer circle the hunters of the party would present their considerable firepower and hope to prevent the Sioux from reaching the main barricade within.

After the seizure of the five scouts, and while the Métis were building their stronghold, three Sioux warriors approached the camp. Ten hunters went out to meet them and prevent them from making any assessment of the defences. The Sioux complained of strangers hunting on their lands, spoke of gifts in compensation and promised to return the next day to deliver up the prisoners in peace. The distrustful Métis were not taken in. They sent two messengers to the main group, battened their defences even tighter, and set an "especial guard."

During the night, Father Lafleche donned his surplice and stole and heard confessions from those who prepared for death on the morrow. In the morning the priest spoke a few words of encouragement, reminding them that the good Lord was on their side. "Fight courageously! It is God who commands you to defend your wives and your children and to protect their lives. Die if you must, but die bravely." With perhaps equal effect, the priest promised that there would be a day of feasting and three high masses if God spared their lives.

That night the hunters stayed up with Father Lafleche to watch the eclipse of the moon he had predicted. It is that eclipse that fixes the date of the wild encounter which followed—July 13, 1851.

One wonders what extra security precautions the Métis might have taken that night. Two years later, Governor Stevens and his party camped near the Red River hunters under their veteran leader, Jean-Baptiste Wilkie. Stevens recorded that, while he detailed 12 sentries in three reliefs, providing only four on watch at a time, the Métis, albeit with a larger camp, had 36 men standing guard all night. And that was at a time of minimal concern for Sioux attacks.[1]

NOTE

1. Isaac I. Stevens, *Narrative and Final Report of Exploration for a Route for a Pacific Railroad 1855*, vol. 13, book 1 (Washington, DC: United States Senate, 1860).

Manpower on the firing line was a problem. The White Horse Plains party had started with only 67 hunters and three of those were now held hostage by the Sioux. But there were 13 boys, down to the age of 13, who could handle a gun. Gabriel Dumont, just turned 14, was one of these. So was his brother, Isadore, who, at 17, was certainly considered mature enough to serve on the defensive firing line. The father, Isidore senior, was understandably hesitant about placing his younger son in a position of such danger, but Gabriel, like all the family members, was inured to the harshness of life on the plains. This was the third year in a row the Dumonts had joined with the summer hunt, and in fact they had been with the great hunt of 1840, 11 years earlier. Isidore weakened as Gabriel insisted. After all, the boy was handy with a gun. So, now there were 77 manned firing pits protecting the women, children, horses and oxen behind the barricades.

The 14-year-old Gabriel Dumont stayed at his front-line post all that long, hot, murderous July day. Gabriel was in his pit when the Sioux came in the morning. He shivered at the might and spectacle of the host of Sioux warriors as they approached in the early sunshine, their war songs ringing in the clear morning air.

The Sioux army halted some distance from the Métis encampment and 30 hunters rode out to meet them. At the head of the Sioux advance guard rode their war chief, White Horse, contemptuously unarmed, shaking a hide-bag rattle and wailing his song. By fateful chance, the hunters from White Horse Plains were threatened by a powerful force under the leadership of a chief bearing the name of their home community.

The Métis offered presents to White Horse and asked him to turn his forces away but their gifts were contemptuously ignored. He had come to take the entire camp, White Horse declared, and could easily do so. His warriors had brought carts to carry off their plunder. During this exchange McGillis broke away and made his wild, successful run to safety. Then White Horse impatiently signalled his warriors forward and the 30 Métis hunters saw their peril. Wheeling their horses, they raced back to the barricades while the Sioux attempted to cut them off. But the Red River ponies won the race, leaping through an opening in the barricades that quickly closed behind them while their riders slipped out to their places on the firing perimeter.

The Sioux warriors rode haughtily forward, confident of an easy victory. Led by a prominent young chief, they charged the Métis encampment. A volley of shots from the firing pits killed the young chief, plus several other warriors, and a number of horses. The Sioux cavalry was surprised at the unexpected defence and wheeled away.

In the confusion of the first charge, Whiteford, still in the hands of the enemy, made a dash for freedom. His guard, a white American living among the Sioux, gave him the opportunity: "If you have a good horse, give it full rein and save yourself. I'll pretend to shoot at you." Whiteford did have a good horse, one of the best buffalo runners on the plains. Lying low on its back, he raced through the ranks of the surprised Sioux warriors. Miraculously, not a shot hit him and he reached the safety of the Métis barricades.

Malaterre followed Whiteford, but had not as fast a steed. Horse and rider went down in a hail of arrows and bullets. The Sioux butchered poor Malaterre and carried body parts on their lances to intimidate the beleaguered Métis.[2] Watching from his firing pit, the young Gabriel Dumont swore that he would not be taken by the Sioux. Fiercely clutching his musket, anxious not to waste ammunition, he waited for a sure shot.

After the first charge, a swarm of Sioux horsemen encircled the Métis and bullets and arrows flew among the defenders. But the effect was minimal. The men on the first line of defence were untouched, and returned the fire with much greater accuracy. Sioux warriors and their horses fell to the prairie and the attackers pulled back out of range. Then, changing tactics, some of the Sioux began to slither through the grass, attempting to steal into sniping range. Others, still mounted, darted at the defences, shooting and swerving away.

The battle was only one degree removed from hand-to-hand combat. The firearms on both sides were single-shot, smoothbore, flintlock muskets, notorious for their short range and poor accuracy. Even the Métis sharpshooters had difficulty hitting a man-sized target at 40 or 50 m (130–165 ft), although the ball or bullet could be lethal at twice that distance. To hit a Sioux warrior astride a charging war pony required more luck than skill, even if the rider was not clinging to the far side of his horse, a favourite technique of the Indian equestrians. Small wonder that the Métis muskets took down many more horses than riders. On the Sioux side, firing a musket from the back of a galloping horse might provide a satisfying sound but had little other effect. Unlike the Métis buffalo hunters, the Sioux had not mastered the technique of reloading while riding and after each shot had to withdraw to recharge their firearms. At the Battle of the Grand Coteau, the rate of musket fire advantage was all with the Métis.

It was different with the Sioux bowmen. They were extremely accurate and could place an arrow where they wanted up to 80 or 100 m (260–330 ft), far better than the musket. The arrow could still be lethal at twice that range, and their rate of fire was up to a dozen arrows in a minute. A devastating technique was the arcing of hundreds of arrows so that they fell like killing hail among the enemy. The Métis lost a number of horses and oxen within their barricade. It could only have been the Sioux arrows that reached the animals. But the arrows were far less effective against the Métis hunters set apart from each other in their firing pits.

The Sioux darted and dashed at the Métis perimeter only to fall to the withering musket fire if they came too close. Frustrated and furious at the defence they failed to understand, they screamed and howled horribly, hoping to frighten the Métis, but with each attack more warriors and horses went down.

The great advantage of the Sioux lay in their numbers. They could have easily overwhelmed the tiny band of defenders in one massed charge, broken through the circled carts and slaughtered at will. But the Indian style of warfare was individual and undisciplined combat. They saw no honour in death and could never accept the carnage inherent in the European style of war. Glory lay in solo feats of bravery.

Within the barricades, Father Lafleche, a tall figure resplendent in white surplice, crucifix in hand, mounted upon a cart in the centre of the circle and prayed and encouraged the defenders. He was not armed, but as a precaution had placed an axe nearby in case the Sioux succeeded in breaching the defences. Pacificism had its limits.

On through the stifling heat of a July day on the plains the battle waxed and waned. The defenders became parched with thirst. Gabriel Dumont could no longer salivate to chew his buffalo jerky. Straining to keep watch through the shimmering, dancing air as the heat rose from the baked ground, his eyes began to play tricks and ghostly Sioux warriors swam across his line of vision.

For six hours the Sioux kept pressing the Métis camp. Finally, toward mid-afternoon, one of the attacking chiefs was heard to cry, "The French have a Manitou with them. We will never be able to harm them. It is impossible to kill them." The Sioux blamed the imposing figure of Father Lafleche for their failure, and the warriors withdrew.

The Métis hunters carefully climbed out of their positions and checked on each other. Not one had been even wounded. Within the barricade, the same. No one had been hurt. But they had lost, or had to destroy, 12 horses and four oxen. As the Sioux pulled away with their dead and wounded on the carts they had brought to carry the plunder to be taken from the Métis, a heavy thunderstorm rolled over the prairie, drenching everyone. Then followed a deep mist that made further engagement impossible.

The victors examined the battlefield. Bloodstains in the grass told them of fallen warriors. The corpse of Malaterre was found, pierced by 67 arrows and three bullets. The hands and feet were missing; the skull crushed and the brains scattered on the prairie. Poor Malaterre was buried where he fell. No monument or dedication marks the spot, unlike Butte de Morale, named for a Métis victim of an earlier encounter with the Sioux, a landmark with an elevation of 525 m (1,724 ft), 8 km (5 mi) west of Wellsburg, North Dakota.

Falcon and Father Lafleche, together with their Métis hunters, pondered what to do. The Sioux had not gone far and there was every reason to think they would return. The two messengers sent to the Saint Boniface/Pembina party had been forced back by Sioux scouts. But that morning two young Métis had panicked and fled, racing away on their fleetest horses. Perhaps they had made it through. But in the meantime, should the Saint François-Xavier band hold its position, or try to retreat? It was decided to stay put for the night and attempt a retreat in the morning, a particularly dangerous manoeuvre.

During the night the Sioux gave every sign that they would be back. Blood-curdling screams out of the darkness, intended to frighten the Métis, and succeeding very well, promised another offensive on the morrow.

When morning came, the Métis moved out, their carts now in four columns so they could be quickly circled by placing two rows on each side and then closing the ends. Four patrols scouted for Sioux, one 1.6 km (1 mi) ahead, another behind, the other two the same distance out on each flank. The traditional signal of danger was two riders galloping past each other on a hilltop.

The camp had been underway barely an hour when the signal came from the rear. The Sioux were coming again. Profiting from the experience of yesterday's battle, the Métis closed their barricade with double rows of carts, then placed the hunters in their hastily scraped-out firing positions at a greater distance, three chains (60 m/200 ft) out from the carts. Digging tools, usually fire-hardened sticks and roots used to excavate the deep-growing wild turnip, were standard equipment for the travelling Métis families. The extended perimeter would make it more difficult for the Sioux to get even within arrow range of the livestock. The Métis had to protect their draft animals; they would be helpless out on the plains without them.

Again the Sioux encircled the camp. Bullets and arrows rained at the Métis, but with even less effect than the previous day because of the greater range forced by the extended defensive perimeter. Again the battle raged throughout the day as the blistering July sun beat down upon the determined defenders. Then, after five hours, one of the Sioux chiefs came forward as if to parley. He demanded entrance to the camp. When the Métis responded that he should leave if he valued his life, the chief then declared that the battle was at an end. The Sioux would retreat and would never again make war against the Métis.

With that, the entire Sioux army suddenly raced forward at full gallop. In single file around the defenders they loosed a tremendous volley of bullets and arrows, the heaviest of the two-day battle. The hunters in their pits returned the fire with a disciplined routine. Aim, fire, charge with powder, load with ball, aim and fire. As the Métis held their ground, the warriors peeled off and streamed over the hillside and away. They were gone.

The Métis were certain they had taken losses from this last charge, but only three, including Gabriel Dumont's father, Isidore, were wounded, and but slightly at that. No livestock were lost this day.

Perhaps the Sioux had reason to withdraw. Only half an hour later the hunters from the main party rode in, accompanied by more than 300 Saulteaux, traditional enemies of the Sioux. The two young Métis riders had slipped past the Sioux. There were tears of joy, for the Saint Boniface/Pembina riders had expected to find only the scene of a massacre. Now with nearly 700 fighting men in all, there was a proposal to follow the Sioux and settle matters permanently. But wiser advice prevailed as again a cooling summer thunderstorm rolled over them.

When the Red River hunters moved on, they left the Sioux a letter attached to a tall pole set in the prairie. In French, the language of the fur trade and the plains, the words of the message have been lost, but, although unpleasant encounters continued, never again did the Sioux test the full might of the Métis nation.

How many Sioux fell to the Métis muskets? Father Lacombe, who was not present for the battle, thought 18. Others claim that 80 of the attackers died, with many more wounded, and that 65 of their war ponies perished. Reality probably lies somewhere in between, but the Sioux would have regarded either end of that estimated range as a punishing loss.

A mere 77 Métis men and boys had vanquished the mighty Sioux, the same warriors of the plains who, 25 years later at Little Big Horn, almost totally destroyed five companies of the United States Seventh Cavalry and its most famous commander. Although contemporary accounts of the battle place the number of Sioux warriors at from 2,000 to 2,500, historians believe those estimates must be severely exaggerated. But with only 1,200 warriors, half the recollected numbers, the Sioux still had a 15 to 1 advantage and the accomplishment of the Métis defenders is not at all diminished.

On the arc of history of the Métis nation, their performance at the Battle of the Grand Coteau stands near the zenith. Here they established their mastery over the Great Plains. Henceforth they roamed at will over what are now the provinces of Manitoba, Saskatchewan and Alberta, and the states of Minnesota, North Dakota and Montana.

And at Grand Coteau, the boy Gabriel Dumont coolly passed a dramatic rite of passage into manhood. Thirty-four years later he was the great commander of the Métis at Batoche when his people last stood in armed defence of their rights.

Gabriel Dumont, as he appeared in later life. The young Dumont was profoundly influenced by the Battle of the Grand Coteau. He would employ the military strategies he learned in the battle during the course of the North-West Resistance of 1885, when he was the military leader of the Métis forces. *Saskatchewan Archives Board R-A6277*

At Batoche, the battle techniques devised at Grand Coteau again prevailed against a superior force—until that force adopted the strategy the Sioux had failed to employ. The shallow depressions on the prairie that had protected the Red River hunters in July 1851, had in May 1885 evolved into cunningly designed rifle pits, 1–1.25 m (3–4 ft) deep with breastworks of earth and logs channelled for shooting ports. For three days at Batoche the Métis defenders held off the modern army brought against them until, on the fourth day, frustrated troops charged and easily overran the resistance.

The circling of the Red River carts that was so effective at Grand Coteau was the spontaneous invention by the Métis of a defensive manoeuvre that developed during the same era among the Conestoga wagon trains crossing the American plains. It was also seen in the laager formed by the wagons of the Boers of South Africa in their battles with the Zulu.

Louise Dumont, mother of Gabriel and Isadore, carefully checked her sons for wounds and thanked God for having spared them. At Batoche, 34 years later, the Dumonts were not so blessed. Although Gabriel, the military leader, was wounded, he survived and escaped; Isadore, the older, was killed in the action.

CHAPTER 10

The End of the Red River Hunt

IN MARCH 1857, ALEX ISBISTER TOOK HIS SEAT BEFORE THE select committee of Parliament in the historic halls of Westminster, overlooking the Thames River, and reflected that he had come a long way, both geographically and socially—a very long way from his birth 35 years earlier at Cumberland House on the Saskatchewan River, the son of Hudson's Bay Company employee and his mixed-blood wife. Even further from his last employment with the Company at its most northern post in all Canada, Fort McPherson, where the Peel River joins the Mackenzie just before it flows into the Arctic Ocean. Isbister was now no longer just the mixed-blood "Son of Rupert's Land," condemned by the fact of that birth to spend his life in the menial service of the mighty Company while real advancement was reserved for those born and educated "outside." In Great Britain he had encountered no racial discrimination and now he appeared before the Committee as Alexander Kennedy Isbister, graduate of the Universities of Aberdeen and Edinburgh (the latter would award him an MA the following year), a prominent educator and scholar, and an author. He was also an articulate voice of the Red River Métis and a large part of the reason the government of Prime Minister Henry Temple (3rd Viscount) Palmerston had struck the Select Committee before which the mixed-blood "Son of Rupert's Land" now began to testify.

Isbister's appearance before the Committee was a challenge to his old employer, the Hudson's Bay Company, and particularly the Company's senior executive in Canada, Governor George Simpson. It was Simpson who had hired the 16-year-old Isbister and assigned him to the far north. It was Simpson who ruled the Company with such an iron grip that he became known as

"The Little Emperor," and who instituted the policy that made Métis "Sons of Rupert's Land," second-class employees, forbidden to rise above junior rank in the Company. It was Simpson who, on hearing of Isbister's intention to resign, wrote to the young man's superior: "Have the goodness to advise him from me not to carry that silly intention into effect, but if he does so, he will have much cause to regret it."[1] Alexander ignored the advice and did resign. Now, 16 years later, he would duel with The Little Emperor before the parliamentarians of Westminster.

Parliament had instructed the Select Committee "to consider the State of those British Possessions in North America which are under the administration of the Hudson's Bay Company, or over which they possess a License to Trade." The venerable Company was at risk. Its licenses for exclusive trade in the Arctic and Pacific watersheds, the territories west of Rupert's Land, were up for renewal and the validity of its Charter was again under consideration. An unsatisfactory report from the Committee back to Parliament could well have serious economic consequences for the 187-year-old monopoly.

Since his failed attempt in 1849, Isbister had become a powerful critic of the Hudson's Bay Company's treatment of Canada's Native peoples, including the Red River Métis with whom he identified. He carried on with their case against the Company as if he were unaware of the Colonial Secretary's rejection of January 23, 1849. He had assistance from two quarters. The Aborigines' Protection Society, formed in 1837, was global in scope, but Isbister was able to bring its focus to bear on the problems of the Natives in the territories under the administration of the Hudson's Bay Company. Isbister became a valuable member of the Society, having witnessed at first hand the starvation, even cannibalism, suffered by the Natives of the far north who, he believed, sacrificed too much of their food-gathering capacity in favour of hunting furs for the Company.

Governor George Simpson was nothing if not a Company man. In his testimony before the Select Committee he did his best to make out the Company's territories in Canada as being barren and valueless, unfit for habitation much less settlement, useless for any purpose other than the production of fur. The entire country was seized with permafrost as far south as Rainy River, Simpson told the Committee. As for the Native population, it was well served by the price certainty of a trade monopoly and freedom from unscrupulous competition. The sale of liquor to the Natives was a necessity forced upon the Company by competitors. The Company had the best interests of the Native population at heart and financially supported the religious missions in

Rupert's Land. Simpson merely waved off as exaggeration evidence of starvation and cannibalism among the Natives.

Alexander Isbister's evidence contradicted Simpson and opened the eyes of the Committee members to the practices of the Hudson's Bay Company. The monies the Company gave to the religious orders in Rupert's Land were actually paid, not to the missions, but to the missionaries individually. The funds were discretionary, Isbister told the Committee, nothing more nor less than a bribe, a "sop," so that they would close their eyes to the Company's less than charitable practices among the Native inhabitants.

It was Isbister's opinion that Red River could quickly become a flourishing settlement and that it should become part of Canada rather than be left under the administration of the Hudson's Bay Company. All British North America should be joined together, and soon, to ward off the threat of annexation by the United States.

The Report of the 1857 Select Committee was a disappointment to everyone. It was the inconclusive, colourless product of a compromise. Since Canada had shown no great interest in taking over the territory, the Report contained no firm recommendation for the future of Rupert's Land. The Company's exclusive licenses to trade would be allowed to expire.

Isbister was sorely disappointed in the outcome, but he had acquitted himself admirably before the Select Committee and came away with his reputation much enhanced. His recommendation that all British North America should be joined in one nation became government policy little more than 10 years later.

It may have been that the cut and thrust of the testimony and cross examination motivated the young scholar to study law. In any event he did, and in 1866 qualified as a barrister, a member of the Middle Temple, one of the Inns of Court. The Métis lad born at Cumberland House became Alexander Kennedy Isbister, M.A., LL.B. He remained in the field of education and became Dean of the College of Preceptors, the body that examined and licenced teachers.

Isbister continued to prosper in London. The royalties from his many books made him a wealthy man but he never discarded his allegiance to Red River. On his death in 1883, he left a major bequest and his 5,000-volume library to the fledgling University of Manitoba. The library was lost in a fire and the funds were embezzled, but Alexander Kennedy Isbister's contributions are still easily recognizable at the University where the most prestigious scholarship bears his name.

THE HUDSON'S BAY COMPANY had survived the Métis assaults against its monopoly and Charter, but the 1860s would be the final decade of its sovereignty over Rupert's Land. Understandably, relations between the Company and the Métis inhabitants continued to be difficult, particularly at Red River, until they finally exploded in 1869.

Métis migration from Red River to the western plains, underway since the late 1840s, accelerated during the 1860s in response to strong economic allure. The price of buffalo robes rose to very attractive levels, bringing as much as $12 at St. Paul in 1866, and many Métis families prospered, earning as much as $1,000 in a year, a substantial income for the time.[2]

The buffalo herds continued to retreat hundreds of kilometres west and south, out of range and spelling the end of the great Red River hunt. By 1866, only 150 carts left the old community seeking buffalo. More and more Métis joined the *hivernants*, the winter settlements, to be nearer the herds. A new hunt, composed of Métis from the several communities along the Qu'Appelle and Saskatchewan Rivers, was organized in 1863 under the leadership of Gabriel Dumont, then living at St. Laurent. It rendezvoused at the Cypress Hills and sought out the herds as far as the Judith Basin, south of the Missouri River. New settlements grew all through the West, as remote from Red River as Victoria (now Pakan) and Lac St. Anne on the North Saskatchewan River system, and even Lac la Biche on the Athabasca drainage. The Red River carts squealed 1,450 km (900 mi) along the Carlton Trail to Fort Edmonton.

The 49th Parallel, ignored and still unmarked, began to make its presence felt in the lives of the Métis. The United States government established a customs house at Pembina and imposed a 10% duty on furs, including buffalo robes. Although enforcement was almost non-existent at first, it was a disincentive to the old freight lines running through Pembina to St. Paul. Further west, at Fort Benton, the head of steamboat navigation on the Missouri River, such niceties as customs duties were still unknown. Good robe prices, still-plentiful buffalo and continued free entry to the American market drew hundreds of Métis away from Red River to the western plains. Still unconcerned about the impact of an international boundary, a good number of Métis settled south of the border, on the Milk River, the Missouri, and as far south as the Judith River.[3] It would not be many years before these Métis would be forcibly brought up against the fact that they were now in a foreign country.

Métis family, with Red River carts, camping on the prairie (no date). *Saskatchewan Archives Board R-A3955*

Until then the border really meant nothing to the Métis, even after the United States Army paid a visit to Fort Garry to warn against further buffalo hunting incursions into American territory. The warning was ignored because the Métis claimed the right to hunt on U.S. soil. They explained this claim to Governor Isaac Stevens when they met on the plains in the summer of 1853. Since there was doubt about the location of the unmarked boundary, and their traditional travels certainly extended into both Canada and the U.S., many of their children had been born out on the plains during the buffalo hunt and were just as likely American citizens as Canadian.[4]

It was no great matter for the Métis to establish themselves in a new location. Jean D'Artigue, a constable with the North-West Mounted Police, described the arrival of a group of Métis buffalo hunters at Fort Saskatchewan in October 1876:

> They carried their luggage in Red River carts, and as many of them had been there the previous year their cabins were ready to receive them, and they had only to take their goods in and settle down; but the newcomers had to build, and this is the way they set about it: Selecting a site well sheltered from the wind, and amply supplied

with wood and water, they felled some trees, and placing the trunks one above another, formed the walls of the new building. The roof was constructed with poles placed in rows and covered with hay and earth. Holes were cut in the walls for door and windows, the latter being closed in when so required with the skins of animals; while the doors were made of slabs of wood split with the axe and fastened together with thongs of rawhide. The chimney was constructed with unburned bricks composed of hay and mud, and the floor formed of hewed logs completed the carpenter work. This done, they plastered the crevices well with mud and the cabin was ready for occupation. The ease with which they are constructed, and the wanderings of game, will account for the number of the cabins to be found throughout the whole North-West.[5]

SOON AFTER THE RIEL-LED uprising of 1869–70 at Red River, a far greater exodus of Métis from the settlement began. Their hard-won achievement of provincial status and recognition of their land entitlement soon curdled. The troops Prime Minister Macdonald had sent west even while negotiations were ongoing in the spring of 1870 were neither professional nor disciplined. Militia and raw recruits, enlisted almost entirely in Ontario, they thirsted to avenge the death of Thomas Scott. When they arrived in the settlement on August 24 and found they were deprived of a battle with Riel, they unleashed their animosity on the Métis in the streets and in their homes. Then began "a reign of terror. Several Métis were slaughtered, Many, hunted like criminals, left their homes and sought refuge in the woods. Even the English-speaking half breeds were subject to indignity."[6]

The troops were followed by settlers from Ontario whose attitude was little better. Land hungry and unscrupulous, far more aware of the value of the Métis lands than the Métis themselves, they invaded and occupied much of the best properties without regard to any previous title or claim. The Métis were forced into the position of having to defend their lands.

The Red River Métis became despondent and demoralized. They felt deceived by their clergy who had preached pacificism and given assurances of the sincerity of the Ottawa government in protecting the rights of its new citizens. An increasing number loaded their carts, turned their backs on their old homes and headed west to begin again.

Several economic factors also turned sour for the Red River Métis after 1870, encouraging them to look westward for better conditions. The United

States imposed the requirement that goods in bond being transported from Eastern Canada through St. Paul into Red River be carried only by bonded carriers, excluding the Métis cart freighters. Hitherto easily avoided, American customs officers became more numerous and vigilant, closing off the buffalo robe traffic to St. Paul. After 1873 the duty on robes doubled from 10% to 20%. Effectively excluded from the American market, the Métis were again restricted to the Hudson's Bay Company as the single market for buffalo robes.[7] Fort Benton beckoned.

Some of the new migrants chose the settlements that had grown up around the fur posts on the Saskatchewan River, such as Cumberland House, Île-à-la-Crosse and Fort Edmonton. There they could maintain themselves by hunting, fishing and trapping fur. Others stayed near the buffalo and turned to the *hivernement* sites, such as Wood Mountain, Qu'Appelle, Cypress Hills, Lac la Biche, and Milk River. The town of Willow Bunch was founded by the Red River Métis in 1870, making it one of the oldest communities on the southern plains. Many adopted new communities in the Saskatchewan valley that took design similar to the river lots of Red River, such as Batoche and St. Laurent, where the annual buffalo hunt ran as it had at Red River, until the buffalo disappeared from the plains.

BEGINNING IN 1871, OTTAWA began negotiating treaties with the several Indian tribes occupying the plains between Lake of the Woods and the Rocky Mountains. The Métis people took a strong interest in these negotiations and served as facilitators at the treaty tables, earning the appreciation of both sides. In spite of the disappointing turn of events at Red River after 1870, prominent members of the Métis community, such as James McKay and Pascal Breland, encouraged their Indian brethren to place their trust in Ottawa's representatives.

There would be no treaties for the Métis; their land rights had been submerged by the 485,640 ha (1,200,000 acres) allotted them at Red River. At the Treaty 4 negotiations at Fort Qu'Appelle, in September 1874, the Cree and Saulteaux spokesmen requested that "the Half-breeds may have the right of hunting." They were assured, "As to the Half-breeds, you need not be afraid; the Queen will deal justly, fairly and generously with all her children."[8]

St. Laurent, on the west bank of the South Saskatchewan River, was the scene of a bold experiment in self-government.[9] On December 10, 1873, a large meeting of Métis from the nearby districts assembled in front of the church at St. Laurent. Gabriel Dumont, then 36 years old and in the prime of his manhood, presided over the meeting. With the guidance of Father Alexis André, and borrowing from the form of regulations employed to govern the buffalo hunt, they chose Dumont as president to serve with eight councillors and agreed to be bound by the laws they enacted.

The assembly then approved 28 basic laws for the governing and policing of the community. These included the traditional rules of the buffalo hunt. The president and his council were authorized to make any additional or supplemental regulations necessary to carry out the purposes already expressed.

During the following year, 1874, the new system worked to everyone's satisfaction and a second assembly was held exactly one year after the first, December 10, 1874. Dumont and his councillors all resigned, but he and most of his council were re-elected.

It was becoming evident to Dumont and his council that the great buffalo herds were diminishing and that care, and even conservation, would be required to maintain the hunt. As might be expected, 1874 had been a bad year, with the huge incursions into buffalo country made by the Boundary Survey and the North-West Mounted Police (NWMP). Accordingly, in January 1875 they revised the rules of the hunt. They provided that in late April the Métis in general assembly would fix the day of departure for the hunt and refreshed the traditional rule prohibiting early starts. Also, for the first time, a rule was enacted forbidding the wasting of animals killed.

In June trouble developed. As Dumont and the St. Laurent brigade were preparing for the hunt, they learned that a party had preceded them 10 days earlier, headed for the same hunting grounds. Dumont sent a message demanding that the jump-starters join his caravan. When they refused, he and 40 of his men rode in pursuit. Overtaking the offenders, Dumont insisted that they break camp and return. When faced with continued refusal, Dumont levied fines on the spot and seized equipment sufficient to make payment.

The lawbreakers had been hunting for the Hudson's Bay Company and promptly complained to Lawrence Clarke, the factor at Fort Carlton. The affair quickly escalated. Clarke saw another attack on the authority of the Company and forwarded an inflammatory account of the incident to Lieutenant-Governor Morris at Fort Garry. Morris, worried that another Red River uprising was in the making, alerted Ottawa and sent an urgent message to NWMP Commissioner French at Fort Livingstone.

The Winnipeg *Daily Press* went over the top with the story:

> Another stand against Canadian authority in the North-West; a Provisional Government at Carlton; M. Louis Riel again to the front; 10,000 Crees on the war-path; Fort Carlton in possession of the Rebels; a number of Mounted Police killed.[10]

With French at his headquarters was Major General Selby-Smythe of the Canadian Militia, on a tour of inspection of the NWMP. The two officers took 50 troopers and made a forced march to Fort Carlton. There they quickly diagnosed the problem as "trivial." When Dumont returned from the hunt he offered apologies and reparations if he had acted improperly.

The overblown affair went all the way to the Colonial Office in London where the Earl of Carnarvon ruled "it would be difficult to take strong exception to the acts of a community which appears to have honestly endeavoured to maintain order by the best means in its power."[11] In the opinion of one eminent historian, "It is quite evident that the Métis attained at St. Laurent, during this period, their highest development, politically, as a distinct race."[12]

The attempt by the Métis of St. Laurent to conserve and preserve the buffalo as a resource failed. The last of the organized hunts went forth in 1881 and the hunters returned only "with light loads of meat."[13] By then the buffalo had all but disappeared from the Canadian plains and the Métis did well to secure any animals.

In July 1879, the existence of the 49th Parallel as an international boundary was harshly brought home to a large group of Métis hunting buffalo along the Milk River in Montana Territory. Some 300 families were arrested by U.S. Army troops under the command of Colonel Nelson Miles who demanded that they identify their home country. Upon the intervention of Inspector James Walsh of the NWMP, 120 families claimed Canadian citizenship and were allowed to return over the border. The remainder identified themselves as American and were sent under military escort to their homes at Turtle Mountain and the Judith Basin.

The buffalo virtually disappeared north of the 49th Parallel after 1879. When starvation followed, those Métis who had been most dependent upon the herds learned that they were in worse circumstances than the Indians suffering beside them. Since they had no treaties, Ottawa took the position that the Métis people were not entitled to assistance in time of famine.

Red River remained the supply centre to the new Métis communities that sprang up in the North-West Territories, and freighting and trading became profitable vocations. In 1875 more than 1,000 Red River carts creaked out of Manitoba heading for the new settlements. The following year over 4,000 carts travelled the trading routes that stretched as far as Fort Edmonton.[14]

Their anchors weakened, the Métis were adrift, clinging to their way of life and avoiding the civilization encroaching from the east. Scattered over the Great Plains between the Missouri and the Saskatchewan, and even north to the Churchill, they lost much of the cohesiveness they had developed over three quarters of a century at Red River. They would not again come together in concerted action until 1885 at Batoche. Then, either forgetting how ephemeral had been their last triumph under his guidance, or in desperation, they turned once more to Louis Riel to lead them in a last defence of their nationhood.

AS A NATION, THE Métis reached only a tiny population. Historians have made estimates of their numbers ranging from 10,000 to 40,000 at the peak of their development in the 1870s, but without providing much census detail in support.[15] The low estimate is clearly incorrect; an 1869 census at Red River alone found 9,800 Métis (5,720 French, 4,080 English) and a white population of 1,600. The high estimate seems equally wrong if only because it is difficult to locate enough population in the settlements outside of Red River to support such a total.

Today the estimates of Canadian Métis population vary widely, from 20,000 to as high as 800,000. In 1996 Statistics Canada reported the number at 210,190 based upon a survey that asked whether people identified themselves as Métis, but of this number more than half lived outside the tradition Métis homeland territory in the West.

The difficulty lies in defining "Métis." There were mixed-blood families literally from coast to coast, wherever fur traders had operated, but many now claim that the only true Métis people are those springing from the early Red River group with its distinct culture. In 2002 the Métis National Council adopted this limited definition: "Métis means a person who self-identifies as Métis, is of historic Métis Nation ancestry, is distinct from other Aboriginal peoples and is accepted by the Métis Nation." Historic ancestry is further defined as deriving from residence in a "Historic Métis Nation Homeland," an "area of land in west-central North America used and occupied as the traditional territory of the Métis, or Half-Breeds as they were then known."

Mixed-blood communities in the eastern Maritime provinces and Pacific coastal areas are excluded from this definition, which has been approved by the five provincial Métis associations that constitute the National Council: Ontario, Manitoba, Saskatchewan, Alberta and British Columbia.

In 2003 the Supreme Court of Canada handed down a decision dealing with Métis hunting rights as an Aboriginal right recognized by section 35 of the Constitution Act, 1982 for "Indian, Inuit and Métis peoples of Canada." The case involved Steve Powley, a Métis from Sault Ste. Marie who, for food but without a license, had killed a moose. The Court held that

The idea that the Métis had become a unique and identifiable race was slow to develop but gradually acquired more than academic acknowledgement. In 2001 the Ontario Court of Appeal gave judicial acceptance to the thesis when it held that the mixed-blood families evolved "into a new and distinct people through a process known as ethnogenesis."[1] And the Royal Commission on Aboriginal Peoples reported in November 1996 that

> The culture of those early forebears [the Métis ancestors] derived from the lifestyles of the Aboriginal and non-Aboriginal peoples from whom the modern Métis trace their beginnings, yet the culture they created was no cut-and-paste affair. The product of the Aboriginal-European synthesis was more than the sum of its elements; it was an entirely distinct culture.[2]

Another feature of the distinctiveness of the Métis people is a unique dialect, *Michif*, a blending of French nouns and Cree verbs that slowly evolved out of the isolation of the Métis communities:

> The impetus for its emergence was the fact that the bilingual Métis were no longer accepted as Indians or French and they formulated their own ethnic identity, which was mixed and where a mixed "language of our own" was considered part of their ethnicity.[3]

The Métis adopted a flag during the time of the troubles that resulted in the Battle of Seven Oaks in 1816. A simple horizontal infinity symbol, or figure eight, white against a blue, or a red, background, it now carries nearly 200 years of tradition.

NOTES
1. R. v. Powley, [2003] 2 S.C.R. 207, 2003 SCC 43.
2. Canada, *Royal Commission on Aboriginal Peoples Report*, vol. 4 (Ottawa: Minister of Supply and Services Canada, 1996), 220.
3. Ibid., 220.

Aboriginal rights are communal rights. They must be grounded in the existence of a historic and present community, and they may only be exercised by virtue of an individual's ancestrally based membership in the present community.[16]

In addition,

the term Métis in section 35 does not encompass all individuals with mixed Indian and European heritage; rather, it refers to distinctive peoples who, in addition to their mixed ancestry, developed their own customs, way of life, and recognizable group identity separate from their Indian or Inuit and European forebears.

The Court decreed that there is no requirement of "a minimum blood quantum," but it is necessary that a person claiming the privilege of section-35 rights must have "a real link, (an 'ancestral connection') to the historic community whose practices ground the right being claimed." And, he or she must have "self-identified" as a member of a Métis community.

Steve Powley was admittedly a Métis with ancestral roots in the historic Métis community of Sault Ste. Marie where hunting for food had been a constant practice. As the moose had been found in the ancestral hunting area, Powley was entitled to take it for food without a license.

The case recognized Métis hunting rights as part of their constitutionally guaranteed Aboriginal rights, but only within the strict limitations outlined. They do not extend to all persons of mixed-blood ancestry and they do not apply in areas where no Métis community had historically hunted for food. The Métis people continue their struggle for self- definition, for recognition of their national identity, and for restoration of their Rupert's Land birthright.

CHAPTER 11

"So Long as the Sun Shines"

WEMYSS MACKENZIE SIMPSON WAS HUMILIATED. AS THE first duly appointed Indian Commissioner of the Dominion of Canada, instructed by the government of Prime Minister John A. Macdonald to negotiate with the Saulteaux band of Ojibway for the surrender of their lands lying between Thunder Bay and Lake of the Woods, he and his proposals had met with outright, even rude, rejection. The chiefs who assembled at Fort Frances in July 1871 to meet with Simpson and his two fellow Commissioners would not even discuss the absolute cession of their domain. A right-of-way through their territory, perhaps, but no more. Simpson and his entourage withdrew, chastened but not entirely surprised.

It was a sorry beginning to the negotiations intended to clear away the Aboriginal title from the Lakehead to the Rockies. On May 5, 1871, Joseph Howe, the responsible minister in Macdonald's government, had instructed Simpson to conclude treaties with the Indians between Thunder Bay and Fort Garry and then, without delay, proceed to deal "with the Indian Tribes to the West."[1] Simpson was to commence at Fort Frances, "for with the Indians in that neighbourhood it will be necessary first to deal."[2]

Wemyss Simpson was a natural choice to bargain on behalf of the Ottawa government with the Indians of the West. Born in London in 1825, at the age of 16 he had come to Canada with the Hudson's Bay Company and achieved the rank of Chief Trader and Chief Factor at the Company's post at Sault Ste. Marie. He retired in 1865 and two years later, as a Conservative, was elected Member of Parliament for Algoma. Simpson had been familiar with the Saulteaux for more than 25 years and although he was not fond of them, he fully respected their strength. He knew they could easily obstruct, and even prevent, travel through their territory, which straddled the 49th Parallel and extended well into the United States.

Ottawa was well aware of the potential barrier presented by the Saulteaux. The previous year, when planning to send the Red River Expeditionary Force under Colonel Wolseley through the region, Macdonald's government engaged Simpson to negotiate safe passage through the Saulteaux lands. On June 21, 1870, the MP met at Fort Frances with some 1,500 Saulteaux, many of them American. The American Saulteaux had already signed treaties and would make certain that their Canadian brothers negotiated terms at least as favourable.

The Saulteaux had no objection to Wolseley and his troops crossing through their lands, they told Simpson at that first meeting. But if the Canadian government continued with its plan to convert the Dawson Route into a permanent water and land access into Red River, they would insist on payment for the right-of-way. And the Saulteaux named their price: $10 per man, woman and child each and every year "so long as the sun shines."

In the manner of the times, Simpson had brought along presents for the Saulteaux. These were rejected, in a manner strikingly similar to another refusal farther west six years later. "They are a bait, and if we take them you will say we are bound to you."[3] Macdonald could send his troops through to Fort Garry, but it would be a different matter when it came time to establish a permanent route into the West.

Less than a year after his first disappointing meeting with the Saulteaux, on April 26, 1871, Simpson resigned his seat in Parliament to accept appointment as Canada's first Indian Commissioner. He did not distinguish himself in that position, but not all the fault was his.

In spite of Simpson's achievements and title, he lacked stature in the eyes of the chiefs with whom he met in conference. Howe was aware that image was a concern and that the Indians expected a representative of the Queen to be suitably attired. Simpson was appointed Lieutenant Colonel of the Algoma Regiment of the Militia and instructed to wear his uniform during all official interviews with the Indians. But the Saulteaux remembered Wemyss Simpson from earlier days.

The Macdonald government had not established an Indian policy, as such, but knew that their "National Policy" of Confederation from the Atlantic to the Pacific could only be fulfilled by clearing away all claims of Aboriginal title to the vast lands between Thunder Bay and the Rocky Mountains. And that could only be accomplished, Macdonald knew, by formal treaty with the several tribes of Indians who inhabited those lands.

The Proclamation of 1763 implied the existence of a valid Aboriginal title that could be dislodged only by treaty, a feature that in Canada received strong judicial endorsement two centuries later. If there was no treaty, the Aboriginal title remained unimpaired.

Just what was meant by "Aboriginal title" was another matter. The Hudson's Bay Company, although granted ownership of Rupert's Land, had acknowledged that the Indian inhabitants had some prior claim to the land.[4] Before the British government had transferred Rupert's Land to Canada, it had first secured a surrender of the interest of the Hudson's Bay Company. Ottawa then looked at the Aboriginal title as in the nature of a cloud upon its own title, a right to possession of the land perhaps, but something much less than full ownership.

Just how the Indians viewed their rights in the lands they occupied is today a matter of debate and litigation. The prevalent opinion is that they believed they were entitled to the use and benefit of the land, in law a *usufruct*, but could not sell or alienate those lands which really belonged to future generations. So the treaty process went forward, with each side holding very different opinions as to what was on the table.

A large number of treaties and land surrenders—123 in all—had been negotiated with the many Indian nations in Eastern Canada, but none since Confederation in 1867, and none ever in the West, with the single exception of a treaty obtained by Lord Selkirk in 1817 to secure his settlements along the Red and Assiniboine Rivers in two-mile strips. As Macdonald explained to the House of Commons on May 2, 1870, during the debate on the Manitoba Act, the reservation to the Métis of 485,640 ha (1,200,000 acres), later increased to 566,580 ha (1,400,000 acres) was

> for the purpose of extinguishing the Indian title and all claims upon the lands within the limits of the Province . . . It is, perhaps, not known to a majority of the House that the old Indian titles are not extinguished over any portion of this country, except for two miles on each side of the Red River and the Assiniboine.[5]

In 1871 Macdonald knew that must change, and change quickly. His plans for the western lands could be stymied by the Indian peoples in possession of those lands. There were not many of them remaining after the smallpox epidemic of the previous year. In the "Fertile Acres," from the Red River west to the Rocky Mountains and between the 49th Parallel and the North Saskatchewan River, only some 15 to 20,000 still existed of the once-mighty buffalo hunting bands that inhabited the Great Plains.[6] In addition, there were about 1,500 Minnesota Sioux on the eastern prairies, refugees of the 1862 Uprising, aptly described by Ottawa officials as "Frontier Wanderers."

Few they might be, but Macdonald needed treaties with those Indians that would give him clear ownership of the vast tracts of the West needed to further his National Policy, a railway to the Pacific. And he needed them soon.

Coincidentally, in 1871, as the young government of Canada opened treaty negotiations with the Indian inhabitants of its new West, the Congress of the United States formally withdrew from any further treaty business with its Indian peoples. There had been many treaties before 1871 and almost all had fallen into difficulty, usually because the American government later found it inconvenient to adhere to their terms. The American Constitution requires that all treaties with other sovereign nations be ratified by the Senate. The approval of the House of Representatives is not needed, a matter that was of some annoyance to its members with respect to Indian treaties. In March 1871, the House of Representatives secured passage of legislation decreeing that "no Indian nation or tribe or power within the territory of the United States shall be acknowledged or recognized as an independent nation, tribe or power with whom the United States may contract by treaty." Thereafter, all agreements America entered into with Indian peoples were in the nature of contracts only, requiring approval from both Houses of Congress and the signature of the President. The United States also adopted a policy of limiting tribal and individual Aboriginal rights. Five years later, in early 1876, the American Indian policy turned entirely militant and responsibility for Indian affairs was turned over to the War Department.

The Macdonald government was well aware of America's difficulties with its Aboriginal peoples: the Indian Removal Act of 1830 that uprooted upwards of 100,000 members of numerous Indian bands from east of the Mississippi River to "Indian Country" in the West; the "Trail of Tears" as President Andrew Jackson ignored a prohibition from the United States Supreme Court and forcibly moved the Cherokees, many in chains, out of their homes in Georgia; the blood that was still being spilled in conflict between the Plains Indians and the United States Army.

Macdonald took some pride in the apparently better relations that had been developed with the Indian peoples of Eastern Canada. Admiring the record of the Hudson's Bay Company, Ottawa determined to adhere to a humane standard in its dealings with the First Nations of the North-West Territories. In June 1871, the Prime Minister explained his policy to Stafford Northcote, governor of the Hudson's Bay Company:

I am very anxious, indeed, that we should be able to deal with the Indians upon satisfactory terms. They are the great difficulty in these newly civilized countries. They are the great difficulty with which the Americans have to contend in their new countries. The Hudson's Bay Company have dealt with the Indians in a thoroughly satisfactory way. The policy of Canada is also to deal with the Indians in a satisfactory manner.[7]

The new government of Canada had inherited a small Indian Branch from the Province of Canada, but none of the half dozen employees had any knowledge of, or experience with, the country west of Lake Superior. Macdonald decided that he needed an Indian Commissioner "to deal with Indian Treaties." Thus, the appointment of Wemyss Simpson and two additional commissioners, Simon J. Dawson, the surveyor of the Dawson Route, and Robert Pither, a former Hudson's Bay Company employee who was familiar with the Saulteaux/Ojibway.

Although Ottawa intended its conduct towards the Indian inhabitants of the West to be fair and honourable, that did not require fiscal altruism. The Commissioners were instructed

to secure the cession of the lands upon terms as favorable as possible to the Government, not going as far as the maximum sum hereafter named unless it be found impossible to obtain the object for a less amount. The number of Indians assumed to inhabit this tract of country, is estimated at about 2,500 and the maximum amount which you are authorized to give is twelve dollars per annum for a family of five ... In fixing this amount, you must not lose sight of the fact that it cannot fail to have an important bearing on the arrangements to be made subsequently with the tribes further West.[8]

As a guideline, the Commissioners were further advised "that in the old Provinces of Quebec and Ontario, the highest price paid for the finest land has seldom, if ever, exceeded four dollars per head per annum, to the Band with which the treaty was made."[9] The first treaty west of the Great Lakes would be vital. As the precedent that would govern the treaties to follow covering the great grasslands between Red River and the Rocky Mountain, its dollar cost must be kept to the minimum.

Wemyss Simpson had been in charge of the Hudson's Bay Company post at Sault Ste. Marie on June 10, 1857 when John Palliser and several members of his expedition arrived *en route* to Thunder Bay and Fort Garry, and from there over the plains. Simpson supplied Palliser and his men with all hospitality and, at the direction of Governor George Simpson (no relation to the Chief Trader), provided the travellers with two 9-m (30- ft) *canots du nord*, each complete with full crews of eight *voyageurs*.

Three weeks later, on July 1, Palliser and his party stopped over at the Company's post on Rainy Lake, Fort Frances.[10] Had the future Indian Commissioner accompanied Palliser on that visit to Fort Frances, he might have formed a very different notion of the magnitude of the task he would face there 14 years later.

Headed by an elderly chief, some 200 Indians, half of them armed, marched into the fort and demanded an interview with Palliser. The spokesman announced that he was accompanied by his chiefs, his soldiers, his young men, and it was by their wish that he addressed Palliser. They had not come to beg, the chief advised. He was the hereditary chief of their band, his father and his father's father had been chiefs

> of this once mighty tribe. Their graves are in our lands, and not far from here . . . All around me I see the smoke of the pale faces to ascend; but my territories I will never part with; they shall be for my poor children's hunting fields when I am dead.[11]

Palliser saw that the Indians were excited and edgy and assured them that he had no designs upon their territory but was merely passing through on his way to more distant lands:

> Our object was neither to take them by force or even bargain with them for the sale of their territories; and moreover, if any body of people should wrest their lands from them, our great Queen would send her soldiers to drive those people back, and would restore their lands to them again.[12]

As Palliser spoke these comforting words, one of the Saulteaux/Ojibway who lived on the United States side of the border stepped beside the old chief. Speaking from experience with the Americans he advised, "Make him put that on paper." But the chief declined. "There is no need of that, what he says he will act up to, for no one who came from the great Queen ever lied."[13]

The chief requested Palliser to tell the Queen of the poverty of his people but to take no stones or plants away with them, "for fear that people far off should think the lands valuable and seize them . . . We will not sell or part with our lands."[14]

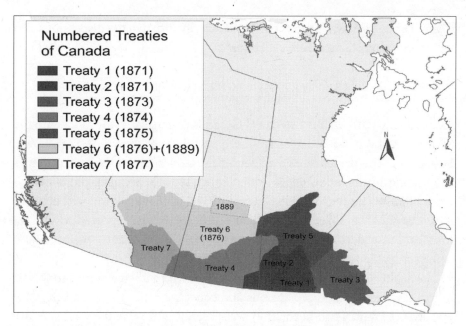

Numbered Treaties
of Canada
- Treaty 1 (1871)
- Treaty 2 (1871)
- Treaty 3 (1873)
- Treaty 4 (1874)
- Treaty 5 (1875)
- Treaty 6 (1876)+(1889)
- Treaty 7 (1877)

The old chief had joined his ancestors when Wemyss Simpson sat down in conference with his successors in another July, 14 years later, in 1871. But the Indian determination not to surrender their lands was just as strong. The Commissioners sent by Ottawa to bargain for those lands were unprepared to deal with such firm resistance and the negotiations were doomed to failure.

Simpson sent a bland report of his failure to the Secretary of State, Joseph Howe. The Indians, he said, "preferred claims in regard to promises which had heretofore been made to them, for 'right of way' through their country."[15] They required time "in which to deliberate calmly on the various points to be embraced in a Treaty." Further meetings would be held the following summer. Then Simpson and his fellow Commissioners hastened to Fort Garry where other tribes were waiting for their treaty negotiations.

Adams Archibald, Lieutenant-Governor of Manitoba and the North-West Territories, had been in residence at Fort Garry since his arrival the previous September. A Nova Scotian lawyer and an active supporter of Confederation, the 59-year-old Archibald had consented to his appointment as Lieutenant-Governor on condition that he be required to serve no more than one year. The one year turned into two, and then stretched out another six months when his appointed successor refused to serve and another had to be found. It was a very eventful two and a half years.

When Simpson, Dawson and Pither arrived in Fort Garry on July 16, Archibald sat them down to develop a strategy for the Indians of Manitoba and surrounding territory, "in the light of the experience gained at Rainy

River." James McKay, a prominent Métis, was included in the discussions. Different and better tactics were called for.

TREATY 1: THE STONE FORT TREATY

ARCHIBALD JOINED THE INDIAN Commissioners when they met with the Saulteaux/Chippewa and Swampy Cree on July 25 at the Stone Fort, Lower Fort Garry. The presence of the Lieutenant-Governor on the government's negotiating team undoubtedly added to its stature. So, also, did a detachment of militia under Major A.G. Irvine that Archibald had ordered up. "Military display always has a great effect on savages,"[16] he reported to Ottawa. Archibald also detailed a force of constabulary as insurance against liquor being smuggled to the Indians.

The Saulteaux/Chippewa and Swampy Cree who gathered at the Stone Fort in July 1871 were even more anxious and concerned than the Saulteaux/Ojibway at Fort Frances had been. They were keenly aware that the Hudson's Bay Company had supposedly sold their homelands and they had been closer to the dramatic events at Fort Garry over the winter of 1869–70. As soon as Archibald had arrived at Fort Garry the previous September, he had been approached by a number of local Indians worried about where they stood in the new order and anxious to have a treaty to settle their affairs. Archibald had told them nothing could be done until the next year, and now that next year had arrived.

Simpson had sent messengers calling the Indians to assemble on July 25, but as several bands were slow in arriving the opening of negotiations was delayed. The Indian Commissioner found himself dipping deeply into department funds to provide food for the gathering multitude. Finally, more than 1,000 Indians assembled, with 200 Métis as very interested observers.

When discussions finally began, Archibald, as befitted his rank, assumed the role of lead spokesman for the government, but turned the treaty details over to Simpson. Archibald did not hesitate to advise the Indians that the proposed treaties were in their best interests. Some of his arguments must have been compelling:

> We told them that whether they wished it or not, immigrants would come in and fill up the country; that every year from this one twice as many in number as their whole people there assembled would pour into the Province, and in a little while would spread all over it, and that now was the time for them to come to an arrangement that would secure homes and annuities for themselves and their children.[17]

Archibald also assured the assembly before him that, under similar treaties, "the Indians in the East were living happy and contented, enjoying themselves, drawing their annuities, and satisfied with their position."[18] Presumably he was referring to the Robinson Treaty of 1850 covering lands around Lakes Superior and Huron that Howe had sent to Simpson as a precedent. But, since none of his listeners had ever been "in the East," or seen any of the Indians of that region, it remains unknown what picture this statement created in their minds.

The Indians advised that there was "a cloud" preventing the proceedings from getting underway. The "cloud" was the jailing of four Swampy Cree who had failed to meet their contracts as boatmen with the Hudson's Bay Company. Archibald promptly ordered that the four be released; the "cloud" was thus cleared away and discussions began.

A major misunderstanding developed almost immediately. Although Archibald had explained that the reserves that would be set aside would only be large enough to provide a farm for each family, the Indian spokesmen returned three days later requesting a land allotment for each family that added up to about two-thirds of the new province.

Archibald and Simpson conferred and decided to take a very firm line. They explained that the terms they offered were the terms that the Queen would approve. Ottawa's treaty was put forward on a "take it or leave it" basis. After deep consideration, the Indians accepted, "acquiesced," as Simpson called it.

On August 3, 1871, nine days after discussions opened, the treaty was signed, the first of the numbered treaties in the West. Altogether, 43,250 km^2 (16,700 mi^2) were surrendered with this treaty, including the new Province of Manitoba plus large tracts of land east, north and west of the provincial boundaries. The treaty provided for a one-time payment, or signing bonus, of $3 to each man, woman and child, and an annual payment of the same amount. Reserves would be on the basis of 65 ha (160 acres) for each family of five.

Simpson immediately set about distributing the cash, a process that required two days as by then nearly 2,000 Indians were present.

TREATY 2: THE MANITOBA POST TREATY

SIMPSON HAD SENT NOTICE of a second treaty meeting to take place on August 17, 1871, at Manitoba Post, at the north end of Lake Manitoba, but he, James McKay and Lieutenant-Governor Archibald, delayed by high winds on the lake, arrived two days late. They found 500 Saulteaux/ Chippewa awaiting them, apparently fully aware of the provisions of the treaty signed less than three weeks earlier, and quite willing to sign a treaty on the same terms.

After only a day or two of discussion, on August 21, Treaty 2 was signed. Payment was handed out the following day. This second surrender encompassed a 97,400-km² (37,600-mi²) tract north of Treaty 1 and so far west as to include the Moose Mountains in present-day southeastern Saskatchewan.

In the words of the treaties, the bands "do hereby cede, release, surrender and yield up to Her Majesty the Queen, and her successors for ever, all the lands included within the following limits." In return, the Indians were to receive "a present" of $3 each, for each family of five an annual allowance of $12 to be paid in "blankets, clothing, prints (assorted colors), twine or traps at the current cost price in Montreal," and be granted reserves based upon 65 ha (160 acres) for each family of five.

With the assistance of Lieutenant-Governor Adams Archibald, Wemyss Simpson had secured two important treaties and the surrender of a huge tract of land. No more negotiations were planned for 1871 and the Indian Commissioner returned to his home at Sault Ste. Marie. It was a mistake, as problems arose almost immediately. During the negotiations, there had been much discussion about the Indians converting to farming, and a number of promises were made which were not included in the text of the treaties. Lieutenant-Governor Archibald had told those assembled at Lower Fort Garry that

> Your Great Mother wishes the good of all races under her sway. She wishes her red children to be happy and contented. She wishes them to live in comfort. She would like them to adopt the habits of the whites, to till land and raise food, and store it up against a time of want. She thinks this would be the best thing for her red children to do, that it would make them safer from famine and distress, and make their homes more comfortable.[19]

Simpson and Archibald had promised the Indians such essentials as breeding stock, plows and harrows to assist them in getting started on their new lives as farmers. No mention of these commitments was made in the written treaties and, although Simpson had mentioned them in his report to Ottawa, no provision had been made to supply these items. When the Indians expressed interest in taking up these promises to be ready for the spring of 1872, there was no one in the West to receive their requests, much less fulfill them. Commissioner Simpson was in Sault St. Marie and no arrangement had been made for the administration of the treaties.

Archibald was concerned. He wrote Ottawa advising that the Indians "recollect with astonishing accuracy every stipulation made at the treaty, and if we expect our relations with them to be of the kind which it is desirable to maintain, we must fulfill our obligations with scrupulous fidelity."[20]

Simpson was slow to see any urgency and did not return to Fort Garry until July 1872, after making another attempt at securing a treaty with the Saulteaux/Ojibway at Fort Frances, and again failing. Archibald sat the Indian Commissioner down with others who had been present during the treaty negotiations and prepared a memorandum outlining the "outside promises," a phrase that rings yet today in debate over the interpretation and application of Western treaties. Still, not until 1875 did Ottawa formally accept the memorandum as properly forming part of Treaties 1 and 2. To offset the loss of goodwill and trust, the fiscal terms of the treaties were improved by raising the annuities from $3 to $5 per head, and adding a new annuity of $20 for each chief.

In August 1875, the amended treaties were carried around to each band with explanations and apologies. Although the bands accepted the revisions, a strong flavour of distrust lingered. And, as Joseph Howe had predicted in his initial instructions to his Indian Commissioners, these first treaties, and the suspicions they created, had "an important bearing on the arrangements to be made subsequently with the tribes further west."

In December 1872, Adams Archibald finally escaped his responsibilities as Lieutenant-Governor of Manitoba and the North-West Territories and was succeeded by Alexander Morris. Morris, a 46-year-old lawyer who once had clerked in John A. Macdonald's law office, had been elected to Parliament in 1867 and taken into Macdonald's cabinet as Minister of Inland Revenue. He resigned in July 1872 to become Chief Justice of Manitoba, then resigned that office in turn just six months later to relieve Archibald.

Morris took an immediate interest in the treaties and became the government's lead negotiator on the next four Western treaties. Wemyss Simpson resigned and, in June 1873, was succeeded by Lieutenant Colonel J.A.N. Provencher. Although the new Indian Commissioner assisted Morris with negotiations, his main responsibility was the administration of the treaties. In the fall of 1873 the new team turned their attention to the situation at Fort Frances where the treaty issue was still outstanding.

TREATY 3: THE NORTH-WEST ANGLE TREATY

OTTAWA HAD BEEN WORKING on the Fort Frances problem and decided that its offer had to be much improved if a deal was to be had. Morris was authorized to increase both the annuities and the one-time cash gratuity. As well, reserves would be allotted on the basis of 260 ha (640 acres) per family of five rather than 65 ha (160 acres) as in Treaties 1 and 2. Also, a look had been had across the border where the Americans were accustomed to showing much greater generosity to the chiefs, a fact very well known to the Saulteaux/ Ojibway at Fort Frances.

As Adams Archibald had, Morris equipped himself with a force of militia, a precaution that greatly contributed to the success of the mission.

After some preliminary skirmishing about location, the participants assembled on September 25, 1873, not at Fort Frances as before, but on the Hudson's Bay Company lands at the North-West Angle of Lake of the Woods, a location that gave its name to the treaty concluded there. The gathering was large and impressive, as some 1,400 Saulteaux from 11 bands attended in addition to the considerable party accompanying the Lieutenant-Governor.

But negotiations were slow to get underway. The various bands spent several days working out a unified position and did not meet with the government team until October 1. Then the chiefs advised Morris that they would not discuss a treaty for their lands until they had been first paid for the passage of the traffic over the Dawson Route. Morris was firm in response; he would make a single settlement only, or he would go home. Morris then put forward the government offer—an annuity of $5 per capita, a signing bonus of $1, and reserve lands based on 2.6 km^2 (1 mi^2) per family of five.

Mawedopenais, the Fort Frances chief, acting as the Saulteaux spokesman, spoke eloquently of their lands in words that strongly indicate they had a good understanding of their bargaining position:

> This is what we think, that the Great Spirit has planted us on this ground where we are as you were where you came from. We think where we are is our property.[21]

Gold had been discovered in the region and the Saulteaux were well aware of that. Another chief spoke of this:

> The sound of the rustling of the gold is under my feet where I stand; we have a rich country; it is the Great Spirit who gave us this; where we stand upon is the Indians' property, and belongs to them.[22]

The Saulteaux were concerned about minerals and wanted to know if they would be entitled to any they discovered. Morris assured them that any minerals found on their reserves would be sold for their benefit, but only with their consent. As for other discoveries, "The Indian is like any other man. He can sell his information if he can find a purchaser."[23]

The chiefs countered with a demand for an general annuity of $10, $15 for warriors, $20 for councillors, $50 for chiefs, and a postponement of the question of land reserves. The negotiations looked headed for failure again when the unified position of the Indians began to break apart.

Not all the bands had the same concerns, but discipline among them had been strong. Morris was sure that without the presence of his militia none of the 11 individual bands would have dared speak out, but the chief of the Lac Seul band came forward, even as others tried to prevent him. His people desired a treaty, he stated. Morris seized upon the weakening in the unity opposite him and declared his willingness to treat with each band individually. Resistance then crumbled and on October 3, 1873, the deal was done. Interestingly, the Lac Seul band did not sign on to the treaty until the next year, June 9, 1874.

The annuity was fixed at $5 and the cash gratuity at $12. Chiefs would be paid $25 each year, and headmen $15. Reserves would be based on 260 ha (640 acres) per family of five, instead of 65 ha (160 acres), and bands would receive agricultural implements, carpenters' tools, seed and cattle. These provisions were written into the treaty document so that there would be no "outside promises" of the sort that caused difficulty with Treaties 1 and 2. The substantial increase in the cash annuities over those provided for in Treaties 1 and 2 were, in 1875, extended to the Indians under the earlier treaties when the "outside promises" made there were finally accepted by Ottawa.

Also included was the provision that "the said Indians shall have right to pursue their avocations of hunting and fishing throughout the tract surrendered" until the lands were taken up for settlement or other purposes. This understanding had been expressed at Treaties 1 and 2 but was not included in the documents. The provision became standard in later treaties.

By this treaty the government secured the surrender of the Indian title to 142,500 km² (55,000 mi²) of lands lying between Lake Superior and those ceded by Treaty 1.

At the formal conclusion of the North-West Angle Treaty, several of the chiefs displayed, with their accustomed eloquence, just how sacred they believed their mutual undertakings to be. Mawedopenais stepped up to Lieutenant-Governor Morris and said,

> Now you see me stand before you all; what has been done here today
> has been done openly before the Great Spirit, and before the nation,
> and I hope that I may never hear anyone say that this treaty has been

done secretly; and now, in closing this Council, I take off my glove, and in giving you my hand, I deliver over to you my birth-right and lands; and in taking your hand, I will hold fast all the promises you have made, and I hope they will last as long as the sun goes around and the water flows, as you have said.[24]

Morris was sincere in response:

I accept your hand and with it the lands, and will keep all my promises, in the firm belief that the treaty now to be signed will bind the red man and the white man together as friends forever.[25]

A number of Métis from Red River had been present during the negotiations and both sides acknowledged the contribution they had made to bringing about the treaty.

The North-West Angle Treaty of October 1873 became Treaty 3, not Treaty 1 of July 1871 as originally intended, but it was the template for the western treaties that followed.

Ottawa now had a clear right-of-way from Lake Superior to Red River, encompassing both the Dawson Route and the route of the railway to the Pacific. It also had, in Morris' words, "an extensive lumber and mineral region."[26]

The way was now open for Prime Minister Macdonald to turn his attention to the Great Plains. But in November 1873 his government fell, victim of a scandal involving the Pacific Railway, and was replaced by the Liberals under Alexander Mackenzie. But there was little change of policy respecting the need to continue the treaty negotiations in the West.

David Laird, a Prince Edward Islander, became Minister of the Interior and responsible for Indian Affairs. For more than 25 years he would play several prominent roles in the negotiation of treaties with the Indians of Western Canada.

TREATY 4: THE QU'APPELLE TREATY

WHEN LIEUTENANT-GOVERNOR ALEXANDER MORRIS settled into his carriage at Fort Garry on August 26, 1874, and headed overland for Fort Qu'Appelle, it must have been with a considerable feeling of trepidation. This was dangerous country he was travelling through, or at least it was in his mind. A year earlier, when Morris received news of what came to be known as the

Cypress Hills Massacre, he had bombarded Ottawa with predictions of Indian uprisings on the plains, of plundered Hudson's Bay Company posts, of the return of Louis Riel with more trouble of the sort seen at Fort Garry in 1869, even of bloodshed on the scale experienced in the Minnesota Uprising of 1862.[27] Morris had demanded police protection for the West and Prime Minister Macdonald had responded by sending 150 North-West Mounted Police out to Fort Garry the previous fall. Now those troops, and 150 more that had arrived at Red River just two months earlier, in June, were now somewhere far out on the plains. Except for a small detachment, an inspector and 14 constables detailed to Fort Ellice, the entire strength of the North-West Mounted Police had marched out on July 8, heading into the far West. Headed to a destination with the unusual name of Fort Whoop-Up, they were too far distant to be of any assistance to the Lieutenant-Governor and his party. Morris believed that even the great expedition of the NWMP was in danger and on his insistence it had taken a route well north of the 49th Parallel to avoid attack by American Sioux.

Ottawa's chief treaty negotiator was taking all precaution with his own modest expedition onto the western plains. Riding ahead of the Lieutenant-Governor and his party were fully 200 troops of the militia from Fort Garry under the command of Lieutenant Colonel W. Osborne Smith.

Morris knew that the treaty negotiations scheduled for him at Fort Qu'Appelle were not going to be simple. His discussions the previous October with the demanding Saulteaux/Ojibway of the Lake of the Woods region had been difficult. The Indians he was going to meet not only had different demands but were also insistent that a treaty be concluded before there were any more incursions into their territory. No more surveyors, no telegraph lines, no settlers. In March, Morris had written to his new minister in Ottawa, pressing the need to proceed with the treaties. Now, in an unusual move, David Laird, Minister of the Interior, had himself appointed one of the three Treaty Commissioners and was riding with Morris.

The third Commissioner, W.J. Christie, knew even better than Morris that the Plains Indians they were about to treat with were seriously discontented. In 1874 Christie was retired, but three and a half years earlier he had been Chief Factor for the Hudson's Bay Company at Fort Edmonton. There, on April 13, 1871, not long after news of the Rupert's Land transfer had raced across the West, Christie received a visitation from several prominent Plains Cree chiefs. Sweet Grass, The Eagle, The Little Hunter, and Short Tail, all from the territory between Edmonton and Fort Carlton, had heard a disturbing rumour. The chiefs wanted to know "whether their lands had been sold or not, and what was the intention of the Canadian Government in relation to them."[28] Christie made the best explanation he could, but the chiefs were not easily satisfied. At the direction of Sweet Grass, the Chief Factor wrote a letter addressed to Lieutenant-Governor Archibald at Fort Garry. All four Cree leaders signed the letter: "We heard our lands were sold and we did not like it; we don't want to sell our lands; it is our property, and no one has a right to sell them."[29] Then, concerned that "our country is no longer able to support us," they expressed a willingness to meet with the Lieutenant Governor. Christie knew the chiefs and thought they were very demanding and on the edge of violence.

Christie had gone on ahead to attend to some matters at Fort Pelly and planned to meet his fellow Commissioners at Qu'Appelle.

Morris made full dramatic use of his militia. Having overtaken Lieutenant Colonel Osborne Smith and his command on the trail, the full party swept impressively into the 10-year-old stockade at Fort Qu'Appelle, beautifully situated on the flat of land between Echo and Mission Lakes. It was September 8, 1874. Morris and Laird had been 13 days on the trail from Fort Garry.

A large number of Cree and Saulteaux, summoned to the treaty discussions, awaited the Lieutenant-Governor and his party. In fact, instead of making their annual hunting trek onto the plains, some had been waiting all summer, to the distress of Father Jules DeCorby of the nearby mission of St. Florent (now Lebret). On July 5, Father DeCorby had written to his Oblate superiors reporting that "many Indian families wait upon the five dollars which the government must bring them. Those miserable five dollars hinder them even more than they help them. Counting on them, they give up hunting to wait, starve to death and encourage others to starve."[30]

But there was much more than $5 on the minds of the Cree, Saulteaux and Assiniboine chiefs who had come to meet with Morris: the £300,000 that the Hudson's Bay Company had received on the sale of Rupert's Land. "We want that money," said the chiefs when the treaty conference began. The lands were theirs, not the Company's, they claimed. They were also upset that, without their permission, the Company had surveyed the area around its post (as it was entitled to do under the terms of its Rupert's Land Agreement). "The Company have stolen our land,"[31] declared The Gambler, a leading Saulteaux spokesman.

It was a rocky beginning to the negotiations. The Saulteaux first insisted that the meeting take place in their tent. Morris rejected that demand but when he learned that they were refusing to meet on Hudson's Bay Company lands a compromise was made and the tent moved. Four days were spent in preliminary skirmishing and it was the afternoon of September 12 when Morris was able to outline his proposals.

Morris got around the Indians' objections to the money paid to the Hudson's Bay Company by explaining that "many years ago the Queen's father's father gave the Company the right to trade in the country"and now the Queen "took all the lands into her own hands and gave the Company a sum of money in place of the rights she had taken from them."[32] That was not a completely frank description of the Rupert's Land agreement. The Company did receive payment for the lands and Morris did not mention the one-twentieth of "the fertile lands" retained by the Company.

The Indians admitted they were confused by the land issue. The Gambler explained that "the Indians were not told of the [Hudson's Bay Company] reserves at all. I hear now, that it was the Queen who gave the land. The Indians thought it was they who gave it to the Company, who are now all over the country. The Indians did not know when the land was given."[33]

There was dissension and drama. The Cree were much more disposed to sign a treaty than the Saulteaux who were so militant that on one day, with full intent to intimidate the proceedings, they placed six men, each armed with both rifle and revolver, in the meeting tent. Lieutenant Colonel Osborne Smith promptly countered by stationing six of his armed troopers across the tent. Between the stern stares of 12 armed men, Morris and the chiefs carried on their discussions.

Much as his predecessor Adams Archibald had done three years earlier at the Stone Fort, Morris related the treaty experiences in Eastern Canada as an example of what the Indians of the Plains could look forward to:

> More than a hundred years ago, the Queen's father said to the red men living in Quebec and Ontario, I will give you land and cattle and set apart Reserves for you, and will teach you. What has been the result? There the red men are happy; instead of getting fewer in number by sickness they are growing in number; their children have plenty.[34]

Morris explained that the Queen was thinking of the future:

> Therefore, the promises we have to make to you are not for today only but for tomorrow, not only for you but for your children born and unborn, and the promises we make will be carried out as long as the sun shines above and the water flows in the ocean. When you are ready to plant seed the Queen's men will lay off Reserves so as to

give a square mile [2.6 km²] to every family of five persons, and on commencing to farm the Queen will give to every family cultivating the soil two hoes, one spade, one scythe for cutting the grain, one axe and plough, enough of seed wheat, barley, oats, and potatoes to plant the land they get ready. The Queen wishes her red children to learn the cunning of the white man and when they are ready for it she will send schoolmasters on every Reserve and pay them.[35]

Morris painted a bleak picture of the Cree and Saulteaux future without a treaty:

We have done all that men who love their red brothers can do; it is for you now to act, on you rests the duty of saying whether you believe our message or not, whether you want the Queen to help you or not, whether or not you will go away and let the days and years go on, and let the food grow scarcer, and let your children grow up and do nothing to keep off the hunger and the cold that is before them.[36]

Finally the assembled chiefs announced that they would accept a treaty on terms similar to those in Treaty 3. On September 15, 1874, the deal was done and Treaty 4 was signed. As in the previous treaties, it provided for a complete cession of territory:

The Cree and Saulteaux tribes of Indians, and all other Indians inhabiting the district hereinafter described and defined, do hereby cede, release, surrender and yield up to the Government of the Dominion of Canada for Her Majesty the Queen and her successors forever, all their rights, title and privileges whatsoever to the lands included within the following limits . . .[37]

The area described was a huge slice of territory reaching from Lake Winnipegosis down to and including the Cypress Hills, most of present-day southern Saskatchewan, some 193,200 km² (74,600 mi²) in all.

The consideration was a signing bonus, or gratuity, of $12 to each individual, $15 for headmen, $25 for each chief. The annuity, which came to be called "Treaty Money," was $5 per capita, headmen (restricted to four per band) $15, and to chiefs $25. Reserves would again be fixed on the basis of 2.6 km² (1 mi²) (260 ha, or 640 acres) per family of five. Morris also agreed to provide carpentry and farming tools and some livestock. A school would be established on each reserve so that the children could learn "the cunning of the white man."

The Saulteaux band at Fort Ellice signed on to the Treaty on September 21, 1874. A year later, on September 8 and 9, 1875, two more groups of Cree, Saulteaux and Assiniboine joined. The latter group included bands led by White Bear, Piapot and Pheasant Rump.

It had been the policy of Prime Minister Macdonald's government to pursue treaties only as the lands were required "for the purposes of the Dominion," and this approach was carried on by the Liberal administration of Prime Minister Mackenzie. So it was that the Cree of the Saskatchewan River district, who had expressed their concerns through W.J. Christie as early as 1871, had to wait until 1876 before they were approached by government treaty negotiators. Others, in particular those farther north, would wait much longer, and suffer accordingly.

Macdonald accepted no responsibility whatsoever towards Indians who had not yet come under treaty and he was interested in making treaty only with the occupants of lands required for settlement or similar purpose. Non-treaty Indians residing in undesirable territory were less than full citizens. When famine struck the Chippewa, Cree and Dene of the Athabasca and Mackenzie districts, Ottawa refused all pleas for assistance on the grounds that they were not under treaty. And there was little likelihood of a treaty in the remote region until interest was sparked by the discovery of oil in the late 1880s.[38] Treaty 8, covering a vast area of the north, was not put in place until 1899, 22 years after the last treaty on the fertile plains where the Pacific railway would run.

Macdonald viewed the Aboriginal inhabitants of the western plains much as did the Canadian public generally. Stereotypically they were indolent, pagan savages whose destiny was to give way before the advancing, superior European Christian civilization. The two leading newspapers of Ontario and Quebec, the Toronto *Globe*, ancestor of today's *Globe and Mail*, and the Montreal *Gazette*, found little, if any, news value in the treaty-making process in the West. The scant coverage explained that the Indians desired treaties and the protection of white society: "Sensible Indians endorsed colonialism—and treaties—as good for them."[39]

TREATY 5: THE WINNIPEG TREATY

IN 1875, SOMEWHAT CURIOUSLY, Ottawa decided it was important to secure the lands to the north of Treaties 2 and 3 and particularly the waterways feeding in and out of Lake Winnipeg. In late September 1875, Morris sailed, by the Hudson's Bay Company steamer *Colville*, up Lake Winnipeg. At

Berens River, Norway House and Grand Rapids he secured Treaty 5, covering a large tract north of Treaties 2, 3 and 4 and reaching as far west as Cumberland House on the Saskatchewan River, about 260,000 km^2 (100,000 mi^2). The negotiations were unusually short; at each site the Saulteaux and Swampy Cree accepted the Treaty on the same day it was presented to them.

The consideration paid here was less than in Treaty 4. The gratuity paid on signing was only $5, not $12, and the reserve allotment was to be calculated on the basis of 65 ha (160 acres) (in some cases 40 ha/100 acres) per family of five. There was little fertile land in the Treaty 5 region and agriculture was not considered as a livelihood for its residents, in the present or the future.

Although Wemyss Simpson spoke the Saulteaux/Ojibway tongue, neither Adams Archibald nor Alexander Morris spoke any Native language. They provided interpreters for their negotiations but just how accurate were their translations is questionable. Some of the misunderstandings that arose might have been caused by the innocent failure of interpreters who had an imperfect knowledge of the different dialects at play.

The government also provided the only written record of the proceedings and the text of the treaties. None of the Indians who negotiated for their people had a written language of their own or any knowledge of the English language. They could not read the documents they signed, nor actually sign their names; they "signed" with an "X," or merely "touched the pen" in the hand of someone else. This reality gave Ottawa a huge advantage, not only during the negotiations but in later decades when the provisions of the treaties were being applied in a modern society not contemplated in the 1870s. The oral history of the Indians was seldom a match for the written record.

The presence of a remarkable man at the Treaty 6 negotiations two years after Treaty 4 would illustrate just how great was the gulf of understanding between the two sides at the treaty negotiations in the Canadian West in the 1870s.

Two momentous events in the history of the North-West Territories would occur before those Treaty 6 negotiations would commence, and both were coming to a conclusion in September 1874, as Lieutenant-Governor Morris left Fort Qu'Appelle on his return trip to Fort Garry. The surveyors of the International Boundary Commission were also returning to Red River after completing their marking of 1,290 km (800 mi) of the 49th Parallel, the border between the United States and Canada. And the North-West Mounted Police, having successfully trekked west to the shadow of the Rocky Mountains, were establishing themselves at Fort Macleod, on the Oldmans River. Political boundaries and law and order were introduced to the Canadian West.

It is tragic that no camera was present to record the history and pageantry of any of the treaty negotiations on the Canadian Plains in the 1870s. Photography was in its infancy, but well enough advanced to capture many of the events of the times. In 1872, four years before the Treaty 6 negotiations, a photographer had crossed the prairies in the company of a survey crew searching out a route for the planned Pacific railway. Another photographer recorded much of the work of the Boundary Commission on the 49th Parallel in 1873 and 1874. One suspects that officialdom did not regard the western treaties as sufficiently important to warrant the trouble and expense. That contrasts with the view of the Plains Indians to whom the treaties were the epic event, not only of their time, but of all their people's history. Still today they look upon their treaties much as English-speaking people look upon the Magna Carta.

TREATY 6: THE TREATIES AT FORT CARLTON AND FORT PITT

A MAJESTIC SIGHT GREETED Peter Erasmus when he arrived at Fort Carlton on Thursday, August 17, 1876. Built by the Hudson's Bay Company in 1810, the trading post looked west over the North Saskatchewan River 90 km (55 mi) upriver from Prince Albert, and on the well-worn cart trail that bore its name. On a grassy plain 3.5 km (2 mi) west of the Fort, 250 tall and graceful tipis were arranged in circles according to the custom of the many Indian bands congregated there. It was a huge assembly, an impressive response to the call that had gone forth advising the Cree of the Saskatchewan that the Queen's representative would meet to negotiate a treaty. The 46-year-old Erasmus had spent his entire life on the western plains but had never before seen such a huge assembly.

The 250 tipis on the Fort Carlton treaty grounds housed some 2,000 Plains Cree of nine different bands. Accompanied by thousands of horses and almost as many dogs, their presence on the southern slope of the North Saskatchewan River was unmistakable. The Queen's representatives on the treaty grounds were fewer in numbers, but not lacking in showmanship. The Treaty 6 negotiations were the first to include the presence of the North-West Mounted Police and 82 officers and men rode onto the scene.[40] Magnificently mounted, resplendent in red serge and white helmets, accompanied by a band, they excited the admiration of the buffalo-hunting Cree, critical equestrians themselves, most of whom had not before seen the new force, in the West just two years.[41]

Erasmus had been engaged by two of the leading Cree chiefs, Ahtahkakoop (Star Blanket) and Mistawasis (Big Child), to serve as an interpreter in the negotiations. They had made a wise choice. Erasmus, born at Red River to a Danish

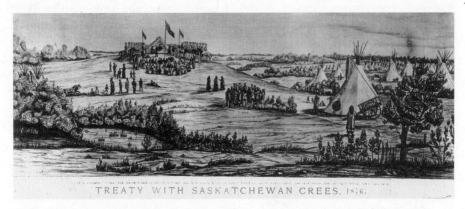

TREATY WITH SASKATCHEWAN CREES, 1876.

Artist's rendering of the signing of Treaty 6 at Fort Carlton, 1876. *Archives of Manitoba N9466*

father and a Métis mother, possessed unusual education and experience. He had studied for the Anglican ministry, served as a school teacher and a missionary, as interpreter with a number of early missionaries throughout the West, and travelled with the Palliser Expedition. An accomplished linguist, Erasmus spoke Swampy Cree and Plains Cree, two almost entirely distinct languages, as well as Ojibway, Blackfoot, Assiniboine (Stoney) and, of course, English.

That Ahtahkakoop and Mistawasis had gone to the trouble of securing the services of their own interpreter speaks loudly as to how seriously they regarded the treaty discussions.

Two other interpreters had been engaged for the negotiations but their inability to properly carry out the task soon became apparent and Erasmus served as official interpreter to the complete satisfaction of both sides. His fortuitous presence at the Treaty 6 assembly later provided the only written account of the background discussions of the Cree participants.[42]

Lieutenant-Governor Morris played his part in the ceremony surrounding the negotiations. On the morning of Friday, August 18, formally and resplendently attired in royal blue uniform trimmed with lace and gold braid, wearing a cocked hat, accompanied by his two fellow Commissioners W.J. Christie and James McKay (who had replaced David Laird), he was driven by carriage from his quarters at Fort Carlton to the council tent erected on the treaty grounds accompanied by a smart escort of NWMP riders.

The grand arrival of the Treaty Commissioners and their retinue was merely the beginning of the pomp and ceremony. The Cree chiefs and councillors approached the council tent behind an intricately choreographed display of equestrianism performed by some 20 young horsemen. Then followed a traditional sacred rite involving a large and beautifully decorated pipestem which was then presented to Lieutenant-Governor Morris and his Commissioners.

The meaning of the pipestem ritual and presentation by the Cree chiefs, and its reception by the Treaty Commissioners, illustrated the gulf of understanding between the two groups.

The secretary to the negotiations, in an account adopted by Morris, described the event thus: "The significance of this ceremony is that the Governor and Commissioners accepted the friendship of the tribe."[43]

Chief Ahtahkakoop's biographer explains that Morris misunderstood:

> According to Indian traditions, in the presence of the sacred pipestem only the truth could be spoken. Men must put aside their differences and work for good things. Thus, for Ahtahkakoop, Mistawasis, and the other leading men, the promises made during the treaty negotiations at Fort Carlton would be considered as binding as those that appeared in the written document.[44]

Erasmus contributed an explanation:

> . . . these ceremonial practices had a deep significance to the tribes and can only be explained as a solemn approach to a serious issue for discussion. ·

> Few people realize that those so-called savages were far more deeply affected and influenced by their religious beliefs and convictions than any comparable group of white people, whose lip service to their religion goes no deeper than that. The forms of ceremonial behaviour with which the Indians approached the Governor's tent were based on practices whose actual meaning has long since been lost. The ceremony in the crowning of the kings and queens of England would have little meaning were it not for the benefit of a written language.[45]

The Plains Cree who gathered on August 18, 1876, to hear the treaty proposals delivered by Lieutenant-Governor Alexander Morris had a very good idea of what the offer would be. It had been two years since Treaty 4 had been signed at Fort Qu'Appelle and its terms had long since been known to the Indians of the Valley of the Saskatchewan. But the Plains Cree who gathered at Fort Carlton had an advantage over their brethren who had signed on to the first five Western treaties. They had been experimenting with agriculture, and had some knowledge of what they might expect when reduced to deriving a living from the tillage of the land.

The bands of Ahtahkakoop and Mistawasis in particular had taken steps in adaptation to a new and different way of life. Near Sandy Lake, west of Prince Albert, John Hines, an Anglican missionary, had introduced the people to the cultivation of potatoes, wheat and barley and had started a school. There had been difficulties, but enough success to promise that there could be life without buffalo. Ahtahkakoop and Mistawasis, the two leading Cree spokesmen at the Treaty 6 negotiations, saw beyond the demise of the great buffalo herds that had sustained them in the past into a future where their children could not only survive but succeed in the way of the white people who now threatened to overrun their lands. These two visionaries looked upon the treaty brought to them as the link that would carry their people into that future.

Morris did not expect the negotiations to go smoothly. He knew there was dissatisfaction among the western Cree about the delay in making treaty with them. A crew laying the telegraph towards Fort Edmonton the previous year had been stopped. The Reverend George McDougall, who had established a Methodist mission at Morleyville, on the Bow River, had been sent into the Cree villages with presents and assurances that the Queen's treaty makers would arrive the following year. McDougall found a hint of trouble when he met Big Bear, a Cree chief whose stature was on the rise. In words similar to those of the Saulteaux of Fort Frances with Wemyss Simpson, Big Bear refused the presents:

> We want none of the Queen's presents. When we set a fox trap we scatter pieces of meat all around but when the fox gets into the trap we knock him on the head. We want no baits. Let your Chiefs come like men and talk to us.[46]

It was an omen. Big Bear would decline the Treaty 6 terms, refuse to sign and hold out for more than six long and often desperate years.

On Friday, after the opening ceremonies and an introductory speech by Lieutenant-Governor Morris, the Indians requested an adjournment until the next day so that they could meet in their own councils and elect their spokesmen.

On Saturday Morris outlined the provisions of the treaty he had come to make. They were as in Treaty 4: reserves would be based on 2.6 km^2 (1 mi^2), or 260 ha (640 acres), for each family of five, and Morris suggested that the Cree not delay in choosing a "home of their own . . . the white man might come and settle on the very place where you would like to be . . . If when a reserve is chosen, a white man had already settled there, his rights must be respected."[47]

There would be schools for the children, tools and implements for those who would farm, as well as seed and livestock.

And there would be a present, or signing bonus, of $12 for every man, woman and child, paid to the head of the family. Thereafter there would be an annual payment of $5 to everyone, increased to $25 for chiefs and $15 for headmen or councillors. There would also be uniforms for the chief and councillors, replaced every three years. Morris assured the Cree that his promises were "not for today or tomorrow only, but should continue as long as the sun shone and the river flowed."[48]

Poundmaker, not yet the great chief he would become, spoke in response to the proposed land allocation: "The governor mentions how much land is to be given us. He says 640 acres [260 ha], one mile square [2.6 km²] for each family, he will give us." Then raising his voice, Poundmaker shouted, "This is our land! It isn't a piece of pemmican to be cut off and given in little pieces back to us. It is ours and we will take what we want."[49]

Erasmus noted "a strong wave of approval" of Poundmaker's words and observed that Morris "was visibly shaken by this demonstration."[50] He had thought his proposed terms had been found acceptable.

Morris responded with care and sincerity, Erasmus recorded, as the Lieutenant-Governor explained that "unless certain lands were set aside for the sole use of the Indians, the country would be flooded with white settlers who would not give the Indians any consideration whatever."[51]

The chiefs requested time to consider the proposals. They allowed Morris' words to percolate throughout the huge Cree encampment all the next day, Sunday. On Monday morning Ahtahkakoop advised the Lieutenant-Governor that his people required a further day to discuss the treaty in council. Peter Erasmus was invited to attend the council and from him we have an account of the deliberations of the Cree leadership at that fateful assembly.

The debate raged all day. Opponents of the treaty, led by Poundmaker and The Badger, were vocal and strong and Erasmus saw little hope of any agreement with the Queen's representatives. Then, late in the afternoon, on a signal from Ahtahkakoop, Mistawasis rose to speak:

> I have heard my brothers speak, complaining of the hardships endured by our people. Some have bewailed the poverty and suffering that has come to Indians because of the destruction of the buffalo as the chief source of our living, the loss of the ancient glory of our forefathers; and with all that I agree, in the silence of my teepee and on the broad prairies where once our fathers could not pass for the great number of those

Chief Poundmaker (no date). *Saskatchewan Archives Board R-B8775*

animals that blocked their way; and even in our day, we have had to choose carefully our campground for fear of being trampled in our teepees. With all these things, I think and feel intensely the sorrow my brothers express.

I speak directly to Poundmaker and The Badger and those others who object to signing this treaty. Have you anything better to offer our people? I ask, again, can you suggest anything that will bring these things back for tomorrow and all the tomorrows that face our people?

I for one think that the Great White Queen Mother has offered us a way of life when the buffalo are no more. Gone they will be before many snows have come to cover our heads, or graves if such should be.

Mistawasis then spoke of the misery inflicted upon the Blackfoot by the American whiskey traders and how the presence of just a few Red Coats had caused those cutthroats and criminals to flee back across the border:

I ask you why those few men could put to flight those bad men who for years have defied the whole of the southern Indian nations? . . .

Let me tell you why these things were so. It was the power that stands behind those few Red Coats that those men feared and wasted no time in getting out when they could; the power that is represented in all the Queen's people, and we the children are counted as important as even the Governor who is her personal speaker . . .

We speak of glory and our memories are all that is left to feed the widows and orphans of those who have died in its attainment. We are few in numbers compared to former times, by wars and the terrible ravages of smallpox . . .

The prairies have not been darkened by the blood of our white brothers in our time. Let this always be so. I for one will take the hand that is offered. For my band I have spoken.[52]

A deep silence followed the eloquence of Mistawasis. Then Ahtahkakoop slowly rose and stood silently with his head bowed. Then he spoke, first of regret at the wars they had waged with the Blackfoot:

If we had been friends, we might now be a host of people of all nations and together have power to demand the things some of you foolishly think you can get, and insist on now demanding.

No, that is not the road we took, but killed each other in continuous wars and in horse stealing, all for the glory we all speak of so freely. The great sickness took half our lodges and the dreaded disease fell as heavily on our enemies. We are weak and my brother Mistawasis I think is right that the buffalo will be gone forever before many snows. What then will be left us with which to bargain? With the buffalo gone we will have only the vacant prairie which none of us have learned to use.

Can we stop the power of the white man from spreading over the land like the grasshoppers that cloud the sky and then fall to consume every blade of grass and every leaf on the trees in their path? I think not. Before this happens let us ponder carefully our choice of roads . . .

Let us not think of ourselves but of our children's children. We hold our place among the tribes as chiefs and councillors because our people think we have wisdom above others amongst us. Then let us show our wisdom. Let us show our wisdom by choosing the right path now while we have a choice.

We have always lived and received our needs in clothing, shelter, and food from the countless multitudes of buffalo that have been with us since the earliest memory of our people. No one with open eyes and open minds can doubt that the buffalo will soon be a thing of the past. Will our people live as before when this comes to pass? No! They will die and become just a memory unless we find another way.

For my part, I think that the Queen Mother has offered us a new way and I have faith in the things my brother Mistawasis has told you. The mother earth has always given us plenty with the grass that fed the buffalo. Surely we Indians can learn the way of living that made the white man strong and able to vanquish all the great tribes of the southern nations . . . I will accept the Queen's hand for my people. I have spoken.[53]

As Peter Erasmus watched, the great majority of the chiefs and councillors signified their agreement with the opinions of Mistawasis and Ahtahkakoop. The council adjourned. The treaty discussions would go forward in the morning.

But the Cree were not yet satisfied with the terms Morris had outlined. They were concerned about food for their people until they successfully made the transition to a farming way of life. An entire day was occupied with the food question. The next morning (Wednesday) Peter Erasmus read to Morris and his Commissioners a list of additional provisions the chiefs wanted included in any treaty. Among their requests were more livestock and farm implements, provisions for the poor, the right to cut timber on Crown lands, a horse and wagon for each chief plus a cook stove, a free supply of medicine and exemption from war service.

Morris responded by granting additional farming supplies and three terms not part of the previous treaties: assistance in the event the Indians were "overtaken by any pestilence, or by a general famine,"[54] a medicine chest to be maintained on each reserve at the house of the Indian agent, and, when they settled on reserves, $1,000 worth of provisions yearly for three years only to tide them over while bringing their lands under cultivation.

The first two of these terms, unique to Treaty 6, would, in the future, attain a significance far beyond that contemplated at Fort Carlton in 1876. The famine clause would be invoked far sooner than anyone present on the treaty grounds could have imagined.

Morris had more than once referred to the treaty he had negotiated at the North-West Angle and its terms, suggesting that the Cree should be satisfied with much the same. His listeners were not without knowledge of conditions at Lake of the Woods. The discussions were on the verge of agreement when one Joseph Thoma rose and, presuming to speak for Chief Red Pheasant of Battle River, pointed out "the quality of the land . . . There is no farming land whatever at the north-west angle, and he goes by what he has done down there."[55] Red Pheasant repudiated Thoma and the proposals Morris made were accepted.

The proposed Treaty 6 had been written out on parchment and the new terms were added by interlineation on the existing sheets and by adding new sheets at the end. The treaty was read and interpreted to the assembly, a process that required the services of all the interpreters. Mistawasis instructed Peter Erasmus to be sure that everything promised had been included in the writing. Assured, Mistawasis, followed by Ahtahkakoop, were the first to "touch the pen" when the treaty was executed at Fort Carlton on August 23, 1876.

On August 28, Treaty 6 was signed by the Willow Indians from Duck Lake and then Morris and his party moved 217 km (135 mi) northwest to Fort Pitt, the second place appointed for the negotiations. Another Hudson's Bay Company trading post, established in 1829 as a halfway point on the Carlton Trail to Fort Edmonton, the fort stood on the north bank of an east-west stretch of the North Saskatchewan River. It was a well-chosen site where the plain slopes gently to the water with none of the usual high banks of the Saskatchewan. There, on September 7 the Treaty Commissioners met with another assembly of Plains Cree, this time under the leadership of Sweet Grass, one of the signatories to the letter written by W.J. Christie at Fort Edmonton in April 1871. Again Peter Erasmus served as interpreter. These negotiation were brief. Sweet Grass and his fellow chiefs signed on to Treaty 6 on September 9, 1876.

Treaty 6 provided for the surrender of a huge territory, reaching from Prince Albert to the Rocky Mountains and down to the Cypress Hills, 313,365 km^2 (121,000 mi^2) in all. The only unceded area remaining on the Canadian Plains was in the southwest corner of the North-West Territories, the lands of the Blackfoot, Blood, Peigan and Sarcee.

Peter Erasmus had so impressed Lieutenant-Governor Morris with his skills that he was taken on by the Indian Department as an interpreter and served for a number of years throughout the West. He had a prodigious memory. Although his account of the Treaty 6 negotiations was not reduced to writing until many years after the event it is regarded as unusually accurate. Peter Erasmus has provided the best record of what was in the minds of the leadership of the Plains Cree as they considered their bleak future and decided to put their faith in Treaty 6.

The new Commissioner of the NWMP, James Macleod, was late in arriving at the Treaty 6 negotiations. Appointed on July 20, 1876, just a month before the great gathering at Fort Carlton, Macleod made a tour of police posts, stopped just overnight at Fort Garry to be married, then moved on to Fort Livingstone. There he arranged to move the NWMP headquarters to Fort Macleod before heading west. He caught up with Lieutenant-Governor

Morris and the other Treaty Commissioners at Fort Pitt in time to place his signature on the second portion of the treaty document.

As he passed through Battleford, Commissioner Macleod received some disturbing news.[56] On June 25, troops of the United States Army 7th Cavalry had suffered serious casualties in a battle with Sioux Indians near the Little Big Horn River. Lieutenant Colonel George A. Custer and 264 of his men had been killed. The Sioux, under the leadership of Sitting Bull, had withdrawn.

Ottawa had been concerned for some months that, if trouble broke out between the Sioux and the U.S. Army, the Sioux might head to sanctuary in Canada. Macleod headed south to Fort Walsh, the NWMP post established in the Cypress Hills just a year earlier.

One of the very early consequences of the disaster at the Little Big Horn was the creation of a "Commission Appointed to Obtain Certain Concessions From the Sioux." Headed by George Manypenny, the Commission had secured an agreement of dubious legality by which the Sioux finally surrendered the Black Hills. Three months after the signing of Treaty 6, President Ulysses S. Grant forwarded the Commission's Report to the Senate and the House of Representatives. In its Report, the Commission was scathingly critical of America's treatment of its Indian peoples, and made comparison with the situation in Canada:

> The fact that the English government in Canada has expended no money in Indian wars since the American Revolution, has lost no lives by massacre, has had no desecrated settlements, and that its Indians are today, as they have always been, loyal to the British Crown, is due to the fact that it has fulfilled its plighted faith, has given to its Indians personal rights of property and the protection of law, and has fostered Christian missions, and has placed over its Indians agents fitted for the task of guiding a savage race to civilization, and who generally hold their office during good behavior.[57]

The future would disclose just how accurate would be this assessment of Canada's treatment of its Indian peoples.

TREATY 7: THE BLACKFOOT TREATY

FATE CONTINUED TO SMILE upon him, James Farquharson Macleod thought on September 12, 1877, as he rode at the head of a troop of 80 officers and men out of Fort Macleod, the headquarters of the NWMP that bore his name. Only four years earlier his appointment to the newly established North-West Mounted Police had rescued him from the tedium and obscurity of life as a small-town lawyer in Ontario and given him a career of adventure and achievement on the western plains. Just three years later he had succeeded to the rank of Commissioner, the top command position of the NWMP. Now his destination was a ford on the Bow River some 130 km (80 mi) to the north-east known as Blackfoot Crossing. Macleod had been chosen by the Canadian government as one of two members of the Commission directed to negotiate a treaty with the Indians of the Blackfoot Confederacy. That treaty would see the Blackfoot surrender their homeland, the last unceded land on the prairies, and give Ottawa clear title to the entire territory stretching from Lake Superior to the Rocky Mountains. Blackfoot Crossing had been chosen as the site of the treaty negotiations, due to commence on Monday, September 17, five days hence.

Macleod's fellow Commissioner for the Treaty 7 negotiations was the Honourable David Laird, the new Lieutenant-Governor of the North-West Territories. Three years earlier, Laird, then the new Liberal Minister of the Interior, had participated with Lieutenant-Governor Morris in the Treaty 4 negotiations. The Prince Edward Islander was so attracted to the West that he had resigned his portfolio to succeed Morris. Macleod rode two days in advance of Laird to prepare their accommodations at the treaty grounds.

Ottawa had chosen wisely in appointing Macleod as one of the treaty negotiators. Assistant Commissioner when the NWMP arrived in the West in the fall of 1874 and put an end to the American whiskey forts that had been preying upon the Blackfoot, Macleod had, in the words of the Honourable David Mills, Minister of the Interior, "acquired the entire confidence and goodwill of the Indian tribes proposed to be dealt with."[58]

The Blackfoot had reason to be grateful. In 1874 they had been destitute, clothed in rags and without horses or guns, all traded for whiskey. But in three short years they had recovered much of their former prosperity and were again well clothed and equipped with good horses and modern rifles. The Blackfoot looked upon Macleod and the NWMP as their saviours. If anyone could induce them to accept Ottawa's treaty terms, it would be Commissioner Macleod.

Like the Saulteaux/Ojibway of Treaty 3, the Blackfoot were as much American as Canadian. They occupied lands that extended down into Montana Territory as far as Three Forks, the beginning of the Missouri River, and were accustomed to roaming back and forth across the border that had not been marked until 1874, just three years earlier. In fact, Blackfoot chiefs had signed treaties with the United States as early as 1855, and again in 1865. Three of their leaders who signed what became known as the Lame Bull Treaty in 1855 would also be present at Blackfoot Crossing in 1877 and would sign Treaty 7 with the Canadian government.

The Blackfoot Confederacy consisted of three tribes, the Blackfoot, the Blood and the Peigan, together with their allies, the Sarcees. All would be present at Blackfoot Crossing, although the Blood and Peigan, annoyed that the location had been chosen to accommodate the Blackfoot, delayed their appearance. Also in attendance, but camped at a safe distance, was an enemy band, the Stoney, a branch of the Assiniboine who occupied the foothills to the west of the other tribes.

Ottawa's policy of negotiating treaties only when it perceived a need for the territory to be surrendered had served it well until 1877. Then events in the United States intervened to make a treaty with the Blackfoot Confederacy a priority. By September it had become a matter of real urgency.

Two missionaries, Reverend John McDougall and Father Constantine Scollen, both familiar with the Blackfoot tribes and their country, had long been urging Ottawa to conclude a treaty as early as possible, while goodwill lasted. Conditions might change and the opportunity be lost. Father Scollen, who had founded the mission, Our Lady of Peace, on the Elbow River in 1873, advised by letter in September 1876, a couple of months after the Sioux victory at Little Big Horn, that the American Sioux had "sent a message to the Blackfeet tribes, asking them to make an alliance offensive and defensive against all white people in the country."[59] Although the Blackfoot claimed they had refused the proposition, that was a condition that might change at any time.

Not long after Father Scollen's letter, some 2,000 Sioux slipped away from the pursuing U.S. Army and into the North-West Territories. The following spring, in May 1877, Sitting Bull arrived and the number of Sioux in Canada rose to 6,000. Their chiefs professed to be interested only in sanctuary, but they presented a major problem to the government in Ottawa and the NWMP in the West. Following up the earlier approach, Sitting Bull sent Crowfoot, chief of the Blackfoot tribe, "a gift of tobacco and other articles, indicating his desire for friendship and peace."[60] Then, in August, just a month before the scheduled Treaty 7 negotiations, he visited Crowfoot at the Blackfoot chief's camp in the Great Sand Hills. The two great leaders held a long discussion and struck a real friendship.[61] Sitting Bull was so taken with the Blackfoot chief that he gave the name Crowfoot to his young son.

The eruption of another problem in the United States added to the urgency of securing a treaty with the Blackfoot. Provoked by a demand that they surrender and vacate their Oregon homeland, the peaceful Nez Perce finally rebelled. Then began an epic march through Idaho and Montana Territories as the Nez Perce, like the Sioux, headed for sanctuary in Canada. It was nothing short of a running battle with the U.S. Army in hot pursuit. More than 800 Nez Perce men, women and children, with all their horses and possessions, defeated and evaded the Army over a course of 1,770 km (1,100 mi) and three and a half months of the summer of 1877. In September the great drama drew within 65 km (40 mi) of the Canadian border when the Nez Perce camped in the Bears Paw Mountains. There they were overtaken and pinned down by the troops. The Nez Perce sent emissaries to Sitting Bull and the Sioux in Canada pleading for assistance. It was an unsettling situation, still very much on the boil, and Macleod was concerned that it would affect the attitude of the Blackfoot.[1]

NOTE

1. Treaty 7 Elders (ed. by Walter Hildebrandt and Sarah Carter), *The True Spirit and Original Intent of Treaty 7* (Montreal and Kingston: McGill-Queen's University Press, 1996), 228–29.

Although Crowfoot and Sitting Bull claimed to wish only peace, even if they were sincere, so long as the Blackfoot remained without a treaty that attitude could disappear overnight.

The Commissioner had another problem on his mind that September morning. The United States had accepted the suggestion from Canada that it offer Sitting Bull and the Sioux amnesty if they would return. President Rutherford Hayes had appointed General Alfred Terry and retired General A.G. Lawrence as a Special Commission to travel into the North-West Territories, meet with Sitting Bull and the other Sioux chiefs, and deliver such a proposal. The Commissioners had requested that the high-level encounter take place at Fort Walsh, the two-year old NWMP post in the Cypress Hills. Terry and Lawrence were already en route and scheduled to arrive on September 29 at the point where the Fort Benton to Fort Walsh trail crossed the border. There they were to be met by a troop of NWMP who would escort them through Canadian territory to Fort Walsh.

Macleod knew that Inspector James Walsh, officer commanding the fort named after him, was busily engaged in making preparations to receive the Presidential Commission, and that included persuading Sitting Bull to attend the meeting. The latter item was no small task. The Sioux were still full of fear and hatred of the Americans and would not easily be convinced to sit down with the two generals, particularly Terry who had been in command of the Army units sent against them at Little Big Horn.

Walsh was an extremely capable officer, but it would be best that Macleod, the senior officer of the NWMP, be in attendance when the President's representatives arrived. Ottawa had instructed Macleod that the government was "most anxious that the United States commissioners should succeed in inducing the hostile Sioux who have come into our territory to return again to the United States." It was feared that conflict would break out with the Blackfoot, Cree and Assiniboine, that the Sioux would carry out raids into the United States, seriously aggravating relations between the two countries, and, if or when the buffalo failed, the Sioux would become "a very considerable expense ... It is therefore important that you should use your influence to promote, as far as you well can, the object of the United States commissioners in securing the return of these Indians to their own reservation."[62]

Fort Walsh was 160 km (100 mi) east of Blackfoot Crossing. It was doubtful that the negotiations with the Blackfoot could be completed in time to allow Macleod to attend at Fort Walsh by the end of September.

Although it would be unfortunate if Macleod was unable to receive the President's Commissioners, it would be far more serious if the negotiations with the Blackfoot failed. Ottawa had made Macleod's priority clear; the Blackfoot treaty was critical.

The Blackfoot had been concerned about being left without a treaty, particularly while their traditional enemies, the Cree and Assiniboine, had been treated with in 1874 and 1876. As early as 1875 their chiefs had stated that there should be no further incursions into their territory until a treaty should be made. At the Fort Pitt Treaty 6 gathering, Reverend John McDougall and Father Constantine Scollen, the two missionaries most familiar with the Blackfoot, had emphasized to Lieutenant-Governor Morris the urgency of carrying the treaty negotiations to the Blackfoot.[63]

The assembly at Blackfoot Crossing was larger than at any of the previous western treaty makings and the pageantry more impressive. Some 5,000 Indians gathered in the wide valley of the Bow River, erecting many hundreds of gaily decorated tipis that stretched for miles on both sides of the river. That the bands had recovered economically from the depredations of the whiskey traders was evidenced by their herds of horses, estimated to number more than 15,000. The missionaries McDougall and Scollen were present, as were many other white people of various occupations. Three prominent trading concerns set up shop, anticipating brisk sales funded by the treaty monies. The Hudson's Bay Company from Fort Edmonton and two Fort Benton merchants,

Painting of the signing of Treaty 7 at Blackfoot Crossing: Crowfoot is speaking. *Glenbow Museum NA-40-1*

I.G. Baker & Co. and T.C. Power & Bro., threw up temporary log and canvas structures and filled them with a wide variety of trade goods. The NWMP provided a strong presence, 108 officers and men, complete with a band and two 9-pounder guns.

On Monday, September 17, the day appointed for the meeting to commence, a blast from one of the NWMP field guns called the assembly into session although not all the Indians were yet present, the Bloods particularly holding back. Lieutenant-Governor Laird addressed the group and then adjourned until Wednesday to give an opportunity for others to arrive.

Peter Erasmus was not called to the Treaty 7 negotiations. The Treaty Commissioners expected Jerry Potts, the NWMP's mixed-blood Peigan scout and guide, to interpret, but, as with the initial Treaty 6 interpreters, Potts was not fully up to the task. James Bird, a Métis who for many years had traded with the American Blackfoot, was conscripted. He spoke five Native languages in addition to French and English, and had worked as an interpreter for explorers, missionaries and the United States government.[64] Bird had lost his eyesight but was able to relay the words and emotions of the Treaty Commissioners.

Like Ahtahkakoop and Mistawasis, Chief Crowfoot of the Blackfoot had his own interpreters at Blackfoot Crossing; Jean L'Heureux, an educated French Canadian who posed as a priest, had been living with the Blackfoot for years. Like Erasmus, L'Heureux was later employed as an interpreter by the Indian department. Father Constantine Scollen *was* a priest, the first English-speaking Catholic cleric in that part of the Territories that later became Alberta, and he also provided the Blackfoot with interpretation and advice.

Wednesday morning saw a brilliant equestrian display as more than 1,000 warriors of the Confederacy, mounted bareback and firing their weapons in the air, surged over the hilltops and swept down upon the NWMP encampment where they reined to a sudden halt. There they stood while Crowfoot stepped out of the mob in front of the official marquee, sat upon a buffalo robe, lighted a ceremonial stone pipe, took a puff and handed the pipe to Lieutenant-Governor Laird. The Blackfoot would meet in council with the Treaty Commissioners.

On Wednesday afternoon Laird opened the negotiations in earnest, even though several principal Blood chiefs were still absent. The Lieutenant-Governor outlined the government's proposals which he said were similar to those adopted by the Plains Cree in Treaty 6. That was true, except for the medicine chest, the famine clause, and the promise of provisions during the first three years of farming. Those three items remained unique to Treaty 6. Laird suggested that the Indians not respond until the next day and the assembly adjourned.

There was much discussion and much dissension in the Indian encampment. The Blackfoot experience with their American treaties had not been good. Many of the minor chiefs and younger warriors were opposed to any more agreements with governments.

On Thursday afternoon, the Treaty Commissioners and the Indians met again, but it was another unproductive day. Invited to express their opinions, the principal chiefs present, Crowfoot for one, Old Sun for another, stated that they would not speak until the next day. They were hesitant, apparently awaiting Red Crow, chief of the Bloods, who had not yet appeared at the treaty grounds. He did arrive on Thursday and went into conference with Crowfoot.

Red Crow also had a friend and advisor at the Treaty 7 negotiations. Charles Conrad, of I.G. Baker, was present and, according to his biographer, studied the treaty terms and conferred with Red Crow. Both agreed that "it treated the Indians fairly, protected their rights, and was as good as they would get."[65]

The discussions went on late into the night. In the end, the chiefs decided to accept the terms of the treaty as outlined by Laird. When the great assembly met on Friday afternoon, Crowfoot stood first. The Blackfoot chief made it plain that he accepted the treaty because it was recommended by Macleod in whom he had great faith:

The advice given me and my people has proved to be very good. If the Police had not come to the country, where would we all be now? Bad men and whiskey were killing us so fast that very few, indeed, of us would have been left today. The Police have protected us as the feathers of the bird protect it from the frosts of winter. I wish them all good, and trust that all our hearts will increase in goodness from this time forward. I am satisfied. I will sign the treaty.[66]

Red Crow followed with similar words. He too put his trust in Macleod:

Three years ago when the Police first came to the country, I met and shook hands with Stamixotokon [Macleod] at Belly River. Since that time he made me many promises. He kept them all—not one of them was ever broken. Everything that the Police have done has been good. I entirely trust Stamixotokon, and will leave everything to him. I will sign with Crowfoot.[67]

That was it. All fell in line behind the great chiefs Crowfoot and Red Crow. While Laird prepared the treaty document for signatures, the various tribes met with Macleod to select their reserves. That was so quickly agreed upon that Laird was able to include the land descriptions of the reserves in the text of the treaty.

On Saturday, September 22, 1877, the signing of Treaty 7 took place. It was a major ceremony with 50 chiefs and councillors of the Blackfoot, Sarcee, Blood, Peigan and Stoney touching the pen or making their mark while David Laird and James Macleod signed on behalf of Her Majesty the Queen. Almost every other literate person present signed as witnesses, NWMP officers, missionaries and wives, to a total of 19. Among the witnesses who put their signatures to the treaty document were Mary Macleod and Charles E. Conrad, the latter "at the insistence of Chief Red Crow"[68]:

Conrad, the Virginian, was joined by three others with American roots in signing Treaty 7. Three Blood chiefs, Medicine Calf, Many Spotted Horses and Father of Many Children, had signed treaties with the United States government in 1855.[69]

The signing was followed by a ceremonial salute of 13 guns. More process and ceremony followed. The first three days of the next week were required to pay out the treaty monies to just under 4,400 chiefs, councillors, men, women and children, a total payout of $53,000. Then, more speeches:

> The Chiefs presented an address to the Commissioners, expressing the entire satisfaction of the whole nation with the treaty, and to the way in which the terms had been carried out. They tendered their well-wishes to the Queen, The Governor, Col. Macleod, and the Police Force. They spoke in the most flattering and enthusiastic manner of the Commissioner, Assistant-Commissioner, officers and the Force in general, and said that it was their firm determination to adhere to the terms of the treaty, and abide by the laws of the Great Mother.[70]

Macleod spoke in reply:

> The Chiefs all here know what I said to them three years ago, when the Police first came to the country—that nothing would be taken away from them without their own consent. You all see to-day that what I told you then was true ... You say that I have always kept my promises. As surely as my past promises have been kept, so surely shall those made by the Commissioners be carried out in the future. If they were broken I would be ashamed to meet you or look you in the face; but every promise will be solemnly fulfilled as certainly as the sun now shines down upon us from the heavens. I shall always remember the kind manner in which you have to-day spoken of me.[71]

That mutual display of grandiloquence concluded Treaty 7 and the import of many of the compelling words would be left to the future. The participants of the last majestic Native assembly in Western Canada broke up the great encampment at Blackfoot Crossing and took their separate trails across the plains. On Friday, September 28, Macleod was finally able to leave for Fort Walsh and the Presidential Commission. The NWMP Commissioner took with him a suitable party of 30 troopers and the doughty Jerry Potts, the guide hired at Fort Benton three years earlier. Potts' talents were quickly called upon. Almost as soon as they set out, the riders were engulfed by a blinding snowstorm that obscured all horizons and landmarks.

TREATY 7 WAS THE last of the prairie treaties Ottawa needed to complete its planned western expansion. The railway route from Lake Superior to the Rocky Mountains was now secure and title had been cleared to the "fertile acres" so that survey and settlement could proceed. Treaty 7 surrendered a final 90,500 km² (35,000 mi²) of territory to Ottawa, bringing the total territorial surrender of the seven treaties to 1,140,000 km² (440,000 mi²), or 114,000,000 ha (281,600,000 acres). That represents a greater surface area than the entire province of Ontario.

Ottawa had been very frugal in dealing with the Indian inhabitants of Western Canada. The initial cost of the seven numbered treaties was modest indeed. The treaties had been a very good deal for Ottawa and others who shared the wealth of the lands surrendered. Under the Rupert's Land transfer agreement, the Hudson's Bay Company was entitled to one-twentieth of the "fertile acres," approximately 2,900,000 ha (7,000,000 acres). Out of the lands cleared by the treaty process "For The Purposes of the Dominion," Ottawa granted some 12,950,000 ha (32,000,000 acres) to the Canadian Pacific and other western railways.

By 1930, sales of Hudson's Bay Company and railway lands together had grossed more than $275,000,000.[72] The land sales profits of the Hudson's Bay Company alone between 1891 and 1930 have been calculated at $96,366,021.[73]

In recent times questions have been raised about just how well the Plains Indians understood the treaties they signed in the 1870s. Did they fully appreciate that they were ceding complete ownership and control of their vast lands? Or did they intend only to allow limited and shared usage?

Today, to be valid and enforceable, a contract between parties of such unequal bargaining power as a national government on the one hand and illiterate, untutored and untravelled Aboriginals on the other would require that the disadvantaged party receive thorough legal advice entirely independent from the dominant party. Advocates on behalf of the descendants of those who signed the treaties now debate whether the very few advisors who were present at the negotiations were truly independent. At Blackfoot Crossing in September 1877, did Reverend McDougall, Father Scollen, Jean L'Heureux, and Charles Conrad truly advise Crowfoot, Red Crow and the other chiefs of the full import of the treaty documents? Or, being Europeans themselves, did they consciously or unconsciously approve of the Ottawa government's proposals as being in the best interests of the people of the Blackfoot Confederacy?

On one feature significantly affecting Treaty 6 and Treaty 7 the government was less than forthcoming. No mention was made of the fact that early in 1876 the Mackenzie government had enacted The Indian Act, 1876. As Minister of the Interior at the time, David Laird had shepherded the bill through Parliament and certainly was familiar with its provisions. As

Lieutenant-Governor and Commissioner at the Treaty 7 negotiations, he said nothing of the legislation that would thereafter govern the lives of the Blackfoot and all Plains Indians.

Not all of the provisions of The Indian Act, 1876 were new; it consolidated a number of pre-existing Acts that mostly applied to the Indians of Eastern Canada. But the legislation was new in the North-West Territories, and earth-shaking in its impact on the Plains Indians.

The proud and able chiefs who signed Treaties 6 and 7 undoubtedly thought they were entering into a form of partnership with the Canadian government, a relationship in which they would be admittedly junior partners, but still equals in many respects. It would have been difficult, if not impossible, for them to knowingly and willingly accept the status accorded to them by The Indian Act, 1876. For they were now legislated into a form of sub-citizen, wards of the state with a ranking somewhat equivalent to that of a minor. They would have no power to deal with the reserves they selected under their treaties; as "Indian Lands," these would be administered by Ottawa. Someone called the "Indian Agent" would enter and control almost every aspect of their lives. They would be prohibited from filing on homesteads when they became available on the very lands they had surrendered. The manner of choosing their chiefs and councillors was imposed upon them.

The Act provided a formula by which an Indian could become "enfranchised," possessed of all the rights taken for granted by other Canadian citizens. That enfranchisement would happen automatically if an Indian attained a medical degree, or became qualified to practise law, or a Notary Public, or became an ordained minister. The successful applicant would then be deemed to be a full citizen of Canada and "no longer an Indian." But the Indians of the North-West Territories were excluded even from this advantage, being considered more lacking in civilized potential than those of Eastern Canada.

Later amendments to The Indian Act added even more paternalistic and offensive features. It became the authority for compulsory attendance at residential schools. To ensure that Indians remained docile, it became an offence to raise money to advance their rights and they were even prohibited from engaging the services of a lawyer. Until well after World War II, in which many Indians served with distinction, they were denied voting privileges. More than a century and a quarter later, The Indian Act remains perhaps the most controversial piece of legislation in Canada.

But little formal objection to The Indian Act, 1876 came from the Indians of the western plains, if only for the simple reason that by the time they learned of its existence they were fully occupied with the struggle to stay alive.

CHAPTER 12

The Boundary Survey

THE SEVERAL FAMILIES OF MÉTIS BUFFALO HUNTERS RESID-
ing in the coulees of the Wood Mountain uplands gathered in won-
derment and apprehension on June 1, 1874. Someone, something,
was approaching their settlement, had been for several hours. At
first they had felt the ground tremble, like distant buffalo. Then came a sound,
a frequent and loud *crack*, like a gunshot, but still unlike any gun they had
ever heard. Now they could hear human voices, loud, coarse and very profane.
The faint tremble had become a rumble they could identify as wheels, heavily
laden wheels. Wagons, but obviously very different from their light, high, two-
wheeled Red River carts. Different even from the heavy wagons the survey
crews had brought with them the previous summer.

Wagons they were, when they finally came into view, but such great, beautiful wagons with bright blue boxes, white canvas tops and vivid red wheels.
Huge transports each with four great broad, iron-shod wheels a full 1.5 m (5
ft) apart at the axle and the rear wheels standing 2 m (6 ft) high. Riding above
those axles were tremendous boxes with nearly vertical sides that reached
more than 3.6 m (12 ft) above the ground. The wagons were in pairs, linked
closely in tandem, each pair drawn by nine double-yoked oxen. The astonished Métis gaped as eight such double units, each with its power supply of 18
plodding oxen, rumbled towards them, each team flanked by foul-mouthed
men with amazingly long black whips that snaked forward and snapped
alongside the ears of the lumbering beasts.

Bull teams at Fort Benton, Montana, 1878. *Glenbow Museum NA-935-6*

A bull train—out of Fort Buford, at the junction of the Missouri and Yellowstone Rivers, 200 km (125 mi) to the southeast.[1] The great transports were Murphy wagons, built in St. Louis and each capable of carrying a payload of four tons. The bull-whackers with the great 2.75-m (9-ft) bull whips and arms like pistons were unaware that they were breaking the sound barrier as their outfits crawled over the plains. The *crack* was made by the tip of their whip as it passed through the speed of sound, the first of man's mechanical contrivances to do so. It was the sonic *crack* that controlled the oxen; the whip seldom touched the animals.

Because the huge, fully loaded wagons, in spite of their broad tires, cut through the dry prairie sod to a depth of 15–20 cm (6–8 in), the teams avoided following each other as they plodded along. When crossing soft, marshy bottoms the wagons might sink to their axles. Then they were separated and sometimes double-teamed so that 36 double-yoked oxen would be strung out in front of the load. The bull-train contractors were of necessity resourceful—and reliable—men.

The great wagons carried 60 tons of oats, bagged and delivered as per the order placed at Helena, in Montana Territory, in the fall of 1873 by the logistics-minded boundary surveyors. Now the Wood Mountain residents knew the purpose of the storage buildings constructed out of poplar logs earlier that spring by the advance crew of Métis directed by the Englishman, George Crompton.[2]

The survey of the international boundary was under way, well under way. At the close of the 1873 season the crews had reached a point 695 km (432 mi) west of the Red River where, before they packed up for the season, they selected the site of the first astronomical station where work would commence in 1874. It was No. 24 and lay just 35 km (22 mi) south of the location on the north slope of the Wood Mountain uplands which had been chosen for a storage depot. The shipment of oats was intended to maintain the 170-odd horses and ponies already hauling men and equipment west from their winter quarters at Dufferin. A further delivery was to be made at another depot 160 km (100 mi) further west.[3]

As it turned out, that shipment of oats would save the horses, lives and reputation of a completely separate expedition also traveling west across the great plains that summer of 1874—the newly-formed North-West Mounted Police on their way to repel the whiskey traders of Fort Whoop-Up.

IN 1818 BRITAIN HAD agreed to a parallel of latitude as a boundary because it was simple, and also it would avoid the expense "of a survey over a tract so little frequented and so little worth submitting at this day to any more precise delimitation than what parallels of latitude may establish."[4] It turned out that taking the graceful line that so neatly circled the globe and marking it across nearly 1,600 km (1,000 mi) of open grasslands would be neither simple nor inexpensive.

To London and Washington the western border remained "so little frequented and so little worth" that no physical marking of its placement was considered necessary. "For the first half century after its creation, the international boundary along the 49th parallel was the imagined glyph of two distant officialdoms."[5]

The inhabitants and the travelers of the grasslands were aware that somewhere on the unbroken plains one country ended and another began, but exactly where was of little concern. The Plains Indians knew that sanctuary from the U.S. Army lay in the land of the Great Mother but when they moved north for security they took no chances and moved well north. When the Santee Sioux crossed from Minnesota in 1862 they stopped only when they reached Fort Garry which clearly was not American. In January 1870, when Mountain Chief and his band of Peigan fled from Major Baker, they moved deep into British territory, well out of the reach of the United States Cavalry.

Only at Pembina was the precise location of the 49th Parallel a matter of importance and this became more so after the United States began to enforce the collection of customs and duties. An 1823 fixing of the border where it intersected the Red River was more or less confirmed by several later calculations, and the Hudson's Bay Company had located its trading post a secure

.4 km (.25 mi) north of that point. In May 1870, a U.S. Army officer took new observations and set the border a full 1,400 m (4,600 ft) north of the previous position. When the Pembina Collector of Customs, armed with the new fix, moved onto the Hudson's Bay Company premises and inventoried the stock, the international border on the plains suddenly became more relevant. The problem at Pembina reached all the way to Washington and London where it occasioned an agreement for a joint survey of the border west of Lake of the Woods. Both governments decided that employing their military would provide the greatest economy.

Britain and Canada agreed to share the cost of their contribution to the survey which gave Prime Minister Macdonald an opportunity to boost his candidate for the position of British Commissioner. He chose Captain Donald Cameron of the Royal Artillery, who happened to be the son-in-law of Dr. Charles Tupper, President of the Privy Council and Minister of Inland Revenue in Macdonald's cabinet. Cameron had acquired some knowledge of the country as a staff member with the unfortunate William McDougall during the failed expedition to assume the Lieutenant-Governor's office at Fort Garry. It was Cameron's wife whom Tupper had journeyed west to rescue. With some reluctance, London agreed to the appointment, which had little to recommend it other than pure politics. Unfortunately, Cameron possessed a difficult personality that did not work well in a three-nation joint undertaking.

The professional qualifications of the British/Canadian Commissioner might have been questionable, but those of his two senior subordinates were not. Captains Samuel Anderson and Albany Featherstonhaugh, both of the Royal Engineers, became Chief and Assistant Astronomer respectively, and both served with great distinction on the boundary survey. Cameron's opposite number on the American team was Archibald Campbell, a West Point graduate more than 20 years older than the British Commissioner with an enviable record of engineering experience.

The British and American parties gathered on the Red River near the 49th Parallel in September 1872. The Americans quartered at their Fort Pembina while the British and Canadian group camped at North Pembina, near the Hudson's Bay Company store. There were few structures other than the Canadian Custom House and the odd log cabin. After the construction of 18 buildings, Cameron named his new community Dufferin, in honour of Canada's then Governor General. The community of Emerson later developed across the river.

Sergeant Kay's Royal Engineers Survey Camp on North Antler Creek, 1873. *Library and Archives Canada / National Archives of Canada fonds C-073303*

The survey teams were just settling into their camp when they were introduced to western weather. A violent three-day blizzard left them blanketed with snow and badly shaken. The residents explained that this was a fortuitous event, that it foretold warm, pleasant weather for the balance of the fall. So it was, and the British enjoyed their first Canadian Indian summer.

The first order of business for the joint survey was to make extremely careful observations and determine finally and forever just where the 49th Parallel lay at Pembina. Only then could it be extended west to the Rocky Mountains. The 49th Parallel also needed to be extended east to connect with the point of the last joint survey, the northwest angle of the Lake of the Woods marked in 1826 by placing a log monument in a swamp.

At Pembina the two Commissions performed independent observations, made careful calculations, and each produced their own fix for the position of the border. When they discovered they were 9.75 m (32 ft) apart, they amiably split the difference and declared the mid-point to be the official location of the 49th Parallel. The Hudson's Bay Company store escaped the clutches of the American customs officer by a scant 230 m (250 yards). Canada's own custom house, however, was found to be well inside United States territory.[6]

Having identified the parallel of latitude, the astronomers set about fixing the meridian of longitude at Red River. To do this, 1,450 km (900 mi) of telegraph line from Dufferin to Chicago were dedicated to the project on a continuous circuit that enabled instantaneous comparison of the times at each end. These were compared with observations of the stars over five successive nights. The mid-winter cold gave near perfect transmissions, broken only by telegraph operators along the line who interrupted with their own messages and complaints of the nonsense being sent over their wires by the astronomers.

The longitude at Red River was determined within a margin of less than 91 m (100 yards), a critical tolerance since it was the point from which the entire boundary to the Rocky Mountains would be measured. In fact, as Anderson pointed out, "it will be the starting-point of all surveys in the central portion of the continent where the accurate geographical position of important points had hitherto been little known."[7]

The site of the 1826 monument at Lake of the Woods was located after clever detective work and found to lie under 1–1.25 m (3–4 ft) of water 42 km (26 mi) north of the 49th Parallel. The monument was re-established and a line run due south to intersect with the border. It was a tough line to run. The first 26 km (16 mi) were swamp and the rest open lake. At the point of intersection with the 49th Parallel the water was 9 m (30 ft) deep. From there west to Pembina, the line ran 145 km (90 mi) through almost continuous swamp, intersected occasionally by belts of timber.

The line from Lake of the Woods to Pembina was surveyed during the winter of 1872–73, the only season when the region was accessible. In the early winter the crews suffered terribly, working waist-deep in the partially frozen swamps. After complete freeze-up, the men contended with a heavy accumulation of snow and temperatures that dropped well below -18°C (0°F), often to -40°C (-40°F) and once to -46°C (-51°F). Observers had to be careful to avoid having their eyelids frozen to the eyepieces of their instruments. A three-day blizzard on January 7–9 paralyzed the entire operation with crews stranded all along the line. No lives were lost, but two men spent two days and nights huddled on the floor of an open sleigh and survived "without having suffered permanent injury."[8] The storm took 80 lives in Minnesota, many of them children trapped on their way home from school.[9] It also took down hundreds of kilometres of the telegraph line that had been used to fix Red River's longitude, putting it out of commission for more than two months. In spite of the hardships, the eastward portion of the boundary survey was completed and the parties were back at Dufferin by April 1, 1873.

PERHAPS PROMPTED BY HIS earlier experience in the West, Cameron implemented one program that greatly contributed to the success of the project: he hired 20 Red River Métis to serve as scouts or guides, also able to pitch in as drovers or teamsters or almost wherever needed. Cameron first engaged William Hallett, an experienced Métis plainsman he had met in 1869 when Hallet had served as a guide to William McDougall. Hallett then selected his troop who, mounted on their own Red River ponies and armed with Spencer carbines, were soon dubbed "The 49th Rangers" and earned the respect of the entire party. The Rangers, under the overall command of Captain Anderson, operated as a reconnaissance unit well in advance of the survey parties, seeking out routes, water, camping and depot sites, wood supplies and hay grounds, all essential to the success and safety of the expedition trekking across hundreds of kilometres of foreign landscape. A reconnaissance map was prepared showing all the important features of the terrain. The Rangers also provided liaison with the bands of Plains Indians.

Unfortunately, Hallett died during the second winter of his command. His position was assumed by D'Arcy East, formerly an officer with the Royal Artillery, with George Crompton, an ex-Royal Navy officer, as second-in-command. The work of the 49th Rangers continued to be vital to the surveyors as they worked their way west over the plains.

Beginning in May, the formidable army of the Joint Boundary Commission moved westward from Pembina. To expedite the work, sections of the line were parceled out among the several parties of both Commissions. Captain Anderson took the 49th Rangers out as far as 160–240 km (100–150 mi) ahead to mark trail, locate water, wood and grazing, and also to indicate where on the boundary astronomical observations were to be taken. This enabled the astronomical parties to proceed directly to their destinations and go to work, again facilitating the enterprise.

The logistics required by the undertaking were considerable. In 1873, the first season west from Red River, 230 officers and men were engaged on the Canadian side: three astronomical parties, three survey parties, one special survey party, one surgeons' party so equipped that it could divide into two complete sections, one geologists' party, a commissariat train party responsible for provisions and transport, one veterinary surgeons' party, and even a party charged with the construction and provision of depots and the cutting of hay. The cautious and experienced planners ensured that among the transport assigned to each field party was at least one water cart.

Just providing for the draft animals was a major responsibility. More than 200 horses, Red River ponies and oxen were utilized in 1873. The next year, 114 horses, 55 ponies, 210 oxen and 112 wagons and carts were required to transport and maintain the survey when it extended approximately 1,300 km (800 mi) west of Pembina. The inventory of equipment and state-of-the-art survey and astronomical instruments, specially designed and built for the project, was as complete as military detail and almost unlimited funding could provide. All in all, two-thirds of the personnel were engaged in supplying and servicing the operations of the expedition's surveyors.[10]

Members of the American Commission, Northern Boundary Survey, West Butte, Sweet Grass Hills, August 6, 1874. Front row, left to right: Captain Gregory, Dr. Elliott Coues, Commissioner Archibald Campbell, Major William J. Twining, Captain Montgomery Bryant. Rear row, left to right: James E. Bangs, Lewis Boss, Lieutenant Francis Vinton Greene, Captain Edwin R. Ames, Charles L. Doolittle, Orrin S. Wilson, Dr. Valentine T. McGillycuddy. *Library and Archives Canada / George M. Dawson fonds C-079630*

The British/Canadian party made do without a military escort, quite certain that the Plains Indians would have no quarrel with them. The Americans were less confident; security was provided by several companies of troops under the command of Major Marcus Reno, whose fame as second-in-command to the ill-fated Colonel George Armstrong Custer at Little Big Horn was three years in the future. Reno commanded one company of infantry and two of cavalry the first season, but five companies of the 6th Infantry plus Reno's two companies of the 7th Cavalry were deemed necessary to guard the extended boundary line the second season. In that summer of 1874, Reno was pleased to learn that Custer was leading a large expedition of exploration into the Black Hills. Such an incursion into the Hills that were so sacred to the warlike Sioux would surely concentrate the Indians' attention away from the plodding invasion of the boundary surveyors.

The surveyors stretched their chains, measurement after infinite measurement, over cactus-infested hills, through stinking sloughs made foul by buffalo excrement, inch-worming towards the ever-receding far horizon of the Great Plains. They encountered mosquitoes in great voracious swarms that caused the men to develop a constant defensive brushing motion; the insects settled on the horses in a writhing film:

> The number of mosquitoes in the summer in these countries is quite incredible, and the reality is worse than the anticipation. It may suffice to say that oxen have been known to be choked by them, and that on a still warm night the noise they make beating against the outside of a tent, resembles that of rain. The only time that there is any relief from them is in the middle of the day, when the heat of the sun prevents their appearing.[11]

But with the mid-day heat came the mirage effect. The instrument men jammed their tripods into the prairie sod, peered into the calibrated lenses of their transit telescopes through the heat waves shimmering above the baking land, and tried to focus on the distant, dancing flagstaff. Frequently they had to abandon their efforts and wait until the prairie cooled—and the mosquitoes returned.

The crews worked and lived in shadeless heat and suffered terribly from lack of any decent water. Good water is always scarce on the surface of the plains, but in 1873 and 1874 almost every waterhole had been rendered muddy and foul by the wallowing, excreting buffalo. When the water carts were unavailable the men drank, gagged, and carried on.

A building crew followed the survey parties, marking the boundary with conical stone cairns or earth mounds, 1.5–2.5 m (5–8 ft) in height, one every 4.8 km (3 mi) across the vastness of the plains, 388 in all. Along the southern boundary of the new Province of Manitoba, iron pins were placed.

As they worked along the boundary, the surveyors detected distinct deflections of the centre of gravity that affected their plumb bobs and levels. This meant that the actual findings did not agree with their theoretical findings. The astronomical stations were placed approximately 32 km (20 mi) apart. If each accurately fixed the location of the 49th Parallel, what about the six monuments in between? It was considered too difficult and costly to attempt to trace on the ground the true arc the 49th Parallel follows around the globe. Instead, by compromise between the Commissions, a series of straight lines was chosen, zigging and zagging from monument to monument "like tracing the course of a drunk between street lights."[12]

Building a boundary mound on the Canadian/U.S. border, c. 1873. *Saskatchewan Archives Board R-A22984*

One result, both of the margin of error inherent in the 1873–74 survey and the compromise adopted, is that at only one monument in a thousand does the line on U.S. and Canadian International Boundary Commission maps coincide with a subsequent geodetic survey of the 49th parallel. That point is at marker 490 in central Montana. The rest of the monuments are at least 30 m (100 ft) off the mark.[13]

Commissioner Cameron resisted the compromise, insisting that the boundary line take the form of a mean parallel, a more perfect curve produced by averaging local variations at all astronomical stations. In so doing he rejected the advice of Chief Astronomer Anderson, and ignored the practicalities of the fact that some 800 km (500 mi) of astronomical parallel had already been surveyed. Cameron was finally overruled by the Astronomer Royal in London. So obstinate was Cameron that Anderson "found it quite impossible to do any business with him except on paper."[14]

The surveyors battled the heat and desolation westward throughout the summer of 1873 and then encountered another peril of the plains. Prairie fires erupted, running at the will of the wind over the open miles of parched grassland. By the end of the summer, with the survey stretched out over almost 640 km (400 mi), several of the parties had desperate experiences rescuing their animals and equipment. One fire, started by the careless match of a crew member, ran eastward for 240 km (150 mi) and then turned south until it was stopped by the Missouri River. As the fires destroyed much of the grazing depended upon for the horses and oxen, the 49th Rangers redoubled their efforts searching out still-available grass that could be mowed and transported back to the main camp.

Because the world is, after all, not flat but round, the shortest distance between two points on the globe is not a straight line, but an arc, a segment of a circle. Today's international travellers are familiar with the great circle routes followed by airliners that appear to take them well off course but in fact cover the shortest distance.

The constant course changes needed to maintain a circle route are today performed by computers fixing on satellites. Global positioning systems are fast, portable and extremely accurate. The state of the surveyors' art in 1873 was more primitive, not much advanced from the astral fixes performed by the early navigators. During the building of the boundary, astronomical surveys were performed by shooting the angles from several chosen stars. Great care was taken to secure the most precise positioning possible. An elevated site was chosen with at least 1.2 km (.75 mi) sight-lines north and south. A special tent was erected to house the zenith telescope and the sod removed to a depth of 45 cm (18 in) to escape ground tremors. The exact time was carried from station to station by special chronometers. Observations were taken after dark, continuously through the night. During the day sextant readings of the sun entered the calculations. The second night another instrument, the theodolite, took bearings on Polaris. Then a fourth instrument, a portable transit, entered the procedure. The readings were computed by reference to a series of astronomical and mathematical tables. The entire process was continued and repeated for a minimum of four days and five nights, but cloudy weather so often prevented the observations that the average time to complete one station was seven days. Twelve days were required to perform the observations at that first station of 1874, No. 24 at Rock Creek in what is now normally sunny southern Saskatchewan. After all that care and effort, a margin of error of 3 m (10 ft) was within accepted tolerances.

Captain Anderson was anxious to find the Wood Mountain uplands. The Métis had told him of the "oasis in the middle of the semi-desert" with its sheltered ravines, or coulees, poplar groves, springs and good pasture. Here was the winter residence of Red River buffalo hunters, relocated closer to the diminishing herds, who traded their pemmican and buffalo robes at Fort Peck and Fort Benton, both on the Missouri River, as well as occasionally back at Fort Garry. The settlement had never been visited by anyone competent to fix its geographical position. Since it was not known for certain if the hills were on the Canadian side of the boundary, Anderson considered it "a matter of the greatest value and importance" to discover their position. Curiously, none of the 49th Rangers were familiar with the location of the settlement, perhaps because the party was south of the uplands and the trail connecting to Fort Garry lay to the northeast.

Anderson and his party worked as far west as the eastern edge of what the Métis called *les mauvaises terres*, a land of weather-sculpted clay buttes and cliffs now known as the Killdeer Badlands, part of the Grasslands National Park. There, George M. Dawson, the head of the geologists' party, would identify dinosaur bones, the first such discovery in Canada.

Just as in their first year on the plains, the boundary surveyors were struck with another early snow storm. This blizzard hit without warning on September 23 and raged for seven days, putting the parties in a very bad way. Unable to secure wood or buffalo chips for fires, the men huddled under blankets in their light canvas tents and waited it out. The horses suffered greatly. The wagons were placed in a horseshoe pattern with canvas sheets strung on the interior providing the animals some protection from the northwest wind, but they were unable to graze. When the storm finally abated, many of the horses were so emaciated that they were unable to work for the remainder of the season.

Several Métis buffalo hunters, caught in the open west of the Wood Mountain hills and unable to make it back to their camps, took shelter under the hides of the buffalo they had just killed, where their frozen bodies were found after the storm.[15]

When the weather finally cleared, Anderson resumed his search for Wood Mountain, but with great difficulty. Some 45 cm (18 in) of snow covered the high ground and the coulees were drifted full. Then, by happy circumstance, he met a group of Sioux who told him they had just left a Métis encampment "a long day's journey to the northward." Following their back track, Anderson located the Wood Mountain settlement where he found that most of the residents were away on the fall buffalo hunt. A sunny day enabled the astronomer to take a fix that placed the site 35 km (22 mi) north of the boundary and 670 km (416 mi) west of Red River. Anderson also determined that he had found a perfect location for a supply depot for the next year.

As in the previous year, another Indian summer followed the great storm, and the boundary surveyors were able to return to Dufferin without difficulty. A blessing from the storm was the great number of pools of sweet meltwater that became available to both man and beast. The last of the British parties made it back on October 31—none too soon, as the Red River had frozen over three days previously, about two weeks earlier than normal. A number of steamers and smaller boats were caught in the ice.

The surveyors spent the winter reviewing their calculations and planning the next year's field operations. Anderson's selection of Wood Mountain as a depot was confirmed and arrangements were made to supply it. An American merchant at Helena, in western Montana Territory, was contracted to supply 60 tons of oats[16] and deliver them to the Wood Mountain site not later than June 15, 1874. Fully aware that their contractor would face numerous perils in moving his wagon trains over a long stretch of country "occupied by Indians unfriendly to United States citizens," the surveyors arranged to freight their principal supply directly from Red River. The success of both deliveries turned out to be a happy circumstance.

On May 20, 1874, the main body of the boundary survey moved out of Dufferin to Wood Mountain to pick up the work where it had been left the previous fall. The 692-km (430-mi) trip was accomplished in 32 days, including several days required to bridge the flooding Souris River.

On their arrival they were pleased to find the 60 tons of oats ordered from Helena neatly stored in the buildings constructed in May by the 49th Rangers. The commissary wagons immediately moved forward to provision a second depot further west. In just two weeks, by July 7, the next supply depot, 240 km (150 mi) west of Wood Mountain, was provisioned. In early August, Commissary Herchmer, with only a single companion, rode 116 km (72 mi) through possible hostile territory down to Fort Benton to arrange for the delivery of another bull train load of oats.[17] The depot at the west butte of the Sweet Grass Hills would provision the horses to the end of the survey and back to Wood Mountain.

With the depots established, the 49th Rangers took on a new duty, that of express riders carrying messages between the camps stretched along the boundary. Then they proved their value in an unexpected way. One of the boundary survey wagon trains spotted a herd of rampaging buffalo approaching from the south. The wagons were quickly circled but the onrushing animals came on at full gallop, heads down and surrounded in such a cloud of dust that it was obvious they neither saw nor cared what lay in front of them. As the paralyzed teamsters stared in horror at the oncoming wall of maddened animals, several of the Rangers present rode straight at the herd, firing their Spencer carbines and causing the beasts to part and pass on each side of the wagons. The cause of the stampede appeared momentarily as the buffalo charged by, and then was enveloped in the dust—a party of mounted Sioux in hot pursuit. The danger over, the Rangers and teamsters finished off the wounded animals and added fresh meat to their menu.

Riding horses over the prairie pockmarked with gopher and badger holes was perilous and falls were not uncommon. Usually the rider suffered nothing worse than bruises and sprains, but only a few days out from Dufferin, Lieutenant Rowe, in charge of the survey party, was not so lucky. When his horse went down, the officer's head struck heavily and he lay still and unconscious. Correctly diagnosing a severe skull fracture, Dr. T.J.W. Burgess decided the man could not be moved. A hospital tent was erected over Rowe where he lay and the doctor and another officer cared for their patient for six weeks before it was safe to take him on to Wood Mountain. At the end of the season, Rowe returned to Dufferin with the survey parties.

The Boundary Commission surveyors carried their work westward up into the Rocky Mountains where they connected with the terminal point erected in 1861 by the former Boundary Commission. The last monument was erected in August. Then, their commission completed, on August 29, 1874, they turned around and headed back to Dufferin, closing up their supply depots as they went along. Ottawa sent a warning by telegraph to Fort Benton that they would be attacked by Cree Indians on their return journey. The surveyors regarded this as probably a false alarm since they were nowhere near Cree country, but they took the precaution of assembling their parties at Wood Mountain and travelling east from there as one huge caravan. They also circled their wagons at night and posted sentries.

There had been some incidents. Some 200 Peigan had visited the depot at Sweet Grass Hills and helped themselves to supplies, the two depot-keepers helpless to prevent them.[18] Disdaining the military protection that accompanied the American parties, the British had a superior attitude about how to conduct relations with the Native residents of the plains. But the British formula of "firmness and tact" was not always successful. When a Sioux chief and his son dropped into the Milk River depot one afternoon and suggested they might help themselves to a fine hunk of bacon, the English caretakers took them firmly by the napes of their necks and tactfully put them out. The chief returned the next day with a party of 100 men, tied up the two Englishmen and set about dividing all the supplies and provisions at the depot into two equal parts. Discovering a box of candles, the interlopers lit 26 of them and danced throughout the night "for the edification of the unfortunate depot keeper." In the morning, the Sioux departed with one equal division of the stores, leaving the other.[19] The Americans were delighted.

On October 11, after a return journey of 43 days and more than 1,300 km (800 mi), the British/Canadian survey parties were back in their quarters at Dufferin. The survey parties had travelled 692 km (430 mi) to reach their project that season and had then performed a difficult and exact survey over a further distance of 578 km (359 mi). They had been out on their trail from May 20 to October 11, nine days short of five months. They established 17 principal astronomical stations, chained 546 km (339 mi) of sight line between those stations, traversed an additional 32 km (20 mi) in the mountains where chaining was impossible, and surveyed the country on each side of the boundary line to a width of 9.5 km (6 mi) as far as St. Mary's River and 5 km (3 mi) from there to British Columbia. They took meteorological observations at Sweet Grass Hills during August and obtained barometrical readings for altitude over the entire route. Then, their work done, they went home. They lost no animals and not one man, in spite of the grievous accident suffered by Lieutenant Rowe.

For the 1874 season, the Boundary Commission had purchased a large number of oxen that were shipped to the end of steel at Fargo/Moorhead. Captain Anderson recorded the

> extraordinary power and endurance of the oxen. They commenced their march from Moorhead in Minnesota early in May, and from that time till their return to Red River on October 5, they marched 2,400 miles [3,860 km] with loaded wagons out and back, at an average rate of travel of 16 miles [26 km] a day. During the whole of this period they had no other food except such pasture as the country afforded on the march.[20]

At Dufferin in the fall of 1874, its work completed, the Boundary Commission disbanded. The crews were paid off, the livestock and equipment sold, and the officers returned home to write their reports. Left behind, stretching more than 1,300 km (800 mi) westward across the plains to the Rocky Mountains, stood the physical evidence of their massive achievement—388 conical monuments proclaiming the longest international boundary in the world on one parallel of latitude.

The newly surveyed boundary came into unexpected prominence just two years after its completion. In late 1876 and early 1877 several thousand American Indians, in flight from the U.S. Army, crossed the new border and sought sanctuary in Canada, provoking a diplomatic duel between Washington and Ottawa that lasted four years.

AS THE WESTERN PLAINS filled with settlers, the Canada/U.S. border achieved only minor significance. After all, it was entirely artificial, tracing an imaginary parallel of latitude. Unlike so many of the boundaries the settlers had known in Europe, this one followed no natural topographical feature— no river, no mountain range, just a thinly placed line of eroding monuments across the prairie. There was no fence, no barricade, and many of the early roads and trails wended carelessly back and forth between the two nations.

By treaty between the United States and Canada in 1925, the boundary was defined as consisting of "straight lines joining adjacent monuments as now established."[1] Thus, the international boundary is now so fixed whether or not it coincides with the 49th Parallel.

• • •

Even today much of the border remains unfenced. Not infrequently an unwary hunter has found that he had inadvertently strayed beyond the limits of his license. Until the advent of computers, a border crossing closed for the night was a minor inconvenience to the locals who knew how to find their way home without the niceties of custom clearances. Off-hours card clearance was introduced for the convenience of those frequently crossing "the Line."

The 49th Parallel became known as "the Longest Undefended Border in the World," a sobriquet that instilled a mild feeling of pride that Canada and the United States could be such good and trusting neighbours. Much of this has changed since September 11, 2001, of course. The 49th Parallel is now a border for real, and the old casual ways have gone, perhaps forever, and perhaps to be forgotten like the men who first traced that Parallel across the dusty plains.

NOTE

1. H. George Classen, *Thrust and Counterthrust, The Genesis of the Canada-United States Boundary* (Toronto: Longmans, 1965), 147.

The border was mostly ignored by those who lived along it. Homesteaders visited, shopped, even received their mail where it was most convenient and it mattered little if that was across "the Line," as it came to be called. Wallace Stegner's family lived winters in Eastend, Saskatchewan, and farmed during the summer along the border, which they recognized almost not at all:

We bought supplies in Harlem or Chinook and got our mail at Hydro, all in Montana. In the fall we hauled our wheat, if we had made any, freely and I suppose illegally across to the Milk River towns and sold it where it was handiest to sell it.[21]

Time soon began to erase not only the monuments of the original survey of 1873 and 1874, but also the triumph of their placement. In only 35 years the elements had so eroded the earthen mounds that in 1908 a new, jointly commissioned boundary crew arrived to replace the original monuments with iron posts. Starting from monument 331 just west of Coutts, Alberta, the 1908 surveyors quickly discovered how forgotten the 1874 boundary had become when "the Line" ran right across the Coutts railway station platform. Undeterred, they painted a white stripe down the platform and carried on.[22]

Again, in 1925 a new and modern geodetic survey was performed along the boundary. By then the men who had first walked that line, with transit, flagstaff and chain, had been long forgotten, as was the epic of their original conquest of that hostile terrain against often adverse weather.

Forgotten as well was the perfection of their planning and the efficient placement and operation of their lines of supply that stretched 1,450 km (900 mi) out into the wilderness, lines of supply that served to rescue another expedition on the western plains from disaster and disgrace.

CHAPTER 13

By Section, Township and Range

T HE MARKING OF THE 49TH PARALLEL OVER THE CANA-
dian plains heralded the arrival of another hallmark of civilization,
a public land survey system.

Fully aware that its clumsy imposition of a land survey had set
off the revolution at Red River in the fall of 1869, Ottawa became more circumspect. In the fall of 1870, when Adams Archibald, Lieutenant-Governor
of Manitoba and the North-West Territories, arrived at Fort Garry he was
requested to make recommendations for a system of township survey for the
new province.

The 1869 survey plan had been adopted on the recommendation of William
McDougall when he was still the responsible minister and was largely based
upon the township survey in use in the United States. That was composed of
a grid of townships 15.5 km² (6 mi²) containing 36 sections in each 1.6 km² (1
mi²). Each such section contained 260 ha (640 acres) and was divided into
quarter-sections of 65 ha (160 acres), which was considered to be the appropriate size of a family farm and a unit suitable for free land grant, or homestead,
to attract immigrant settlers.

McDougall, however, altered the American system in two major ways.
He thought 80 ha (200 acres) would be more familiar to immigrants from
Ontario and the larger unit would also attract settlers away from the United
States. Accordingly, he instructed that the sections contain 325 ha (800 acres).
Also, McDougall disapproved of the American survey making no allowance
for roadways which were constructed on land taken from the settler, and pro-
posed a public appropriation for roads.

Archibald disagreed with McDougall's main amendment to the American system. He was satisfied that 65 ha (160 acres) easily met an immigrant family's needs for farm purposes. The 260-ha (640-acre) section had worked well in the United States for 75 years and had peopled half a continent. The American and Canadian systems would come together along the 49th Parallel and should mesh as much as possible. Although Archibald did agree that allowances for public roadways should come from the public lands, not those of the settlers, he thought a 20-m (66-ft) (1-chain) road allowance would suffice where McDougall had proposed 30 m (99 ft) (1.5 chains). Archibald's plan proposed a road allowance every mile, both north, south, east and west.

McDougall, after his ignominious retreat from Pembina, had returned to his seat in the House of Commons. There, fiercely defending every action he had taken respecting Red River and the North-West Territories, he battled in support of both the 325-ha (800-acre) section and the 30-m (99-ft) road allowance. He also proposed a $5 homestead application fee, instead of the $10 charged in the United States, and a three-year proving-up, or residency, period rather than five years. These inducements, he insisted, would attract many immigrants out of the United States.

One feature of Archibald's recommendations proved impervious to McDougall's attack. An old politician himself, Archibald had calculated that the 2,125,000 ha (5,250,000 acres) open for the Manitoba township survey would produce 32,800 homesteads of the 65-ha (160-acre) variety, but only 25,000 of the 80-ha (200-acre) size. That simple arithmetic settled the issue of the section size, but McDougall came away with his 30-m (99-ft) road allowance.

So it was that the Dominion Land Survey, fixed by Order in Council on April 25, 1871, provided a township grid of 36 260-ha (640-acre) sections, divided into 65-ha (160-acre) quarters,[1] amply supplied with road allowances of 30 m (99 ft) on each side of every section. Rather than adopt the county, township and concession method of land identification that had developed in Eastern Canada, Ottawa decided that Western lands, both townships and sections, would be identified by numbers. Townships were numbered from south to north and divided by ranges numbered from east to west commencing from a series of seven meridians, north-south planes running from pole to pole. The First, or Prime, Meridian had been fixed on the 49th Parallel 16 km (10 mi) west of Pembina in the fall of 1869.

Perhaps because of the unsettled situation at Pembina and Red River in the fall of 1869, the First Meridian was placed at an odd line of longitude, 97° 27' 28.41" West. The other six meridians are all placed 4 degrees apart, at 102°,

106°, 110°, 114°, 118° and 122°. Thus, there are 30 9.5-km (6-mi) ranges along the 49th Parallel between all meridians except the First and Second where 34 ranges are numbered. The entire survey west to the Pacific is tied to the First, or Prime, Meridian.

In July 1871, 13 survey parties under the direction of Lindsay Russell, Inspector of Surveys, commenced laying out the Dominion Land Survey in Manitoba. On July 10, the first monument was placed on the First Meridian near Headingly, west of Winnipeg.

The surveyors did not have an easy time of it. Equipping and provisioning themselves at Fort Garry they were met with exorbitant prices. Out on the plains they experienced an unusually severe and perilous fire season that rendered their instruments nearly useless and made them fear for their lives. As Russell reported to Parliament:

> Even before they reached any particular section heavy smoke darkened all the country alike and effectually prevented the surveyors from taking anything but exceedingly short and unprofitable sights. Sometimes obliging them through the impossibility of seeing a Picket at all to cease work until a favorable wind would spring up to dissipate the densely hanging fog of smoke and ashes.[2]

Even worse, fires swept over the surveyors' camps:

> Two of the parties, that of Mr. Wagner, and Mr. F.H. Lynch Staunton, were completely burnt out, losing all their provisions, tents, equipage, clothing, some of their instruments and barely escaping with their lives. Mr. Milner Hart, though successful in saving his effects under the like circumstances, had with his party even a narrower escape from suffocation and burning.[3]

The surveyors persevered and returned in the following year, 1872, and every season thereafter until the huge task was completed and more than 80,940,000 ha (200,000,000 acres) had been brought under the township system in what is today Manitoba, Saskatchewan, Alberta and parts of British Columbia. An astute land-seeker with shoulder-borne spade searching out the best soil, or a traveler uncertain of his whereabouts, need only refer to one of the survey posts fixed at the corners of every section to determine his location with an exactitude equal to today's satellite-driven global positioning system. Unfortunately, Prime Minister Macdonald, serving as Minister of the

Interior, failed to appreciate the disadvantages of wooden survey posts which soon rotted in some soils and far more quickly disappeared in prairie fires. Many, the surveyors believed, were utilized for campfires. Not until 1881 were iron posts finally approved.

The survey system adopted and implemented in 1871 continued until 1879 and became known as the First Survey. All of the southern portion of present-day Manitoba, a narrow strip along the southeast boundary of present-day Saskatchewan, and a few townships in central Saskatchewan, chiefly between the North and South Saskatchewan Rivers south of Prince Albert, were included in the First Survey. In 1880 a modification was introduced by running all section lines true north and south rather than parallel to the eastern boundary as in the First Survey.

In 1881 the Third Survey was introduced with major modifications to the road allowances. All road allowances were reduced to 20 m (66 ft) (1 chain) and the east-west road allowances in each township were reduced from six to three. North-south road allowances remained 1.6 km (1 mi) apart but the east-west road allowances were now every second 1.6 km. These changes effected considerable economy in the amount of public lands required for roadways, a benefit to Ottawa. They also reduced the eventual cost burden of actually constructing and maintaining a usable road on the allowances, a benefit to the local governments of the future. The Third Survey, the most generally utilized of the several survey systems, was applied to almost all of the future settlement areas of what became Saskatchewan and Alberta. It was also employed in those areas of Manitoba north of the First Survey.

The Dominion Lands Act of 1872 confirmed the survey system and provided the regulations for the free homesteads that were expected to attract people to the western lands coming under the survey. A male applicant, 21 years old with a $10 fee, could file on a 65-ha (160-acre) homestead that would be titled to him after a residency period, initially set at five years but later much reduced.

The free homestead program in Canada was patterned closely on the system that had been operating in the United States for a number of years. The requirements were modified many times to eliminate fraud and make the program more attractive to immigrant settlers. Even so, free homesteads produced no immediate tide of settlement until the railways finally entered the West.

In March 1871, even before opening negotiations with British Columbia, Ottawa had made provision for land grants to support the construction of an "Inter-Oceanic Railway." Three full townships on either side of the route finally chosen were to be withdrawn for that purpose and the free homestead system was to be suspended, "if necessary." The first Canadian Pacific Railway Act, passed in 1872, proposed to set aside a colossal 20,235,000 ha (50,000,000 acres), more than the total size of New Brunswick, Nova Scotia and Prince Edward Island. That would have been a full one-quarter of all the surveyed land in Western Canada.

Like the free homestead program, the Canadian Pacific Railway land grants went through several manifestations before crystallizing in final form.

In administering its public lands, Ottawa provided for all its obligations, past, present and future, by a scheme applied to each township of 36 sections. Only 16.25 of those sections would be available to homesteaders. Sixteen sections, all but two of the odd numbered, were reserved for railway lands, and 1.75 sections (a full two sections in every fifth township) were dedicated to the Hudson's Bay Company to fulfill the one-twentieth of the fertile lands it retained upon the surrender of its charter.

With admirable foresight, Ottawa reserved the remaining two sections as an endowment for public schools. The sale of these lands would cover the cost of building schools, although maintenance costs and teachers' salaries would have to be paid out of land taxes. Sections 11 and 29 were dedicated as school lands so that, hopefully, no child would have to walk more than 6.5 km (4 mi) to school.

The Dominion Lands Act of 1872 had made careful provision for the system of township survey that was working its way across the West. But one fundamental element was lacking: all measurements to the west were tied to the First, or Prime, Meridian and great care had been taken to ensure it had been accurately placed. As for measurements to the north, the regulations for the Dominion Land Survey provided that "The International boundary shall form the base line for Townships 1 and 2." The 49th Parallel, the chosen boundary with the United States, was to be the benchmark from which the survey lines would run as far north as the Churchill and the Peace Rivers. The Prime Meridian was extended northward by careful sighting and astronomical measurement, but there was no similar extension westward along the 49th Parallel. So long as the 49th Parallel remained an imaginary line, the 1,290 km (800 mi) of grasslands west of Red River remained undisturbed.

When the boundary surveyors decamped in August 1874, the illusionary line that circled the globe had been captured and imprisoned where it crossed the western plains so that it could be seen and identified by all. Soon men carrying tripods, transits and chains returned to the prairies. Before them lay a gigantic undertaking, to lay down the Dominion township survey over 1.3 million km² (500,000 mi²) of empty land.

There was much similarity between the township survey systems adopted by Canada and the United States, but there was one huge difference. The American expansion to the Pacific had been accomplished in piecemeal fashion, requiring many different base lines and more than a score of meridians. Canada's westward extension was achieved in one enormous gulp. This meant that "a uniform and integrated survey was feasible throughout a quarter of the continent."[4] The newly established 49th Parallel became the single base line from Red River to the Rocky Mountains, and later, after 1846, through to the Pacific Ocean.

As Prime Minister Macdonald proudly stated, his government had "the advantage of having one great country before us to do as we like," and "one vast system of survey, uniform over the whole of it."[5]

CHAPTER 14

The North-West Mounted Police

I T WAS A GRAND SPECTACLE, THE LIKES OF WHICH HAD NEVER before been seen anywhere on the western plains. And would never be seen again.

Formed up as if on parade before a reviewing stand, 275 mounted officers and men of the North-West Mounted Police,[1] resplendent in red tunics and white helmets, divided in six troops, each mounted on horses of identical colour, rode in formation. They were followed by 73 freight wagons, 114 Red River carts, two field guns, two mortars, and field kitchens, all drawn by 142 oxen and three dozen horses handled by 20 Métis drivers. At the tail, very much out of formation, a herd of 93 cattle bellowed and complained.

Of the NWMP's total strength only a few men and horses stationed at Fort Ellice and Dufferin were missing. In close order, as it was on this one and only occasion, the expedition stretched 3.2 km (2 mi) across the prairie. Close order would last only until the start command was given. Then the units quickly straggled out over 6.4 km (4 mi), and then much more. As it worked its way west, the expedition was usually spread out over 16 km (10 mi) of prairie—dust-covered, weary, plodding.

But today the Force put on a fine display. Commissioner French rode at the head of the great formation. Then came "A" Troop mounted on dark bay horses, then "B" on dark browns, "C" on bright chestnuts, also with the field guns, "D" on greys and buckskins, "E" on blacks, and, finally, "F" on light bays.

It was July 8, 1874. The NWMP was riding out of Dufferin, on the Red River, where it had been drilling and organizing since the last units arrived from the east on June 19. Their destination was Fort Whoop-Up, 1,290 uncharted kilometres (800 mi) into the western plains. The Great Trek, as it came to be called, was underway, with the stated mission to deliver law and order to the new Canadian West.

Prime Minister Macdonald's government had received a number of reports about the need for a police force in the West. In 1870 Captain William Butler had warned of a complete lack of "law, order, or security for life and property" and recommended the creation of a police force.

Three years later, Colonel Patrick Robertson-Ross of the Canadian militia confirmed Butler's assessment and recommended sending into the West a regiment of mounted riflemen, 550 strong. Robertson-Ross also reported that American whiskey traders were operating well inside Canada with the largest of their operations at the junction of the Belly and Bow Rivers (which join at that point to become the South Saskatchewan River). This last was a piece of misinformation that complicated matters for the NWMP the following year.

Finally responding to the reports from the West, on May 23, 1873, Prime Minister Macdonald introduced legislation providing for the "Establishment of a Police Force in the North-West Territories." Macdonald contemplated only a small force centred in the developing agricultural region around Fort Garry, and even that sometime in the future, but events in the West forced his hand.

On June 1, 1873, as the boundary surveyors were moving west from Dufferin, a shootout broke out in the Cypress Hills 965 km (600 mi) to the west between a band of American wolfers on the trail of some stolen horses and Little Soldier's band of Assiniboines from the Wood Mountain district. Both groups had been drinking heavily, the Assiniboine men so intoxicated as to be barely able to defend themselves, when the Americans, armed with Henry repeating rifles, opened fire on them. The firefight that followed took the lives of some 22 Assiniboine men, women and children, including Little Soldier. The Americans decapitated Little Chief and mounted his head on a lodge pole. Only one wolfer died.[2]

News of the Cypress Hills Massacre, as it was almost immediately described, was slow to seep out of the West. It reached Ottawa two months later, in early August, via diplomatic channels—Washington to London to Ottawa. About the same time, the report reached Fort Garry where it threw Lieutenant-Governor Alexander Morris into a state of near panic.[3] He wanted protection in the West and he wanted it now. The NWMP was recruiting 150 men in Ontario but Macdonald's plan was to keep them at Toronto over the winter for drilling and training. Morris insisted they be sent west immediately, before the Dawson Route closed for the winter.

Lieutenant Colonel James F. Macleod, North-West Mounted Police, March 1879. *Glenbow Museum NA-354-1*

The Lieutenant-Governor was fearful that a bloodbath equal to the Minnesota Uprising that cost the lives of hundreds of settlers might break out in the North-West Territories. He bombarded Macdonald with predictions of Indian depredations, of plundered Hudson's Bay Company posts, of a "movement" by the "Riel party" that promised a repeat of the 1869 troubles at Red River, and generally of "grave disaster."[4] On just one day, September 20, 1873, Morris fired off to Macdonald one letter and two telegrams, all on the same subject.

Macdonald succumbed to the pressure. Ottawa was a lot further from the Cypress Hills than Fort Garry, but the political risk became too great:

> It would not be well for us to take the responsibility of slighting Morris' repeated and urgent entreaties. If anything went wrong, the blame would be at our door. I shall hurry the men off at once. No time is to be lost. The Dawson route is not open after the middle of October.[5]

The Dawson Route was no idyllic avenue at any time of the year, but in late fall it provided additional hardship and misery to its travellers. It ran 877 km (545 mi) over land, rock and water from Prince Arthur's Landing (later Port Arthur, now Thunder Bay) to Fort Garry. The portages were almost beyond counting.

In three contingents, the 150 raw recruits from Ontario were quickly transshipped across the Great Lakes. The first two made the crossing in good weather and carried on overland in good time, reaching Fort Garry on October 22, 1873. The third contingent, delayed by a vicious storm on Lake Superior, was caught by the onset of winter and suffered blizzards, deep snow and freezing temperatures before reaching Red River, minus much of their gear. Fortunately for the men of that third contingent they were commanded by James Macleod, whose acumen and experience on the trail led them safely through a dangerous situation. Macleod had made the crossing three years earlier as a staff officer to the 1870 Wolseley Expedition and had been decorated for his demonstrated superior command performance on that mission. Macleod was one of the first nine officers commissioned in the NWMP.

The officers and men of the new police force were quartered in the Stone Fort, the Hudson's Bay facility at Lower Fort Garry, leased by Ottawa for their use. A Commissioner for the NWMP had been selected back in Ontario but the news had not yet reached Red River and on November 3, the men were sworn in by the temporary Commissioner, Lieutenant Colonel W. Osborne Smith of the Canadian Militia, stationed at Winnipeg. A regimen of training and drill for the still-raw recruits was immediately instituted.

An embarrassment occurred on the swearing-in when 12 of the men recruited in Ontario and transported to Fort Garry refused to take the oath. Since the legislation contained no authority to do otherwise, Smith authorized their discharges with full pay from the date of their engagement.[6] This inadequacy received greater exposure the following year.

On October 16, 1873, Lieutenant Colonel George Arthur French became the first official Commissioner of the NWMP. An Irishman by birth, the 32-year-old French had experience in the Royal Irish Constabulary, which the Canadian government looked to as a model for its new force. An officer of the Royal Artillery, he had been seconded to the Canadian Militia in 1871 and appointed Commandant of the School of Gunnery at Kingston, later the Royal Military College. On assuming his command, French hastened to Fort Garry to inspect his force already quartered there, and assess his needs for the next year.

Commissioner French travelled through the United States, but before he reached Fort Garry in late November 1873, the continued existence of the NWMP came into question in Ottawa. On November 5, Prime Minister Macdonald's government resigned in the face of the Pacific Scandal and was succeeded by a Liberal government under Alexander Mackenzie. Prime Minister Mackenzie was very dubious about the wisdom of incurring the heavy cost of attempting to police the vast western plains. The financial panic of 1873 had thrown both the United States and Canada into a depression and government expenditures were being cut across the board.

Mackenzie made a startling proposal to Governor General Dufferin. Instead of a Canadian expedition to clear the whiskey traders from the plains, how about arranging with Washington to have the U.S. Army come up to the North-West Territories to look after the problem? "Saskatchewan" Taylor at Winnipeg and Senator Alexander Ramsey in Minnesota would have cheered this suggestion.

Dufferin was properly horrified that Mackenzie had so little appreciation for the value of Canadian sovereignty. He assured the Prime Minister that the

Colonial Office in Whitehall would have nothing to do with any such plan and pointed out the advantages of a Canadian force in the West. The Governor General added that, "as the Americans are abhorred by the whole Indian people, it might be a doubtful policy for us to become identified with them in anything like a military policy."[7] Mackenzie relented and the NWMP went on into the West and later to fame and glory as Canada's national police force.

When Commissioner French reached Fort Garry he found that Lieutenant-Governor Morris was not fully comforted by the arrival of the 150 NWMP recruits; he continued to see Indian troubles. Morris would successfully instill in French some of his distorted perception of conditions in the West. But to be fair to Morris, the West was far from tranquil.

About the time news of the Cypress Hills Massacre broke upon the world, another firefight had taken place on the Canadian plains. Although the fatalities were almost as great, only the participants were aware of the event until the evidence was discovered a year later. Even then, the affair received little or no attention.

In the autumn of 1873, 20 American Crow Indians crossed the huge Blackfoot reservation in northern Montana and travelled north across the unmarked border into Canada where they successfully appropriated a number of Peigan/Blackfoot horses. Escaping with their booty, the Crow were overtaken by a number of pursuing Blackfoot. A battle ensued, but as the Crow attempted to dig in for defence, they were overrun and slaughtered. Scalped, stripped and mutilated, the Crow were left on the plains, where their desiccated bodies were discovered the following year by the boundary surveyors near the Sweet Grass Hills but north of the border (see p. 99). The bodies had been collected together in such a way that it appeared to the surveyors that their conquerors had held a victory dance around them. All the elements of an international incident were present, but it is a comment upon the attitude of the time that it received only casual mention in the surveyors' reports.[8]

Commissioner French spent December 1873 and January 1874 at Red River sizing up the magnitude of the task to move the NWMP several hundred kilometres into the uncharted West. He met at Dufferin with the boundary surveyors, Commissioner Cameron, Captain Anderson and Lawrence Herchmer, the head of the Commissary Party who himself would later serve as a Commissioner of the NWMP. French needed to learn as much as possible about what he might expect. His decisions the next year raise questions about just how much attention French paid to the advice boundary surveyors must have given him.

French would have been told about the work of the 49th Rangers and the importance of having advance scouts to locate camps where there was water, wood and grazing. Surely he would have asked about the availability of experienced plainsmen who could serve as guides. French must have inquired about equipment and animals. The surveyors had found that the Red River cart was fine for nomadic wanderers, but broke down too frequently and required far too much repair to be suitable for expeditions. Modern wagons were far superior, although a few carts were useful for light work. The power and endurance of oxen far exceeded that of horses, and the boundary survey was converting its wagons as much as possible to oxen, reserving horses for riding; 210 oxen would be used in 1874 instead of the 48 in yoke the previous year. As well, oxen required no food other than natural pasturage while horses needed 4.5 kg (10 lb) of oats per day. The surveyors had also learned that the Red River pony had far more endurance than the Canadian horse and, like the ox, rustled for itself out on the trail, requiring and receiving no oat ration.

Commissioner French and the boundary surveyors certainly would have discussed such matters as the nature of the terrain to the west, the weather that might be expected and the location of existing Métis settlements and trails. Captain Anderson did tell French of the supply depot that would be established at Wood Mountain and the shipment of oats ordered for spring delivery. French was also made aware of the Métis village of Willow Bunch that had taken root three years earlier, in 1870, just east of the Wood Mountain uplands. They might even have discussed tents because the surveyors were switching to bell tents. The old Hudson's Bay Company wall tents were fine in the bush but they collapsed before the winds of the open plains.

And water. French must have inquired about the availability of water out on the plains. The boundary surveyors, if asked, would have reported that in their first season west of Dufferin they had experienced an ugly shortage of good water.

APPARENTLY HAVING ACQUIRED A sufficient understanding of the requirements of his force, in early February 1874 French headed back East to purchase the animals and equipment needed for a major expedition and, hopefully, to recruit more men. He had recommended doubling the size of his command to 300 men and was pleased to learn that the Mackenzie government had agreed.

Before leaving Fort Garry French revealed some of the misinformation he had absorbed from the alarmist Lieutenant-Governor Morris. In a letter to the Deputy Minister of Justice, he wrote:

There will be hot work for us next summer. The governor has had reliable information that there are five forts between the Milk River and Edmonton, one of them containing 100 outlaws and desperadoes, and mounting several guns. The manner in which they got the guns will give you some idea of the ruffians we will have to deal with; it was simply this: they assaulted an army train which the U.S. Government was sending to one of their western forts, captured the guns and ran them across the line. They boldly give out that they will fight it out with any force that goes to disturb them, and as most of them have been outlawed in Montana, I think it is possible they mean what they say. *I hope so* [emphasis added].[9]

Surely someone in Ottawa must have wondered at the judgment of both Morris and French in so casually accepting that a band of outlaws could, with apparent ease, seize cannons from the U.S. Army, known to be quite capable of defending itself, and then *run* those cannons, not the most mobile of armament, across the border. Nothing, obviously, had been heard of this from the American authorities who were not slow in complaining about lawbreakers taking sanctuary in Canada. And the new commander of the NWMP was expressing something akin to joyous anticipation of a serious battle.

The consequence of this belief was that, at terrible cost to their horses, French and his troops would haul over the plains two 9-pounder muzzle-loading field guns and two brass mortars. The whiskey traders would be blasted from their fortresses.

In Ontario over the winter, Commissioner French recruited 217 officers and men and selected transport wagons and equipment. He also purchased 278 Ontario horses, claiming that none were available at Fort Garry. In fact, French turned his nose up at the Red River pony. He wanted his troopers to be mounted on the larger and more attractive Canadian horses, and he carefully chose only bloodstock of matching colours. A cruel future awaited French's fine horseflesh.

The rate of pay for recruits was substantial for the time and would be later reduced: constables, $1 per day; sub-constables, 75¢ per day. As an added inducement a 65-ha (160-acre) land grant was available to those who completed their three-year hitch satisfactorily. The land grant also was later removed.

Men, horses, wagons and equipment all travelled by rail to Fargo on the Red River about 260 km (160 mi) south of Dufferin, arriving on June 12, 1874. This Ontario wing assembled its wagons and moved overland to Dufferin, leaving much of its heavy equipment to be later shipped by steamer. The six-day march to Dufferin was a precursor of what lay ahead on the far plains; on the fifth day a number of played-out horses were left behind and several more died.[10] The arrival of 25 fresh horses from Dufferin, thanks to Macleod's foresight, was more than welcome.

Arriving at Dufferin on June 19, the Ontario recruits joined up with the other half of the Force that had spent the winter at the Stone Fort. By July 8, the entire expedition was ready to march west, minus another exodus of recruits who suffered a change of mind.

French contributed to these late departures. Rather than have misfits failing out in the wilderness, he warned his troops of the dangers and hardships that lay ahead. Thirty-one constables and sub-constables heeded the Commissioner's warning and took, as it were, "French leave." As with the earlier group at the Stone Fort, there was little the Force could do but grant discharges and pay them up to date.[11]

French's instructions from Ottawa were to take his force directly to the forks of the Bow and Belly Rivers where Robertson-Ross had reported the American whiskey traders to be operating, establish a post there and another at Fort Edmonton, then return with the remainder of his troops to Fort Ellice, the Hudson's Bay trading post on the Assiniboine River, about 290 km (180 mi) west of Fort Garry. That site had been chosen as the headquarters of the Force; the government would arrange for the construction of suitable buildings while French was out on the plains. French had never seen Fort Ellice but sent a dispatch to Ottawa strenuously objecting to its suitability as a headquarters and claiming that Lieutenant-Governor Morris agreed with him.[12]

The natural and practical route for the expedition to follow was the boundary trail established by the surveyors who were then several hundred kilometres west of Dufferin and, in fact, French's initial instructions were to do exactly that. Ottawa, however, excited by information provided by Lieutenant-Governor Alexander Morris at Fort Garry, instructed French to avoid the boundary.

Morris, an educated and otherwise level-headed man, perhaps had not been long enough on the frontier to learn how to discount its rumour and exaggeration. A month before French and his troops arrived in Dufferin, Morris had reported to Ottawa that 1,000 lodges of Sioux had moved north of the Missouri River and were heading to the border with hostile intentions towards the boundary survey. Morris was so concerned about a collision between the NWMP and the Sioux that he recommended that the Force take the well-travelled Carlton Trail to Edmonton and then move south to the confluence of the Bow and Belly Rivers. Ottawa chose a middle course.[13]

French was instructed to follow "the most direct route possible but as far north of the U.S. boundary as was feasible, to avoid contact with aliens."[14] After consulting with Morris, French decided his best course was to follow the boundary trail "for about 150 to 200 miles [240–320 km] and then strike in a northwesterly direction towards Qu'Appelle but before reaching that turning still more westerly towards the Cypress Hills."[15]

Morris assured French that such a route would take him through "good country in which he would find adequate feed for his livestock."[16] That statement was not only untrue, but irresponsible. Morris and French had no map more recent than Palliser's, more than 15 years old, and next to useless because Palliser had never set foot in the region. More current and better information was available. The exploratory survey for the intended Pacific railway had passed through the plains in 1872. The information gathered was displayed on a map published in 1876. Clearly shown is a trail called the Traders' Road running from Fort Garry through Wood Mountain to the Cypress Hills.

The Traders' Road had been in use for years by the Métis traveling west out of Red River to Willow Bunch, Wood Mountain and the Cypress Hills. Jean-Louis Légaré, and others, had been trading with the Métis settlement at Wood Mountain for at least three years, freighting their wares from Fort Garry and Pembina over the trail that became known as Traders' Road. From Wood Mountain the trail continued almost due west to the Métis *hivernants'* settlement of Chimney Coulee in the Cypress Hills.

The Traders' Road was perfectly situated for the NWMP Expedition. Some 55–65 km (35–40 mi) north of the 49th Parallel, it was secure from cross-border attack, and it followed by far the best terrain for horse-drawn wagons. The route Commissioner French planned to take intersected with the Traders' Road, but, unfortunately for his command, he would reject the marked trail and lead his troopers over the most difficult landscape in the region.

Morris showed admirable foresight in arranging to warn the Blackfoot and other tribes in the region of the coming intrusion into their territory of both the Boundary Survey and the NWMP. Through the Hudson's Bay Company a message was forwarded out to the Reverend John McDougall, who maintained a Wesleyan Mission at Morleyville in the foothills of the Rockies and enjoyed good relations with the Stoneys and Blackfoot. McDougall was requested to explain the coming expeditions and emphasize that they came with good will. The Hudson's Bay Company was authorized to provide $1,500 in presents for distribution at McDougall's discretion. Similar requests went to the Hudson's Bay Company at Qu'Appelle and Fort Edmonton.[17]

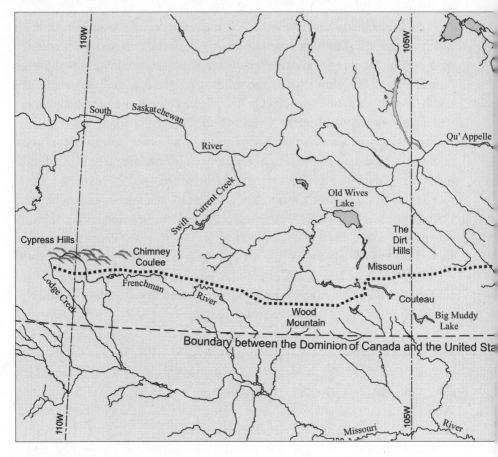

Traders' Road. *Map by Diane Perrick, GIS Information Services, CPRC*

Commissioner French did not command by consensus. Neither did he make good use of his officers when planning the NWMP expedition. His most capable officer, James Macleod, had far more experience than French in moving troops through the primitive conditions of the West. The Wolseley Expedition had involved the transit of some 1,600 personnel and not a man was lost. Macleod had again acquitted himself well the previous fall when he brought the third contingent safely through the extreme weather conditions encountered on the Dawson Route.

Not only did French ignore Macleod during the planning of the NWMP expedition, he passed him over when requested by Ottawa to nominate one of his officers to be Assistant Commissioner and recommended a much junior officer.[18]

Fortunately for the NWMP expedition, Macleod had friends in high places and a well-deserved reputation for military competence. A lawyer, Macleod

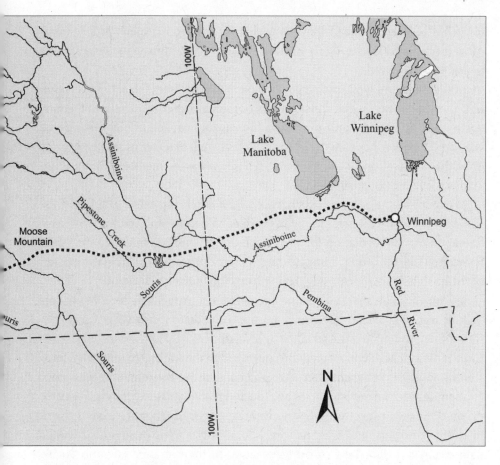

had become acquainted with Prime Minister Macdonald as early as 1869 when the Wolseley Expedition was formed.[19] Macdonald was out of office in the spring of 1874 when French made his attempt on Macleod's career, but Macdonald's brother-in-law, Colonel Hewitt Bernard, had been kept on as Deputy Minister of Justice. Macleod was well-known to Bernard.

Word came back from Ottawa on June 1, 1874. James Macleod was appointed Assistant Commissioner of the NWMP and instructed to accompany the expedition into the West. It was a serious affront to French, who had been Commissioner for only six months. Macleod knew that, although he had received a coveted promotion, he dared not cross French in any way if he wished to continue with the NWMP. And Macleod did desperately wish to retain his position. He was engaged to marry a girl in Winnipeg, and needed the job. Macleod also had bitter personal experience to guide him. Sixteen years earlier, as a young lieutenant in the Militia he had made the mistake of criticizing the competence of a senior officer and nearly lost his commission.[20] Macleod was not about to jump off that cliff a second time. There was nothing for it but to keep his head down, see that the Commissioner's orders were carried out, hold his thoughts to himself, and make himself as nearly indispensable as he could.

In this Macleod would succeed. Although at first French treated his Assistant Commissioner like an enlisted man, before the expedition had reached its destination he would admit to Ottawa the wisdom of their choice: "Macleod is a capital fellow; he is my right hand. I wish we had a few more like him."[21] After the completion of the expedition, French's assessment of his Number Two was even more positive.

Macleod's decision to avoid conflict with French was wise. The Commissioner brooked no questioning of his orders. When he ordered his troops to line up in parade formation for the march out of Dufferin and into the West, Inspector Charles Young, commanding "B" Troop, remonstrated in the matter of the horses. French dismissed Young from the Force on the spot.

The magnificent spectacle of the entire NWMP expedition parading in formation out of Dufferin had not been the immediate result when Commissioner French signalled the advance by lowering his upraised sword. Assistant Commissioner Macleod relayed the command to the waiting troops in his best stentorian voice, the trumpeter gave a blast, and the consequence was pure pandemonium; the restive horses bucked and reared and did their best to rush off on their own trajectories. Scores of inexperienced troopers were thrown from their mounts, and wagons careened about as their unseasoned teams kicked and did their best to rid themselves of their strange encumbrances. After a couple of hours of shouting and exertion, the men managed to align themselves into something of the formation desired by the Commissioner.[22]

French was satisfied. "The column of route presented a very fine appearance," he reported.[23] It was indeed a splendid sight and it is unfortunate that no photographer was on hand to provide a visual record of one of Canada's great historic moments.

The column of route that Commissioner French had ordered was a formal order of march, magnificent to watch but militarily and practically foolish. It was inefficient and worked an unnecessary hardship on both men and animals. Rather than husband the energy and strength of the resources of his command, the vainglorious French insisted upon a military show that had no place on the open prairie. Worse, the formation unnecessarily rendered the expedition vulnerable to attack by hostile Indians, a threat that was considered to be very real.

The departure from Dufferin was a "Hudson's Bay Start," a technique borrowed from the experience of the *voyageurs*, a shakedown beginning of short duration and distance intended to identify problems and shortages while there was still opportunity to correct them. It was also useful to get the men out of town and away from the grog shops and give them an opportunity to sober up before undertaking the voyage in earnest. French managed to move his expedition out of Dufferin about 5:00 p.m. and camped for the night after travelling only 3.2 km (2 mi). It was about all they could have managed anyway.

The next morning, July 9, the expedition rested. It had been a bad night. Fifty oxen had strayed and a number of horses stampeded, but all were recovered. Another debate on the subject of horses broke out. Ignoring Macleod's good advice to let the Commissioner have his head, Inspector Theodore Richer of "F" Troop, insisting that they had far too few horses, protested French's order to turn over his spare riding horses for use as draft animals pulling wagons. The Commissioner responded by placing Richer under arrest. Richer stormed out of camp heading back to Dufferin on foot, swearing to bring French's incompetence to the attention of the authorities in Ottawa and the public generally. It was not a morale booster. Two out of six troop commanders were gone before the expedition really got under way.

Sergeant Major Sam Steele, writing 40 years later when he was Colonel S.B. Steele, explained the disagreement between French and his officers over the endurance and feeding of horses:

> Erroneous reports of travellers in the northern part of the prairie region had been made to the effect that horses could do 40 miles [65 km] a day on grass. The people forgot to say that they had ridden and driven on horseback and in buck-boards with a herd of acclimatized native ponies behind them, and none of them were obliged to be under saddle or in harness for more than a couple of hours a day at most.[24]

French checked his cargo and sent two wagonloads of syrup and the like back to Dufferin to be replaced with oats. As an omen of what was to come, that first day on the trail one horse died and three wagons broke down and were abandoned.[25]

Macleod had found that he could be most useful shepherding the rear of the great caravan, rendering assistance where needed and ensuring that stragglers were not abandoned. His greatest challenge was with the Métis drivers. These free souls cared not a whit for the Commissioner's discipline or order of march and travelled according to their own rhythm. With blandishment and humour Macleod was usually able to keep the Red River carts in reasonable proximity to the rest of the expedition.

The troopers quickly learned to turn to Macleod when they had a problem. Writing to Mary Drever only two days out of Dufferin he described having to get three ox teams unstuck and complained, "I have been called out of my tent about 50 times since I commenced this stupid letter, and I am in very bad humour."[26] The Assistant Commissioner became the man who kept Commissioner French's show on the road.

On July 12, the expedition was visited by a swarm of Rocky Mountain grasshoppers that filled the air and covered the ground, the tents, the wagons, the equipment, everything. The pests proceeded to devour the camp: "Even the paint and woodwork of the waggons, and our carbines were not free from their attacks, and our tents had to be hurriedly packed away to save them from destruction."[27]

Commissioner French had made little or no attempt to duplicate the 49th Rangers of the Boundary Survey and relied upon Lieutenant-Governor Morris to provide him with guides and scouts. Morris sent out a party of six Métis, headed by Pierre Leveille, who joined the NWMP on the trail six days out of Dufferin. They would prove to be less than entirely reliable.

Perhaps because of the lack of competent scouts, or perhaps because of French's style of march, night camp was often made without access to water. On July 17 they camped without water or pasturage and only later discovered that Whitewater Lake was only a few kilometres away. The next day the horses began to give out and two were left behind as "unfit for further travel." The day after that (July 19), two more horses were abandoned and two more died.

Dry camps were no minor inconvenience. The journal kept by Lieutenant Francis V. Greene of the U.S. Army, who was out on the western plains with the American Boundary Survey that season of 1874, tells us of his experience:

> These dry camps for travelers not provided with water carts or casks are a terrible thing. Night finds them almost parched with thirst from the day's tramp over dusty and often alkaline plains, tired also, and hungry. Eating only increases the thirst, which is so great as to prevent sleep. I made a camp of this kind last autumn and shall not forget it.[28]

Already French must have regretted one of the most critical omissions in his planning. Not only did his expedition include no bulk transport of water, his men were not even equipped with canteens, an item that had been standard military equipment for at least 10 years. After a full day under the broiling sun of July and August on the western plains, a dry camp meant that no one drank—not a horse, not an ox, not a man. This was no oversight; before departure French had warned his recruits that "they would be often without water."[29]

Instead of sending advance units, including the field kitchens, out early each morning to scout out a site for that evening's camp and prepare to feed the oncoming troopers, French insisted on maintaining his column of route. The result was that the field kitchens were often so late in reaching camp that the men were already asleep without a meal. The cattle, intended to be a travelling commissary, were the slowest element of the expedition and so many kilometres behind as to be inaccessible for butchering.

On July 18 the expedition reached the Souris River, where they found plenty of wood and good water. French ordered two days of rest but even this did not restore the horses. On July 21, the day they left the Souris, 15 sick horses "failed to reach camp." The riders were ordered to walk every alternate hour to relieve their mounts.

By July 22, just two weeks on the trail, the oat supply was completely exhausted, even with the two additional wagonloads French had ordered as an afterthought. One wonders what the initial provision was, remembering the 4.5 kg (10 lb) per day allowance of the boundary surveyors.

On July 24, the expedition once more came upon the Souris River, this time at Roche Percée, near Estevan in today's Saskatchewan. Here again there was good water, wood and pasture, but the horses were in terrible shape, many of them lying down, unable to rise. The trail behind was "strewn with broken carts and horses and oxen overcome with hunger and fatigue."[30] At this point the expedition had covered 435 km (270 mi) from Dufferin.

Just before he trooped out of Dufferin, Commissioner French had received from Ottawa an inexplicable amendment to his instructions. The plan to establish a police post in the region of the whiskey forts was cancelled. After dispatching the American whiskey traders, the Commissioner was to position half his force at Edmonton and return with the other half to Fort Ellice. But at Roche Percée, just a couple of weeks into his ordeal, French was forced to the realization that he had already lost the capability to meet his original objective of taking his entire force west to deal with the whiskey forts. The Commissioner's transport had so broken down, and several of his men become so incapacitated, that a radical change of plan had become essential.

French decided to divide his troops then and there, sending half directly to Edmonton while he carried on to the West with the other half. The Commissioner meant to strengthen his force by discarding the infirm horses and men as well as many of the cattle and much of the provisions.

Accordingly, "A" Troop under Inspector William D. Jarvis was detailed to Fort Ellice and on to Edmonton. He was given the 55 weakest horses while his best were divided among the other troops. Colour coordination had long since been discarded. Jarvis was also assigned six additional men, 12 Métis, 24 wagons, 55 carts, 62 oxen and 50 cows and calves as well as agricultural implements and stores not deemed essential to the main body. In addition, he was to deliver to Fort Ellice half a dozen sick men and three wagons.

Jean D'Artigue, a visitor from France who had joined the NWMP out of a spirit of adventure, and one of the troopers assigned to Jarvis, believed that the arrangement was "the most unreasonable and incredible plan that ever originated in any man's brain."[31] It was about 1,045 km (650 mi) to Edmonton via Fort Ellice, but D'Artigue, who thought it was 1,450 km (900 mi), complained, "traveling 900 miles [1,450 km] with sick horses and heavy wagons was a very different thing from traveling 270 miles [435 km] with horses that were at least in good condition at the outset."[32] D'Artigue was convinced that their little caravan could not reach Edmonton before winter, if at all, and that French really intended them to make it only as far as Fort Ellice, 210 km (130 mi) distant.

To Roche Percée the expedition had been following the main boundary surveyors' trail. At Wood End, a Commission depot at the last crossing of the Souris River a few miles west of Roche Percée, that trail swung southward across the border where it remained for several miles before it turned back. It then carried on northwesterly along the east slope of the Missouri Coteau to a point about 65 km (40 mi) north of the border where it joined the Traders' Road that ran west through a gap in the Coteau to Wood Mountain and on to Cypress Hills. Commissioner French with his pruned-down troops, but still dragging the guns, left the trail where it turned south and took a course to the northwest, following Long Creek.

Two days later, on August 1, French had reconnected with the main boundary surveyors' trail and stayed with it for three days until it joined the Traders' Road. At that point, the Traders' Road would have been impossible to miss; the heavy wagons of the boundary surveyors had been over it in June, leaving their unmistakable ruts on top of the gouges created by years of Red River carts.

Then, on August 4, French made the decision that nearly brought his expedition to ruin. He started the day mistaking a small range of hills for the Missouri Coteau, which he would not encounter for two more days, "Ascended the coteau about 8:30 a.m., and halted at 9:30." Then, still on the Traders' Road/Boundary Commission Road:

North-West Mounted Police crossing the Dirt Hills (Saskatchewan), August 4, 1874. *Glenbow Museum NA-361-10*

As our road was to break off from the Boundary Commission Road at this point, sent Macleod and six carts to Wood Mountain by this road, for pemmican. We struck in a N.N.W. direction, making a road for ourselves over a very rough undulating country, descending the coteau, which we need not have ascended if the guides knew the country properly.[33]

French knew the trail led to Willow Bunch and Wood Mountain when he sent Macleod to procure pemmican from the buffalo hunters there. Inexplicably, he struck off on his own towards a very desolate section of the Missouri Coteau. His decision here guaranteed his force a cruel march over just about the most difficult terrain that lay between Red River and Cypress Hills.

Two days later his horses were straining up the Dirt Hills that French estimated were "1,000 feet [305 m] above the adjoining plain; very severe work on horses, especially the gun horses."[34] The next day, August 7, the Commissioner had to order a day's rest for the played-out horses.

Such extreme exertion would have been avoided if French had remained on the Traders' Road. It followed a pass through the hilly Missouri Coteau, "The Gap," a prominent feature so well-known that the NWMP Métis guides must have been aware of it.

Today, Saskatchewan's Highway 13, which takes advantage of the easy passage through the Missouri Coteau is called, for tourist purposes only, "The Red Coat Trail." The Gap, north of today's community of Ceylon, is recognized in the name of the rural municipality in which it lies, R.M. of The Gap No. 39.

Another calamity awaited the NWMP horses as French pushed them over the Coteau. He was delighted to reach Old Wives Lake, an alkaline water. French, an equestrian, naïvely thought the water beneficial, "slightly brackish, just enough so to purge some of the weaker horses," and he ordered another day of rest. A day later, August 10, the Commissioner recognized his mistake. "The saline water and bad feed is telling on the horses."[35] They were stricken with copious diarrhoea and were so weakened by the alkali that they died during the winter.

Alkali was an unknown hazard to the Eastern greenhorns riding with the NWMP. Certainly Sub-inspector Cecil E. Denny,[36] a 23-year-old English immigrant, had never heard of the mineral salt that collected in shallow evaporation basins. Riding in pursuit of some antelope, Denny suddenly found his horse floundering and sinking in a patch of soft, whitish mud. By the time he extricated himself from the quicksand-like alkali and reached solid ground, his horse had sunk so deeply that only the head appeared above the surface. Deeply chagrined at his predicament and the likely loss of his horse, Denny marked the site and set out on foot for help. Miles later he encountered Assistant Commissioner Macleod, who by good fortune was leading a second horse and carrying a lasso. Denny, able to re-locate the spot, was pleasantly surprised to see his horse still alive with his head showing. The horse came free after much effort but was so exhausted by the ordeal that he was unable to work for weeks. Amazingly, when so many of the expedition's horses were lost, Denny's survived the entire journey and the two rode together for some years after.[37]

Three days northwest of Roche Percée French found that Pierre Leveillé and the Métis guides supplied by Lieutenant-Governor Morris knew nothing of the country that lay ahead. Not surprisingly, none of them had any experience so far off the established trails. French was on his own. He was navigating by a primitive process known as "dead reckoning," using a compass and keeping track of the distance travelled by means of a counter attached to the wheel of his wagon, confirming his position from time to time by astronomical observation. His only map was the one prepared by Palliser, who had not entered the region French was crossing. The map was based on hearsay and consequently seriously distorted.

The expedition met a party of Métis hunters, who told French that the whiskey traders had spent the summer preparing to defend against the NWMP artillery. Five hundred strong, the Americans had constructed underground galleries that would withstand bombardment. In a dispatch he was able to get off to Ottawa, French reported the threat as it had come to him; only later did he treat the story as the nonsense it was.[38]

Macleod caught up with the expedition at Old Wives Lake. He carried 2,130 kg (4,700 lb) of pemmican and dried buffalo meat and the news that the Boundary Commission had a surplus of oats at Wood Mountain.

French's diary for August 14 contains this statement: "Have heard that the Boundary Commission have oats to spare at Wood Mountain, and have dispatched Macleod with 16 carts to get some." "Have heard." Later it would be contended on French's behalf that he intended all along to supply his units this way. It was a vital point. The NWMP expedition was then on the point of paralysis and surely would have failed without the oats which became available only because of the fortuitous oversupply caused by the caution of the boundary surveyors.

Macleod rejoined the expedition on August 17 with 120 sacks of oats loaded on his carts and some wagons borrowed from the Boundary Commission at the Wood Mountain depot. He also brought with him Lawrence Herchmer, the officer in charge of the commissary supplying the survey parties and who had easily provided the oats. Herchmer had accepted Macleod's invitation to accompany him back to negotiate the terms of sale directly with Commissioner French.

On August 18, 1874, three Commissioners of the North-West Mounted Police, one currently holding the office and the other two destined to succeed to that rank in the future, sat in a tent at the Force's campsite by the Wood River (which French called Old Wives Creek). Not two years later French, the first Commissioner, would resign under fire and be replaced by Macleod.[39] Ten years later, in 1886, Herchmer would become the fourth Commissioner. But on that August day the three officers bargained and haggled over price and terms like Persian traders at a *caravanserai*. A deal was quickly reached.

Herchmer advised French that he was well-supplied with oats and could spare a good quantity. In truth, although he probably did not reveal the fact, because of the double delivery in June he was overstocked and wanted to dispose of at least 27,000 kg (60,000 lb), about half of the American order, or he would have to transport his surplus back to Dufferin and sell it there. On the other side, French needed every bushel Herchmer could spare; his diary admits that, to his horses, "oats, at any price, is a Godsend."

Since the oats Herchmer was selling had been purchased in the United States, he quoted his price, 8.5¢ cents a pound, in American funds. French thought the price was high, and it was. Assuming an average weight of 15.5 kg (34 lb) to a bushel it was equivalent to $2.90 a bushel, not far off market value 130 years later.[40] But French had no choice if he was to save his expedition. They settled at 7.5¢ cents for 27,000 kg (60,000 lb) with a provision that, if the NWMP actually took a lesser quantity, the Boundary Commission would have the "discretionary power to charge a price not exceeding 8.5 cents." That clause would later cause difficulty.

This was not to be a handshake transaction. Macleod, the lawyer, wrote the contract out by hand. Expressed to be between "Lt. Col. French and Lawrence A. Herchmer," it stated that it was "signed at Old Wives Creek, August 18, 1874." The contract stated that Macleod had already taken delivery of 7,165 kg (15,800 lb), another 9,000 kg (20,000 lb) would be taken at Wood Mountain, 5,450 kg (12,000 lb) at the Boundary Commission depot at White Mud (Frenchman) River, and "the balance from Boundary Commission trains coming East provided NWMP can conveniently intercept these trains."[41]

Obviously Macleod was still walking on eggs around French and was careful not to presume upon the Commissioner's authority when it came to such a major commitment as the purchase of 27,000 kg (60,000 lb) of expensive oats. He had brought Herchmer to French and let the two of them make the deal. Yet, French's diary entry for 18 August reads: "I find *he* [Macleod] has purchased 60,000 pounds [27,000 kg] of oats from the Boundary Commission, and, although the price is high, I approved *his* purchase" (emphasis added).

French and Macleod also bought a horse and a pony from Herchmer and were able to pick up five more ponies from an accompanying Métis. The deplorable state of the NWMP expedition was obvious to the Métis horse trader; when he returned to Fort Qu'Appelle he gave his opinion that they would be unable to march another 65 km (40 mi).[42]

Herchmer told French that several of the whiskey traders who had been operating north of the boundary were holed up in Fort Benton expecting the arrival of the NWMP, and were promising to return to their operations as soon as the Force left the area. French sent off with Herchmer a dispatch to Ottawa recommending that, to prevent this, a portion of his command be stationed in the vicinity. He requested a reply be sent to him at Fort Benton.[43]

Herchmer's report was likely accurate. The NWMP expedition was a matter of deep interest as it crawled its way westward:

In Fort Benton, westerners who followed their painful progress across the plains through reports brought in by Indians were appalled by the succession of blunders that marked their course. And they marvelled at the raw courage which kept the column slowly moving westward along a trail strewn with broken carts and abandoned animals . . . Shadowy, unseen Blackfoot scouts silently watched the strange cavalcade as it fought its way through an unknown and hostile land . . . Who were these red-coated invaders and what was their purpose? . . . Who were these men who knew so little of the country that their horses starved while they were forced to make dry camps unable to find water?[44]

In spite of his desperate need, before he distributed any of the oats Macleod had carted from Wood Mountain the fastidious French attempted to check the weights of the 120 sacks, a difficult feat out on the trail. He calculated a total of 6,648 kg (14,655 lb), not the 7,170 kg (15,800 lb) claimed by Herchmer, and made a notation to that effect on his copy of the contract.[45]

It was a lifesaving deal for the NWMP expedition. Macleod made several more trips to pick up the rest of the contracted oats and by the end of August, according to Boundary Commission records, the NWMP had secured a total of 25,630 kg (56,505 lb), or about 1,662 bushels.

After he completed the contract with Herchmer, French moved his troops a couple of miles further up the Wood River to a point 11–12 km (7–8 mi) north of today's town of Gravelbourg. Here the Commissioner again lightened his load by establishing what he called a "Cripple Camp," where he left seven men, five of them quite ill, a Métis, 26 worn-out horses, 12 wagons and some superfluous stores, all to be picked up on the return to Fort Ellice. On August 20, the expedition moved out west. Five days later they reached the Cypress Hills.

On September 2, the troops encountered buffalo and enjoyed the fresh meat. That luxury soon demanded a price. The buffalo had so grazed the little grass in the area that nothing was left for the expedition's horses and they again began to fail. Once more French and his troops were in serious difficulty.

By September 6, "for practical purposes the command was lost."[46] Searching for the forks of the Bow and Belly Rivers where they expected to find a major whiskey fort, the force struggled westward in the vicinity of today's Medicine Hat. The weather turned wet and cold. Many of the horses were in serious condition. On September 9, five horses died; the next day, two more. French realized that his horses, and likely many of his men also, would lose their lives if they were hit with a snowstorm of the sort that had crossed the plains each of the last two Septembers. As it was, his diary noted: "Horses starving, the oats just keeping them up."

French found the junction of the Bow and the Belly, but the fortifications there consisted of three rude log huts without roofs, occasionally used by transient wolfers. He sent reconnaissance parties searching for whiskey forts, but none were found. Perhaps that was just as well; the Force was in no condition to deal with a band of armed desperadoes. The men were faced with the problem of their own survival.

The situation was so desperate that French became willing to accept advice. He called his officers into council to discuss their predicament. The consensus was to strike for the Sweet Grass Hills, visible to the south, where water, wood and plentiful pasture were assured. No matter that the Hills lay across the border in United States territory; formalities would be discarded in favour of survival.

Inspector Walsh, with 70 men and 57 horses, had been detailed to Edmonton but, taking the advice of Pierre Leveillé and listening to his own common sense, French countermanded his order and called Walsh back as the entire expedition headed to sanctuary.

It was a near-run thing. Horses dropped in their tracks and even the oxen were too weak to move. When Walsh came in he had lost six of his 57 horses. Dismounted, chilled by driving sleet, weary and hungry themselves, the men placed their own blankets around the starved and staggering horses and encouraged them onward. Five miserable days, but they made it through to West Butte, the most westerly of the Sweet Grass Hills.

The cost was huge: many more horses died "from general debility and complete prostration." Henri Julien, an illustrator accompanying the expedition, noted in his diary entry of September 17: "We lost 18 horses from the 9th of September, making 48 since we left Toronto." Yet the cumulative total from French's diary seems far higher, at least 75. Even 12 hardy oxen died "from want of feed and water." The veterinary surgeon, John Poett, supervised the men as they tried to keep the horses on their feet so he could treat them, but several were unable to stand even with assistance and were lost. Poett was disturbed at the experience: "The debilitated state of the horses generally at this place was a sight that will not soon be forgotten."[47]

Dead Horse Coulee (Alberta), September 19, 1874. *Glenbow Museum NA-361-21*

Fittingly, the troops christened their camping site "Dead Horse Coulee." Unfortunately, it was an old Indian camping ground and everyone became infested with body lice. Surgeon John Kittson resorted to an experiment with his stock of oil of juniper. A parade was ordered, every man appeared in the nude and was swabbed down with the oil. All clothing and bedding was similarly treated. It worked. (It is interesting to note, in light of the Force's activities a century later, that one of Surgeon Kittson's most commonly used medications was opium.)

French was entirely aware of how soon winter could arrive on the western plains. After allowing four days for the horses to recover, he ordered Inspector Jacob Carvell to move slowly eastward with "D" and "E" Troops and this time to use the Boundary Commission trail. French intended to catch up to Carvell but meanwhile he and Macleod with a small party left for Fort Benton, on the Missouri River. French expected a telegraphed response to his request to be allowed to leave a strong party on the Bow River. It was waiting for him on September 24 and Ottawa approved his plan.

Fort Benton offered everything that could be expected of a lawless frontier town, and a good deal more. Present were all the Wild West essentials of cattle ranching, gold mining, Indian fighting, and wagon trains, with the added dimension of the Missouri River and steamboating. Known as the head of navigation on the Missouri, it was frequently beyond even that. Steam boats could make it up the river as far as Fort Benton only during the high water of spring and early summer. When the water dropped, freight was deposited at Cow Island, about 195 km (120 mi) downstream, for later shipment upriver by smaller boats.

Lieutenant Francis V. Greene of the American Boundary surveyors arrived in Fort Benton on September 11, two weeks ahead of French and Macleod. Greene was not impressed:

> Fort Benton is a row of whisky shanties along the river front and a few adobe buildings in the background—by all odds the lowest of all the low places I have seen on the frontier. At the other end of the "town" is a stockade of adobe garrisoned by a Company of the 7th Inf'y—the quarters propped up with sticks and so shaky and full of vermin that the men sleep outdoors and the officers seek refuge with one of the two respectable traders in town . . . There are two legitimate licensed traders in the place; but the main commerce is in whisky, this being the grand depot for the whisky which is carried over the line near the mountains & traded to the Indians there.[48]

Along Fort Benton's dusty main thoroughfare fronting the Missouri and the steamboat landing were the two mercantile firms mentioned by Greene: I.G. Baker & Co. and T.C. Power & Brother—remarkable, full-service operations that could meet any need and deliver anywhere within several hundred kilometres. American entrepreneurship, hustle and initiative, was everywhere. Fort Benton's commercial activity was likely unequalled anywhere in the West. An early resident gave this description:

> It began merely as a trading post, but as the country began to be wrested from the Indians and herds of buffalo, it became a centre of commerce and the head of navigation on the Missouri River. Although it continued to be a mere village in size, in a commercial way it was the Chicago of the Plains. It was the door through which the country to the east, west and north of it was entered. It was the door, also, through which entered all gold hunters, adventurers, speculators, traders, land seekers, big game hunters, fugitives from justice, desperados and all the mean Indians on top of the earth. Yes, it was a busy scene. A great scene. So great that I can't paint it for you as I would like to.[49]

Fort Benton was a lifesaver for French and his men. Almost before French and Macleod dismounted and tethered their horses, John Glenn, a local opportunist, had loaded a light wagon and dashed off to Dead Horse Coulee camp at West Butte. There he earned a quick and tidy profit selling food and delicacies to the half-starved troopers who grudgingly paid Glenn's exorbitant prices. Especially in demand was syrup, the commodity French had sent back to Dufferin two and a half months earlier.[50]

Thanks to a fortuitous reference in the East, Ottawa had selected I.G. Baker as the supplier to the NWMP, even though by 1874 the founder had sold a majority interest in the business and had returned to his home in St. Louis and the management of the firm's offices there. Charles and William Conrad, well-born Virginians, had acquired control of the operation and were building it into a commercial empire. Not yet in 1874, but within a few years, I.G. Baker had "offices in Toronto, a store in Montreal, and business offices in Helena, St. Louis and other cities, while operations were conducted from Fort Benton as headquarters."[51]

The connection between the NWMP and the Conrads was fortunate to both. Charles Conrad was very knowledgeable about the Canadian West, where for four years he had been living and carrying on business. Recognizing an opportunity when the Hudson's Bay Company's monopoly ended with its sale of Rupert's Land, in 1870 the Conrads moved into the fur trade, building as many as eight trading posts in Canada, reaching as far north as Great Slave Lake. Two of their posts, Robbers Roost and Slough Bottom, were maintained on the Oldman River where the NWMP was headed.[52]

By good fortune, Charles Conrad was in Fort Benton when French and Macleod rode in and he promptly took them under his wing. A survivor of the Civil War, where he spent two years on horseback with Mosby's Raiders, his knowledge of the West was invaluable to the novices of the NWMP. Standing 1.75 m (6'3"), slender and handsome, fluent in several Indian dialects and graced with courtly Southern manners, Conrad was a commanding presence. His reputation for personal courage and square dealing had earned him the trust and confidence of the Indians.[53] And his firm could deliver the goods. To operate its bull trains, I.G. Baker maintained "500 yoke of oxen and several hundred head of mules."[54] After 1875 it owned and operated steam boats hauling freight and passengers up the Missouri to Fort Benton.

I.G. Baker became a full-service supplier to the NWMP, building and supplying its forts on the Canadian plains, handling mail and telegraph messages, acting as the force's banker, providing transportation for personnel; whatever Canada's western police force needed, I.G. Baker supplied. Later, the Canadian Indian Affairs department also came to depend on I.G. Baker, particularly when it became necessary to supply rations to thousands of Treaty Indians.

The Conrads were already competing with the Hudson's Bay Company in Canada and the arrival of the NWMP gave them a springboard to a greater economic presence. As quickly as the new police force established posts in the West, I.G. Baker followed with its stores.

The NWMP business was tremendously profitable. In 1875, its first year of service to the NWMP, I.G. Baker billed the government $122,771, and the following year $122,057, huge amounts in those days.[55] In fact, the arrival of the NWMP lifted the entire town of Fort Benton out of an economic slump suffered when the gold mines it serviced became exhausted.

The first order of business for I.G. Baker was to rush some food out to the men camped at Dead Horse Coulee and fast horse-drawn light wagons quickly put John Glenn out of business. Slower bull trains followed.

At Fort Benton French learned of Ottawa's decision to change the location of the headquarters of his force. Fort Ellice was out and a new site had been chosen 160 km (100 mi) further north. To be called Fort Livingstone, it would be situated on the Swan River near Fort Pelly. French and the troops returning east with him were expected to winter at the new location.

Although there was a certain plausibility to the choice of Fort Livingstone as NWMP headquarters, it was a decision that could only be made by bureaucrats 3,200 km (2,000 mi) removed. Fort Livingstone did not then exist, but the site was on the line then projected for the Canadian Pacific Railway and Ottawa had contracted to run the Dominion Telegraph to that point. Ottawa must have selected the headquarters site considering that there were good timber supplies nearby and it was in reasonable proximity to a number of existing settlements such as those at Qu'Appelle, Fort Ellice and nearby Fort Pelly, Prince Albert and Fort Carlton, and the Métis communities along the South Saskatchewan River. But the new police force would be conducting most of its business in Blackfoot country west of the Cypress Hills, 800 crow-flying kilometres (500 mi) to the southwest, and there would be no communication from the new headquarters into that region. French would protest against this senseless choice, so much that it would cost him his command two years later.

Instructions to proceed with the erection of the buildings at the new headquarters site were issued to the Department of Public Works in Ottawa on July 9, 1874.[56] That was one day after Commissioner French had led his expedition out of Dufferin still in the belief that Fort Ellice was to be his final destination and winter quarters.

At Fort Benton, French, totally exasperated by the incompetence of the guides he had been provided, engaged a good one. Charles Conrad recommended Jerry Potts, the orphaned son of a Scots fur trader and a Peigan woman, the same Jerry Potts who had participated in the Battle of the Belly River four years earlier. Potts signed on to lead the NWMP across the western plains. Although not the only competent plainsmen at Fort Benton, to the green Eastern police Potts was a miracle man and he became part of the legend that grew around the Force.

French and Macleod also stocked up on horses and ponies, oats, a wagon and incidentals. French was chagrined to learn that his force was camped only a few kilometres from the well-travelled trail to Fort Whoop-Up, at the junction of the St. Mary's and Belly Rivers, not the Bow and the Belly as Robertson-Ross had reported.

Commissioner French performed another subdivision of his command. Macleod was assigned to proceed to Fort Whoop-Up, conduct such investigations as he considered appropriate, to choose a location for a post and construct winter quarters. "B," "C" and "F" Troops, with a sprinkling of "A," would accompany the Assistant Commissioner. The bull trains of I.G. Baker would freight supplies and provisions to Macleod and his new command.

The two officers reverted to their status as police and opened an investigation into the Cypress Hills Massacre. As with the location of Fort Whoop-Up, the identity of the perpetrators was an open secret in the rough-and-tumble town. Arrests and a trial would follow, but with little success.

On September 26, French departed Fort Benton to catch up with Carvell and left Macleod to deal with Whoop-Up. It was the last time the two would meet as officers of the NWMP.

Commissioner French had succeeded in leading his expedition through to its destination—almost—but the hardship endured by his men had not endeared them to their commander. Constable James Finlayson wrote in his diary: "September 29. If Canadians knew what his expedition will cost I think Col. French would very soon get his discharge. He left here with the best wishes of the men. That he may never come back."[56]

At Fort Benton there had been another report of an imminent Indian attack upon the boundary surveyors. Ottawa had telegraphed a warning to the Boundary Commission, but the source of the information is not known. French, reconnected to Carvell and perhaps by this time fed up with the frontier's wild rumours, stayed on the boundary road as he continued east.

When they reached the White Mud (Frenchman's) River, the troops encountered grisly evidence that animosity still prevailed between the buffalo-hunting Métis and the Sioux. The body of a Métis man, caught alone on the prairie, was found stripped naked and tied to a tree beside the stream. The branches of the tree had been lopped off to allow the sun full play on the man whose agonized death from thirst, starvation and exposure was apparent on his features.

By October 7, French reached the depot at Wood Mountain that had provided his life-saving oats. With admirable foresight, he purchased the building, some corrals and several tons of hay, and dropped off a few of his weaker animals. Two men were assigned as caretakers for the depot. The hastily built log building would before long be converted to the Wood Mountain post of the NWMP and play a central role in some dramatic historical events. The obscure Métis encampment would become well-known as far away as Ottawa, Washington and London.

After leaving Wood Mountain, French gathered up his Cripple Camp and pressed on, following a northeasterly course that would take him to the Hudson's Bay Company post at Fort Pelly and his nearby headquarters at Fort Livingstone still under construction. En route, he stopped briefly at Fort Qu'Appelle where he was able to replenish some of his horse transport and detail a few troops east to Fort Ellice. The Commissioner, anxiously watching the weather, encountered a new concern: the prairies were on fire all around.

On October 21, French arrived at his new headquarters only to find that his horizon had again receded. The site, poorly chosen, was on a rocky outcrop fully exposed to the prevailing northwesterly winds. The contractor was nailing up green spruce boards as fast as they could be planed at his sawmill in the nearby woods, either unaware or unconcerned that shrinkage would soon open the walls to the elements. Worse, a prairie fire that had been stopped only 6 m (20 ft) short of the buildings had destroyed half the winter hay supply. French decided that Fort Livingstone, or, as it came to be known, Swan River Barracks, could not accommodate all his command through the coming winter.

Once again, the Commissioner summoned his officers into conference to deal with a serious emergency. The consensus was to leave a much-reduced troop at Swan River and press on to Dufferin with the remainder. Inspector Carvell and part of "E" Troop were detailed to remain.

On October 24, French and the rest of his command set out for Dufferin via Fort Ellice and Winnipeg. The weather turned cold with blowing snow and once again the men faced a desperate march, but they made it through, arriving in Winnipeg on November 7. Veterinary Surgeon Poett declared the horses to be "very much run down in condition" with some sick. It was several weeks before the final march to Dufferin was accomplished.

When French and his troops finally reached Dufferin, they had travelled 2,900 km (1,800 mi) since leaving on July 8—1,257 km (781 mi) out to Belly

River and 1,800 km (1,119 mi) on the circuitous route back via Swan River Barracks. Another 258 km (160 mi) had been covered on the march from Fargo to Dufferin in June. It was, as Commissioner French described it, "one of the most extraordinary marches on record." It was also to become one of the most controversial.

THE WINTERY SNOW SQUALLS that brought misery to French and his men en route to Winnipeg had several days earlier hit the troops under Inspector Jarvis, 80 long days beyond Roche Percée but still out on the Carlton Trail, struggling towards Edmonton. Jean D'Artigue's opinion that it was utter folly to expect Jarvis and his men to cover the kilometres from Roche Percée to Edmonton before winter set in was not at all an unreasonable point of view. They very nearly did not.

Jarvis was a fine leader of men and he knew the route from Fort Ellice to Edmonton, having travelled it just the year before. He also had an unusually competent non-commissioned officer, Troop Sergeant Major Samuel B. Steele. "Sam" Steele would write his own chapters in the legends of the West.

D'Artigue was full of praise for his new superior and his style of command:

> He was as fond of short marches as Colonel French was of long ones; and he was right; for the proverb "slow but sure" is always the safest to follow on long marches. Taking advantage of the best camping places to be found, Inspector Jarvis would order a halt, four or five times a day in order to give the horses and oxen time to feed. And the result of such a course was soon felt; the animals began to recover rapidly, and even most of the sick men were soon able to resume their duties.[57]

Even so, two horses died and at Fort Ellice several sick men and weaker horses were dropped off. On August 18, the remaining party that decamped and headed for Edmonton consisted of 20 officers and men, 30 horses, 69 oxen hauling 65 carts and wagons, 13 Métis and 20 head of cattle. It was a gruelling journey for man and beast. When they reached Fort Carlton on September 11, Jarvis commented that, if the horses were his and not government property, he would put several out of their misery, such was their condition. Three days later the Métis cart drivers went on strike, stating "they'd had enough." Much persuasion was required to induce them to continue.

By October 1 the draft horses could not get up in the mornings without help and their legs needed to be massaged to restore circulation. The troops were now losing both horses and oxen; some dying, some unable to continue and abandoned on the trail. Three weeks later the expedition was still crawling onwards, lifting fallen horses to their feet and then walking beside the suffering animals with hands at their heads and shoulders, holding them upright.

The Carlton Trail was in wretched condition, far worse than Jarvis had found it the year before. To enable their wagons and weakened animals to cross mud holes and streams, the men felled trees and built corduroy roads and bridges. Jarvis estimated that several miles of corduroy were constructed.

Ice now formed on the ponds. Both horses and oxen were trapped when they fell through, too weak to escape without assistance. On October 27, now only 20 km (12 mi) out of Fort Edmonton, Steele organized two rows of fires and had the horses washed, dried and rubbed down so that they could stagger that last distance. The column was so scattered that seven days were required to bring in all the stragglers.

The Hudson's Bay Company post, Fort Edmonton, was a huge structure. Behind its 6-m (10-ft) palisades were stables for the NWMP animals and plenty of cottages with fireplaces and bunk beds for the men. Jarvis and his men were secure for the winter. Unfortunately, most of the horses they had carried through with them were so used up that they failed to recover and died before spring.

Jarvis and his troops had been on the trail a total of 88 days, 60 of them travelling days, and had covered 1,046 km (650 mi), an average of 18 km (11 mi) per day. Another NWMP epic had been written.

CHARLES CONRAD AND JERRY Potts led Assistant Commissioner Macleod out of Fort Benton and on to Fort Whoop-Up at the St. Mary and Belly Rivers. It was no great trick. The trail was an overland highway. That summer when geologist George Dawson of the Boundary Commission saw the Whoop-Up trail where it crossed the border it was a major thoroughfare. He found it

> deeply worn & wide & shows evidence of recent & very heavy teaming being done over it. Ashe saw yesterday a party of traders going N. They had several heavy freighting waggons drawn by mules & horses & heavily laden.[58]

In fact, the rutted trail was still easily visible 60 years later, long after it had fallen into disuse and become overgrown with grass.

Whoop-Up, first named Fort Hamilton, had been in business since January 1870. Financed and supplied by the very mercantile firms in Fort Benton the NWMP was now contracting with, Whoop-Up was merely the largest, most

Model of Fort Whoop-Up, 1870–74. *Glenbow Museum NA-1181-2*

successful and permanent of several similar enterprises that had been operating on the Canadian side of the border for about six years when the police
arrived. Those few years of whiskey trade had been enough to reduce the once
proud, prosperous and noble Blackfoot nation to abject poverty and misery.
As the American bootleggers preyed upon their weakness for the poisonous
"firewater," the Blackfoot sank into debauchery, drunken brawls and impoverishment. "Chiefs lost control over their followers, inter-tribal disputes arose
as drunken killings resulted in acts of revenge, and people were afraid to meet
each other on the trails."[59]

Unlike so many "forts" in the West which were nothing more than simple
log structures thrown together for temporary occupation, Whoop-Up was a
fort worthy of the name. Well-placed between the rivers, it was constructed
of 6,000 cottonwood logs, with huge palisades and even two ancient muzzle-loading cannon. The entrance was secured by massive outward-swinging
gates beside which was a wicket door for trading.

When Macleod and his men arrived at Whoop-Up on October 9, the
American flag flew above the fort and the main gate stood open. Macleod first
positioned his artillery and his troops and then, with Potts at his side, strode
through the gate and knocked loudly upon the door of the nearest building.
A grey-haired veteran responded and invited Macleod to enter. There were
only half a dozen other men, a few Indian women and several children on
the premises. No 500 armed desperadoes, no underground galleries, and no
liquor, as a thorough search soon established. Well aware of the impending
arrival of the NWMP, the resident whiskey traders had scarpered and taken

their stock in trade with them. Macleod and his troopers greedily accepted an invitation to stay to dinner and sat down to a hearty meal of buffalo, vegetables and canned fruits. Potts then took the NWMP to a second notorious whiskey fort, Slide-Out, which was equally barren of liquor.

Macleod needed to choose a site for his post and it seemed to him that Fort Whoop-Up would serve admirably. Its location was excellent and its fortifications and accommodations were all the NWMP would need. Assuming that the Fort Benton owners would have little further use for their facility, Macleod offered to take it off their hands but must have been shocked when he was quoted a price of $25,000.[60] That number was generally viewed as unrealistic but perhaps it confirmed the rumour current when Whoop-Up had been built five years earlier that the construction costs had run to $25,000. Conrad recommended that Macleod reject the offer.[61] I.G. Baker could build a fortification for the NWMP at a cost much less than $25,000.

Conrad and Potts knew of a choice location on the Oldman River and Macleod agreed when he first viewed it on October 13. I.G. Baker supplied workmen, materials and provisions for the project. With Macleod's troopers in support, construction raced against the weather. Living quarters, hospital, storehouses, kitchens, stables and a blacksmith's shop were built, all facing an enclosed square. It was a large undertaking and the western winter came on early. The troops were barely under roof when the temperatures dropped to -35°C (-30°F) accompanied by a record snowfall. Then, at the beginning of December, the Easterners experienced their first Chinook when the temperature soared overnight from -29°C to 7°C (-20°F to 44°F) and the snow disappeared.

Even before the fort was finished, I.G. Baker had completed and stocked a store nearby to supply the needs of Macleod and his men.[62] Provisioned and supported by I.G. Baker, Macleod and his troops were secure for the winter. Not so with the horses. Hay was in short supply and it was too late in the season to put up a sufficient store. Macleod ordered in 9,000 kg (20,000 lb) of oats but could see no way to maintain his entire herd over the winter. Accordingly, he ordered Inspector James Walsh to take 64 horses, 20 oxen and 10 beef cattle 320 km (200 mi) south to winter at Sun River, in Montana.

It was a busy winter at the western outpost of the NWMP, but Ottawa had neglected to make arrangements to pay the troopers following their arrival out on the western plains. Pay fell seven months in arrears. On one Saturday evening in March 1875, 15 of Macleod's 140 men deserted and three more followed later. Macleod was thunderstruck. He admitted he had been unaware that his troops were so dissatisfied. Ottawa quickly responded to the emergency and arranged to enable the Assistant Commissioner to draw $30,000 on the Bank of Montreal to pay his men and purchase supplies and clothing.[63] Macleod had to travel down to Helena, Montana Territory, to draw the funds, which he did in early April. He deposited half with I.G. Baker and headed back to Fort Macleod with the other $15,000 in cash in his saddle bags. The Assistant Commissioner was guilty of some understatement when he described his four-day ride through the lawless Montana Territory as "a matter of no little risk."[64]

Macleod paid off his men and morale improved remarkably, with some residual griping about how they had been gouged by traders with whom they had been forced to deal on credit. That fact was acknowledged and compensation was granted later. But life in the West outside the NWMP was no bed of roses either. While Macleod was in Helena, four of his deserters came to him and applied to be allowed to return. The Assistant Commissioner consented, understanding how his troops had been provoked by Ottawa's laxness. The penalties were modest considering the gravity of the offence.

Gracing the parade square of Fort Macleod were the two 9-pounder field guns and the two brass mortars, dragged at huge sacrifice all the way from Dufferin to never fire a shot except once or twice during the trek to signal troopers lost on the plains.

WHILE THE NWMP WERE struggling across the western plains, a number of letters and articles appeared in newspapers describing the expedition as a failure, with its horses lost and its men stranded and facing death by starvation and exposure. The discharged Inspector Richer, and others, had done their work well. Newspapers as far away as New York and London reported that the NWMP was plagued by bad management, desertion and death. A Canadian paper claimed that the officers were "incapable" and "inexperienced," the men "careless" and "disheartened," and predicted that "the expedition will fail in the accomplishment of its objective."[65] The criticism reached beyond Commissioner French to the government, accused of incompetent management and direction of the NWMP. The issue reached Parliament in 1875.

Mackenzie's government did deserve some censure for its part in the near-failure of the NWMP expedition and escaped only because the Opposition had too little knowledge of what had actually happened in the West. Something was known about the shoddy construction at Fort Livingstone, and that was raised in the House, but Prime Minister Mackenzie's denial ended the matter.

Ottawa's cavalier, almost capricious, last-minute amendments to the marching orders of the huge NWMP expedition displayed an uncaring obliviousness to the immensity of the western plains. The orders to abandon the initial plan to station half his force near the Belly and Bow Rivers, and instead send those troops on to Edmonton—almost 480 km (300 mi) to the north— added considerably to the challenge facing French. Since the whiskey traders were known to be operating and supplied out of Montana, it was unreasonable of Ottawa to expect that their illegal activities along the border could be policed by men stationed in Edmonton.

Similarly, the decision to abandon Fort Ellice as the headquarters site in favour of the non-existent Fort Livingstone put another 160 km (100 mi) of travel before the second half of French's force. As it turned out, the fact that the Swan River Barracks were not completed in time required French to travel an additional 560 km (350 mi) to winter sanctuary at Winnipeg. Later, in January 1875, he moved another 105 km (65 mi) back to Dufferin. Ottawa seems to have assumed that the horse-mounted troops of the NWMP could be moved about the Great Plains as easily as relocating pins on a map.

Unaware that French was logistically unprepared for the original plan of march, Ottawa imposed last-minute changes upon him when he had no spare capacity to comply. French's planning was inadequate and arrogant. He had almost no intelligence that the nature of the terrain he would be crossing was woefully inadequate. He based almost the entire supply requirement of his men and his horses on the faulty premise that he could operate as a self-sustained unit; much of the men's food supply would come from a herd of cattle travelling with them, and the horses and oxen would subsist by grazing the prairie grasses. No provision whatever was made for transporting water. The decision not to equip the men with canteens could only have been made by one assuming they would be crossing a somewhat idyllic terrain. It went hand in hand with the assumption that the horses would require little or no transported feed.

The Commissioner's first plan was to travel west on the Boundary Commission trail along the border. That was sensible. Then, shortly before taking his force out of Dufferin, he was instructed by Ottawa to use a more northerly route to avoid trouble. French accepted the altered route without any change in his logistical planning. Also, the abandonment of the plan to leave troops in the Fort Whoop-Up neighbourhood, and instead send half to Edmonton and return with the other half, seemed to warrant no increase in his supply requirement.

Without any personal experience, without anyone on his staff who had spent time on the far western plains, and without accepting any input from officers such as Macleod who had at least some understanding of the region, French believed it was possible to cross the prairies as a self-supporting expedition. But the NWMP concept of a travelling commissary in the form of an accompanying cattle herd was almost a total failure. On many days the column was stretched 16 km (10 mi) across the grassland with the cattle far in the rear, making it impractical to bring them up for butchering. It was impossible in camps without wood or water.

The Commissioner neither explained nor apologized for his men not having been provided with canteens or any means of carrying decent water. Instead, he took pride in their ability to make do:

> The Force ever pushed onward, delighted when occasionally a pure spring was met with; there was still no complaint, when salt water or the refuse of a mud-hole was the only liquid available. And I have seen this whole Force obliged to drink liquid, which when passed through a filter was still the color of ink.[66]

French did not mention the heavy incidence of typhoid fever, dysentery and diarrhoea suffered by his men as a result of drinking such contaminated water.[67]

Perhaps French's greatest mistake was his assumption that the eastern horses he had imported could subsist on the western grasslands while carrying men and hauling equipment. They failed utterly to stand up to the ordeal. The horses would have performed better had French been more solicitous of them, scouting out water and grass in advance of making camp and then giving the animals time to rest and graze. One pioneer historian noted that the NWMP

> had little knowledge of the relative food value of the grasses [and] purposely camped in the neighbourhood of sloughs thinking, no doubt, that the pasturage there was better. The buffalo had been very thick over the country and the prairie grass in many places was pretty well eaten up or tramped out, but even in that condition it would have been much more nutritious than the slough or pond grass. French evidently did not think so. He probably did not know that it was only necessary to give the horses time enough to fill themselves with the grass on the ridges to enable them to stand the trip in first class condition.[68]

The Commissioner was an equestrian, but he displayed little knowledge of the care and keeping of horses, at least in western conditions. Exposing the expedition's horses to the alkaline water of Old Wives Lake was a mistake with near-catastrophic consequences. Veterinary Surgeon Poett stated that the water "produced copious diarrhea amongst the horses of every Division in the force." Poett administered "anti-purgatives and other astringent medicines." The NWMP horses left the "rest camp" in worse shape than they had arrived, carrying a condition that caused many of them to die over the winter. In December, Assistant Commissioner Macleod reported that several of the horses left with him had never recovered and "succumbed notwithstanding their being treated with the greatest care."[69] And Inspector Walsh reported that the horses he had taken south to winter at Sun River had been diagnosed as "alkalied" and were expected to die before spring.[70]

French was sensitive to the charge that he had imported horses unsuitable in the West instead of acquiring local animals. His first Annual Report as Commissioner, in January 1875, contained much explanation and defence: "It is an admitted fact that almost all Canadian or American horses fail during the first season they are fed on prairie grass, and therefore it is little to be wondered at that ours should have failed."[71] As to the vaunted superiority of the Red River ponies, "When a Red River pony is thin, he is very useless, he cannot do much work, and he certainly won't try." On the other hand, French claimed, "Canadian horses will work till they drop."[72]

A few years later, in 1882, Frank Oliver, the pioneer publisher of the Edmonton *Bulletin* (and later Minister of the Interior in the government of Sir Wilfrid Laurier), expressed a very different opinion of the western pony, or cayoose (also cayuse):

> Ordinary horses were not of sufficient powers of endurance, and they required some kind of grain feed in order to produce satisfactory results in the way of work, but the cayoose left nothing to be desired. All the outfit he required was a shaganappi harness and a Red River cart for the summer or the simplest kind of sled for the winter ... Thus equipped he proved himself able to draw a load of 800 or 900 pounds [360–410 kg] from Winnipeg to the Rocky Mountains. He was, moreover, so tractable and obedient that only one man was required for the management of every four or five carts. When a river too deep to be forded was encountered the wheels with the cart cover underneath them were improvised into a raft and he swam the stream with this load tied to his tail. In return he asked for nothing. Some neighbouring pond or creek gave him a drink; the tall prairie grass with its pea vine and vetches was his fodder ... He covered his fifty miles [80 km] a day and kept it up for weeks. If the traveller became tired of riding in the buckboard and wished to ride on horseback, he was ready for that

too. His untiring "lope" was the easiest gait for riding in the world and the horse seemed to enjoy it ... [H]is flanks would indeed get thinner before the journey was over, but it was hard treatment indeed that forced him to give up, and even if turned out on the prairie to forage for himself, two or three weeks sufficed to regain his flesh and spirit and get him ready for another trip ... The cayoose has deserved well of the country. His wants were few and his services many and varied. If speed, sure footedness and courage were required he filled the bill as a buffalo hunter; if strength and endurance were required he was the freighter's standby."[73]

In response to the criticism of its management of the NWMP, in 1875 the Mackenzie government sent the commander of the Canadian Militia, Major-General E. Selby Smith, into the West to look into the efficiency and operation of the Force. Smith provided just the sort of opinion the government needed. After his tour of inspection, accompanied part of the way by French, the Major General issued a statement at Fort Carlton:

I am now satisfied, and I never doubted it, that the defamatory letters which have from time to time appeared in the press were written by ill-disposed persons, and did not give a true statement of this Force— probably by deserters, who, having broken their oath of allegiance, did not scruple to write untruths when they found the Police Force was not the holiday pastime they had anticipated.[74]

Smith filed two reports with the government. One was a general account of his findings and recommendations. The second was a confidential report to the Minister of Justice respecting the performance of the Commissioner. It completely exonerated French. Smith, specifically addressing the Commissioner's procurement of the Boundary Commission oats, admitted that "this of course saved his horses from starvation." But, the inspecting general went on to say, "I have reason to know that he had from the first calculated on procuring large quantities of supplies from the Boundary Commission ...[;] he had pre-considered it."[75]

Smith did not identify the source of his knowledge. Since it could only have been French, Smith's report smacks of senior military officers closing rank. Perhaps Smith was feeling some guilt over the fact that Robertson-Ross of his command had so egregiously mis-identified the location of Fort Whoop-Up, and with such serious consequences to French and his expedition.

In his 1875 Annual Report, written before the appointment of Smith, French does not claim that the purchase of the oats was "pre-considered." There he states only, "Hearing that there was a probability of obtaining some oats from the Boundary Commission at Wood Mountain, I despatched the Assistant Commissioner thither with a party to obtain some."[76] If French intended to later secure supplies from the Commission depot at Wood Mountain, as he in fact did, the question arises, why did he take his party 65–80 km (40–50 mi) to the north, away from that source of supply?

French could not have "pre-considered" the acquisition of oats from the Boundary Commission before he took his expedition out of Dufferin. It was only because of the fortuitous circumstance of the double delivery caused by the cautious prudence of the surveyors that the oats became available. That double delivery became known to the boundary surveyors only when their outward-bound parties reached Wood Mountain on June 22. It would not have been a known fact in Dufferin when French completed his logistical procurement between his arrival there on June 19 and his departure on July 8.

Major-General Smith extended himself somewhat in endorsing Commissioner French's chosen route for the expedition:

> In the first place, he had intended to follow the boundary track, and had he been permitted to do so, he would have been in no want of food for his horses or cattle, but, being diverted from that line, by unavoidable circumstances he was forced to make his way further north by the aid of sextant and compass, over the trackless prairie, devoid for days together of wood and water and frequently of any nourishing grass.[77]

Smith did not explain where French would have found the "food for his horses or cattle" on the boundary track. He must have assumed that the pasturage there was adequate, or, perhaps, French would have been better placed to draw on the Boundary Commission supplies. The question remains: If French was "forced to make his way north . . . over the trackless prairie," why did he not increase his provisions to accommodate the necessities of the new route?

What Smith did not touch upon at all was why, on August 4, French ignored the obviously suitable Traders' Road and continued further north into "the trackless prairie." French knew the Traders' Road was there; he took advantage of it to send Macleod to Willow Bunch for pemmican.

There was a good reason why the Dirt Hills and the Cactus Hills were "trackless." They were avoided by knowledgeable prairie travellers. There the Missouri Coteau was every bit as tough as Smith described it, with the added disadvantage of presenting sharply sloped hills that were murder for horses and oxen hauling heavy wagons and field guns.

French did not profit greatly from his consultations with the Boundary Commission officers at Dufferin in the fall of 1873. Much of the knowledge they had acquired during their summer on the plains was harshly learned again by French. The Red River cart, French discovered for himself, was "one of the impositions of the country." Money spent on modern wagons "would be infinitely more advantageously laid out than in perpetuating the construction of a style of vehicle more in accordance with the 1st than the 19th century."[78] Also, French came around to the point of view, already held by the boundary surveyors, that oxen were more suitable than horses for hauling freight. As for the Hudson's Bay Company wall tents French selected, Henri Julien, an illustrator accompanying the NWMP, considered that on the prairie they were "a fraud."

In the way of greenhorns, the members of the NWMP, overlooking their brush with failure, were prideful of their achievement. More experienced residents of the West were unimpressed. At Edmonton, Inspector Jarvis, with a lack of modesty understandable in his case, recounted the story of his journey to the Reverend John McDougall, a missionary who had been on the plains for a dozen years. In fact, McDougall, whose mission was then at Morley, in the valley of the Bow River, had been commissioned by Lieutenant-Governor Morris to prepare the way for the approaching NWMP by explaining their purpose to the various camps of Blackfoot. The Reverend alerted Jarvis to the reality of prairie life:

Nine or ten miles [14.5–16 km] north of Edmonton there dwells, when at home, a French half-breed who, when the spring comes, will load his carts with his winter's trade and catch of furs and pemmican, and with his wife and children, will take the trail you came by, crossing all the streams you crossed. In due time he will reach Fort Garry; then he will sell his furs and robes, and purchase his fresh supply of goods and articles of trade, load these on to his carts, turn his face westward, recross all the streams, now at their highest, reach his home north of Edmonton, put up several stacks of hay, fix up his winter quarters, mend his carts and harness, and having carefully stored his goods, he and his family, with the same horses and carts, will cross the Saskatchewan and travel out from two to three hundred miles [320–480 km] on to the plains ... run buffalo, stand on guard day and night, make many bales of meat, make many bags of pemmican, and finally ... return over the long journey to their home north of Edmonton. And still, it is not yet winter; and thus this native has travelled about three times the distance you and your party did ... and they had no government behind them, and what they have done is a common occurrence in this Western country.[79]

Although McDougall himself was thoroughly acquainted with hardship, he was a little unfair with the chastened Jarvis. The gentle Reverend could not have known the burden that had been placed upon the Inspector by his superior back at Roche Percée and the incredible fortitude displayed by Jarvis and his men in carrying out their orders.

It had not been a well-run affair, but Jarvis and the rest of the North-West Mounted Police had succeeded in their long march into the West. Shortcomings at the command level there had been, but grit and determination among the men had carried them through. Quick learners, they were soon proficient plainsmen and ably carried out their assignment to introduce law and order to the new lands of Canada.

Before taking his force on its great trek, Commissioner French had displayed commendable foresight in inviting the *Canadian Illustrated News* to send an artist to accompany the expedition. Henri Julien received the assignment and made the round trip with French, arriving back in Dufferin on November 24, 1874. Julien's sketches are the entire visual record of the great event. But why an illustrator instead of a photographer? Here the Boundary Commission was again ahead of Commissioner French. Photographers accompanied the surveyors across the West with the result that several hundred excellent photographs recording their work are now held by the National Archives.

The visual record remains, but there is no "Legend of the Boundary Survey." There is, instead, the "Legend of the Long March West" of the North-West Mounted Police. The surveyors came, carried out their duties with efficiency and dispatch, and left. The NWMP marched somewhat ineptly into the West, and stayed. The glory went to those who remained on the plains. And perhaps deservedly so. For those who did stay in the West to overcome the early inadequate planning and carry the bold concept into the triumph of the North-West Mounted Police were truly heroic. Failure was unacceptable to men of the calibre of James Macleod, James Walsh, Sam Steele and many others.

The men of the North-West Mounted Police had barely established themselves on the western plains when their mettle was thoroughly tested by events entirely unseen when they left Eastern Canada.

CHAPTER 15

The Buffalo

C APTAIN W.J. TWINING STARED IN WONDER AT THE GREAT stream of buffalo as it moved over the plain before him. Shuffling slowly southward as if to a common destination, the shaggy beasts stretched from horizon to horizon without visible beginning or end. To count or even estimate their numbers was impossible.

Perhaps no feature of the great West provoked more hyperbole than the buffalo. Campfires and saloons heard countless "one-better-than-that" first-person accounts of herds so huge as to crowd the otherwise limitless prairies, accounts that survive even today. They entertain but provide little in the way of accurate statistics.

Captain Twining was different. No teller of tales, he was a man of science, the chief astronomer of the United States Boundary Survey, and he recorded his observations in his official records. And on that late August day, 1874, those observations were made from an unusual coign of vantage. Twining stood 550 m (1,800 ft) above the plain, on the most westerly butte of the Sweet Grass Hills, giving him a bird's-eye view of the buffalo-filled prairie. And still he could see neither end of the streaming herd.[1]

Had Twining remained on his butte for another three weeks, he would have witnessed the sorry arrival of the tattered North-West Mounted Police expedition, for it was to the western butte of the Sweet Grass Hills that the desperate troopers coaxed the pitiful survivors of their horses, hoping to save enough of them to ensure their own survival. But when the almost-lost patrol straggled in on September 18, the boundary survey crews on both sides of the line were long gone. Their work finished, they were well on their way back east, all their horses and oxen alive and well. The troopers scavenged through the supply depot vacated by the survey crews, and found some sugar and syrup, which "almost started a war" since they "had not seen anything of the sort for weeks."[2]

Like Twining, the NWMP also encountered a multitude of buffalo in the area. Inspector Denny, on patrol along the Bow River, witnessed "thousands of buffalo, swimming the Bow" and, later, more thousands, "on a stampede, going south."[3] On September 23, Commissioner French and Assistant Commissioner Macleod, travelling to Fort Benton, saw "immense quantities of buffalo," a herd they estimated at 70,000–80,000 animals.[4]

Twining's observation post was only a few hundred metres south of the recently surveyed international boundary and he could see well into Canada, where the great herd originated. The buffalo, of course, paid no heed to the earthen monuments erected at 4.8-km (3-mi) intervals by the survey crews to mark the border, and continued on their journey into the United States, just as they had done for centuries. They would return when the mood struck them.

Now that the boundary was surveyed and staked, the age-old movement of the buffalo gave rise to questions of international importance. To which nation did they belong? And, more importantly, who was entitled to hunt them? Did the marking of the border mean that the Plains Indians, accustomed to hunting the herds wherever they went, could no longer follow the buffalo across that "Medicine Line"?

Twining's snapshot of uncountable buffalo, and the NWMP observations of many thousands, are consistent with the healthy state of the herds in the northern plains as late as 1874. But although still numerous in 1874, the herds were nothing like they had been five years earlier. In July 1869, Isaac Cowie of the Hudson's Bay Company encountered a huge mass of buffalo at the north end of Last Mountain Lake:

> we fell in with buffalo innumerable. They blackened the whole country, the compact moving masses covering it so that not a glimpse of green grass could be seen. Our route took us into the midst of the herd, which opened in front and closed behind the train of carts like water round a ship, but always leaving an open space about the width of the range of an Indian gun in front, rear and flanks. The earth trembled day and night, as they moved in billow-like battalions over the undulations of the plain. Every drop of water on our way was foul and yellow with their wallowings and excretions. So we travelled among the multitude for several days, save when we shot a fat cow for food, or a bull made a charge and perhaps upset a cart before he was shot

down, neither molesting nor molested. . . . we reached the scattered
fringe of the mass through which we had journeyed, marvelling at its
myriads and their passive indifference to us.[5]

By 1879, just five years after the arrival of the NWMP in 1874, the supply of
animals was failing and by the end of the decade had almost completely disappeared in Canada. The tens of millions of buffalo that once roamed the plains
had shrunk to the point of imminent extinction, while at about the same time
the passenger pigeon that once darkened the sky with flocks estimated in the
billions disappeared.

HOW MANY TENS OF millions of buffalo actually did roam is still a matter
of debate. Usually thought of as solely a creature of the Great Plains, where
they certainly did thrive, the buffalo once ranged North America almost as far
east as the Atlantic seaboard, west to the Rocky Mountains, and from Mexico north to the shores of Great Slave Lake.[6] Not really a buffalo, but a bison
(*bison bison*), it was particularly suited to the short grass prairie of the Great
Plains, where it achieved a legendary population. The buffalo is the largest of
the North American animals, with bulls 152–182 cm (5–6 ft) at the shoulders,
275–305 cm (9–10 ft) in length, weighing 725 kg (1,600 lb) and occasionally
reaching 900 kg (2,000 lb). Cows are somewhat smaller and average 315–545
kg (700–1,200 lb). Belying their appearance, buffalo are fast on their feet,
reaching speeds over 65 km (40 mi) per hour and maintaining that rate for
long distances.[7] Only the fleetest of horses could serve as buffalo runners, and
if a rider had not caught up to his prey in 450–550 m (500–600 yards) he was
wise to break off the chase.[8]

The naturalist Ernest Thompson Seton, writing in 1929, calculated that
the buffalo achieved a population of 75 million before its range was reduced
by European settlement, their numbers then decreasing to about 40 million
by 1800.[9] An unusual Canadian historian, Frank Roe, in a work that is still
the most comprehensive on the subject, drew extensively on contemporary
accounts and concluded that Seton had been too conservative.[10]

More recent studies have examined the carrying capacity of the Great
Plains and established that it could have supported a population of about 30
million animals, with admitted fluctuations according to variations in rainfall and resultant grazing conditions.[11] One such calculation estimates that
one buffalo required 4 ha (10 acres) of tallgrass prairie and 18 ha (45 acres) of
shortgrass prairie, or an average of 10 ha (25 acres) per animal across the Great
Plains. Again, this approach results in an estimated population of 30 million.[12]

Still, 30 million was a lot of buffalo, and Chief Spotted Eagle, in Canada in 1879, can be forgiven for dismissing warnings of pending doom with the statement, "I can and do not believe that the buffalo will ever disappear." He was only expressing the belief generally held by the Plains Indians that the buffalo were limitless and would exist forever. Mythology held that the herds were annually replenished by great wellsprings variously situated in caves, great holes in the earth, or beneath lakes from which each spring issued torrents of animals that then spread over the plains. Depending on the tribes, these magic sources were

Spotted Eagle, Sioux Chief, 1880. *Glenbow Museum NA-207-15*

believed to be caves on the Staked Plains of Texas, or, in Canada, a lake far southwest of Battleford, or great springs near Jackfish Lake.[13] Occasionally, also, the buffalo returned to their sources, swallowed up by the earth. This explained the times of want when animals were scarce. But always the herds would return. Chief Plenty-coups of the Crow witnessed the happening in a vision:

> I saw a Buffalo bull . . . I got up and started to go to the Bull, because I knew he was the Person who wanted me . . . Then he shook his red rattle and sang a queer song four times. "Look!" he pointed.

> Out of the hole in the ground came the buffalo, bulls and cows and calves without number. They spread wide and blackened the plains. Everywhere I looked great herds of buffalo were going in every direction, and still others without number were pouring out of the hole in the ground to travel on the wide plains.[14]

Even as clear evidence mounted of a shrinking supply, the Indians of the Plains clung to the belief of their ancestors that they could depend upon the Great Spirit to cause the buffalo to come again. It was not an unreasonable belief. Even today it seems inconceivable that such huge numbers of animals could be almost totally annihilated in only a few years.

Watercolour painting by Peter Rindisbacher (1806–34), c. 1822: "Indian Hunters Pursuing the Buffalo Early in the Spring when the Snow is Sufficiently Frozen to Bear the Men but the Animal Breaks Through and Cannot Run." *Library and Archives Canada / David Ives Bushnell Collection of Canadiana C-114467*

From the Rio Grande to the Saskatchewan, and from the Mississippi to the Rockies, the buffalo was one of the primary food sources for a number of tribes who lived either on the Great Plains, or on its margins. The Cheyenne, Omaha, Pawnee, Assiniboine, Sioux, Crow, Blackfoot, Gros Ventre, Plains Cree and others preyed upon those herds that came into their territories. Until the arrival (more accurately, the return) of the horse to the Great Plains in the 1700s,[15] the tribes were afoot, with no beast of burden other than their dogs, and had not yet become fully dependent upon the buffalo.[16] Yet, as pedestrian hunters they brought their ingenuity to bear and developed several methods of taking the fleet buffalo that were quite successful. In spite of their elementary appearance, these hunts demanded great skill and discipline.

The "Surround" required a herd of manageable size, quietly grazing or, better yet, lying down. By stealth, the hunters would encircle the buffalo at sufficient distance to avoid detection, then slowly tighten the ring. When the herd became alerted to danger, usually by the animals' keen sense of smell, and began to move off it would find the way blocked. Continually frightened back to the centre, the buffalo would mill about in confusion, enabling the attackers to reach the killing range of their bows and spears. As many as possible would be taken before the terrified animals succeeded in breaking through and escaping.

Evidence of the slaughter: buffalo bones near Lloydminster, from Chief Poundmaker's last great corral, c. 1874. *Library and Archives Canada / Ernest Brown Collection C-004817*

The "Pound" and the "Jump" were variations of the same theme, driving the buffalo into an enclosure where they were slaughtered, or over a cliff of sufficient height that the fall would kill or cripple them. Both methods required careful site selection, preliminary construction, detailed planning, and rigid discipline among the many participants.

Lengthy drive-lines, marked at intervals of decreasing distance by rock or brush-pile "deadmen," were laid out in a huge "V" focusing on the pound or jump. These drive-lines might extend as far as 16 km (10 mi) across the plains, usually into a prime grazing area. The deadmen would themselves serve to deter the buffalo from swerving from their desired course but many would conceal tribal members whose duty was to frighten wayward animals back on track. These were communal hunts and all members of the band were pressed into service—men, women, and children of sufficient age to accept discipline.

It was usually necessary to entice herds from some distance into the reach of the drive-lines. This was accomplished by appealing to the buffalo's curiosity. The most experienced hunters, disguised in animal skins, moved out in front of the herd, first attracting its attention, then enticing it forward by imitating the bleating of a calf in distress. As the chosen herd approached the drive-lines, other hunters would move into position behind to cut off retreat.

When the buffalo were judged to be close enough to the pound or jump, they would be panicked by hunters behind and along the drive-lines, driving them forward in a terrified rush that carried them into the pound or over the jump, the animals in the rear forcing those in front into the enclosure or over the cliff.

If the cliff was high enough, most of the buffalo would be killed in the fall and only a few crippled survivors would need to be dispatched. At the pound, however, all the animals were fully alive, full of terror, and would need to be killed as quickly as possible lest they break free. The ensuing slaughter was grisly indeed. Professor H.Y. Hind of Toronto, on his expedition of exploration to the West, witnessed the conclusion of a successful pound hunt in late July 1858, near the elbow of the South Saskatchewan River. His account, although a bit more judgmental than one would expect from a man of science, does provide a graphic description of the event:

> A dreadful scene of confusion and slaughter then begins; the oldest and strongest animals crush and toss the weaker; the shouts and screams of the excited Indians rise above the roaring of the bulls, the bellowing of the cows, and the piteous moaning of the calves. The dying struggles of so many huge and powerful animals crowded together create a revolting and terrible scene, dreadful from the excess of its cruelty and waste of life, but with occasional displays of wonderful brute strength and rage; while man in his savage, untutored, and heathen state shows both in deed and expression how little he is superior to the noble beast he so wantonly and cruelly destroys.[17]

Some 240 buffalo had been successfully trapped and killed, and Professor Hind described the scene a week later when the butchering of the chosen animals was completed and the pound still contained some 200 carcasses, surplus to the Indians' wants:

> From old bulls to calves of three months old, animals of every age were huddled together in all the forced attitudes of violent death. Some lay on their backs, with eyes starting from their heads and tongue thrust out through clotted gore. Others were impaled on the horns of the old and strong bulls. Others again, which had been tossed, were lying with broken backs, two and three deep. One little calf hung suspended on the horns of a bull which had impaled it in the wild race round and round the pound. The Indians looked upon the dreadful and sickening scene with evident delight, and told how such and such a bull or cow had exhibited feats of wonderful strength in the death-struggle. The flesh of many of the cows had been taken from them, and was drying in the sun on stages near the tents. It is needless to say that the odor was overpowering, and millions of large

blue flesh-flies, humming and buzzing over the putrefying bodies, was not the least disgusting part of the spectacle.[18]

Perhaps Professor Hind might have been similarly repulsed by a visit to the killing floor of an 1858 Toronto slaughterhouse.

There were hundreds of jump sites on the northern plains and perhaps almost as many pound sites, but the pound enclosures, mostly crude wooden corrals bolstered with earth, have rotted and eroded out of existence. Jump sites were, of course, permanent installations and over time those with the best natural features were developed into killing fields that were marvels of cunning complexity. The best preserved and most elaborate jump site in North America is Head-Smashed-In, below a rimrock in the Porcupine Hills, near Fort Macleod, in southern Alberta. Here archeologists have identified buffalo kills made as early as 6,000 years ago and "an intricate labyrinth of more than thirty intersecting drive lines, containing an estimated 12,000 to 30,000 cairns."[19] Head-Smashed-In, a UNESCO World Heritage site, now has an interpretive centre, itself an architectural marvel that rises from the jump floor to the top of the cliff.

Ulm Piskun, near Great Falls, Montana, bills itself as perhaps the world's largest jump site and also has an interpretive centre. The Gull Lake site in southern Saskatchewan, the largest in the province and used over 1,600 years, has been carefully studied but remains undeveloped.

After a successful hunt, the processing of the animals began. The tribe might be camped at the jump or pound site for many days as the buffalo were skinned and dismembered, the meat cut into strips and hung for drying or smoked over a fire, and the hides tanned. The recipe for pemmican was discovered about 2,000 years ago, enabling surplus meat to be preserved for future use or trade.[20] In a much later century the demand for this high-energy portable food would contribute to the near-extinction of its source, the buffalo.

THE BUFFALO PROVIDED NOT only what today would be the big-ticket items of food, shelter and clothing, but also bedding, tools, household utilities, rope, sinew for stringing bows and snowshoes, packing containers for travelling, and much more. The comprehensive list of the uses made of the various parts of the buffalo is a testament to human ingenuity.

The tanning of buffalo hides, whether with the hair removed for tipi covers and clothing, or with the hair retained for bedding or trade, was a laborious process assigned to the women. Summer hides that were lighter and carried less hair were used for tipi covers, and cow hides were preferred as they were thinner and of more even thickness. Hides taken at the beginning of winter, November and into December, before the heavy coating of hair had been damaged, were tanned for robes. The work required to prepare hides for tipi covers was considerable:

> Every hide had to be staked out, cleaned and fleshed, then dried for several days, turned over and the hair scraped off. Then it was turned again flesh side up and the heavy, thick skin on the shoulders and hump had to be scraped and flaked until the entire hide was of uniform thickness—all strenuous, back-breaking work. Next it was soaked in water for a couple of days and when thoroughly softened, was treated with a preparation of brains and liver, thoroughly worked into it. Rolled up and laid aside for several days, it then had to be dried by stretching, pulling and sawing over a sharp-sided stake, or through a heavy rawhide rope loop, until soft and velvety. The main ingredient in Indian tanning was elbow grease and lots of it . . . the sign for work in the sign language of the Plains refers to the scraping of a hide![21]

The finished tipi cover was pure white and of very light weight for its size, perhaps as little as 45 kg (100 lb) for a 5.5-m (18-ft) cover.[22] When new, it was buttoned up tight and a smudge fire built inside so that the smoke would permeate the hides. This added to the waterproofing and ensured that the cover would remain soft and pliable after a soaking. The smoking turned the finished product a beautiful cream colour.[23]

Since at least 8–10 tanned buffalo hides were required to construct a small tipi of about 3.5 m (12 ft) in diameter, the Plains Indians were restricted to very small tipis so long as they were dependent upon dogs for transport. With the arrival of the horse, tipis, or lodges, grew larger, the average being 4.25–4.85 m (14–16 ft) across and utilizing 12–14 hides. Wealthy families with many horses would often reside in large tipis of from 22 to 25 hides.[24] Crowfoot, the great Blackfoot chief, had a 30-hide tipi, so large and heavy that it was constructed in two sections, each being a full load for a horse-drawn travois when moving.[25]

Council lodges for special occasions were sometimes very large tipis or, frequently, were constructed by joining several tipis together. The result could be very commodious. When Lewis and Clark encountered the Sioux on the Missouri in September 1804, they met in a council lodge with some 70 chiefs and elders of the tribe.[26] On October 24, 1879, Abbot Martin Marty, visiting the American Sioux in Canada, addressed a gathering of 200 in Spotted Eagle's council tent.

Estimates of the usual number of inhabitants occupying a tipi vary widely. Since it was customary to assess the population of a camp by counting only the tipis, or lodges, it is still today difficult to know with any degree of certainty what the true population was. Lewis and Clark provide the first description by an American of the plains tipi, and one of the highest estimates of occupation. They found the Sioux camp "was handsum made of Buffalow Skins Painted different Colour, all compact & handSomly arranged, their Camps formed of a Conic form Containing about 12 or 15 persons each and 40 in number."[27]

The tipi was a marvel of function and design. Light, easily transported, quick to assemble (or disassemble in an emergency), it was a secure, comfortable and well-ventilated dwelling for family groups averaging six to eight persons, or more. It was warm in winter, cool in summer and able, by reason of its conical shape, to withstand the powerful winds of the plains. To properly accommodate the smoke-hole, the tipi was constructed as a cone tilted slightly to the back so that the hole extended down the front from the apex. Adjustable external flaps, or ears, drew the smoke away or could close the hole entirely in inclement weather.[28]

When furnished with robes, backrests and usually a skirt lining around the cover bottom, the tipi interior was spacious and comfortable.[29] Often brightly decorated, the tipi was a thing of beauty standing proudly on the prairie. Tipi rings, circles of rocks that had once been placed to hold down a tipi cover, can still be found at many locations on the plains.

The origin of the tipi is lost in time. Coronado, the Spanish explorer, found them in use among the Apaches of the southern plains in 1540–42.[30] These were transported by dogs, and another early Spanish explorer reported seeing "five hundred dogs in one train, following one another."[31]

After the arrival of the horse, the tipi came into general use by all the buffalo-hunting tribes and by 1840 was found all over the Great Plains, including Canada.[32] The poles supporting the tipi cover, usually 6–7.5 m (20–25 ft) in length, became the travois poles during transportation. Differing styles and methods of construction suggest the portable dwellings originated, or at least developed, along separate paths.

The tipi of the plains is to be distinguished from the wigwam utilized by the inhabitants of the eastern and northern woodlands. "Wigwam is a word from a tribe far to the East, in Massachusetts, and refers to the dome-shaped round or oval shelter, thatched with bark or reed mats, used by the people of the Woodland area."[33] The wigwam was far less portable than the tipi, but the woodland dwellers were much less nomadic than the Plains Indians.

THE ARRIVAL, OR, MORE correctly, the return of the horse transformed life on the Great Plains. Not only the tipi dwelling, but also hunting and warfare changed suddenly and forever as a new, exciting and prosperous, but short-lived, culture evolved based upon a swiftly adopted equestrian lifestyle.

The Spanish Conquistadores who plundered the Americas in the 1600s were well named. Conquerors they were, and their cruel treatment of the Native inhabitants they subjugated made the French and English who invaded North America look benign in comparison. In 1680 the Pueblo Indians of what is now New Mexico rebelled against more than 80 years of Spanish oppression, killing several hundred settlers and forcing more than 2,000 to flee, leaving behind their livestock, including many horses. By the time the Spaniards reconquered the region at the end of the century the Pueblos had a well-established inter-tribal trade in horses.[34] Fifty years later, by 1750, the horse had reached the northern plains and the buffalo hunters were afoot no longer.

The Plains Indians adapted to the horse with astonishing alacrity, putting aside their initial fear and ignorance and becoming world-class equestrians:

> Rapidly the Indian became an expert horseman, and while he did not handle his horse with the brusque impetuosity of the Spaniard, proba-bly since he commonly had no saddle, nevertheless, in certain respects he was more clever. His ingeniousness may be explained by two prin-cipal factors: first, a saddle was lacking; and second, the hands were seldom used to guide a trained horse. The fighting native needed both hands to shoot his bow and arrow, and as a result he became a marvel-ous rider. Actions such as dropping on the far side of a galloping horse and shooting under the neck at the enemy, mounting and dismount-ing at a dead run, and picking up a fallen comrade without stopping the horse were all common feats. When it is considered that the Indi-ans accomplished these feats without any saddle to support them and without holding the reins, guiding the horse entirely with the knees, the extraordinary skill of the Indian riders can be appreciated.[35]

A Commissioner of the NWMP despaired of his troops ever achieving a level of equestrian ability that might match that of the Plains Indians:

> to make our men effective to fight on horseback against such enemies as we might meet in the North-West, they will have to be engaged as children and made to ride every day until they grow up.[36]

The Great Plains had never seen much equilibrium among the inhabiting tribes who continually jostled and jousted for territory, but such equilibrium as then existed was severely disrupted by the arrival of the horse. The first to possess this new technological advance did not hesitate to put it to full advantage. Thus, for a time the northwestern plains were dominated by the horse-mounted Crow and Shoshone who drove the pedestrian Blackfoot and Gros Ventre bands all the way to the North Saskatchewan River.[37]

Obviously, acquisition of the horse became supremely important and thus was born the honourable sport of horse theft. At first, this was necessary business, vital to the security of the tribe. Thus, the Blackfoot raided the Crow for horses, the Assiniboine stole from the Blackfoot, and the Sioux in turn took them from the Assiniboine.[38]

After the horse population on the plains increased to the point that most tribes had a surplus, horse theft continued as a means of achieving honour and stature, a feature that dismayed and infuriated Europeans with their more developed sense of property and ownership. And, in truth, the loss of a horse out on the plains might be a matter of life or death. But, as one writer put it, to the Indian the successful theft of a horse was roughly equivalent to stealing home base.

The early gains achieved by the Crow and Shoshone were soon erased by the arrival on the plains of another technological advance, this time from the north and east. The firearm, the ubiquitous trade musket, traded its way into the hands of the Plains Indians. The Cree and Assiniboine middlemen, dealing with both the Hudson's Bay Company and the North West Company, brought the smooth-bore muzzleloader to the Blackfoot. By then also equipped with horses, the Blackfoot and their allies soon recovered the territory that had been lost to the Crow and Shoshone.[39]

The horse freed the plains tribes from sedentary or village life of any permanence and enabled them to follow the buffalo out onto the open prairie. They were encouraged in this by the smallpox pandemic of 1780–81. The mortality in the horticultural villages along the Missouri River occupied by the Arikara, the Mandan and the Hidatsa was extreme; the nomads on the plains suffered far less severely. Until the epidemic, the Cheyenne and many of the Sioux lived in villages; these were now abandoned and the survivors took to the open country. On the southern plains the Comanche did the same. The Omaha followed after another outbreak of smallpox in 1801–02 reduced their numbers to just a few hundred.[40]

Buffalo being driven off a "jump" by mounted Indians (no date). *Saskatchewan Archives Board R-B3382 (Original painting in the possession of Library and Archives Canada)*

By 1800 the Indians of the Great Plains were equipped with both horse and gun and enjoyed almost sole possession of the vast western rangeland stocked with millions of buffalo. They were entering upon their wealthiest and most idyllic period—the apogee of their horse/buffalo culture. Sadly, it would last little more than two generations and then be rudely wrenched from them by forces they could neither control nor understand.

Securing all their needs from the vast herds of buffalo, the Plains Indians enjoyed an enviable freedom and apparent independence but in truth had rendered themselves cruelly vulnerable. All skills unrelated to the buffalo, such as fishing and trapping, were abandoned and then lost.[41] Totally reliant upon a single food source, they were not unlike the Irish peasantry, who in the same period lived solely upon the potato and starved miserably when their single crop failed.

The missionary John McDougall, who lived among the Blackfoot, saw their vulnerability:

> These men were thoroughly buffalo Indians. Without the buffalo they would be helpless, and yet the whole nation did not own one. To look at them and to hear them, one would feel as if they were the most independent of all men; yet the fact was they were the most dependent among men ... In short, they lived and had their physical being in the buffalo.[42]

The horse transformed the buffalo hunt on the plains, not so much so the gun. Quickly mastering the equestrian arts, the Plains Indians found they could take buffalo almost at will. The surround was still used, but with horses was far more efficient. Hard-riding hunters more easily turned the animals back in upon themselves, shooting as they did so.[43] The pound fell into disuse, and the jump less so. There, too, horses were more effective in herding the panicked buffalo in the desired direction.

Now with fast horses the hunters could run the buffalo, riding alongside and most often shooting the animal of choice, the cow. And such a chase was far more exhilarating and provided more opportunity for individual prowess. Unlike the communal hunts of the past, the women and children were now excluded and relegated to the processing of the kill.[44]

The Plains Indians never achieved the proficiency with the muzzle-loading musket that the Red River Métis enjoyed, and stayed with their first choice, the bow and arrow, until they acquired the breech-loading repeating rifle after the American Civil War. With a bow each hunter could easily kill two or three buffalo in one run. A total kill of 200 or 300 in a day was not uncommon.[45]

Contemporary observers estimated that each Plains Indian, man, woman and child, consumed each year about six or seven buffalo for food, clothing and shelter. More would be taken for inter-tribal trading. In 1859, a prominent Missouri trader calculated that, for subsistence and trade, the buffalo-hunting tribes took a total of 450,000 animals each year. Even such a huge number was likely still within the annual increase of the total plains herd and caused no overall shrinkage, even though a disproportionate number of cows were taken.[46]

But not for long were the Plains Indians the only consumers of the North American buffalo. Well before 1859 other interests were competing for the resource. As the fur trade extended its reach, the demand for pemmican increased year by year. The opening of the Upper Missouri River to steamboat transportation created a strong market for buffalo robes. "Sport hunting" was a misnomer for an activity that killed as many animals as possible for the sheer pleasure of the killing. The last demand, and the one that spelled the end of the great herds, was the discovery about 1870 that the buffalo hide had a unique value as industrial belting.

Man was not the only cause of mortality among the buffalo. Life on the vast western plains was a hazardous affair, even for a buffalo. The great herds were continually harassed by wolves that attacked the calves, the weak, and the aged. As many as 1.5 million wolves[47] prowled the plains, a population that provided a lucrative income for a class of men known as "wolfers," whose method was to leave a poisoned buffalo carcass on the prairie and return to collect the victims. The now extinct but once common plains grizzly bear was also a buffalo predator. A fearsome creature weighing as much as 450 kg (1,000 lb), the grizzly preferred to scavenge upon the already-dead carcasses, but was quite capable of killing aged and young animals. Fire was also a common danger on the plains, particularly in the late fall before the snows came, and again in the early spring. Occasionally even the fleet buffalo were overtaken by a raging prairie fire and reduced to charred corpses scattered over the blackened landscape.

A sudden winter thaw followed by a sharp frost creates a crust over the snow that can be difficult for even a buffalo to paw through to reach the grass beneath. In 1841 such an event in Wyoming caused tremendous mortality: "By spring there were millions of fresh bison bones in Wyoming, but no living bison."[48]

The buffalo's trait of travelling in herds frequently brought them quick death when crossing rivers. In March 1879, a herd of 2,500 was lost when traversing the ice on the Missouri near Cow Island. Their combined weight was too much for the weakened ice which gave way beneath them; the animals sank into the swift current and were dragged under. In less than a minute not one buffalo remained.[49] This was such a common event that nearly every spring carcasses would be seen along the Missouri shorelines.[50] John McDonnell of the North West Company travelling on the Qu'Appelle River counted in one day (May 16, 1795) 7,360 drowned buffalo.[51]

But drowned buffalo were a total loss only if the carcass could not be recovered. Submerged animals that had reached the point of putrefaction were often preferred. An early trader on the Missouri River recorded that buffalo were frequently driven onto weakened ice where they would fall through and drown, then be recovered after a suitable period:

> When the skin is raised you will see the flesh of a greenish hue, and ready to come alive at the least exposure to the sun; and is so ripe, so tender, that very little boiling is required.

Soup made from such a carcass was "bottle-green and reckoned delicious."[52]

The mass production of pemmican, mostly by Métis hunters, consumed a huge number of buffalo. The cow was preferred for meat as well as for hides and robes, and it was estimated that the flesh from one and one-half cows was required to produce one 40–45 kg (90–100 lb) bag of pemmican. The standard weight was 40 kg (90 lb), since that was the assigned weight of one "piece" of cargo carried by the *voyageurs* over portages, but some pemmican makers preferred the larger unit.

Pemmican manufacture and packaging was a labour-intensive process. The downed animal was skinned and the meat cut into strips and hung on wooden racks to dry in the sun. Then, placed on a clean hide, it was pounded or flailed until it crumbled. Norbert Welsh, a Métis hunter and trader on the Canadian plains, gave his recipe:

> I should explain how the pemmican was prepared. I took a big Hudson's Bay copper kettle that held about ten gallons. I mixed that full of tallow and fat. I melted it over a fire. I let it boil. Then onto a buffalo hide I spread the cut-up dried buffalo meat which had been pounded into shreds or flakes with a flail. Next I took a small kettle, and out of the large kettle of boiling fat I dipped and poured the boiling fat over the buffalo meat, and mixed it properly, using a shovel. It took two people to make pemmican, one to pour, one to mix.

Welsh also gives us a description of the packaging process:

> We took a buffalo hide and stretched it out properly, then ripped it in the centre to make four pieces out of it. Then we took one piece and doubled it evenly. We cut this piece a little round at the corners, and sewed the two bottom corners with sinew. The top was left open. Then we packed the bag half full of pemmican, pounding it down with a wooden mallet, adding more pemmican, and pounding that down until the bag was full. I could guess fairly well when there were a hundred pounds [45 kg] in the bag. When the bag was full, we lapped it over at the top and cut the corners round. Then we took a needle full of sinew and sewed it up. The bag was now thrown on the ground, flattened with a mallet and made into a nice shape, not too fat, not too thin. If you want to eat something that will stay with you, eat pemmican. A pemmican bag held about a hundred pounds [45 kg], and was three feet [1 m] long, and solid when packed.[53]

A Fort Garry resident, writing in 1879, provides a somewhat cynical appraisal of the edibility of pemmican:

> Take the scrapings from the driest outside corner of a very stale piece of cold roast-beef, add to it lumps of tallowy, rancid fat, then garnish all

with long human hairs, on which string pieces, like beads upon a neck-lace, and short hairs of dogs or oxen, or both, and you have a fair imita-tion of common pemmican. Indeed, the presence of hairs in the food has suggested the inquiry whether the hair on the buffaloes from which the pemmican is made does not grow on the inside of the skin. The abundance of small stones or pebbles in pemmican also indicates the discovery of a new buffalo diet heretofore unknown to naturalists. . . .

Carefully made pemmican, flavored with berries and sugar, is nearly good; but of most persons new to the diet it may be said that, in two senses, a little of it goes a long way . . .

The flavor of pemmican depends much on the fancy of the person eat-ing it. There is no other article of food that bears the slightest resem-blance to it, and as a consequence it is difficult to define its peculiar flavor by comparison. It may be prepared for the table in many dif-ferent ways, the consumer being at full liberty to decide which is the least objectionable. The method largely in vogue among the *voyageurs* is that known as "pemmican straight," that is, uncooked. But there are several ways of cooking which improve its flavor to the civilized pal-ate. There is *rubeiboo*, which is a composition of potatoes, onions, or other esculents, and pemmican, boiled up together, and, when prop-erly seasoned, very palatable. In the form of *richot*, however, pemmi-can is best liked by persons who use it, and by the *voyageurs*. Mixed with a little flour and fried in a pan, pemmican in this form can be eaten, provided the appetite be sharp, and there is nothing else to be had. This last consideration is, however, of importance.[54]

The voracious demand made on the buffalo stock to satisfy the pemmi-can needs of the fur trade in Canada was more than equalled by the demand from the American traders for buffalo robes. It was not that the Hudson's Bay Company had no desire for robes, just that it was uneconomical to transport them out the river system to Hudson Bay. Compared to beaver or other pel-tries, the buffalo robe was both bulky and heavy, unsuitable cargo for canoes or even York boats. The steamboats that conquered the Upper Missouri River in the early 1800s easily accommodated the traffic, and buffalo hides tanned with the hair retained began to move to meet the Eastern demand. Robes also moved overland from Red River as the cart trail from Fort Garry to St. Paul developed. Buffalo robes were used for bed covers and became standard equipment to protect the passengers on horse-drawn winter sleighs, the customary method of travel in the 1800s and later. The buffalo overcoat, a much-desired item of winter wear, was regular issue to the United States Army and later to many Canadian police forces, including the RCMP, until the middle of the 1900s.

Buffalo shed their heavy coats in the spring and they assist the process by rubbing against anything handy. With few trees on the prairie, erratics, large free-standing rocks left by the glaciers, became favourite rubbing sites and many were worn smooth by the attention of thousands of buffalo over the years. When telegraph poles were first placed across the plains, the buffalo were delighted, but the poles tended to give way when leaned into by 680-kg (1,500-lb) animals. The telegraph companies, not amused at losing miles of line, countered by installing bradawls, sharp pointed spikes intended to discourage buffalo rubbing. It was a mistake, as reported in a Kansas newspaper:

> For the first time they came to scratch sure of a sensation in their thick hides that thrilled them from horn to tail. They would go fifteen miles [25 km] to find a bradawl. They fought huge battles around the poles containing them, and the victor would proudly climb the mountainous heap of rump and hump of the fallen and scratch himself into bliss until the bradawl broke, or the pole came down. There has been no demand for bradawls from the Kansas region since the first invoice.[55]

The best buffalo robes were those taken in November and December when the heavy winter coat had fully developed but had not yet become damaged or worn.

The tanning of buffalo robes was only slightly less laborious than preparing hides for tipi covers and again was women's work. Ten robes in a year, in addition to her other duties, was about the limit of one woman's output. Polygamy had always existed among the plains tribes, but became more pronounced as, to process robes, successful hunters took additional wives, often as many as six or seven.[56]

THE ROBE TRADE CAUSED the Plains Indians to convert from subsistence hunting of buffalo to commercial hunting. The naturally resulting impact on the herds became significant, particularly after 1830 when "the bison's skin became the most marketable natural resource in the plains."[57] The numbers of buffalo robes that travelled down the Missouri River increased to 110,000 annually by 1847.[58]

The Red River Métis recognized the opportunity presented by the robe trade and improved their lifestyle immeasurably. After the Sayer Decision in 1849 (see p. 120), the traffic in robes and furs moving overland to St. Paul grew quickly. By 1865 1,400 cartloads with a value of $300,000 travelled to St. Paul, where a prime buffalo robe brought a price of $12. The price out on the plains was only $2.50 to $3. Many Métis robe traders achieved incomes of $1,000, or more[59]; $1,000 was the annual salary of a sub-inspector in the NWMP in 1874.

In 1869, the Union Pacific Railroad that had been pushing west from Omaha, Nebraska, since 1865, joined the Central Pacific at Promontory, Utah, and opened for cross-country traffic. The line and its construction effectively sliced the great American buffalo herd in two. Seriously reduced in total population, the now two herds still numbered in the millions. The southern herd was estimated to contain at least 3 million animals[60] or perhaps as many as 15 million.[61] The northern herd ranged over a larger territory but was thought to be somewhat smaller.

Other railroads entered the West; the Kansas Pacific reached Denver in 1870 and the Atchison, Topeka and Santa Fe reached Dodge City, Kansas, in 1872. The buffalo range became easily accessible and economical transportation was now available to facilitate the slaughter of the southern herd. Railroad construction on the northern plains remained a few years behind. The Northern Pacific was stopped at Bismarck, in Dakota Territory, in 1873, by a financial panic. The resultant depression prevented further construction until 1879. In 1867 General William Tecumseh Sherman spoke of the future to a peace council with the Indian tribes in Nebraska Territory:

> We build iron roads, and you cannot stop the locomotive any more than you can stop the sun or moon, and you must submit and do the best you can . . . If our people in the east make up their minds to fight you they will come out as thick as a herd of buffalo, and if you continue fighting you will all be killed. We advise you for the best. We now offer you this, choose your own homes, and live like white men, and we will help you all you want.[62]

It was a bitter prophecy, but becoming more true every year.

Sherman might also have told his Indian listeners that his people had other uses in mind for their buffalo range. In 1868, 800 Texas cattle were trailed into Nebraska. By 1870 the cattle herd was up to seven thousand, with a smaller number of sheep. The buffalo were being displaced.[63]

North-West Mounted Police hunting buffalo in 1874. *Library and Archives Canada / Royal Canadian Mounted Police fonds PA-201325*

In 1870 a tanning process was developed that produced out of buffalo hides leather uniquely suited to industrial belting for which the industrial revolution under way in Eastern United States provided a huge demand.[64] Now there was a market, and a steady one, for buffalo hides without concern for the quality of the hair. Until 1870 the commercial market had been restricted to robes, and because of the laborious tanning process these were supplied almost exclusively by Native hunters, the Plains Indians and the Métis. For belting, the hides could be taken in any season, dried and shipped east for tanning. The opportunity attracted hundreds of hide hunters.

The American firearm industry was up to the challenge. By the end of the Civil War the Springfield Arms Company was producing a breech-loading .50-calibre rifle that was quite an adequate buffalo gun. In 1872 the Sharp Rifle Manufacturing Company came up with a .50-calibre rifle that fired 450 grain lead bullets propelled by 90 grains of powder. With the Sharps Big 50 hunters could kill buffalo at distances of 450 m (500 yards) or more and a new method of hunting, the "still hunt," came into general use.[65]

Small teams of buffalo hunters flooded onto the southern plains. One marksman, two skinners and a cook were considered the most efficient operation, unless the marksman was particularly good, in which case more skinners might be required.[66] In the morning, approaching stealthily and on foot, the shooter would position himself downwind as close as he dared to an unsuspecting herd. Using a "dead rest" for the heavy rifle and a telescopic sight, he would first shoot the herd leader, usually the oldest cow, and then continue, picking the animals that looked most ready to flee. As the herd milled about in confusion, unable to identify what was happening, the shots would continue at a rate of about one per minute. An experienced shooter would often keep the animals within range for an hour or more and kill up to 50 buffalo. Claims were made of having killed as many as 91 and 120 in not more than one hour of shooting.[67]

Shooting was discontinued at noon to provide time to skin the animals before dark. In the first year or two of the slaughter, shooting was so careless and skinning carried out so crudely that three or four animals or hides were lost for every one that made it to market.[68] Even so, the statistics of the hide slaughter of the southern herd are scandalous.

Colonel Richard I. Dodge, who witnessed the carnage, provided some statistics of the total kill in the years 1872, 1873 and 1874 that were used in presenting these calculations:

> Total hides shipped by railroads (actual and estimated).... 1,378,359
> Total number killed and wasted... 1,780,461
> Total slaughter .... 3,158,730[69]

In addition to this total, Dodge estimated another 1,215,000 buffalo were killed by the Indians for their needs and to supply the robe market, for a grand total of 4,373,730 slaughtered in three years. Even these startling numbers did not reflect the total kill, as many hunters hauled their hides to market by wagon, a movement that did not appear in any statistics.[70]

As the hunt continued it became more efficient. An expert marksman would kill 75–100 animals a day and an average shot about 50. A smaller kill was hardly enough to make expenses. Skinners became skilled enough to handle 60–75 buffalo in a day.[71]

Most hunters wasted no time attempting to preserve the meat. Not only was the market glutted, with buffalo steak worth only 1¢ to 2¢ per .45 kg (1 lb),[72] but taking the meat slowed down the operation. The plains reeked with the stench of rotting carcasses.[73]

Like the numbers of the buffalo themselves, the true totals of their slaughter merely for their hides will never be known. But they were far greater than the herds could stand. By the end of the hunting season of 1875 the southern hide hunt was over; the herd had ceased to exist. All that remained were a "few bands of stragglers."[74] The northern buffalo herd survived a few more years in the drainage of the Yellowstone and Missouri Rivers, but was equally doomed.

Buffalo were not only useful for their meat and hides. Here, buffalo chips are being gathered for fuel during the North American Boundary Commission (1872–1875). *Library and Archives Canada / Natural Resources Canada fonds C-004209B*

The production of tanned robes on the northern plains had reached serious levels. As well as the Plains Indians, the Métis, now settled in communities throughout the West, had become dependent upon the European goods they acquired with the proceeds of their robe sales.[75] In 1875 the production of Native-tanned buffalo robes from the West finally exceeded the Eastern demand, and prices began to fall. To maintain their accustomed level of income, the Métis increased their output until the supply of buffalo on the Canadian prairie suddenly was exhausted.[76]

The traders at Fort Benton handled most of the robes coming out of Canada as well as the production of the Montana Indians. In 1876 some 75,000 robes moved through Fort Benton alone; by 1880 the trade had fallen off to 25,000. In 1883 no more than 5,000 robes were handled and that was the end; in 1884 no robes came to market.[77] Hide hunting was not practised in Canada, but the robe trade and pemmican production, on top of subsistence hunting, were together quite sufficient to wipe out the herds north of the border. Except for a small band here and there, by the end of 1879 the buffalo was finished in Canada.

Large numbers of animals remained in the northern herd in the United States, but there, too, oblivion approached. Many of the southern hide hunters moved in upon the northern herd, attracted by hide prices that were two or three times what they had brought in the south. By 1880 prices reached from $1.50 to $3.50, and the summer slaughter recommenced.[78] Soon the ugly statistics that had been seen in the south were repeated. The Northern Pacific Railroad reached Glendive and Miles City in 1881 and carried out some 50,000 buffalo hides and robes. The next year 200,000 were shipped, but in 1883 the volume dropped to 40,000. In 1884 the Northern Pacific carried only one carload of buffalo hides out of the Territories; the great northern herd, in its turn, had been annihilated.[79]

A few small bands survived for a very few years, but the commercial hunting of the buffalo had come to a permanent end. So, too, had the subsistence hunting of those one-time monarchs of the prairie, the Plains Indians, now thrown upon the mercies, and the meager rations, of the Canadian and United States governments.

As the once mighty buffalo approached complete extinction, no ground-swell of concern to preserve the species arose; instead a grotesque desire to be part of the impending catastrophe manifested itself. So-called hunters aspired to the honour of having killed the last buffalo, and scores claimed the title.[80] The phenomenon was not confined to the United States. In October 1884, a report of seven surviving buffalo in the Cypress Hills attracted between 50 and 100 hunters who crowded onto a Canadian Pacific train running east-bound out of Calgary. The hunters, equipped with rifles and gear, were all heading to Maple Creek, the nearest point to the Cypress Hills. Supposedly they were unsuccessful.[81]

In early 1886 the chief taxidermist of the Smithsonian National Museum awoke to the strong likelihood that his institution would not be graced with an exhibit of the *bison bison* that had once ranged the plains of North America in such vast numbers. Accordingly, William T. Hornaday mounted an expe-dition into Montana Territory to secure specimens for his museum. After considerable effort and expense, 25 of the very few surviving buffalo were killed. Of these, six were selected and preserved for an exhibit that opened in March 1888, to an enthusiastic public. In a reaction that today seems some-what strange, "The Buffalo Group quickly achieved acclaim as a symbol of the early conservation movement."[82]

Hornaday became something of an authority on the subject of buffalo and in 1889 published a comprehensive but overly judgmental study entitled *The Extermination of the American Bison*. At that time he estimated the total wild population of buffalo in the United States at 85. Another 550 wood buffalo (a different sub-species) lived in northern Canada, for a total of 635 in the wild; 456 more lived in captivity for a total world population in 1889 of 1,091,[83] likely the lowest ebb of the species.

Hornaday's Buffalo Group was also hailed as a "triumph of the taxidermist's art," but by 1957 it had become somewhat shopworn and was removed in favour of new-ly killed specimens. Discarded and separated, the exhibit was later recovered and rehabilitated and now can be seen at Fort Benton in the Montana Agricultural Cen-ter and Museum.[1]

NOTE

1. *Smithsonian Magazine*, "Last of the Wild Buffalo" (February 2000).

As early as the 1870s, crossbreeding the buffalo with cattle was undertaken in the hope of producing a marketable animal carrying the best traits of both.[84] The "cattalo" was not a success. Similar efforts a century later promoted the "beefalo," that also soon disappeared in Canada but continues in the United States. One perhaps unfortunate result of the crossbreeding attempts was the introduction of the cattle gene into the wild genetic makeup of the buffalo so that today, although the total buffalo population in Canada has recovered to some quarter of a million animals, "only about 1,000 are pure descendants of the original wild ones."[85]

The carnage on the American plains during the hide-hunting years did not escape public clamour. In 1874 the *New Mexican*, a newspaper published in Santa Fe, New Mexico, spoke out:

> The buffalo slaughter, which has been going on the past few years on the plains, and which increases every year, is wantonly wicked, and should be stopped by the most stringent enactments and most vigilant enforcement of the law. Killing these noble animals for their hides simply, or to gratify the pleasure of some Russian duke or English lord, is a species of vandalism which can not too quickly be checked. United States surveying parties report that there are two thousand hunters on the plains killing these animals for their hides. One party of sixteen hunters report having killed twenty-eight thousand buffaloes during the past summer. It seems to us there is quite as much reason why the Government should protect the buffaloes as the Indians.[86]

Some feeble attempts were made in the United States Congress to protect the herds by legislation and in 1874 one bill actually was passed but President Ulysses Grant killed it with a pocket veto. More bills were introduced, but none received approval and after 1876 no further moves were made to prevent the slaughter.

In Canada concern for protection of the buffalo was raised in the House of Commons in 1876 and again in March 1877 by John Schultz, MP for Lisgar, Manitoba. Schultz quoted Father Lacombe, who estimated 80,000 buffalo were being taken in the summer, and an equal number in the winter, a rate that would render the herds extinct in eight years—total optimism, as it turned out. Father Lacombe proposed a closed season from November 1 to May 1 in every year, and on calves at all times. The Liberal government agreed that "the buffalo were rapidly diminishing," but thought enforcement of any law would be "a formidable undertaking" and "had better be left to be dealt with by the government of the North-West Territories . . . it being on the spot and more familiar with the matter."[87]

In fact, at the time of the debate in the House of Commons, an Ordinance along the lines proposed by Father Lacombe had already been enacted by the Council of the North-West Territories, on March 22, 1877. The use of pounds and buffalo jumps were prohibited, as was killing buffalo merely for their hides or choice cuts. Cows were protected between November 15 and August 14, as were calves under the age of two years. Indians were granted certain exemptions during the winter months and "in circumstances of pressing necessity."[88]

Ottawa's judgement turned out to be correct; enforcement was impractical and almost impossible. The Métis objected to the preference given to the Indians and pointed out that the closed season on cows included the best period for securing good robes. Offence was also taken by the Indians who resented the white man's attempt to interfere with the buffalo that providence had placed on earth for them.[89] "When did the Almighty give the Canadian Government the right to keep the Indians from killing the buffalo," inquired Sitting Bull from Wood Mountain.[90]

The Ordinance was repealed at the next session of the North-West Council and the buffalo on the Canadian plains were abandoned to their fate.

IN 1883, THE FEW buffalo herds remaining on the Montana plains vanished so abruptly that to some minds it did not seem possible that hunting alone could have been responsible. The theory that disease was the final factor in the demise of the buffalo took root. In his 1951 epic, Frank Roe gave the possibility his usual thorough examination. He worked from the reasonable assumption that any

> epidemic disease on a scale sufficiently large to constitute any appreciable force in the extermination of the buffalo must surely have left some visible indications of its ravages in large masses of dead carcasses.[91]

Having uncovered not "the least hint or allusion to such conditions," Roe concluded that there was no substance to the disease theory.

Writing more than 30 years after Roe, Dr. Rudolph W. Koucky again advanced the disease theory. It had been in his mind since 1926 when he encountered a cluster of buffalo skeletons out on their former range "arranged much like a herd of cows lying on a meadow." A trained pathologist, Koucky examined the skeletons and found no evidence that they had been killed. "They had simply laid down and died. Obviously, the entire herd had been sick."[92]

Koucky theorized that the herds of domestic cattle that first came into contact with the buffalo in Montana in 1880–81 carried a disease that was then called "tick fever." Whatever the disease actually was, it was one to which the buffalo had no immunity and were "virgin soil." The fever raced through the few remaining herds with devastating effect. Koucky provided no evidence of carcasses other than his 1926 observation.

Professor A.S. Morton of the University of Saskatchewan questioned Frank Roe's conclusion and referred to a group of buffalo skeletons found on a farm near Kamsack, Saskatchewan, not far from Fort Pelly. Like Dr. Koucky's skeletons, these were so numerous as to indicate a sudden disaster. Nearby tree branches had been chewed and stripped of bark, suggesting starvation in a hard winter as a possible cause of death, but disease seems more likely.[93]

None of the three writers—Frank Roe, Professor Morton or Dr. Koucky— were aware of the experience of H.M. Starkey who, in the summer of 1883, worked on his father's survey crew creating the township plans in what is now western Saskatchewan, mid-way between today's towns of Eston and Eatonia. In September the crew encountered buffalo:

> [F]our different herds and several small bunches from six to ten in number. . . . On one of our lines we found a bunch of dead buffalo whose hides were still intact. They were lying close enough so that a person could jump from one carcass to another. We did not take time to count them, but they covered several acres. They did not die in winter as they were in summer fur. When I reported it at night they thought I had been drinking the Frenchman's brandy but my crew verified my statement. I made a record of it in my field notes. I have told this to a great many people and they always ask the same question. What killed them? The same thing killed them as all through the west—some disease.[94]

AFTER THE GREAT BUFFALO herds had passed into history, the finger-pointing began. Who had been responsible for the wholesale destruction of such a magnificent animal?

From the Smithsonian, William Hornaday, overlooking his own predation among the few buffalo remaining in Montana, took aim at the Métis of the Red River hunt:

> Probably never before in the history of the world, until civilized men came in contact with the buffalo, did whole armies of men march out in true military style, with officers, flag, chaplains, and rules of war, and make war on wild animals. No wonder the buffalo has been exterminated. So long as they existed north of the Missouri in any considerable number, the half-breeds and Indians of the Manitoba Red River settlement used to gather each year in a great army, and go with carts to the buffalo range. On these great hunts, which took place every year from about the 15th of June to the 1st of September, vast numbers of buffalo were killed, and the supply was finally exhausted. As if Heaven had decreed the extirpation of the species, the half-breed hunters, like their white robe-hunting rivals farther south, always killed *cows* in preference to bulls so long as a choice was possible, the very course best calculated to exterminate any species in the shortest possible time.[95]

Utilizing some statistics from Alexander Ross's account of the Red River hunt from 1820 to 1840, Hornaday calculated that 652,275 buffalo had been taken in this 20-year period.

Frank Roe, in a paper presented to the Royal Society of Canada,[96] demolished Hornaday's thesis by a withering examination of his assumptions and self-contradictions, combined with a detailed presentation of contrary evidence. But Roe had to acknowledge the inescapable fact that the Red River Métis killed an impressive number of buffalo. The demand for pemmican to provision the burgeoning fur trade industry undoubtedly contributed to the destruction of the great herds.

The United States Army was a natural and usual suspect, and with good reason. The General of the Army from 1869 to 1883 was William Tecumseh Sherman, who brought to his command the same strategy that he employed when he laid waste the state of Georgia during the American Civil War. The destruction of the buffalo, the primary food source of the Plains Indians, Sherman believed, would shatter their ability to resist.

General Phil Sheridan, commanding the Military Division of the Missouri, held similar beliefs. An oft-quoted, but perhaps apocryphal account, has

Sheridan addressing the Texas state legislature in 1875 in support of the hide hunters then cleaning out the southern buffalo herd:

> These men have done in the last two years, and will do more in the next year, to settle the vexed Indian question, than the entire regular army has done in the last thirty years. They are destroying the Indians' commissary; and it is a well-known fact that any army losing its base of supplies is placed at a great disadvantage. Send them powder and lead, if you will; but for the sake of a lasting peace, let them kill, skin, and sell until the buffaloes are exterminated.[97]

Six years later Sheridan is quoted as confirming his Texas opinion:

> If I could learn that every buffalo in the northern herd were killed I would be glad. The destruction of this herd would do more to keep Indians quiet than anything else that could happen, except the death of all the Indians. Since the destruction of the southern herd . . . the Indians in that section have given us no trouble.[98]

The Army supported the hide hunters but did not itself conduct an overt campaign against the buffalo, other than to organize and participate in a number of "sporting" hunts. VIP tourists were routinely treated to buffalo hunts by Army officers. In 1872, Sheridan entertained Grand Duke Alexis, son of the Czar of Russia:

> A military escort consisting of two companies of infantry, two of cavalry, and the Second Cavalry's regimental band, along with teamsters and cooks, completed the assemblage. All boarded a special train provided by the Union Pacific Railroad and headed for North Platte, Nebraska. In five days of exuberant hunting the party slaughtered hundreds of buffalo.[99]

Although the work of the white hide hunters certainly finished off the buffalo, in the opinion of at least one authority death began when the Plains Indians themselves succumbed to the temptations of the trading posts and began preparing buffalo robes for sale:

> By the middle of the nineteenth century, the changing American legal and economic order had helped to transform Plains Indian societies

into market-driven societies. Under the pressure of the market, plains nomads began to hunt the bison into extinction. Decades before white hunters, armed with powerful, accurate rifles, delivered the coup de grace to the herds, plains nomads' exploitation of the bison for trade had already proved to be unsustainable ... From 1840 until the 1870s, plains nomads traded more than 100,000 robes each year to Missouri River merchants. The opening of the market in buffalo robes hastened the commercialization of Plains Indian culture and led to increasingly heavy pressure on buffalo herds.[100]

This view runs contrary to the myth of the American Indian as conservationist, one who traditionally, and by culture, took only such game as was reasonably needed for sustenance. Nothing was wasted and killing for joy was sinful.

RECENT ANTHROPOLOGICAL RESEARCH HAS established the myth of the Aboriginal conservationist to be nothing more than sentimental nonsense. Early human societies are now known to have wantonly hunted many species into extinction. Whatever was available was taken if only because frequently nothing was available. North America was once home to a number of long-extinct animals, many of them gigantic. The horse, camel, sabretooth tiger, a giant beaver and a giant bison as well as the mighty mammoth and mastodon all lived here until about 13,000 years ago. Difficult as it is to believe that such huge creatures could fall prey to early man equipped only with spears, excavations have proved just that.

Somewhere about 12,500 years ago a band of North American big-game hunters invented a new weapon, the Clovis point:

These magnificent fluted stone spearheads are of distinctive design, ranging from around four to twenty-three centimetres [1.5–9 inches] in length. Highly functional, they are also works of art.[101]

Their makers, naturally, are now known as the Clovis people and they ranged over the entire continent in pursuit of their prey.

Coincident with the operations of the Clovis people, the large animals of North America passed out of existence and a growing body of opinion holds

human hunting to be responsible ... [for] the black hole theory of extinction, which suggests that ... all of those huge mammoths, sloths, camels and mastodons disappeared into a black hole. Not any black hole, mind you, but that very discerning one lying between nose and chin on the Clovis physiognomy.[102]

About 12,000 years ago spear hunting of the bison was replaced by the more efficient drive-hunt and, perhaps inevitably, waste appears in the archeological sites. "At the Olsen-Chubbuck site in eastern Colorado nineteen of the 193 bison killed were not even touched by the hunters while another thirty were only partially butchered."[103] In 1858 Professor Hind counted 200 animals wasted at the pound kill he witnessed. When running a herd of panicked buffalo off a cliff or into a pound, little thought would be given to the actual needs of the moment. And the hunters had no choice over the actual numbers; they took whatever was available. Their belief that a buffalo that escaped would warn its fellows against being trapped again justified taking every last animal.

Still, many animals were slaughtered only for the choice cuts, the tongue, hump or fetus. The trader Charles McKenzie recorded in 1804–05 that the Gros Ventre daily killed whole herds only for the tongues, leaving the rest of the carcasses to rot in the sun. McKenzie accompanied a band of Cheyenne who killed "250 fat Cows which they left on the field as they fell; excepting the Tongues which they dried for a general feast they were to make."[104] And Peter Fidler of the Hudson's Bay Company observed in February 1793 that the Peigan hunted the cow buffalo only for the fetus carried at that season of which they were "remarkable fond."[105]

In Europe several of the jump sites disclose slaughter on a tremendous scale: 1,000 mammoths at Piedmont, in the Czech Republic, more than 100,000 horses at Solutre, in France. "A bad smell of extinction follows *homo sapiens* around the world."[106]

The buffalo in North America proliferated because of the unique suitability of the great plains and the scarcity of cliffs to be run over. But even the great herds could not prevail after the arrival of the horse and the gun. Even after the Plains Indians began to see the buffalo as supplying a tradeable commodity, they continued in their belief that the buffalo herds were replenished from a wellspring beneath the earth and their numbers could not be diminished, let alone exhausted. With no concept of a finite resource, there was no wrong in killing as many as possible, more than could be utilized.

Some of the accounts of excessive slaughter are startling. In May 1832, when George Catlin, an American artist and writer visited Fort Pierre, on the Missouri River, he was told by the *bourgeois* and his clerks of just such an incident that had occurred a few days earlier:

When an immense herd of buffaloes had showed themselves on the opposite side of the river, almost blackening the plains for a great distance, a party of five or six hundred Sioux on horseback forded the river about mid-day, and spending a few hours among them, recrossed the river at sun-down and came into the Fort with *fourteen hundred fresh buffalo tongues*, which were thrown down in a mass, and for which they required but a few gallons of whiskey, which was soon demolished, indulging them in a little, and harmless carouse . . . not a skin or a pound of the meat (except the tongues) was brought in.[107]

Even when it became impossible to escape the knowledge that the buffalo was not a limitless resource but, instead, on the point of extinction, the killing continued whenever an opportunity arose. In the summer of 1882 a great slaughter took place near the Standing Rock Sioux Reservation when a herd of buffalo appeared where none had been seen for years. Major James McLaughlin, the Indian Agent, organized 600 Sioux hunters to ride after the herd. Two thousand animals were taken the first day and the hunt did not stop until "five thousand buffalo were slain."[108]

Disregarding the fact that they had pretty well cleaned out the last decent herd in existence, McLaughlin claimed that "The slaughter had been awful but not wanton," and that "I never have known an Indian to kill a game animal that he did not require for his needs."[109]

MORE RECENT TIMES HAVE witnessed incidents of Natives taking far more game animals than required for subsistence and wasting huge quantities. Each fall the Beverly barren-ground caribou herd traditionally migrates south from the North-West Territories into the boreal forest of northern Saskatchewan, where it is hunted by local Chipewyan, Cree and Métis residents. During the winter of 1979–80 the herd, then made up of little more than 100,000 animals, travelled further south than usual, arrived early, about November 1, and remained almost six months, until mid-April, providing a unique opportunity to the Saskatchewan hunters. A wanton slaughter ensued. Utilizing modern rifles, wheeled vehicles, snowmobiles and aircraft, hunters attacked the helpless caribou out in the open on such huge lakes as Wollaston, Reindeer and Black with little regard to the recovery and preservation of the carcasses. Pregnant cows carrying the prized fetus were the favourite target. A huge number of animals were crippled and abandoned.

Wildlife officials attempting to regulate the hunt were harassed and prevented from performing their duties. When it was all over, carcasses littered shorelines after spring break-up and lost animals rotted in the bush, as did much of the meat recovered but not properly preserved. The official estimates of the total kill was 17,295, including a modest 15% crippling loss. The actual kill will never be known. Admitted individual kills ranged as high as 80 animals.[110] This was at a time when the Beverly herd was in decline and wildlife biologists feared that it might suffer the same fate as the Kaminuriak herd of the Keewatin District, which had dropped 75% in numbers. The near extermination of the buffalo serves as a powerful warning that even the great herds of caribou in northern Canada are not immune from a similar fate.

On the Great Plains the destruction of the once-mighty herds of the magnificent buffalo was a crime of monstrous proportions, on a scale so huge that it could be committed only by many perpetrators, each contributing a share of culpability. And it was not a sudden event:

> The near extermination of the American buffalo did not happen overnight, nor was one generation of human beings fully responsible for clearing the plains and prairies of this most noble animal.[111]

Buffalo skull, March 1873. *Library and Archives Canada / Topley Studio fonds MIKAN 3506423*

CHAPTER 16

The Road to Little Big Horn

O N JUNE 25, 1975, THE 99TH ANNIVERSARY OF THE BATTLE of Little Big Horn, the United States Court of Claims handed down a decision in a case considering the conduct of the government of the United States in its relations with the Sioux Indians at the time of the conflict. The Court was caustic: "A more ripe and rank case of dishonorable dealings will never, in all probability, be found in our history."

This highly unusual judicial opinion was later tacitly approved by the Supreme Court of the United States when the case came before it for review, and remains undisturbed. It stands as a scathing indictment of the violation of the rights of the Sioux Nation, rights those Sioux who were at Little Big Horn were fully entitled to fight to defend.

It was the determination of the United States to secure the 2,832,900 ha (7,000,000 acres) making up the Black Hills of what is now South Dakota, and the tenacious resolve of the Sioux to protect their sacred Hills, that brought about the conflict and doomed the Sioux. It all began in September 1851, a quarter of a century before the bloodletting at Little Big Horn, at Horse Creek, near present-day Morrill, Nebraska.

FATHER PETER DE SMET was delighted to receive the invitation and not in the least daunted by the assignment it involved, even though it would have chilled the heart of a lesser mortal. Likely no man had as much experience in the American West, or was as knowledgeable about its many Indian tribes, as the Jesuit priest. Certainly no one was as well respected by those Indians.

But the 50-year-old Belgian-born De Smet was stuck in an office job, procurator of the Missouri Vice-Province of the Jesuit Order at St. Louis, and he yearned to be back out on the plains, carrying the word of God among his beloved Indians.

It was April 1851, and the message that set De Smet free came from the government of the United States. Concerned about the safety of the thousands of westward-bound emigrants crossing what was then called the Great American Desert on the Oregon, Mormon and California Trails, Washington had called a council of all the Indian tribes living between the Missouri River and Texas. The assembly was to be held at Fort Laramie, Wyoming Territory, at the beginning of September 1851. Anxious to ensure good representation at the council, and well aware of the priest's reputation among the Indians of the Upper Missouri, the superintendent of Indian Affairs at St. Louis inquired if Father De Smet would assist. Specifically, would he travel up the Missouri River to Fort Union and along the way invite the tribes to participate in the meeting? It was understood, of course, that preaching the faith as usual would be part of the priest's activities. Once arriving at Fort Union, would Father De Smet then be good enough to gather a representative group of chiefs from the northern tribes and escort them overland to Fort Laramie and assist at the great council? And then, as a government envoy, provide such further assistance as might be appropriate during the deliberations?

Would he? Father De Smet leaped at the opportunity. It was hardly necessary for the superintendent to assure the priest that "[t]he objects of the government are just and humane, and intended entirely for the benefit and future welfare of the Indians."[1]

De Smet had been grounded in the St. Louis offices of the Jesuit Order because his superiors disapproved of his solitary travels, but they could hardly refuse to allow their priest to accept such an invitation. They could, however, and did assign another priest to accompany De Smet and ensure that he adhered to official protocol. Father Christian Hoecken was directed to join De Smet on the journey.

It was not a modest undertaking that the government asked of De Smet. The *St. Ange*, a stern-drive steamboat, would carry the two Jesuits from St. Louis up the Missouri to Fort Union, a trip that in itself would be five tedious weeks. And between Fort Union and Fort Laramie lay nearly 1,300 km (800 mi) of uncharted prairie with no trails to mark the route. But Father De Smet had first embarked upon a Missouri River steamboat almost 25 years before, and heading into unknown country was an old experience. Five years earlier he had walked through the early snows of the winter of 1845–46 over the

Rocky Mountains onto the western plains, spent the winter with the Hudson's Bay Company at Fort Edmonton, and recrossed the mountains in the spring of 1846.

Still, the river trip to Fort Union in the summer of 1851 was no picnic. Only four days out of St. Louis cholera broke out on the *St. Ange* and the first victim died. Before they reached Fort Union on July 14, the disease took more than 20 passengers and crew, including Father Hoecken. De Smet was left to make the cross-country journey alone.

At Fort Union, De Smet assembled a group of chiefs from the region— Mandan, Assiniboine, Arikara, Crow and Minnetare—and persuaded them to accompany him across the plains to the conference. Since the government had agreed to underwrite his expenses, the priest had brought with him on the steamboat a number of wagons and carts and for these he secured horses and hired Métis drivers. His party had grown to some three dozen men by the time they got underway on July 31, aiming through the wilderness for Fort Laramie. The destination was not unknown to De Smet. He had travelled the Oregon Trail westward twice 10 years earlier, in 1840 and 1841.

Navigating by dead reckoning the priest overshot his mark and came upon the Oregon Trail several days travel west of Fort Laramie. There was no difficulty recognizing the Trail. It was a packed and rutted highway littered with the cast-off equipment and garbage of the thousands of emigrants who eagerly followed it each year, heading to a new life in the West. De Smet's Indians were amazed.

When his party reached Fort Laramie, Father De Smet found that the conference site had been moved some 56 km (35 mi) further east, to Horse Creek, near present-day Morrill, Nebraska.

When the government negotiators arrived at Fort Laramie in August, they were surprised by the response to their invitations and unprepared for the numbers of guests. Every tribe in the region had turned up, some 10,000–12,000 men, women and children accompanied by 30,000 horses and uncounted numbers of dogs. It was the largest assembly of Plains Indians known to that time and was rivalled only by two later huge gatherings of Sioux, the last one 25 years later, at Little Big Horn.

The logistics of providing for such a multitude were intimidating. To secure forage for the huge horse herd and fresh ground for the encampment, a move was necessary. There was another reason for the change of locale. The several tribal villages had been in place for several days and the pristine purity of Fort Laramie and its immediate environs had been severely displaced. Picture Woodstock without any sanitation facilities whatsoever and add 30,000 horses and at least as many dogs. The emissaries from Washington heeded their nostrils and called for a fresh site. Horse Creek was a good location and proceedings there got underway on September 7, 1851.

Among those present must have been some of the Sioux who two months earlier had been bloodied in an encounter on the Grand Coteau with the Métis from Red River (see Chapter 9). Perhaps the story of that engagement, as it passed through the lodges at the Fort Laramie conference, made a small contribution to the treaty process. The discussions went on for 10 days, accompanied by numerous feasts, dances and ceremonies. Father De Smet took full advantage of the opportunity presented by the huge gathering to preach the word of his Christian God and claimed 1,856 converts.[2]

Finally, on September 17, 1851, eight Indian nations and the United States government entered into a short and simple treaty. They agreed "to abstain in future from all hostilities whatever against each other, to maintain good faith and friendship in all their mutual intercourse, and to make an effective and lasting peace." For this security the government agreed to pay the sum of $50,000 annually for 50 years, in the form of rations and supplies. A government caravan of 27 wagons arrived on September 20 with the first installment and a great celebration ensued.

The Treaty also laid out the agreed territory of each of the participating tribes, and here Father De Smet made an invaluable contribution. Drawing upon his intimate knowledge of the country and the lands occupied by the various tribes, he prepared a map outlining the territory assigned to each. The Sioux territory was a huge tract west of the Missouri River with the Black Hills pretty much dead in the centre. The 1851 Fort Laramie Treaty clearly acknowledged Sioux ownership of the Black Hills.

When Father De Smet returned to St. Louis on October 22, he calculated that on his round trip he had travelled a total of 8,782 km (5,457 mi),[3] much of it on foot and on horseback—not bad for a portly priest carrying 100 kg (220 lb) on a 170 cm (5'7") frame.

THE GOVERNMENT ALMOST IMMEDIATELY encountered trouble with the Treaty. The United States Senate, finding the 50-year term too rich, unilaterally amended the Treaty by limiting the obligation to 10 years, with another five years at the discretion of the President. It was not thought necessary to bring the change to the attention of the Sioux, or the other participating tribes, all of whom believed the original term was in force. This breach of the deal made on the ground was later identified as a major cause of the Powder River War that broke out in 1866.[4]

The Treaty of 1851 bought only three years of tranquility to the plains before it fell victim to misunderstandings and breaches. Tribal conflict again became the norm. Firefights between the Army and the Sioux broke out, and the Sioux made life miserable for trading posts and wagon trains throughout their territory. Attempts were made to secure new treaties, but no success was achieved.

In 1862 the formerly peaceful Santee Sioux in Minnesota broke into open warfare and several hundred white settlers were murdered. In spite of the Civil War on its hands, the Army regained control and forced the surviving Santee west into Dakota Territory. There the war spread to the Teton, or Lakota, Sioux.

The Sioux determination to resist the incursion of the settlers was stiffened by the development of the Bozeman Trail, or Powder River Road, which ran through Sioux territory to the gold finds of western Montana. In 1866, the year the Treaty of 1851 expired (the Senate's 10-year term, plus the permitted five-year extension which had been invoked by President Abraham Lincoln), the conflict again became deadly. On December 21, near Fort Philip Kearny, an army post on the Bozeman Trail, Crazy Horse and a band of Oglala Sioux administered the worst defeat the Army had until then suffered on the western plains. The entire command of Lieutenant Colonel William Fetterman was wiped out, a loss of 81 officers and men. The affair was the "Fetterman Massacre" to the white community, the "Battle of the Hundred Slain" to the Sioux. The Powder River War was well underway and the Bozeman Trail was effectively closed.

A century later, the United States Supreme Court described the Powder River War of 1866–67 as "as series of military engagements in which the Sioux tribes, led by their great chief, Red Cloud, fought to protect the integrity of earlier-recognized treaty lands from the incursions of white settlers."[5] Different characterizations were applied in 1876.

Nonetheless, the conflict led to a new Fort Laramie Treaty, signed in April and May 1868 and, lastly and finally, by Red Cloud in November. Again there was peace on the plains. Not all the Sioux signed on to the Treaty. Two groups refused, Oglalas led by Crazy Horse, and the Hunkpapa band of Sitting Bull. A growing number of Sioux remained opposed to any treaty with the intruding whites and moved behind the leadership of Crazy Horse and Sitting Bull.

The Fort Laramie Treaty has been described as a complete victory for Red Cloud and the Sioux. It might even have been "the only instance in the history of the United States where the government has gone to war and afterwards negotiated a peace conceding everything demanded by the enemy and exacting nothing in return."[6]

Certainly the Fort Laramie Treaty of 1868 contained a number of grave commitments on the part of the United States. It established the Great Sioux Reservation, a huge tract of land including approximately half of what is now the state of South Dakota, plus a strip of land west of the Missouri and north of today's border between North and South Dakota. Again, the Black Hills were well within the boundaries of the Sioux lands.

The undertaking given by the United States respecting the Reservation was clear and strong: no unauthorized person "shall ever be permitted to pass over, settle upon, or reside in" the Reservation.[7] It was also agreed that members of the Sioux tribes could select lands within the Reservation for agriculture and, to assist them in becoming civilized farmers, the government promised to provide necessary services and materials, and subsistence rations for four years.

In return, the Sioux agreed to relinquish their rights under the 1851 Treaty to occupy territories outside the Reservation, while reserving their "right to hunt on any lands north of North Platte, and on the Republican Fork of the Smoky Hill river, so long as the buffalo may range thereon in such numbers as to justify the chase." The Sioux also agreed to the building of railroads outside their reservation, to discontinue attacks on settlers, and that the government could retain the military posts and roads that had been established south of the North Platte River.[8]

The Treaty contained a major provision that was to haunt the United States ever after:

> No treaty for the cession of any portion or part of the reservation herein described which may be held in common shall be of any validity or force as against the said Indians, unless executed and signed by at least three fourths of all the adult male Indians, occupying or interested in the same.

In practical terms, this provision cast the boundaries of the Great Sioux Reservation in stone for all time. Jealousy and bickering was as normal a condition among the several disparate tribes making up the Sioux Nation as would be expected in any such loose confederation. The government representatives must have known that the likelihood of ever securing 75% unanimity among this group was close to zero. This clause was to form one of the central issues in litigation between the United States and the Sioux a century later.

After the Powder River War, a concerned Congress appointed a mixed military and civilian commission to inquire into the causes of Indian complaint. The result was perhaps surprising: "After the most careful examination into the causes of this war, these gentlemen declare that we alone are responsible." It was less surprising that the commission found "the Indians were not willing to make another treaty unless they could have the pledge that no white man should ever enter the territory guaranteed to them."[9]

The Commission's comment on the Powder River War itself was strongly critical:

> The results of the year's campaign satisfied all reasonable men that the war was useless and expensive. To those who reflected on the subject, knowing the facts, the war was something more than useless and expensive: it was dishonorable to the nation and disgraceful to those who originated it.[10]

These strong words did not bring about any discernible or profound change in the approach of the United States towards its Indian population.

In spite of its commitment to prevent encroachment upon the Sioux lands, in 1874 the government itself sent a large expedition into the Black Hills to explore their value, with a particular interest in gold. The expedition, under the command of Lieutenant Colonel George Armstrong Custer, reported the discovery of gold and from then on even the United States Army could not protect the Hills from eager prospectors.

In 1875 the United States attempted to negotiate the purchase of the Black Hills from the Sioux but was refused. Early the next year, 1876, the Army opened hostilities against the Sioux and in June met defeat at Little Big Horn. Then the government suspended rations called for by the 1868 Treaty until the Sioux should give up the Hills. A number of Sioux (only 10%) capitulated and signed the new treaty put to them in the fall of 1876. The next year, Congress enacted legislation ratifying the acquisition and the United States had the Black Hills.

But let the United States Supreme Court tell the story. Historians delving into the murky past frequently emerge with different, often contradictory, versions of ancient events. Not often do we enjoy the advantage of history judicially determined as the result of extensive litigation between two well-matched, thoroughly researched and vitally interested parties. Here the Supreme Court of the United States has provided just such an official account of the Sioux conflict of the last half of the 1800s.

In 1920, the United States Congress provided special jurisdiction for the Court of Claims to hear "[a]ll claims of whatsoever nature which the Sioux Tribe of Indians may have against the United States." In 1923, the Sioux commenced action claiming compensation for the improper taking of the Black Hills.

The lawsuit was initially badly handled by the attorneys retained by the Sioux, and dragged on for decades, prompting one judge to comment dryly in 1975, "The instant claim has had a long history and, as an occasion for lawyers' work and effort, a distinguished one. For the Indians it has so far been unrewarding."[11]

But the Sioux eventually achieved success that, in 1980, was confirmed by the Supreme Court of the United States. What follows are the historical facts covering the years following the Fort Laramie Treaty of 1868, as determined initially by the United States Court of Claims and subsequently approved by the Supreme Court. In the words of the Supreme Court:

> The years following the treaty brought relative peace to the Dakotas, an era of tranquillity that was disturbed, however, by renewed speculation that the Black Hills, which were included in the Great Sioux Reservation, contained vast quantities of gold and silver. In 1874 the Army planned and undertook an exploratory expedition into the Hills, both for the purpose of establishing a military outpost from which to control those Sioux who had not accepted the terms of the Fort Laramie Treaty, and for the purpose of investigating "the country about which dreamy stories have been told."[12] Lieutenant Colonel George Armstrong Custer led the expedition of close to 1,000 soldiers and teamsters, and a substantial number of military and civilian aides. Custer's journey began at Fort Abraham Lincoln on the Missouri River on July 2, 1874. By the end of that month they had reached the Black Hills and by mid-August had confirmed the presence of gold fields in that region. The discovery of gold was widely reported in newspapers across the country. Custer's florid descriptions of the mineral and timber resources of the Black Hills, and the land's suitability for grazing and cultivation, also received wide circulation, and had the effect of creating an intense popular demand for the "opening" of the Hills for settlement. The only obstacle to "progress" was the Fort Laramie Treaty that reserved occupancy of the Hills to the Sioux.

Having promised the Sioux that the Black Hills were reserved to them, the United States Army was placed in the position of having to threaten military force, and occasionally to use it, to prevent prospectors and settlers from trespassing on lands reserved to the Indians. For example, in September, 1874, General Sheridan sent instructions to Brigadier General Alfred H. Terry, Commander of the Department of Dakota, at Saint Paul, directing him to use force to prevent companies of prospectors from trespassing on the Sioux Reservation. At the same time, Sheridan let it be known that he would "give a cordial support to the settlement of the Black Hills" should Congress decide to "open up the country for settlement, by extinguishing the treaty rights of the Indians." Sheridan's instructions were published in local newspapers.

Eventually, however, the Executive Branch of the Government decided to abandon the Nation's treaty obligation to preserve the integrity of the Sioux territory. In a letter dated November 9, 1875, to Terry, Sheridan reported that he had met with President Grant, the Secretary of the Interior, and the Secretary of War, and that the President had decided that the military should make no further resistance to the occupation of the Black Hills by miners, "it being his belief that such resistance only increased their desire and complicated the troubles." These orders were to be enforced "quietly," and the President's decision was to remain "confidential." [Letter from Sheridan to Sherman.]

With the Army's withdrawal from its role as enforcer of the Fort Laramie Treaty, the influx of settlers into the Black Hills increased. The Government concluded that the only practical course was to secure to the citizens of the United States the right to mine the Black Hills for gold. Toward that end, the Secretary of the Interior, in the spring of 1875, appointed a commission to negotiate with the Sioux. The commission was headed by William B. Allison. The tribal leaders of the Sioux were aware of the mineral value of the Black Hills and refused to sell the land for a price less than $70 million. The commission offered the Indians an annual rental of $400,000, or payment of $6 million for absolute relinquishment of the Black Hills. The negotiations broke down.

In the winter of 1875–76, many of the Sioux were hunting in the unceded territory north of the North Platte River, reserved to them for that purpose in the Fort Laramie Treaty. On December 6, 1875, for reasons that are not entirely clear, the Commissioner of Indian Affairs sent instructions to the Indian agents on the reservation to notify those hunters that if they did not return to the reservation agencies by January 31, 1876, they would be treated as "hostiles." Given the severity of the winter, compliance with these instructions was impossible. On February 1, the Secretary of the Interior nonetheless relinquished jurisdiction over all hostile Sioux, including those Indians exercising their treaty-protected hunting rights, to the War Department. The Army's campaign against the "hostiles" led to Sitting Bull's notable victory over Custer's forces at the battle of the Little Big Horn on June 25.

The reserved and precise language of the Supreme Court deprives the reader of all feeling for the fear and agony suffered by the Sioux on the ground who were the object of this distasteful intrigue and the subsequent military incursions.

The Allison Commission, mandated to somehow acquire the Black Hills, whether by purchase or lease, actually met with the Sioux in September 1875, and quite a meeting it was. The second of the three huge assemblies of Plains Indians turned out. An even larger congregation than appeared at Fort Laramie in 1851, as many as 20,000 Sioux, appeared before the Commissioners. A delegation from Crazy Horse's band, 300 hostile warriors headed by Little Big Man, raced into the deliberations and threatened to kill "the first chief who speaks for selling the Black Hills."[13] Not surprisingly, the negotiations broke down and Allison reported his failure to President Ulysses S. Grant who then took a different tack to secure the Hills.

The Supreme Court was very circumspect with its comments on the conduct of President Grant. The Court of Claims had been a little more forceful:

We take judicial notice of certain documents which show that President Grant on November 3, 1875, secretly ordered the Army to make no further resistance to the miners going in. At the same time, he decided not to rescind orders theretofore issued forbidding them to occupy the Black Hills country, but in the absence of enforcement, this was ineffectual. The dependence of the Sioux on Government rations was relied on to prevent their making trouble.[14]

The official United States Army version of their instructions to "commence military operations" against the Sioux, written, of course, well after the events, is wonderfully self-justifying:

> In November, 1875, Indian Inspector E.C. Watkins reported to the Commissioner of Indian Affairs the attitude of certain wild and hostile bands of Indians, under the leadership of various chiefs or headmen, who were roaming about Dakota and Montana.
>
> Some of these bands had never accepted the reservation system, would not recognize the authority of the government, and insisted upon remaining wild and perfectly free from control. Of this class was "Sitting Bull," who was not a chief, but a "head-man," and whose immediate following did not exceed thirty or forty lodges.
>
> Among the Indians referred to were some who had not only attacked settlers and emigrants, but who had also been in the habit of making war upon the Mandans, Arickarees, and other tribes who were friendly to the whites. Inspector Watkins recommended, therefore, that troops should be sent into the country inhabited by these wild and roving bands, to punish and reduce them to submission.[15]

As a *casus belli*, this was thin stuff. The various Indian tribes in the West had been skirmishing and raiding each other long before the whites knew of their existence. Now the United States was going to war against one tribe of Indians to protect another tribe of Indians?

Why name only Sitting Bull? Crazy Horse was also out in the territory, was known to be more militant, and had a much larger following. This turned out to be one of the very early shots, in a campaign of a different sort, to cast Sitting Bull as the villain of the piece, deserving of all action brought against him. Much more of the same would follow.

The Army obviously did not expect the Sioux to comply with the directive to return to the reservations; planning for a campaign against them began on December 13, 1875, even before the messengers left for the territory. On February 7, 1876, a week after the passing of the impossible deadline imposed, "authority was received to commence operations against the hostiles."[16]

That the deadline fixed at January 31, 1876, was next to impossible for the Indians to meet was exposed by the Sioux Commission who treated with them in September of that year. It found that none of the messengers sent out by the agents to notify the hunting Indians of the edict "was able to return to his agency by the time which had been fixed for the return of the Indians."[17] Although some reports state that a few bands did come back into the reservations, the winter was severe. The snow in Minnesota was so deep no trains were running. In February, Colonel Custer, the commander of the 7th Cavalry, had difficulty returning from the East to his regiment at Bismarck.[18]

No matter what the weather, it was unlikely that any of the leading Sioux had any intention of obeying the instructions, certainly not Crazy Horse or Sitting Bull. Sitting Bull, however, responded diplomatically to his message to come into the agency. He did not refuse, merely stated that he could not return just now—perhaps in the spring, perhaps later.

In spite of the winter, some units of the Army were prepared, ready and quick off the mark. On March 1, 1876, 10 troops of the 2nd and 3rd Cavalry and two companies of infantry moved out of Fort Fetterman "in search of the hostiles." On March 17, the expedition found and attacked a large village consisting of 105 lodges of Sioux and Northern Cheyenne near the mouth of Little Powder River, Montana. All the lodges were destroyed, with ammunition and stores. The large horse herd was captured but later recovered by the Indians. The Army mistakenly thought (and officially recorded) the encampment to be Crazy Horse's village.

The severity of the winter caused Generals Terry and Crook, commanding the two Army departments in charge of the offensive, to discontinue operations until spring. There was no further encounter between the Army and the Indians until summer.

The tough winter was no impediment to the gold rush in the Black Hills. By the time the Army marched out of Fort Fetterman on March 1, there were 15,000 prospectors swarming through the forbidden territory. The boomtowns of Deadwood and Custer City (named after the soon-to-be-deceased officer) sprang up overnight.[19]

By June 1876, the Army was ready and three major columns moved into position to attack the Sioux who were believed (correctly, as it turned out) to be congregated in the valley of the Little Big Horn River. On June 17, the units under General Crook, moving along the Rosebud River, encountered a force of Sioux and Cheyenne warriors under Crazy Horse. Crook was bloodied and withdrew.

On June 25, Lieutenant Colonel George Armstrong Custer, in command of the 7th Cavalry, accompanied by Major M.A. Reno and Captain Frederick W. Benteen, made his fateful charge against a large encampment of Indians on the Little Big Horn River. The fate of Custer and his 7th Cavalry at Little Big Horn did nothing to deter the United States from its determination to acquire the Black Hills, the main purpose of the military campaign.

The provision in the Fort Laramie Treaty requiring the government to provide subsistence rations for four years was, after eight years, beginning to rankle among members of Congress. In 1876 the Commissioner of Indian Affairs reported that his office had been "seriously embarrassed by inadequate and delayed appropriations." In January, he complained, Congress was told that provisions on the two major Sioux reserves, Spotted Tail and Red Cloud, were almost exhausted. Special appropriations were requested; none were forthcoming. In April, $150,000 was approved but, the Commissioner stated,

> relief had been so long delayed that, although the utmost expedition was used, supplies failed to reach the agencies until the Indians were in almost a starving condition, and until the apparent purpose of the Government to abandon them to starvation at their agencies had induced large numbers to go north and join the hostile bands under Sitting Bull.

In July, the Commissioner reported, the same thing occurred, and again, "many Indians, rendered excited and suspicious by the war in the north, abandoned their agencies to take part in hostilities."[20] This confirmed the complaint of the Army commanders that they were meeting in the field large numbers of Indians who were supposed to be quietly residing upon the reservations.[21]

On August 15, 1876, Congress finally addressed the matter of appropriations for the sustenance of the Sioux Indians who had accepted reservation life. As found by the Court of Claims, "Incensed by [the defeat of Custer on June 25], Congress attached a rider to the Appropriations Act of August 15, 1876, cutting off the Sioux rations until they ceded the Black Hills. Since they could not hunt, until they yielded they would starve."[22] Congress requested the President to appoint yet another commission to negotiate with the Sioux for the surrender of the Black Hills, now that the stakes had been considerably raised.

It was done. The new commission, headed by George Manypenny, arrived in Sioux country in early September, bringing a treaty prepared in advance. The principal provisions of the new treaty put before the Sioux required them to relinquish their rights to the Black Hills, plus other lands, as well as their right to hunt in the unceded territories to the north—all this in exchange for subsistence rations for as long as they would be needed to ensure the survival of the Sioux. The commission required signatures, enough signatures to give the process some semblance of legitimacy, because "the commission ignored the stipulation of the Fort Laramie Treaty that any cession of the lands contained within the Great Sioux Reservation would have to be joined in by three-fourths of the adult males."[23]

"You have come to save us from death," Chief Red Cloud told the commissioners when they arrived at his agency on September 7, 1876. Indeed, the commissioners assured Red Cloud and his headmen, they came with "a plan to save their people from death."[24] Surely never in history was a more flagrant example of unequal bargaining power so casually exposed going into a deal.

Even so, Red Cloud and his councillors were slow to accept the terms of the deal that had been fixed by Congress. After the provisions were "carefully explained and interpreted," the Sioux retired into council while the commission waited. After seven days, the commission requested an answer. Chief Little Wound came out of council and told the commissioners:

> You are wise men and you have had time. Our councils may not seem
> of much importance to you, but to us it seems a very serious matter to
> give up our country. You must have patience and bear with us.[25]

The "agreement" was not signed until September 20, after almost two full weeks of consideration. "When do we eat?" Red Cloud is reported to have asked, as soon as the signing was complete.

After Red Cloud, things went more quickly. The last three bands of the seven on the commission's list required only one day to sign on. "The treaty was presented just to Sioux chiefs and their leading men. It was signed by only 10% of the adult male Sioux population."[26] The three-fourths requirement was ignored.

The Manypenny Commission was not instructed as part of its mandate to inquire into and comment upon the causes of the conflict that had erupted with the Sioux earlier in 1876, but it did so anyway. What the commissioners heard from the many chiefs they "negotiated" with impressed them mightily:

> At times they told their story of wrongs with such impassioned earnestness that our cheeks crimsoned with shame. In their speeches,
> the recital of the wrongs which their people had suffered at the hands

of the whites, the arraignment of the Government for gross acts of injustice and fraud, the description of treaties made only to be broken, the doubts and distrusts of present professions of friendship and good-will, were portrayed in colors so vivid and language so terse, that admiration and surprise would have kept us silent had not shame and humiliation done so.[27]

One chief inquired of the commissioners: "If you white men had a country which was very valuable, which had always belonged to your people, and which the Great Father had promised should be yours for ever, and men of another race came to take it away by force, what would your people do? Would they fight?"[28] Another made a caustic observation:

I hear that you have come to move us. Tell your people that since the Great Father promised that we should never be removed we have been moved five times. I think you had better put the Indians on wheels and you can run them about wherever you wish.[29]

The Commission questioned the authority of the Army to conduct the war against the Sioux, referring to the Constitution, statements of the Supreme Court respecting treaties, and the ordinance of July 1787, which declared that Indians "shall never be invaded or disturbed, unless in just and lawful wars *authorized by Congress*" (emphasis in original).[30]

As to the present war, the Commission noted that the original communication from Indian Inspector Watkins was a complaint about Sitting Bull and other Indians with him and a recommendation that "a force of one thousand men should be sent to compel them to submit to the Government." In all of the correspondence of the War and Interior Departments the only reference the Commission found to hostile Indians was to the "followers of Sitting Bull." This gave rise to the obvious question as to how a request for such a limited engagement was converted by the Army into a full-scale declaration of war against all Indians found off reservations. The Commission did not question the appropriateness of action against Sitting Bull, but did state: "We do deplore any action which makes no discrimination between friends and foes, and which overwhelms the innocent with the guilty."[31]

As to the war itself, still very much underway when its report was delivered on December 19, 1876, the Commission repeated the words of the military review of the Powder River War written in 1868:

the war was something more than useless and expensive: it was dishonorable to the nation and disgraceful to those who originated it.[32]

And they added more:

> We hardly know how to frame in words the feelings of shame and
> sorrow which fill our hearts as we recall the long record of the broken
> faith of our Government. It is made more sad, in that the rejoicings
> of our centennial year are mingled with the wail of sorrow of widows
> and orphans made by a needless Indian war, and that our Govern-
> ment has expended more money in this war than all the religious bod-
> ies of our country have spent in Indian missions since our existence
> as a nation.[33]

The Commission concluded its report with a passionate plea:

> Our country must forever bear the disgrace and suffer the retribu-
> tion of its wrong-doing. Our children's children will tell the story in
> hushed tones, and wonder how their fathers dared so to trample on
> justice and trifle with God.[34]

But the Manypenny Commission brought back the bacon. The "agreement"
was signed, if only by the chiefs and headmen, just 10%, not 75% as required by
the Fort Laramie Treaty. Congress resolved the question of the illegitimacy of
the document signed in September 1876. On February 28, 1877, it enacted the
1876 "agreement" into law, by abrogating the Fort Laramie Treaty and imple-
menting the terms of the Manypenny "agreement." The United States had the
Black Hills, 2,972,585 ha (7,345,157 acres) of unsurpassed mineral and agricultural wealth.[35]

Of this sequence of events, the United States Court of Claims 100 years
later, in 1975, held that:

> A Treaty was tendered the Sioux for adhesion in 1876. However,
> breach of the obligation to protect the Indians' lands from unwanted
> intruders, as promised in the 1868 Treaty, reneged on another special
> relationship. The duplicity of President Grant's course and the duress
> practised on the starving Sioux, speak for themselves. A more ripe
> and rank case of dishonorable dealings will never, in all probability,

be found in our history, which is not, taken as a whole, the disgrace it now pleases some persons to believe.[36]

The army's campaign continued until the Sioux had been totally and finally defeated. In 1877, the year after Little Big Horn, the last of the Sioux in the United States surrendered and were placed on reservations. In 1881 the few who remained of several thousand more who had fled into Canada returned and delivered themselves up. In 1890 the army turned its artillery on a Sioux encampment at Wounded Knee Creek, South Dakota, and killed more than 150 men, women and children. There was no further resistance from the Sioux Nation.

Criticism similar to Manypenny's came two years later from a strange source, the same Lieutenant General Phil Sheridan who had conspired with President Grant to open the Black Hills:

> in 1877 the great country . . . which, in 1869, belonged to the Indians, and extended from the line of the British possessions on the north, and almost to the Gulf of Mexico on the south, had passed into the hands of the whites, with the exception of the limited reservations assigned to the Indians, and with no compensation beyond the promise of religious instruction, schools, supplies of food and cloth- ing, and an opportunity of learning the ways in which the white man cultivated the ground—most of which promises have never been ful- filled. In other words, we took away their country and their means of support, broke up their mode of living, their habits of life, intro- duced disease and decay among them, and it was for this and against this they made war. Could any one expect less? Then, why wonder at Indian difficulties?[37]

THE SIOUX LITIGATION AGAINST the United States government was enor- mously complex and seriously constrained by unfortunate decisions made by the first attorney on the case. The government defended vigorously. A major defence was the claim for an offset against any judgement awarded the Sioux for the cost of rations supplied over the many years, more than $43 million, a sum far greater than the value of the Black Hills in 1877. The Sioux con- tended that the government had pursued a policy of western settlement that destroyed the buffalo herds upon which the tribes depended for their exis- tence and then used the offer of food as a means to coerce the starving natives into surrendering their lands. Congress agreed with the Sioux, and by legislation removed offset from the government's defence.

On June 30, 1980, the Supreme Court handed down final judgement in the case. It awarded the Sioux $17.5 million for the 1877 value of the Black Hills plus interest over all the intervening years, a total of almost $106 million. It had been the longest-running case in United States history, 57 years. In 1987, the Sioux secured judgement for another $40 million in a related case having to do with the 1868 Treaty. The Sioux have refused to touch a dollar of either judgement. The funds still remain in the United States Treasury, running at interest.

During the many years consumed by the lawsuit, a new generation of Sioux came to power in the tribal councils. The Black Hills, they decided, were not for sale at any price and they demanded return of the land itself. They take the view that to accept the money awarded by the judgements would be tantamount to acknowledging the validity of the United States' title to the Hills.

At the time of writing, 128 years after the taking of the Black Hills, more than half a billion dollars now sits running at interest in the United States Treasury to the credit of the Sioux Nations while the dispute runs on, now incapable of settlement. Return of the lands is impossible, while money alone will not expiate the guilt of a nation. The poverty and misery on the Sioux reservations continues.

CHAPTER 17

The Events of 1876–77

AMERICANS WERE CELEBRATING THEIR FIRST CENTENNIAL on July 4, 1876, when the news burst out of Montana Territory. The 7th Cavalry of the United States Army had been defeated, almost destroyed, by Sioux and Cheyenne Indians. Ten days earlier, on June 25, near the Little Big Horn River,[1] Lieutenant Colonel George Armstrong Custer and five companies of his command had been wiped out to the last man. The rest of the regiment had been badly mauled. The army suffered total fatalities of 265 officers, enlisted men and civilians. The Indians, led by Sitting Bull and Crazy Horse, had disappeared into the wilderness.

The impact upon the 45 million Americans of the time was no less than the shock wave that followed the destruction of the New York Trade Towers 125 years later.

The public reaction was immediate. "MASSACRE," cried the New York *Herald* and claimed that

> Never since the time of the rebellion has there been such a warlike sentiment abroad among the people . . . On one position all seemed agreed—to wit, that the policy of the government should be made one of deadly aggression, looking to the total extermination of the treacherous Indians of the plains.[2]

The shock was nationwide. In Washington, "A thrill of horror ran through the whole community." There was great excitement in San Francisco and a meeting was called to organize a company of military. In St. Louis, the news created "an appalling sensation."[3]

Stories out of Little Big Horn, casualty lists, maps of the campaign, and biographies of the participants, particularly Custer and Sitting Bull, occupied the front page of the *Herald* all the month of July. The public was whipped into a vicious mood. The U.S. Army ordered Colonel Nelson Miles to bring his 5th Infantry regiment up from Leavenworth, Kansas, to replace the decimated 7th Cavalry. Travelling by train, the troops passed through town after town draped in black crêpe. Station platforms were crowded with well-wishers urging the soldiers on against the Sioux[4]:

> Reaction throughout the country was no different in 1876 than it is today upon receipt of similar news: shock, followed by disbelief, fury and a slavering appetite for revenge ... Like cats hit with a spade, wits addled, state after state joined the national ululation. The Fort Smith, Arkansas, *Herald*, yowled with inchoate desire that thousands of rebels would respond to any call. Tennessee sang to the moon, pledging the terrible swift might of the Jackson Guards, the Chicksaw Guards, the ex-Confederate Irish Volunteers, and an unspecified Negro company. Ex-rebel General Jo Shelby of Missouri telegraphed Ulyssess Grant for permission to enlist one thousand Indian fighters. Atlanta's Cleburne Rifles yearned for retribution.[5]

Following the dramatic events at Little Big Horn, American outrage centred upon Sitting Bull as the Sioux leader most responsible for the disaster. For a time, the Army belittled Sitting Bull, claiming that he was not even a chief, merely a "head man" with a following of only 30 or 40 lodges,[6] but the press of the day howled for his head.

The media, the public, and even the Army, who should have known better, assumed that Indians conducted warfare with the same command and control hierarchy utilized by the modern military. Chiefs, it was believed, developed battle plans and directed their warriors just as did the officers of the U.S. Army. Sitting Bull was seen as the evil mastermind who coached the Sioux and Cheyenne to victory at Little Big Horn. He became "General Sitting Bull" to some newspapers, and the rumour grew that he was a graduate of the U.S. Military Academy at West Point and a military strategist the equal of Napoleon. The "Napoleon of the Sioux," rang the headlines.

The Sioux did have a traditional hierarchy of leadership, partly based along hereditary lines and partly granted according to prowess in battle and wisdom

Gall, Sioux war chief, c. 1870s. *Glenbow Museum NA-1196-7*

in council. Sitting Bull had achieved unusual stature among the seven tribes that made up the confederacy. Proven bravery had taken him to the rank of war chief of his Hunkpapa band and, in about 1869, he had been chosen as the supreme chief of the entire Sioux confederation,[7] a rank that had never before existed, and, with final defeat of the Sioux, never would again. Although Sitting Bull's supreme leadership was not acknowledged by all Sioux, he was clearly the most prominent among all the chiefs of the seven tribes of the confederation and an understandable target of the American media and Army. Remarkably, this illiterate Hunkpapa Sioux would, in a very few years, receive delegations from the heads of state of both the United States and Canada.

But no Indian commanded another in battle. Sitting Bull's voice in council might be decisive on the issue of war or peace, but once battle was engaged each warrior fought as an individual, a feature that often proved fatal to developed strategy. Many an ambush failed when a hot-blooded young brave could not resist an opportunity for glory.

At Little Big Horn the Sioux and Cheyenne had no defensive battle plan. Although they knew Army units were in the vicinity, they were surprised, first by Reno's attack and then by Custer's, and rushed to defend their camp. Battle groups developed around Gall, a Hunkpapa chief, and Crazy Horse of the Oglalas, two fighters with reputations that attracted followers. Historians credit Crazy Horse and Gall with the Sioux success that hot June day.

Sitting Bull was likely 45 years old in 1876,[8] a senior chief not expected to engage in front-line battle. His responsibilities were to ensure that the women and children were protected and then to provide encouragement to the fighters. His main contribution to the struggle at Little Big Horn may have been to convince the warriors to discontinue their assault on the troops dug in with Reno and Benteen.[9] But, regardless of the nature of his participation at Little Big Horn, Sitting Bull was the chosen villain of the piece.

Sitting Bull. *Saskatchewan Archives Board R-B11365*

If the attack the United States Army made against the Sioux and Cheyenne Indians camped in the valley of the Little Big Horn River[10] had come off as planned, the battle would have produced a very different result, but likely no less shedding of blood. That blood, however, would have been Sioux and Cheyenne blood, not that of troopers and officers of the U.S. Army. The attack was intended to go forward on June 26, 1876, but the impetuous George Armstrong Custer, in command of the 7th Cavalry, jumped the gun and rushed into battle a day early, on Sunday, June 25. He was riding for glory but found instead death and immortality as the commander of the most ignominious defeat ever suffered by the American military.

Custer carries the blame for the debacle, but not all of the responsibility was his. Major General Alfred H. Terry, commanding the U.S. Army Department of the Dakota, had designed a three-pronged attack on the Sioux and Cheyenne, whom he believed, correctly as it turned out, were camped somewhere along the Little Big Horn. One column of 450 men under Colonel John Gibbon approached from the west. Another, consisting of 1,000 men under Major General George F. Crook, marched from the south. Terry, with Custer under him, commanded another 925 officers and men moving from the east. The planned pincer movement, if properly executed, would have trapped the Sioux and Cheyenne with no escape route.

But on June 17, on the Rosebud River only 40 km (25 mi) short of the Little Big Horn, Crook's column was attacked by Sioux led by Crazy Horse. After a fierce, six-hour engagement, the Sioux broke off the fight, leaving Crook so seriously bloodied that he withdrew his troops. Their consequent absence from the field was an immense factor in the events on the Little Big Horn a week later. On June 25, the day Custer and his command were crushed, Crook's officers were leisurely fishing for trout in the mountain streams.[11]

It seems fair to say that Terry and his officers did not anticipate that there might be quite so many Indians camped along the Little Big Horn. Not a sinister assembly, this was a social event: the annual get-together for visiting and dancing, including the serious and spiritual Sun Dance. It was a huge gathering with tipis, or lodges, filling the valley for a full 5 km (3 mi). Estimates of the numbers of Indians in the encampment have, over the years, become more conservative. It was once thought that there were as many as 15,000, of whom 3,000 to 4,000 were warriors.[12] Twenty years later, after exhaustive research, the same writer calculated that the valley contained "from 450 to 1,000 lodges, from 3,000 to 7,000 people, from 800 to 1,800 fighting men."[13] Whatever the number, Custer and Company ran into far more defenders than they expected, or had ever before experienced. The Army complained afterwards that many Indians had left the reserves to join the encampment and that they had not been informed. But it was not the number of Sioux and Cheyenne warriors that took the 7th Cavalry by surprise that hot and dusty June day; it was the fact that, instead of fleeing before the attacking horsemen as Custer expected, they stood their ground and fought fiercely. Emboldened by their success against Crook on the Rosebud the week before, the warriors not only defended, but attacked, and did so with disciplined and coordinated movements—for them an innovation.

Terry sent Custer and the 7th Cavalry south up the Rosebud River on June 22. He was to cross to the Little Big Horn and attack on June 26, the day Gibbon was expected to reach the scene. Custer pushed his troops, covering 53 km (33 mi) on June 23, 45 km (28 mi) on June 24, then a night march of a further 16 km (10 mi), stopping for coffee from 2:00 a.m. to 5:00 a.m. on June 25 and then continuing the march until 8:00 a.m. Finally, with his men and horses exhausted, he pressed an attack against the huge village. In doing so he breached elementary military doctrine by splitting his command. He sent three companies under Captain Frederick W. Benteen to scout to the left, or south, and three more under Major Marcus A. Reno to attack the village from the south. With five companies under his direct command, Custer moved straight against the encampment. An hour after engaging the Sioux and Cheyenne warriors, Custer, together with 13 of his officers and 189 men, lay dead, their bodies scattered across a dusty Montana hillside looking far less heroic than they were later depicted in countless artistic renderings of "Custer's Last Stand." Four civilians with Custer also died, including a Canadian, Mark Kellogg, a journalist with the Bismarck *Tribune* who had been expected to provide the reportage of the flamboyant Custer's triumph, dispatches that would be also carried in the New York *Herald*.[14]

Major Reno charged the Indian village as instructed, but the Sioux defenders nearly overwhelmed his command. Under withering fire, he retreated to the top of a bluff and in the process lost 32 officers and men, plus several wounded.

Captain Benteen and his units joined Reno on the bluff where, until 9:00 p.m., the nearly 400 survivors of the 7th Cavalry desperately fought off a furious assault that killed another 18 of them and wounded 46 more. After only a short respite, at 2:30 a.m. the defenders came under a terrific rifle fire that continued unrelentingly for seven hours and was then followed by a charge that very nearly overran their position. The attack eased and then ceased, but bloodshot eyes remained watchful and close to their rifle sights. Finally, in the early evening the besieged cavalrymen saw the Indian encampment move away towards the Big Horn Mountains and only then were they able to send parties down to the river for water to slake the thirst that threatened their sanity. The next morning, June 27, brought Gibbon's troops, accompanied by General Terry, and final relief.

Horse and hand litters were built to transport the wounded men out to the steamer *Far West* at the mouth of the Little Big Horn. The trip took three days and must have been excruciating agony for the many of the injured who were strapped to Indian-style travois and dragged by horses over the rough terrain. On June 28, Major Reno and the surviving members of his command set about the grisly task of burying the 204 bodies of Custer and his command they found strewn about the hillside, many of them stripped and mutilated.

The officially reported U.S. Army casualties at Little Big Horn were 15 officers, 245 men, and five civilians dead, and two officers and 41 men wounded.[15] The Sioux and Cheyenne losses were not, of course, statistically identifiable but were small in comparison. Some of their dead were quickly buried; others, dressed for death, were left behind in lodges that were ransacked for souvenirs and poles to make litters for the wounded. Best estimates of the U.S. Army, not always noted for reticence in calculating body counts among enemy forces, was "a loss of about forty warriors killed."[16] This number was secured from later interviews among Indian participants in the battle.[17]

The outcome of the war between the Sioux and the United States Army was inevitable. After Little Big Horn, heavy reinforcements for the Army in Montana, Dakota and Wyoming Territories were mobilized, some from as far away as New York. Units were ordered into pursuit of the Sioux and Cheyenne, a pursuit that continued relentlessly even over the harsh winter of 1876–77. The Indian success at Little Big Horn was followed by another Trail of Tears as the tribes were hounded throughout the Territory until they either surrendered or fled the country.

Colonel Nelson A. Miles and his 5th Infantry Regiment became the Sioux nemesis. Miles was intensely ambitious, vain, jealous, as much a glory-hound as Custer had been, but a capable and determined officer. He would give no quarter.

Less than three years after the Little Big Horn disaster on the American Plains, Africa witnessed another bloody clash between an imperialistic modern army and Aboriginals defending their homeland. In January 1879, a British Expeditionary Force marched into Zululand determined to destroy all military capability possessed by the Zulus. With tactics reminiscent of Little Big Horn, the British army divided its forces as it probed and searched for the Zulu forces.

On the morning of January 22, Captain George Shepstone of the 24th Regiment chased several Zulu herdsmen to the edge of a ravine. Shepstone peered into the ravine and recoiled in horror. There before him was the main Zulu army, 20,000 warriors, crowded over the entire floor of the ravine. Undetected, they had approached within 8 km (5 mi) of Shepstone's units. With magnificent discipline the Zulus waited in total silence, intending to attack the next day with the rising moon. Their discovery advanced that plan.

Shepstone raced back to camp, blabbering incoherently and pointing wildly behind him. His colonel was slow to believe the story, but did send a messenger up to his commander and ordered his troops into defensive positions. Defence was futile against such overwhelming numbers. It was all over in two hours and the bodies of 1,329 British soldiers littered the Isandhlwana Plain.

It was different a few hours later when a smaller Zulu army attacked the British post at nearby Rorke's Drift. There the tiny command of 140 troopers, more than 30 of whom were patients in the post hospital, made the most of their defensive position and their new Martini-Henry breech-loading rifles. The Zulus withdrew after a 10-hour battle that left more than 2,000 of their warriors either killed or wounded. The British lost 15 men. Modern weaponry had triumphed over primitive arms.[1]

NOTE

1. Eleven Victoria Crosses, Britain's highest award for valour, were awarded to the defenders of Rorke's Drift. In December 1890, at Pine Ridge, South Dakota, troops of the American Army used artillery during an unprovoked attack that killed and wounded more than 200 Sioux. Twenty Congressional Medals of Honour, the United States' highest award, were issued for this engagement.

The United States Congress responded with unusual alacrity. Less than a month after Little Big Horn, on July 22 it approved funding for two more military forts in the Yellowstone country and decreed that there would be no more rations for the many surrendered and peaceable Sioux until they gave up all claim to the Black Hills, an open admission of the true motive for the war upon the Sioux.

The huge Cheyenne and Sioux encampment moved away from Little Big Horn into the mountains and there broke up as the individual bands went their own ways. It was logistically difficult to maintain such a large assembly for long. Grass for the thousands of horses, wood for the cooking fires, and game to feed such a multitude were soon exhausted. Traditionally, the summer was spent in hunting buffalo and preparing for the coming winter. Meat and berries had to be dried and hides tanned for clothing and lodges. But there was little time for such activities during the summer of 1876 after the Army regrouped and began searching out and attacking the camps. There were several encounters during July and August and by fall the Indians were sorely pressed by troops of both cavalry and infantry.

On September 9, at Slim Buttes, north of the Black Hills, units of the 2nd and 5th Cavalry surprised a village of Sioux at dawn, ran off the horse herd and shot up the camp, driving the men, women and children from their beds. The lodges were destroyed, along with a considerable supply of food, and the poorly clad survivors were left to fend for themselves. Several of the captured horses carried the brand of the 7th Cavalry indicating they had been with Custer at Little Big Horn. Also found was a 7th Cavalry guidon and a pair of gauntlets bearing the name of Captain M.W. Keogh, who had been killed at Little Big Horn. The evidence infuriated the troops, and the style was set for the engagements to come.

Then, in October, on the Yellowstone River in Montana Territory, a bizarre diplomatic encounter took place between Sitting Bull and two senior Army officers, first with Lieutenant Colonel E.S. Otis, and then with Colonel Nelson Miles. A supply train that Otis had been trying to get through to a post on the Tongue River came under attack by several hundred warriors from Sitting Bull's camp. The Sioux were driven back even after they set a prairie fire that overran the wagon train. The next day Sitting Bull attempted an unusual overture. One Johnny Bruquier, of mixed-blood ancestry, and who had once served as an army scout and interpreter, had moved in with the Sioux while waiting out a matter of homicide. At Sitting Bull's direction, the semi-literate Bruquier wrote a very strange diplomatic communication that was placed on the trail for Colonel Otis:

Yellowstone

I want to know what you are doing travelling this road. You scare all the buffalo away. I want to hunt in this place. I want you to turn back from here. If you don't I will fight you again. I want you to leave what you have got here and turn back from here.

I am your friend.
Sitting Bull

I mean all the rations you have got and some powder. Wish you would write as soon as you can.[18]

This was followed by two warriors carrying a flag of truce. The Sioux were hungry, they said, and tired of the war. They wished for peace. Sitting Bull wanted to meet Colonel Otis outside the protection of the military escort. Otis declined, but offered to meet inside his line of troops. Sitting Bull refused this proposal, but did send three chiefs. Otis advised that he had no authority to treat with the Sioux and suggested they go to the Tongue River post to negotiate a surrender. The Colonel gave them 68 kg (150 lb) of hard bread and a couple of sides of bacon and moved his transport train onward.

Colonel Nelson Miles and his 5th Infantry Regiment showed up a few days later, and again Sitting Bull signalled a desire to parley. Miles agreed and the two met between the lines of troops and warriors. Sitting Bull's request was simple: the Sioux had no wish for more war. They wanted to be free to hunt buffalo and would not fire upon the troops if they were not molested. Not good enough, Miles replied. The Sioux must place themselves under the authority of the Army. They agreed to talk again the next day, but Miles took the opportunity to move his 400 rifles between the Sioux camp and their anticipated destination.

On October 21, Miles and Sitting Bull met again. Their differences were irreconcilable. Sitting Bull "said he would come in to trade for ammunition, but wanted no rations or annuities, and desired to live free as an Indian."[19] Still not good enough, Miles insisted. The government's conditions were "that he should either camp his people at some point on the Yellowstone River, near to the troops, or go into some agency and place his people under subjection to the government."[20] Non-acceptance of the government's terms would be considered an act of hostility, Miles concluded.

With those words the battle was on. The troops drove the Sioux out of their campground and pursued them 68 km (42 mi) to the banks of the Yellowstone, forcing them to abandon tons of dried meat, many lodge poles, camp equipment and a number of horses. Several warriors were killed.

Miles' tactics produced some desired results a week later when 2,000 Sioux men, women and children turned themselves in to Miles rather than face a starvation winter. But Sitting Bull and his band did not surrender. They moved north to the Missouri River where they were joined by more Sioux under Gall and several other chiefs. Miles organized a force of 434 rifles and moved out in pursuit, but the trail disappeared under the snow. Undeterred,

Miles and his units continued their campaign, in spite of blizzards and record low temperatures. A winter of horror had just begun.

The natural and probable consequences of sending the United States Army against the Sioux, that they might be driven to escape into Canada, appears not to have occurred to the American authorities, but it had become obvious in faraway Ottawa as early as May. On May 26, H. Richardson, Deputy Minister of Justice, wrote NWMP Assistant Commissioner A.G. Irvine, warning that the operations might result in the Indians "being driven for shelter into the Territories." With uncanny foresight Richardson predicted "The place for which these escaping parties (should the suspicions I have expressed prove correct) would make, might be somewhere in the vicinity of Wood Mountain."[21] The NWMP were instructed to keep a sharp lookout and advise Ottawa immediately if any escaping Indians entered the North-West Territories.

Great Britain also took note of the unhealthy situation developing in the American West. Sir Edward Thornton, head of the British Legation in Washington, reported to London with a copy of the 1868 Fort Laramie Treaty being breached by the army's attack upon the Sioux. In July, after Little Big Horn, concern that the war might spill over into Canada was raised on the floor of the House of Commons at Westminster.

The 4,000 well-armed and equipped troops the U.S. Army had mobilized continued to press the campaign against the Sioux and Cheyenne even as a brutal winter descended upon the western plains. Colonel Ranald Mackenzie, who had won renown against the Comanche and Kiowa, had been ordered into Wyoming Territory with his 4th Cavalry. There, on November 25, in a surprise dawn attack on a village of Cheyenne under Dull Knife, the cavalrymen seized the herd of 500 horses and shot up the camp. The Cheyenne were driven on foot into the bitter cold while Mackenzie torched 173 lodges together with their contents, clothing, utensils and artifacts. Large quantities of dried buffalo meat and many buffalo robes, plus all the camp's ammunition, also disappeared into the flames. Equipment with 7th Cavalry markings was recovered.

At least 25 Cheyenne were killed. The survivors fled, without food and without protection from the fierce cold. Only a few had moccasins. For three horrifying weeks they struggled through the wilderness. Unable to withstand the -34°C (-30°F) temperatures, 11 babies perished in their mothers' arms. Finally, the destitute band reached a camp of Oglala Sioux with Crazy Horse and received the meagre succour available there. Their spirit broken, the Cheyenne continued on south to Nebraska, where they surrendered at Camp Robinson.

Meanwhile, Mackenzie and the 4th Cavalry returned to Fort Reno. There it was decided "The thermometer was so far below zero [-18°C] that further active field operations, in such weather, were considered impracticable, and they were, therefore, suspended for the winter."[22]

Not so with Colonel Nelson Miles. Jealous of Mackenzie's success, he kept his troops on operations. On December 18 the 5th Infantry surprised Sitting Bull's camp near the head of the Redwater River and captured 122 lodges, all their contents, the food supply and a number of horses and mules. The Sioux scattered with little but what they had on their persons. On December 29 Miles moved out from his post at the mouth of the Tongue River with 436 officers and men and two artillery pieces. Moving south up the Tongue he forced more than 600 lodges out of their winter camp. On January 8, 1877, near Wolf Mountain, the Sioux put up a fierce defence that lasted for hours until a blizzard blew up that so blinded both sides that they withdrew, but not before the superior weapons of the troopers worked heavy casualties among the Indians.

Suffering severely in the harsh conditions, the Sioux struggled into the Big Horn Mountains, where fortunately they found buffalo and were able to replenish their food, clothing and shelter. The bands of Sitting Bull and Crazy Horse met here, and later were joined by several other bands until the gathering became immense. Much time was spent in council. The Sioux were defeated and they knew it. The majority opinion was that surrender could not be avoided, and the debate moved on to the question of where they could secure the best deal, from Miles to the north or from General Crook at the agencies in Nebraska to the south. The Sioux began to negotiate. Miles, anxious to have the glory of the surrender, sent captives back to testify that they were well treated and invited a delegation of chiefs to meet with him at Fort Reno. In February the bands split up, taking separate directions to their common destiny. Crazy Horse moved south, towards Nebraska and Camp Robinson. Sitting Bull went north to the Missouri River. But his real destination was Canada.

Sitting Bull had been considering his options since Little Big Horn, well aware of the consequences that would follow the Sioux victory. He soon concluded that he would not be allowed to live in freedom in the United States and declared that there were only two routes to sanctuary, "one to the country of the Great Mother, the other to the Spaniards."[23] Between Canada and Mexico, Canada was the obvious choice, and Sitting Bull was not the only Sioux to reach that decision.

Perhaps Sitting Bull and the other Sioux leaders had considered Canada as a place of refuge before the battle at Little Big Horn made sanctuary an immediate imperative. Or, perhaps they had planned to enlist the Indians in Canada, particularly the Blackfoot, to a confederacy designed to drive the whites from the West on both sides of the border, and return the Great Plains to its rightful owners.

THERE IS SOME EVIDENCE to support both theories, as impossible as it is more than 125 years later to divine the thoughts and plans of such complex men (strategy being the preserve of men alone), when those thoughts and plans were entirely unrecorded other than in the writings of the few literate Europeans in the vicinity, most of whom were adversaries, or nearly so, and who could only pretend to surmise the real thinking behind the conduct they observed and the few words they heard.

We do know that there was a "Great Indian Gathering at Cypress Hills"[24] in June 1876, sometime prior to the encounter at Little Big Horn. This was reported by the Toronto *Daily Globe*'s correspondent from Fort Macleod, someone obviously very closely connected to, or even a member of, the NWMP. There were two reports, dated at Fort Macleod on June 27 and July 1, 1876, when they were likely sent overland to Helena, in Montana Territory, to be telegraphed to Toronto. By neither date had the news reached Fort Macleod of the disaster at Little Big Horn on June 25.

The initial report described the assembly as huge, 3,000 lodges, which would make it three times larger than the congregation at Little Big Horn. Later, after inspection by a troop of NWMP under Assistant Commissioner A.G. Irvine, the estimate was reduced to 1,000 lodges, still as large, or perhaps larger than the summer camp that overwhelmed Custer.

According to the *Daily Globe*'s correspondent, the gathering consisted of "North and South Peogans [*sic*], Blackfeet, Bloods, Assiniboines, besides Gros Ventres, Crows and Sioux from the American side." It went on, "it is reported, and generally believed here, that the Sioux, who planned and carried out this meeting of the different tribes, will attempt to sow the seeds of dissension and distrust amongst the other Indians with a view to a general rising hereafter against the whites." Whatever the plan, such an assembly, even if only half as large as reported, was exceedingly unusual, and the more so if it brought together such traditional enemies as the Sioux and the Crow, not to mention other reliable hostilities.

Almost the only other piece of evidence is the report of Inspector Cecil Denny dated August 22, 1876. Dispatched to the Blackfoot camp he found them "about thirty miles [48 km] above the mouth of the Red Deer River," in the vicinity of today's Alsask and quite happy to see an officer of the NWMP. The chiefs invited Denny to a council, where they reported that about a month earlier they had received a messenger from the Sioux. The message was accompanied by tobacco, the traditional gift to seal a bargain, and was theirs to smoke if they were willing to come across the line and join the Sioux in fighting the Crow Indians, and other tribes with whom they were at war; and also the Americans whom they were fighting at the same time:

> The Sioux promised to give the Blackfeet, if they would join them, plenty of horses and mules they had captured from the Americans; they also told the Blackfeet that they had plenty of white women, whom they had taken prisoners, and they promised to give them to the Blackfeet if they would join them.

> They also told the Blackfeet that if they would come to help them against the Americans, that after they had killed all the Whites they would come over and join the Blackfeet to exterminate the Whites on this side.

> They also told him that the whites on this side were weak, and that it would take them but a short time to take any forts that they had built here, as they had taken many strong stone forts from the Americans, at small loss to themselves.[25]

The messenger the Blackfoot sent back to the Sioux refusing the offer had just returned prior to Denny's arrival on the scene. He reported that the Sioux had been angry at the refusal and threatened to come against the Blackfoot just as soon as they were finished with the Americans. Crowfoot and his chiefs were upset at this news and wanted assurance that the NWMP would come to their aid in the event of such an attack.

When Denny calmed the Blackfoot with his promise that the NWMP would protect them, Crowfoot reciprocated with his pledge that 2,000 warriors would come to the assistance of the police if they came under attack by the Sioux. Strangely, the Blackfoot had not returned the tobacco to the Sioux, as protocol required when refusing the offer it accompanied. They showed it to Denny. Strange also that in 1939, when Inspector Denny, then Sir Cecil E. Denny, Bart., wrote his memoir, *The Law Marches West*, he made no mention of this incident other than to quote from his 1876 report.

Did Sitting Bull and the Sioux leadership hope in the summer of 1876, both before and after Little Big Horn, to organize a great uprising of all the Indian tribes in the West to drive out the whites and regain their homelands? Or was this merely the interpretation of the whites who were most fearful of just such at attempt?

ON THE BITTERLY COLD afternoon of December 17, 1876, Jean-Louis Légaré spotted horsemen out his Wood Mountain window. Twelve riders, swathed in buffalo robes, sat silently staring at the door to Légaré's log home that doubled as his trading post. The Quebec-born Légaré, trading in the West for 12 years and wise in the ways of Indians, paid no attention. After a long half hour, one of the riders dismounted, opened the door and stared silently into the room before entering and seating himself on the floor. Légaré and his several companions were ignored. Then the first visitor called to his companions one by one and each joined him until all 12 sat cross-legged on Légaré's floor. Still no one spoke. The door remained open.

After two hours of uncomfortable silence, the leader, who turned out to be the Sioux chief Little Knife, leaped to his feet and, followed by his companions, cheerfully shook hands with Légaré and the others. A speech was made: "We left the American side because we could not sleep. We heard that the Big Woman was very good to her children and we came to this country to sleep quietly."[26]

The first of the Lakota Sioux had arrived in Canada. And, as predicted by Richardson seven months earlier, they had made precisely for Wood Mountain.

After securing some provisions from Légaré, the Sioux left but returned the next day in full force. When NWMP Inspector James Walsh arrived at Wood Mountain on December 21 to investigate the situation, he found 109 lodges crammed with a remarkable number of Sioux, almost 3,000. He counted "500 men, 1,000 women and 1,400 children, 3,500 horses and 30 United States' Government mules."[27]

The 49th Parallel was about to face its first real test as an international boundary. The camp of the fugitive Sioux was only 30 km or so (20 mi) inside Canada. Could the two-year-old earthen monuments, whose three-mile spacing kept them below the horizon even on the great western flatland, ensure sanctuary from the pursuing United States Army?

THE NEWLY ARRIVED LAKOTA moved in beside the camp of Minnesota Santee Sioux under White Eagle living 6.5 km (4 mi) east of the Boundary Survey buildings that soon became the NWMP Wood Mountain Post. It had been 15 years since the Minnesota Uprising that brought White Eagle and his people to Canada, and they had fitted in very well. The 150 lodges of Santee were not greatly pleased to see their Lakota cousins. The good life they enjoyed north of the border might be jeopardized by the demands of too many refugees. But the buffalo in the vicinity were more plentiful than they had been in years and there would be enough for everyone—for now.

North-West Mounted Police post, Wood Mountain, c. 1877. *Glenbow Museum NA-2003-49*

White Eagle's people had been included in a reserve in Canada granted in 1874 and 1875. Their Oak River Reserve No. 58, consisting of 3,238 ha (8,000 acres) about 32 km (20 mi) west of Brandon, was occupied by a few families, but most of the band remained out on the plains so long as the buffalo were plentiful. When the Lakota sought similar reservations, Ottawa refused, with the rationale that the Santee had greater rights since they had come into the West before it had been acquired by Canada. It was a distinction not well understood by the Lakota Sioux who arrived after Little Big Horn.

White Eagle wanted Walsh to explain the rules to the newcomers. The Santee were familiar with the law in Canada and were anxious that the Lakota who had joined their camp have the same understanding. Walsh was pleased to have the opportunity and addressed an assembly of the Lakota chiefs called by White Eagle. Here for the first time he met Black Moon, Little Knife, Long Dog, the Man Who Crawls, and others.

The NWMP officer outlined the basics of the Canadian law the Sioux would be expected to observe, the two important features being that there was one law for all, whether Indian or white, and that horse stealing was a serious crime. Then he wanted to know why the Sioux had come to Canada.

They had been driven from their homes by the Americans and had come to look for peace, the chiefs replied. Their grandfathers had told them that they would find peace in the land of the British; their brothers the Santees had found it years before and they had followed them. They had not slept soundly for years and were anxious to find a place where they could lie down and feel safe. They hoped that the Great Mother would have pity on them.

The chiefs assured Walsh that they had no intention of recrossing the Medicine Line to make war on the Americans. But the Lakota were in desperate need. Without ammunition for their rifles they had been killing buffalo with bows and arrows, with knives tied to lances, and even by lassoing the huge animals. Their horses were used up and could no longer match the buffalo. They required ammunition. Walsh agreed to instruct Jean-Louis Légaré to issue them limited quantities of shells, but only for hunting. None was to go over the border. With that, the first of the refugee Sioux settled in to life in Canada. More were on the way.

In early March Walsh met with Four Horns, chief of the Hunkpapa Sioux and senior even to Sitting Bull, who had just crossed the border with 57 lodges and camped on the Frenchman River 193 km (120 mi) east of Fort Walsh. The band, 25 days on the trail from Powder River, south of the Missouri, had been so hard pressed by the Army that they had been unable to hunt and were forced to butcher their horses.

Walsh gave Four Horns the same lecture he had delivered at Wood Mountain and received the same explanation for the Sioux coming in to Canada; they wanted peace and security from the American soldiers. Four Horns claimed that they were British Indians, that 65 years earlier (after the War of 1812) was the first their fathers knew of being under the Americans. Why the British had given their country to the Americans they did not know, but their fathers had been told that if they did not wish to live under the Americans they could move northward where they would find the land of the British.

It had been Four Horns, Sitting Bull's uncle and leader of the Hunkpapa Sioux, who, concerned about the succession to the Sioux leadership, had arranged Sitting Bull's elevation to supreme chief. Now the old chief had fled to sanctuary in Canada while Sitting Bull and his followers remained on the Missouri River near Fort Peck, seemingly reluctant to take the final step of leaving the United States. When a sudden breakup of the river and an ice jam sent a flood rushing into the camp the Sioux barely escaped with their lives, leaving many lodges and most of their possessions to the river.

As spring advanced, the options open to the Sioux took on dreadful clarity. They could either surrender, fight to the death, or flee the country. In early April Sitting Bull and a number of other chiefs gathered between Fort Peck and the border to again discuss their plight. Once more Sitting Bull declared his intention to move into Canada. He would not surrender.[28]

But more and more Sioux bowed to the ultimatum issued by Colonel Miles. On April 22, chiefs Two Moons and Hump led 300 followers into surrender at Fort Reno. Others drifted into the agencies and military posts to the south.

Then, on the morning of May 6, the unthinkable happened: Crazy Horse surrendered. The great leader of the Oglala Sioux, 11 months on the run following the battle at Little Big Horn, had been so relentlessly hounded by the Army over the long and bitter winter that he could no longer endure the suffering of his people. On a flat plain 3.2 km (2 mi) north of Camp Robinson, the U.S. Army post in northwestern Nebraska, Lieutenant Philo Clark and a small group of fellow officers, with several enlisted Indian scouts, watched as the 36-year-old warrior chief rode, still proudly, at the head of a column of 900 ragged and hungry followers, accompanied by more than 2,000 horses. Crazy Horse stopped before Clark, turned and surveyed the survivors of his band. His headmen were in front, dressed in warrior regalia, while the women and elderly still straggled through the hills. All were singing their death songs, the chant ringing eerily in the morning air.

Then Crazy Horse dismounted and loosened the knots in his horse's tail, signifying that its warrior rider was no longer at war. Then he seated himself on the greening prairie in front of Clark, and extended his left hand, by custom the one closest to the heart. "I want to shake hands while seated because that means our peace will last," he told Clark, who also sat before taking the outstretched hand.[29] Thus did the great Oglala chief surrender his freedom, and that of his people, for life on the reservation. It was an epic and heartrending event, sufficiently momentous to be reported in the *Times* of faraway New York on May 8, 1877.

Crazy Horse had been the real military genius of the Sioux Nation and deserved most of the credit for the victory over the 7th Cavalry, although Sitting Bull was cast by the American press as the prime villain.

Miles' ultimatums were no idle threats. On May 7, the day after the Crazy Horse surrender, he attacked the camp of Lame Deer near the head of the Rosebud River. Lame Deer attempted to surrender but he was misunderstood and killed. His people fled into the hills and the village of 51 lodges was sacked; 450 horses and mules were captured.

That same week Sitting Bull finally made his move. His camp of 135 lodges and almost 1,000 Sioux travelled up the valley of the Frenchman River into Canada and on to Pinto Horse Butte, an upland 225 km (140 mi) east of Fort Walsh. For a third time Inspector James Walsh saddled up and rode forth to read the Canadian laws to Sioux refugees from the United States.

As Walsh, accompanied by an escort and three Métis scouts, followed the fresh trail, Sioux riders appeared on both skylines, obviously picquets, or sentries. As they approached the camp more and more riders appeared until the NWMP party was surrounded by Sioux. Walsh continued riding to the edge of

North-West Mounted Police Inspector James Morrow Walsh (no date). *Library and Archives Canada / Library and Archives Canada published holdings project C-17038*

the camp where he and his men dismounted and were immediately met by several chiefs who announced that this was indeed Sitting Bull's camp. The chiefs told Walsh that never before had any white men, soldiers or scouts ridden in so casually.

Walsh held council with Sitting Bull and his fellow chiefs, particularly Spotted Eagle, and delivered his standard message. Like the earlier arrivals, these chiefs also claimed British connections and assured Walsh that they sought only peace. Sitting Bull claimed that he was having the most wonderful experience of his life, feeling that he was in another world, among white men who were different from any he had ever seen. Yesterday, he said, he had been fleeing white men and cursing them as he went, but today they ride into his camp and offer him their hand. Walsh, not initially impressed with Sitting Bull, thought he was making a political speech, was full of revenge, and likely to recross the border to attack the American troops any time he was able.[30]

Walsh and his troop spent the night in the Sioux camp. The next morning the NWMP scouts spotted some obviously stolen horses in the possession of White Dog, an Assiniboine who had just arrived at the camp. Three of his horses belonged to Reverend Jules DeCorby, the Oblate priest from St. Florent (Lebret) in the Qu'Appelle Valley who was then serving the Métis camps at Wood Mountain and in the Cypress Hills. Walsh ordered White Dog's arrest as if the horde of Indians surrounding him did not exist. White Dog, assuming he would be supported by the Sioux, became belligerent. Walsh cooly forced White Dog to surrender the horses and apologize for his conduct as hundreds of amazed Sioux watched this example of Canadian justice. It was a good beginning for the reputation of the NWMP.

Later in May, Walsh pulled off a remarkably daring and successful arrest. A camp of 250 lodges of American Assiniboine had moved in near the Cypress Hills and their 200 warriors had terrorized a small camp of Saulteaux. The Assiniboine chief, Crow's Dance, openly challenged the authority of the NWMP. With an escort of 15 men Walsh rode into the Assiniboine camp at dawn and arrested Crow's Dance, several other chiefs and 18 warriors. The officer then addressed the remaining chiefs on the reasons for his action and the necessity of obeying Canadian law. Then he took 11 Assiniboine the 80 km (50 mi) back to Fort Walsh for trial. Crow's Dance was sentenced to six months at hard labour, another chief to two months, and the rest were released. Walsh's actions cemented throughout the West the NWMP reputation for unwavering courage and fair and firm justice.

James Morrow Walsh was a man who had achieved his destiny, but only after more than a few failed attempts. Ontario-born, with minimal education, he had worked variously as a machinist, a railwayman, a sales clerk, a broker and a hotel manager before discovering the militia. Along the way he had developed connections to the Conservative Party that secured him appointment to the newly formed NWMP in 1873. There he quickly displayed such aptitude that he was promoted to inspector. Thirty-six years old when he met Sitting Bull, Walsh, although a bit of a swashbuckler, was a supremely confident officer, the perfect fit for his unique position on the western plains.

The NWMP were too few to properly police the huge territory for which they were responsible. About June 23, four traders from Winnipeg, the West Brothers and two others, were approaching Wood Mountain when they were accosted by a party of 27 Sioux warriors. The Sioux wanted gun powder and musket balls for which they proposed to exchange several horses. But the traders noticed that the horses carried brands identifying them as the property of the U.S. Army and declined the offer. The Sioux then forcefully helped themselves to three kegs of powder and a bag of bullets. The nearest police were more than 240 km (150 mi) away, too far to travel to even file a complaint.[31]

The presence of the American Sioux in the North-West Territories was a serious problem for the government of Canada. The process of clearing away the Indian title to the western plains was not yet completed and suddenly several thousand new Indians had taken up residence there, claiming a very plausible right to do so. Also, the Sioux were traditional enemies of the Cree, Assiniboine and Blackfoot whose homelands were being intruded upon, not to mention the Métis who also depended on the western buffalo herds. Trouble was very likely. The Sioux had settled from Wood Mountain to the Cypress Hills, all on Treaty 4 lands, but they could be expected to move about at will, especially in search of buffalo.

David Laird, then occupying the dual positions of Lieutenant-Governor and Indian Superintendent of the North-West Territories, was quick to see the problem. On March 22, 1877, he wrote Ottawa expressing his concerns.

He pointed to the obvious solution, that the Sioux return to the United States, and suggested that communications be opened to persuade Washington to induce that result.[32]

The diplomatic channels at the time were stilted and slow. Canada, still a colony of Great Britain, was not in charge of its external affairs. These were handled by the Colonial Office in London. Accordingly, dispatches went through the office of the Governor General in Ottawa to London and then to Britain's *chargé d'affaires* in Washington, who would carry them to the American Secretary of State, and then back along the same route. With the speed of the mails at the time, it was laborious and frustrating, provoking a Canadian minister to cut through the formal protocol, incurring serious criticism but achieving good results.

Just how many Sioux were on Canadian soil was difficult to estimate accurately. It was usual to count the number of lodges, and then apply a standard factor of inhabitants per lodge. In normal times each lodge would contain just one family, perhaps three to five individuals. But the U.S. Army had destroyed lodges more quickly than the Sioux could replace them, and two and three families were crammed into one lodge.

Ottawa's early estimates were somewhat exaggerated. On June 1, Governor General Dufferin reported to London: "I am sorry to say the Sioux are pouring into our territory. We have already got 10,000 on our side of the line—the greater proportion being women and children."[33]

In the summer of 1877, Pascal Breland, a Red River Métis and an experienced plainsman and member of the North-West Council, made a calculation of the number of Sioux in the West, both the Minnesota Santee and the recently arrived Lakota. Breland identified 350 lodges of Minnesota Santee, 127 lodges of Dakota who had been in the Territory for some time, and 800 lodges of Lakota. He assumed seven inhabitants in each lodge, resulting in an estimate of 5,600 Lakota Sioux who had come into Canada in 1876 and 1877.[34]

But the total of all Sioux in the Territories was likely 1,277 lodges holding 8,399 men, women and children. That was perhaps one-half, or certainly one-third, of the total Canadian Indian population covered by Treaties 1 through 6, including the Blackfoot who would come under Treaty 7 later in 1877. Those were numbers that caused real concern in Ottawa. The Santee Sioux had been granted reserves on the basis of 32 ha (80 acres) per family of five, half that allotted under the land surrender treaties. To extend that consideration to 5,000 newcomers would require some 32,376 ha (80,000 acres) of land, more charity than Ottawa could contemplate.

Late in May Sitting Bull sent messengers to Fort Walsh advising that three unwelcome visitors from the United States were in his camp. NWMP Assistant Commissioner A.G. Irvine was at Fort Walsh when the messengers arrived and accompanied Inspector Walsh and two other officers on their patrol to the Sioux village 225 km (140 mi) to the east which they reached on June 2.

The Americans were the Benedictine Abbott Martin Marty, who was accompanied by an interpreter, and one John Howard, an Englishman by birth who served as chief scout to Colonel Nelson Miles, a fact known to the Sioux, who looked upon the three with deep suspicion.

Abbott Marty had been appointed Vicar General of Dakota Territory just the year before, in 1876, in response to a call from the Bureau of Catholic Indian Missions to provide Catholic leadership on the Indian frontier. Believing it was his duty to induce Sitting Bull and his followers to return peacefully to the United States, the priest had, with more faith than good sense, travelled into Canada to meet with the Sioux.

Sitting Bull was apologetic about calling upon the police. Had Walsh not requested to be advised if anyone came over the border, the chief would have looked after the matter himself, by dispatching Marty's two companions and sending the priest himself packing.

The Sioux took advantage of the presence of four officers of the NWMP to conduct a formal assembly. When the large council lodge was erected and filled with a number of chiefs and more than 100 observers, the meeting commenced with a prayer and the pipe ceremony. Then Sitting Bull and a number of other chiefs spoke of their treatment at the hands of the Americans, their loss of the Black Hills, their grandfathers' connection to the British, and their desire to now live in peace in the Great Mother's country. Sitting Bull said that he did not throw their land away: "Crazy Horse is still holding it. He is looking at me to see if it is good here."[35]

Marty, who carried letters of authorization from his superiors and the Commissioner of Indian Affairs, claimed that he had come to invite the Sioux to return to the United States. Sitting Bull did not believe the priest, whose story had been inconsistent. In the end, Marty told the Sioux that he thought they were better off "on British soil." And with this statement the priest was perhaps representing the true desire of the American government.

Irvine was much taken by Sitting Bull:

> He is a man of somewhat short stature, but with a pleasant face, a mouth showing great determination, and a fine high forehead. When he smiled, which he often did, his face brightened up wonderfully

... he spoke as a man who knew his subject well, and who had thoroughly weighed it over before speaking. He believes no one from the other side, and he said so. His speech showed him to be a man of wonderful capability.[36]

Sitting Bull apparently recognized that the Assistant Commissioner was a man of more influence even than Walsh. About 11:00 p.m. he visited Irvine in his tent, where he spent several hours sitting on the officer's bed telling of his experiences at the hands of the American Army. Sitting Bull gave a glorified description of the events at Little Big Horn and his participation that could only have been intended to impress Irvine.

The Canadian government was perplexed by the presence of the American Sioux. After considering Irvine's account of the council on June 2, he was instructed not to allow them "to believe that they will be allowed permanent residence or treated as Canadian Indians."[37] At Canada's behest, F.R. Plunkett, the British *chargé d'affaires* at Washington, had written William Evarts, the American Secretary of State, requesting "that the United States Government will be so good as to use their best endeavors to induce those Indians to return to their own country."[38] In other words, "please get your Indians out of Canada."

But the United States was not nearly as unhappy with the fact its Sioux were in Canada. When Plunkett had received no reply to his request by July 24, he marched over to Evarts' office. The Secretary explained that they were having some difficulty deciding how to deal with the problem. He assumed that Canada would not appreciate the American army crossing the border after the Sioux, nor would it want to drive the Sioux back by force. Plunkett thought that it would only be necessary for the United States to offer the Sioux "favourable terms on which to return." In his view the Indians were not citizens but merely wards of the United States without political privileges and the government had more direct power over them. Evarts demurred. In his view,

the United States Government could not be expected to hold out great temptations to return, in the case of savages whom they were only too happy to have got rid of, and who had committed all sorts of crimes before quitting the United States . . . if the United States troops ever caught hold of those among the savages who had robbed and murdered on American territory before they crossed into Canada, they would probably shoot them.[39]

It was obvious to the Canadian government that a quick solution to the problem of "the Sitting Bull Sioux," as they were becoming known, would not be coming from Washington. Frustrated by the impasse and the cumbersome diplomatic protocol, the Liberal government of Alexander Mackenzie decided to attempt an unorthodox "can do" approach befitting a frontier nation. They would slice through the formalities. Their decision was made easier by the absence from Ottawa of Governor General Dufferin. Ignoring protocol, David Mills, Minister of the Interior, headed for Washington.

Early in the morning of August 8, Mills appeared at the offices of the British Legation in Washington and asked to see Mr. Plunkett. It was far too early for a respectable British diplomat to be found in his offices, so Mills headed for the Plunkett residence, where he presented himself to the astonished *chargé d'affaires*.

Plunkett was good enough to take Mills over to the offices of the Secretary of State. Evarts was out of town but Mills spoke with the Under-Secretary who thought the problem belonged with the Department of the Interior. When Mills arrived at the office of Interior Secretary Carl Schurz, Schurz listened carefully and then took the Canadian over to the White House and introduced him to President Rutherford Hayes. Arrangements were made to meet the next day with Secretary Schurz and the Secretary of War, George McCrary.

The next morning, August 9, when President Hayes sat in on the meeting, the Canadian minister knew he had captured the attention of the Washington decision-makers. Schurz thought the Sioux were political offenders who had made war on the United States and retired under arms across the border and that Canada was obliged to disarm them. Mills replied as gently as he could that, from the Sioux point of view, the hostilities had been commenced by the United States, not the Sioux. Since the United States had certain treaty obligations to the Sioux, he went on, it might be best to consider making some concessions to conciliate them and induce them to return to their reservations.

The thought of Sitting Bull and the Sioux moving back across the border while still in possession of their rifles was unacceptable to the American officials. They must first surrender their arms and their horses as a condition of returning. If the Sioux refused, would the Canadian government be prepared to disarm them?

Mills explained that the Sioux had no ammunition other than the small amount the NWMP allowed them for hunting. If they could not hunt, they would starve. Also, to disarm them would leave them at the mercy of the Canadian Blackfoot and Cree who very much resented the Sioux presence.

Further, seizing the Sioux firearms would not elevate their level of trust. Mills thought the solution was to show consideration to Sitting Bull and the other chiefs by providing them with superior weapons and distinctive uniforms.

President Hayes commented that he understood Mills to be saying that, to the Sioux, firearms were merely tools by which they secured their living and the Canadian was proposing that the United States "buy up" Sitting Bull and the Sioux leaders. Mills agreed, but "by doing them justice, and by securing . . . their goodwill and friendship."

Mills went on to plead the Sioux cause. Sitting Bull and his people never desired war, but the lands reserved only for them had been invaded by whites and when the Sioux complained the government took action against them, forcing them to defend themselves. But, Shurz wanted to know, "How do you keep your whites in order?" The United States, he intimated, had not been able to prevent white invasion of the Indian territories.

In the end, President Hayes and his two secretaries agreed to appoint a commission to visit Sitting Bull and the Sioux in Canada with the view of persuading them to return to the United States. Mills warned them that, if the United States insisted upon disarming the Sioux and seizing their horses, there would be little likelihood of success. The President thought that, if such were the case, the commission might at least learn what terms and conditions the Sioux would be willing to accept.[40] The Canadian mission succeeded in convincing the American government that it had some responsibility for the Sioux, and that action should be taken to bring them home.

The British, however, were not amused at Canada's audacity. Governor General Dufferin described the circumventing of his office as "a very pernicious precedent," and remonstrated with Prime Minister Mackenzie.[41] The Colonial Secretary in London, Lord Carnarvon, followed with another rebuke. While agreeing that the Mills visit had produced excellent results, he emphasized that independent action of that sort could not be permitted because of the possible effect on other areas of the British Empire. The Mackenzie government meekly acquiesced.[42]

Not long after Mills had returned to Ottawa, Washington began to wonder just how much success it desired for the commission the President had agreed to appoint. On August 14 the Cabinet approved the concept of a commission but refused to provide any funding and directed that the two commissioners should come from the Army and the Indian Department. General Terry was selected as military representative and to be the head commissioner, a feature that assured limited success for the mission. Terry had commanded many of the units that fought against the Sioux, including Custer and the 7th Cavalry at Little Big Horn.

Cabinet further agreed that the commission would be instructed to request that Sitting Bull and the Sioux surrender and agree to be placed on a reservation, a proposition that admittedly had little hope of success. Which would be just fine. "In fact, it would be pleasing to this Government if the proposition did not succeed, as Sitting Bull is not a denizen to be desired by any country."[43] If the expected failure occurred, the United States would then "make a demand on the Canadian authorities to remove him and his Band from our borders . . . based upon the principles of international law, that foreign territory cannot be made the basis of hostile operations."[44]

Ottawa was alert to the thinking in Washington. On August 20, David Mills advised NWMP Commissioner Macleod of the likely result and predicted that the United States would thereafter demand reparations from Canada for any injuries or damages that the Sioux might cause on raids across the border. Mills instructed Macleod to compile as much information as possible about American breaches of treaties with the Sioux and the frauds worked upon them by corrupt Indian Agents—all with the view of defending the expected American claims by counterclaiming for the expense Canada had been put to by reason of the ill treatment of the Sioux:

> when the misgovernment of any portion of that population is notoriously such as to give rise to civil war on our border, to force a portion of that population upon our territory, and to impose upon us additional expense, we certainly have a right to remonstrate.[45]

Washington's decision to provide no funding for the commission had the expected result of making it difficult to find someone willing to serve. Terry was under orders and on pay and allowances but other candidates were reluctant to undertake a 3,200-km (2,000-mi) trip into the western wilderness and back in the hope that the Government would retroactively cover the cost. "The Sitting Bull Epidemic Affecting Everybody Who Is Called Upon To Act On The Commission," the *National Republican* observed, as two retired Army generals used illness as an excuse for declining appointment to the commission.[46]

The American government found the delay in getting the commission under way quite acceptable. In fact, as fall approached, Interior Secretary Schurz suggested that it might be best if the project did not go forward until the next year. Then reports came in to Washington from Colonel Miles on the frontier claiming that, after a disagreement between the Canadian authorities and Sitting Bull and his followers, the Sioux had returned to the United States, 1,300 warriors strong, equipped with plenty of ammunition and ready to fight. Miles requested more troops and orders to move against the Sioux. There was, of course, no point in sending a commission into Canada to negotiate with Sitting Bull if he was back in the United States. The project was again delayed until the NWMP reported that the Sioux were, as usual, camped near Wood Mountain.

The *National Republican* was no fan of the proposed commission. It hoped that the Sioux were back in the United States:

> [I]t will save our Government the humiliation of sending Commissioners to that untamed barbarian, who has twice badly defeated our military forces, and who is now asking us for terms of surrender ... we should not condescend to make any treaty with that savage until he has been thoroughly thrashed, for if we were to do so, he would take it as an evidence of fear and weakness, and we could not expect him to observe any treaty obligation in good faith.
>
> We hope, therefore, that the talk about a treaty with Sitting Bull will be abandoned. Such a policy may be well enough for the Canadian Government, but our relations with the Indians are quite different. It will not do for us to humiliate ourselves by treating with a Chief who has twice defeated us ... We should, therefore, only treat with Sitting Bull by a force strong enough to compel him to accept such terms as our Government may see proper to dictate. Treaties with Indians are, at the best, worth but little, and the fewer we have of them, the better it will be for all concerned.[47]

Since the *National Republican* was close to the administration of President Rutherford Hayes, it can be assumed that it expressed the opinions of many in that government.

William T. Sherman, General of the Army, was in favour of a commission being sent to offer the Sioux safe conduct to their assigned reservations, but only as a concession prior to demanding that Canada expel them:

> General Terry is with me, and we have discussed this matter freely, and we agree that the English authorities should *now* elect to adopt these refugee Indians as their own or force them back to our side of

the line before they recuperate their ponies and collect new supplies of ammunition.[48]

The Sitting Bull Commission, as it was called, was finally made complete by the appointment of retired General A.G. Lawrence as second Commissioner, and Lieutenant Colonel H.C. Corbin, as Secretary. The Commissioners rendezvoused at St. Paul and then, on September 14, headed into Montana Territory, travelling by Union Pacific Railroad to Corinne, Utah, and by stage coach to Helena. Then they would ride to Fort Shaw and Fort Benton before moving on to the Canadian border, which they expected to reach on September 29. They were accompanied by two newspaper correspondents, Jerome Stillson of the New York *Herald*, and Charles Diehl of the Chicago *Times*. A third correspondent, from the Fort Benton *Record*, would join them at Fort Benton. There was great public interest in Sitting Bull and the Commission going to meet him.

At St. Paul the Commissioners reviewed their instructions and agreed that they were, in at least one particular, completely impractical. Sitting Bull and the Sioux could accept the proposal being made to them only if they surrendered all their firearms, ammunition and horses at the border. Only the "aged and infirm" would be permitted the use of a horse; the able-bodied would be required to "march on foot to the reservation." Since any reservation selected would certainly be several hundred kilometres south of the border, this condition, in the opinion of the Commissioners, would be "very embarrassing to both the troops and the Indians." General Terry sent off a telegram requesting a modification to the instructions that would permit the Sioux to ride to their final destination. A telegram of approval awaited the Commission when they reached Helena.

While Generals Terry and Lawrence, and their retinue, made their way through the West, another great council with Sioux delegates took place in Washington. Inviting the Indian leaders to the capital was a favourite ploy. Travelling by train through the eastern cities, the chiefs could not fail to be impressed with the white man's numerical and technological superiority.

On September 27, a large delegation of chiefs from the surrendered bands at the Agencies arrived at the White House to meet with President Hayes to discuss the location of the reservations they were to occupy. All in full regalia except the two great leaders, Red Cloud and Spotted Tail, they were ushered into the East Room where they sat down not only with the President but also Secretary of State Evarts, Secretary of War McCrary, the Postmaster General and several other officers and officials.

Red Cloud had led the Sioux in the Powder River War that secured the 1868 Fort Laramie Treaty guaranteeing the Black Hills, but had long since decided that further struggle was useless. This was his third trip to the White House. He wanted to locate his people on the Tongue River and wished his request granted in return for the ceding of the Black Hills. The next day he increased his demand. "Half the Black Hills had not been paid for," he said, and he wanted the Indians to have "$40 apiece and overcoats and trunks." "If you were in our country," Red Cloud told the President, "and looked at our people, the water would come into your eyes."

Spotted Tail also spoke about the loss of the Black Hills. He had signed the surrender out of fear, he said. He did not understand about the land:

> I know one thing, and that is whenever the whites own a piece of land and it belongs to them, they put a fence around it, and it is theirs as long as he don't sell it; that is the way the white man lives. Your people who come out into my country, ask no questions of anybody, but impose on us and take our lands away.

The Sioux who had chosen peace with the Americans were far from content. Sitting Bull was determined not to follow their path and there was little to point to that might change his mind. The terms General Terry carried with him were laughably inadequate.

OUT ON THE WESTERN plains, in Montana Territory and the North-West Territories straddling the boundary, a high drama was building. As the Presidential Commission worked its way west and then north towards Fort Walsh, it encountered unexpected trouble. And on the Canadian side of the border the officers of the NWMP were experiencing great difficulty in making arrangements to receive the distinguished American emissaries.

It had all begun four months earlier, in the first week of May 1877, with three incidents, all widely separate geographically, that set in motion trains of circumstance that converged that October in the remote and primitive corner of the Canadian West: Fort Walsh.

On May 3, 1877, at Fort Walla Walla, in Oregon, General Oliver O. Howard of the United States Army met with the leaders of the Nez Perce Nation and delivered a fateful decision of his government—the Nez Perce were to abandon and vacate their homeland in the beautiful Wallowa Valley. It was the last straw for the Nez Perce. Hostilities broke out, and a month later the Nez Perce and the United States were at war, a running battle that traversed through the

Idaho and Montana Territories as the Nez Perce desperately sought to reach refuge in Canada.

On May 6, 1877, Crazy Horse and his band rode proudly into captivity at Fort Robinson. Then, in that same week, Sitting Bull, the only high-profile Sioux leader still at large, thwarted the Army units that had been pursuing him all that same winter and slipped over the border into Canada. The epics of the Nez Perce, of Crazy Horse and of Sitting Bull all came together at Fort Walsh that fall of 1877.

Throughout the summer of 1877, the Nez Perce, desperately seeking the same refuge and freedom in Canada that so many of the Sioux had secured, continued to elude the pursuing troops of the United States Army under General Howard. Several hundred men, women and children with all their lodges and household effects, plus about 2,000 horses, battled their way towards sanctuary. Their incredible feat extended over more than 1,770 km (1,100 mi) through the mountains and onto the Montana plains. As the Nez Perce drew closer to the border, the Americans became concerned that the Sioux in Canada would come to their aid.

Then, on September 5, 1877, occurred one of the great tragedies that so frequently visited the struggle between the American military and the Sioux Nation. At Fort Robinson, Crazy Horse, who had been living quietly on his reservation, was bayoneted and killed by soldiers during a trumped-up arrest. As news of the killing of the great Oglala leader spread like wildfire across the western plains, many Sioux who had been chafing at reservation confinement began to break away and head north, encouraged by word that "on his deathbed Crazy Horse himself had urged a general flight to Grandmother's Land."[49] Over that fall and winter as many as 2,000 joined the Sioux already in Canada.[50]

In Montana, the Nez Perce crossed the Missouri River at Cow Island, about 195 km (120 mi) east of Fort Benton. Since they were well ahead of the pursuing troops, they relaxed their relentless pace. On September 29 they reached the north slope of the Bears Paw Mountains, relaxed and settled into camp. It was a heartbreaking mistake. The Nez Perce were only an easy day's ride short of the border and just 112 km (70 mi) south of Fort Walsh as all available units of the U.S. Army raced to intercept them.

At Fort Walsh, preparations for the meeting between President Hayes' Commissioners and the Sitting Bull Sioux were not going well. The spit-and-polish cleanup of the fort itself and the surrounding grounds had been carried out so that the whitewashed buildings and stockade fairly shone. But ensuring the presence of the intended participants was another matter.

Commissioner Macleod and his party, having completed the Treaty 7 negotiations, were somewhere between Blackfoot Crossing and Fort Walsh, struggling through a raging blizzard. And, when Inspector Walsh had ridden over to the Sioux encampment at Pinto Horse Butte at the western end of the Wood Mountain uplands to invite the chiefs to Fort Walsh, he was met with an absolute refusal. The Sioux chiefs had nothing but enmity and contempt for the Americans and saw no purpose in such a meeting. Why would the Sioux sit down with the same General Terry who had sent the Army units against them at Little Big Horn? The story of the killing of Crazy Horse likely would have made its way into Canada by then and was certainly no inducement to the Sioux leaders to place their lives in the hands of the American Army.

Fortunately, down in Montana, the U.S. Commissioners were forced off their intended schedule. When they dismounted from the stagecoach at Helena, they discovered that the military escort that had been planned to take them to Fort Benton and then on to the Canadian border had been pre-empted by an unforeseen emergency. The army units were over at the Bears Paw Mountains doing battle with the Nez Perce. Generals Terry and Lawrence, and their entourage, were forced to sit and wait.

On September 30, two days after Commissioner Macleod rode away from Blackfoot Crossing headed for Fort Walsh, the Nez Perce were discovered and pinned down at their camp at the Bears Paw Mountains. Units of the U.S. Army under Colonel Nelson Miles cut off the escape route to Canada. A fierce battle ensued as the Nez Perce, only 65 km (40 mi) short of the border, desperately tried to break free. They sent word to Wood Mountain, asking the Sioux camped there to come to their aid.

When the messengers from the embattled Nez Perce arrived at Pinto Horse Butte, Inspector Walsh was still trying to convince Sitting Bull to meet with the Terry Commission. That discussion was immediately derailed. The young Sioux warriors raged to ride to the assistance of the Nez Perce and take vengeance on the hated U.S. Army. Walsh warned that, if they did ride, they would forfeit the sanctuary they enjoyed in Canada. The deliberations continued for two full days. It was a close decision, but finally the Sioux concluded that they dared not cross the border to help the Nez Perce.

But that did not make them any more inclined to sit down with Generals Terry and Lawrence. Walsh needed all his powers of persuasion to convince Sitting Bull and the others that no harm and perhaps some good would come from such a meeting. The Sioux, concerned that the Long Knives, as they called the U.S. cavalry, would come after them into Canada, grudgingly and reluctantly accepted Walsh's assurances of protection. But their decision was shaky, and there was much reconsideration.

On October 5, it was finally all over for the Nez Perce at the Bears Paw Mountains. After a heroic defensive stand that was a fitting climax to their four-month saga of out-running, out-witting and out-fighting the United States Army, Chief Joseph surrendered his people with the famous and moving words that concluded: "Hear me, my chiefs. I am tired; my heart is sick and sad. From where the sun now stands I will fight no more forever." Not all the Nez Perce fell into the hands of the U.S. Army. Chief White Bird and approximately 200 men, women and children slipped through the army lines and escaped into Canada.

The next day, October 6, Generals Terry and Lawrence made it through to Fort Benton, where they found for a second time that no military units were available for escort duty. The Fort Benton garrison also was away doing battle with the Nez Perce. The news of the surrender at the Bears Paw did not reach Fort Benton until two days later. The President's Commissioners were more than a week behind schedule, but it was just as well that they were. In Canada the NWMP were not nearly prepared to receive the delegation.

Fort Benton, Montana, 1878. *Glenbow Museum NA-2246-11*

At Pinto Horse Butte, on the morning the trip to Fort Walsh was to begin, scouts reported a large body of horsemen approaching from the south. The news threw the Sioux into a panic. Disbelieving Walsh's assurances, they were certain that the Long Knives were on the attack. The move to Fort Walsh was abandoned and excited preparations for defence begun.

But the approaching body was not the U.S. Cavalry. It was the Nez Perce refugees who had evaded the American Army and made it through to Canada. Men, women and children, they were in pitiful condition, shot to pieces, horribly wounded. The Sioux took the suffering Nez Perce into their lodges and ministered to them as best they could. Their people were well experienced in gunshot wounds.

The plight of the Nez Perce again threw open the decision to meet with the Terry Commission. The condition of the refugees awakened all the Sioux fury at the U.S. Army that could so callously shoot women and children. Again Walsh patiently marshalled his reasoned argument and finally he was able to get Sitting Bull and some 20 other chiefs on the trail west to Fort Walsh. Still, the Inspector was frustrated when the Sioux frequently stopped, sat down, smoked and debated again and again the wisdom of what they were doing.

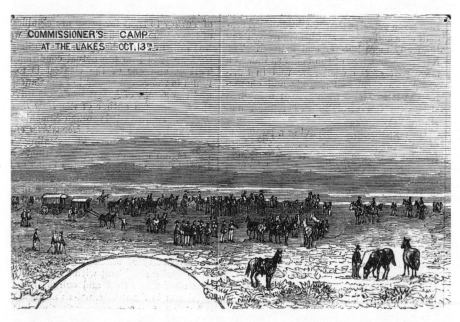

Commissioner's camp during the "Sitting Bull Commission," Fort Walsh, October 13, 1877. *Glenbow Museum NA-1406-228*

The unerring instincts of Jerry Potts had carried Commissioner Macleod and his party four days through the blinding snowstorm and into Fort Walsh on October 1. They found all in readiness but lacking actors. When word came that the U.S. Commissioners were stalled at Fort Benton, Macleod rode on to Pinto Horse Butte to see if he could assist Walsh in persuading the Sioux to meet with the Americans, whenever that would happen. Halfway there he met Walsh escorting the Sioux, whose doubts and fears were growing. Macleod was able to provide additional assurance that the U.S. Army would not dare to cross the border and the chiefs stayed on the trail. They finally arrived at Fort Walsh on October 12 and reluctantly settled in to await the American Commissioners.

On October 15 the Presidential Commission finally reached the Canadian boundary. Macleod was there to greet them. The NWMP put on a bit of a show for the Americans, who were duly impressed. Jerome Stillson of the New York *Herald* described the scene:

> Colonel Macleod, whose fame as a gentleman and officer had reached the commission far below this latitude of 49 degrees north, approached General Terry on horseback, and clad in his scarlet uniform at the head of a small but brilliant retinue, passed the stone monument on the left of the road and paused on United States soil to receive his American guests. Very soon the escort of lancers brought down by Colonel Macleod were seen advancing, their red uniforms and the red and white pennons affixed to their lances contrasting beautifully with the monotonous dun colour of the plains. Halting, they formed on one side of the road and presented lances to the commission as it passed them.[51]

The Americans with their NWMP escort rode swiftly on to Fort Walsh, arriving in the evening of October 16. Stillson was again impressed, but subtly critical of the military merit of the facility:

> Suddenly Fort Walsh came into view, lying low in a charming valley. No more romantic spot, no wilder scene could impress a traveller at the end of a monotonous journey than the one that met our eyes. The fort, built by Major Walsh only two years ago, is notwithstanding its excellence of a form and aspect so quaint and old as to remind one of the stories of the early Kentucky stockades. It is in fact an irregular stockade of upright logs enclosing all the offices and buildings, which are likewise built of logs, necessary for the accommodation of a garrison. Whitewashed on every part except the roof, the fort nestles

between the surrounding heights. A scraggly but picturesque little settlement adjoins it.[52]

Finally, the next day, October 17, 1877, at 3:00 p.m., the long-awaited drama opened in the ante-room to Inspector Walsh's quarters that doubled as the Fort's officers' mess. There were three interpreters present: Baptiste Shane brought by the U.S. Commission, another brought by Sitting Bull, and the official interpreter at the Fort. There was also a stenographer, and Sub-Inspector Dalrymple Clark of the NWMP was skilled in shorthand.

Generals Terry and Lawrence were seated behind a table at one end of the room, with the journalists at an adjoining table. Walsh escorted Sitting Bull into the room. With Sitting Bull were Bear's Cap, Spotted Eagle, Flying Bird, Whirlwind Bear, Medicine Turns-around, Iron Dog, Bear that Scatters, The Crow, Little Knife, Yellow Dog and about 12 lesser chiefs. Notably missing were several powerful chiefs such as Four Horns, Gall and Black Moon. It is not known whether they had refused to attend or somehow were not aware of the event.

Sitting Bull and his group seated themselves on the floor but rose again when Macleod and several of his officers entered. Sitting Bull shook hands warmly with Macleod, then disdainfully passed Terry and Lawrence before returning to his seat on the floor opposite them. He then demanded that the generals also sit on the floor as he could not see them. Terry and Lawrence compromised by moving their chairs in front of their table. Other than the encounter on the Yellowstone a year earlier between Sitting Bull and Colonel Miles, this was the first time any of the American officers had laid eyes upon the great Sioux chief. The newsmen furiously scribbled descriptions for their papers.

Significantly, there was no pipe ceremony, almost an absolute requirement to open formal councils. Presumably the Sioux, holding the opinion they did about the Americans, saw no point in asking them to engage in a sacred ceremony that bound all participants to the truth.

General Terry stood and read a prepared message:

The President has instructed us to say to you that he desires to make a lasting peace with you and your people. He desires that all hostilities shall cease, and that all shall live together in harmony . . . [I]f you return to your country and refrain from further hostilities, a full pardon will be granted to you and your people for all acts committed in the past . . . [N]o attempt will be made to punish you or any of your people; what is past shall be forgotten, and you will be received in as friendly terms as other Indians have been received . . . The President

cannot nor will not consent to your returning to your country prepared for war. He cannot consent to your returning prepared to inflict
the injuries you have done in the past. He invites you to come to the
boundary of this country, and give up your arms and ammunition and
go to the Agencies assigned for you, and give up your horses except
those required for peace purposes.

Sitting Bull was the first to reply:

For 64 years you have kept and treated my people bad; what have we
done that caused us to depart from our country? We could go nowhere,
so we have taken refuge here . . . We did not give you our country; you
took it from us; see how I live with these people [the police]. Look at
these eyes and ears; you think me a fool, but you are a greater fool than
I am . . . you come to tell us stories and we do not want to hear them. I
shake hands with these people; that part of the country we came from
belonged to us, and you took it from us, now we live here.

Other chiefs spoke in similar terms. Then, in an intended insulting breach of
protocol, a woman spoke, a squaw, the wife of Bear That Scatters:

I wanted to raise children in your country but you gave me no time; I
come to this country to raise my children; I will stay with these people here and raise my children.

Terry inquired if he was to tell the President that his offer was refused. Sitting Bull replied,

I could tell you more, but that is all I have to tell you. If we told you
more—why, you would not pay any attention to it. That is all I have
to say. This part of the country does not belong to your people. You
belong on the other side; this side belongs to us.

The Crow embraced Macleod and Walsh and said:

This is the way I like these people . . . What mean you to come here
and talk to us? All this country belongs to this people [the police] that
is the reason we come here . . . You can go back to where you came
from and stay there.

The Terry Commission, with Sitting Bull and Sioux Indians at Fort Walsh, 1877. *Provincial Archives of Alberta B 1050N*

The Sioux then asked Terry if he had anything more to say. The Commissioner, acknowledging the hopelessness of the situation, replied that he had nothing more. Doomed from the start, doomed by more than 10 years of bloodletting and broken promises, the conference ended.[53]

The next morning, with an escort of NWMP, the Commissioners and their party rode back to the border. At Fort Benton they embarked in mackinaw boats down the Missouri River to Fort Buford, then rode in Army ambulances to Bismarck where the Northern Pacific Railroad carried them to St. Paul. There a letter from Commissioner Macleod awaited them. Macleod, as requested by Terry, reported on a further discussion he had held with the Sioux after the Commission left Fort Walsh.

Macleod wrote that he had told the Sioux of the importance of the decision they had given to Terry and Lawrence. Although they claimed to be British Indians, the Canadian government looked upon them as American Indians who had taken refuge on Canadian territory. They could expect no support in Canada other than protection. They must not cross the border with hostile intent for, if they did, they would have not only the Americans for enemies, but also the NWMP and the Canadian government. Macleod concluded by stating that the Sioux had unanimously reaffirmed the response they had given the President's Commission.[54] The NWMP Commissioner did not tell Generals Terry and Lawrence that he had requested the Sioux to give him a complete account of the grievances they had against the Americans.

It had been a very frank discussion with Sitting Bull and the other chiefs. Macleod pointed out that the buffalo would not last long and then the Sioux would have to find another method of living as the Canadian government would not support them. He then asked them to state their account of the misconduct they had suffered that "has caused you to leave your country."

Sitting Bull spoke bitterly about the Black Hills:

> The Americans tried to get our country from us; our country was full of gold, I mean the Black Hills country . . . I did not give them the land, no more than you would have given it . . . The Americans kill ten or twenty of my children every day for nothing . . . All of the Americans robbed, cheated and laughed at us . . . I could never live over there again. They never tell the truth . . . If they liked me why did they drive me away; for my part they can stop on the other side of the line with their big guns; I stay on this side without being afraid.

Spotted Eagle spoke in the same tone:

> We did not give them our land; we did not take annuities from them; they stole our land from us; the Americans are liars; they pretend to know how many of us they killed, but they do not; I know, I was there . . . the Americans say the prisoners they took they treated well; this is a lie; they kill plenty of us, but we kill plenty of them too.

When three other chiefs echoed those complaints, Macleod then asked, "Then I am to understand that you have been driven from your country?" With this all the chiefs agreed. The Sioux, it would seem, could be regarded as legitimate refugees, in every sense of the term.

The Sioux did not believe that the buffalo would disappear. There had always been buffalo. There would always be buffalo. "God Almighty gave us lots of buffalo to live long," Sitting Bull said. "I wish there be lots of buffalo for a long time to come."[55]

While at Fort Walsh, the two journalists, Stillson and Diehl, had each secured, with Walsh's help, a private interview with Sitting Bull. Their account of the conference, together with stories and sketches of the great Sioux chief, were carried in newspapers all over America.[56] Sitting Bull had now attained an international profile as the personification of all the Sioux Indians. The formal account of their mission by Generals Terry and Lawrence was headed "The Sitting Bull Indian Commission." The Government Printing Office in Washington set up the cover page this way:

REPORT

of

THE COMMISSION

appointed by direction of the

PRESIDENT OF THE UNITED STATES

under instruction of

THE HONORABLES THE SECRETARY OF WAR

AND THE SECRETARY OF THE INTERIOR

to meet

THE SIOUX CHIEF, SITTING BULL

with

a view to avert hostile incursions into the territory of the
United States from the Dominion of Canada

"SAVING CORPORAL RYAN"

As the Sitting Bull Indian Commission made its way home from Fort Walsh, General Terry fell into conversation with Baptiste Shane, the Métis interpreter he had engaged. Shane told Terry that during the previous spring he had visited Sitting Bull's camp and there met a captive, a white man who said he was Martin Ryan, a survivor of Little Big Horn. Ryan had been a corporal in the 7th Cavalry serving under Custer. Captured, he had been held a prisoner ever since. His several attempts at escape had failed. Shane described Ryan as so painted up by the Sioux as to be almost unrecognizable as a white man. Ryan said that he had been forced into a marriage with a daughter of Spotted Eagle, the prominent Sioux chief. This was all Shane had been able to learn from Ryan before Sitting Bull himself interrupted their conversation and ordered Shane away.

General Terry was an educated man and a good judge of character. He found Shane to be "a truthful and trustworthy young man." Terry checked the Little Big Horn casualty list and discovered that a Corporal Ryan, of Company "C," 7th Cavalry, was shown as killed in action.[1]

Terry's report went up through channels, to the General of the Army, the Secretary of War and over to the Secretary of State. From there a demand went forth to Sir Edward Thornton, head of the British Legation in Washington, and on to Lord Dufferin, the Governor General of Canada. The demand was loudly echoed by the American press: "Save Corporal Ryan."

NOTE

1. NA, RG 7, Series G21, vol. 319, Terry to HQ, Military Division of Missouri, November 16, 1877.

Ottawa was disappointed, but not surprised, that the Terry and Lawrence mission had failed to induce the Sioux to return to the United States. The likely consequences of the Sioux remaining permanently in Canada were all bleak. So bleak, in fact, that when the Ottawa *Free Press* picked up a story out of the New York *Herald* alleging that Sitting Bull had not fully comprehended the Terry proposition and might have agreed with it if he had, David Mills promptly instructed Commissioner Macleod to check this out. If there was any chance that the story might be correct, Sitting Bull should be invited to visit Washington to discuss the matter directly with the President.[57]

There was no such luck. Sitting Bull and his fellow chiefs were very firm in their decision. Canada was stuck with the Sioux. In addition to handling the problems that had brought them into the West three years earlier, the 300 men of the NWMP would now have to contend with 6,000 volatile and dangerous American Sioux camped on the western plains. It was a sudden coming of age.

CHAPTER 18

Canada Versus the United States

T HE REPORT OF CORPORAL RYAN'S IMPRISONMENT IN SIT-
ting Bull's camp reached NWMP Headquarters at Fort Macleod
at the arrival of the New Year, 1878. Commissioner Macleod forwarded it on to Assistant Commissioner Irvine at Fort Walsh with
instructions to immediately conduct a search.

Irvine found the Sioux camp to be about 95 km (60 mi) from Fort Walsh
and only 4.8 km (3 mi) from his Eastend outpost at the eastern edge of the
Cypress Hills. There Sitting Bull assured Irvine that the story was untrue; no
prisoners were taken at Little Big Horn and none were in his camp. Nonetheless, the officer hunted unsuccessfully through the 30-odd lodges in the village
and then rode further east to Spotted Eagle's larger camp. Spotted Eagle also
denied any knowledge of Corporal Ryan, and certainly not as a son-in-law for
he had no daughters.

Baptiste Shane's story was utter nonsense, another of the wild rumours
that burst fully formed and hyperactive out of the West and caused much
anguish in faraway Washington and Ottawa until the patient officers of the
NWMP knocked them on the head. Disregarding Irvine's report, belief in the
imprisoned Corporal Ryan continued in the United States, fed by a press
unwilling to let go of a good story.

Before the NWMP report negating the Corporal Ryan rumour was received,
more gossip was picked up by Colonel Miles' headquarters, given some credibility and forwarded on to Washington. A report had come in that Sitting
Bull had assembled a large force made up of some seven different tribes and
was planning an attack into the U.S. The Army judged its garrison at Fort Peck

to be in danger and began defensive preparations. Telegrams flew and again Commissioner Macleod was instructed to investigate.

Irvine, who had just returned from his Corporal Ryan inquiries, was able to kill this new rumour without leaving his office. Sitting Bull, he reported, was "quietly camped with about thirty lodges three miles [4.8 km] from our post at end of Cypress Hills ... No foundation whatever for rumours...."[1]

The American Army had demonized Sitting Bull to the point that they could not believe that he was quietly living in Canada and happy to have seen the last of the Long Knives. As for Sitting Bull, his great fear was that the Americans would kidnap him. For this reason, Macleod advised David Mills in Ottawa, the suggestion that the Sioux chief be offered a trip to Washington to speak to the President should be quickly dropped as Sitting Bull would "imagine that we wanted to place him within the power of his enemies."[2] That this was not an irrational fear on Sitting Bull's part later became apparent when a suggestion along this very line came out of Washington.

Much of the constant rumour of imminent invasion out of Canada was invented in Fort Benton to support its hope for a military garrison with the usual spinoff economic benefits. And Colonel Miles, chafing under his instructions to remain south of the Missouri River, was receptive to any report that would provide an excuse to move his troops against the Sioux. Miles even proposed that he be permitted to take his units over the 49th Parallel into Canada, as the American Army had in 1873 crossed the Mexican border on a punitive expedition against Kickapoo Indians. But Mexico was not the British Empire, as General Sherman firmly reminded his ambitious officer.[3]

After Sitting Bull's humiliating rejection of the Presidential Commission at Fort Walsh in October, Superintendent Walsh accompanied the Sioux leaders on their return to their encampment at Pinto Horse Butte. There was great rejoicing at their arrival, for most had believed that Generals Terry and Lawrence were nothing more than a ruse by which Sitting Bull and the other chiefs would be handed over to the American Army.

At the Sioux camp Walsh found 200 newly arrived Nez Perce refugees and held a council with them along the now well-rehearsed lines. The Nez Perce had been a prosperous tribe, they told Walsh, raising cattle and breeding horses. They lived in houses like white people and went to church on Sunday. Chief White Bird explained how they had been forced from their homeland and had chosen to fight rather than accept confinement on a reservation. He spoke movingly of the Nez Perce plight:

We who yesterday were rich are beggars today, made so by the orders of a Christian white chief. We have no country, no people, no home. We do not desire longer life, and we pray day and night that the Great Spirit will remove us.[4]

Walsh was sympathetic but could do little but issue the same advice he had so frequently given the Sioux; the Nez Perce could remain in Canada and would be protected from the Americans, but must obey the law.

THE SANCTUARY THAT CANADA had become continued to attract fugitives from the United States over the winter of 1877–78. The followers of the lamented Crazy Horse kept slipping over the line until by spring they numbered about 240 lodges. Among them were chiefs Red Bear and Big Road who had visited the White House in September.[5] The total Lakota Sioux and Nez Perce population in the North-West Territories reached more than 5,000, not including the 1,500 Santee Sioux between Wood Mountain and Fort Garry. With the Sioux was their wealth of horses, between 12,000 and 15,000 head.

The western plains were graced by an unusually benign winter that first year of the Sioux hegira. The temperatures were moderate, even mild. The buffalo were plentiful and there was very little snow to impede travel and hunting. Horses grazed without difficulty. With their camps scattered on the prairie between the Cypress Hills and Wood Mountain, the Sioux and Nez Perce enjoyed a bountiful season and took many buffalo robes, enough to replenish their needs and more for trading.

The buffalo were plentiful, except in the foothills of the Rocky Mountains, the hunting ground of the Blackfoot. There, wildfires had destroyed the grasslands and the buffalo abandoned their usual winter haunts. The freeze-dried buffalo grass took on the quality of tinder so that a careless spark caused a fire that ran before the wind for kilometres. In a harbinger of events soon to come, the Blackfoot were forced to travel eastward to find game, a move that brought them perilously close to their traditional enemy, the Sioux. And the additional demands of the Sioux upon the already dwindling herds of buffalo accelerated the decline of the food supply upon which all the tribes depended.

In the third week of April, as if to compensate for the mild winter, a fierce, two-day blizzard struck the Cypress Hills region. A camp of Métis lost 100 horses to the storm, while two of their hunters, caught out on the prairie, perished.

The NWMP, still with a total strength of only 330 officers and men spread over the entire Canadian West, were required to frequently adjust the placement of their resources to meet the constantly shifting contingencies that faced them. In 1876, headquarters had been moved from the unsatisfactory location at Swan River to Fort Macleod. Just a year later the tremendous influx of Sioux and Nez Perce into the region between Cypress Hills and Wood Mountain dictated that units be moved closer to what suddenly became a very volatile situation. In May 1878, the headquarter units were again transferred, this time 290 km (180 mi) east to Fort Walsh, where additional barracks and stables were constructed. The three-year-old post became even more prominent in the turbulent affairs of the new West.

The North-West Mounted Police outpost at Fort Walsh, 1878. *Glenbow Museum NA-2003-52*

A town sprang up beside the NWMP stockade in the Cypress Hills and quickly grew to some 500 residents, the largest settlement between Fort Garry and Vancouver, a distinction that had been held briefly five years earlier by Wood Mountain. The hub of the many trails crossing the plains, its life was short but colourful. Métis buffalo hunters with their Red River carts, heavy Murphy wagons hauled by bull teams from Fort Benton, and the travois of the ever-present Indians all mingled on the rough streets. In the winter, dog teams yipped through. Buildings were thrown up: a dance hall, a billiard hall and barber shop, even a hotel. In spite of the sharp eye of the NWMP, enough

Montana Redeye came into the community to enliven such social events as dances, card games, minstrel shows, theatrical performances and concerts where the post band performed. A Black woman who set up as a laundress and, naturally for the times given the sobriquet "Nigger Molly," claimed the distinction of being the first *white lady* in the Cypress Hills even though she had arrived as one of a small group of Blacks. Molly's companions, given equal nomenclature, were "Nigger Annie," "Nigger Jess" and "Nigger Tom."[6]

Both of the major Fort Benton trading firms, I.G. Baker & Co., and T.C. Power and Bro., placed stores near the stockade. Charles Conrad of I.G. Baker, who had held the inside track with the NWMP since its arrival in 1874, and still did almost all of the Force's business at Fort Benton, had the effrontery to name one of his Missouri River steamboats *The Colonel Macleod*. Whether or not the Commissioner granted permission to have the boat bear his name, there is no evidence that objection was raised to what surely was the first commercial exploitation of the reputation of the Force.

At Fort Walsh, I.G. Baker found the competition from T.C. Power and Bro. bothersome. That was quickly solved when the two firms quietly entered into a price-fixing agreement that ensured that the Canadian government would contribute handsomely to both their profit lines.[7]

Becoming famous as Sitting Bull's Canadian address, the Wood Mountain post was also bolstered by more men and improved facilities, including four 7-pound cannon, and Superintendent Walsh moved his headquarters over from Fort Walsh. Here, too, was a settlement, but it dated back before 1870 when many of the first Métis to leave Red River had been attracted to the sheltered coulees and springs of the Wood Mountain uplands. Today's town of Willow Bunch, on the eastern slope of Wood Mountain, dates its origin from 1870, making it one of the oldest communities in the West.

Hardy Oblate priests from their mission at St. Florent in the Qu'Appelle Valley (now known as Lebret) followed their flock, and one of the first to winter with the Wood Mountain Métis was the same Father Jean-Joseph Lestanc who had represented the absent Bishop Taché during the time of the Riel Provisional Government at Fort Garry in 1869. After the arrival of the Ontario militia in 1870, Lestanc became such a target of Protestant abuse that his superiors transferred him to the safety of the plains, where for many years he served faithfully among the buffalo-hunting Métis.

Métis continued to migrate to Wood Mountain so that by the winter of 1872–73 the uplands had become home to 175 families,[8] a total population of at least 750, far more than any other settlement on the plains west of Red River. But the Métis were still nomadic. Only three years later they almost totally abandoned Wood Mountain and established new settlements in the Cypress Hills to be closer to the buffalo.[9] But the winter of 1878–79 saw 150 families again settled in the Wood Mountain coulees.[10]

The NWMP experienced plenty of hardship during patrols between their posts in the Cypress Hills and Wood Mountain, particularly in the winter. Walsh provided a telling description:

> An undulating bare plain for a distance of one hundred and twenty miles [193 km], covered with snow, devoid of timber or wood of any kind, streams frozen to the bottom and no shelter but what the broken banks of a coulee could afford. Men had to melt snow and horses eat it to quench thirst, wood had to be carried to melt the snow and heat water for tea. Most sparingly was this wood handled and when the little fire was made the poor half frozen party would gather around it to catch the smallest radiated spout of heat to try and warm their shivering bodies. But at a temperature of twenty-five degrees below [-32°C] the little fire only made one feel more severely the want of timber. There was no such thing as feeling comfortably warm on one of those trips from the time Cypress Mountain was departed from until Wood Mountain was reached and you can imagine what joy it brought to every heart after five or six days through snow without water or fire when "Indian Cliff" in Wood Mountain on the butte, or "The Three Pines" in Cypress Mountain would be sighted, either of them affording a haven of rest.[11]

The arrival of the Sioux caused a huge increase in the local Native population and attracted a number of new traders to Wood Mountain to compete with the long-established Jean-Louis Légaré. Leighton and Jordan, a Montana firm with posts along the Missouri River, put Gus Hedderich in charge of their Canadian branch. Hedderich got along so well with Sitting Bull that he was able to teach him how to sign his name in English, an ability that the chief later turned to his advantage when his fame created a demand for his autograph.

The paranoia caused by the presence in the North-West Territories of more than 5,000 refugee Sioux, Cheyenne and Nez Perce was not confined to the United States. Ottawa also worried, but there the concern at first was more economic than military; the Canadian government did not want to be trapped into having to take responsibility for the welfare of the American Indians.

The question of the expense incurred by the Sioux incursion into Canada was raised in the House of Commons on February 18, 1878, provoking an infantile exchange between Prime Minister Mackenzie and Sir John A. Macdonald, then Leader of the Opposition. The Prime Minister explained to the House that, although Sitting Bull had caused Canada some expense, and might yet cause more, he did not think the government was justified in making demand for recompense from London. Macdonald interjected, "I do not see how a Sitting Bull can cross the frontier." "Not unless he rises," the Prime Minister responded. "Then he is not a Sitting Bull," Macdonald concluded.[12]

In June 1878, Sitting Bull pulled off by far his best caper to date. A report circulated that he and a band of warriors had slipped over the border, kidnapped Benjamin Potts, the Governor of Montana Territory, and taken him back into Canada, where they were holding him hostage. In the style of terrorist actions of a later century, Sitting Bull demanded the freedom of Nez Perce Chief Joseph as the price of the governor's release. When Governor Potts returned to Helena from a visit to his sheep farm, untouched and the last to learn of his wild adventure, the embarrassment was only short-lived.[13]

Alerted to the fact that conspiracies were fomenting in the West, the NWMP kept their ears close to the ground and soon secured an advantage. Commissioner Macleod hired an informant, surely the first in the history of the Force, a Métis named Joseph LaRivière, who enjoyed the confidence of the Sioux and was able to travel freely among their camps. LaRivière's regular reports greatly improved the NWMP intelligence on the movements and plans of the Indians.

Many of the Nez Perce who, with Chief White Bird, slipped through the encirclement at Bears Paw Mountains in the fall of 1877 and made it through to Canada, did not remain long north of the border. Although Sitting Bull's camp took in the new refugees and cared for them, it was an uncomfortable situation for traditional enemies who did not share a language. In the spring of 1878 several groups of the Nez Perce quietly crossed back into the United States, where further bloody encounters with the U.S. Army ensued. Captured, most of the returning Nez Perce were sent to join Chief Joseph and the other Bears Paw prisoners where they had been placed in Indian Territory (Oklahoma).[14]

In the summer of 1878, another official American delegation travelled north to negotiate the return of Indians who had taken sanctuary in Canada. And again NWMP Commissioner Macleod convinced reluctant refugees to meet U.S. Army officers at Fort Walsh.

Colonel Nelson Miles sent his aide, Lieutenant George W. Baird, two interpreters, and three Nez Perce prisoners to induce White Bird and his followers to accept surrender terms. Concerned that the presence of the Americans might incite trouble, Macleod denied the party permission to approach the Sioux encampment that included the Nez Perce. Instead, he directed Assistant Commissioner A.G. Irvine to invite White Bird to come to Fort Walsh. Irvine succeeded, overcoming strong advice the Nez Perce received from the Sioux as well as White Bird's own reluctance to meet with any American. In the end, White Bird and seven of his fellow chiefs and headmen attended at Fort Walsh.

The discussions took place over two days, July 1–2, 1878. Lieutenant Baird did not distinguish himself:

> At the opening of the meeting, July 1, Baird lied outright to White Bird, extending to the chief the likelihood that he and his people would be allowed to return to their Idaho homeland, although he knew that the opposite was true.[15]

Colonel Miles had made the same promise to Chief Joseph when he surrendered at the Bears Paw battlefield, but had been overruled by his superiors. "When will these white chiefs speak the truth?" Joseph wondered when he heard the news.[16]

White Bird saw through Baird's perfidy. He knew Chief Joseph had not been returned to the Wallowa Valley. The Nez Perce did not like being camped with the Sioux, but they could sleep well where they were. White Bird refused even Macleod's encouragement to accept the American offer. "We will not go," he declared.[17] The second American mission to Fort Walsh also ended in failure.

THE SIOUX AND THE Crow, whose territory lay in Montana just below the border, had been implacable enemies for many generations, and any alliance between the two was unthinkable. But, improbable or not, word came to the NWMP that the Nez Perce, who got along with both, had brokered a pact that included all three tribes, a pact that would see the Crow join the Sioux in Canada. Although the Crow had accepted a huge reservation, they retained their horses and guns and lived by the hunt. Fear that they were to be disarmed and dismounted, as the reservation Sioux and Cheyenne had been, made them think of Canada. Sitting Bull was reported to have sent messengers to the Crow with a gift of tobacco as an offering of peace and with an invitation to join his camps north of the border, where they would find plentiful buffalo and freely traded guns and ammunition.

The proposed Sioux/Crow alliance quickly came unstuck—and in the usual way—when a band of Crow raided the Sioux and ran off a herd of horses. Sitting Bull was furious and blamed the American Army with whom the Crow served as scouts and auxiliaries. He immediately formed a war party to retaliate. Word came to Walsh at Wood Mountain in January 1879, and he promptly saddled up and went searching for Sitting Bull. He found the Sioux and Nez Perce camped together on the Frenchman River a couple of kilometres into Montana.

When accused by Walsh, Sitting Bull admitted what he had been up to and what his intentions were:

> I never deny anything I do. I did send messengers to the Crows asking them to leave their Reservation and to join the Sioux camp north of the line; I did tell them they could purchase guns and ammunition . . . It was my wish to try to get every man that lived by the bow and arrow to confederate, but while I was endeavouring to get them to shake hands, the Americans appeared [by the Crow] and stole my horses. The Americans have beat me. There is no man in the American country that wears trousers that is not a rascal . . . I wish you to tell the White Mother that I will do to the Americans as they have done to me. It is not my wish to go to war, but I must.[18]

Walsh advised Sitting Bull to "think well" about what he was going to do, that his action might bring great trouble to his people. But it was Walsh's assessment that Sitting Bull did not have the support to carry out his intentions; a number of lodges were leaving his camp and more were planning to do so, anxious to avoid any conflict. It was also Walsh's opinion that hostility between the Sioux and the Crow was good news, certainly a better state of affairs than the alliance that had been attempted. But it was a dangerous situation, Walsh reported:

> [T]hose who listen to Sitting Bull, in their hearts have no more love for the whites in Canadian territory than they have for those in the United States Territory; their true hatred is not against the Americans, but against the white man generally.[19]

The enmity between the Sioux and the Crow intensified a few days later. In the first week of February, a hunting party of Sioux, camped and asleep about 25 km (15 mi) south of the border, was attacked by Crow. One Sioux was killed and three others badly wounded while the Crow ran off 19 horses. Buffalo were becoming scarce north of the border and, as they had always done,

Sir John A. Macdonald. *Library and Archives Canada /
Harold Daly fonds C-002829*

the Indians from Canada had travelled south in search of the herds. Through British channels, Washington brought the situation to Ottawa's attention and a new dimension to the diplomatic dilemma opened.

Sir John A. Macdonald's Conservatives had returned to power in October 1878, and Macdonald retained for himself the Interior portfolio. He also moved responsibility for the NWMP back into Interior from Secretary of State. As Minister of the Interior, Macdonald prepared a lengthy response for transmission to Washington.

It was Macdonald's opinion that, if Canadian Indians were in the United States, it was a matter of necessity "in order to procure food for themselves and their families, the herds having been driven south by the incessant warfare waged upon them for actual subsistence by the large number of foreign Indians at present within Canadian territory, in addition to our own Indians." The problem, he said, would become more critical as the numbers of buffalo decreased. They were not expected to last more than five years.

Besides, the Sioux were a problem not of Canada's making:

> The Indians in question were driven into Canadian territory after having been worsted by United States troops, with whom they had come into collision, in consequence, it is said—whether rightly or wrongly—of difficulties arising out of unjust treatment they had received at the hands of agents of the Government in the matter of treaty promises.

The solution, Macdonald concluded, was for Washington to make further efforts to induce the Sioux to return. Feelings of animosity, he thought, had now had time to soften and

> a different spirit might be exhibited by Sitting Bull and the other leading chiefs, were they approached at the present time in a friendly way

by the Government of the United States with propositions of a similar, and, if possible, more lenient character that those formerly rejected.[20]

Before a response could be received, a further complaint came from Secretary of State Evarts in Washington. He claimed there were "about twenty-five hundred armed and hostile Indians at present under the command of Sitting Bull near the border . . . hostile demonstrations will be made by this force during the coming spring." And, again, "Sitting Bull has sent emissaries to all the various affiliated tribes in Montana and Dakota Territories for the purpose of enlisting them in his behalf, should actual hostilities occur." Evarts wanted the Canadian government to "take all necessary precautions . . . to avert the consequences arising from the possible outbreak of an Indian war."[21]

Evarts' information was once more without foundation. Perhaps reports about Sitting Bull's state of mind back in January had just filtered through to Washington, with the usual exaggeration attached, but that was old news. Sitting Bull had taken Walsh's advice and simmered down. On March 20, he and several other Sioux chiefs visited Walsh at Wood Mountain and stayed several days. While there Sitting Bull explained that in January he had not meant to say that he wanted to make war, only to defend himself. He had thought that as the Crow had commenced war on him, they would continue it.

But Ottawa had no reason not to accept Evarts' report as accurate. Before Walsh could file his report on his meeting with Sitting Bull, Macdonald decided to bring to bear the highest level of diplomatic authority. Governor General Lorne would send a strong communiqué directly to Sitting Bull to be delivered by the officer commanding the NWMP. For the second time the Sioux chief out on the western plains would receive the envoy of a head of state.

24 March, 1879.

The Governor General desires that you should convey to Sitting Bull and the other chiefs of the foreign Indians his desire that the shelter enjoyed during their residence north of the frontier line be not used for hostile preparations against the Queen's allies.

If they do not act peaceably in accordance with the wishes of the Queen, the safety they have hitherto found will no longer exist.

Lorne[22]

Washington was immediately advised of the serious action Canada had taken to ward off the Indian war feared by Secretary Evarts.

Although fired into the West by telegraph, Helena was still the closest any telegraph line ran to Fort Walsh and the Governor General's instructions reached NWMP headquarters only on April 13. Assistant Commissioner Irvine was in command and advised that he would personally convey the message to Sitting Bull.[23] This he was able to do on April 27 at Wood Mountain where he found an encampment of 250 Sioux lodges. When Irvine read the Governor General's edict to Sitting Bull and the other Sioux chiefs, all solemnly assembled, they unhesitatingly gave their assurance that no campaign would be launched across the line.

The Sioux, Irvine reported on his return, were planning to move north to the Great Sand Hills where buffalo had been reported.[24] Sitting Bull himself with a camp of only five lodges was also planning to go to the Sand Hills. There was no evidence of any plans to take hostile action into the United States. Only four months later the Sioux, hotly provoked, would have made just such an incursion against the American Army. Only the command from the Governor General and the promise exacted by Irvine stayed their hand.

In Washington, Sir Edward Thornton called on Evarts to discuss the latter's fears that Sitting Bull was planning to lead the Sioux back across the border "with hostile intentions." Evarts made it clear that he regarded Sitting Bull as a very dangerous man,

> a man of action and energy, the leader of the disoriented Indians, both of his own and other tribes, and that the cause of all hostilities [were] centered in him. If he could be got hold of and prevented from doing mischief, there would be no danger to his followers.[25]

The United States Secretary of State gave Thornton a simple solution: invite Sitting Bull to Ottawa and then arrest him. Sitting Bull's paranoia about the Americans was well-founded.

At Wood Mountain, during their March meeting, Walsh and Sitting Bull had a very thorough discussion. On his arrival, Sitting Bull, who was noted for his generosity to the less fortunate, confessed that he was now without provisions and his family had not eaten for more than a day. Walsh quickly ordered up food and made sure that Sitting Bull was well enough victualled to carry him back to his camp. After two days in council with his headmen, Sitting Bull and several other chiefs gathered at Walsh's quarters. He had come, he said, to dispel a rumour that he had sent agents into the United States to bargain for surrender:

> I have but one heart and it is the same as when I first shook your hand ... I came to the White Mother's country to sleep sound and ask her to have pity on me. That I never would again shake the hand of an American. I went at your request to the White Mother's Fort to meet the Americans [the Terry Commission] but I will never meet them again ... I am looking to the north for my life [Joseph Manzione used this line as the title of his excellent account of Sitting Bull's years in Canada] and hope the White Mother will never ask me to look to the country I left, although mine, and not even the dust of it did I sell, but the Americans can have it ... I told you before and I tell you now that I am never going to leave the White Mother's country.

"Those who wish to return to the Americans can go," Sitting Bull told Walsh, a significant change of policy. Until then, the *akicita*, the camp police, had forcibly prevented any Sioux from slipping away to surrender:

> Those who wish to remain here, if the White Mother wishes to give them a piece of land, can farm, but I will remain what I am until I die, a hunter, and when there are no buffalo or other game, I will send my children to hunt and live on prairie mice, for when an Indian is shut up in one place his body becomes weak.

His people were then camped and hunting on the American side of the line, Sitting Bull reported. They needed to stay close to the buffalo because their horses were no longer strong enough to hunt from the Canadian side. "But I will not remain south of the line one day longer than I can help, for I wish to be as far away from the Americans as I can get and live." The Sioux chief concluded with a plea for his people: "You have for many months been advising us to think of getting our living from the ground. Will you tell me where we will find the ground?"

This was a sensitive subject. Walsh knew that although Ottawa had granted reserves to the Santee Sioux there was little likelihood that this policy would be extended to the Lakota Sioux. He told Sitting Bull that the United States offered far more advantages than Canada to Indians wishing to farm. Walsh stated that he "did not know whether the White Mother would give those who were determined never to return to the United States a piece of land or not."[26]

Washington was far from satisfied with Ottawa's response to its complaints. Although the NWMP continued to report that the Sioux were "scattered in small camps north of line and between [Fort Walsh] and Wood Mountain,"[27] different reports were coming out of the Indian agencies in Montana. The Indian Agent at Fort Peck had been complaining monthly that "Sitting Bull Indians" were camped all over from Milk River to Wood Mountain, driving the buffalo and making hunting difficult for his Indians. On April 19 he reported:

> I believe there is no doubt at all that Sitting Bull is now on American soil, and has been camped south of the boundary line since the middle of February last, and that practically all his Indians are now south of the northern boundary, there being, as they claim, no game for their subsistence on the Canadian side.[28]

Secretary Evarts lost his patience. On May 27, in a missive he forwarded to Ottawa through the British minister, he barely restricted himself to diplomatic language. Evarts repeated the complaint from the Indian agent at Fort Peck and warned that if something was not done the United States would resort to armed force even if it might seriously affect relations with Great Britain. Any Indians who crossed the border, "with or without apparent hostile intent," might be compelled to submit to U.S. forces and any who sought asylum across the line would require "the British Government to repulse them, or to disarm, disable and sequestrate them under a due responsibility for them as a component part of the territorial population of the British American dominion."

That led Secretary Evarts to the contention that the Sioux were now British Indians. They had, he claimed,

> in the most formal manner possible to their savage state renounced their rights in the one country and rejected terms of security, subsistence and peace to seek and receive asylum in the other . . . The significance of their acts of submission to British protection, as they themselves understood and intended them, admit of no doubt as to the extent of their intention to assume the character of inhabitants of British domain and their belief that they had done so.

The American government, Evarts concluded, "is bound now to regard the Indians of Sitting Bull's command as British Indians." As the Secretary then pointed out, if the now-British Sioux crossed the border into the United States, very serious consequences might follow.[29]

This was hardly a useful contribution to the dilemma in the West. There was no possibility of restraining the Indians in the North-West Territories, whether Sioux, Blackfoot, Cree or Assiniboine, from following the buffalo into Montana Territory, just as there was no way of preventing the American Crow and Peigan from crossing in the other direction. The Plains Indians had followed the buffalo for generations and they would not be deterred by the building of a few marker mounds along the imaginary Medicine Line. The NWMP certainly did not have the troops to control the movements of several thousand Indians over hundreds of kilometres of open border.

And there were no buffalo in Blackfoot country. In April, Assistant Commissioner Irvine reported that large numbers of Blackfoot, Peigan and Blood were at Fort Macleod in "a starving condition." They needed help quickly "as the buffalo have entirely disappeared."[30]

The situation was so desperate that Irvine made a highly unorthodox proposal to alleviate the distress of the Blackfoot. By telegram he requested approval to

> raise a troop of Blackfoot Indians, one hundred strong, to be attached to the police force. Will furnish their own horse and rifle. Government to ration and give them twenty-five cents a day. They are now badly off. This would strengthen their friendship with us as they are selling their horses and rifles for food.[31]

Irvine was apprehensive. A week later he sent off another wire recommending that he be given another 200 troopers.[32]

An unusual letter made its way out of the North-West Territories to Sir John A. Macdonald in Ottawa, from one Watagola who introduced himself as the nephew of Sitting Bull. Dated May 10, 1879, it was a crudely written plea for help:

> Will the Canadian Government help us in any way when the Buffalo die out and our children are starving for food. Will your Government grant to us any land so that we could sow and seed if we wanted to and will it grant us seed or not will it help us in any way or not ... On your answer will Depend a great deal as to whether we will stay that is most of the Indians on this side of the line or not.[33]

Macdonald accepted the letter as authentic and as an opportunity to officially advise the Sioux of the position of the Canadian government. He prepared a report to the Privy Council:

> But one reply can be given to the enquiry, viz. that the serious respon-
> sibility and heavy expenditure which devolve upon the Dominion in
> connection with the carrying out of the Treaties made with our own
> Indians who number many thousands . . . the Government cannot
> afford the slightest aid to the Sioux by the granting of land, or of seed
> grain, nor can they in any other way encourage them in the belief that
> they may look forward to making permanent homes on Canadian soil.

Macdonald recommended that the Sioux be informed

> that they ought no longer to delay in making overtures to the Govern-
> ment of the United States to be allowed to return and settle in their
> own country . . . as the only alternative to prevent the death by starva-
> tion of themselves, their wives and their children.[34]

The Prime Minister's report was, as a matter of course, accepted by cabinet.
This approval took place on June 28, 1879. From then on the firm policy of the
government of Canada towards the American Sioux refugees was, starkly put,
"Get out, or starve."

Meanwhile, out in Montana Territory, the "serious consequences" predicted by Secretary Evarts were coming to pass. Washington decided to
unleash Colonel Nelson Miles. On June 5, orders went forth to Miles directing him to

> move north of the Missouri, to separate our friendly from the hostile
> Sioux Indians, and to clear out those who had moved south of the
> boundary line; after driving them back, to establish a summer camp
> north of the Missouri.[35]

Miles was in trouble before he left his quarters at Fort Keogh. Two ranchers
had been murdered and one wounded during a stock raid on the Yellowstone
River in March. Miles believed that the offenders were Indians from Canada
and that the survivor, by the name of Sterns, could identify the murderers and
the stolen stock. In June Miles sent Sterns, then recovered, escorted by one of
his officers, Lieutenant J.C.T. Tillson, north to Fort Macleod. Tillson carried

the reports and a request from Miles to NWMP Commissioner Macleod for assistance in apprehending the murderers.

When Washington learned of Miles' actions there was hell to pay. On July 24, General of the Army William T. Sherman was called on the mat by President Hayes and Secretary of War Schurz. Miles' dispatches to Fort Macleod were "beyond the limits of his own command" and a complete explanation was required immediately. Every effort was to be made to intercept Tillson before he crossed the border, even sending a courier after him if necessary.

But the President and War Secretary were more concerned that the impetuous Miles was likely to provoke an Indian war north of the Missouri River and that was definitely not a desired event, particularly if it involved the Sioux from Canada. Sherman issued orders directing Miles to restrict his operations south of the Milk River, and not beyond. "He should not approach the National Boundary in a threatening manner to provoke hostilities by Indians resident beyond who have come a short distance south in hunting."[36] Rather lamely, Sherman explained that the real object in having Miles north of the Missouri was to protect navigation on the river. Steamboats had been running freely on the Missouri for 20 years.

But the horse was out of the barn. Tillson had crossed the border before he could be stopped. Miles had assembled his considerable command and headed north. By July 12 he was on the north side of the Missouri River with a force of cavalry, infantry and artillery, consisting of 33 officers, 643 enlisted men and 143 Crow and Cheyenne scouts and auxiliaries. In case the Sioux decided to stand and fight, Miles' superior, General Terry, had equipped the artillery with four Hotchkiss breech-loading cannon and one Hotchkiss revolving cannon.

Sitting Bull and a large party of Sioux were south of the border hunting buffalo. On July 17 they had scored a large kill along Beaver Creek, a northern tributary of the Milk River. The women had commenced to butcher the animals while the main party withdrew in search of another herd. Advance units of Miles' force, led by the Crow auxiliaries, surprised the Sioux and opened fire, killing two. The dozen or so Sioux men who were present, including Sitting Bull, held off the attack while the women escaped.

At this point an extraordinary encounter occurred. A prominent Crow named Magpie sent a messenger forth under a white flag carrying a challenge. Would Sitting Bull meet in a duel, just the two of them, one against one. Without hesitation Sitting Bull accepted. Like two medieval knights, the two headed their horses directly at the other as if jousting, but aiming rifles instead of lances. Magpie shot first but his rifle malfunctioned. Sitting Bull carried the latest model of Winchester carbine and he made no mistake. His shot took Magpie in the head, killing him instantly. Sitting Bull dismounted and took the scalp, then mounted Magpie's superior horse and rode back among the Sioux defenders.[37]

Whatever might be said about Sitting Bull, no one questioned his personal bravery. And among the Sioux, even after attaining great rank and stature, one's courage was always on the line.

When news of the army's attack reached the main Sioux party, about 60 of the hunters raced back and put up a strong fight until the artillery arrived. The Sioux retreated to their camp at the head of Rock Creek in the badlands north of the border, leaving their dead. Ignoring his orders, Miles pursued, following the trail right to the markers of the 49th Parallel. There he stopped as his troopers gazed north into Canada, which they contemptuously called "Europe."

Partly to allay the criticism of his actions, and partly out of characteristic exaggeration, Miles reported that he had defeated a force of "400 hostile Sioux" and killed eight of them. His casualties were three killed and three wounded.[38]

Washington's sensitivity to the volatility along the 49th Parallel was realistic on this occasion. The Hayes Administration fully believed that Sitting Bull and the Sioux intended, when ready, to attack the U.S. Army. They were encouraged in this belief by "Saskatchewan" Taylor, still the Americans' man in Winnipeg, who included in his reports any published editorial or military opinion that supported this view. In fact, Sitting Bull had no such plans, but, enraged by Miles' attack at Beaver River, the Sioux leader came close to striking back.

Miles likely never knew how near he had come to provoking another bloody battle on the scale of Little Big Horn, perhaps with similar results. He was badly outnumbered by the Sioux just over the border who, smarting from their losses, were barely restrained from surging south in revenge. Later that summer, several of the Sioux who had been across the line with Sitting Bull told Indian Commissioner Edgar Dewdney that, but for the promise made to Irvine when he delivered the Governor General's edict, "they would have exterminated Miles and his force." Dewdney stated that he confirmed that fact "from other sources."[39]

Superintendent James Walsh, on the scene at Wood Mountain, thought the Sioux were on the verge of attack and that Miles would have been defeated, but stated that he was responsible for saving the day. Writing of the incident 11 years later, he immodestly claimed that he had "saved General Miles from destruction." Walsh explained that "When Bull saw Miles was not going to cross into Canada he wanted to attack him at the line." But the NWMP officer "defeated Bull in the Council at Medicine Lodge Buttes and prevented an attack upon Miles' Command in camp at the International line."[40]

The battle at Beaver River gave Walsh another diplomatic problem. Lieutenant Tillson and Sterns had made it through to Fort Macleod where they were directed on to Wood Mountain. Now they were with Walsh on their mission to identify and arrest the men accused of murder on the Yellowstone River. An American Army officer in the vicinity of the Sioux villages was suddenly very much *persona non grata*, even more than usual, and Tillson requested a police escort back to Miles' camp. Walsh, having no men to spare to protect Tillson, took the two Americans with him while he visited the Sioux camp in search for the accused murderers. Walsh estimated that there were "at least two thousand warriors present at the time."[41] Unfortunately, Tillson's thoughts as he rode among this throng of bitter enemies were unrecorded.

When Sterns was unable to make the identification, Walsh enlisted "six reliable young warriors" to help him protect the two Americans as he escorted them back to the United States. The party found Miles camped on Rock Creek a mile south of the border. Walsh wisely left the Sioux escort at the border when he took Tillson into Miles' encampment. Again unfortunately, Colonel Miles did not record his thoughts when he learned that his junior officer had been returned safely to his command under the protection of six Sioux warriors.

Walsh took the opportunity of this meeting to assure Miles that the Sioux had no desire to make war with him but were "clamorous for peace." Walsh did not tell Miles, but he and other NWMP officers considered that this new U.S. Army attack on the Sioux would serve only to strongly reinforce both their hatred of the Long Knives and their determination to stay in Canada.

The units under Miles then patrolled east and west from Rock Creek and came upon some camps of buffalo-hunting Métis. They "arrested" some 300 families, 829 men, women and children, whom Miles claimed were "intruders upon our Indian reservation." The Métis sent word to Wood Mountain and again Walsh rode down to meet with Colonel Miles. The NWMP officer negotiated the release of 130 Métis families who wanted to return to Canada. Those who claimed Turtle Mountain as their home were sent under escort to Fort Buford and the remainder were shepherded, again under escort, south of the Missouri River to the Judith Basin, the drainage valley of the Judith River.

Miles and his units were then ordered to once more withdraw south of the Missouri River. Perhaps considering that its point was now firmly made, Washington did not use the clash between the Army and the Sioux as an excuse for further escalation of the diplomatic row. And less objection was made when buffalo-hunting Indians from Canada crossed into the United States.

The message was clear out on the western prairie. The American plains were now closed, even to the nomadic buffalo-hunting Red River Métis. The 49th Parallel had become the first fence erected on the great western grasslands.

Sir Edgar Dewdney, Ottawa, April 1879. *Library and Archives Canada / Topley Studio fonds PA-26629*

ON MONDAY EVENING, JUNE 9, 1879, Edgar Dewdney stood on the deck of the steamboat, *Red Cloud*, 14 days out from Bismarck, as it approached the landing at Fort Benton, Montana Territory. He was not impressed with what he saw. "The same as all western towns," he noted in his diary.[42]

Dewdney was a 43-year-old English immigrant but he was no tenderfoot and Fort Benton was by no means his first experience with a primitive community. Fifteen years in British Columbia, working as a surveyor, engineer, explorer, road builder, prospector and gold miner had stripped away the greenness, leaving a tough and seasoned frontiersman. Dewdney possessed the physique for the rough outdoors. Tall, large-framed and powerful, he was now more distinguished, with imposing white mutton chops connected by a full moustache.

A term in the British Columbia Legislature when it approved Confederation with Canada, followed by six years as the Member of Parliament for Yale, had given Dewdney a wider, national perspective. A loyal Conservative, he was a strong supporter of Prime Minister John A. Macdonald. All of which went to explain why Edgar Dewdney was on board the *Red Cloud*, preparing to disembark at Fort Benton on his way into the North-West Territories.

When Macdonald retained the portfolio of Minister of the Interior on his return to power in 1878, he found that affairs in the West were becoming very complex, particularly with respect to the Indian population and the recently concluded Treaties. David Laird, Lieutenant-Governor of the North-West Territories, had also served as Indian Superintendent but, finding the latter responsibilities too heavy, had resigned the superintendency in February 1879. From their posts in the West the NWMP reported disappearing buffalo and looming starvation among the Indians, particularly at Fort Macleod in

Blackfoot country. NWMP Commissioner Macleod had warned of this a year earlier when he delivered his Annual Report for the year 1877:

> I am bound to confess a fear that we are soon to be brought face to face with a danger which may involve very serious complications, indeed in some portions of the Territories the danger is already imminent ... in some parts of the country they [the Indians] are already brought face to face with starvation ... Hungry men are dangerous whether they be Indians or Whites."[43]

The situation was aggravated by the American refugee Sioux, Macleod claimed. They not only killed immense numbers of buffalo for their own use that would otherwise have been available to the Canadian Indians, but by their presence interfered with the movement of the herds, preventing them from reaching the Indians residing along the North Saskatchewan.

Macleod's prophesy had come to pass and now it was on Macdonald's plate. Needing a strong man to go into the West fully authorized to deal with the problem, Macdonald created the new position of Indian Commissioner and, to fill it, looked for someone experienced with the plains Indians. When several knowledgeable former Hudson's Bay Company men declined the proffered appointment, the prime minister called on the Member of Parliament for Yale. At first Dewdney demurred; he had never seen the prairies, or met any of the Indians there, but Macdonald reminded him that he had for years worked with the Indians of British Columbia. "Indians are all alike,"[44] the Prime Minister pronounced, and that was that. Freshly appointed, the new Commissioner was on his way into the West to take up his duties and see for himself how the plains Indians were faring under their Treaties.

Dewdney had been travelling for nearly three weeks and was still a few days from his destination. He travelled by train from Toronto to Collingwood, where he boarded the lake steamer *City of Owen Sound* for the four-day trip through the Great Lakes to Duluth. He then went by Great Northern Railroad to Bismarck where he boarded the *Red Cloud* on May 26. This route through the United States was the fastest way to reach the Canadian West. The all-Canada route through the Great Lakes, over the Dawson Route to Fort Garry and from there overland, was difficult and ponderously slow.

Dewdney had for travelling companions NWMP Commissioner James Macleod and Mrs. Macleod, and 83 recruits with as many horses, all heading for Forts Walsh and Macleod. The NWMP relied upon the Missouri River transportation system to support and supply its posts in the Territories.

Also on the journey were Thomas Wright and J.J. Taylor, two Ontario practical farmers hired by Ottawa and sent West to create and operate farms that would, hopefully, supply much of the food needed by the Blackfoot under Treaty 7. Thirteen more farmers were to follow and set up at the other agencies throughout the West. The 15 farms were also intended to serve as examples and schools of instruction where the Indians would learn how to support themselves from the land.

The new Indian Commissioner knew he had taken on a difficult assignment. Both Macdonald and his deputy minister, Colonel J.S. Dennis (he of the 1869 surveys at Fort Garry), had made that plain. Dewdney carried with him lengthy and detailed written instructions provided by Dennis.[45] Some food supplies, in the form of cattle and flour, had been placed at Fort Macleod and Fort Walsh. Dewdney was to distribute the food among those Indians who were in need, choose locations for the farms, and get them into operation.

Dewdney was also instructed to meet with Sitting Bull and the other Sioux chiefs and "note carefully the disposition and movement of these refugee Indians, and keep the Minister constantly advised thereof."[46] Dennis emphasized the policy of the government towards the Sioux:

> so long as they remain on our soil, they will not be permitted to be molested, provided they obey the laws of Canada, and are not guilty of making the Dominion a base for organizing or executing raiding expeditions into the territory of the United States.[47]

But there was to be no food for the Sioux. Dennis made that very clear in further instructions a month later when he stated that he hoped "Sitting Bull and his people, seeing that the buffalo is failing them in our territory, will go back to their own country, the only other alternative being starvation for themselves, their wives, and their families."[48] Dennis used almost the exact words that his minister had employed two days earlier in recommending to the Privy Council what became the official policy of the Canadian government. Probably the deputy minister himself had prepared the earlier recommendation. In any event, the new Indian Commissioner was clearly instructed that starvation was to be used as a lever to force the Sioux back out of the country, notwithstanding their admitted refugee status.

After spending several days in Fort Benton outfitting himself and his two farmers, Dewdney set forth on the 260-km (160-mi) trail north to Fort Walsh. Along the way, his diary notes, he was "continually meeting hungry Indians." On the trip up the Missouri River Dewdney had seen several herds of buffalo and complained to his diary about "ruffians" shooting them from the decks of the *Red Cloud* with no hope of recovering the carcass. But as he drove into his new domain he saw none. Ominously, however, there were "Lots of old dried carcases [*sic*] all over the prairie."

Several bands of Cree, Assiniboine and Blackfoot were waiting at Fort Walsh to meet the new representative from the Great Mother whom they promptly dubbed "Whitebeard," in reference to Dewdney's bushy mutton chops. Dewdney encountered concern here, and hunger, but no outright starvation. He explained that the policy of his government was to assist the Indians to become self-supporting and that farm instructors would soon arrive to show them how. Rations would be made available only when clearly needed and then only to those who would settle on their reserves and work at farming.

But when Dewdney moved farther west into Treaty 7 territory he found a much different scene awaiting him. At Fort Macleod he received a letter from Reverend Constantine Scollen describing the plight of the Blackfoot in strong terms. Dewdney considered the letter "very impertinent" but soon learned that Scollen told the truth. Jean L'Heureux, who had participated in the Treaty negotiations in the fall of 1877, was still residing with the Blackfoot and gave Dewdney a "gloomy" report of conditions at Blackfoot Crossing.

Dewdney headed for Blackfoot Crossing followed by a wagonload of provisions and several driven cattle. He found that Scollen and L'Heureux had not exaggerated the plight of the Indians. The beautiful flat held Crowfoot's village of 1,500 lodges but there were no signs of life. No one was in sight, no children were at play, no smoke rose from the lodges. No dog barked at the approach of strangers. There was no sound. Dewdney's party drove to the centre of the camp and an interpreter called out. An old man with only a blanket for covering appeared and, when asked for Crowfoot's lodge, gave directions.

Crowfoot was found sitting forlornly in his lodge, the very picture of despair. His favourite dog was the only one in the camp; all the others had long since been sacrificed for food. When introduced to Dewdney as sent by the Great Mother, Crowfoot held out his hand. "I am glad to see you and so are all my people. They are hungry—look at their lodges. They have no fire for there is nothing they can cook."[49] When the wagon appeared, Dewdney asked Crowfoot if its contents should be distributed immediately or would his people prefer to wait until the cattle arrived. "Give them something at once—they are starving," Crowfoot replied, and called loudly to his camp which quickly came alive. Wood was gathered, fires lighted and food distributed. Then three head of cattle were butchered and the feast was on. "And a happier lot of men, women and children you could hardly conceive," Dewdney related later.[50]

The happiness was but a fleeting reprieve from the misery Dewdney saw all about him. "Strong young men were now so weak that some of them could hardly walk—often who last winter were fat & healthy are now skin and bone."[51] Dewdney noted the plea of one Blackfoot mother: "If I can't get any food for my two children, I must kill myself. I live only for them and I can't bear to see them starve."[52]

The wealthy Blackfoot of less than two years earlier were no more. At the making of Treaty 7 they owned 15,000 horses, buffalo robes, firearms, and clothing. Now they were destitute, almost all their possessions gone, traded for food at outrageous rates of exchange dictated by unscrupulous traders. (A horse brought only a few cups of flour from the trader at Blackfoot Crossing.[53]) The once-proud people had been reduced to eating badgers, gophers and mice. Dewdney was told that many had died before his arrival, but he made no attempt to identify the number.

The plight of the Blackfoot had been predicted by Crowfoot three years earlier, in July 1876, when he told NWMP Inspector C.E. Denny: "We all see that the day is coming when the buffalo will all be killed, and we shall have nothing more to live on, and then you will come into our camp and see the poor Blackfoot starving."[54] Crowfoot defended his having taken his people under the Treaty two years before. If they had not taken the Treaty, he pointed out, how could they now beg the government for food to ward off starvation?

Dewdney had been told by his superiors in Ottawa that he would find the Blackfoot "in a starving condition" due to the disappearance of the buffalo, but he was unprepared for the extent and severity of the crisis he encountered on the western plains. The famine was not confined to Treaty 7 but extended well north to the valley of the Saskatchewan River and east into the Qu'Appelle where the Cree of Treaties 6 and 4 were also desperate. As Dewdney moved further into the West, visiting Fort Edmonton, Battleford and Prince Albert, he found that the plains were empty, not only of buffalo, but of all other game animals. The deer and elk had already been cleaned up. Dewdney also found that the food supplies that had been sent into the North-West to meet the emergency were entirely inadequate.

Although only Treaty 6 contained the so-called "famine clause" that required the government to provide sustenance, morally and practically Ottawa could not avoid caring for all its Treaty Indians equally. But the concept of welfare as an obligation of society had not yet entered the national conscience and, in fact, was repugnant to a wide segment of political thought. This made it difficult for Macdonald's government to boldly step forward and meet the crisis in the West.

But there was an overriding practical consideration that forced Ottawa's hand; it was obviously cheaper to feed the Indians on the Plains than to fight them. And no one doubted that the proud inhabitants of the West would fight before they would starve. At Qu'Appelle the previous spring, when some 400 destitute Cree had been refused food supplies at a government depot, they took what they needed at gunpoint.

Dewdney also found that the citizens of the several communities along the North Saskatchewan were in a state of considerable alarm, fearful of what action the starving Indians might resort to. The government was urged not only to implement a food program,[55] but also to provide better security for the local population.

Responding to urgent reports from Lieutenant-Governor Laird in August 1879, the federal government summoned its senior officials in the West to a council at Battleford, the seat of the Territorial government. The council was instructed to develop measures "to avert the apparently impending calamity of famine among the Indians."[56] Those directed to attend were Lieutenant-Governor Laird, Indian Commissioner Dewdney, NWMP Commissioner Macleod, Stipendiary Magistrate Richardson, Indian Agent Dickieson, and Pascal Breland, a prominent Métis and member of the Territorial Council.

The Battleford Conference confirmed the state of crisis facing the Territories. Unless the government made a major effort to feed the Indian population, massive starvation would result:

> Should this state of affairs arise, and it appears to the Conference to be inevitable, it will be fraught with such dire consequences not only to the Indians themselves, but to the many settlers scattered throughout the Territories, that immediate steps should be taken to avert, if possible, so great a calamity.[57]

This verdict was unsettling to Ottawa. An Indian uprising in the West was not only possible, but probable, perhaps even "inevitable," but how far it might spread was unknown. The Treaty Indians, the largest group, should be the least likely to revolt, particularly if adequate food supplies could reach them. But there were a large number of holdouts to the treaties, led by chiefs such as Big Bear, who could be expected to be troublesome, and who would not be granted rations. There were the American Sioux, wild cards certainly, and to whom there would definitely be no food supplied. Finally, there were the Métis, also starving and not included in the rationing program. It was a volatile mix.

Pascal Breland arrived late for the Battleford Council, but approved all the action taken except that he felt a far larger quantity of provisions was called for. His advice was taken, but it was soon apparent that feeding even the Treaty Indian population would be an immense undertaking. Fortunately many still followed the buffalo for, as Dewdney later noted, the 700 tons of food Ottawa managed to ship into the Territory for the winter of 1879–80 was woefully insufficient. "If it had been found necessary to feed three fourths of our Indians, this would not have lasted more than a month."[58] The Indian Commissioner encouraged the Indians to follow the buffalo wherever possible, even if that meant crossing the 49th Parallel.

Ottawa agreed that the situation called for stronger security. On September 5, a telegram, in cypher, was sent to Lieutenant-Governor Laird:

> It is proposed, as a precautionary measure, in view of the situation in Northwest, especially as regards Sioux, to organize and arm, but not at present to uniform, three troops and two infantry companies of volunteers under Militia Act at Prince Albert and vicinity, and one company of infantry at Battleford. Is this in opinion of yourself and Council expedient and necessary?[59]

There were enough residents in the region to supply that much manpower. Settlers were quickly taking up land in the West, particularly along the North Saskatchewan River. From the NWMP detachment at Fort Saskatchewan, Superintendent Jarvis reported that in 1880 he expected to be able to fill his requirements of flour from local grist mills. Dewdney was impressed with the number of farmers he found between Prince Albert and Battleford. He was not, however, impressed with the courage of the residents at Battleford whom he declared "have shown a great deal of unnecessary nervousness."[60]

By September 24 Dewdney was back at Fort Walsh. He was shortly to be provided with an excuse to avoid making the journey over to Wood Mountain to meet with Sitting Bull as he had been instructed.

The determined Reverend Abbott Martin Marty was on his way back into the North-West Territories, this time armed with Canadian authorization. He had visited Ottawa, secured an interview at the Interior Department and contended that he had a good chance of convincing Sitting Bull to return. The Abbott admitted his earlier failure, but claimed to have good reason to believe that many of the Sioux chiefs now wished to go home and the scarcity of food on the plains would tip the decision in their favour. Macdonald was in England, but his officials were quick to approve Abbott Marty's proposal.

"The Government of Canada would gladly give assent to any scheme by which the return of the Sioux to their own country could be effected in a peaceable and proper manner."[61] This time Abbott Marty was more careful in arranging his visit to the Sioux. When he arrived at Fort Walsh on September 30, he was given an impressive NWMP escort for what he termed his "pastoral visit," a strange description of a clergyman accompanied by 16 armed men.

NWMP Inspector John Cotton and 15 constables rode with Marty over to Wood Mountain, but there Walsh directed them back to the Sioux camp at the intersection of the White Mud (Frenchman) River and the border. After 12 days on the trail, Cotton and Marty came upon Spotted Eagle's camp of about 200 lodges; Sitting Bull, losing influence and stature among his people, was elsewhere with his much smaller band.

Spotted Eagle called for the erection of the great council tent and, on October 24, some 200 chiefs and headmen assembled to hear what Inspector Cotton and Abbott Marty had come to tell them. Cotton explained that the American Sioux were in a different position from the Canadian Indians who had surrendered their lands and taken Treaty. Now that the buffalo were failing, many Canadian Indians were in a bad way, particularly to the west and the north. The Great Mother was obliged to furnish her Indians with provisions for the coming winter but there could be no help for the Sioux. But the Americans were bound, and willing, to pay the Sioux for the lands taken from them and provide them with food and necessaries.

Abbott Marty, who was fluent in Siouan, described the conditions at the Dakota agencies where the friends and relatives of his listeners now lived. Yes, he admitted, they had no guns, but guns were now useless without buffalo to hunt, and only horses enough to do their work, but they were being provided for. He had not come, the priest said, to prescribe a course for them, but to hear their own wishes and opinions. He called on them to give their view on the question of the greatest importance to them and their families: "What are we going to do when there will be no more buffalo?"

Four chiefs in turn rose and spoke for their people. Marty summarized their position:

1. The Sioux full understood that the Queen owed them nothing and they claimed nothing but asylum on good behaviour, and free trade;

2. They expected nothing good from the Long Knives and were fully determined never to trust their promises or submit to their control;

3. There was no chance of returning to the Long Knives because the Sioux were fully convinced that there would be buffalo as long as there should be Indians.

Abbott Marty tried to explain that the Long Knives were not anxious to have the Sioux return because so long as they stayed in Canada the Americans were relieved of the obligation to pay for the Sioux lands.

But the Abbott failed again. The Sioux had no more interest in his message than they showed on his first visit in 1877. Their stubborn belief that the buffalo would always be there for them was confirmed by Spotted Eagle, who paid Cotton and Marty a farewell visit that evening:

I can not and do not believe that the buffalo will ever disappear. I have seen so many this summer and therefore I shall never be compelled to accept the hard conditions of the Long Knives.[62]

Spotted Eagle's people had been more fortunate than the other residents of the Canadian plains. For them buffalo had indeed been plentiful during the summer. At the end of July 1879, Captain Eli Huggins, one of Miles' officers at the U.S. Army encampment on the Milk River, just across the border from Spotted Eagle's camp, wrote to his family that "thousands of buffalos have crossed the line going north during the last few days."[63] But Spotted Eagle's luck was about to run out. The buffalo began to desert his region also and during the harsh winter of 1879–80 starvation crept into the lodges of his people. Just a year after he so loftily dismissed Abbott Marty, Spotted Eagle made the acquaintance of Captain Huggins. It was to the young cavalry officer that the great Sioux leader and some 500 of his followers abjectly surrendered in late October 1880.

While Abbott Marty was heading into the Canadian West to meet with the Sioux, Secretary of State Evarts visited Toronto where, on September 11, 1879, he discussed with Governor General Lorne several topics of concern to both the United States and Canada. The presence of the American Sioux in the North-West Territories headed the list. To read the account of the conversation is to wonder at the lack of understanding of the West displayed by the American Secretary of State.

Evarts was presented with the most recent NWMP reports, from Commissioner Macleod and Superintendent Walsh. After reading the reports, Evarts observed, with an innocence perhaps feigned, that Canada seemed to be anticipating trouble with the Sioux. Well, yes, Lorne agreed. Canada was sufficiently anxious about its own Indians on the verge of starvation without several thousand American Indians stuck in the middle of a very volatile situation. Still playing the innocent, Evarts said that the American government always fed its Indians and Canada should do the same. To this Lorne explained that Canada, at huge cost, was attempting to do just that but the United States was making it impossible for the Sioux to return home. Evarts then fell back on his often-stated position: Canada should, as international law required, disarm the Sioux and intern them.

Lorne pointed out that it was a bit unreasonable to expect the strict application of the letter of international law along a frontier of 1,600 km (1,000 mi) "where large armed bodies of wild Indians had been for generations in the habit of living upon the moving herds of buffalo, following them in their migrations southward and northward." Canada, Lorne went on, had no military force in the North-West sufficient to intern the Sioux and, he noted, the Americans with much superior military capability had found it impossible to keep their Indians on their reservations.

How many troops did Canada have? Evarts inquired, as if the Sioux-in-Canada question had not been debated between the two nations for at least two years and his office at the forefront of the debate. Not more than 300 to 400 Mounted Police in the entire North-West, Lorne replied with diplomatic patience. Then he went on to make three strong requests that Canada wished the American government to consider. First, reports from the West claimed that General Miles had stationed his forces along the boundary line to prevent the buffalo from coming north. There should be no impediment to the migration of the buffalo. Second, according to the same reports, General Miles had ordered that no "white man, half-breed or red man" should cross into the huge Indian reservations that lined the border in Montana Territory. Since Canada placed no prohibition on southern Indians coming north, the northern Indians should also be allowed to follow game across the line. Third, the American requirement that the Sioux give up both their guns and their horses if they returned was unreasonable as to the horses and made surrender unthinkable to such a nomadic people.

The discussion closed with Evarts diplomatically agreeing to consider Canada's concerns and discuss them with Secretary of War Schurz. But it might well be that Lorne succeeded in lowering the level of belligerence from the office of the Secretary of State in Washington, at least on the subject of Canadian Indians hunting buffalo in the United States.

Out in the West, at Fort Macleod in that fall of 1879, Indian Commissioner Edgar Dewdney, knowing nothing of the conversation between Evarts and

Lorne, was about to test the tolerance of the Americans to the presence in their territory of Indians from north of the border. On October 11, Dewdney again visited Crowfoot and his people at Blackfoot Crossing and found the situation as desperate as it had been in July. Again all was silent and no smoke rose from the lodges. Another death occurred the afternoon of Dewdney's arrival.

The Indian Commissioner was under strict instructions from Ottawa to exercise the utmost economy in dealing with the famine in the West and he fully appreciated the magnitude of the problem. It was there in front of him, in stark reality. Dewdney could also see that feeding the thousands of starving treaty Indians on the plains would require a massive and hugely expensive program, all because of the disappearance of the buffalo. But there were buffalo still, just not in Canada. In the United States the herds were still strong. Prime Minister Macdonald had wanted an Indian Commissioner who would make decisions on the ground and in Edgar Dewdney he had his man.

To Dewdney the solution was simple. The presence of an international boundary in the form of the lightly marked 49th Parallel was no obstacle at all. Neither was Washington's sensitivity to the matter of Indians from Canada hunting buffalo on American soil. The Indian Commissioner strongly encouraged Crowfoot to take his people to where the buffalo were, in Montana, and issued provisions for the journey. Late that fall of 1879 the Blackfoot trekked south until they found ample supplies of buffalo between the Little Rockies and the Bears Paw Mountains. There they found other Indians from north of the border, including Big Bear and his band of Cree, holdouts from Treaty 6. A very large number of Canadian Indians, treaty and non-treaty, spent the winter of 1879–80 in Montana; just how many was never defined. The Canadian estimate is 8,000, but Colonel Thomas Ruger, commanding the U.S. 18th Infantry at Helena, Montana Territory, thought 17,000.[64] The usual penchant of the American Army to exaggerate the numbers of Indians it faced might in this case be offset by Ruger's superior proximity to the area occupied by the refugees from north of the border.

Whatever the number, Edgar Dewdney considered this to be quite a satisfactory state of affairs. As long as the Blackfoot were in Montana they were off his payroll. As for Big Bear and his people, so long as they stayed off-treaty, and out of the country, they were of little concern. Dewdney later estimated that his stratagem saved the Canadian government at least $100,000.[65]

But the cost to the Blackfoot was enormous. The whiskey traders who had plundered Crowfoot's people until the arrival of the NWMP in 1874 still operated in Montana, and immediately they again set upon their prey. Once again the Blackfoot camps were debauched, their possessions sold and their women prostituted. Thus, we have the spectacle of one agency of the Canadian government, the Indian Commissioner, undoing much of the good accomplished by another agency of the same government, the NWMP.

On November 2, when Dewdney, intending to cross the visit with Sitting Bull off his list, set out for Wood Mountain, only a few kilometres down the trail he encountered Inspector Cotton and his men returning from escorting Abbott Marty. After listening to Cotton's account of the meeting with Spotted Eagle, Dewdney concluded "that it would be useless and unwise to visit them so soon after their interview with the Bishop." The Indian Commissioner certainly knew that Marty and Cotton had not met Sitting Bull, but, never mind, Spotted Eagle would do. Quite relieved to be presented with a reason to abort his mission, Dewdney turned around and accompanied Cotton back to Fort Walsh. With a satisfied feeling of accomplishment, by November 8 Dewdney felt he could leave his theatre of responsibility for the winter and return to his wife and home in Ottawa, not to mention the fine dining and gracious society offered by Canada's capital city.

With navigation on the Missouri River closed for the season, there was no stateroom on a steamboat for Dewdney as he headed home in early November. Instead he crammed into overloaded stagecoaches from Fort Assiniboine, the American Army post on the Milk River, to Fort Benton, Helena, and on to Ogden, Utah, the terminus of the Union Pacific Railroad. The Indian Commissioner was back in Ottawa on November 25 after a trip that was about a week shorter than his journey into the West.

Jay's Treaty of 1794, in addition to sorting out boundary imprecisions and other problems arising from the Treaty of Paris acknowledging American independence, provided that British subjects and United States citizens and "Indians dwelling on either side of the said boundary line [might] pass and repass ... into the respective territories and countries of the two parties." The Treaty was not mentioned in the debate over the Plains Indians following the buffalo, it being then assumed that it was no longer effective, as supplanted by later treaties, particularly the Treaty of Ghent that closed the War of 1812. This provision from Jay's Treaty has current recognition in United States immigration rules but not in Canada, where it is a subject of litigation.

CHAPTER 19

Fire and Starvation

sitting bull
. . . .
in wood mountain—
what did he feel or think
smelling the southern plains burning above the missouri
wood mountain incised by the moving sword of fire
may have looked like a sundancer
beneath heatwaves
the dancing plains fastened by smoke coiling to
the dark orange moon
while he and his people fled to seek refuge
in the wood mountain post
. . . .[1]

THE FIRES RAGED OVER THE PLAINS "FROM WOOD MOUN-
tain on the east to the Rocky Mountains on the west," a distance
of 560 km (350 mi), and "north of the boundary line as far north
as the latitude of Qu'Appelle," another 210 km (125 mi). The fires
"were started at different points almost simultaneously, as by some recon-
structed arrangement."[2] So reported Indian Commissioner Edgar Dewdney
in his December 31, 1880, account to Parliament on the past year's activities of
his department. The conflagration, he said, occurred after his departure from
the Territories in November 1879. The result of the grass being destroyed over
such a huge swath of territory was to "keep the buffalo south" of the border.
By this Dewdney meant away from the Indians in Canada.

Although since thoroughly debunked,[3] in Dewdney's time, and for much
later, it was believed that the buffalo was a migratory animal, with regular north

and south movements of the herds. The destruction of the grass over such a vast range would render it barren and inhospitable until at least late in the following spring when new growth was established. The northern "migration" would thus be interrupted. The fires "were started at different points almost simultaneously, as by some preconstructed arrangement." In other words, deliberately and by plan intending to deprive the Blackfoot, American Sioux and other Indians in the region of buffalo to hunt, thereby reducing them to starvation.

Who would commit such a monstrous crime? Someone on the American side, of course, since according to Dewdney only the grass north of the boundary was fired. Prime suspects were the U.S. Army, the American hide hunters operating in Montana Territory, and the American Indians wanting to keep the diminishing herds to themselves. Strangely, the NWMP at Fort Macleod blamed the Blackfoot themselves as they went south over the border in search of the herds.[4]

The NWMP were not alone in assigning blame to the Blackfoot. W.L. Lincoln, the United States Indian Agent at Fort Belknap, on the Milk River in Montana Territory, reported on October 6, 1879, that

> the country has been ravaged by fires in all directions ... The country is so thoroughly burnt over that there is barely enough grass left upon which to herd our cattle. The setting of fires is presumably the work of northern British Indians. Since about the 20th they have been passing here every day in large numbers.[5]

The U.S. Army, which wanted the Sioux forced back over the border, was a natural suspect and reasonably so since it was known to have employed fire as a tactical weapon. In 1865 in Nebraska Territory, hoping to burn out Sioux and Cheyenne war parties, the military set a prairie fire along a 480-km (300-mi) front.[6] Colonel Nelson Miles, whose units were well placed to arrange a huge fire along the border, did propose burning over the entire country north of the Missouri River but was denied permission by his superiors, "except as a last resort."[7]

But why would the Army extend the fire all the way west to the Rockies over the territory of the Blackfoot? The U.S. military had no interest in the Blackfoot. Firing the range from the Cypress Hills to Wood Mountain would have confined the resulting misery to the Sioux who were the Army's target. In Ottawa, Macdonald's cabinet believed that some agency of the American government was already responsible for fires along the border intended to prevent the movement of the buffalo. On September 22, 1879, the Privy

Council adopted a four-point strategy that it hoped the United States would accept and thereby ease the return of the Sioux; point three proposed that "the Americans must cease burning the grass along the forty-ninth parallel to keep the buffalo south."[8]

If no other culprit could be found, Louis Riel was available. The infamous leader from Red River had that winter of 1879–80 joined the Métis community in Montana Territory[9] and was a "usual suspect" in a number of rumours that swirled about the West.[10]

Such deliberately ignited fires were not unheard of on the plains. A year earlier just such a fire raged for 64 km (40 mi) west from the Missouri River near the Rosebud Agency in Dakota. A U.S. Army officer on the scene reported that the prairie was "set on fire at innumerable points almost simultaneously, and at places but a few rods apart, with the manifest determination to make the work of destruction thorough and complete."[11] Officials concluded that the fire was set in an attempt to corner the local transportation market, and it did cause difficulty in maintaining the supply line to the Rosebud Agency with its population of 13,000. The teams crossing the 64 km (40 mi) of blackened landscape were required to carry corn sufficient to feed their draft animals along the way.

Captain Samuel Anderson of the Boundary Commission described the great fire that attacked several of their survey parties in the late summer of 1874:

> The heat of the sun and the excessive drought during the summer had completely parched the prairie-grass, and the soil was fissured in all directions. Although the greatest vigilance was practised, the occurrence of prairie-fires seemed inevitable, and towards the end of August a pillar of smoke visible to the north, a great distance off, gave warning that before many days were past, the whole of the Great Plains would be swept by fire. The course of the fire was most capricious, and often turned by a ravine, or by a slight change in the wind, into a new course. The onward progress of the fire was noticed for many days by the gradually-increasing temperature of the air, and soon by the smell of the burning grass. The various parties of the Boundary Commission being scattered over 400 miles [643 km] of longitude at the same time, experienced very varied fortune in their encounter with the fire ... The result of all these prairie-fires, which raged in different localities between the middle of August and middle of September, was that the general appearance of the county was now changed from the universal yellow tint to a dismal black, and the whole surface of the plains was as bare of herbage as the sand on the sea-shore.[12]

PRAIRIE FIRE

John Palliser, in *Solitary Rambles*, the account of his wanderings in Eastern Montana in 1847–48, 10 years before his expedition across the Canadian Plains, included a vivid description of a prairie fire experienced by a sportsman friend shortly after Palliser had returned to Ireland:

We had seen, during the latter part of our day's journey, a remarkable appearance in the eastern horizon; and during supper observed a smell of burning, and a few light cinders fell about the camp, and presently we remarked that the luminous appearance in the east had very much augmented. There being a little hill in front of us, we could not see distinctly what caused it; but having consulted together, we agreed that it proceeded from a prairie on fire, which, however, was a long way off. About eight o'clock the smell of burning and the glare having materially increased, we walked up to the top of the hill, when a spectacle presented itself to us the most grand that can well be conceived. The whole horizon, from north to south, was one wall of fire, blazing up in some places to a great height, at others merely smouldering in the grass. It was, however, at least eight miles [12.8 km] off; but the wind seemed to set in our direction, so we instantly returned, and took measures to preserve the camp.... In about twenty minutes, however, it approached so near, that there was no time to be lost, and all hands were immediately employed in burning a road across the face of the hill, so as to stop the fire at that part. ... The night was very dark, but as far as the eye could reach, all across the horizon, about four miles [6.4 km] in front of us, was a broad, bright, lurid glare of fire, with a thick canopy of smoke hanging over it, whose fantastic wreaths, as they curled in the breeze, were tinged with the red reflection of the flames. Even at that distance we could hear the crackling and rushing of the fire, which, as it advanced, caused a strong wind, and every now and then a brighter flame would shoot high up into the black cloud of smoke over the top of the hill, illuminating for an instant our tents and wagons in the dark hollow, and giving a momentary glimpse of the horses which were picketed on the side of the rise, on the crest of which the figures of the men engaged in lighting the opposition fire (which, as it became too extended, they beat down with blankets, only suffering it to burn a space about twelve feet [3.6 m] broad, right across the line of the advancing conflagration,) stood out in strong relief against the glowing wall of light beyond them; and as they ran about tossing their arms and waving the blankets and little torches of lighted grass, they looked in the distance like demons rather than men.

We had no time to look at the picturesque, however, for every moment... became more pregnant with danger, and by the time they had burned as much as would only about half cover the camp, the fire was raging in the bottom at the other side of the hill. I ran up for an instant to the top, and shall never forget the scene. Although still half a mile [.8 km] off, the fire seemed close to me, and the heat and smoke were almost intolerable, while the dazzling brightness of the flames made it painful to look at them; they were in three lines nearly parallel, the first of which was just below me, burning with a rushing noise, and crackling as it caught the dry grass, that gave an idea of total destruction which it is impossible to convey, and stretching away over the hill and dale for twelve or fourteen miles [19–22 km] on each side of me, lighting up the sides of the hills and the little groves of wood far away. The two lines in the rear were not so much connected, and seemed rather licking up any little spots of grass which had escaped at first.

Every now and then a prairie hen would flirr past, flying in a wild uncertain manner, as if fear had almost deprived it of the use of its wings; while all the songsters of the grove were wheeling about among the trees, uttering the most expressive cries of alarm, and the melancholy hooting of several owls, and wailing yells of the wolves, together with the shouts and cries of the men almost drowned occasionally by the roaring of the flames, added to the savage grandeur of the scene, and one could have fancied the end of all things was at hand.

On returning to the camp, I found all hands cutting the lassoes and halters of the mules, some of which galloped off instantly into the river, where they remained standing till the hurricane of flame had passed over; the others, seemingly trusting themselves instinctively more to man than to their own energies in such an emergency, followed us up the space which we had burned, and remained quietly there, trembling indeed, but without an effort to escape. By the time the animals were collected in this spot, the fire was blazing on the top of the hill, and we all rushed away with blankets to arrest its progress, if possible, at the part which we had left unguarded; all our efforts would have been in vain, however, and our tents and everything else must have been consumed, but that, just at that weak point, the grass suddenly became thin and scanty, with much stony ground, and we had the satisfaction of seeing the flames stopped there and turned off to the northward along the edge of the brushwood. It was really terrific to be, as we were, trying to break it down in the very middle of the blaze (which, after all, was so narrow that where the flames were not high, you could jump across it); we were, indeed, nearly suffocated by the smoke and heat.

As soon as we perceived the fire turned off we returned to the camp and horses; and all danger was over, but the sight of the three lines of fire stretching up the rising grounds behind the camp, just like the advance of a vast army, was magnificent; and it was still more extraordinary to watch the manner in which the fire passed itself on, as it were, over the tops of the highest trees, to the height of at least forty or fifty feet [12–15 m].

The whole scene lasted altogether about two hours, and nothing could be conceived more awfully grand. The extraordinary rushing and crackling sound of the flames was one of the most terrific parts of it, and when one considers that the grass is no where more than five or six feet [1.5–1.8 m] high, it is difficult to imagine how the flame blazes up to such a vast height as it did.

The contrast presented, two hours afterwards, was most striking. Instead of the brilliant glare of the fire, and lurid appearance of the sky, there reigned an impenetrable darkness, earth and sky being alike shrouded in a black gloom, which could almost be felt; not a star was to be seen, and the air retained a suffocating, sulphureous smell, as if Satan himself had passed over the earth. We could not distinguish objects at ten paces distance, and were right glad when a fresh breeze came gently breathing over the prairie, dissipating the murky vapours still hanging in the atmosphere; and a fine starlit sky with a sharpish frost at length relieved us from the close choking feeling we had experienced for hours before. This prairie fire had travelled at the rate of five miles [8 km] an hour, bringing with it a strong gale of wind; for otherwise the night was quite calm, both before and after it had passed over.[1]

NOTE

1. John Palliser, *Solitary Rambles and Adventures of a Hunter in the Prairies* (Edmonton: Hurtig, 1969), 90–95.

There is ample evidence of extensive prairie fires in the fall of 1879, but not all of them were in November. The fire at Wood Mountain broke out on October 3 and destroyed 25 tons of hay.[13] No fires are mentioned in the NWMP reports from Fort Walsh in the Cypress Hills, which would have been right in the middle of the fire described by Dewdney.[14]

In early October, John Macoun and his assistant, carrying out a geological and botanical survey of the western plains, were caught by a prairie fire while camped 160 km (100 mi) southwest of Battleford. Fortunately, they spotted the oncoming flames in time to take precautions by moving their camp and horses to a patch of nearly-bare ground. Macoun described the experience:

A few moments more and the fire has passed the last ridge, and with the speed of a fast horse it bears down upon us. As it came near us the whirling smoke and leaping flames seemed to take the forms of living things that were in terrible agony and added largely to the sublimity of the spectacle. When it reached our oasis it swept past on either side, and a few gulps of smoke, accompanied with a strong hot wind, were the only discomforts it caused us. When it was past we saw that it kept an even front, and wherever the grass was long and thick the flames continued for some time after the first rush was past.[15]

Two nights later the same fire swept over a NWMP camp while the men were asleep and destroyed their tent and camp while they barely escaped with their lives.[16] Ten days later Macoun crossed the area ravaged by the fire and found the grass destroyed for 38.5 km (24 mi).[17]

Fires there certainly were, but not quite as reported by Edgar Dewdney. Prairie fires were not uncommon events in the late fall, usually started by lightning or carelessness. Sometimes they would run for hundreds of kilometres and were dreaded by the Indians. A severe fire would destroy winter grazing and ensure that there would be no buffalo to hunt.[18] Wildfires occurred in the spring also. In that same year 1879, on April 9, a fire swept upon the Sioux camp at Wood Mountain so suddenly that eight lodges and two lives were lost.[19]

The fall of 1879 was an unusually destructive fire season. In Montana ranchers were so concerned that they banded together and placed advertisements in the Fort Benton *Record* offering rewards of $500 and $700—huge for the time—for "the arrest and conviction of any person or persons found setting fire to any cattle range or prairie."[20] Even so the fires continued, and the *Record* reported that

> In spite of the large reward offered by the cattle dealers of the Sun River basin for the apprehension of prairie burners, the fires still continue in the destruction of the cattle ranges of this county . . . The recent fire which destroyed a large portion of the best ranges in this county was thought to have been the work of Peigan Indians who recently passed over the Missouri en route to the buffalo grounds in the Judith Basin, but so far from being the cause of the fire, these Indians informed the settlers along the route that they had received instructions from their agent to exercise the greatest caution in regard to fires, and that they would not even camp where there was any danger of burning the prairie.[21]

The editor of the Deadwood *Pioneer* provided a colourful description of his experience with prairie fire while travelling by train through Dakota Territory in that fall of 1879:

> My trip from Fargo west was through a land of fire and smoke and blackness. I now know where the Indian summer smoke comes from. Millions on millions of square miles of rank grass and weeds and woods ablaze night and day, from the Rocky Mountains to the great lakes, and from the Saskatchewan to the Arkansas, furnish smoke

enough to hang a drapery of blue and lavender haze over the whole continent for weeks at a time, and it would seem that such a vast area of roaring furnace fires would be sufficient to account for the warmer temperature that always accompanies the autumnal season of atmospheric crape and dreamy langour. No one who has never seen these limitless oceans of conflagration can form any conception of their terrible grandeur while aflame, or of the gloomy desolateness of the swept regions after the lurid glow is gone. The fires this fall have been more widespread and destructive than ever before in the memories of a score of oldest inhabitants tied together.[22]

As if anticipating the disastrous fire season about to begin, on September 26, 1879, the Council of the North-West Territories enacted an ordinance "For The Prevention of Prairie and Forest Fires." Open fires were prohibited, except for "camp or domestic purposes . . . in the months of December, January, February, March or April." Strangely omitted were the months of October and November, which saw the worst of the great fires on the plains.

Evidence of a fire of the magnitude reported by Dewdney was discovered by Professor Henry Youle Hind on an expedition through the West in 1858:

From beyond the South Branch of the Saskatchewan to Red River all the prairies were burned last autumn, a vast conflagration extended for one thousand miles in length and several hundreds in breadth. The dry season had so withered the grass that the whole country of the Saskatchewan was in flames. The Rev. Henry Budd, a native missionary at the Nepowewin [Nipawin], on the North Branch of the Saskatchewan, told me that in whatever direction he turned in September last, the country seemed to be in a blaze; we traced the fire from the 49th parallel to the 53rd, and from the 98th to the 108th degree of longitude. It extended, no doubt, to the Rocky Mountains.[23]

There was no fire of the sort reported by Dewdney, one that was "started at different points almost simultaneously." The fall of 1879 was just an unusually severe fire season. The disappearance of a once abundant species seems to prick a human need for an extraordinary explanation. When the billion-bird flocks of passenger pigeons vanished thirty years later, scientific journals variously reported them in the Arizona desert or east of Puget Sound. Henry Ford was convinced they had perished in the Pacific Ocean en route to Asia.

There are several accounts, some a bit fanciful, alleging that steps were taken on the American side to prevent the northern movement of the buffalo in 1879.

Mari Sandoz,.an early historian of the era, wrote in 1954 that the U.S. government was embarrassed by the escape into Canada of the Sitting Bull Sioux and

> worked to get him back. By 1878 they were ready to starve him and his followers into surrender. A line of men, breeds, Indians and soldiers, was set to turn the buffaloes back whenever they started to cross the border, and it was there, some said, shut in by this line of prairie fire and guns, that the greatest slaughter of the northern herd took place.[24]

C.M. MacInnes, an Oxford-educated historian writing in 1930, somewhat earlier than Sandoz, provides an account suspiciously similar:

> In 1878 the United States government decided to starve Sitting Bull and his followers into surrender. A cordon of half-breeds, Indians and American soldiers was therefore formed, and ordered to drive the buffalo back whenever the herds started to come north; and it was there, shut in by this cordon from their favourite grazing grounds on the Bow River that the last great slaughter of the bison took place.[25]

If MacInnes' "cordon" actually existed, and took the usual form of a human chain, it should have settled once and for all the debate as to whether anything would deter an onrushing herd of buffalo from their chosen course:

> When once a column is in full career, it goes straight forward regardless of all obstacles; those in front being impelled by the moving mass behind. At such times they will break through a camp, trampling down everything in their course.[26]

Dr. A.O. MacRae, writing in 1912, was a bit more circumspect, but he, too, provides a likely invented version, attributed to one who should have been more restrained:

> The year 1879 was a sad one for the Indians; the buffalo were disappearing altogether. The exact cause for the astonishing rapid decrease has never been satisfactorily determined. Many have thought that some epidemic peculiar to cattle carried off the buffalo; others say it

was the wholesale slaughter by the Indians and whites for the valuable robes. Colonel Herchmer, the ex-commissioner of the Royal Northwest Mounted Police, told the author that he believed it was the work of the United States Government; they sent out sharpshooters, with long Winchester rifles, and deliberately destroyed the buffalo, in order to force the Sioux and kindred warlike tribes to sue for peace and mercy because of starvation.[27]

In 1983, a medical doctor, Rudolph W. Koucky, while advancing the thesis that the disappearance of the northern buffalo herd in 1881–82 was caused by disease, states as a matter of fact: "In 1878 large prairie fires drove the buffalo from northern Alberta southward into the Missouri River valley."[28]

Certainly the buffalo had disappeared from their usual Canadian range by the fall of 1879. Perhaps it was natural to cast about in search of some intervention that had brought about this phenomenon. In Ottawa, the Macdonald government suspected that the Americans were behind the buffalo shortage. In its September 22, 1879 report, the Privy Council complained:

> The buffalo which forms the staple of consumption amongst the Indians of British North America is diminishing rapidly in numbers and their migration northward into Canadian Territory has, your Committee are informed, latterly been arrested (as far as it could be) by United States troops stationed along the Border.[29]

Prime Minister Macdonald told the House of Commons that "the utter disappearance of the buffalo" was caused by "the action of the American Government which formed a perfect *cordon* to prevent buffalo from crossing the line."[30]

Ottawa had some reason for its belief that the American Army was impeding the movement of the herds. On July 30, 1879, in Washington, *The Post* carried a story out of St. Paul stating that Colonel Nelson Miles was on the Frenchman River and had "succeeded in placing his command between the Indians and the buffalo, which movement will, he says, force the hostiles to attack him in his chosen position or retreat across the border."[31]

Whatever the cause, the buffalo did not return to the Canadian plains that winter of 1879–80, and starvation and great suffering befell the resident Indian population. It struck the northern plains first. As early as June 1879, Lieutenant-Governor David Laird reported from Battleford that "scarcely a buffalo can be found north of the Red Deer and South Saskatchewan Rivers." Hunters returned from the plains empty-handed and in need of assistance:

For the last two months, on an average, about one thousand Indians have frequented this place, and I hear that in all the settlements along the Saskatchewan there are Indians begging for food . . . Notwith-standing the assistance the Indians receive from the Government stores, they are continually begging around among the settlers, their craving for animal food is so great that they hope to procure morsels by going from house to house.[32]

Farther south, in his camp near the border, by mid-winter the confidence Spotted Eagle had expressed to Bishop Marty in the fall evaporated as the Sioux struggled to stay alive. By spring they were reduced to scavenging the carcasses of horses that had died of scabies the previous fall. Not surprisingly, an epidemic with many fatalities was the result. At the Wood Mountain NWMP Post, the men saved table scraps and shared their rations with the women and children. Superintendent Walsh, in disregard of orders, raided the Force's store of provisions to assist the desperate Sioux.[33]

In Ottawa, concern for the difficulties in the Territories received mention in the Speech from the Throne on February 12, 1880, but its placement and tenor speak to the attitude of the times. The plight of the Indians starving on the Canadian plains was of less concern than the suffering in Ireland, caused again by failure of the harvests. After an opening paragraph expressing gratitude for an abundant harvest in Canada and a prosperous economy, the Speech turned to the "less fortunate circumstances of our fellow subjects in Ireland, where so much destitution prevails" and invited "means of showing our practical sympathy with their distress." The last paragraph of the introduction referred to the similar situation on the western plains, but now the concern was for the cost. "In consequence of the entire failure of the usual food supply of the Indians in the North-West, a large expenditure has been necessarily incurred to save them from starvation." The government hoped that its efforts to induce the bands "to betake themselves to the cultivation of the soil may prevent the necessity of similar calls for relief in the future."[34]

It was not only the Sioux in the vicinity of Wood Mountain who suffered cruelly in the early winter of 1880. At Fort Walsh some 500–600 Canadian Indians congregated, destitute and helpless, their horses so weak they were unable to even carry provisions, making it necessary for the NWMP to deliver food to the Indian camps. To alleviate the drain on his meager supplies, Superintendent Crozier set up a fishing operation on nearby lakes, providing nets and instruction from some of his men who were experienced fishermen; the buffalo hunters had no knowledge of the art of catching fish. In February 1880,

Crozier advised that buffalo were reported "on both sides of the Missouri, and heading north," but "[t]he Indians find it difficult to follow buffalo, owing to deep snow and the poor condition of their horses and are said to have very little provisions."[35]

In April, many of those who had crossed into Montana Territory in search of buffalo began straggling back, all starving, so feeble that many were unable to continue the journey without assistance. Crozier kept men and teams steadily on the road with food for the wretched travellers; the stream continued until Fort Walsh was surrounded by 5,000 starving Indians.[36]

The lack of buffalo meant not only a shortage of food but also of hides that could be tanned and used to replace clothing and tipi covers. The constant moving of the camps in search of the herds caused heavy wear and tear on both clothing and tipi covers. Such heavy usage could wear out a tipi cover in one year[37] and in the valleys of the Saskatchewan and the Qu'Appelle Rivers most of the Cree bands had not seen buffalo for much longer than a year. The result was that the people were nearly naked and unable to maintain their shelters. Unable to leave camp to fish or hunt, they were forced to eat their horses and dogs.[38] At White Bear's reserve in the Moose Mountains, the lack of skins forced the Cree and Assiniboine to attempt plastering their tipi poles with mud.[39]

From Edmonton, Indian Agent James Stewart reported that in his long residence in the country he had never seen anything like it:

> It was not only the want of buffalo, but everything else seemed to have deserted the country; even fish were scarce. Fur-bearing animals, from which the Indians might have supplied themselves with clothing etc. were not to be had. In some cases some hunting might have been done, but the poor people were naked, and the cold was intense, and remained so during the whole winter . . . They ate many of their horses, and all the dogs were destroyed for food.[40]

At Qu'Appelle the situation was much the same. The nearly naked people had been unable to fish the frozen lakes and little improvement came with spring. They clustered about the agency, "quite bewildered, not knowing what to do; to return to the plains was sure starvation, and every likelihood of the few horses they had being stolen from them."[41] Warned that no rations could be provided until they moved onto their reservations, they found little succour when they accepted the condition. Then, having nothing to depend upon for a living, until they produce something for themselves they must look for a liberal supply from a generous Government for support. Many of them have hardly enough to cover their persons, still they are willing to work and to learn.[42]

The famine engulfing the entire western plains almost rendered moot Ottawa's policy of starvation towards the Sioux refugees from the United States, but the policy began to bear fruit. Solidarity weakened as some of the bands, desperate to survive, broke away, slipped over the border and surrendered to the U.S. Army.

At the time of Abbott Marty's visit to Spotted Eagle's camp in October 1879, the American Sioux in Canada had recovered the prosperity they had enjoyed prior to the Battle of the Little Big Horn. Their numbers were strong as was their determination to retain their freedom. Colonel Nelson Miles, prowling below the border, had for three years been gathering intelligence on the Sioux numbers from all the sources he considered reliable: men who had visited their camps, traders, Métis hunters and the NWMP. In September 1879, Miles estimated that his enemy's strength was "between 6,000 and 8,000 souls, with between 12,000 and 15,000 horses."[43] The U.S. Army also noted that, since the battles of 1876, the Sioux had been able to "repair all the losses of arms, horses and equipments which they suffered in the campaign of that year, and to completely prepare themselves again for war."[44]

It was a time of great prosperity for the buffalo-hunting Plains Indians, perhaps the greatest they ever enjoyed. Briefly poised on the knife edge between their old world and the onrushing new world, they capitalized on both. Supplying some of the demand for buffalo robes gave them a cash income with which to indulge in the trappings of modern civilization: firearms, tools, utensils and the like. The United States Indian Agent at the Crow Agency in Montana calculated the wealth of the 3,500 residents of his reservation:

Horses, 14,000 @ $20.00 .... $280,000.
Buffalo robes, 10,000 @ $4.00 .... 40,000.
Cattle, 600 @ $18.00 .... 10,800.
Peltries, 50,000 lbs. @ 25 cents .... 12,500.
Other furs and peltries .... 5,000.
TOTAL .... $348,300.

These substantial holdings, which did not take into account more personal assets such as tipis, firearms, or articles of adornment, meant that "in per capita wealth they compare favourably with their pale-faced brothers in this or any other country."[45]

Miles identified that the Sioux were "divided into four large camps: The Uncapapas, under Sitting Bull, Black Moon, Long Dog, and Pretty Bear; the Minneconjoux, under Black Eagle; the Sans Arcs, under Spotted Bear; and the Ogalallas, under Big Road, or Broad Tail."[46] Sitting Bull remained far and away the most famous of the Sioux leaders but had lost much of his following. Correctly perceiving Sitting Bull to be a lightning rod for controversy and unwanted attention, particularly from the American Army, hundreds of the expatriates quietly attached themselves to Spotted Eagle, a handsome, intelligent and eloquent leader who, although a leading war chief, was gentle in his manner.

Although very much down on their luck in 1876 and 1877 when they crossed into Canada, by 1879 the Sioux were no longer impecunious. They had, as they promised, asked for nothing from the Great Mother other than free access to the plentiful supply of buffalo which had enabled them to become very much self-supporting and hardly less wealthy than the Crow across the border. As time had passed, and the American Army had not followed them into Canada, the Sioux felt more secure and content in their new homeland.

All that suddenly changed over the harsh, bitterly cold winter of 1879–80 when the buffalo deserted and starvation beset the camps. At first, horses were slaughtered, a dreadful alternative to a people who valued their ponies so highly, but then disease attacked the horses. The snow that year arrived in November and was so deep that the Indians at the Fort Peck Agency, then situated at the confluence of the Poplar and Missouri Rivers, Montana, about 185 km (115 mi) south and east of Wood Mountain, were unable to travel on the prairie to hunt.[47] The heavy snow was a barrier to grazing and the weakened animals of the Sioux in Canada succumbed to the onslaught of scabies and perished. Continuing to consume the diseased horse-flesh provoked an epidemic that took the lives of many of the starving people.[48]

Towards the end of January 1880, the first of the destitute and starving Sioux from Wood Mountain arrived at the Fort Peck Agency. Forty-one families, most of whom had struggled on foot through the wind-hardened drifts, had chosen surrender and survival over freedom and starvation.[49]

Like the Canadian government, the American government had also chosen to employ starvation as a lever in dealing with the Sioux escapees. Learning of the possibility that at least some of the "Sitting Bull Indians" might be disposed to surrender, on June 25, 1879, President Hayes issued an order directing the Indian agencies to "hold out no inducements to them" but "if they come in and surrender their arms and ponies, and submit as prisoners of war, it must be without conditions."[50] The agencies were also instructed that "everyone of them if fed must be made to earn his rations by work in some capacity for the government."[51] There was to be no compromise.

And so it was at Fort Peck. After the first group in January, starvation continued to drive Sioux into the agency until the end of April. By then a total of 1,116 had surrendered: 109 men, 209 women, 424 boys and 374 girls. They had with them, and turned over, only 43 ponies, 40 rifles and 7 revolvers.[52] A small number surrendered at other agencies.

Superintendent Walsh claimed a good deal of credit for the Sioux decision to give themselves up that winter: "It was always my opinion that it was only necessary to induce a few families to surrender themselves & that then a larger no. would follow."[53] To that end he concentrated his attention on the Minneconjoux, a group with whom he felt he had considerable influence, and not only convinced them to turn themselves in at Fort Peck but travelled down with them, "without letting the U.S. Authorities know anything of my mission."[54] Walsh's theory proved out, as "since that time they have been gradually going themselves in small parties of from 20 to 50 lodges strong, and a few days ago a report reached me from Milk River that a party numbering 100 lodges had gone in to declare their intention to surrender."[55]

Walsh reported that only 200 lodges of Sioux remained: 50 hunting along the Milk River valley and 150 at Wood Mountain. The principal chiefs camped near the Post were Broad Tail, Pretty Bear, Spotted Eagle, Sitting Bull, Little Knife, Hairy Chin, Red Horn, Lame Brule, Long Dog, Stone Dog, Four Horns and Dull Knife.[56]

The misery of that January of 1880 seems to have shaken the resolve even of Sitting Bull himself; he tested the waters on his own behalf at another U.S. Indian Agency. An emissary appeared at Fort Belknap, on the Milk River, Montana, about 80 km (50 mi) south of Wood Mountain, and inquired of the agent, W.L. Lincoln, the terms of surrender. A pipe and a hatchet accompanied the overture, tokens of friendship to be returned in the event of rejection. When he reported the proposal to his superiors, Lincoln was instructed to "abstain from any communication with [Sitting Bull] as the government did not wish to make any terms."[57] The pipe and hatchet were returned. Similar inquiries on behalf of the Sioux generally were made at the Pine Ridge Agency, in Dakota Territory, and were rebuffed there also.[58]

Louis Riel, who had been living for several years in the eastern United States, moved to Montana in 1879, joining the Métis community on the Fort Belknap Reservation. Almost immediately rumours swirled through the region; Riel was forging an alliance of all the Métis and Indians in the West, intending to drive out the whites and form a new provisional, all-Aboriginal government. Sitting Bull and the Sioux featured prominently in these stories.

Riel did have plans, but only to induce the Sioux to surrender to the American Army and thereby lessen the competition facing his Métis people when hunting the disappearing buffalo. If success in this endeavour resulted in increased prominence for Louis Riel, so much the better.

In March 1880, Riel approached the commanding officer at Fort Assiniboine, Lieutenant Colonel H.M. Black, claiming to be authorized to negotiate the surrender of Bull Dog and some 57 lodges of his followers. A pipe and a knife were offered as tokens of good faith. When Black requested that Riel put his proposal in writing, he did so, in three letters dated March 16 and 18, 1880, two of which have just recently been discovered. The Sioux wanted improved terms of surrender, provisions, even ammunition, and the continued possession of their horses and firearms. Riel claimed that Sitting Bull and the other Sioux remaining in Canada were watching with interest and would also surrender if the proposed terms were acceptable.[59]

They were not. The U.S. Army's position remained firm. Unconditional surrender, including relinquishment of horses and guns. The pipe and knife were returned.

The unrelenting attitude of the Americans began to wear upon the Sioux refugees. Their determination to maintain a solid front on their intention to remain in Canada, enforced when necessary by the *akicita*, the camp police, had fractured. Sitting Bull recognized this and removed the restriction. He advised Superintendent Walsh at Wood Mountain that "[t]he people of my camp who wish to return to the agencies can do so, I will place no obstacle in their way."[60] On May 19, 1880, Sitting Bull advised Walsh that only 150 lodges of the refugee Sioux remained in Canada; the rest had crossed over the line with a view to surrendering.[61] In fact, Spotted Eagle and his followers had not yet decided to deliver themselves up.

Sitting Bull had a particular concern about his own welfare. He knew that the Americans held him responsible for their defeat at Little Big Horn and he fully believed that a special fate awaited him after capture or surrender, a very public hanging. He pleaded with Walsh, asking if "the White Mother is determined to drive me out of her country, and force me into the hands of people I know are but awaiting, like hungry wolves, to take my life?"[62]

A unique relationship had developed between the Sioux leader and the officer. When he crossed into Canada three years earlier, Sitting Bull brought with him a deep hatred of uniforms acquired out of his experiences with the

American Army. It had been a shock to meet the officers of the NWMP and learn for the first time of honour, trust and the even-handed enforcement of laws that made no distinction for colour. Walsh had demonstrated that he was both brave and compassionate but above all a man of his word. Although he did not always see eye-to-eye with the officer, and had a serious altercation with him that spring of 1880, Sitting Bull had come to rely on Walsh's advice and considered him a friend. As the sands of time began to run out for the Sioux leader, he clung desperately to one last and only hope—that his Canadian friend would in the end be able to save him. In doing so, he unwittingly caused Walsh to suffer loss of reputation and advancement.

Sitting Bull was not the only Sioux leader who feared his fate if he fell into the hands of the American Army. Broad Tail, Dull Knife, Stone Dog and Little Hawk of the Oglala approached Walsh in early July with the idea that he negotiate the terms of their surrender with President Hayes. They refused his advice that they surrender unconditionally. They would never, they insisted, accept assignment to the Red Cloud or Spotted Tail agencies where lived the chiefs who had traitorously sold the sacred Black Hills. In passing the request up to Commissioner Macleod, Walsh recommended the small concession but, of course, nothing came of it.[63]

Understandably, the United States Army in 1880 had little time for considerations as delicate as requested by the Oglala chiefs exiled in Canada. It was still fully engaged upon its campaign to subdue the Indians on the Great Plains. From Montana to Texas, the military endured guerilla attacks while it carried out its search and destroy missions. Fifty-one "Actions With Indians" were recorded during the calendar year.[64]

Indian Commissioner Edgar Dewdney returned to the Canadian West in April 1880. Since his area of responsibility had been extended to include Treaties 1, 2, 3 and 5, Dewdney travelled directly to Winnipeg, mostly by train via Chicago and St. Paul. He spent several weeks there familiarizing himself with conditions on the reserves in southern Manitoba and northwestern Ontario, leaving the problems on the western plains to his assistant, Elliot Galt.

Elliot was the son and only child of Sir Alexander Galt, a colleague of Prime Minister Macdonald, a Father of Confederation and Canada's first Minister of Finance. At Sir Alexander's behest, the previous year his son had been wrenched from what his father considered to be an addicting life of indolence and self-indulgence and sent West to be hardened.[65] Appointed Dewdney's secretary, the 29-year-old Galt had travelled into the North-West by the Missouri River route and met the Indian Commissioner for the first time on August 19 during Treaty payments at Sounding Lake.[66]

Athletic, lean and tall (190.5cm/6' 3"), Elliot Galt adapted well to life on the plains and made himself so nearly indispensable to the Indian Commissioner that the next season Dewdney had no reservation about sending his assistant alone to supervise the agencies in the vast area encompassed by Treaties 4, 6 and 7.

Wanting to reach Fort Walsh early, Galt set out on the overland route well before navigation opened on the Missouri. Soon after March 16, when he stepped off the Utah and Northern Railroad at its terminus 322 km (200 mi) south of Helena, Elliot might well have reflected back upon his former life of indolence and luxury. A heavy snowstorm had closed the route ahead to wheeled stagecoaches and a sleigh was substituted. Galt was one of 17 passengers "jammed up like herrings in a box and exquisitely uncomfortable."[67] Constantly required to dismount and dig their horses out of the heavy drifts, the unhappy wayfarers spent more than 20 hours covering just 48 km (30 mi), but they finally broke free of the snow and were pleased to upgrade to a covered stagecoach. But again there was no semblance of luxury as, to Galt's disgust, the stage was seriously overloaded with passengers:

> They bundled 11 of us into the inside, three on each seat, one on my lap & one on the knees of another man. Fourteen more got on the roof, besides the driver & any amount of luggage . . . We had not been going more than a few hours before the roof began to crack & evidenced signs of coming through with all the passengers on top . . . whenever we came to a rough piece of road, the 11 of us would put our arms up & try to support the roof as well as we could."[68]

But the stagecoach made it through to Helena in three days without mishap (the passenger riding on Elliot's knees disembarked after five hours, to the great relief of both of them). Galt carried on to Fort Benton where he met NWMP wagons and crews for the five-day journey to Fort Walsh, the last day through a blinding snowstorm. (The wagons doubled as sleighs, with either the runners or the wheels carried in the box as conditions required.) The cruel winter that had caused such suffering among the destitute Indian population had not released its grip when Elliot Galt finally reach the Canadian prairie; he reported temperatures of -29.5°C to -25.5°C (-21°F to -14°F) on April 5 and 6 and very deep snow for at least 80 km (50 mi) west of Fort Walsh.[69]

By 1880 practically all of the Indians on the western plains were, as Dewdney admitted in his annual report, "entirely dependent upon the Government for their existence."[70] Worse, their weakened condition rendered them susceptible to disease, and epidemics of measles and scarlet fever broke out with unusual rates of mortality; 100 deaths occurred in one camp alone.[71] At Fort Walsh, a camp of 1,500 Cree came down with dysentery and diarrhoea and NWMP medical officer George Kennedy found himself treating 150 cases a day. He reported that "quite a number, principally children, died."[72] Dewdney admitted that much of this was due to "the scanty fare they received from the Government."[73]

The cost of rationing almost the entire Indian population of the North-West Territories was of prime concern to the Macdonald government, and to the Liberal opposition that scrutinized every expenditure. All agencies were instructed to keep their expenses as low as possible. They complied, and frequently issued to each individual only .22 kg (.5 lb) each of meat and flour daily, a diet that NWMP surgeon Dr. Norman Kittson considered entirely inadequate:

> Gaunt men and women with hungry eyes were seen everywhere seeking or begging for a mouthful of food—little children . . . fight over the tidbits. Morning and evening many of them would come to me and beg for the very bones left by the dogs in my yard.[74]

Even the larger issue of .35 kg (.75 lb) of both beef and flour daily cost the government only 8¢ per head per day at a time when the same department was spending 50¢ per day to feed white farm labourers.[75]

Even so, the Liberals, led by former Interior Minister David Mills, continually scrutinized, and criticized, the expenditures being made to sustain the Indian population of the North-West Territories. Even the 8¢ per day translated into almost $30 a year for an individual and was attacked as extravagant:

> The Indians of the North-West are costing us today, in the matter of food, upwards of $100 per family. These Indians are being pensioned on the public Treasury; instead of being taught habits of self reliance, they are being taught habits of dependence, and, at this hour, they are more dependent on the Government for their means of subsistence than they have been at any former period.[76]

Small wonder that Dewdney continued to encourage Crowfoot and his Blackfoot to remain with the buffalo in the United States. As he admitted, "The bulk of the Indians belonging to Treaty 7 have been making their living in American Territory, as well as a large number of the Crees and Treaty half-breeds."[77] On his journey through Montana Territory in March, Galt had met at Helena with Colonel Thomas H. Ruger, commanding the 18th infantry battalion stationed there. Galt reported to Dewdney that Ruger had informed him "that it was absolutely necessary that we should make our Indians go home as soon as possible as they were in a very bad way with neither food, there being very few buffalo left in that part of the Country, nor clothing."[78] Ruger admitted that the Canadian Indians had so far behaved well, but he "fears they may commit some indiscretion in which case they would have to be driven back by force."[79]

Chief Crowfoot. *Provincial Archives of Alberta P129*

Ruger estimated that there were about 17,000 Canadian Indians in Montana, "Bloods, North Blackfeet, North Peigans, North Assiniboines, Crees, and others."[80] Although perhaps exaggerated, this number was almost equal to the total number of Indians in the area of Treaties 4, 6 and 7 being rationed by the government of Canada.[81]

Ottawa had no intention of complying with Ruger's edict and thus acquiring several thousand more mouths to feed. In fact, Dewdney was "in dread of our Indians" returning from the United States because he "saw no means of providing for the feeding of so large a number."[82] Instead, Dewdney was instructed to notify all Indian Affairs agents or employees not to discuss with officials of the American government or officers of the American Army the subject of "Canadian Indians crossing the American line."[83]

Elliot Galt, ambitious and hoping to secure appointment as Assistant Indian Commissioner (his ambition was realized the next year, 1881), knew that the road to success lay in finding economies in the Indian rationing system. Beef had been the first and obvious substitute when the buffalo failed, but bacon, even though more expensive per .45 kg (1 lb) (17.5¢ versus 7.25¢), had the advantage of being easier to ship and store. Fresh beef, unless delivered on the hoof, was very susceptible to spoilage. And, the assumption that .45 kg (1 lb) of bacon had the nutritional equivalent of 1.1 kg (2.5 lb) of beef increased the economic benefit of bacon over beef. Galt carried out several arithmetical calculations designed to demonstrate the savings the government could achieve feeding bacon instead of beef.

There was one problem, a major one: the Indians hated bacon. The adjustment to beef after so many years on a pure buffalo diet had been difficult enough; bacon was much too much—it made them gag. Nonetheless, bacon began to supplement, then supplant, beef in the Indian rationing, finally provoking Crowfoot and other prominent chiefs to formally complain to Commissioner Dewdney. They had, they claimed, agreed to accept bacon only in the spring when beef was more difficult to secure.[84]

The soon-to-be Assistant Indian Commissioner, so recently removed from his life of indolence and luxury, had little sympathy for the western Indians who were his new responsibility. In that summer of 1880, while travelling to Shoal Lake, his department's agency at the eastern edge of Treaty 4, he met with the chiefs of one Indian band and was glad he did not see more, "as they are very poor, & almost entirely destitute." But Galt did listen to the chiefs' lengthy account of "all their grievances and ills" and found it "most disagreeable" when the children of the camp were brought to him to demonstrate how thin they were. He expressed his views in a letter to his mother:

> These Indians have only themselves to thank for being so poor & hungry, as if they would do as the government wants them to, they would work on their Reservations & receive a regular ration of beef and flour; but the trouble is, they do not like the idea of settling down to work on their Farms & prefer to roam over the prairies with their women & children in search of game. The latter has become very scarce, there being next to no buffalo.[85]

NWMP Commissioner Macleod with Crowfoot, and Superintendent Walsh with Sitting Bull, had each earned the trust of the leading chiefs of the Blackfoot and the Sioux, making them unusually valuable officers; those two tribes were unquestionably the potentially most dangerous the Force had on its hands. But in 1880 both officers lost the confidence of Prime Minister Macdonald and were removed from any further responsibility in the areas where they wielded the greatest influence.

Walsh went first, in July, transferred from Wood Mountain next to the Sioux encampment, to Qu'Appelle, a quiet post supposedly elevated to headquarters of the new "Eastern Division," which was to include Shoal Lake and Swan River, both reduced to a non-commissioned officer and several constables. It was a demotion in all but name. Walsh spent little time at Qu'Appelle. After checking the facilities of his new command, he took medical leave and returned to his home in Brockville, Ontario, where he remained until the

Sitting Bull Sioux affair finally came to an end. Macdonald, believing that Walsh was responsible for Sitting Bull's refusal to surrender, removed him from the scene so that there would be no further interference with his desire to see the Sioux leader out of Canada.

Macleod went next, at the end of October. A good friend to Macdonald, to whom he owed his appointment in the NWMP, and the promotion to Assistant Commissioner when French would have preferred otherwise, Macleod had made the mistake of standing in the way when the Prime Minister proposed a patronage appointment to the force.[86] Overworked, serving as Stipendiary Magistrate as well as Commissioner, on October 31, 1880, Macleod was relieved of his command and appointed Stipendiary Magistrate for the Bow River judicial district, an area that included Fort Calgary, Fort Walsh and Edmonton with headquarters at Fort Macleod, the post and growing community that bore his name.[87] Macleod was succeeded on November 1 by Assistant Commissioner Acheson G. Irvine, who quickly demonstrated that he fully understood the necessity of pleasing his political master.

When Walsh left Wood Mountain on July 15, Sitting Bull was deeply saddened. Although there had occasionally been altercations between the two, including an armed stand-off just a month earlier, the Sioux chief had developed great admiration for the officer and placed much confidence in his ability and his word. He had one final and urgent request to make: would Walsh intercede on his behalf with the President of the United States? Sitting Bull still feared the fate that he was sure awaited him if, or when, he surrendered to the American Army. Taking Walsh by the hand, he pleaded, "Friend, I put myself in your hands. Do with me as you like. If I am to die in the chains, let it be so, but find a home for my children."[88]

Walsh, who in turn had a high regard for Sitting Bull, agreed that, if the Canadian government would grant him permission, he would speak to the President. On parting, Sitting Bull presented Walsh with his headdress, or war bonnet. "Take it my friend," he said "and keep it. I hope never to have use for it again. Not a feather there but marks some deed done in war while yet the Sioux were strong."[89]

The promise Walsh made to Sitting Bull out of compassion would be misinterpreted and cost him his career in the NWMP. On his return to Ontario he did secure an audience with the Prime Minister who, naturally enough, had no desire to have a mere officer of police interceding with the President of the United States. Macdonald did not share, nor understand, Walsh's sympathy for Sitting Bull, someone the Prime Minister had never met but who had been the cause of a great deal of anxiety to his government. Besides, the Prime

Minister had received reports from the West that told him Walsh was deliberately subverting attempts to remove Sitting Bull from Canada.

At Wood Mountain, Sitting Bull awaited word from Walsh on the success of his mission. He told Superintendent Lief Crozier, who succeeded Walsh as officer commanding the Wood Mountain Post, that Walsh had agreed to see the President of the United States on his behalf and that no decision on surrender could be made until word came back from Walsh.

Crozier thought Walsh's conduct was out of line, and said so in his report to NWMP headquarters at Fort Walsh where Irvine commanded. Crozier added his opinion that, but for Walsh, Sitting Bull would have surrendered some time ago. Irvine agreed with Crozier and, no friend of Walsh's, took the opportunity to share Crozier's report and concern with Indian Commissioner Dewdney, who was at Fort Walsh preparing to return to Winnipeg for the winter. As Irvine must have expected, Dewdney quickly passed this poison to the Prime Minister in a letter written from Chicago where he changed trains.[90]

Dewdney also relayed Crozier's view that Ottawa should quickly and formally advise Sitting Bull that Walsh had no authority to plead for him in Washington. The Prime Minister agreed and directed that a message be promptly sent to the new Commissioner for delivery directly to Sitting Bull telling him this and advising that his best, and only, course of action was to surrender to the American authorities, and the sooner the better. Macdonald also instructed Irvine that "Walsh is not to return to Wood Mountain."[91] The Prime Minister sent Dewdney a copy of his telegram to Irvine and assured him that Walsh would not be going to Washington or allowed to interfere in any way.[92]

At Fort Walsh, Irvine decided it would give the edicts greater emphasis if he delivered them himself and rode over to Wood Mountain, arriving on November 22.[93] The next day, in council with Sitting Bull and some 30 of his headmen, the Commissioner "explained, most minutely and carefully" Ottawa's hard-line position.

Irvine then set about searching out further evidence against Walsh. He interrogated Sitting Bull about whether "Superintendent Walsh had ever held out any encouragement which was calculated to lead him [Sitting Bull] to believe he would eventually obtain a reserve in Canada, or, if any inducement was held out to him [Sitting Bull] by that Officer to remain in Canada."[94] With some reluctance, Sitting Bull replied that "Superintendent Walsh had gone to Canada to see the Queen, and if necessary the President of the United States, that Walsh would give him advice as what was best for him to do." He then related that, before Walsh left,

> I told him I did not know what to do, I was like a bird on the fence, not knowing on which side to hop. I meant on which side of the line to live. I was inclined to surrender to the United States. Walsh told me to wait here in Canada until he returned and he would then advise me what to do.[95]

Irvine pressed further. He had heard a rumour that Walsh had planned to take Sitting Bull on exhibition throughout Canada and the United States. Was this true? Sitting Bull provided nothing on this, but his cryptic comment that his body was considered "like silver and gold" was all the confirmation Irvine needed. He found more from Charles Thompson, a former member of the NWMP then living with the Sioux. Thompson, known to Irvine as a "bad character" who had served a sentence of imprisonment for desertion,[96] stated that he expected to accompany Sitting Bull and Walsh on an exhibition tour. Irvine then gathered up from Wood Mountain residents a number of letters from Walsh supposedly containing messages to be given to Sitting Bull. One letter to the trader Fred Cadd requested that tobacco be given to Sitting Bull. Such a gift, Irvine claimed, "would be accepted as a pledge of good faith in previous promises made."[97]

The new Commissioner was pleased with himself. In reporting to Macdonald he claimed that only he could have uncovered "the dishonest representations made Sitting Bull by Supd't Walsh, all calculated to lead to the belief that Supd't Walsh and he alone was the man in whom Sitting Bull generally should place his confidence." But for Walsh's conduct, "Sitting Bull would have surrendered at once." Nonetheless, due to Irvine's efforts, "matters are now in a favourable condition as regards a speedy surrender."[98]

Superintendent Walsh had been the darling of the American press; they dubbed him "Sitting Bull's Boss," and he loved it. A true glory hound, he corresponded with journalists as far away as New York until he was called to the mat by Commissioner Macleod over several letters that appeared in the New York *Herald*. Then the steel-nerved officer who had faced down the fiercest of Sioux warriors behaved like a chastened schoolboy. "He begged me to forgive him, to trust him again and promised I should never find him tripping up again," Macleod later described the interview.[99]

The attention paid to the flamboyant Walsh, who had himself photographed in buckskins but whose deeds of derring-do were unassailably genuine, must have rankled with his fellow officers. Among them he lost much respect because of his penchant for taking Native women to his bed, particularly when overnighting in Indian encampments. Few accepted Walsh's view that it was rude to refuse the host's offer of female companionship, and that it was an opportunity to prove one's "manliness."

In the spring of 1878, Walsh returned west from a visit to Ontario, travelling up the Missouri by steamer accompanied by a number of recruits and by Frederick White, the Ottawa bureaucrat most closely associated with the NWMP since its formation in 1873. White, who two years later in 1880 became the Comptroller of the Force, was making his first journey of inspection into the West. In a remarkable display of poor judgement brought on by his bravado and conceit, Walsh tried to convince the staid White that protocol would require him to accept Native women in his bed when offered. Fred White and John A. Macdonald were very close and this information undoubtedly passed to Macdonald when he returned as Prime Minister a few months later, if not before.[100]

Macleod considered Walsh to be "not a gentleman," and suspected him of attempting to "undermine me in a sneaking way."[101]

Irvine, Macleod's successor as Commissioner, did not intend to give Walsh an opportunity to cause him any difficulty. He set about debunking the Walsh reputation and showing him to have improperly induced Sitting Bull to remain in Canada.

The Prime Minister had already decided upon Walsh's guilt. On November 24, 1880, he wrote Governor General Lorne stating that Walsh was responsible for Sitting Bull's continued presence in Canada:

> Walsh undoubtedly has influence with Bull, which he tried to monopolize in order to make himself of importance and is, I fear, primarily responsible for the Indian's unwillingness to leave Canada.[102]

Two months later the Prime Minister was even more convinced of Walsh's guilt. On January 25, 1881, he again wrote the Governor General:

> I greatly fear that Major Walsh is pulling the strings through Thompson, the deserter, to prevent "Bull" from surrendering. Walsh is still at Brockville and I have given him two months more leave to keep him there lest he might return and personally influence Sitting Bull. I regret much being obliged to play with this man Walsh, as he deserves dismissal. But if he were cashiered, he would (for he is a bold and desperate fellow) at once go westward and from mere spite urge the Indians to hostile incursions so as to cause an imbroglio. When this is over I shall recommend Your Exy. to dismiss him most summarily.[103]

Whether Walsh knew it or not, his career as the most celebrated officer in the NWMP was already over.

The Prime Minister had refused him permission to visit Washington, but Walsh had already succeeded in making one high-level plea on behalf of his friend at Wood Mountain. While passing through Chicago on his journey out of the West and back to Ontario he had luckily met with U.S. General Phil Sheridan and secured an assurance that Sitting Bull would receive treatment equal with all other surrendering Indians. This would have to do, Walsh knew. To get the word back to Sitting Bull at Wood Mountain, Walsh wrote Jean-Louis Légaré, who had just moved his store to Willow Bunch, 64 km (40 mi) east of Wood Mountain. In a later account of the affair, Walsh stated that his letter requested Légaré to pass the message to Sitting Bull through Joseph Morin, a local Métis who had worked with Walsh as a scout. The letter, Walsh claimed, received an entirely different and false interpretation and was used to destroy his reputation.[104]

The letters Crozier and Irvine collected might have been no more than friendly interest in people and events at Wood Mountain. One who received a letter from Walsh was NWMP sergeant Henry Hamilton who had served under Walsh. Hamilton replied on September 30, 1880:

> I received your kind letter today. The only Indians I cont. see of those you named was Sitting Bull . . . Sitting Bull said altho you were far away his heart was with you, that sometimes he had words with you that he thinks of now and is sorry for, as he now sees you were always doing the thing that was right. He evidently intends to stop on this side.[105]

Sergeant Hamilton's assessment of Sitting Bull's intention appears to have been correct. No record exists of him ever acknowledging having received assurances from Walsh that he would be well treated upon surrender to the Americans. To the bitter end the Sioux leader continued to view with deep repugnance any thought of delivering himself into the hands of the U.S. Army.

Sitting Bull and Walsh never met again as they tracked into their futures on widely divergent paths.

CROSS-BORDER PROBLEMS WERE NOT confined to the western portion of the 49th Parallel. In the late summer of 1880, a band of Chippewa/Ojibway Indians limped into Fort Ellice. They were in dreadful condition, due they said to having been attacked by American Indians somewhere between

Roche Percée and Moose Mountain. Now it was Canada's turn to complain of the depredations of U.S. Indians crossing the border, and the diplomatic channels heated up. An explanation was demanded.[106]

That explanation, when it was received from the U.S. Indian Agent at Fort Berthold, established that the Canadian Indians were somewhat less than blameless. On August 28, 1880, Walking Wolf, a resident of the Fort Berthold Agency, was shot and killed while herding horses, and a party of some 50 Gros Ventre from the Agency set out in pursuit of the killers. They found the trail and followed it, but on overtaking the supposed perpetrators they were immediately fired upon. The Fort Berthold Indians claimed that two of their party were killed before a shot was fired in return. In the ensuing firefight five Fort Berthold Indians were killed and six wounded. Driven from the field, the Americans claimed to have no knowledge of how much damage they inflicted on the Canadians.[107] Canada dropped its complaint.

Crowfoot and his Blackfoot followers remained in Montana Territory where they had gone in 1879 on Dewdney's advice. In the fall of 1880 they sent a messenger to the Indian Commissioner asking his advice as to whether they should return to Canada to receive their treaty payments. Again they were told to stay with the buffalo, as Dewdney "saw no means of feeding them if they returned."[108] He would hold their annuity money for them until they returned. The Blackfoot took Dewdney's advice and stayed in Montana, a move that he claimed "saved the gov't $100,000 at least."[109]

The likely savings were potentially much greater. In addition to the Blackfoot, Big Bear and his Cree also remained camped in Montana. Although Big Bear had not yet signed a treaty, as long as he remained out of the country he was not a problem. As soon as he returned to Canada and took treaty he and his people would be entitled to rations, an inducement Dewdney had promised. Just how many Canadian Indians were over the border was, according to Elliot Galt, "impossible to estimate correctly" but he did "not think ten thousand (10,000) would be an over estimate."[110]

Sitting Bull and the few Sioux remaining in Canada were of far more concern to the American government than the thousands of Canadian Indians hunting buffalo in the Judith Basin. Sitting Bull himself had become an elusive trophy. The glory that would come to his captor gleamed in the imagination of the army officers stationed south of the border and continued to attract civilians as well.

In that fall of 1880 a glory-hound named E.H. ("Scout") Allison either came close to bringing about the surrender of Sitting Bull, or stampeded the Sioux leader away from the firm intention to give himself up, depending on which of several versions of the event is accepted. Allison, fluent in Siouan, had worked with the U.S. Army as an interpreter and sometime scout. He claimed to be a friend of Gall, the Sioux chief who had generalled so well at Little Big Horn and who was in Canada with Sitting Bull. Allison developed the notion that he could induce the Sioux to surrender and took his plan to Major David Brotherton, commanding officer of Fort Buford, on the Missouri River. Brotherton, anxious to be the officer to receive the Sitting Bull surrender, authorized Allison to head up to Wood Mountain and see what he could accomplish.

Taking advantage of jealousies and divisions that he found in the Sioux encampment, Allison succeeded in convincing a good number of Sioux to surrender. Gall and Sitting Bull in particular had fallen out and a large portion of the band followed Gall across the border with the intention of travelling to Fort Buford. On November 25 they stopped at the Fort Peck Indian Agency on the Poplar River, about 105 km (65 mi) west of Fort Buford.[111]

Allison stayed at Wood Mountain where he met several times in council with Sitting Bull, urging the Sioux to follow Gall's example. Superintendent Lief Crozier, commanding the Wood Mountain NWMP Post, attended some of the sessions. On December 11, Sitting Bull and his followers packed up and crossed the border with the avowed intention of surrendering. They set up camp at the mouth of the Milk River, about 80 km (50 mi) further west from the group at Fort Peck. There they found buffalo and settled in while Sitting Bull sent emissaries to Fort Buford to negotiate terms of surrender.[112]

With the exception of a few stragglers, all the American Sioux had left Canada with the declared intention of surrendering to the United States authorities. Allison had done good work. But the Sioux had not yet actually handed over their horses and guns, the terms of surrender insisted upon by the United States. It was a delicate situation that called for tact and diplomacy. The American Army was not nearly up to the task.

Allison had recommended that the Army beef up its strength at Fort Peck and by December 24, eight companies of infantry under Major Guido Ilges had moved into position around the Indian encampment of 400 men, women and children. When Ilges met in council with Gall and the headmen he found little unanimity on the issue of surrender. Some wanted to surrender now but most wanted to wait until spring; some preferred to go to Fort Keogh rather than Buford and some wished to stay at the Fort Peck Agency. Ilges had received orders forbidding him to negotiate and instructing him "to compel the surrender of The Gall and his people by such means as may seem best adapted to that end."[113] Accordingly, on December 31, Ilges gave the Sioux an ultimatum: they must be ready to move to Fort Buford on the morning of January 2, 1881, or he would move against them. Not surprisingly, this threat provoked threats in response.

At noon on January 2, Ilges sent his troops into the Sioux encampment, opened fire with his field guns on the woods where the men, women and children fled, and ordered the destruction of the tipis. His official report reveals the sentiment of the U.S. Army of the day:

> I directed him [Captain Read] to open fire upon a number of bucks who were seen running from the rear of the right village towards the agency, and across the Missouri. They soon dropped out of sight among the willows. What execution was done among them is not known.[114]

When it was over, Ilges had over 300 prisoners and their horse herd of about 200 animals. He thought about 60 escaped, some to Sitting Bull's camp.

The treatment received by Gall and his followers had an immediate effect upon Sitting Bull's surrender intentions. He headed straight back to Canada. The Army sent units out of Fort Assiniboine to cut him off, but by the time they arrived the Sioux had slipped back over the border.

But not all of them. Another dispute arose in the band and more than half under Crow King decided to carry on to Fort Buford. They had a dreadful journey across the open prairie in the middle of January. Even the Army's official report evokes sympathy: "Their progress was very slow; they were nearly destitute of food, they had but few horses, they were half naked, and the cold was excessive."[115] Rations were sent out, and horses and wagons for the women and children, and finally, on February 10, 325 of the Sioux made it through to Buford, although "in a deplorable condition."[116]

The Army considered it had done good business. With the roundup of a few more small parties, by May 26 Fort Buford held "1,125 Indian prisoners of war."[117]

In Ottawa on February 11, Governor General Lorne reported to Macdonald that Secretary Evarts in Washington again complained that Canada should solve the problem out on the western border by arresting Sitting Bull. Lorne responded by noting that Canada's starvation policy "succeeded in inducing the American Sioux to move to the frontier with a view of surrendering" but many were prevented from doing so by the actions of the American Army. Sitting Bull's surrender, Lorne advised, could "be secured without bloodshed, a result which will be more easily attained if the United States be moved to prevent further measures of intimidation, leaving hunger to do its work."[118]

Hunger was, indeed, "doing its work." The few Sioux who had returned to Canada were hard-pressed to keep body and soul together. The western plains are harsh and desolate at the tail end of winter and offer nothing of sustenance until well into spring, when the ice leaves the ponds and migrating waterfowl return. Unless a good Samaritan could be found, the desperate people would not escape the stark choice between death and surrender.

Sitting Bull might still be at large, but his following was so greatly reduced that the United States no longer regarded him as any kind of a threat. Allison offered to make one more trip to Wood Mountain to try for the trophy, but the Army declined, no longer worried about the Sioux leader. "His power for evil being entirely destroyed, it was a matter of indifference to our government if he never came in."[119] In fact, with only 43 lodges, the tiny band was vulnerable to attack from other tribes, such as the Blackfoot, Assiniboine or the Cree, or even the Métis, all of whom were enemies of the Sioux. Just two months following Sitting Bull's return to Canada, such an attack occurred. On March 17, 1881, without apparent fear of retaliation, a war party of Assiniboine jumped 17 Sioux hunting just across the line from Wood Mountain and killed 15 of them, only two escaping.[120]

NWMP Superintendent Crozier at Wood Mountain not only gave Allison no credit for the Sioux surrender; he blamed him for Sitting Bull's change of mind. The Sioux, Crozier claimed, "with good reason" have no confidence in the American Army scouts:

> There is not the slightest doubt in my mind but that Sitting Bull, when he left here last December, was fully determined to have given himself up. But unfortunately one of these scouts joined the camp, and after getting within one or two day's march of an American post, Wolf Point, old Bull declined going any further with him.[121]

Problems presented by the presence of the American Sioux in the Canadian West were diminishing, but Indian Commissioner Dewdney saw new difficulties arising. He was now quartered for the winter at Winnipeg, in response to criticism of the Indian Commissioner luxuriating during the off-season at Ottawa so far removed from his responsibilities. There Dewdney worried that his Canadian treaty Indians might revolt against the privations being forced upon them by the parsimony of the Macdonald government.

The ration allowance was meager enough, but the policy of "no work, no rations" was causing undue hardship. For the simple fact was that the Indians had no clothing and it was raw cruelty to force nearly naked men and women into bitterly cold weather to perform hard labour in order to qualify for a subsistence food ration. "Women worked out with the thermometer 40 below zero [-40°C] with nothing on but a shift made of flour sacks."[122] Complaints were coming to Dewdney, not only from the Indians, but from missionaries and settlers. "The Indians that come in from the Plains wear nothing but a breech clout and a blanket or robe thrown over them. The women are almost naked and every rag and old flour sack is seized on to make some covering for the children."[123]

The Indian Commissioner did not think that his government appreciated the gravity of the situation with the Indians. Expensive it might be, but it was essential that better preparations be made to feed the Indian population. And it would be dangerous not to do so. "As long as there is food in the country and they are starving, they will have it."[124] It was Dewdney's firm opinion that the government was not yet in full control of the West. "In a year or two with the railway in the centre of the continent we shall be in a position to dictate to the Indians; we are not so now, and any outbreak occurring this year or next would be most disastrous."[125] The real crisis would come, Dewdney knew, when the Americans finally evicted the Canadian Indians still hunting the buffalo in their territory and those thousands of hungry mouths descended upon his ill-prepared agencies.

His concerns were causing the Indian Commissioner many a sleepless night. That they were not frivolous concerns would become frighteningly apparent in the early summer of 1881.

CHAPTER 20

Surrender

JOHNNY CHARTRAND CLAMBERED TO THE SUMMIT OF HEART Butte and cursed softly as he peered out over the empty and silent plains. Gone was his hope to spot a landmark or some recognizable feature that would tell him where he was. Below him the countryside in every direction lay shrouded under a heavy mist. Even his horse, tethered at the base of the Butte, was nearly invisible as the fog swirled about it.[1]

Off to his left a growing pink from the not-yet-risen sun identified east, but the Métis plainsman's uncanny sense of direction had little need of that confirmation. What he needed to find was the Missouri River, somewhere out in front of him. How far had he ridden in his breakneck ride through the night? Where was Fort Buford? Chartrand knew the mid-July sun would soon burn away the night mist, but he had no time to wait.

Johnny Chartrand was one of 12 Métis riders enlisted by Jean-Louis Légaré of Willow Bunch to assist with the transportation of Sitting Bull and his camp of about 200 Sioux down to Fort Buford, where they were to surrender to the U.S. Army. Légaré's caravan had covered less than half the 240-km (150-mi) journey when he became worried about running out of food and losing his passengers. Chartrand, a good horseman, was secretly sent away at dusk to ride the 130 km (80 mi) to Buford and convince the U.S. Army to send enough provisions back to Légaré to enable him to complete the trip. And he was supposed to get it done in only a day and a half—a heroic time frame, but essential if the Sioux paranoia about the Americans was to be kept in check. No soldiers must accompany the wagons carrying the food or the Sioux were sure to panic. Chartrand had no time to spare.

He had ridden hard. The first of the two good saddle-horses he started with had played out, so used up that Chartrand had left it behind on the prairie. He hoped to pick it up on the return journey, but was afraid it might not live. His remaining horse had stood up well, but could not be expected to cover many more kilometres.

How far to the fort? Johnny Chartrand peered into the rising mist.

EARLIER THAT YEAR, WHILE Sitting Bull and his people were still camped about the NWMP Post at Wood Mountain, Superintendent Crozier had attempted to allay their fears of the treatment they would receive from the U.S. Army if they gave themselves up. Crozier made a determined effort to persuade the Sioux to surrender, providing feasts and even sending his second-in-command, Inspector Alex MacDonell, to accompany a delegation to Fort Buford to inspect conditions there and report back. Sitting Bull had demanded written assurance that he and his Sioux would receive humane treatment, and MacDonell returned with a letter from Major David Brotherton, the commanding officer at Fort Buford, guaranteeing just that. Sitting Bull led Crozier to believe that they were on the verge of surrender but needed full stomachs to reach a decision. When the NWMP obligingly provided another feast the Sioux tucked away as much as they could eat and then announced that their position was unchanged; they did not trust the Americans and would stay in Canada. Crozier was furious. He washed his hands of Sitting Bull, telling the Sioux leader and his headmen that they could all "go to hell,"[2] and ordering them away from the Wood Mountain Post.

On April 20, 1881, the Sioux moved 64 km (40 mi) east to Willow Bunch, where Jean-Louis Légaré had established his trading post the previous fall, closing the store he had operated for 10 years at Wood Mountain. The well-respected trader now had 500 impoverished people looking to him for sustenance. A letter from Crozier asking him to do what he could to induce the Sioux to return to the United States was cold comfort. If the resources and prestige of the NWMP failed to move the Sioux, what hope had a poor French Canadian trader?

Légaré's years on the plains had taught him to deal with the problem first, leaving the cause for later. And he knew how to deal with the Sioux; he threw a feast. As he explained later under oath, "I wanted to get them surrendered to the United States and the only way to get an Indian to do what you want is to feed him well before talking to him. I gave the feast to induce them to surrender."[3] It was an expensive feast: 225 kg (500 lb) of pemmican, 15 sacks of flour, four bales of dried meat, 13.5 kg (30 lb) of sugar, 4.5 kg (10 lb) of tea and 1.4 kg (3 lb) of tobacco, worth altogether about $350 at that time.[4]

Jean-Louis Légaré. *Saskatchewan Archives Board R-A47*

Légaré spoke to the Sioux like a Dutch uncle: "You have no friend but me. The mounted police have sent you away, and the Queen is not willing to give you land in this country. If you want your children to live longer, you should take my advice and go back to the other side."[5] The Sioux replied that Légaré's word was good, but that they had no faith in the Americans. After much parley, it was agreed that a delegation would accompany the trader down to Fort Buford to meet the commanding officer, Major David Brotherton. The Sioux wanted a promise of amnesty and good treatment. To meet the concern that Brotherton would lock up the delegation and not let them return, Légaré promised that if that happened he would stay with them.

On April 26, with his carts, horses and provisions, Légaré and 30 Sioux set out for Fort Buford, 240 km (150 mi) and eight days' travel away. On the first day out, 14 lost their nerve and turned back, but the trader and the remaining 16 made it through to the U.S. Army post on the Missouri River.

Major Brotherton's first action was to place the 16 Sioux in custody, stating that his orders were to keep them at his post. When Légaré related the promise he had made to the Sioux and explained that he would be in personal danger if he failed to keep his word, the officer telegraphed his superior. Légaré's reputation as an honourable man saved the day. Orders came back to give the Canadian trader a free hand in working with the Sioux to surrender. Légaré's passengers were returned to him, but only four chose to return to Willow Bunch; the others found the situation to their liking and surrendered then and there.

When Légaré and his shrunken delegation arrived back at Willow Bunch on May 12, he found that Sitting Bull and about 20 lodges with most of the principal Sioux chiefs had decamped for Qu'Appelle. Although Sitting Bull undoubtedly hoped to find Superintendent Walsh and learn the result of his petition to the President, he had other plans also. Before leaving he announced that "The Santee Sioux and Pheasant Rump the Assiniboine have secured reservations in this country and I am going to try for one also."[6] Failing that, he would move in with the Santee Sioux on their reservation.[7]

In May the still-frustrated Crozier was not displeased when he was trans-ferred from Wood Mountain to Fort Macleod. He handed command over to MacDonell and told his successor that "whatever glory there was in Sitting Bull's surrender he would leave to someone else."[8]

Sitting Bull was greatly disappointed not to find Walsh at Qu'Appelle but he achieved an audience with Indian Commissioner Dewdney, who came over from Shoal Lake to meet with the Sioux. Dewdney hewed to the gov-ernment's tough line; there would be no reservation and there would be no provisions. Dewdney did offer to provide food and escort to the Sioux if they would return to the U.S. via Fort Ellice and Pembina. Sitting Bull tried a repeat of the gambit that had worked with Crozier and requested 200 cart-loads of grub while they thought over the proposition. Dewdney refused to bite, telling Sitting Bull that "he had deceived one of the Queen's Officers and I did not intend he should me."[9]

The Indian Commissioner reported that the Sioux were "getting lots of ducks and selling horses for flour and old people are at the doors of settlers continually begging for food."[10] It was Dewdney's opinion that because of the small numbers of his followers, Sitting Bull was "quite harmless, having very few able bodied men with him . . . Our Crees are very hostile to the Sioux and it is the impression of a good many that should Sitting Bull go south our Indians will destroy him."[11] Any chance of the Sioux joining the Santee Sioux on their reservation near Qu'Appelle[12] was lost, as "they would not speak to the Sitting Bull lot."[13]

The Indian Commissioner was not kind to Sitting Bull. In his report to the Prime Minister, he stated:

> He feels very small now, and if the outsiders would leave him alone he would find out he was not such a big man as he has been led to think he is. I hear some parties have lately gone up to try and induce him to exhibit himself in Canada. This makes him think he is a big man & says his carcass is worth its weight in gold & that all who are endeav-ouring to get him to return want to make money out of him.
>
> I told him I did not consider his carcass worth 10c. He was much annoyed at this & got up and left the council, much to the amusement of the other Indians.[14]

Dewdney's assessment of their vulnerability might have been shared by the Sioux themselves. They refused to leave Qu'Appelle even after it became obvious that no assistance would be forthcoming and that Superintendent Walsh would not be returning. Not only would no reservation be granted to them, but they were not welcome at the Santee Sioux Standing Buffalo reservation.

Finally, the NWMP offered to provide escort if the Sioux would return to Wood Mountain, where Indian Affairs would provide some sustenance, and this was accepted. Although a few remained at Qu'Appelle, Sitting Bull and the majority rode dejectedly back south under the protection of the Red Coats.[15] The thoughts of the once-mighty Sioux during this humiliating journey were not preserved.

At Wood Mountain the Sioux found that the Indian Agency was not prepared to assist them and that Crozier's departure had not changed the hardness of the NWMP when it came to handing out provisions. So, at the beginning of July they turned again to Willow Bunch and Jean-Louis Légaré, their first friend in Canada and now apparently their last.

At Willow Bunch Sitting Bull discovered that his people had been surviving on Légaré's compassion and his inability to extricate himself from the problem of several hundred Sioux starving on his doorstep. The trader had been doing his best to convince the Sioux that their only hope for survival was to surrender to the American authorities, but so far with minimal success. The good report from the four Sioux who had returned with Légaré from Fort Buford resulted in another 32 deciding to surrender, and Légaré had taken them down at the end of May. But the remainder refused to budge until Sitting Bull returned.

Sitting Bull was distressed to learn that his daughter, Many Horses, had taken advantage of his absence to slip over the line with her betrothed. Reports claimed that the U.S. Army had immediately thrown her into prison. At Sitting Bull's request, Légaré provided another feast, and the starving Sioux spent an entire afternoon gorging themselves. Their host claimed that a hungry Indian could consume more than 30 kg (20 lb) of buffalo in one sitting.

The Sioux leader told Légaré that Dewdney had offered to escort him to Pembina but that he had replied, "If I do surrender at all, I will go with Jean-Louis."[16] Légaré was running out of provisions and told Sitting Bull that he could not wait much longer. He would be taking his carts to Fort Buford for supplies in seven days and anyone willing to go along should be ready.

In the early morning of July 11, 1881, Légaré arrived in Sitting Bull's camp with 37 carts, horses, drivers and provisions for the trip. He was ignored in a silent standoff that lasted two hours. Finally, when Légaré announced he was leaving, 20 lodges agreed to join him, but Sitting Bull remained adamant. The expedition headed out, but Légaré left 17 carts behind for Sitting Bull and the others should they change their minds. They did. They first loaded themselves in the carts and headed west towards Milk River, but in the middle of the night they moved into Légaré's camp.

The Sioux were truculent and abusive, continually demanding more provisions. When Légaré stopped one man from removing a sack of flour, the Sioux threw it at the trader's feet and shot twice into it. Then the Sioux refused to move further, angry at being refused free access to the provisions. For two hours they sat silently upon the prairie, only 25 km (15 mi) out of Willow Bunch. Finally, late in the morning of July 12, the caravan again began to move towards Fort Buford. It was a difficult and unpleasant journey, and the next day Légaré worried about what would happen if his provisions ran out. He called Johnny Chartrand to his side.

ON HEART BUTTE, JOHNNY Chartrand started in surprise as a sound like thunder rolled towards him. Yet there was not a cloud in the sky. Then another sound, faintly heard through the fog. A musical note. A bugle. The morning cannon at Fort Buford, and reveille. Chartrand fixed the direction of the sounds in his mind and headed for his horse.

At the fort, Chartrand ran into another problem. The Métis plainsman spoke French, Cree and some Siouan, but no English, and he was unable to make the sentries understand him. But they allowed him entry and Chartrand hunted up a French cook he knew who worked in the kitchen. "Hola, Johnny! You go and get lost? What you doing here?" The weary Chartrand explained that he had no time for talk. He gave the cook Légaré's letter to Major Brotherton, found a bed and sank into sleep. He had been in the saddle for thirteen and a half hours and had covered 129 km (80 mi). It was Thursday, July 14, 1881.

Brotherton instantly recognized the urgency and opportunity in Légaré's report. He organized a wagon train with provisions and sent it north early the next morning with instructions to report to Légaré. Johnny Chartrand served as guide. The post commander also sent a letter back to Légaré:

> Your messenger with your good news arrived last night. I sent out a train this morning with rations, at your request. I sent a few soldiers to take care of wagons on the road; did not send an officer, as I thought from your letter that you didn't want any. The men in charge will be directed to report to you so that you can dispose and issue the rations as is best. Have sent a small present for each of the six chiefs, as you wished, which you can give to them. You can say to them that

I am told by my department commander to say to them all, Sitting Bull included, that they will be well treated here, and they need fear nothing in coming in. Wagons will travel as fast as they can towards you. Shall be glad to see you when you get here.[17]

Except for the few men guarding the wagons, Brotherton acceded to Légaré's stipulation that there be no troops. But the post commander was first and foremost an officer of the U.S. Army, and he had no intention of letting Sitting Bull change his mind and again slip over the border. At 3:00 a.m. the next morning Brotherton sent Captain Walter Clifford and a small mounted detail up the trail. Ten years earlier, Clifford had served as an Indian agent at Fort Berthold, in Dakota Territory, and had there become acquainted with Sitting Bull. Clifford's orders read:

Sitting Bull and other Sioux chiefs are *en route* to this post to surrender. You will meet him and bring his party into Buford. Captain Clifford will use the utmost discretion in carrying out his delicate and important mission and allow nothing or any person to interfere with him to prevent his success.[18]

Légaré's caravan and Brotherton's rescue wagons came together about noon on July 16, some 95 km (60 mi) out of Fort Buford, not far from today's Plentywood, Montana.[19] There was an immediate issue of food and it was some time before the combined expedition got under way again.

Captain Clifford and his men joined Légaré the next afternoon. The officer was pleased that Sitting Bull recognized him and was pleasant in his greeting, but it soon was apparent that the Sioux leader was fearful of being imprisoned upon surrender and deeply concerned about the welfare of his daughter. Clifford assured Sitting Bull that he would not be harmed and that Many Horses was just fine and not in shackles as the rumour reported. But, mindful of his orders, Clifford did not let Sitting Bull out of his sight for the remainder of the journey.[20]

The pending surrender of the most famous Indian leader in North America was of urgent interest to many in the West. NWMP Inspector Alex Mac-Donell had been ordered by Commissioner Irvine to ride from his post at Wood Mountain down to Fort Buford by a route different from Légaré's. If the surrender actually took place, MacDonell was to promptly telegraph the news to the East.

Another trader friend of Sitting Bull's followed the Légaré caravan as it wended its way over the plains. Gus Hedderich, who managed the Wood Mountain store for Leighton and Jordan, whose main operation was at Fort Buford, was determined to be in on this historical event.[21] It was Gus who had taught Sitting Bull to sign his name, an ability that would soon be put to good use.

After camping overnight just 3.2 km (2 mi) from the fort, in mid-morning of July 19, Sitting Bull and several other chiefs, mounted on their gaunt ponies, led their bedraggled procession into Fort Buford and set up camp. To the watching officers the 188 Sioux who surrendered that day were clearly an impoverished and destitute people.

One of Sitting Bull's most admired attributes was his refusal to seek or accept any personal advantage from his great stature. His possessions were as meager as those of anyone in the band. For the formality of the surrender, Sitting Bull's garments were as ragged as those of his people. He wore "a dirty calico shirt, plain black leggings, a calico kerchief tied around his head, and a simple woolen blanket wrapped loosely around his waist."[22]

The Sioux's horses and firearms were confiscated. Sitting Bull, however, turned over a smooth bore musket and requested permission to deliver up his Winchester the following day, after he had rested and eaten. Brotherton granted the request, not knowing that there was a reason behind it.

The telegraph wires out of Fort Buford were busy. Brotherton sent a terse message to General Terry, "Sitting Bull and following surrendered to me at noon today."[23] A Minneapolis reporter filed a longer account to his paper and MacDonell, as instructed by Irvine, wired Washington and Ottawa.

The next day, July 20, in the late morning, Sitting Bull with some thirty of his chiefs and headmen, filed into Brotherton's quarters. On hand, in addition to the post commander, were a number of officers, including Major Guido Ilges who had caused the imbroglio at Fort Peck in January. Légaré and Mac-Donell represented Canada. With Sitting Bull was his 6-year-old son, Crow-foot, named after the great Blackfoot leader.

After Brotherton outlined the already-understood terms of surrender, it was Sitting Bull's turn. After a few words to his followers, he turned to his captors and gestured to Crowfoot. The boy picked up his father's Winchester Model 1866 .44-calibre carbine and silently handed it to Brotherton.[24] Sitting Bull then spoke, through the post interpreter:

> I surrender this rifle to you through my young son, whom I now desire to teach in this manner that he has become a friend of the Americans.

I wish him to learn the habits of the whites and to be educated as their sons are educated.

Then came the reason for the request for the delay in delivering up the weapon: "I wish it to be remembered that I was the last man of my tribe to surrender my rifle."

The Sioux leader then went on:

This boy has given it to you, and he now wants to know how he is going to make a living . . . I now wish to be allowed to live this side of the line or the other as I see fit. I wish to continue my old life of hunting, but would like to be allowed to trade on both sides of the line. This is my country, and I don't wish to be compelled to give it up. My heart was very sad at having to leave the Grandmother's country. She has been a friend to me, but I want my children to grow up in our native country, and I also wish to feel that I can visit two of my friends on the other side of the line—Major Walsh and Captain Mac-Donell—whenever I wish, and would like to trade with Louis Légaré, as he has always been a friend to me . . .

Then, speaking directly to Brotherton, Sitting Bull said, "You own this ground with me and we must try and help each other."[25]

The pitiful condition of Sitting Bull and his followers when they reached Fort Buford excited the sympathy of the base commander. On July 21, two days after the surrender, Brotherton sent a plea to St. Paul:

Would the Department Commander object to making application for a small amount, say $3.00 per head, toward clothing the Indians who came in with Sitting Bull? They are, some of them, literally naked, and with most of them the clothing is falling off them from pure rotten-ness. They certainly need something and this amount would perhaps suffice to cover their nakedness, until they get to where supplies will be issued to them by the Officer or accredited agent of the Interior Department.[26]

The indomitable spirit of the Sioux leader is reflected in his surrender speech as he claimed continued privileges and freedoms that he surely knew were unattainable. Perhaps his mind had not yet accepted how complete and irreversible was his capitulation. Two weeks later, as he was being transported to his assigned agency, the awful realization did sink in and Sitting Bull broke down. A fellow chief found him on the steamer sobbing uncontrollably and took him in his arms, where he continued to weep like a child.[27] Sitting Bull's bravery and ability to withstand excruciating physical pain had been demonstrated in a score of Sun Dances, but the emotional agony of the loss of freedom was more than he could bear.

Ten days later Sitting Bull and his people were sent by steamer down the Missouri to Fort Yates. A stop was made at Bismarck, where they were treated as celebrities and given a tour of the city followed by a great dinner at the leading hotel when for the first time they tasted ice cream. Sitting Bull put Gus Hedderich's teachings to good profit, charging from $2 to $5 for his autograph.[28]

The U.S. Army turned its collection of captive Sioux over to Indian Affairs at Fort Yates, the agency maintained at Standing Rock, Dakota Territory. The Indian Agent logged 2,858 men, women and children received as "prisoners of war." The names of the chiefs among them still ring down through the history of the Sioux Nation: Gall, Hump, Fool Heart, Bull Dog, Spotted Eagle, Circle Bear, Rain-in-the-Face, Crow King, Big Road, Low Dog, Crawler.[29]

The name of Sitting Bull is missing from the list. In spite of its standing offer of amnesty, renewed at Fort Buford by Major Brotherton, the U.S. Army imprisoned Sitting Bull and 137 of his more immediate followers at Fort Randall.

NOT QUITE A MONTH before Sitting Bull's son, Crowfoot, surrendered his father's rifle at Fort Buford, the other Crowfoot, the great Blackfoot chief for whom the boy was named, trudged wearily into Fort Walsh with more than 1,000 of his people. For almost two years, on the advice of Indian Commissioner Dewdney, they had survived by following the buffalo in Montana Territory, but now even that last, great herd had failed, and Crowfoot was forced to lead his band back home.

The Blackfoot sojourn in Montana had been a wretched experience. The prosperity they had won back after the NWMP freed them from the whiskey traders in their homeland had again been taken from them by the same merchants of grief operating across the border. Debauched, impoverished and sick, their horses traded for the vile firewater, their trek on foot north to their homeland was an epic of endurance. The savings Dewdney achieved for Prime Minister Macdonald's treasury by sending the Blackfoot into Montana had been paid for in the misery of Crowfoot and his people.[30]

The Blackfoot had been streaming into Fort Walsh since early May, long before Crowfoot himself arrived. Indian Agent Edwin Allen told Dewdney that "large numbers are daily arriving from the direction of the Missouri in a most destitute condition, in many instances assistance has to be sent to them to enable them to reach this place."[31] Allen noted that the Stockmen of Montana, a prominent cattlemen's association, were demanding that the U.S. Army remove all Canadian Indians from south of the line and in consequence he expected "a very large number of Indians at this place at an early date and the government will have to make some arrangement for the transportation of a large number of them to their different reservations as no doubt many of them will be destitute of horses or other means of conveyance."[32] The agent hoped that Dewdney would make arrangements for the feeding of the approaching multitude.

The nightmare that had cost the Indian Commissioner sleepless nights had become a reality. On May 18, his Inspector of Agencies, J.P. Wadsworth, telegraphed from Fort Macleod that there were "six thousand Indians now in."[33] Wadsworth, too, wanted arrangements made to keep the agency in supplies.

On June 19, Dewdney advised Macdonald of the problem and alerted him to the coming horrendous expense:

> Our Indians by this time I expect are all back on our side of the line and the consumption of food is going to be something terrific . . . We are for the first time brought face to face with our Indians of the North West and while a few of them are in a position to eke out an existence, eight tenths of them are helpless. We cannot find work for them all and they must not be left to starve . . . A small regular ration will satisfy them, but with so large a number a small ration counts up—but as I feel it has come to this a system should be agreed upon . . . and one sufficiently liberal to satisfy the Indian—the difference between what you might get along with without raising a row & what would be sufficient to satisfy them would not be much, & the result I am sure of inducing them to help themselves would be much surer of being obtained.[34]

There was a wild card in the volatile situation facing the Indian Commissioner. Big Bear and his huge following of 480 lodges of Cree were also reported on their way back from Montana. Since they were still holdouts from Treaty 6, Dewdney would continue to refuse them rations, but they would be a very large additional complicating factor. Then another report came in that added to the Indian Commissioner's woes:

> I have just heard that Crowfoot, the head chief of the Blackfoot & Big Bear, a non-treaty Cree but to whom all the Crees look up to as their chief and who has more influence than any Indian on the Plains, are together, crossing the Missouri River on their way north. This looks as if an understanding had been come to between the Cree and the Blackfoot, & if that is the case the more difficult will be our dealings with them.[35]

Elliot Galt, promoted to Assistant Indian Commissioner, with Dewdney in their Winnipeg offices, was determined to keep the expense as low as possible. When Agent Allen at Fort Walsh advised that he was "compelled to purchase from Baker and Co. supplies for issue as required,"[36] Galt promptly told Wadsworth to put an end to the practice, establish a fixed ration and "stop the issuing of anything but flour and bacon, or beef, as the case may be, except when it is considered advisable to issue a little tea now and again to sick people or to Indians who are really doing well on their Reserves." The government wanted the Indians settled on their reservations, and Galt proposed to accomplish this by allowing only reduced rations "for those who won't go home . . . If they choose to roam about the country they must not be permitted to think that they can go to any Post and receive a similar ration to those Indians who belong there."[37]

The next economy measure provoked a strongly negative reaction from the field. Dewdney had the previous fall established the ration allowance at .45 kg (1 lb) each of flour and of beef to each individual. From the security and remoteness of Winnipeg, instructions were sent to Agent Allen at Fort Walsh "to issue half rations to non working Indians"[38] and to Agent Macleod at Fort Macleod "to issue half rations to women and children and to let the able bodied Indians hunt small game for a living."[39]

At Fort Walsh, NWMP Commissioner Irvine intervened and decreed that "it would be very unwise at this critical period, when the Indians are about settling on their Reservations, to reduce their rations."[40] Irvine countermanded the order for reduced rations and Wadsworth agreed when he arrived on the scene.

At Fort Macleod, Agent Macleod on his own initiative refused to implement the order for reduced rations and fired back to Dewdney:

Fort Macleod, 1878. *Library and Archives Canada / Royal Canadian Geographical Society collection PA-210466*

I considered the consequences to the Public would be of so serious a nature if I acted on your Telegram that I declined to carry it out and that if you considered my action as a disobedience of orders, that I must beg to be relieved in my duties here. The number of Indians now assembled in the several Reserves in this Treaty is so very great that utter destitution and the absolute lack of small game would leave the Indians no other recourse than raiding the cattle of the settlers in the neighbourhood and I do not feel inclined to take this responsibility.[41]

The directive that all Indians should proceed to their own reserves extended to Crowfoot and his Blackfoot people, who were drawing rations at Fort Walsh. In July they obediently shuffled on westward towards Fort Macleod. In spite of Agent Allen's naïve expectation that the government "would have to make some arrangement for their transportation," the horseless Blackfoot trudged on foot over the searing prairie. Hugh Dempsey, Crowfoot's biographer, described their journey:

> The meager reserves of pemmican were doled out, a tiny morsel having to last all day. But even with this rigid rationing, the food supplies were gone long before they reached Fort Macleod. The daily trek had slowed to a few miles; the young men as well as the old were unable to keep up a steady pace. There were frequent rests, but even this slow pace was too much for the starving people. Each day, new voices wailed the Death Songs as the spirits of their loved ones departed for

the Sand Hills. The wooded coulees and the bare hilltops along the route were dotted with the graves of those who died. Finally, after almost six weeks of walking and starving, the Blackfoot at last saw the palisaded walls of Fort Macleod. And there, camped along the river bottom, was the remainder of the tribe still waiting for their chief.[42]

The Blackfoot made it back home on July 20, 1881. Agent Macleod recorded the event:

> Crowfoot arrived here on the 20th ulto with 1,064 followers, all in a most destitute condition. A large proportion of his followers consisted of old men, women and children. They were nearly all on foot.[43]

The Indian Commissioner's experiment in saving money by sending Treaty Indians into the United States was over. The cost to the Blackfoot had been huge, in human suffering and lost lives:

> Scores of fresh graves dotted the countryside from the Oldman River to the Missouri. Warriors who had defeated every enemy in battle were reduced to bony derelicts before starvation and disease carried the life from their bodies. No one knows exactly how many people from the Blackfoot tribe died during those starvation years, but from 1879 to 1881 at least one thousand members of the nation in Canada perished.[44]

NWMP Commissioner Irvine's opinion in June that the situation at Fort Walsh was "critical" was elevated considerably in August when his headquarters were temporarily blockaded by unruly Indians and Métis. Irvine responded by placing the Fort on high alert.

While J.P. Wadsworth, Inspector of Indian Agencies, was making Treaty 4 payments at Fort Walsh, a deputation of Métis came to him and demanded to be put under the Treaty. When Wadsworth necessarily refused to do so, the Métis succeeded in inciting the Indians encamped nearby. Led by Chiefs Lucky Man and Little Pine, the Cree refused to accept their treaty payments and declared they would force him to "pay every native of this country."[45] The Cree became very excited and "liable to do almost anything."[46]

Irvine also became excited, so much so that he battened down the hatches at the fort. He closed the gates, confined all troops to barracks, placed them on full alert and issued extra rifles and ammunition. The bastions, casually used to store oats, were emptied in short order. A squad was drilled in the use of the four 7-pounder field guns preparatory to placing two of the guns in each bastion to cover all four sides of the stockade.[47]

Elliot Galt, a civilian and a budding bureaucrat, proposed that Fort Walsh simply be abandoned. Presumably he intended that the NWMP march out, carrying with them anything of value, and leave the rest to the Cree and the Métis. Commissioner Irvine, with his military background, was shocked at Galt's suggestion. The abandonment of the fort would reflect very seriously upon the reputation of his Force with the Indians. In their minds the NWMP had been invincible. How would the Force be able to handle the Indians after such a humiliating capitulation?

Wadsworth, another bureaucrat, disagreed with Irvine. He thought that the Commissioner

> cannot be aware that the Indians have the greatest indifference for the force here, on account of the comparatively few men; they keep upon their good behaviour only as long as it suits them, their manner is defiant, they think they are the stronger.[48]

The standoff was defused when reports came in of a great herd of buffalo nearby. The Cree and the Métis raced off to the hunt and the demand for inclusion of the Métis in the treaty was forgotten. With the "blockade raised," Elliot Galt withdrew his "proposition of abandoning this place, at present."[49]

It was not a good summer for the Governor General to visit the western plains, but Lord Lorne, 9th Duke of Argyll, husband of Princess Louise, fourth daughter of Queen Victoria, and resident at Rideau Hall since 1878, intended to do just that. The office of the Indian Commissioner and the NWMP were required to devote much of their attention to the logistics and planning of the great event.

At Qu'Appelle in June, upon hearing the news of the royal visit from Dewdney, the Cree scolded the Indian Commissioner:

> You told us just now that the Great Chief and a daughter of the Great Mother would probably visit us this summer. The daughter of the Great Mother would surely not like to see the Great Mother's Children hoeing potatoes in the fields naked, and that is what she will see if you don't send us some clothing.[50]

CHAPTER 21

1881: The End of the Old West

Lo! The poor Indian, whose untutored mind sees
God in clouds, or hears him in the wind.

—ALEXANDER POPE, 1688–1744

QUEEN VICTORIA'S DAUGHTER DID NOT SEE NAKED INDIANS hoeing potatoes in their fields that summer of 1881, only because she did not accompany Governor General Lorne on his trip into the West. Seriously injured in a sleighing accident, Princess Louise returned to England to recover, leaving her husband to make his promotional tour without her.

A promotional tour it clearly was. It was Lorne's purpose to advertise to the world, and particularly to prospective farmers in England and Scotland, the many opportunities of Canada's new agricultural lands. Among the invited guests were correspondents and artists from three leading London and two Edinburgh newspapers. The Governor General was well equipped to entertain the journalists as they travelled the barren plains; his personal attendants included a French chef, six servants, three aides-de-camp, a military secretary and a medical doctor.[1]

The expedition's route had been well laid-out. Carried by the Canadian Pacific Railway to its end of steel 71 km (44 mi) west of Portage La Prairie, the entourage then travelled by the steamer *Manitoba* up the Assiniboine River to Fort Ellice. They there became the responsibility of the NWMP under the command of Superintendent W.H. Herchmer, formerly the commissary officer of the Boundary Commission. The touring dignitaries put a considerable strain upon the resources of the Force, requiring 96 horses, 27 wagons and carriages, and 21 tents, all handled by 47 troopers.[2]

From Fort Ellice the party travelled overland to Qu'Appelle and on to St. Laurent on the South Saskatchewan River, where it was ferried across by Gabriel Dumont in his single scow, an operation that required more than a few crossings. Dumont then enlisted a mounted escort of Métis who accompanied the Governor General as far as Duck Lake and Fort Carlton. They went to Prince Albert on the steamer *Northcote* that, thanks to Dumont, would achieve a certain ignominy four years later,[3] and back to Battleford on the S.S. *Lily*. There the Governor General and his party were guests of David Laird, Lieutenant-Governor of the North-West Territories, at the new Government House.

This unabashed boosting of the new West was somewhat tarnished when the vice-regal party was confronted with the misery of its former owners. Along his route, at Fort Ellice, Qu'Appelle, Fort Carlton and Battleford the Governor General received delegations of the Cree chiefs who had signed on to Treaties 4 and 6 and was subjected to a litany of grievances about life under those Treaties. The Blackfoot chiefs were met at Blackfoot Crossing and Fort Macleod. To assist in understanding and responding, Elliot Galt, by then promoted to Assistant Indian Commissioner, travelled with the vice-regal party. Indian Commissioner Edgar Dewdney joined at Battleford.

At every council, the single refrain from the Cree chiefs was their lack of food and clothing, followed by their need for proper farm implements if they were expected to succeed at farming. At Qu'Appelle, Yellow Quill spoke plainly:

> I was glad to hear you were coming. I think my women and children will live now. Let us see the kindness you will show us here. Our forefathers could see buffalo and game all round. We used to live at that time. I am asking you and what is it that I ask? I do not understand the Treaty. Now I see what has been done to us. Our property has been taken from us. I cannot live by what I was then told. You do not see horses because I have eaten them. We have also eaten our dogs. That is what your work has done for me. I shall not be able to live by the good words that are told me. You see me naked as I am . . . We think that because this excellency has the power he can do what we ask. The reason is we cannot live by the first Treaty; we shall die off. Provisions are the only thing that will enable us to live long. They cannot hold to the Treaty that was made before.[4]

There would be no changing of the Treaties. On that the Governor General was firm. The thing to do was work, work at the farming:

> I have heard very eloquent speeches. I am quite sure that men who speak so well can work as well as their red brethren in the East. Hands were not given by Manitou to fill pipes only but also to work. I am sure that red men to the East when they work do well and do not starve and I have heard that the men who talk most and ask most do not work.[5]

At Carlton, Mistawasis did not yet regret having supported Treaty 6, but spoke with deep melancholy:

> Many a time I had no provisions, was deprived of them, but I was never angry. The agent has been kind to us and was acting to his instructions. I felt there was no use to grumble. Many a time I was very sad when I saw my poor people ill, starving, and I could do nothing for them . . . At the time of the Treaties it was mentioned that while the sun rose and set and the water ran the faith in the Treaties was to be kept.[6]

Ahtahkakoop also spoke at Carlton:

> I am a poor man . . . but as I look around I do not see anything I could live by. I see nothing. All that I used to live by has gone. Where I used to get my game was the animals of the buffalo, and also I had horses. Now the buffalo and the horses have left me. I say with that I am a poor man.
>
> You may have seen the poverty of the land as regards the animals. That was my hunting ground. I used to find there all I wanted. Now it is a solitary wilderness. I find nothing there. When I look at all this I see but one thing left—that is to work the ground.

His people would farm, Ahtahkakoop stated, but to do so they needed cattle and implements, a threshing machine. They lost too much of their wheat threshing with a flail.

The chiefs should not ask too much, Lorne warned:

You must remember that you are numerous, that it costs the government much money to help, and that the Queen has to take care of all her children, and some white men as well as red, and I have heard where the sun rises that the white men complain that too much is given to her red children and not enough to white.[7]

Poundmaker spoke at Battleford. After reluctantly signing on to Treaty 6 in August 1876, he had held out from selecting a reserve for three years, but was supportive. He, too, was willing to work at farming, "But I am short of implements. I mean the same things used by the white man—a reaper mower . . . we don't know the use of the flail and when good crops come we want a thresher."[8] Lorne's words at Battleford were platitudinous and disjointed:

That I have come so far is a proof of the love of the Queen. I have come all this way to show that the Queen loves you and that I have seen under the Treaties that many of them are getting a living by farming and those who help themselves.

That sometimes they open their hands too wide, but I am pleased to see that some of you are reasonable.[9]

On September 1, after two days at Battleford, the Governor General and his party headed out to Calgary. Two colourful guides scouted the trail, the Cree chief Poundmaker, the adopted son of Crowfoot, and John Longmore, a Métis who was better known as "Johnny Saskatchewan." Superintendent Herchmer had planned to take the expedition directly to Calgary, but, behind schedule and short of provisions, he changed course for Blackfoot Crossing. That caused a problem. Crowfoot and his people, little more than a month returned from Montana, were camped at the Crossing and there was nothing for it but to quickly arrange a council. A marquee was raised and seats provided for the Governor General and his dignitaries while the NWMP speedily turned out an impressive guard of honour. After an equestrian display by the Blackfoot warriors, Crowfoot and his fellow chiefs, Old Sun, Heavy Shield and Bull Head, each bearing a Union Jack, came forward to shake the vice-regal hand. A ceremonial pipe was smoked and then Crowfoot arose to address the Queen's representative.

Clad only in rags, he delivered an eloquent and passionate plea for his destitute people who had turned their lands over to the white man and no longer had the buffalo. "I find myself very poor now—since I signed the Treaty I get poorer and poorer." His arm outstretched, Crowfoot held forth a tin cup. "You see what we have. That is the measure which each person receives and they cannot live on that alone." More rations were direly needed, Crowfoot urged, and assistance to learn the art of farming. Sydney Hall, artist for the *London Graphic*, captured the poignant scene. Lord Lorne is portrayed lounging beneath the marquee, Dewdney beside him, while the great Blackfoot chief, supported by a staff, holds forth a tin cup as a symbol of the misery and need of his people.

The Reverend Dr. James MacGregor of Edinburgh, an old friend of Lorne's and his guest on the expedition, described the moment:

> I have rarely seen a more touching sight than the poor infirm chief, with his finely chiselled countenance and bright smile, as, leaning on his staff, and worse clad than any of his followers, he moved forward to his place; the shabby clothes, which the poorest artisan would be ashamed to wear, contrasting sadly with the Victoria medal he wore on his breast, the remainder, and almost the only remnant of the high position which he once occupied.

Seemingly less taken with Crowfoot's words, MacGregor continued, "It was touching, too, to hear the earnest way in which he pled for greater help from the Government for his starving people."[10]

When Crowfoot pressed the Governor General for a commitment to more and better rations, the response was condescending. "He must remember that there are other poor, poor whites and poor Indians who have to be helped." "Everywhere they only think of grub," Crowfoot replied. The famine, he knew, was not confined to the Blackfoot. With that, the unplanned formalities were over. The vice-regal expedition took down its marquee and departed that same afternoon for Calgary. The Blackfoot returned to their lodges, their stomachs empty. There was no feast at Blackfoot Crossing to celebrate the visitation of the Queen's representative.

There was one more council to be endured by the touring dignitaries, at Fort Macleod where Red Crow and his fellow Blood and Peigan chiefs made their plea. Plea it was, as Red Crow made plain in his opening. "Great Chief who has come into this country, take pity on us. God takes pity. Do you take pity?" The response from Lord Lorne was as it had been at the earlier councils. He had not come to change the Treaties, but "to see that the Treaties are well kept and that the government will always keep the Treaties and promises."[11]

Lord Lorne was not impressed with what he had heard at the five great councils. In his experience, Natives were continually beseeching for something or other. He and the Reverend MacGregor were not alone in missing the agony and sincerity in the eloquent supplications of the Cree and Black-foot chiefs. Indian Commissioner Dewdney and other representatives of the Ottawa government also failed to detect the desperation behind the words of the eminent leaders of the Plains Indians and recognize that a serious and significant concern was growing.

After the vice-regal party moved on to Calgary, Poundmaker remained behind at Blackfoot Crossing for several days as a guest of Crowfoot, his adopted father. There is, of course, no record of the discussions between the two chiefs, but they must have compared notes of their experiences under their Treaties, 6 for Poundmaker, 7 for Crowfoot. Both had placed their faith and trust, and the welfare of their people, in Ottawa's hands; both were experiencing a cruel new reality. Their last meeting, five years in the future, would be deeply tragic.

The Governor General's promotional tour of the West was considered a great success. The accompanying correspondents "were enthusiastic about the rich soil, the ranching possibilities of southern Alberta, the vacant lands which could accommodate many hard-pressed farmers from Europe, and the remarkable climate during the fall season." Back in the Old Country, the Edinburgh *Scotsman* opined that the publicity "opened up to our distressed farmers a land of promise, where they could take refuge from high rents, bad harvests, sunless skies, and destructive tempests, in a land of vast area, rich soil, sunny clime, and serene air."[12]

That year, 1881, was only seven, five and four years respectively after the signing of Treaties 4, 6 and 7 that surrendered the *Scotsman*'s "land of promise," but the Cree, Assiniboine and Blackfoot who had signed those Treaties were already surrounded by powerful evidence that a new order had come. Just what their place would be in that new order was less clear, and very worrisome.

Sir John A. Macdonald ensured that Ottawa retained ownership of all the lands of the North-West Territories, to be used for the "purposes of the Dominion," roughly synonymous with his National Policy. Once the Treaties cleared away the title of the Plains Indians, the Prime Minister set about developing the western plains. The barren prairies had little value in their primal state. To extract their wealth they must be developed, converted to agriculture, hundreds of thousands of individual farms, all occupied by hardworking families, all contributing to Canada's gross national product, all requiring goods and services to be supplied by the manufacturers of Ontario and Quebec and delivered by the Canadian Pacific Railway, under construction.

The process of "development" differed very little from that followed today by those who create residential subdivisions out of raw land. First, send in the surveyors to lay out the individual parcels of land intended to be sold, and the roadways to provide access to those parcels. Next, install the services the parcels will enjoy, construct the access roads, and hang up the "For Sale" sign.

So it was on the western plains in that summer of 1881. Survey crews fanned out as far west as Calgary, slicing and dicing the great western commons into the 65-ha (160-acre) parcels considered to be marketable as give-away homesteads. It was the end of the freedom era on the Great Plains, when the vast wealth of grass and game, wood and water, was open to all who came. The wild wilderness was no more. The great expanse of prairie that belonged only to future generations was swiftly being transformed into a huge grid of tiny parcels, each to be allocated to individuals, each to be possessed of something called "property rights."

It was the golden age of land surveying. The survey parties that were scattered across the prairies in 1881 were merely harbingers of what was to come. The following year saw 92 parties working on the township plan, and in 1883, 119 survey parties subdivided a total of 10,926,900 ha (27,000,000 acres), ready for settlement.[13] That translated into 168,750 farms of 65 ha (160 acres) each, which would, according to the calculations of an Ottawa bureaucrat, support "a purely agricultural population of 506,250, allowing an average of only three souls per farm."[14]

Indian Commissioner Dewdney's concern that the government would not be in full control of the Plains Indians until the railway arrived was being addressed. The steel of the Canadian Pacific Railway extended west of Brandon in 1881, but the next year would leap across the prairies under the whirlwind command of its new general manager, William Cornelius Van Horne. At the close of construction in 1882, the line snaked clear across Saskatchewan and well into Blackfoot country in today's Alberta.

None of this had been in the contemplation of any of the Plains Indians when they accepted the terms of Treaties 4, 6 and 7. Their former homelands were being transformed so rapidly that only a perspicacious few could understand what was happening all around them.

Poundmaker was one whose foresight told him what had befallen his people. The up-and-coming chief who raised such troubling questions at the Treaty 6 negotiations had come to appreciate the inevitability of the new order and in 1879 had accepted a reservation on the Battle River west of Battleford. At the New Year of 1881 he spoke to his people and advised them to work hard at farming and accept the new way of life:

> Next summer, or at latest next fall, the railway will be close to us, the whites will fill our country, and they will dictate to us as they please.

It is useless to dream that we can frighten them; that time is past; our only resource is our work, our industry and our farms. Send your children to school . . . if you want them to prosper and be happy.[15]

Poundmaker's faith and willingness to dedicate himself to a future in the white man's ways would wither before Ottawa's parsimony in meeting its treaty obligations. Just four years into that future the great Cree chief would meet an ignoble fate.

The Métis in their several communities across the West also struggled to adapt as their traditional way of life fell away. 1881 was the last year of the annual buffalo hunt. That fall Gabriel Dumont led his people onto the plains, but they returned with empty carts. No food, no robes or pemmican for sale or barter. Like their Treaty Indian brethren, the Métis were forced to turn to the land for a living.

That raised an old problem, one that was an echo of troubles at Red River in 1869. The Dominion township survey of square, 260-ha (640-acre) sections excluded the river lots the Métis had established and settled along the South Saskatchewan River. At Prince Albert in 1878, surveyors accommodated the Métis land use pattern and laid out lots 201 m (660 ft) in width facing the river and 3.2 km (2 mi) in length. But Ottawa refused to extend the survey of river lots to the community at St. Laurent.

Worse, much of the lands the Métis had settled on years earlier was not available to them even as homesteads if they fell within sections reserved for the Canadian Pacific Railway, the Hudson's Bay Company, or schools. Finally, even if their homes were open for homesteading, the Métis were required to file and wait the requisite three years before qualifying for title. And, if they were slow to file, a stranger might well jump their claim and take the land out from under them.

It was an unhappy situation crying for a quick and imaginative solution. None was forthcoming. Once again warnings from the West fell upon deaf ears in Ottawa.

In the view of the public east of the Great Lakes, the great plan for the western plains was unfolding as it should. The Plains Indians had signed Treaties and were penned up on their reserves where they were out of sight, out of mind, and out of the path of progress. That the residents of those reserves were coping with squalid conditions on subsistence rations barely enough to keep them alive was not a matter of public concern.

There was little, if any, public sympathy in Canada for Sitting Bull and the Sioux during the years they sought sanctuary north of the 49th Parallel, and certainly none in the West where they were most unwelcome. The American Indians had intruded into the territory between Wood Mountain and the Cypress Hills already uneasily shared by the Métis, White Eagle's band of Santee Sioux from Minnesota, the Plains Cree and the Assiniboine, with the Blackfoot looking hungrily in from the western edge. The Oblate priests, with their missions at St. Florent, in the Qu'Appelle Valley, at Wood Mountain, Cypress Hills and Milk River, were right in the centre of the situation and came down firmly, even harshly, on the side of their Métis parishioners. An early Church history described the dispute between the United States and the Sioux in terms decidedly unsympathetic to the Sioux:

> [The United States] had tried in vain to make these Indians sign a treaty by which they would renounce their territory and would consent to move to the new reservation assigned to them. The majority of the Indians, under the influence of the great chief Sitting Bull, obstinately refused to any compromise. In desperation the American[s] ... saw themselves forced to tell the Redskins that, if on January 1, 1876, they had not entered the specified reservation, they would be treated as enemies. It was war.[16]

The Church held a poor opinion of the Sioux:

> These people were barbarians. Their clothing consisted of a buffalo skin tied by a cord at the waist, without headdress, shirt or trousers. They wore moccasins and chaps, and their guns never left them ... When the bisons became scarce, the Indians began to steal in order to sustain themselves. They made frequent expeditions across the frontier, raiding the herds. They forced the Canadian traders to give them their merchandise without hope of payment; they went so far as to mistreat the resistors and threaten to kill them.[17]

Even the peace-loving Nez Perce came off badly:

> a once numerous tribe who, after having pillaged and massacred everything in certain districts of Oregon, and in its flight to Canada [a distance of 2,400 km/1,500 mi] had clashed with the American cavalry at the border before coming to our Montagne. These unfortunates came to us in a deplorable state, weakened, without shoes, without clothing, without provisions, almost all suffering with bleeding wounds.[18]

The priests on Canada's western plains were, of course, unaware of the 1876 report of the Manypenny Commission that took an entirely different view of the conduct of the United States government in its relations with the Sioux:

> Our country must forever bear the disgrace and suffer the retribution of its wrong-doing. Our children's children will tell the story in hushed tones, and wonder how their fathers dared so to trample on justice and trifle with God.

Little wonder that the lay members of the Canadian public had no greater concern for the once proud Plains Indians who had been shunted onto reservations, reduced to penury and isolated from society.

Canadian public opinion towards the Plains Indians was less harsh than in the United States, but that is indeed faint praise. One American historian explained the Eurocentric attitude:

> The dominant white society justified its violent campaigns against the Indians by first vilifying them because of their race, then claiming the whole race to be inferior, and, finally, to be less than human. Once the Indian was conceived of as stereotype (shiftless, a hunter, incapable of rational thought, childlike, and so on) instead of an individual, the dehumanization process was complete and violence against him was made acceptable to respectable people.[19]

The American press frequently employed a distortion of the Alexander Pope quotation, "Lo! The poor Indian, whose untutored mind sees God in clouds, or hears him in the wind." Treating the exclamation mark as if it were a comma, "Lo" became a derisive descriptor of the Indian people, as in, "Lo should be taught a lesson," or "The Lo family must learn."[20]

The Macdonald government made no attempt to disguise its policy of starvation as the lever used to force Sitting Bull and the Sioux refugees out of Canada, and drew little, if any, criticism of its actions. Ottawa then turned the same strategy against its Treaty Indians. Until they surrendered their nomadic freedom and accepted life on the reservations, there would be no food. Even then, to qualify for rations they must bow to the dictate that they labour in the fields, learning the new and strange ways of farming. Again there was no criticism of this policy, only concern for the cost of feeding the multitude on the prairie. It was the temper of the times.

Macdonald's government described the dreadful conditions on the western plains in another Throne Speech, on December 9, 1880, at a session of

Parliament called to approve the contracts for the building of the Canadian Pacific Railway. The Speech explained that the contracts were essential because "no permanent arrangement for the organization of a systematic Emigration from Europe to the North-West Territories, can be satisfactorily made until the policy of Parliament with respect to the Railway has been decided." Then, after some housekeeping matters, the Speech went on:

> I greatly regret being obliged to state that the entire failure of the usual food supply of the Indians in the North-West, to which I called your attention last Session, has continued during the present season, and has involved the necessity of a large expenditure in order to save them from absolute starvation. Several of the Bands have, however, already applied themselves to the cultivation of their reserves and the care of their cattle. No effort will be spared to induce the whole of the aboriginal population to betake themselves to agricultural pursuits.[21]

Farming, as practised under Ottawa's direction, was labour-intensive to a high degree, very little advanced from Biblical times. Sowing was performed by broadcast, reaping by scythe and cradle, and threshing by flail. These primitive methods would be entrenched by a terribly misguided policy based on the conviction that the Indians could not advance directly to mechanized farming, but must evolve from hand tools slowly, in stages as the Europeans had over centuries. As well, labour-saving machinery would only enable the slothful Indians to sit about in idleness, their preferred condition.[22]

In Macdonald's view, his approach to the plight of the Indians who had taken his Treaties was not oppressive but benevolent. In response to an accusation that poor-quality food was being distributed, he explained:

> It cannot be considered a fraud on the Indians because they have no right to that food. They are simply living on the benevolence and charity of the Canadian Parliament, and, as the old adage says, beggars should not be choosers.[23]

The Prime Minister's benevolence did not, however, extend to non-Treaty Indians such as those of the Peace, Athabasca and Mackenzie River systems. For years Vital Grandin, Bishop of St. Albert, pleaded with Macdonald to relieve the suffering along the Peace River but was told only that the government could do nothing for those Indians since they were not under treaty.[24] And Macdonald refused to extend treaties over territory not needed for his National Policy. Even Lawrence Vankoughnet, the long-serving Deputy Superintendent of Indian Affairs whose parsimony ensured no more than starvation-level rations on the plains, was touched by the misery of the northern Indians. He recommended that the government proceed to negotiate a treaty: "it is in the interest of humanity very desirable that the Government should render them assistance, as their condition at many points is very wretched." Macdonald rejected the proposal until "there is a likelihood of the country being required for settlement purposes."[25]

To be sure, the hard-hearted attitude Macdonald's government displayed towards Canada's Native population was not much more severe than that directed to residents of European descent. Humanitarian sensibilities had not then evolved into the concept of social welfare as a public responsibility.

The Plains Indians were considered to be several rungs down the ladder of biological and cultural development. They were non-persons by legislative enactment. The Indian Act of 1876 provided the definition: "Person" means an individual other than an Indian.[26] The Indian could not vote or conduct his own financial affairs. The Indian Act provided a method by which one could become enfranchised, by attaining university education or membership in a professional society, but this escape route was available only to the Indians of the East. Those on the western plains were considered to be incapable of such self-improvement. In this way Ottawa presumed to classify Canada's aboriginal residents somewhat as did the American Department of Indian Affairs in 1872 when it broke down its Indian population as: "Civilized, 97,000; semi-civilized, 125,000; wholly barbarous, 78,000."[27]

None of this policy originated in Ottawa, or even in North America, but devolved from Great Britain. It was in keeping with the Victorian philosophy that governed Britain's relations with the Aboriginal peoples that had come under its dominion during the expansion of the empire. Believing in a natural hierarchy of societies that placed the British firmly at the top, and that graded downwards through Latins and Asians to Aboriginals at the very bottom, the notion or concept of racial supremacy became a moral responsibility, not a self-serving attitude. What followed was the Christian duty of the superior Victorian civilization to exercise a wardship over the pagan Aboriginals. This sentiment was neatly captured at the end of the 19th century by Rudyard Kipling in his poem, *The White Man's Burden*.[28]

Following the 1859 publication of Charles Darwin's *On the Origin of Species*, his theory of natural selection was seized upon as further validation of the Eurocentric attitude towards Aboriginal peoples, and the phrase Social Darwinism entered the lexicon of anthropologists and social theorists. Survival of the fittest was taken to mean, in North America, that the Indian could not survive the collision with the European in-migration.[29]

By 1880, the 49th Parallel as an international boundary was dividing two cultures developing on diverging tracks, often described as the "mild" Canadian West as distinct from the "wild" American West. A perhaps too simple explanation suggests that the early arrival of the NWMP in the Canadian West, before the influx of settlers, assured minimal conflict between those settlers and the Indians who had been displaced from the lands being homesteaded. By contrast, settlers frequently raced into the American West well ahead of law and order, often resulting in clashes with the Indian residents. Whatever the reason, certainly the entire Canadian West experienced no fatal encounters to compare with those in Montana described by Robert Vaughn in his memoirs, *Then and Now, or, Thirty-Six Years in the Rockies*: more than 121 settler deaths in 14 years. Of course, no count was kept of the Indian fatalities suffered in those encounters.

By 1881 Ottawa's problem with its Treaty Indians was considered to be well in hand, so much so that additional duties were assigned to Indian Commissioner Dewdney. He was appointed Lieutenant-Governor of the North-West Territories in succession to David Laird, an arrangement worked out by Macdonald to entice Dewdney to stay on the job. The appointment meant another $2,000 per annum, and the prestige of the position. But Dewdney had other affairs on his mind as well—his own affairs.

The new appointment was an excellent fix for Dewdney. As Lieutenant-Governor, he would have a good deal to say about the location of the new capital city of the Territories along the right-of-way of the Canadian Pacific Railway to be constructed in the next year. That was important to Dewdney because he and a number of well-placed friends had formed syndicates and purchased 28 sections of land along that future route. Assistant Indian Commissioner Elliot Galt was also a member of the syndicates.[30]

Many expected that Fort Qu'Appelle, in its beautiful valley, would be the choice for the capital city, but the selection went to an unattractive locale known as Pile o' Bones with a later name change to Regina. Not surprisingly, the spot selected was almost on top of Dewdney's land interests. He scored a quick and certain profit, but his reputation suffered. Dewdney was savaged by the Toronto *Globe* and by the Liberal opposition in the House of Commons, where Macdonald stood by his man.[31]

The nature of the criticism directed at the Lieutenant-Governor/Indian Commissioner is telling. He had improperly used his public office to secure to himself a personal profit. The accusation did not extend to his shirking the responsibility of devoting full time and attention to the plight and needs of the Treaty Indians, his wards under the Indian Act. Dewdney's land speculation was not confined to Regina. He played in the Winnipeg land boom of 1881 and gambled on the location of the Canadian Pacific Railway terminus on the Pacific. Other and more local investments in farms and transportation companies were less than successful.[32]

What with his new responsibilities as Lieutenant-Governor and his extensive and time-demanding investment activities, Dewdney had little of himself left to devote to the condition of the Plains Indians. Assistant Indian Commissioner Elliot Galt was also busy outside his official duties. He had spotted the coal deposits at the Coal Banks on the Belly River (Lethbridge) and drawn them to the attention of his businessman father. The Galts formed a company to develop the deposits.

But the situation on the western plains was not tranquil, not even superficially. Discontent was well-nigh universal among the Métis and Treaty Indians of the North-West Territories, a fact that was no secret to a number of well-placed observers. As had been the case with the Red River troubles, Ottawa received excellent advice about the growing problem, some of it from the same sources that had been ignored more than 10 years earlier.

Macdonald's deputy minister in the Interior Department was the same Colonel J.S. Dennis whose survey chain had been stepped upon by Louis Riel and his Métis at Red River in 1869. Dennis retired in 1881, but on leaving office he strongly recommended to Macdonald that the Métis land claims be attended to: "He thought that if the land question were dealt with imaginatively, what was now a situation of potential conflict could be turned to advantage in establishing peace in the West."[33]

Archbishop Taché, who had been cold-shouldered by Macdonald's government in 1869, but then brought back from Rome to rescue Ottawa's chestnuts from the Red River conflagration, again proffered excellent advice, this time in writing:

> The formidable Indian question has not yet arisen in our midst, owing largely to the influence of the Halfbreed element. The disappearance of the buffalo and especially the extension of the settlers into the Indian country, are preparing difficulties which may be avoided, I hope, but which would otherwise involve such terrible and expensive results that it is the duty of all the friends of the Government and of the country to do all in their power to prevent such misfortune.

The result depends in a great measure on the way the Halfbreeds would be treated. Friendly [*sic*] disposed, they will mightily contribute to the maintenance of peace; dissatisfied, they would not only add to the difficulty, but render the settlement of the country the next thing to an impossibility.

The Halfbreeds are a highly sensitive race; they keenly resent injury or insult, and daily complain on that point. In fact, they are daily humiliated with regard to their origin by the way they are spoken of, not only in newspapers, but also in official and semi-official documents.

It is desirable that the Halfbreed question should be decided upon without any further delay. The requisite legislation ought to be passed in the coming session of the Legislature . . . There is no doubt the difficulties increase with delay.[34]

Warnings showered on Ottawa. In August 1878, the North-West Territories Council adopted a resolution calling for immediate attention to the Métis land question. Former Lieutenant-Governors Alexander Morris and David Laird both urged that action be taken.

At the close of the 1870s, the Great Lone Land envisaged by Captain William Butler 10 years earlier had become stark reality. Life on the Canadian plains bore little resemblance to its earlier condition. The buffalo were gone, the nomadic Plains Indians were penned up on their reservations and the once free-roving Métis were confined to a hated community life. As an eminent historian has observed, the Indians of Eastern Canada had 200 years to accommodate and adapt to the European takeover of their lands, but those in Western Canada had only 20 years. In truth, almost all of that transition was forced upon the Plains Indians, and Métis, in a mere 10 years, the decade of the 1870s.

As the new decade of the 1880s opened, famine and fear stalked the reservations and Métis settlements along the valley of the Saskatchewan Rivers. Once again the Métis were threatened with loss of their lands and culture, but there was no further hinterland into which they might escape. The Plains Indians also were discontented, starving, torn from their traditional way of life, angry at the non-fulfillment of the promises of their Treaties. The spectre of a great western confederation rising in defiance of the national authority hovered over the plains.

A fuse smouldered in the West. It led to an explosive charge very similar to that which had erupted at Red River 10 years earlier, but now was larger, and more widespread.

As Ottawa remained obdurate and oblivious, the fuse continued to smoulder, growing shorter. It was a long and slow-burning fuse, but it did have an ending. That ending was reached at Duck Lake, on March 26, 1885.

CHAPTER 22

Epilogue: After Events

MARCH 26, 1885, WAS THE DAY THE FIRST SHOT WAS fired in the North-West Rebellion. That shot killed Isidore Dumont, brother of Gabriel, in a parley that went badly, 34 years after the two brothers had fought side by side against the Sioux on the Grand Coteau.

The firefight that followed between a combined NWMP and volunteer force directed by Superintendent Leif Crozier and a band of armed Métis commanded by Gabriel Dumont resulted in 17 fatalities, 12 of them among the troops led by Crozier, the same officer who had been outsmarted by Sitting Bull at Wood Mountain in 1871. Crozier, criticized for not awaiting the imminent arrival of NWMP Commissioner A.G. Irvine with a large force of reinforcements, was passed over for promotion and resigned his commission the next year.

Irvine's performance during the Rebellion also came under criticism and he, too, resigned in 1886, the third Commissioner of the NWMP and the third to leave office under fire. He served as warden of the penitentiaries at Stoney Mountain and Kingston and died at Quebec City in 1916.

Lieutenant Colonel George Arthur French, the first Commissioner of the NWMP,[1] annoyed the Mackenzie government with his complaints about the conditions at Swan River Barracks and his reluctance to follow orders from Ottawa. Contrasting French's attitude with that of Macleod, who was "cheerfully" meeting far greater obstacles out on the plains, the Commissioner was dismissed on July 22, 1876, and Macleod was appointed in his place.[2] Later, on October 7, 1876, the government allowed French a face-saving resignation that enabled him to return to his career in the Imperial Army.[3] There, French served successfully, retiring in 1902 with the rank of Major-General and a knighthood.

James Farquharson Macleod, the second Commissioner, was relieved of his command on October 31, 1880, when he resisted Prime Minister Macdonald in a proposed patronage appointment to the Force. He continued as Stipendiary Magistrate until 1887, when his position was converted to Justice of the newly formed Supreme Court of the North-West Territories. Until 1890, Macleod also served as an *ex officio* member of the North-West Territorial Council, a position he had held since his appointment as Commissioner in 1876.

Macleod died on September 5, 1894, somewhat suddenly and prematurely, just short of his 58th birthday. He was financially unprepared for death. Although Macleod was a well-paid jurist, raising and educating the five children of his 18-year marriage, some attending schools as far away as Toronto, had prevented the accumulation of savings, and he left his widow with only a very few dollars in the bank.[4] Pensions were then still a novelty, viewed by some as designed only to ensure the retention of incompetent employees. Macleod's salary ceased with his death, there was no pension for his widow, and Mary found herself destitute with five children not yet fully educated.[5]

A petition seeking a pension for Macleod's widow went to Ottawa, supported by a number of influential friends of the family. That Canada owed a great debt of gratitude to Macleod for his 20 years of outstanding public service was unquestioned. His unique contribution to the making of Treaty 7, the Blackfoot Treaty, alone had been of inestimable value to the government. But Ottawa refused to grant any financial relief to Macleod's family, because to do so would establish a dangerous precedent. The same refusal was met by the Marquess of Lorne, the former Governor General who toured the West in 1881, and the Earl of Dufferin, also a former Governor General, when they petitioned the British government for at least enough financial support to meet the school bills for the Macleod children.[6]

Mary Macleod became a seamstress. A strong and noble lady, she survived her husband by almost 40 years. She died in 1933 at the age of 81.

This account, unthinkable today, goes far in explaining the wretchedness on the Cree and Blackfoot reservations. If the family of Scottish-born James Macleod, well-deserving and well-connected, could not cut through officialdom's antipathy towards public assistance, or welfare, what hope had the friendless and unloved Plains Indians?

After their surrender at Fort Buford on July 19, 1881, Sitting Bull and his Sioux followers were taken by steamer down the Missouri River to Fort Yates, in today's North Dakota, the administrative site for the Standing Rock Reservation. For three weeks the United States Army reconsidered its guarantee of amnesty and then reneged. From the Secretary of War came the order—there would be no amnesty for Sitting Bull and his immediate following. Sitting Bull was furious, but resistance was futile. At bayonet point he and his people were herded back aboard the steamer and taken farther down the Missouri to the military post of Fort Randall, on the southern border of South Dakota. There, under loose confinement, they were maintained as prisoners of war. Not until May 1883 were they returned to Fort Yates and allowed to join the remainder of their people on the Standing Rock Reservation.

Sitting Bull established himself on the Grand River and challenged the farming life, with some success. He developed a fair herd of both cattle and horses, raised chickens, oats, corn and potatoes. On travels to Bismarck and St. Paul, the famous Sioux chief displayed such star power that an exhibition tour was arranged for him. During the fall of 1884, the "Sitting Bull Combination," made up of Sitting Bull, half a dozen other chiefs, and their wives, drew thousands in New York and Philadelphia.[7]

The next year Sitting Bull toured with the flamboyant William F. Cody in his Buffalo Bill's Wild West Show, appearing in more than a dozen cities, half of them in Canada.[8] After that, James McLaughlin, the Indian Agent at Standing Rock, decided Sitting Bull was becoming too prominent and put a stop to any further tours.

In 1890 an Indian messiah, Wovoka, a Paiute holy man, spoke of a new faith that would carry all believers to a new land, a place that would be pristine, full of buffalo and other game, and devoid of all white people. Believers should dance a Ghost Dance that would put them on the road to this utopia. Those who wore a special Ghost Shirt would be protected from the firearms of the white man.

Wovoka's doctrine was seized upon by the impoverished and suffering Sioux, who saw their traditional culture slipping away from them. By the fall of 1890 the Ghost Dance religion was on the verge of destabilizing Sioux reservations in Nebraska and the Dakotas. White communities grew fearful and the Indian Office sought the assistance of the army.

On Standing Rock, McLaughlin saw an opportunity to rid himself of Sitting Bull and convinced his superiors that arresting and imprisoning the Sioux leader would end the Ghost Dance craze.

In the early morning of December 15, 1890, McLaughlin's agency police, themselves Sioux, attempted to arrest Sitting Bull at his cabin on Grand River. It was a bungled affair. Sitting Bull was killed, together with several followers who attacked the police when the shooting started—some 15 fatalities in all, including six police.

Crowfoot, Sitting Bull's 14-year-old son, named after the great Blackfoot chief back in Canada, and who had surrendered his father's rifle at Fort Buford in July 1881, was dragged from under a blanket and murdered.

When he heard of the death of Sitting Bull, former superintendent James Walsh noted:

> I am glad to learn that Bull is relieved of his miseries even if it took the bullet to do it. A man who wields such power as Bull once did, that of a King, over a wild spirited people cannot endure abject poverty, slavery and beggary without suffering great mental pain and death is a relief ... Bull's confidence and belief in the Great Spirit was stronger than I ever saw in any other man. He trusted to him implicitly ... History does not tell us that a greater Indian than Bull ever lived, he was the Mohammed of his people, the law and king maker of the Sioux.[9]

Following the surrender of Sitting Bull, in July 1881, Walsh, still on extended leave in Ontario, was finally permitted to return to his command at Qu'Appelle, but there was little time remaining to him in the NWMP. During the construction season of 1882, when more than 640 km (400 mi) of steel were laid across the prairies, Walsh made the acquaintance of W.C. Van Horne, the CPR General Manager. The two men got along famously, so much so that they were reportedly seen near Maple Creek joy-riding in a CPR locomotive, Van Horne on the throttle and Walsh working the brake. Van Horne sent Commissioner Irvine a letter thanking the NWMP for its assistance, specifically commending Walsh,[10] but Irvine continued in his campaign to see Walsh ousted from the Force. Prime Minister Macdonald had not forgotten his intention to fire the man he held responsible for Sitting Bull's reluctance to leave Canada and Walsh accepted the inevitable. He resigned effective September 1, 1883. In accordance with the policy of the day, Walsh received for his 10 years of outstanding service the one-time gratuity of $1,166.66. The official history of the NWMP records,

> Of all the officers in the Mounted Police none had given better service to Canada in the great western transition than had Major Walsh. In fact, between 1875 and 1883, no man wearing the red tunic had been called upon to exercise a greater degree of courage, tolerance and tact.[11]

Embittered at the forced termination of his career, Walsh went into business and became the manager of Dominion Coal, Coke and Transportation Company in Winnipeg. His friendship with Van Horne brought him contracts to supply coal to the CPR and Walsh prospered. He became a friend to a rising Liberal politician, Clifford Sifton, appointed Minister of the Interior when Wilfrid Laurier became Prime Minister in 1896. When Walsh supplied Sifton with a memorandum outlining his views on the NWMP, his criticism fell on receptive ears. The Liberals, suspicious that they were dealing with an overly politicized institution that had outlived its usefulness, came close to ordering the dissolution of the Force.[12]

Walsh returned to the NWMP, in a fashion, during the Gold Rush of 1897, when Sifton appointed him Commissioner of the Yukon District and Superintendent of the 250-man force in the Yukon, but reporting directly to Sifton as minister, rather than to the NWMP Commissioner. Walsh's tenure in the Yukon was brief and less than successful. He resigned in under a year amid a storm of political controversy.

Walsh built a fine home in Brockville which he named Indian Cliff, after a prominent feature of the Wood Mountain Uplands, the landmark that he searched for on bitter winter patrols from Fort Walsh. There he died on July 25, 1905, at the age of 65.

The Rebellion that erupted along the valley of the Saskatchewan Rivers in the spring of 1885 first seared, and then shortened, the lives of two of the greatest chiefs ever of the Cree nation, Poundmaker and Big Bear. Both men were unfairly blamed for crimes committed by members of their bands incited by the Métis-inspired but futile protest against injustice. Both were imprisoned, a tragic fate for such noble and freedom-loving souls, and one that destroyed their health and spirit and hastened their deaths.

Poundmaker was charged with complicity in three events, the looting of Battleford, a battle with the Militia under Colonel Otter at Cut Knife Hill, and the capture and robbing of a wagon supply train. The plea that Poundmaker had not ordered or directed any of the incidents, but instead had done his best to dissuade the guilty hot-heads from their actions, failed in the face of his reputation as a powerful leader. At his trial in Regina in August 1885, the eloquent chief spoke on his own behalf:

> I am not guilty. Much that has been said against me is not true. I am
> glad of my works in the Queen's country this spring. What I did was
> for the Great Mother. When my brothers and the pale faces met in
> the fight at Cut Knife Hill I saved the Queen's men. I took their arms

from my brothers and gave them up at Battleford. Everything I could do was done to prevent bloodshed. Had I wanted war, I would not be here now. I would be on the prairies. You did not catch me. I gave myself up. You have got me because I wanted peace.[13]

Sentenced to three years in Stoney Mountain Penitentiary, Poundmaker was released little more than six months later, on March 4, 1886, because of his obvious declining health. After a few weeks of rest on his own reserve, in May Poundmaker headed south to Blackfoot Crossing to visit Crowfoot, his beloved adoptive father. There he met an emotional welcome from Crowfoot, whose lodge was filled with sorrow. In just the last month the Blackfoot chief had lost two sons to disease and his only other natural son was going blind. Poundmaker was Crowfoot's only surviving son who had achieved manhood, and his return was a miracle.[14] In declining health himself, Crowfoot perked up at Poundmaker's appearance and seemed to recover. Poundmaker, too, grew stronger as father and son feasted on each other's company.

It was not to last. On July 4, 1886, during the annual Sun Dance ceremonies, Poundmaker choked on saskatoon berry soup, hemorrhaged and died within minutes. His tuberculosis had killed him at the age of 44.

Big Bear's trial took place at Regina in September 1885, a month after Poundmaker's. His charges related to the killing of nine white people at Frog Lake, the seizing and sacking of the Fort Pitt Hudson's Bay Post, and the battle with the Alberta Field Force at Frenchman's Butte. These actions had been carried out by or under the direction of the Warrior Society who had seized control of Big Bear's band, but the prejudice aroused by the "massacre" at Frog Lake rendered it useless for Big Bear to contend that he had done everything in his power to prevent the crimes. As with Poundmaker, Big Bear's reputation as a powerful chief worked against him.

Big Bear, too, spoke with great eloquence in his own behalf:

I think I should have something to say about the occurrences which brought me here in chains. I knew little of the killing at Frog Lake beyond hearing the shots fired. When any wrong was brewing I did my best to stop it in the beginning. The turbulent ones of the band got beyond my control and shed the blood of those I would have protected . . . When the white men were few in the country I gave them the hand of brotherhood. I am sorry so few are here who can witness for my friendly acts. Can anyone stand out and say that I ordered the death of a priest or an agent? You think I encouraged my people to take part in the trouble. I did not. I advised against it.

The old chief then pleaded for his people, "starving and outcast. If the government does not come to help them before the winter sets in, my band will surely perish."[15]

Big Bear's fate was three years in Stoney Mountain. There he, too, lost his health, but Ottawa did not relent and allow his early release until January 27, 1887. By then the 62-year-old chief was bedridden. Sick, tired and broken in health, body and spirit, Big Bear made his painful way back to Little Pine Reserve, west of Battleford. There, the last of the great chiefs of the western plains to submit to the white man's treaty, he survived one long and humiliating year, abandoned by his band, his wife and most of his family, until death finally released him on January 17, 1888.

During their last and tragically ended visit, Crowfoot and Poundmaker surely discussed how close the older chief had come to being implicated in the North-West Rebellion, in the way Poundmaker had been. Perhaps only the distance between the Blackfoot reservations and the troubles along the North Saskatchewan River enabled Crowfoot and Red Crow to keep their hot-blooded youth out of the insurrection. That and the age-old Blackfoot enmity for the Cree. To the elders it was unthinkable that they could fight side by side with their mortal enemies, even against the whites. An immediate increase in the rations also helped to pacify the situation, but it had been a near-run thing.

Macdonald and Dewdney had worried that the insurrection on the Saskatchewan would spread to the Blackfoot reservations. That fear was shared by the residents of what became southern Alberta. The streets of Fort Macleod and Calgary were barricaded and patrolled by Home Guards. The women and children from Fort Macleod were moved into Calgary.[16]

All this might have been with good cause. The young men on the Blackfoot and Blood reserves were anxious to fight and were dissuaded only with difficulty, but distance and traditional enmity kept them out of the fray.

Thus, Crowfoot and Red Crow and the other Blackfoot and Blood chiefs were counted as loyal, but perhaps for the wrong reasons. No matter. Prime Minister Macdonald was grateful and said so.

Two weeks after Poundmaker's death, Macdonald and Mrs. Macdonald, on their way to Victoria on the newly completed CPR that ran through the northern portion of the Blackfoot Reservation, stopped at Gleichen to pay their respects. Again Crowfoot assembled his fellow chiefs and waited upon a plenipotentiary from Ottawa. As he had been when he addressed Governor

General Lorne, the Blackfoot chief was dressed in rags, this time as mourning for Poundmaker, but once more the Blackfoot chief seized an opportunity to plead for food for his people.

Crowfoot was impressed that the Prime Minister had come to call and expressed a desire to return the visit in Ottawa.[17] Before long, he was given that opportunity. In gratitude for their loyalty, Macdonald invited several Blackfoot, Blood and Cree chiefs to Ontario in the fall of 1886, ostensibly to participate in the unveiling of a monument to honour Joseph Brant, the Six Nations chief who had distinguished himself in the War of 1812. Crowfoot and Red Crow were included, as were Mistawasis and Ahtahkakoop. Escorted by Father Lacombe, Crowfoot was lionized in Montreal, Quebec City and Ottawa.

The travel confirmed Crowfoot's belief in the numerical and technological superiority of the white race, and that he had made the right decision in taking his people under Treaty 7. But he returned to Blackfoot Crossing tired, weakened, and with his illness again in ascendancy. Crowfoot died on April 25, 1890, at the age of 60.

When he refused the American delegation at Fort Walsh in July 1878, White Bird had with him 32 lodges, or about 120 people, but slowly they continued to drift back into the United States. Those who remained moved to Pincher Creek, built strong cabins, and took what employment they could find in order to survive. In 1892, White Bird was murdered by another Nez Perce. After that tragedy, the small settlement broke up, some of its residents crossing the border. By 1900 there were no Nez Perce remaining in Canada.[18]

In the spring of 1884, Gabriel Dumont led a three-man delegation into Montana to invite Louis Riel to come to Batoche and assist the Métis with their protests to Ottawa. When Riel accepted and moved to Batoche, matters soon escalated beyond what many of the Métis had in mind. Thinking to follow the script that had been so successful at Red River in 1869–70, in March 1885 Riel declared another Provisional Government. It was a serious mistake that led rapidly to a clash of arms and defeat.

Louis Riel was the inspiration of the North-West Rebellion of 1885, but Gabriel Dumont was its military commander. After the Métis were defeated at Batoche on May 12, 1885, and Riel surrendered, Dumont made the wise decision to decamp for the United States. Travelling at night, with one companion, in late May he slipped into Montana.

In the summer of 1886 Dumont signed on with Buffalo Bill's Wild West Show, just a year behind Sitting Bull. He toured with the show as a trick shot artist briefly during the next two years and then spent some time in Quebec. Although Dumont had been included in an 1886 Amnesty Proclamation covering the combatants in the Rebellion, he was slow to return to the West and wandered between Montana and Quebec until 1893, when he finally moved back to the Saskatchewan. He built a small log cabin on a relative's farm south of Bellevue, about 16 km (10 mi) from Batoche, where he lived in solitude until his quiet death on May 19, 1906, at the age of 68.

Even though the North-West Rebellion broke out on his watch, Edgar Dewdney carried on as Lieutenant-Governor and Indian Commissioner, retaining Macdonald's full confidence. In the aftermath of the Rebellion, Dewdney acted firmly, perhaps harshly, in regaining control of the Indian situation in the West and ensuring that there would be no further outbreaks.

In the summer of 1888 Dewdney resigned as Lieutenant-Governor and Indian Commissioner and re-entered active politics as the MP for Assiniboia East. He joined Macdonald's cabinet as Minister of the Interior and Superintendent General for Indian Affairs.

In November, 1892, Dewdney returned to British Columbia as Lieutenant-Governor, retiring in 1897 at the end of his five-year term. In spite of his land speculations and years of good salaries, he was not well-to-do and in 1901 returned to surveying. He died at Victoria in 1916 at the age of 80.

Jean-Louis Légaré, after delivering Sitting Bull and his followers to Fort Buford on July 19, 1881, turned his caravan around and headed back to Willow Bunch. His head was full of numbers. Major Brotherton had promised to see that Légaré was "recompensed" if he was able to bring Sitting Bull in to surrender, and now that the deed was done it was time to render an account.

The Willow Bunch trader was substantially out-of-pocket for the care, feeding and transport of 248 Indians for the best part of four months, and the United States government should have been duly grateful to have the elusive Sitting Bull handed over without a shot being fired. Surely Canada, too, would be anxious to show its appreciation for the final departure of the desperate Sioux from its territory. It was a golden opportunity.

Jean-Louis Légaré severely overestimated the gratitude of both the American and the Canadian governments. His bill to the United States War Department was $13,412, and to Ottawa an astounding $48,891, a total of $62,303 in 1881 currency, the equivalent of more than $1,250,000 in 2006 dollars. Not surprisingly, Légaré experienced difficulty in collecting.

A year after the surrender, Ottawa voted $2,000 for Légaré's services, in full payment. Légaré promptly credited his outstanding account with the payment and resubmitted the bill, claiming the balance of $46,891.

The American Army was shocked at the size of Légaré's account. Major Brotherton thought $2,000 would cover all expenses and leave enough for a reasonable bonus, which he agreed was deserved. But Légaré was determined. In 1887, he retained an American attorney and sued the United States government. The proceedings exposed the cost of living on the western plains in 1881. Pemmican was worth 15¢ per .45 kg (1 lb), dried buffalo meat from 10–12¢ according to quality, a sack of flour was $12, tea was $1.50 per .45 kg (1 lb), sugar was 35¢ per .45 kg (1 lb), and tobacco was $1.50 per .45 kg (1 lb). Buffalo hide tipis, or lodges, sold from $10 to $20, according to size.[19]

In 1905, the United States paid Légaré $5,000, again in full settlement. Today the descendants of Jean-Louis Légaré still press for payment of what they contend is the properly due and owing balance of the accounts in both the United States and Canada.

Légaré lived out his life as a prominent member of the Willow Bunch community, a cattle and horse rancher and a businessman. He died there on February 1, 1918 at the age of 76. A nearby regional park has been established in his honour, and a plaque commemorating his life was erected in 1970 by Canada's Historic Sites and Monuments Board. In 1993 the Saskatchewan Legislature enacted The Jean-Louis Légaré Act, stating:

> The people of Saskatchewan hereby recognize the heroic efforts, humane compassion and personal financial sacrifice made by Jean-Louis Légaré with respect to Chief Sitting Bull and his people during their years of refuge in what is now the Province of Saskatchewan.

Not all the Sioux followed Jean-Louis Légaré and Sitting Bull to surrender at Fort Buford. As many as 150 lodges remained at Wood Mountain, most of them drifting back across the line during the next year until only a small band under Black Bull were left. Eking out a living as best they could, they spent long periods camped near Moose Jaw, where they found some employment as labourers. In 1910 Ottawa relented and granted the survivors a small reserve near Wood Mountain (IR 160), where their people had first sought refuge in 1876 and 1877.

Wood Mountain is the last of several Sioux reserves established in Manitoba and Saskatchewan. Beginning in 1874, the early Dakota Sioux refugees from the 1862 Minnesota Uprising were granted reserves based upon 32 ha (80 acres) for each family of five. In Manitoba, Dakota Tipi (IR 1) and Dakota Long Plain (IR 6), near Portage La Prairie, Birdtail Creek (IR 57 and 57A), Oak River (Sioux Valley) (IR 58) and Oak Lake (IR 59), all west of Brandon. A 260-ha (640-acre) reserve (IR 60) on the north slope of Turtle Mountain was dissolved in 1909.

TREATIES: THEN AND NOW

A 1973 Supreme Court of Canada decision in a case brought by the Nisga'a Indians of the Nass Valley in northern British Columbia prompted Ottawa to concede that Aboriginal title might well exist, and to agree that the question should be settled by negotiation. That process with the Nisga'a began in 1976 and brought to the table with the Nisga'a Tribal Council both the government of Canada and the government of British Columbia. Each of the three parties was supported by vast teams of lawyers, consultants, specialists and advisors. In 1998, an agreement was achieved. The contrast between the sophistication and reach of the Nisga'a Treaty, and Treaties 4, 6 and 7 negotiated in mere days on the western plains more than 120 years earlier, is remarkable and worthy of comment. A very small sample of comparisons between Nisga'a of 1998 and Treaty 7 of 1877:

Size and Coverage: The text of Treaty 7 consists of 22 paragraphs easily printed on four pages and just nine of those paragraphs were needed to cover the promises of the Queen. The Nisga'a Treaty, with side agreements and appendices, consists of more than 1,500 pages of sophisticated provisions covering in detail such subjects as land ownership, resources (forest, water, mineral, fish, fur, migratory waterfowl), environment, government, taxation, administration of justice, etc.

Land Surrender: Treaty 7 surrendered 90,650 km^2 (35,000 mi^2) to Ottawa. Under Nisga'a, Ottawa and British Columbia grant full fee simple ownership of 1,992 km^2 (770 mi^2) to Nisga'a, including forest and mineral resources.

Governance: Unknown to the bands who signed Treaty 7, they were already wards of the federal government under The Indian Act, 1876. Nisga'a provides that the Nisga'a people are to be self-governing and may operate their own justice system.

Consideration: Under Treaty 7, Ottawa paid annually $5 to each band member ($15 to Councillors, $25 to Chiefs), $2,000 annually to the band for ammunition, plus some tools, cattle breeding stock, farm implements and the like. Under Nisga'a, Ottawa agreed to pay $190 million over 15 years.

This is a slight illustration of what would be involved if treaty negotiations were required to be undertaken today to extinguish the Aboriginal title on the Canadian Plains. For more than 10 years, the governments of Canada and Saskatchewan and the Federation of Saskatchewan Indian Nations have been engaged in a process to achieve agreement on what should be a fair and proper understanding and interpretation of the Saskatchewan treaties in the modern world.

In Saskatchewan, the Standing Buffalo (IR 78), abutting Echo Lake in the Qu'Appelle Valley, and White Cap (IR 94), along the eastern bank of the South Saskatchewan River south of Saskatoon, were taken up in the late 1870s by bands of Dakota Sioux who had been in Canada since 1862. In 1894 a small reserve named Wahpeton (IR 94A) was established north of Prince Albert to accommodate a number of Dakota Sioux who had settled there.

Although the Sioux in Canada were granted these reserves, and in a few cases some tools and implements to enable them to begin farming, this was by way of gift and not as of right. They were not regarded as possessing any Aboriginal rights in Canada, were not included in the Canadian Treaties, and received none of the benefits that were paid to Canadian Indians.

For 20 years after the signing of Treaty 7 in 1877, Ottawa negotiated no further treaties for the simple reason that it had no need for the northern lands that were unsuitable for agriculture and settlement. Finally, in 1899 Treaty 8 was negotiated, covering what six years later became the northern half of Alberta, much of northern Saskatchewan, and the North-West Territories. In 1905 and 1906, Treaty 9, the "James Bay Treaty," took in all of northern Ontario to the shores of Hudson and James Bay. Also in 1906, Treaty 10 covered the remaining portion of northern Saskatchewan. Then, in 1921, Treaty 11 reached north to the Arctic Ocean east of Yukon Territory, and Ottawa considered that it had completed all treaties that would be required of it.

When British Columbia entered Confederation in 1871, since none of its lands were taken for "the purposes of the Dominion," it was not thought necessary to negotiate treaties with the many bands of Indians in the province. Thus, except for some very early treaties on Vancouver Island, the entire territory of the huge province remained unaffected by land surrenders. Ottawa and Victoria carried out their programs under the assumption that any Aboriginal title had somehow been lost without the necessity of formal surrender. In 2014 the Supreme Court of Canada held that Aboriginal title to ancestral land is still owned by native Canadians.

The site of the 1876 encounter between units of the United States Army under the command of Lieutenant Colonel George Armstrong Custer and the Sioux and Cheyenne Indians continues to change in name and character. First designated as a *National Cemetery* it later converted to the *Custer National Cemetery*, then to *Custer Battlefield National Monument*. Then, in 1991, recognizing that there were two sides to the engagement, it became the *Little Bighorn Battlefield National Monument*.

Finally, in 2013, in acknowledgement of the many Indians who lost their lives in the battle, but not without dissension, a permanent *Indian Memorial* was dedicated on the site.

. . . .

sitting bull

. . . .

while he rose to
crumple to the ground with his son
did his life really flow before the darkening light
his years in these southern hills
older than the meaning of name
and the gods i will never know
or the lying faces of men who betrayed him
giving him an ultimatum:
starve or surrender to the enemy

. . . .

he may not have had time to remember
the words he left us with at wood mountain:
the great spirit provided for both white and red men
but white man has grown powerful
and defies the gods—
is trying to undo all that wakantanka has done

—from Andrew Suknaski, "Poem to Sitting Bull
and his son Crowfoot," *Wood Mountain Poems*
(Toronto: Macmillan, 1976)

ENDNOTES

ENDNOTES TO PREFACE (PP. XIII–XVIII)

1. Royal was added in 1904. The Force became the Royal Canadian Mounted Police in 1920 when it assumed national policing responsibility.
2. Replicas of the original NWMP buildings have since been created at this site, which is now maintained as a provincial historic site.

ENDNOTES TO CHAPTER 1 (PP. 1–14)

1. Affidavits of Lydia B. Johnson and Charlotte Johnson Opheim, South Dakota State Historical Society, Pierre, South Dakota, August 6, 1943.
2. Francis Parkman, *La Salle and the Discovery of the Great West* (New York: New American Library, 1963), 228–29.
3. The Missouri was measured at 4,097 km (2,546 mi) in 1895. Subsequent engineering has removed many of these kilometres and the length today is considered to be 3,767 km (2,341 mi).
4. Stephen A. Ambrose, *Undaunted Courage: Meriwether Lewis, Thomas Jefferson, and the Opening of the American West* (New York: Simon & Schuster, 1996), 105, 202.
5. James A. Hanson, *When Skins Were Money: A History of the Fur Trade* (Chadron, NE: Museum of the Fur Trade, 2005), 104.
6. Harold A. Innis, *The Fur Trade in Canada: An Introduction to Canadian Economic History* (1930; Toronto: University of Toronto Press, 1970), 95.
7. Hanson, *When Skins Were Money*, 62.
8. Ibid., 65.
9. The full title of the corporation was The Governor and Company of Adventurers of England Trading into Hudson's Bay.
10. Douglas MacKay, *The Honourable Company: A History of the Hudson's Bay Company* (Toronto: McClelland and Stewart, 1966), 39.
11. Cumberland House is often described as the first inland trading post of the Hudson's Bay Company, but that title properly belongs to Henley House, established on the Albany and Kinogami Rivers much earlier, in 1744, according to Dennis F. Johnson, *York Boats of the Hudson's Bay Company* (Calgary: Fifth House, 2006), 12. According to Innis, Henley House dates back to 1720. See Innis, *The Fur Trade in Canada*, 144, note 91.
12. Marjorie Wilkins Campbell, *The North West Company* (Toronto: Macmillan, 1957), 81.

13. Hanson, *When Skins Were Money*, 104.

14. Ibid., 105.

15. Ambrose, *Undaunted Courage*, 185.

16. Ibid., 187.

17. Innis, *The Fur Trade in Canada*, 237–38.

18. Robert M. Utley, *After Lewis and Clark: Mountain Men and the Paths to the Pacific* (Lincoln: University of Nebraska Press, 2004), 11, 12.

19. Joel Overholser, *Fort Benton: World's Most Innermost Fort* (Fort Benton: River & Plains Society, 1987), 6.

20. Robert Vaughn, *Then and Now: Thirty-Six Years in the Rockies, 1864–1900* (Helena: Farcountry Press, 2001), 75–83.

21. Overholser, *Fort Benton*, 7–9.

22. Brock Silversides, *Fort de Prairies: The Story of Fort Edmonton* (Surrey, BC: Heritage House Publishing, 2005), 19.

23. Robert C. Carriker, *Father Peter John De Smet, Jesuit in the West* (Norman: University of Oklahoma Press, 1995), 93.

ENDNOTES TO CHAPTER 2 (PP. 15–24)

1. John E. Parsons, *West on the 49th Parallel: Red River to the Rockies, 1872–1876* (New York: William Morrow and Company, 1963), 4.

2. *The Convention respecting fisheries, boundary, and the restoration of slaves between the United States and the United Kingdom of Great Britain and Ireland*, also known as the *London Convention, Anglo-American Convention of 1818, Convention of 1818*, or simply the *Treaty of 1818*, was a treaty signed in 1818 between the United States and the United Kingdom. It resolved standing boundary issues between the two nations, and allowed for joint occupation and settlement of the Oregon Country, see especially Article II.

3. In 1846 the United States and Britain extended the 49th Parallel as boundary to the Strait of Georgia and left Vancouver Island as British Territory. The waters between Vancouver Island and the mainland remained in a confused state for another 25 years.

4. The device caught on. In 1858 the northern boundary of the colony of British Columbia was fixed at the 55th Parallel and in 1863 moved to the 60th Parallel. The 60th was also employed as the northern boundary of Alberta and Saskatchewan when they were formed in 1905, and of Manitoba when it was extended northward in 1912. The 4th Meridian became the boundary between Alberta and Saskatchewan, a decision that was criticized for not taking geography into account.

5. Irene M. Spry (ed.), *The Papers of the Palliser Expedition 1857–1860* (Toronto: The Champlain Society, 1968), liii.

6. Mary Beth LaDow, "The Medicine Line: Nations and Identity on the Montana-Saskatchewan Frontier, 1877–1920" (PhD dissertation, Brandeis University, 1994), 30.

7. Francis M. Carroll, *A Good and Wise Measure: The Search for the Canadian-American Boundary, 1783–1842* (Toronto: University of Toronto Press, 2001), 123.

8. Wallace Stegner, *Wolf Willow: A History, A Story, and A Memory of the Last Plains Frontier* (New York: Viking Press, 1962), 84.

9. Joseph Kinsey Howard, *Strange Empire: A Narrative of the Northwest* (New York: William Morrow and Company, 1952), 25 and 49.

10. Two hundred years later, the Lewis and Clark adventure has been ranked as "the greatest expedition ever undertaken in the history of this country (the U.S.)." Ambrose, *Undaunted Courage*, cover, a sweeping statement that takes in even the 1969 moon landing. Yet, more than 75 years ago, a pre-eminent historian and writer on the American West found considerable fault with Lewis and Clark: "The journals of the Lewis and Clark expedition are, however, meager and unsatisfactory. Why a man of (President) Jefferson's philosophical and scientific turn of mind should have been unable to select more capable men for the enterprise, keen observers with trained minds, is hard to understand. Throughout the journal there is a lack of specific detail, a vagueness, an absence of names of persons and places in connection with episodes related. The records fail to reveal in their authors much knowledge of geology, physical geography, botany, zoology, or anthropology. Of course the fact remains that the expedition succeeded in its main objective: it went to its destination and returned, and this success tends to obscure the imperfections of the report." Walter Prescott Webb, *The Great Plains* (Boston: Ginn and Company, 1931), 143–44.

11. Sheila McManus, *The Line Which Separates: Race, Gender, and the Making of the Alberta-Montana Borderlands* (Edmonton: University of Alberta Press, 2005), 4.

12. D'Arcy Jenish, *Epic Wanderer: David Thompson and the Mapping of the Canadian West* (Toronto: Doubleday Canada, 2003), 214.

13. Doug Owram, *Promise of Eden: The Canadian Expansionist Movement and the Idea of the West, 1856–1900* (Toronto: University of Toronto Press, 1980), 67.

14. Ibid., 68.

15. Canada, Parliament, *Sessional Papers, 1872*, Paper No. 22, 14.

16. Sherm Ewing, *The Range* (Missoula: Mountain Press, 1990), 121.

17. See for example Vanguard, Saskatchewan, July 3, 2000.

18. *New York Times* (April 28, 2002).

19. Denver *Rocky Mountain News* (June 22, 1999).

20. Quoted in Irene M. Spry, "Early Visitors to the Canadian Prairies," in Brian W. Blouet and Merlin P. Lawson (eds.), *Images of the Plains: The Role of Human Nature in Settlement* (Lincoln: University of Nebraska Press, 1975) 175.

ENDNOTES TO CHAPTER 3 (PP. 25–38)

1. Ambrose, *Undaunted Courage*, 74–75.

2. Ibid., 77.

3. H. George Classen, *Thrust and Counterthrust: The Genesis of the Canada-United States Boundary* (Toronto: Longmans, 1965), 115.

4. Lower Louisiana, including New Orleans, was transferred at New Orleans on December 20, 1803.

5. http://memory.loc.gov/ammem/amlaw.louisianapurchase.html

6. *The Times Atlas of World History* (London: Times Books, 1984), 220.

7. Alvin C. Gluek, Jr., *Minnesota and the Manifest Destiny of the Canadian Northwest: A Study in Canadian-American Relations* (Toronto: University of Toronto Press, 1965), 215.

8. Ibid., 193.

9. Ibid., 206.

10. Ibid., vii.

11. Ibid., 206–07.

12. Webb, *The Great Plains*, 153.

13. Owram, *Promise of Eden*, 76.

14. Ibid., 77.

15. W.L. Morton, *The Critical Years: The Union of British North America, 1857–1873* (Toronto: McClelland and Stewart, 1964), 212.

16. Ibid., 223.

17. British North America Act, 1867, 30–31 Vict., c. 3 (U.K.) section 146.

18. "John A. Macdonald, Campaign Speeches, August 1867," in D. Owen Carrigan, *Canadian Party Platforms, 1867–1968* (Toronto: Copp Clark, 1968).

19. Peter C. Newman, *Empire of the Bay: The Company of Adventurers that Seized a Continent* (Toronto: Penguin Books, 1998), 575–76.

20. When the western provinces were surveyed for settlement, a township plan was utilized that created sections of 260 ha (640 acres) divided into quarter sections of 65 ha (160 acres). Each township contains 36 sections, numbered consecutively. In each township, Section 8 and all but the northeast quarter of Section 26, were granted to the Hudson's Bay Company (in every fifth township the Company received all of Section 26). The Company gradually sold these holdings; by 1928 only 1,011,750 ha (2,500,000 acres) remained. The last lands were disposed of in 1984.

21. "Leveraged buy-out" usually describes a technique where the assets of the acquired property are utilized to fund their own purchase.

22. A later example would be the funding of the Canadian Pacific Railway by the grant of more of the fertile lands of the west. A much later example, in the minds of many westerners, was the National Energy Program of 1980, by which the government in Ottawa transferred control of the oil and gas industry to the federal government.

23. Lewis Herbert Thomas, *The Struggle for Responsible Government in the North-West Territories, 1870–97* (Toronto: University of Toronto Press, 1956), 14.

24. "Fertile acres" was a defined term in the transaction, covering the area described in the text.

25. Newman, *Empire of the Bay*, 575–76.

26. Chester Martin, *Dominion Lands Policy* (Toronto: McClelland and Stewart, 1973), 9.

27. Margaret A. Ormsby, *British Columbia: A History* (Toronto: Macmillan, 1964), 244.

28. Alexander Begg, *History of British Columbia from its earliest discovery to the present time* (Toronto: William Briggs, 1894), 393.

29. Canada, Parliament, *Sessional Papers, 1872*, Paper No. 22, 60.

ENDNOTES TO CHAPTER 4 (PP. 39–58)

1. Georgetown is about 32 km (20 mi) north of present day Fargo/Moorhead, North Dakota.

2. Colonel Wolseley on his arrival in 1870, quoted in Douglas Hill, *The Opening of the Canadian West: Where Strong Men Gathered* (New York: John Day Co., 1967), 89.

3. Gerhard J. Ens, *Homeland to Hinterland: The Changing World of the Red River Métis in the Nineteenth Century* (Toronto: University of Toronto Press, 1996), 140.

4.   Howe to Macdonald, October 16, 1869. Quoted in Joseph Pope, *Memoirs of the Right Honourable Sir John Alexander Macdonald, G.C.B., first Prime Minister of the Dominion of Canada* (Toronto: Musson, n.d.), 415.

5.   Canada, *Sessional Papers, 1870*, 5. McDougall despatch, October 31, 1869.

6.   Canada, House of Commons, *Debates*, February 21, 1870, 87.

7.   Canada, *Sessional Papers, 1870*, 11.

8.   Joseph Howe, letter to McDougall, October 31, 1869. Pamphlet, *Red River Insurrection, Hon. Wm. McDougall's Conduct Reviewed* (Montreal: Lovell, 1870), 15.

9.   Morton, *The Critical Years*, 240.

10.   Alexander McArthur, *On the Causes of the Rising in the Red River Settlement, 1869–70* (Winnipeg: Manitoba Historical and Scientific Society, Publication No. 1, 1882), 2.

11.   Robert Machray, *Life of Robert Machray, D.D., LL.D., D.C.L., Archbishop of Rupert's Land, Primate of all Canada, Prelate of the Order of St. Michael and St. George* (Toronto: Macmillan Co. of Canada, 1909), 168.

12.   Canada, *Journals of the House of Commons*, vol. 8, 1874, Appendix no. 6, "Report of the Select Committee on the Causes of the Difficulties in the North-West Territory in 1869–70," Taché deposition, 9.

13.   Ibid., 10.

14.   Morton, *The Critical Years*, 240.

15.   Joseph Andrew Chisholm, *The Speeches and Public Letters of Joseph Howe*, vol. 2 (Halifax: Chronicle Pub. Co., 1909), 595. Howe spoke to the House on February 21, 1870.

16.   Canada, *Sessional Papers, 1870*, No. 12, "Dennis Memorandum of Facts and Circumstances connected with the active opposition by the French half-breeds in this settlement to the prosecution of the Government surveys, Fort Garry, 11 October, 1869."

17.   Ibid.

18.   Morton, *The Critical Years*, 240.

19.   William Preston, *The Life and Times of Lord Strathcona* (London: Eveleigh Nash, 1914), 171–72.

20.   Chisholm, *Speeches and Public Letters*, 594. This version differs somewhat from that contained in Hansard, but Chisholm states (at 593) that "His (Howe's) speeches, however, were not fully reported." Howe's distance estimate was exaggerated. Fort Abercrombie was 400 km (250 mi) south of Fort Garry. See J.J. Hargrave, *Red River* (Montreal: Lovell, 1871), 503.

21.   Chisholm, *Speeches and Public Letters*, 594.

22.   Ibid., 596.

23.   Howe to Edward O'Brien, October 23, 1869. Quoted in Beckles Willson, *The Life of Lord Strathcona and Mount Royal* (London: Cassell and Company, 1915), 175–76.

24.   Chisholm, *Speeches and Public Letters*, 585. In his by-election, Howe publicly took credit for have secured for Nova Scotia some $220,000 annually for a ten-year term, all being improved terms of Union due to the protest he led.

25.   Ibid., 590.

26.   Alexander Begg, *The Creation of Manitoba; or, A History of the Red River Troubles* (Toronto: Hunter, Rose, 1871), 33.

27.   Canada. *Sessional Papers, 1870*, 20.

28.   Macdonald to Sidney Smith, July 12, 1869. Quoted in Thomas, *The Struggle for Responsible Government*, 15.

29.   Ibid.

30. Macdonald to J.Y. Brown, October 14, 1869, quoted in D.N. Sprague, *Canada and the Métis, 1869–1885* (Waterloo: Wilfrid Laurier University Press, 1988), 30.

31. Gluek, *Minnesota and the Manifest Destiny*, 210–11.

32. Taylor letter of December 17, 1861, to United States Secretary of War, Chase, quoted in Leonard Bertram Irwin, *Pacific Railways and Nationalism in the Canadian-American Northwest, 1845–1873* (New York: Greenwood, 1968), 67.

33. Ibid., 68.

34. Gluek, *Minnesota and the Manifest Destiny*, 218–19.

35. George F. G. Stanley, "The 1870s," in J.M.S. Careless and R. Craig Brown (eds.), *The Canadians 1867–1967* (Toronto: Macmillan, 1967), 46.

36. Hamilton Fish to J.W. Taylor, December 30, 1869, quoted in George Stanley, *The Birth of Western Canada: A History of the Riel Rebellions* (Toronto: University of Toronto Press, 1960), 59–60 and 416.

37. Morton, *The Critical Years*, 240.

38. George Stanley, *Louis Riel* (Toronto: Ryerson, 1963), 81.

39. James G. Snell, "American Neutrality and the Red River Resistance, 1869–1870," *Prairie Forum* 4, no. 2 (1979): 183, 189.

40. Stanley, *The Birth of Western Canada*, 58. Joseph Kinsey Howard, *Strange Empire: A Narrative of the Northwest* (New York: Morrow, 1952), 135. Howard states that Taché revealed the American offer in "official testimony," but there is no identification of where and when this testimony was given. Howard died before his work was published and his editor was unable to include annotations, 4-5.

41. Ibid.

42. Howard, *Strange Empire*, 135.

43. Dale Gibson, *Attorney for the Frontier: Enos Stutsman* (Winnipeg: University of Manitoba Press, 1983), 5.

44. St. Paul *Pioneer*, January 21, 1870, as quoted in Gibson, *Attorney for the Frontier*, 136.

45. Gibson, *Attorney for the Frontier*, 104.

46. Ibid.,109.

47. Ibid., 110.

48. Stanley, *The Birth of Western Canada*, 71.

49. Gibson, *Attorney for the Frontier*, 117.

50. Canada. *Sessional Papers, 1870*, Vol. 5, No. 12, 21.

51. William McDougall, *Eight Letters to Hon. Joseph Howe, Secretary of State for The Provinces* (Toronto: Hunter, Rose & Co., 1870), 36–37.

52. Canada, *Sessional Papers, 1870*, Vol. 5, No. 12, Braun to Dennis, October 4, 1869.

53. Howard, *Strange Empire*, 104–05.

54. Stanley, *Louis Riel*, 79.

55. Canada, *Sessional Papers, 1870*, Vol. 5, No. 12, 4.

ENDNOTES TO CHAPTER 5 (PP. 59–64)

1. "Spectator" to St. Paul *Daily Press*, December 4, 1869, published December 21, 1869, as quoted in Gibson, *Attorney for the Frontier*, 122.

2. Donald Creighton, *John A. Macdonald: The Old Chieftain* (Toronto: Macmillan Co. of Canada, 1955), 48.

3. Ibid., 51.

4. *Minutes of the Executive Council of Canada*, February 18, 1857, as quoted in Irwin, *Pacific Railways and Nationalism*, 44.

5. Macdonald to Rose, December 5, 1869, as quoted in Creighton, *John A. Macdonald*, 49.

6. Stutsman to Grant, November 2, 1869. Quoted in Beckles Willson, *The Life of Lord Strathcona & Mount Royal* (London/Toronto: Cassell, 1915), 291.

7. Gibson, *Attorney for the Frontier*, 120.

8. Ibid., 124.

9. *Red River Insurrection*, 47.

10. Macdonald to John Rose, December 31, 1869, as quoted in Pope, *Memoirs of the Right Honourable Sir John Alexander Macdonald*, 414–16.

11. Macdonald to C.J. Brydges, January 28, 1870, as quoted in Creighton, *John A. Macdonald*, 54–55.

ENDNOTES TO CHAPTER 6 (PP. 65–76)

1. Canada, *Sessional Papers, 1870*, Vol. 5, No. 12, 95. McDougall to Louis Riel, Esq., December 13, 1869.

2. Howe to McDougall, December 10, 1869, as quoted in Preston, *The Life and Times of Lord Strathcona*, 212.

3. Preston, *The Life and Times of Lord Strathcona*, 211.

4. St. Paul *Pioneer*, January 4, 1870, as quoted in Gibson, *Attorney for the Frontier*, 128.

5. Snell, "American Neutrality and the Red River Resistance," 189.

6. Gluek, *Minnesota and the Manifest Destiny*, 269.

7. Ibid., 269.

8. Stanley, *The Birth of Western Canada*, 103.

9. Stanley, *Louis Riel*, 117.

10. Gluek, *Minnesota and the Manifest Destiny*, 276–77.

11. Creighton, *John A. Macdonald*, 54.

12. Gluek, *Minnesota and the Manifest Destiny*, 283.

13. Snell, "American Neutrality and the Red River Resistance," 183.

14. Ibid., 185.

15. Ibid., 186.

16. Macdonald to Rose, February 23, 1870 as quoted in Stanley, *Louis Riel*, 141.

17. Stanley, *Louis Riel*, 141.

18. W.L. Morton, *Manitoba: The Birth of a Province* (Winnipeg: Manitoba Record Society, 1965) 47.

19. A.C. Gluek, *Manitoba and the Hudson's Bay Company* (Winnipeg: University of Winnipeg Press, 1973), 2.

20. Snell, "American Neutrality and the Red River Resistance," 193.

21. The western boundary of the new province of Manitoba. Portage la Prairie was not included in the first draft of the Manitoba Act, but the boundary was altered in response to Opposition criticism.

22. W.L. Morton, "The Bias of Prairie Politics," in Donald Swainson (ed.), *Historical Essays on the Prairie Provinces* (Toronto: McClelland and Stewart, 1970).

23. George Woodcock, *Gabriel Dumont: The Métis Chief and His Lost World* (Edmonton: Hurtig, 1975), 19.

ENDNOTES TO CHAPTER 7 (PP. 77–101)

1. Robert M. Utley, *Frontier Regulars: The United States Army and the Indian, 1866–1890* (New York: Macmillan, 1973), 198.

2. Stan Gibson and Jack Hayne, *Notes on an Obscure Massacre*, IM Diversity Inc. at http://www.imdiversity.com/article_detail.asp?Article_ID=1536

3. Ibid.

4. Jared Diamond, *Guns, Germs, and Steel: The Fates of Human Societies* (New York: W.W. Norton & Company, 1999), 213.

5. Ibid., 210.

6. Quoted in Robert Boyd, *The Coming of the Spirit of Pestilence: Introduced Infectious Diseases and Population Decline among Northwest Coast Indians, 1774–1874* (Vancouver: University of British Columbia Press, 1999), 14.

7. Francis Jennings as quoted in James Wilson, *The Earth Shall Weep: A History of Native America* (New York: Grove Press, 1998), 77.

8. Charles C. Mann, "1491," *The Atlantic Monthly* (March 2002): 44–45.

9. E. Wagner Stearn and Allen E. Stern, *The Effect of Smallpox on the Destiny of the Amerindian* (Boston: Bruce Humphries, Inc., 1945), 42.

10. Ibid., 47.

11. Arthur J. Ray, *Indians in the Fur Trade: Their Role as Trappers, Hunters, and Middlemen in the Lands Southwest of Hudson Bay, 1660–1870* (Toronto: University of Toronto Press, 1974), 105.

12. Elizabeth A. Fenn, *Pox Americana: The Great North American Smallpox Epidemic of 1775–1783* (New York: Hill and Wang, 2001), 193.

13. Ibid.

14. Ibid.

15. Mary Helen Richards, "Cumberland House, Two Hundred Years of History," *Saskatchewan History* 27, no. 3 (Autumn 1974): 109.

16. Daniel Francis, *Battle for the West: Fur Traders and the Birth of Western Canada* (Edmonton: Hurtig, 1982), 42.

17. Edwin Thompson Denig, *The Assiniboine* (Regina: Canadian Plains Research Center, 2000), 5.

18. David Thompson, *David Thompson's Narrative, 1784–1812* (Toronto: Champlain Society, 1962), 323, 336.

19. Michael K. Trimble, *An Ethnohistorical Interpretation of the Spread of Smallpox in the Northern Plains* (Columbia, MO: Department of Anthropology, University of Missouri-Columbia, 1979), 38.

20. Wilson, *The Earth Shall Weep*, 263.

21. Bernard DeVoto, *Across the Wide Missouri* (Boston: Houghton Mifflin, 1947), 287.

22. Ibid., 289.

23. Ibid., 297.

24. Edwin Thomas Denig, *Five Indian Tribes of the Upper Missouri: Sioux, Arickaras, Assiniboines, Crees, Crows* (Norman: University of Oklahoma Press, 1961), 71.

25. Issac I. Stevens, *Narrative and Final Report of Explorations For a Route For a Pacific Railroad*, vol 12, book 1 (Washington, DC: United States Senate, 1855, 1860).

26. Trimble, *An Ethnohistorical Interpretation*, 74–75.

27. DeVoto, *Across the Wide Missouri*, 295.

28. Ray, *Indians in the Fur Trade*, 188–91.

29. John Maclean, *McDougall of Alberta: Life of Rev. John McDougall, D.D., Pathfinder of Empire and Prophet of the Plains* (Toronto: Ryerson, 1927), 38.

30. Ibid., 207.

31. Ibid.

32. William Butler, *The Great Lone Land: A Narrative of Travel and Adventure in the North-West of America* (Edmonton: Hurtig, 1968), 369.

33. MacGregor, *Father Lacombe*, 205.

34. Butler, *The Great Lone Land*, 370.

35. Gary Abrams, *Prince Albert, The First Century, 1866–1966* (Saskatoon: Modern Press, 1976), 11.

36. Butler, *The Great Lone Land*, 369

37. Ibid., 372.

38. Isaac Cowie, *Company of Adventurers: A Narrative of Seven Years in the Service of the Hudson's Bay Company during 1867–1874 on the Great Buffalo Plains* (Lincoln: University of Nebraska Press, 1993), 382.

39. John Upton Terrell, *Land Grab: The Truth About "The Winning of the West"* (New York: The Dial Press, 1972), 175–77.

40. DeVoto, *Across the Wide Missouri*, 296–97.

41. Gerald L. Berry, *The Whoop-Up Trail (Alberta-Montana Relationships)* (Edmonton: Applied Art Products, 1953), 15.

42. Butler, *The Great Lone Land*, 360.

43. DeVoto, *Across the Wide Missouri*, 283.

44. Howard, *Strange Empire*, 258.

45. John Macoun, *Manitoba and the Great Northwest* (Guelph, ON: World Publishing, 1882), 111, 112.

46. Maclean, *McDougall of Alberta*, 43.

47. Butler, *The Great Lone Land*, 369.

48. Hugh A. Dempsey, *Firewater: The Impact of the Whisky Trade on the Blackfoot Nation* (Calgary: Fifth House, 2002), 60.

49. Thomas, *The Struggle for Responsible Government*, 47.

50. E.H. Oliver, *The Canadian North-West: Its early development and legislative records: minutes of the councils of the Red River Colony and the Northern Department of Rupert's Land*, vol. 2 (Ottawa: Government Printing Bureau, 1915), 977.

51. Dempsey, *Firewater*, 61.

52. Cowie, *Company of Adventurers*, 313–15.

53. John S. Milloy, *The Plains Cree: Trade, Diplomacy and War, 1790 to 1870* (Winnipeg: University of Manitoba Press, 1988), 115.

54. Butler, *The Great Lone Land*, 368.

55. Ibid., 371.

56. William Pearce, "unpublished manuscript," National Archives of Canada, C.F. 5574, P4, vol. 2, 181–82.

57. C.A. Magrath interview, *The Last Great (Inter-tribal) Indian Battle* (Lethbridge: Lethbridge Historical Society, Occasional Paper No. 30, 1997), 8.

58. Ibid., 13.

59. Ibid.

60. Ibid., 21.

61. Cowie, *Company of Adventurers*, 414.
62. MacGregor, *Father Lacombe*, 206.
63. Arthur J. Ray, Jim Miller and Frank J. Tough, *Bounty and Benevolence: A History of Saskatchewan Treaties* (Montreal: McGill-Queen's University Press, 2000), 94.
64. John McDougall, *In the Days of the Red River Rebellion* (Toronto: William Briggs, 1911), 130.
65. James Mooney, *The Aboriginal Population of America North of Mexico* (Washington: Government Printing Office, 1928), as quoted in Andrew Isenberg, *The Destruction of the Bison: An Environmental History, 1750–1920* (Cambridge: Cambridge University Press, 2000), 59.
66. James G. MacGregor, *Vision of an Ordered Land* (Saskatoon: Western Producer Prairie Books, 1981), 50.

ENDNOTES TO CHAPTER 8 (PP. 103–121)

1. Eric W. Morse, *Fur Trade Canoe Routes of Canada/Then and Now* (Ottawa: Queen's Printer, 1969), 87–88.
2. Marjorie Wilkins Campbell, *The North West Company* (Toronto: Macmillan, 1957), 44.
3. James P. Ronda, *Astoria & Empire* (Lincoln: University of Nebraska Press, 1990), 88–92.
4. Hanson, *When Skins Were Money*, 46.
5. Ibid., 96.
6. Harold A. Innis, *The Fur Trade in Canada* (Toronto: University of Toronto, 1970), 238.
7. Ens, *Homeland to Hinterland*, 42.
8. Alexander Ross, *The Red River Settlement* (Edmonton: Hurtig, 1972), 249.
9. Father George Belcourt, "Hunting Buffalo on the Northern Plains: A Letter from Father Belcourt," *North Dakota History* 38, no. 3 (Summer 1971): 335.
10. Johnson, *York Boats of the Hudson's Bay Company*, 30.
11. Ibid., 50.
12. Ross, *The Red River Settlement*, 374.
13. Stanley, *Louis Riel*, 15.

ENDNOTES TO CHAPTER 9 (PP. 123–132)

1. This account is based mainly upon the following works: L'Abbé G. Dugas, *Histoire de l'Ouest Canadien de 1822 à 1869* (Montreal: Librairie Beauchemin, 1906), 119–30; William L. Morton, *The Battle at the Grand Coteau, July 13 and 14, 1851* (Winnipeg: Papers of the Historical and Scientific Society of Manitoba, Series III, Number 16, 1961); George Woodcock, *Gabriel Dumont* (Edmonton: Hurtig, 1975), 55–63.
2. On his return to his parish of St. François Xavier, Father Lafleche recorded the following entry: "On July 13, 1851, we have buried near the Cheyenne River, the body of Jean Baptiste Mal a Terre, slaughtered the same day by (Sioux). We regained the cut off feet and hands, the chopped off hair and the cracked skull, and the brains scattered on the soil, having buried the body and also three bullets and 67 arrows planted in the body. Being present at the internment Pascal B—— and Charles Montaine who have undersigned and others who have not signed. *Louis Lafleche*." Manitoba Archives, St. Francis-Xavier Parish, 1834–1850 Register, MG 7, D 6, M 38–39, sheet/page 55.

ENDNOTES TO CHAPTER 10 (PP. 133–144)

1. Simpson to Lewes, June 28, 1841, as quoted in Barry Cooper, *Alexander Kennedy Isbister: A Respectable Critic of the Honourable Company* (Ottawa: Carleton University Press, 1988), 19.
2. Ens, *Homeland to Hinterland*, 76.
3. Ibid., 79.
4. Stevens, *Narrative and Final Report*.
5. Jean D'Artigue, *Six Years in the Canadian North-West* (Belleville, ON: Mika, 1973 [orig. pub. 1882]), 125.
6. Marcel Giraud, *The Métis in the Canadian West*, vol. 2, (Edmonton: University of Alberta Press, 1986), 377.
7. Ens, *Homeland to Hinterland*, 150–51.
8. Alexander Morris, *The Treaties of Canada with the Indians of Manitoba and the North-West Territories, including the negotiations on which they are based, and other information relating thereto* (Saskatoon: Fifth House, 1991 [orig. pub. 1880]), 123.
9. This account is based upon that found in Woodcock, *Gabriel Dumont*, 93–110.
10. Stanley, *Louis Riel*, 182.
11. Woodcock, *Gabriel Dumont*, 110.
12. Ibid., 181.
13. Ibid., 118–19. In his later years Gabriel Dumont thought he led the last hunt in 1880, but it seems that 1881 was the final year.
14. Giraud, *The Métis in the Canadian West*, 387.
15. Woodcock, *Gabriel Dumont*, Howard, *Strange Empire*, and Stegner, *Wolf Willow*.
16. R. *v.* Powley, [2003] 2 S.C.R. 207, 2003 SCC 43, 51.

ENDNOTES TO CHAPTER 11 (PP. 145–184)

1. Canada, Parliament, *Sessional Papers*, *1872*, Paper No. 22, Howe to Simpson, May 5, 1871.
2. Ibid.
3. Ibid., Simpson to Howe, 9.
4. Ray, Miller and Tough, *Bounty and Benevolence*, 3.
5. Canada, House of Commons, *Debates*, vol. 1, May 2, 1870 (Ottawa: Canadian Government Publishing, 1997), 1292–93.
6. Census of Canada, 1871.
7. Ray, Miller and Tough, *Bounty and Benevolence*, 69–70.
8. Canada, Parliament, *Sessional Papers*, *1872*, Paper No. 22, Howe to the Commissioners, May 6, 1871, 6.
9. Ibid.
10. In 1832 Governor Simpson had renamed this post after his European wife. Simpson did not honour any of the two or three Native women he had established relations with in violation of his own order prohibiting such fraternization.
11. Spry (ed.), *The Papers of the Palliser Expedition*, 77.
12. Ibid.
13. Ibid., 78.
14. Ibid.
15. Canada Parliament, *Sessional Papers*, *1872*, Paper No. 22, Simpson to Howe, p. 9.

16. Morris, *The Treaties of Canada*, 32.

17. Ibid., 34.

18. Ibid., 35.

19. Ibid., 28.

20. Canada, Parliament, *Sessional Papers, 1873*, No. 23, Archibald to Joseph Howe, February 12, 1872.

21. Morris, *The Treaties of Canada*, 59.

22. Ibid., 62.

23. Ibid., 70.

24. Ibid., 75.

25. Ibid.

26. Ibid., 51.

27. John Leonard Taylor, "The Development of an Indian Policy for the Canadian North-West, 1869–79" (PhD dissertation, Queen's University, 1975), 111–12.

28. Morris, *The Treaties of Canada*, 168.

29. Ibid., 170.

30. Letter dated July 5, 1874, Jules DeCorby to his superiors. Original in possession of Joann Decorby Blaise, Carlyle, Saskatchewan.

31. Morris, *The Treaties of Canada*, 101.

32. Ibid., 106.

33. Ibid., 104.

34. Ibid., 95.

35. Ibid., 96.

36. Ibid., 116.

37. Ibid., 331.

38. René Fumoleau, *As Long As This Land Shall Last: A History of Treaty 8 and Treaty 11, 1870–1939* (Toronto: McClelland and Stewart, 1973), 30–38.

39. Mark Anderson, "Two Newspapers, One Solitude: Canada's First Nations in the 1873 Press," unpublished paper (Regina: University of Regina, 2005), 11; available at http://www.cst.ed.ac.uk/2005conference/papers/M_Anderson_paper.pdf

40. John Turner, *The North-West Mounted Police, 1873–1893* (Ottawa: King's Printer, 1950), 271.

41. Peter Erasmus, *Buffalo Days and Nights* (Calgary: Fifth House, 1976), 239.

42. Ibid., 239.

43. Morris, *The Treaties of Canada*, 198.

44. Deanna Christensen, *Ahtahkakoop: The Epic Account of a Plains Cree Head Chief, his People, and their Struggle for Survival, 1816–1896* (Shell Lake, SK: Ahtahkakoop Publishing, 2000), 236.

45. Erasmus, *Buffalo Days and Nights*, 240.

46. George McDougall to A. Morris, October 23, 1875, as quoted in Hugh A. Dempsey, *Big Bear: The End of Freedom* (Vancouver: Douglas & McIntyre, 1984), 63.

47. Morris, *The Treaties of Canada*, 204–05.

48. Ibid., 208.

49. Erasmus, *Buffalo Days and Nights*, 244.

50. Ibid.

51. Ibid., 245.

52. Ibid., 246–49.

53. Ibid., 249–50.

54. Morris, *The Treaties of Canada*, 354.

55. Ibid., 220.

56. Michael Craufurd-Lewis, *Macleod of the Mounties* (Ottawa: Golden Dog Press, 1999), 194.

57. U.S. Commissioner of Indian Affairs, *Annual Report* (1876), 345.

58. Morris, *The Treaties of Canada*, 246.

59. Ibid., 249.

60. Hugh A. Dempsey, *Crowfoot: Chief of the Blackfeet* (Edmonton: Hurtig, 1972), 91.

61. Ibid., 91.

62. Turner, *The North-West Mounted Police*, 358.

63. Hugh Dempsey, *Treaty Research Report, Treaty Seven (1877)* (Ottawa: Indian and Northern Affairs, 1987), 6–7.

64. Ibid., 54.

65. James Murphy, *Half Interest in a Silver Dollar: The Saga of Charles E. Conrad* (Missoula: Mountain Press Pub. Co., 1983), 47.

66. Morris, *The Treaties of Canada*, 272.

67. Ibid., 273.

68. Murphy, *Half Interest in a Silver Dollar*, 47.

69. Dempsey, *Treaty Research Report*, 3.

70. Morris, *The Treaties of Canada*, 274.

71. Ibid., 275.

72. Chester Martin, *Dominion Lands Policy* (Toronto: McClelland and Stewart, 1973), 231.

73. Ray, *Bounty and Benevolence*, 57.

ENDNOTES TO CHAPTER 12 (PP. 185–201)

1. Fort Buford is approximately 35 km (22 mi) west of Williston, North Dakota.

2. Captain S. Anderson, "The North American Boundary from the Lake of the Woods to the Rocky Mountains," *Journal of the Royal Geographic Society of London* 46 (1876): 249.

3. Ibid., 248.

4. Classen, *Thrust and Counterthrust*, 123.

5. Ladow, "The Medicine Line," 30.

6. Anderson, "The North-American Boundary," 231.

7. Ibid., 238.

8. Ibid., 236.

9. Captain A. Featherstonhaugh, *Narrative of the Operations of the British North American Boundary Commission, 1872–76* (Woolwich, England: A.W. & J.P. Jackson, 1876), 33.

10. Anderson, "The North-American Boundary," 257.

11. Featherstonhaugh, *Narrative of the Operations*, 37.

12. LaDow, "The Medicine Line," 33.

13. Parsons, *West on the 49th Parallel*, 150.

14. Classen, *Thrust and Counterthrust*, 138.

15. Anderson, "The North-American Boundary," 247.

16. Ibid., 249. Featherstonhaugh, *Narrative of the Operations*, 41, states the order was for "29,000 bushels of oats" but this must be in error. At 35 pounds per bushel this would be more than 500 tons.

17. Parsons, *West on the 49th Parallel*, 109.
18. Ibid., 121.
19. Ibid., 122.
20. Anderson, "The North-American Boundary," 256.
21. Wallace Stegner, *Wolf Willow* (New York: Viking Press, 1962), 83.
22. Frederick M.J. Fulford and Robert Lee Jewett, "Recollections of a Monument Setter," *Beaver* (Spring 1976): 11.

ENDNOTES TO CHAPTER 13 (PP. 203–208)

1. A further subdivision was provided. Each section contained sixteen Legal Subdivisions (LSDs), four to each quarter, 16 ha (40 acres) each. It was possible to divide the LSDs into quarters, producing identifiable parcels of only 4 ha (10 acres).
2. Canada, Parliament, *Sessional Papers, 1872*, Paper No. 22, 16.
3. Ibid.
4. Martin, *Dominion Lands Policy*, 17.
5. Canada, House of Commons, *Debates* (1883), 874.

ENDNOTES TO CHAPTER 14 (PP. 209–248)

1. The Force was initially called Mounted Police. Although the full title North-West Mounted Police, and the acronym NWMP, did not come into existence until 1879, both are used here for ease of reference.
2. There are many lurid and inaccurate versions of the tragedy at Cypress Hills. Philip Goldring provided an authentic account in "The Cypress Hills Massacre: A Century's Retrospect," *Saskatchewan History* 26 (Autumn 1973): 81.
3. Hugh A. Dempsey, *Firewater: The Impact of the Whisky Trade on the Blackfoot Nation* (Calgary: Fifth House, 2002), 128.
4. Alexander Morris to Sir John A. Macdonald September 20, 1873 as quoted in Taylor, "The Development of an Indian Policy," 112.
5. Sir John A. Macdonald to Lord Dufferin September 24, 1873 as quoted in ibid., 113.
6. E. Morgan, "The North-West Mounted Police: Internal Problems and Public Criticism, 1874–1883," *Saskatchewan History* 26 (Spring 1973): 41.
7. National Archives of Canada, Dufferin Papers as quoted in Roderick Charles Macleod, "The North-West Mounted Police, 1873–1905" (PhD dissertation, Duke University, 1971), 38.
8. Anderson, "The North-American Boundary," 253.
9. Turner, *The North-West Mounted Police*, 106.
10. "Fred Bagley Diary," Glenbow Archives, M44, June 18, 1874.
11. Morgan, "The North-West Mounted Police," 44.
12. Turner, *The North-West Mounted Police*, 120.
13. S.W. Horrall, "The March West," in Hugh A. Dempsey (ed.) *Men in Scarlet* (Calgary: Historical Society of Alberta/McClelland and Stewart West, 1974), 20.
14. Turner, *The North-West Mounted Police*, 122.
15. French to Richardson, June 30, 1874, as quoted in Horrall, "The March West," 21.
16. Ibid., 21.

17. Turner, *The North-West Mounted Police*, 115–16.

18. Craufurd-Lewis, *Macleod of the Mounties*, 143.

19. Ibid., 104.

20. Ibid., 65.

21. French to Department of Justice, August 12, 1874, in Turner, *The North-West Mounted Police*, 115–16.

22. Joseph Carscadden Diary, as quoted in David Cruise and Alison Griffith, *The Great Adventure: How the Mounties Conquered the West* (Toronto: Penguin, 1996), 180.

23. Commissioners of the Royal North-West Mounted Police, "1874 Report," in *Opening Up the West: Being the Official Reports to Parliament of the Royal North-West Mounted Police From 1874–1881* (Toronto: Coles Publishing Company, 1973), 10.

24. S.B. Steele, *Forty Years in Canada: Reminiscences of the Great North-West with Some Account of his Service in South Africa* (Toronto: Prospero Books, 2000), 67. Steele died in 1919 as Major General S.B. Steele, K.M.G.

25. Turner, *The North-West Mounted Police*, 131.

26. Macleod to Drever, July 10, 1974 as quoted in Cruise and Griffith, *The Great Adventure*, 184.

27. Steele, *Forty Years in Canada*, 65.

28. John E. Parsons, *West on the 49th Parallel* (New York: Morrow, 1963) 171.

29. Commissioners of the Royal North-West Mounted Police, "1874 Report," in *Opening Up the West*, 9.

30. Turner, *The North-West Mounted Police*, 133.

31. Jean D'Artigue, *Six Years in the Canadian North-West* (Belleville, ON: Mika Pub., 1973 [orig. pub. 1882]), 56.

32. Ibid., 57.

33. Commissioners of the Royal North-West Mounted Police, "1874 Report," in *Opening Up the West*, 39.

34. Ibid.

35. Ibid., 40.

36. Years later, in February 1922, then resident in Alberta, Denny inherited his father's title and became Sir Cecil E. Denny, Baronet.

37. See Cecil Denny, *The Law Marches West* (Toronto: Dent, 1972).

38. Turner, *The North-West Mounted Police*, 139, and Commissioners of the Royal North-West Mounted Police, "1874 Report," in *Opening Up the West*, 14.

39. French was actually the second Commissioner. Lieutenant Colonel W. Osborne Smith held the position in a temporary capacity for less than a month prior to French's appointment on October 17, 1873.

40. Herchmer was not gouging French. Over the next two years, and longer, the NWMP purchased significant quantities of oats at Fort Benton, Montana Territory, at 6.5¢ a pound.

41. National Archives of Canada, RG 18, Vol. 3, File 393-75, Dufferin Correspondence.

42. Commissioners of the Royal North-West Mounted Police, "1874 Report," in *Opening Up the West*, 19.

43. Ibid., 16. Although French does not identify Herchmer as the source of his information, it appears unlikely that it was anyone else.

44. Paul F. Sharp, *Whoop-Up Country: The Canadian-American West, 1865–1885* (Norman: University of Oklahoma Press, 1973), 83.

45. During the following winter at Dufferin, Commissioner Cameron, busying himself with the Boundary Commission accounts, billed the NWMP for 25,630 kg (56,505 lb) of oats at 8.5¢. French objected, claiming the lesser weight he had found on the first delivery and contending that the Boundary Commission had been unable to deliver the full 27,216 kg (60,000). Cameron also ignored the provision in the contract stating that the price was in American funds and charged in Canadian, then a superior currency.

46. Turner, *The North-West Mounted Police*, 145.

47. Commissioners of the Royal North-West Mounted Police, "1874 Report," in *Opening Up the West*, 73.

48. Parsons, *West on the 49th Parallel*, 174–75.

49. W.S. Stocking, November 30, 1906. Stocking arrived in Fort Benton in 1865. Museum of the Upper Missouri, Fort Benton.

50. Sharp, *Whoop-Up Country*, 87.

51. Murphy, *Half Interest in a Silver Dollar*, 27.

52. Ibid., 26–27.

53. Ibid., 6, 23, 39.

54. Ibid., 27.

55. J.F. Klaus, "Fort Livingstone," *Saskatchewan History* 15 (Autumn 1962): 97.

56. National Archives of Canada, MG 29, F-4, Diary of Constable James Finlayson, 15.

57. D'Artigue, *Six Years in the Canadian North-West*, 60–61.

58. George M. Dawson diary as quoted in Dempsey, *Firewater*, 94.

59. Dempsey, *Firewater*, 223.

60. Overholser, *Fort Benton*, 363.

61. Murphy, *Half Interest in a Silver Dollar*, 37.

62. Ibid., 38.

63. Morgan, "The North-West Mounted Police," 41.

64. National Archives of Canada, RG 18, Vol. 7, File 393-75, Macleod to French, April 22, 1875.

65. French to the Minister of Justice, January, 1875, as quoted in Commissioners of the Royal North-West Mounted Police, "1874 Report," in *Opening Up the West*, 24–25.

66. Ibid., 27.

67. Report of Surgeon John Kittson, M.D. in *A Chronicle of the Canadian West, North-West Mounted Police Report for 1875* (Calgary: Historical Society of Alberta, 1975).

68. National Archives of Canada, William Pearce Unpublished Manuscript, Vol. 2, 164–65.

69. Commissioners of the Royal North-West Mounted Police, "1874 Report," in *Opening Up the West*, 62.

70. Ibid., 66.

71. Ibid., 11.

72. Ibid., 23.

73. As quoted in MacGregor, *Vision of an Ordered Land*, 15, 16.

74. *The Daily Globe*, Toronto (Tuesday, August 31, 1875), 2.

75. Report of Surgeon John Kittson, M.D. in *A Chronicle of the Canadian West*, 31.

76. Commissioners of the Royal North-West Mounted Police, "1874 Report," in *Opening Up the West*, 12.

77. Report of Surgeon John Kittson, M.D. in *A Chronicle of the Canadian West*, 31.

78. Ibid., 26.

79. As quoted in Douglas Hill, *The Opening of the Canadian West: Where Strong Men Gathered* (New York: John Day Co., 1967), 135.

ENDNOTES TO CHAPTER 15 (PP. 249–280)

1. Archibald Campbell and Captain W.J. Twining, *Reports upon the survey of the boundary between the territory of the United States and the possessions of Great Britain from the Lake of the Woods to the summit of the Rocky Mountains authorized by an act of Congress approved March 19, 1872*. United States Northern Boundary Commission (Dept. of State Washington: G.P.O., 1878).

2. Denny, *The Law Marches West*, 37.

3. Ibid., 36.

4. Commissioners of the Royal North-West Mounted Police, "1874 Report," in *Opening Up the West*, 50.

5. Cowie, *Company of Adventurers*, 373–74.

6. F.G. Roe, *The North American Buffalo: A Critical Study of the Species in its Wild State* (Toronto: University of Toronto Press, 1951), 204.

7. Andrew C. Isenberg, *The Destruction of the Bison: An Environmental History, 1750–1920* (New York: Cambridge University Press, 2000), 22.

8. Colonel Richard Irving Dodge, *The Plains of the Great West*, as quoted in Roe, *The North American Buffalo*, 152.

9. As quoted in Roe, *The North American Buffalo*, 492–93.

10. Roe, *The North American Buffalo*, 489–520. Roe had immigrated to Canada from Britain with his parents and after several years on the family homestead in the Alberta foothills, he became a locomotive engineer. After retirement he turned to history and produced a number of well-regarded books and articles on the early years of the West.

11. Isenberg, *The Destruction of the Bison*, 25.

12. Dale F. Lott, *American Bison: A Natural History* (Berkeley: University of California Press, 2002), 74–75.

13. Roe, *The North American Buffalo*, 643–44, quoting, respectively, Col. Richard I. Dodge, Sir William Butler, and Rev. John McDougall.

14. Valerius Geist, *Buffalo Nation: History and Legend of the North American Bison* (Saskatoon: Fifth House, 1996), 23, quoting from Frank Bird Linderman, *Plenty-Coups, Chief of the Crows: The Life Story of a Great Indian* (London: John Day Company, 1930).

15. The horse originated in North America, but became extinct there after it migrated to Asia, likely over the Bering land bridge. The horse flourished in Asia and Europe, then returned to North America with the Spanish Conquistadores in the 1500s. See Frank G. Roe, *The Indian and the Horse* (Norman: University of Oklahoma Press, 1955)

16. Isenberg, *The Destruction of the Bison*, 38.

17. Henry Youle Hind, *Narrative of the Canadian Red River Exploring Expedition of 1857 and of The Assiniboine and Saskatchewan Exploring Expedition of 1858* (Rutland, Vermont: Charles E. Tuttle, 1971), 356–57.

18. Ibid.

19. Heather Pringle, *In Search of Ancient North America: An Archaeological Journey to Forgotten Cultures* (New York: Wiley, 1996), 155.

20. Ibid., 160.

21. Reginald and Gladys Laubin, *The Indian Tipi: Its History, Construction, and Use* (Norman: University of Oklahoma Press, 1977), 205.

22. Ibid., 209.

23. Ibid., 202.

24. Ibid., 201.

25. Dempsey, *Crowfoot*, 63.

26. Ambrose, *Undaunted Courage*, 173.

27. Ibid., 162.

28. Laubin, *The Indian Tipi*, 15–16.

29. Ibid., 56–57.

30. Ibid., 4.

31. Ibid., 7.

32. Ibid., 11.

33. Ibid., 15.

34. Isenberg, *The Destruction of the Bison*, 40.

35. Robert Moorman Denhardt, *The Horse of the Americas* (Norman: University of Oklahoma Press, 1947), 105–06 as quoted in Frank Gilbert Roe, *The Indian and the Horse*, 186.

36. Commissioners of the Royal North-West Mounted Police, "1878 Report," in *Opening Up the West*, 24.

37. Theodore Binnema, *Common and Contested Ground: A Human and Environmental History of the Northwestern Plains* (Norman: University of Oklahoma Press, 2001), 93.

38. Isenberg, *The Destruction of the Bison*, 46.

39. Binnema, *Common and Contested Ground*, 94.

40. Isenberg, *The Destruction of the Bison*, 58–60.

41. Roe, *The North American Buffalo*, 611.

42. John McDougall, *Saddle, Sled and Snowshoe: Pioneering on the Saskatchewan in the Sixties* (Toronto: W. Briggs; 1896) as quoted in Roe, *The North American Buffalo*, 610.

43. George Arthur, "The North American Plains Bison: A Brief History," *Prairie Forum* 9, no. 2 (1984): 284.

44. Isenberg, *The Destruction of the Bison*, 96.

45. Ibid., 88.

46. Ibid., 83.

47. Ibid., 26.

48. Lott, *American Bison*, 75.

49. *Bismarck Tribune*, March 29, 1879.

50. Isenberg, *The Destruction of the Bison*, 26.

51. Roe, *The North American Buffalo*, 168. Shepard Krech III, *The Ecological Indian: Myth and History* (New York: Norton, 1999), 133.

52. Krech, *The Ecological Indian*, 133.

53. Mary Weekes, *The Last Buffalo Hunter* (Calgary: Fifth House, 1994), 60.

54. H.M. Robinson, *The Great Fur Land* (Toronto: Coles Canadiana Collection, 1972), 118–20.

55. Leavenworth, Kansas, *Daily Commercial*, March 1869, as quoted in Arthur, "The North American Plains Bison," 283.

56. Isenberg, *The Destruction of the Bison*, 100.

57. Ibid., 105.

58. Ibid., 106.

59. Ens, *Homeland to Hinterland*, 84.

60. William T. Hornaday, *The Extermination of the American Bison: With a Sketch of its Discovery and Life History* (Washington: Government Printing Office, 1889), 493.

61. Isenberg, *The Destruction of the Bison*, 138.

62. Stephen E. Ambrose, *Nothing Like It in the World: The Men Who Built the Transcontinental Railroad, 1863–1869* (New York: Simon & Schuster, 2000), 266.

63. Ibid., 267.

64. Isenberg, *The Destruction of the Bison*, 131.

65. Ibid.

66. Hornaday, *The Extermination of the American Bison*, 495.

67. Ibid., 470.

68. Ibid., 494.

69. Richard Irving Dodge, *The Plains of the Great West and Their Inhabitants* (New York: Archer House, 1959), 142.

70. Isenberg, *The Destruction of the Bison*, 138.

71. Ibid., 136.

72. Hornaday, *The Extermination of the American Bison*, 501.

73. Roe, *The North American Buffalo*, 418.

74. Ibid.

75. John E. Foster, "The Métis and the End of the Plains Buffalo in Alberta" in John E. Foster, Dick Harrison, I.S. MacLaren (eds.) *Buffalo* (Edmonton: University of Alberta Press, 1992), 73.

76. Ibid., 72–73.

77. Hornaday, *The Extermination of the American Bison*, 506.

78. Ibid., 509–10.

79. Ibid., 513.

80. Ibid., 521.

81. Roe, *The North American Buffalo*, 486.

82. "Last of the Wild Buffalo," *Smithsonian Magazine* (February 2000).

83. Hornaday, *The Extermination of the American Bison*, 525.

84. Ibid., 514.

85. Candace Savage, "Back Home on the Range," *Canadian Geographic* 125, no. 1 (January/February 2005): 54.

86. Hornaday, *The Extermination of the American Bison*, 516.

87. Canada, *Journals of the House of Commons*, Vol. 3 (March 26, 1877), 993.

88. Stanley, *The Birth of Western Canada*, 223.

89. Ibid.

90. Ibid.

91. Roe, *The North American Buffalo*, 829.

92. Rudolph Koucky, "The Buffalo Disaster of 1882," *North Dakota History* 50 (Winter 1983): 28.

93. Henry Bayne Macdonald, "The Killing of the Buffalo," *The Beaver* 3 (December 1935): 22.

94. H.M. Starkey, "A Survey in Saskatchewan in 1883," *The Canadian Surveyor* 6, no. 5 (July 1938): 26. The Starkey crew was working in townships 25 and 26, ranges 22, 23, 24 and 25, West of the Third Meridian.

95. Hornaday, *The Extermination of the American Bison*, 474.

96. F.G. Roe, "The Red River Hunt," *Transactions of the Royal Society of Canada* (Ottawa: Royal Society, 1935), 171.

97. David D. Smits, "The Frontier Army and the Destruction of the Buffalo: 1865–1883," *Western Historical Quarterly* 25, no. 4 (1994): 313, 330.

98. Ibid., 337.

99. Ibid., 315.

100. Andrew C. Isenberg, "Towards a Policy of Destruction: Buffaloes, Law and the Market, 1802–83," *Great Plains Quarterly* 12, no. 4 (Fall 1992): 227, 235. The author does not mention the substantial robe trade moving overland to St. Paul during these years.

101. Tim Flannery, *The Eternal Frontier: An Ecological History of North America and Its Peoples* (New York: Atlantic Monthly Press, 2001), 181.

102. Ibid., 187.

103. Ibid., 221.

104. Krech, *The Ecological Indian*, 134–35.

105. Ibid., 135.

106. Ronald Wright, *A Short History of Progress* (Toronto: Anansi Press, 2004), 37.

107. George Catlin, *Letters and Notes on the North American Indians* (North Dighton, MA: JG Press, 1995), 289. The incident is also mentioned by Edwin Thompson Denig, for many years a trader in the region although Denig, writing years later, placed the happening in 1830 and recalled 1,500 tongues. Denig, *Five Indian Tribes of the Upper Missouri*, 30.

108. James McLaughlin, *My Friend The Indian* (Seattle: Superior Publishing, 1970), 30.

109. Ibid. Sitting Bull has been frequently accused of leading this hunt, but he was at Fort Randall at the time.

110. J.B. (Red) Wilkinson, *Western Sportsman* (Regina) 12, no. 2, (Summer 1980): 4, and vol. 13, no. 2, (Summer 1981): 4 and 55.

111. D.A. Dary, *The Buffalo Book* (Chicago: Swallow Press, 1974) as quoted in Arthur, "The North American Plains Bison," 281, 285.

ENDNOTES TO CHAPTER 16 (PP. 281–298)

1. Robert C. Carriker, *Father Peter John De Smet, Jesuit in the West* (Norman: University of Oklahoma Press, 1995), 127.

2. Ibid., 134.

3. Ibid., 137.

4. "Report of the Sioux Commission, December 18, 1876," attached to Annual Report of the Commissioner of Indian Affairs, 1876, 338–39.

5. United States *v.* Sioux Nation of Indians, 448 U.S. 371 (1980).

6. D. Robinson, "A History of the Dakota or Sioux Indians," *South Dakota Historical Quarterly* (1904) as quoted in United States *v.* Sioux Nation of Indians, 448 U.S. 371 (1980).

7. Ibid.

8. Ibid.

9. "Report of the Sioux Commission," 339.

10. Ibid., 343.

11. United States *v.* Sioux Nation of Indians, United States Court of Claims, 25 June, 1975, 518 Federal Reporter, 2d Series, 1298, 1300.

12. The quotation is from the 1874 Annual Report of Lieutenant General Philip H. Sheridan, Commander of the Military District of the Missouri, to the Secretary of War.

13. Edward Lazarus, *Black Hills White Justice: The Sioux Nation Versus the United States, 1775 to the Present* (New York: HarperCollins, 1991), 81.

14. United States *v.* Sioux Nation of Indians, United States Court of Claims, 25 June, 1975, 518 Federal Reporter, 2d Series, 1299.

15. "Record of Engagements With Hostile Indians," United States of America Headquarters, Military Division of the Missouri, 49.

16. Ibid., 50.

17. "Report of the Sioux Commission," 342.

18. Stephen Ambrose, *Crazy Horse and Custer: The Parallel Lives of Two American Warriors* (Garden City New York: Doubleday, 1975), 370.

19. Lazarus, *Black Hills White Justice*, 85.

20. United States of America, *Annual Report, Commissioner of Indian Affairs, 1876*, iv.

21. "Record of Engagements," 52.

22. U.S. Court of Claims, 1300. The Supreme Court was more reserved on this point. "The chronology of the enactment does not necessarily support the view that it was passed in reaction to Custer's defeat at the Battle of the Little Big Horn on June 25, 1876, although some historians have taken a contrary view." United States *v.* Sioux Nation of Indians, 448 U.S. 371 (1980), 6.

23. United States *v.* Sioux Nation of Indians, 448 U.S. 371 (1980), 6.

24. "Report of the Sioux Commission," 335.

25. Ibid., 335.

26. United States *v.* Sioux Nation of Indians, 448 U.S. 371 (1980), 6.

27. "Report of the Sioux Commission," 337.

28. Ibid.

29. Ibid.

30. Ibid., 340.

31. Ibid., 341.

32. Ibid., 343.

33. Ibid., 343.

34. Ibid., 347.

35. The Court of Claims determined that the fair value of the Black Hills at the time of the taking in 1877 was $17.5 million. The Supreme Court held that interest of 5% a year since 1877 was also payable, totalling about $106 million. At date of writing, 2007, the Sioux have refused money for the Black Hills, demanding that the land be returned. While the U.S. Supreme Court attempted to resolve past injustices with its award, the lands lost from the Sioux and the crimes committed by the U.S. government cannot now be repaid. Homestake Mining Company, the largest operator, has extracted approximately $1.5 billion of gold from its Black Hills mines.

36. U.S. Court of Claims, 1302. The Supreme Court did not comment directly upon this opinion. But, it restated the fundamental appellate principle that a reviewing court generally will discard findings of a lower court only when they are clearly erroneous and unsupported by the record. Then the Court went on to state, "No one, including the Government, has ever suggested that the factual findings of the Indian Claims Commission and the Court of Claims failed to meet that standard of review."

37. United States of America, *Report of the Secretary of War*, 1878, 36.

ENDNOTES TO CHAPTER 17 (PP. 299–337)

1. Little Big Horn was the spelling on the 1876 maps. Little Bighorn is now the official name of the battlefield site, by Act of the United States Congress in 1991, replacing Custer Battlefield, thought to be somewhat prejudiced in not acknowledging the presence of the victorious Sioux.
2. New York *Herald*, July 7, 1876.
3. Ibid.
4. Nelson A. Miles, *Personal Recollections and Observations of General Nelson A. Miles* (New York: Werner Co., 1896), n.p.
5. Evan S. Connell, *Son of the Morning Star* (New York: Harper Perennial, 1991), 330–31.
6. "Record of Engagements," 49.
7. Robert Utley, *The Lance and the Shield: The Life and Times of Sitting Bull* (New York: Henry Holt, 1993, 87.
8. Sitting Bull's birth date is uncertain, but 1831 is generally accepted. See Utley, *The Lance and the Shield*, 3.
9. Utley, *The Lance and the Shield*, 160.
10. In 1876 maps and military despatches used "Big Horn." Later usage developed "Bighorn." For years the battle was known as "Custer's Massacre." This bias was removed by Act of Congress in 1991 which officially designated the event, and its site, as "The Battle of the Little Bighorn."
11. Charles M. Robinson III, *A Good Year to Die: The Story of the Great Sioux War* (Norman: University of Oklahoma Press, 1995), 220.
12. Robert M. Utley, *Frontier Regulars: The United States Army and the Indian, 1866–1890* (New York: Macmillan, 1973), 266.
13. Utley, *The Lance and the Shield*, 142.
14. Kellogg was not the only Canadian to die at Little Big Horn. Custer's adjutant, Lieutenant William Winer Cooke, of Hamilton, Lieutenant Donald McIntosh, of Montreal and Vancouver, and Sergeant John Vickery, were also from Canada, as were a number of the 7th Cavalry's enlisted men, Richard Saunders, Darwin Symms, Andrew Snow and Edmond Tessier. Six other Canadians survived the action at Little Big Horn. Gontran Laviolette, *The Dakota Sioux in Canada* (Winnipeg: DLM Publications, 1991), 187.
15. United States of America, *Chronological List of Actions, &c., With Indians*, from January 1, 1866, to January, 1891, Adjutant General's Office, E 83,866 U5 R., 39.
16. "Record of Engagements,"
17. Nonetheless, a visitor to the Interpretive Centre at the Little Bighorn Battlefield might, as the author did in the summer of 1999, hear an account of the battle that suggests Indian losses of between 400 and 600.
18. "Record of Engagements," 62.
19. Ibid., 63.
20. Ibid.
21. National Archives Canada (NA), RG 7, Series G21, Vol. 319, Richardson to Irvine May 26, 1876.
22. "Record of Engagements," 65.
23. NA, RG 7, Series G21, Vol. 319, Affidavit of Gabriel Solomon, August 18, 1876.
24. *The Daily Globe*, Toronto (Monday, July 24, 1876): 4.

25. Commissioners of the Royal North-West Mounted Police, "1876 Report," in *Opening Up the West*, 21–22.

26. Turner, *The North-West Mounted Police*, 303.

27. NA, RG 7, Series G21, Vol. 319, Walsh to Macleod, December 31, 1876.

28. Utley, *The Lance and the Shield*, 181.

29. Jeffrey V. Pearson, "Tragedy At Red Cloud Agency, The Surrender, Confinement and Death of Crazy Horse," *Montana: The Magazine of Western History* (Summer 2005).

30. Turner, *The North-West Mounted Police*, 313.

31. NA, RG 7, Series G21, Vol. 319, Taylor to Seward, July 24, 1877.

32. Ibid., Laird to Minister of the Interior, March 22, 1877.

33. C.W. de Kiewiet and F.H. Underhill (eds.) *Dufferin-Carnarvon Correspondence, 1874–1878* (Toronto: Champlain Society, 1955), 353.

34. NA, RG 7, Series G21, Vol. 319, Alexander Morris to Secretary of State, July 21, 1877, with clipping from *Daily Free Press*.

35. Ibid., Irvine to Scott, June,6 1877.

36. Ibid.

37. Ibid., White to Irvine, August 14, 1877.

38. Ibid., Plunkett to Evarts, June 20, 1877.

39. Ibid., Plunkett to the Earl of Derby, July24, 1877.

40. NA RG 7, Series G21, Vol. 319, Memorandum of David Mills, August 23, 1877. The above account and quotations are taken from this document.

41. de Kiewiet and Underhill, *Dufferin-Carnarvon Correspondence*, Dufferin to Carnarvon, August 25, 1877.

42. NA, RG 7, Series G21, Vol. 319, Report of Privy Council approved October 8, 1877.

43. Ibid., Extract from Washington *National Republican*, August 15, 1877.

44. Ibid.

45. Ibid., Mills to Macleod, August 20, 1877.

46. Ibid., Extract from the *National Republican* August 24, 1877.

47. Ibid., Extracts from the *National Republican* August 30, 1877.

48. NA, RG 7, Series G21, Vol. 319, Sherman to Secretary of War, July 16, 1877.

49. Kinglsey M. Bray, "We Belong to the North," *Montana: Magazine of Western History* (Summer 2005): 28, 34.

50. Utley, *Frontier Regulars*, 291. A marker on the Frenchman River west of Eastend, Saskatchewan, erected by the local historical society, states that the Crazy Horse refugees camped in the river valley nearby.

51. Turner, *The North-West Mounted Police*, 363.

52. Ibid., 364.

53. NA, RG 7, Series G21, Vol. 319, The Sitting Bull Commission, October 17, 1877, and Report of The Sitting Bull Commission.

54. Ibid., Macleod to Generals Terry and Lawrence, October 17, 1877.

55. Ibid., Interview between Lieut.-Col J. F. Macleod and Sitting Bull and other Chiefs of the Sioux Nation, Fort Walsh, October 17, 1877.

56. Utley, *The Lance and the Shield*, 197.

57. NA, RG 7, Series G21, vol. 319, Mills to Macleod, December 6, 1877.

ENDNOTES TO CHAPTER 18 (PP. 339–369)

1.   NA, RG 7, Series G21, Vol. 319, Irvine to Scott, February 2, 1878.
2.   Ibid., Macleod to Mills, March 11, 1878.
3.   Utley, *The Lance and the Shield*, 204.
4.   Turner, *The North-West Mounted Police*, 374.
5.   Utley, *The Lance and the Shield*, 200.
6.   Turner, *The North-West Mounted Police*, 489.
7.   Agreement—Fort Walsh Interpretive Center.
8.   Rev. Clovis Rondeau, *La Montagne de Bois, 1870–1920* (Winnipeg: Canadian Publishers Limited, 1970), 53.
9.   Ibid., 62.
10.   Ibid., 85.
11.   James M. Walsh, Letter to Cora, Royal Canadian Mounted Police Museum, Regina, 3. On retirement, Walsh took up residence in Brockville, Ontario where he named his home "Indian Cliff."
12.   Canada, House of Commons, *Debates*, February 18, 1878.
13.   Helena *Herald*, June 18, 1878, and Joseph Manzione, *I am Looking to the North for My Life: Sitting Bull, 1876–1881* (Salt Lake City: University of Utah Press, 1991), 125.
14.   Jerome A. Greene, *Nez Perce Summer, 1877* (Helena: Montana Historical Society Press, 2000), 343.
15.   Ibid., 344.
16.   Ibid., 336.
17.   Ibid., 346. Turner, *The North-West Mounted Police*, Vol. 1, 399.
18.   NA, RG 7, Series G 21, Vol. 319, Walsh to Irvine, January 25, 1879.
19.   Ibid.
20.   NA, RG 7, Series G 21, Vol. 319, Department of the Interior Memorandum, February 28, 1879.
21.   Ibid., Evarts to Thornton, March 15, 1879.
22.   NA, RG 7, Series G 21, Vol. 318, File 2001, Pt. 3b, 1878–1879.
23.   Ibid., Irvine to Dennis, April 13, 1879.
24.   Ibid., Irvine to Dennis, April 28, 1879.
25.   NA, RG 10, vol. 3652, file 8589, Thornton to Salisbury, March 28, 1879.
26.   NA, RG 7, Series G 21, Vol. 318, File 2001, PT. 3b, 1878-1879, Walsh to Irvine, March 25, 1879.
27.   Ibid., Irvine to Dennis, May 19, 1879.
28.   United States of America, *Report of the Secretary of War*, 1879, Bird to Commissioner of Indian Affairs, 70.
29.   NA, RG 7, Series G 21, Vol. 318, File 2001, PT. 3b, Evarts to Thornton, May 27, 1879.
30.   NA, RG 10, Vol. 3691, File 13,893, telegram, Irvine to Dennis, April 14, 1879.
31.   Ibid., telegram, Irvine to Macleod, April 14, 1879.
32.   Ibid., telegram, Irvine to Macleod, April 22, 1879.
33.   NA, RG 7, Series G 21, Vol. 318, File 2001, PT. 3b, 1878–1879, Watagola to Minister of the Interior, May 10, 1879.
34.   Ibid., Department of the Interior Memorandum, June 21, 1879.
35.   United States of America, *Report of the Secretary of War*, 1879, 71.
36.   Telegram, Sherman to Sheridan, July 24, 1879.
37.   Utley, *The Lance and the Shield*, 208.

38. *Report of the Secretary of War*, 71.

39. NA, RG 10, Vol. 3704, File 17,858, Dewdney Report, 103.

40. Royal Canadian Mounted Police Museum, Regina, Walsh letter to Cora, May 21, 1890, 1 and 18.

41. Commissioners of the Royal North-West Mounted Police, "1879 Report," in *Opening Up the West*, 14.

42. NA, GAI, Edgar Dewdney Papers, 1879 Journal, Monday, June 9.

43. Commissioners of the Royal North-West Mounted Police, "1877 Report" in *Opening Up the West*, 22.

44. NA, Edgar Dewdney Papers, *Memo of My Appointment as Indian Commissioner in 1879*, 1.

45. Ibid., Dennis to Dewdney, May 31, 1879, 180.

46. Ibid.

47. Ibid.

48. Ibid., Dennis to Dewdney, June 23, 1879, 1184.

49. Ibid., *"First Meeting With Crowfoot,"* 32.

50. Ibid.

51. NA, GAI, Edgar Dewdney Papers, 1879 Journal, Monday, July 17,.

52. Ibid., July 19.

53. Canada, Parliament, *Sessional Papers*, 1880, Vol. 3, 78.

54. Commissioners of the Royal North-West Mounted Police, "1876 Report," in *Opening Up the West*, 22.

55. *Saskatchewan Herald* (n.d.).

56. NA, RG 10, no volume, Privy Council to Minister of Interior, August 4, 1879.

57. NA, RG 10, no volume, Minutes of Battleford Council.

58. NA, RG 10, Volume 3704, file 17,858, Dewdney Report, 109.

59. NA, RG 10, Volume 3691, File 13,802, Department of Interior to Laird, September 5, 1879.

60. NA, RG 10, Volume 3704, file 17,858, Dewdney Report, 99.

61. NA, RG 10, Volume 3693, file 14,837, pp. 502–03, Report of the Department of the Interior to the Privy Council, August 13, 1879. (C.O. 42/757)

62. NA, RG 7, G 21, Volume 319, File 2001, part 3c, 1879–1885, Marty to Dennis, October 31, 1879.

63. Francis Haines, "Letters of an Army Captain on the Sioux Campaign of 1879–1880," *Pacific Northwest Quarterly* 39, no. 1 (January 1948): 39, 45, Captain Eli Huggins, July 28, 1879.

64. United States of America, Report of the Secretary of War, 1880, Vol. I, Ruger to Headquarters District of Montana, 21 September, 1880, 77.

65. NA, RG 10, Volume 3751, file 30249, Dewdney letter to D.L. McPherson, August 4, 1881.

ENDNOTES TO CHAPTER 19 (PP. 371–401)

1. From Andrew Suknaski, "The Teton Sioux and 1879 Prairie Fire," *Wood Mountain Poems* (Toronto: Macmillan, 1976).

2. Canada, Parliament, *Sessional Papers*, Annual Report 1880, Department of Indian Affairs, 93.

3. Roe, *The North American Buffalo*, presents in 150 pages of his epic work an exhaustive compilation of historical data on the movements of the buffalo and concludes with this statement, on pp. 671–72: "First and foremost, if our evidence can be considered to bear any meaning whatever, it has been demonstrated beyond disproof the inapplicability to the buffalo species, even to the degree of absurdity, of any theory of uniformity or regularity in their habits."

4. Commissioners of the Royal North-West Mounted Police, "1879 Report," in *Opening Up the West*, 10.

5. NA, RG 7, G21, Vol. 320, file 2001, Pt. 4b, 1879–1880, W.L. Lincoln to Commissioner of Indian Affairs, October 6, 1879.

6. David Dary, *The Oregon Trail: An American Saga* (New York: Knopf, 2004), 294.

7. NA, RG 7, Vol. 319, file 2001, vol. 3 (c), General A. Terry to Colonel N.A. Miles, September 22, 1880.

8. NA, RG 7, G 21, Vol. 320, file 2001, Pt. 4b, 1879–1880, Report of Committee of Privy Council, September 22, 1879.

9. Stanley, *Louis Riel*, 238.

10. Turner, *The North-West Mounted Police*, 409.

11. United States of America, Commissioner of Indian Affairs, Annual Report (1878), xxxi.

12. Anderson, "The North-American Boundary," 245–46.

13. Ibid., 15.

14. Ibid., 17.

15. John Macoun, *Manitoba and the Great North-West* (Guelph: World Publishing, 1882), 652.

16. Ibid.

17. Ibid.

18. Isenberg, *The Destruction of the Bison*, 71.

19. United States of America, Commissioner of Indian Affairs, Annual Report (1879), 13.

20. Fort Benton *Record*, November 21, 1879.

21. Ibid., October 24, 1879.

22. Manitoba *Daily Free Press*, November 14, 1879.

23. Hind, *Narrative of the Canadian Red River Exploring Expedition*, 292.

24. Mari Sandoz, *The Buffalo Hunters: The Story of the Hide Men* (New York: Hastings House, 1954), 340.

25. C.M. MacInnes, *In the Shadow of the Rockies* (London: Rivingtons, 1930), 146.

26. Washington Irving, as quoted in Roe, *The North American Buffalo*, 131. See Roe, *The North American Buffalo*, 131–38, on the evidence for and against the turning of buffalo.

27. Archibald Oswald MacRae, *History of the Province of Alberta* (Calgary: Western Canada History Co., 1912), 377.

28. Koucky, "The Buffalo Disaster of 1882," 23.

29. NA, RG 7, G 21, Vol. 320, file 2001, Pt. 4b, 1879–1880, Report of Committee of Privy Council, September 22, 1879.

30. Canada, House of Commons, *Debates*, May 9, 1880.

31. Washington *Post*, July 30, 1879.

32. *Battleford Historical Society Publications* 1, no. 1 (1926): 58, 59, Laird to Minister of the Interior, June 30, 1879.

33. Commissioners of the Royal North-West Mounted Police, "1879 Report," in *Opening Up the West*, 27.

34. Canada, House of Commons, *Debates*, 1880, Volume One, 3.

35. NA, RG 7, Vol. 319, File 2001, vol. 3 (c), February 3, 1880. Crozier to Dennis.

36. Commissioners of the Royal North-West Mounted Police, "1880 Report," in *Opening Up the West*, Crozier Report, December 1880, 30–31.

37. Laubin, *The Indian Tipi*, 201.

38. Maureen K. Lux, *Medicine That Walks: Disease, Medicine and Canadian Plains Native People, 1880–1940* (Toronto: University of Toronto Press, 2001), 36.

39. Ibid.

40. Canada, Parliament, *Sessional Papers*, Annual Report 1880, Department of Indian Affairs, 102.

41. Ibid., 104.

42. Ibid., 105.

43. United States of America, Report of the Secretary of War, 1879, Vol. I, 62.

44. Ibid., 63.

45. United States of America, Annual Report, Commissioner of Indian Affairs, Washington, 1881, A.R. Keller, Crow Agency.

46. Ibid.

47. United States of America, Commissioner of Indian Affairs, Annual Report 1880, 112.

48. Commissioners of the Royal North-West Mounted Police, "1880 Report," in *Opening Up the West*, 27

49. United States of America, Annual Report, Commissioner of Indian Affairs, Washington, 1880, 13.

50. Ibid., xlviii.

51. Ibid., 113.

52. Ibid.

53. Manitoba Provincial Archives, Walsh Papers, Walsh to Macleod, April 4, 1880, 384–87.

54. Ibid.

55. Ibid.

56. Ibid.

57. United States of America, Commissioner of Indian Affairs, Annual Report (1880), 116.

58. Ibid., 39.

59. David G. McCrady, "Louis Riel and Sitting Bull's Sioux: Three Lost Letters," *Prairie Forum* 32, no. 2 (Fall 2007): 213.

60. Commissioners of the Royal North-West Mounted Police, "1880 Report," in *Opening Up the West*, 27.

61. Ibid.

62. Ibid., 28.

63. Turner, *The North-West Mounted Police*, 520.

64. United States of America E 83,866, U.S.R., Chronological List of Actions With Indians, January 1, 1866, to January 1891, United States Adjutant General's Office, 48–50.

65. A.A. den Otter, "Letters From Elliott Galt: Travelling The Prairies, 1979–80," *Alberta History* 26, no. 3 (1978): 21.

66. Canada, Parliament, *Sessional Papers*, Department of the Interior Annual Report, 1879, 84.

67. den Otter, "Letters From Elliott Galt," 27.

68. Ibid., 28.

69. Ibid., 28–29.

70. Canada, Parliament, *Sessional Papers*, Department of the Interior Annual Report, 1880, 91.

71. Ibid., 92.
72. Commissioners of the Royal North-West Mounted Police, "1880 Report," in *Opening Up the West,* 47.
73. Canada, Parliament, *Sessional Papers,* Department of the Interior Annual Report, 1880, 92.
74. NA, RG 10, vol. 3726, file 24,811, Kittson to Macleod, July 1, 1880 as quoted in Lux, *Medicine That Walks,* 38.
75. Noel Dyck, "The Administration of Federal Aid in the North-West Territories, 1879–1885" (MA thesis, University of Saskatchewan, 1970), 42.
76. Canada, House of Commons, *Debates,* May 3, 1882, 1290.
77. NA, RG 10, Volume 3751, file 30,249, Dewdney to MacPherson, June 8, 1881.
78. Saskatchewan Archives Board, R-182, File 121007, Galt to Dewdney, March 22, 1880.
79. Ibid.
80. United States of America, Report of the Secretary of War, 1880, 77.
81. Dyck, "The Administration of Federal Aid," 42.
82. NA, RG 10, Volume 3751, file 30,249, Dewdney to MacPherson, June 8, 1881.
83. David McCrady, "History of the Canadian Plains Since 1870," in Raymond J. DeMallie (ed.) *Handbook of North American Indians,* Vol. 13 (Washington: Smithsonian Institution, 2001), 316.
84. Valerie Jobson, "The Blackfoot and the Rationing System," *Alberta History* 33, no. 4 (1985): 14.
85. den Otter, "Letters From Elliott Galt," 30.
86. Craufurd-Lewis, *Macleod of the Mounties,* 216–18.
87. Turner, *The North-West Mounted Police,* 541.
88. Walsh to Taylor, September 1, 1888. In Edward A. Légaré, *Sitting Bull and Jean-Louis Were Friends* (self-published by the author, 2004).
89. Turner, *The North-West Mounted Police,* 520 (the headdress was later presented to the Royal Ontario Museum, Toronto).
90. NA, Macdonald Papers, MG26A, Dewdney to Macdonald, October 23, 1880, 89371–77.
91. Ibid., 89377.
92. Glenbow Musuem, Edgar Dewdney fonds, Series 8, M 320, November 1, 1880, Macdonald to Dewdney, 382.
93. NA, Royal Canadian Mounted Police, RG 18, B 3, U.2185, Irvine to Macdonald, December 8, 1880.
94. Ibid.
95. Ibid.
96. NA, Royal Canadian Mounted Police, RG 18, B 3, U.2185, Irvine to Macdonald, November 12, 1880.
97. NA, Royal Canadian Mounted Police, RG 18, B 3, U.2185, Irvine to Macdonald, December 8, 1880.
98. Ibid.
99. Craufurd-Lewis, *Macleod of the Mounties,* 258. Macleod revealed these thoughts in a letter to his wife, July 17, 1878.
100. Ibid., 258. Frederick White was appointed by Macdonald to be one of the executors of his estate.
101. Ibid., 259.
102. NA, Lorne Papers, Macdonald to Lorne, November 24, 1880, 186.

103. NA, Lorne Papers, Macdonald to Lorne, January 25, 1881, 195–96.
104. Walsh to Taylor. In Légaré, *Sitting Bull and Jean-Louis Legaré Were Friends* (no date).
105. Royal Canadian Mounted Police Museum, Regina, 72.55.20, Hamilton to Walsh, September 30, 1880.
106. NA, RG 10, Indian Affairs, File 23, 896-2.
107. Ibid., Jacob Kaufman to Commissioner of Indian Affairs, Washington, January 8, 1881.
108. NA, Macdonald Papers, MG26A, Dewdney to MacPherson, July 4, 1881, 89477–88.
109. Ibid.
110. NA, Macdonald Papers, MG26A, Galt to Macdonald, May 30, 1881, 89435–45.
111. E.H. Allison, *Surrender of Sitting Bull* (Dayton, OH: Walker Litho and Printing, 1891), 50.
112. United States of America, Report of the Secretary of War, 1881, Volume I, 106.
113. Ibid., 102.
114. Ibid., 103.
115. Ibid., 107.
116. Ibid.
117. Ibid.
118. NA, RG 10, Volume 3652, file 8509, part 1, "Confidential Memorandum on the subject of the Sioux Indians for the consideration of the Honourable the Privy Council," February 11, 1881.
119. Allison, *Surrender of Sitting Bull*, 84.
120. NA, RG 10, Volume 3744, file 29506-1, Crozier to Irvine, March 28, 1881.
121. Turner, *The North-West Mounted Police*, 548.
122. NA, Macdonald Papers, MG26A, Dewdney to MacPherson, July 4, 1881, 89477–88.
123. Ibid.
124. Ibid.
125. Ibid.

ENDNOTES TO CHAPTER 20 (PP. 403–417)

1. This account is based upon Jean Chartrand's recollection of the event recorded in 1944 when he was "considerably over 80 years," Saskatchewan Archives Board. In fact, Chartrand was accompanied by another Métis, Ambroise Delorme, and perhaps a Sioux guide. Turner, *The North-West Mounted Police*, 582. United States Court of Claims No. 15713, Legare v. United States, Deposition of Jean-Louis Légaré, Regina, August 17, 1888.
2. Turner, *The North-West Mounted Police*, 568.
3. United States Court of Claims No. 15713, Deposition of Jean-Louis Légaré, 26.
4. Ibid.
5. Ibid., 8.
6. NA, RG10, no file, 06942, Crozier to Irvine, May 1, 1882.
7. Ibid., no file, 07035, Crozier to Irvine, May 4, 1882.
8. United States Court of Claims No. 15713, Légaré v. United States, Deposition of Alexander R. MacDonell, Regina, August 25, 1888, 101.
9. NA, Macdonald Papers, MG26A, Dewdney to Macdonald, June 19, 1881, 89450.
10. Ibid.
11. Ibid.
12. The Standing Buffalo reservation.

13. NA, Macdonald Papers, MG26A, Dewdney to Macdonald, June 19, 1881, 89450.

14. Ibid.

15. Turner, *The North-West Mounted Police*, 580.

16. United States Court of Claim No. 15713, Deposition of Jean-Louis Légaré, 13.

17. Ibid., Brotherton to Légaré, July 15, 1881, 116–17.

18. Turner, *The North-West Mounted Police*, 583.

19. A historical marker at Plentywood commemorates the meeting "near this site."

20. Paul L. Hedren, "Sitting Bull's Surrender at Fort Buford: An Episode in American History," *North Dakota History* 62, no. 4 (Fall 1995): 2, 7.

21. Ibid.

22. Ibid., 8.

23. Ibid., 10.

24. The musket Sitting Bull handed over on July 19 was deposited with the Smithsonian Institute in 1894 by Major James L. Bell, who had been one of the officers present at Fort Buford when the surrender took place. The musket was authenticated as "surrendered by Sitting Bull." The fine Winchester carbine apparently disappeared into the private collection of Major Brotherton, from whence it reappeared in 1946. The rifle, manufactured in 1875, was then a state-of-the-art firearm, efficient and expensive. It is not known how Sitting Bull acquired such a fine weapon. Undoubtedly this was the rifle that Sitting Bull used to dispatch the Crow, Magpie, at their duel on July 17, 1879, at Beaver Creek.

25. Hedren, "Sitting Bull's Surrender at Fort Buford," 11–13. Sitting Bull's words are as recorded by the reporter for the *Saint Paul and Minneapolis Pioneer Press*, and carried in its issue of July 1, 1881.

26. Mark Harvey, "Securing the Confluence: A Portrait of Fort Buford, 1866–1895," *North Dakota History* 69, nos. 2, 3 and 4 (2002): 24, 45.

27. Ibid., 14.

28. Ibid., 13.

29. United States of America, Report of Commissioner of Indian Affairs, 1881, 57.

30. Dempsey, *Crowfoot*, 131.

31. NA, Indian Affairs, RG10, Vol. 3744, file 29506-1, Allen to Dewdney, May 8, 1881.

32. Ibid.

33. NA, Indian Affairs, RG10, Vol. 3744, file 29506-1, Wadsworth to Dewdney, May 18, 1881.

34. NA, Macdonald Papers, MG26A, Dewdney to Macdonald, June 19, 1881, 89450–62.

35. NA, Macdonald Papers, MG 26A, Dewdney to MacPerson, July 4, 1881, 89477–88.

36. NA, Indian Affairs, RG 10, Vol. 3744, file 29606-1, Allen to Galt, June 27, 1881.

37. Ibid., Galt to Wadsworth, July 3, 1881.

38. Ibid., Allen to Galt, June 27, 1881.

39. NA, Indian Affairs, RG 10, Vol. 3744, file 29506-1, Macleod to Dewdney, June 24, 1881.

40. Ibid., Allen to Galt, June 27, 1881.

41. Ibid., Macleod to Dewdney, June 24, 1881.

42. Dempsey, *Crowfoot*, 133.

43. Macleod to Dewdney, August 4, 1881 as quoted in Dempsey, *Crowfoot*, 134.

44. Dempsey, *Crowfoot*, 134.

45. NA, Indian Affairs, RG 10, Vol. 3744, file 29506-1, Wadsworth to Galt, August 8, 1881.

46. Turner, *The North-West Mounted Police*, 607. Diary of Cst. "Bob" Wilson.

47. Ibid.

48.   NA, Indian Affairs, RG 10, Vol. 3744, file 29506-1, Wadsworth to Galt, August 8, 1881

49.   NA, Indian Affairs, RG 10, Vol. 3744, file 29506-1, Telegram, Galt to Vankoughnet, August 20, 1881.

50.   Ibid., Dewdney to MacPherson, July 4, 1881.

ENDNOTES TO CHAPTER 21 (PP. 419–434)

1.   Turner, *The North-West Mounted Police*, 591.

2.   Ibid.

3.   During the North-West Rebellion, on April 9, 1885, the *Northcote*, somewhat fortified, was sent into action at Batoche against the Métis commanded by Gabriel Dumont. The Métis simply lowered the ferry cable, shearing her mast and funnels, and the disabled vessel drifted helplessly downstream and out of the action.

4.   NA, Indian Affairs, RG 10, Volume 3768, file 33642. Reports of different Councils which His Excellency, the Governor General, held with the Indians while in the Northwest Territories, 1881.

5.   Ibid.

6.   Ibid.

7.   Ibid.

8.   Ibid.

9.   Ibid.

10.   Rev. James MacGregor, "Lord Lorne in Alberta," *Alberta Historical Review* 12, no. 2 (Spring 1964): 1, 7.

11.   Ibid.

12.   Ibid., 1.

13.   MacGregor, *Father Lacombe*, 63 and 78.

14.   Canada, Parliament, *Sessional Papers*, February 29, 1884, Vol. 7, no. 12, Department of the Interior, Report of Deputy Minister.

15.   Ibid., 233.

16.   Rondeau, *La Montagne de Bois*, 71.

17.   Ibid., 75–76.

18.   Ibid., 66.

19.   Lynne B. Iglitzin, *Violent Conflict in American Society* (San Francisco: Chandler Publishing, 1972), 83, as quoted in *Journal of American Indian Education* 17, no. 2 (January 1978): 2.

20.   This usage abounded in newspaper reportage, but also made its way into larger works. See John F. Finerty, *War-Path and Bivouac or, The conquest of the Sioux: a narrative of stirring personal experiences and adventures in the Big Horn and Yellowstone Expedition of 1876, and in the campaign on the British border in 1879* (Norman: University of Oklahoma Press, 1961).

21.   Canada, House of Commons, *Debates*, vol. 1, December 9, 1880.

22.   Sarah Carter, *Lost Harvests: Prairie Indian Reserve Farmers and Government Policy* (Montreal: McGill-Queens University Press, 1990).

23.   Canada, House of Commons, *Debates*, April 15, 1886.24. Fumoleau, *As Long As This Land Shall Last*, 31.

25.   Ibid., 35.

26.   Statutes of Canada, 1876, 36 Vic, c. 18.

27. J.E. Chamberlin, *The Harrowing of Eden* (Toronto: Fitzhenry & Whiteside, 1975).

28. Published in 1899 as a commentary on the American takeover of the Philippines after the Spanish-American War. The first stanza illustrates:

> Take up the White Man's burden
> Send forth the best ye breed
> Go bind your sons to exile
> To serve your captives' need:
> To wait in heavy harness,
> On fluttered folks and wild,
> Your new-caught sullen peoples,
> Half-devil and half-child.

29. The above too-brief description of 19th-century public policy is drawn from Robert J. Nestor, "Hayter Reed, Severalty, and the Subdivision of Indian Reserves on the Canadian Prairies" (MA thesis, University of Regina, 1997).

30. Pierre Berton, *The National Dream: The Great Railway 1871–1881* (Toronto: McClelland and Stewart, 1970), 115.

31. Brian E. Titley, *The Frontier World of Edgar Dewdney* (Vancouver: University of British Columbia Press, 1999), 85–86.

32. Ibid., 85.

33. Woodcock, *Gabriel Dumont*, 123.

34. Ibid., 124–25.

ENDNOTES TO CHAPTER 22 (PP. 435–447)

1. French is generally regarded as the first commissioner of the Force, although technically he was the second. Lieutenant Colonel W. Osborne Smith, commanding the Canadian Militia at Fort Garry, served as interim commissioner until the appointment of French on October 16, 1873.

2. NA, Royal Canadian Mounted Police, RG 18, Vol. 3436, O/C #104 as quoted in Craufurd-Lewis, *Macleod of the Mounties*, 187.

3. NA, Royal Canadian Mounted Police, RG 18, Vol. 3436, O/C #1 as quoted in Craufurd-Lewis, *Macleod of the Mounties*, 187.

4. Craufurd-Lewis, *Macleod of the Mounties*, 248.

5. Prime Minister Macdonald introduced pensions to the NWMP in 1889, an innovation that met strong resistance from the Liberal opposition. R.C. Macleod, "The Mounted Police and Politics," in Hugh A. Dempsey (ed.) *Men in Scarlet* (Calgary: Historical Society of Alberta/McClelland and Stewart West, 1974), 103–04.

6. Craufurd-Lewis, *Macleod of the Mounties*, 248.

7. Utley, *The Lance and the Shield*, 263.

8. Ibid., 265.

9. Ibid., 307.

10. Turner, *The North-West Mounted Police*, Vol. II, 2.

11. Ibid., 25.

12. Roderick Charles Macleod, "The North-West Mounted Police 1873–1905" (PhD dissertation, Duke University, 1971), 61.

13. D'Arcy Jenish, *Indian Fall: The Last Great Days of the Plains Cree and the Blackfoot Confederacy* (Toronto: Viking, 1999), 228.

14. Dempsey, *Crowfoot*, 199.

15. Blair Stonechild and Bill Waiser, *Loyal Till Death: Indians and the North-West Rebellion* (Calgary: Fifth House, 1997), 207.

16. Jack Dunn, *The Alberta Field Force of 1885* (Calgary: Jack Dunn, 1994), 25.

17. Dempsey, *Crowfoot*, 201.

18. Jerome Greene, *Nez Perce Summer, 1877: The U.S. Army and the Nee-Me-Poo Crisis* (Helena, MT: Montana Historical Society Press, 2000), 349.

19. Saskatchewan Archives Board, Accession no. R-125, Collection no. R - E3219, Deposition of Jean-Louis Légaré, Regina, August 17, 1888.

BIBLIOGRAPHY

Abrams, Gary. 1976. *Prince Albert, The First Century, 1866–1966*. Saskatoon: Modern Press.

Allison, E.H. 1891. *Surrender of Sitting Bull*. Dayton, OH: Walker Litho and Printing.

Ambrose, Stephen E. 1975. *Crazy Horse and Custer: The Parallel Lives of Two American Warriors*. New York: Doubleday.

———. 1996. *Undaunted Courage: Meriwether Lewis, Thomas Jefferson, and the Opening of the American West*. New York: Simon & Schuster.

———. 2000. *Nothing Like It in the World: The Men Who Built the Transcontinental Railroad, 1863–1869*. New York: Simon & Schuster.

Adams, Howard. 1989. *Prison of Grass*. Saskatoon: Fifth House.

———. 1995. *A Tortured People*. Penticton: Theytus Books.

Ahenakew, Edward. 1995. *Voices of the Plains Cree*. Regina: Canadian Plains Research Center.

Anderson, Gary Clayton. 1986. *Little Crow*. St. Paul: Minnesota Historical Society Press.

———. 1996. *Sitting Bull and the Paradox of Lakota Nationhood*. New York: Harper Collins.

Anderson, Harry. N.d. "A Sioux Pictorial Account of General Terry's Council at Fort Walsh, October 17, 1877," *North Dakota History*.

Anderson, Mark Cronlund. 2005. "Two Newspapers, One Solitude: Canada's First Nations in the 1873 Press." Unpublished paper available at http://www.cst.ed.ac.uk/2005conference/papers/M_Anderson_paper.pdf

Anderson, Samuel (Captain). 1876. "The North-American Boundary from the Lake of the Woods to the Rocky Mountains." *Journal of the Royal Geographic Society of London* 46: 228-262.

Andrist, Ralph K. 1964. *The Long Death*. New York: Macmillan.

Arthur, George. 1984. "The North American Plains Bison: A Brief History," *Prairie Forum* 9, no. 2 (Fall).

Babe, Robert E. 1990. *Telecommunications in Canada: Technology, Industry and Government*. Toronto: University of Toronto Press.

Bailey, John W. 1979. *Pacifying the Plains*. London: Greenwood Press.

Baker, William M. 1998. *The Mounted Police and Prairie Society, 1873–1919*. Regina: Canadian Plains Research Center.

Beal, Merrill D. 1963. *"I Will Fight No More Forever."* Seattle: University of Washington Press.

Begg, Alexander. 1871. *The Creation of Manitoba; or, A History of the Red River Troubles*. Toronto: Hunter, Rose & Company.

———. 1894. *History of British Columbia from its earliest discovery to the present time*. Toronto: William Briggs.

———. 1895. *History of the North-West*. Toronto: Hunter, Rose & Company.

Belcourt, George Antoine (Reverend). 1971. "Hunting Buffalo on the Northern Plains: A Letter from Father Belcourt," *North Dakota History* 38, no. 3.

Berger, Thomas R. 1991. *A Long and Terrible Shadow.* Vancouver: Douglas & McIntyre.

Berry, Gerald L. 1953. *The Whoop-Up Trail.* Edmonton: Applied Art Products Ltd.

Berton, Pierre. 1970. *The National Dream: The Great Railway 1871–1881* . Toronto: McClelland and Stewart.

——. 1971. *The Last Spike.* Toronto: McClelland and Stewart.

Binnema, Theodore. 2001. *Common and Contested Ground: A Human and Environmental History of the Northwestern Plains.* Norman: University of Oklahoma Press.

Binnema, Theodore, Gerhard J. Ens and R.C. MacLeod (eds.). 2001. *From Rupert's Land to Canada.* Edmonton: University of Alberta Press.

Blaise, Joann Decorby. 2000. *My Residence is My Carriage.* Privately printed.

Blanchard, Jim (ed.). 2002. *A Thousand Miles of Prairie.* Winnipeg: University of Manitoba Press.

Bonnichsen, Robson and Stuart J. Baldwin. 1978. *Cypress Hills Ethnohistory and Ecology: A Regional Perspective,* Archaeological Survey of Alberta, Occasional Paper No. 10, Alberta Culture, Historical Resource Division, December. Edmonton.

Boyd, Robert. 1999. *The Coming of the Spirit of Pestilence: Introduced Infectious Diseases and Population Decline among Northwest Coast Indians, 1774–1874.* Vancouver: University of British Columbia Press.

Bray, Kingsley M. 2005. "We Belong to the North," *Montana: The Magazine of Western History* 55, no. 2 (Summer).

——. 2006. *Crazy Horse: A Lakota Life.* Norman: University of Oklahoma Press.

Brown, Dee. 1972. *Bury My Heart at Wounded Knee.* Toronto: Bantam Books.

——. 1974. *The Westerners.* New York: Holt, Rinehart and Winston.

Brown, Mark H. 1967. *The Flight of the Nez Perce.* Lincoln: University of Nebraska Press.

Bumsted, J.M. 1999. *Fur Trade Wars.* Winnipeg: Great Plains Publications.

——. 2001. *Louis Riel v. Canada.* Winnipeg: Great Plains Publications.

Bureau of Catholic Indian Missions. 1878. *Annals of the Catholic Indian Missions of America* 2, no. 1 (January). Washington, DC..

Burnet, Robert. 1996. *Canadian Railway Telegraph History.* Etobicoke, ON: Telegraph Key & Sounder.

Burt, A.L. 1940. *The United States, Great Britain and British North America.* Toronto: Ryerson.

Butler, William. 1968. *The Great Lone Land: A Narrative of Travel and Adventure in the North-West of America.* Edmonton: Hurtig.

Calloway, Colin G. 2003. *One Vast Winter Count.* Lincoln: University of Nebraska Press.

Camp, Gregory S. 2002. "The Dispossessed: The Objibwa and Metis of Northwest North Dakota," *North Dakota History* 69, nos. 2–4.

Campbell, Archibald and W.J. Twining. 1878. *Reports upon the survey of the boundary between the territory of the United States and the possessions of Great Britain from the Lake of the Woods to the summit of the Rocky Mountains authorized by an act of Congress approved March 19, 1872.* Washington: G.P.O.

Campbell, Marjorie Wilkins. 1950. *The Saskatchewan.* Toronto: Rinehart.

——. 1957. *The North West Company.* Toronto: Macmillan.

Carley, Kenneth. 1976. *The Sioux Uprising of 1862.* The Minnesota Historical Society.

Carrigan, D. Owen. 1968. *Canadian Party Platforms, 1867–1968.* Toronto: Copp Clark.

Carriker, Robert C. 1995. *Father Peter John De Smet, Jesuit in the West.* Norman: University of Oklahoma Press.

Carroll, Francis M. 2001. *A Good and Wise Measure: The Search for the Canadian-American Boundary, 1783–1842*. Toronto: University of Toronto Press.

Carter, Sarah. 1990. *Lost Harvests. Prairie Indian Reserve Farmers and Government Policy*. Montreal/Kingston: McGill-Queen's University Press.

——. 1999. *Aboriginal People and Colonizers of Western Canada to 1900*. Toronto: University of Toronto Press.

Catlin, George. 1995. *Letters and Notes on the North American Indians*. North Dighton, MA: JG Press.

Chamberlin, J.E. 1975. *The Harrowing of Eden*. Toronto: Fitzhenry & Whiteside.

Chambers, Ernest J. (Captain). 1973 (1906). *The Royal North-West Mounted Police*. Montreal: Mortimer Press.

Chisholm, Joseph Andrew. 1909. *The Speeches and Public Letters of Joseph Howe*, 2 vol. Halifax: Chronicle Publishing.

Christensen, Deanna. 2000. *Ahtahkakoop: The Epic Account of a Plains Cree Head Chief, his People, and their Struggle for Survival, 1816–1896*. Shell Lake, SK: Ahtahkakoop Publishing.

Classen, H. George. 1965. *Thrust and Counterthrust: The Genesis of the Canada-United States Boundary*. Toronto: Longmans.

Commissioners of the Royal North-West Mounted Police. 1973. *Opening Up the West: Official Reports of the RNWMP, 1874–1881*. Toronto: Coles.

Connell, Evan S. 1991. *Son of the Morning Star*. New York: HarperPerennial.

Cooper, Barry. 1988. *Alexander Kennedy Isbister: A Respectable Critic of the Honourable Company*. Ottawa: Carleton University Press.

Coward, John M. 1999. *The Newspaper Indian*. Chicago: University of Illinois Press.

Cowie, Isaac. 1993. *Company of Adventurers: A Narrative of Seven Years in the Service of the Hudson's Bay Company during 1867–1874 on the Great Buffalo Plains*. Lincoln: University of Nebraska Press.

Craufurd-Lewis, Michael. 1999. *Macleod of the Mounties*. Ottawa: Golden Dog Press.

Creighton, Donald. 1955. *John A. Macdonald—The Old Chieftain*. Toronto: Macmillan.

Cruise, David and Alison Griffiths. 1996. *The Great Adventure: How the Mounties Conquered the West*. Toronto: Viking/Penguin.

Cumberland House Bicentennial Committee. 1974. *A History of Cumberland House, 1774–1974*. Northern News Services, Department of Northern Saskatchewan.

Cushman, Dan 1966. *The Great North Trail*. New York: McGraw-Hill.

D'Artigue, Jean. 1973 [1882]. *Six Years in the Canadian North-West*. Belleville, ON: Mika.

Dary, David A. 1974. *The Buffalo Book*. Athens, OH: Swallow Press/Ohio University Press.

——. 2004. *The Oregon Trail: An American Saga*. New York: Knopf.

Daschuk, James W. 2002. "The Political Economy of Indian Health and Disease in the Canadian Northwest" (PhD dissertation, University of Manitoba).

De Brou, Dave and Bill Waiser (eds.). 1992. *Documenting Canada*. Saskatoon: Fifth House.

Decker, Jody F. 1988. "Tracing Historical Diffusion Patterns: The Case of the 1780–82 Smallpox Epidemic Among the Indians of Western Canada," *Native Studies Review* 4, nos. 1–2.

de Kiewiet, C.W. and F.H. Underhill (eds.). 1955. *Dufferin-Carnarvon Correspondence 1874–1878*. Toronto: The Champlain Society.

DeMontravel, Peter R. 1982. "The Career of Lieutenant General Nelson A. Miles from the Civil War through the Indian Wars" (PhD dissertation, St. John's University, New York).

Dempsey, Hugh A. 1972. *Crowfoot: Chief of the Blackfeet*. Edmonton: Hurtig.

—— (ed.). 1974. *Men in Scarlet*. Calgary: Historical Society of Alberta/McClelland and Stewart West.

——. 1980. *Red Crow*. Saskatoon: Western Producer Prairie Books, Saskatoon.

——. 1984. *Big Bear: The End of Freedom*. Vancouver: Douglas & McIntyre.

——. 1987. *Treaty Research Report, Treaty Seven (1877)*. Ottawa: Indian and Northern Affairs, 1987.

——. 1993. "The Tragedy of White Bird," *The Beaver* 73, no. 1 (February/March).

——. 2002. *Firewater: The Impact of the Whisky Trade on the Blackfoot Nation*. Calgary: Fifth House.

——. 2003. *The Vengeful Wife, and Other Blackfoot Stories*. Norman: University of Oklahoma Press.

—— (ed.). 2006. "To Fort Benton and Return, 1873, Diary of the Rev. George McDougall," *Alberta History* (Spring).

Denig, Edwin Thompson. 1961. *Five Indian Tribes of the Upper Missouri: Sioux, Arickaras, Assiniboines, Crees, Crows*. Norman: University of Oklahoma Press.

Denig, Edwin Thompson. 2000. *The Assiniboine*. Regina: Canadian Plains Research Center.

Denny, Cecil E. (Sir). 1972. *The Law Marches West*. Toronto: Dent.

den Otter, A.A. 1978. "Letters From Elliott Galt: Travelling The Prairies, 1979–80," *Alberta History* 26, no. 3.

DeVoto, Bernard. 1947. *Across the Wide Missouri*. Boston: Houghton Mifflin.

Dewar, Elaine. 2001. *Bones: Discovering The First Americans*. Toronto: Vintage Canada.

Diamond, Jared. 1999. *Guns, Germs, and Steel: The Fates of Human Societies*. New York: W.W. Norton & Company.

Dick, Lyle. 1996. "The Seven Oaks Incident and the Construction of a Historical Tradition, 1816 to 1970." In Catherine Cavanaugh and Jeremy Mouat (eds.), *Making Western Canada: Essays on European Colonization and Settlement*. Toronto: Garamond Press.

Dickason, Olive Patricia. 1992. *Canada's First Nations*. Toronto: McClelland & Stewart.

Dobak, William A. 1995. "The Army and the Buffalo," *Western Historical Quarterly* 26, no. 2.

——. 1996. "Killing the Canadian Buffalo, 1821–1881," *Western Historical Quarterly* 27, no. 1.

Dodge, Richard Irving. 1959. *The Plains of the Great West and Their Inhabitants*. New York: Archer House.

"The Dominion Telegraph." N.d. *Canadian North-West Historical Society Publications* 1, no. 6. Battleford, SK.

Dugas, L'Abbé G. 1906. *Histoire de l'Ouest Canadien de 1822 à 1869*. Montreal: Librairie Beauchemin.

Dunlevy, Ursula (Sister). 1941. "The Canadian Halfbreed Rebellions of 1870 and 1885," *North Dakota Historical Quarterly* 9, no. 1 (October).

Dunn, Jack. 1994. *The Alberta Field Force of 1885*. Calgary: Jack Dunn.

Dyck, Noel Evan. 1970. "The Administration of Federal Indian Aid in the North-West Territories, 1879–1885 (MA thesis, University of Saskatchewan).

Elias, Peter Douglas. 2002. *The Dakota of the Canadian Northwest*. Regina: Canadian Plains Research Center.

Ens, Gerhard J. 1996. *Homeland to Hinterland: The Changing World of the Red River Métis in the Nineteenth Century*. Toronto: University of Toronto Press.

Erasmus, Peter. 1976. *Buffalo Days and Nights: As Told to Henry Thompson*. Calgary: Fifth House Publishers.

Ewing, Sherm. 1990. *The Range*. Missoula, MT: Mountain Press Publishing.

Farr, William E. N.d. "Going to Buffalo," *Montana: The Magazine of Western History* 53, no. 4 and 54, no. 1.

Featherstonhaugh, A. (Captain). 1876. *Narrative of the Operations of the British North American Boundary Commission, 1872–76*. Woolwich, England: A.W. & J.P. Jackson.

Fenn, Elizabeth A. 2001. *Pox Americana: The Great North American Smallpox Epidemic of 1775–1783*. New York: Hill and Wang.

Ferguson, Barry (ed.). 1991. *The Anglican Church and the World of Western Canada, 1820–1970*. Regina: Canadian Plains Research Center.

Finerty, John F. 1961. *War-Path and Bivouac or, The conquest of the Sioux: a narrative of stirring personal experiences and adventures in the Big Horn and Yellowstone Expedition of 1876, and in the campaign on the British border in 1879*. Norman: University of Oklahoma Press.

Flannery, Tim. 2001. *The Eternal Frontier: An Ecological History of North America and Its Peoples*. New York: Atlantic Monthly Press.

Foster, John, Dick Harrison and I.S. MacLaren (eds.). 1992. *Buffalo*. Edmonton: University of Alberta Press.

Francis, Daniel. 1982. *Battle for the West: Fur Traders and the Birth of Western Canada*. Edmonton: Hurtig.

——. 1992. *The Imaginary Indian*. Vancouver: Arsenal Pulp Press.

Francis, R. Douglas. 1987. "From Wasteland to Utopia, Changing Images of the Canadian West in the Nineteenth Century," *Great Plains Quarterly* (Summer).

——. 1989. *Images of the West*. Saskatoon. Western Producer Prairie Books.

Fraser, Marian Botsford. 1989. *Walking the Line*. Vancouver: Douglas & McIntyre.

Friesen, Gerald. 1984. *The Canadian Prairies*. Toronto: University of Toronto Press.

Friesen, Jean. 1986. *Magnificent Gifts: The Treaties of Canada with the Indians of the Northwest 1869–76*. Toronto: Proceedings and Transactions of the Royal Society of Canada.

Friesen, John W. 1999. *First Nations of the Plains*. Calgary: Detselig Enterprises.

Fulford, Frederick M.J. and Robert Lee Jewett. 1976. "Recollections of a Monument Setter," *The Beaver* (Spring).

Fumoleau, René. 1973. *As Long as This Land Shall Last: A History of Treaty 8 and Treaty 11, 1870–1939*. Toronto: McClelland and Stewart.

Gard, Wayne. 1959. *The Great Buffalo Hunt*. Lincoln: University of Nebraska Press.

Geist, Valerius. 1996. *Buffalo Nation: History and Legend of the North American Bison*. Saskatoon: Fifth House.

Getty, Ian A.L. and Antoine S. Lussier (eds.). *As Long as the Sun Shines*. Vancouver: University of British Columbia Press.

Gibson, Dale. 1983. *Attorney for the Frontier: Enos Stutsman*. Winnipeg: University of Manitoba Press.

Gibson, Dale and Lee Gibson. 1972. *Substantial Justice*. Winnipeg: Peguis.

Gibson, James R.. 1997. *The Lifeline of the Oregon Country, The Fraser-Columbia Brigade System, 1811–47*. Vancouver: University of British Columbia Press.

Gillman, Rhoda R., Carolyn Gillman and Deborah M. Stultz. 1979. *Red River Trails*. St. Paul: Minnesota Historical Society.

Giraud, Marcel. 1986. *The Metis in the Canadian West* (translated by George Woodcock). Edmonton: University of Alberta Press.

Gluek, Alvin C., Jr. 1965. *Minnesota and the Manifest Destiny of the Canadian Northwest: A Study in Canadian-American Relations*. Toronto: University of Toronto Press.

——. 1973. *Manitoba and the Hudson's Bay Company*. Winnipeg: University of Winnipeg Press.

Goldring, Philip. 1973. "The Cypress Hills Massacre: A Century's Retrospect." *Saskatchewan History* 26 (Autumn).

Gough, Barry. 1997. *First Across the Continent*. Norman: University of Oklahoma Press.

Goulet, George R.D. 1999. *The Trial of Louis Riel: Justice and Mercy Denied*. Calgary: Tellwell.

Grant, George M. (Reverend). 1967. *Ocean to Ocean*. Edmonton: Hurtig.

Gray, John Morgan. 1963. *Lord Selkirk of Red River*. Toronto: Macmillan.

Greene, Jerome A. 2000. *Nez Perce Summer, 1877: The U.S. Army and the Nee-Me-Poo Crisis*. Helena: Montana Historical Society Press.

Grobsmith, Elizabeth S. 1981. *Lakota of the Rosebud*. Orlando, FL: Harcourt Brace.

Hackett, Paul. 2002. *A Very Remarkable Sickness*. Winnipeg: University of Manitoba Press.

Haines, Francis. 1948. "Letters of an Army Captain on the Sioux Campaign of 1879–1880," *Pacific Northwest Quarterly* 39, no. 1 (January).

Hamilton, Zachary Macaulay and Marie Albina Hamilton. 1948. *These are the Prairies*. Regina: School Aids and Text Book Publishing Co. Ltd.

Hanson, James A. 2005. *When Skins Were Money: A History of the Fur Trade*. Chadron, NE: Museum of the Fur Trade.

Hardorff, Richard G. 2001. *The Death of Crazy Horse*. Lincoln: University of Nebraska Press.

Hardy, W.G. 1959. *From Sea Unto Sea*. New York: Doubleday.

Hargrave, Joseph James. 1871. *Red River*. Montreal: John Lovell.

Harvey, Mark. 2002. "Securing the Confluence: A Portrait of Fort Buford, 1866–1895," *North Dakota History* 69, nos. 2–4.

Hedren, Paul L. 1995. "Sitting Bull's Surrender at Fort Buford: An Episode in American History." *North Dakota History* 62, no. 4.

——. 1996. *Traveler's Guide to the Great Sioux War*. Helena: Montana Historical Society Press.

Higham, Carol and Robert Thacker. 2004. *One West, Two Myths*. Calgary: University of Calgary Press.

Hill, Douglas. 1967. *The Opening of the Canadian West: Where Strong Men Gathered*. New York: John Day Co.

Hind, Henry Youle. 1971. *Narrative of the Canadian Red River Exploring Expedition of 1857 and of The Assiniboine and Saskatchewan Exploring Expedition of 1858*. Rutland, VT: Charles E. Tuttle Company.

Historical Society of Alberta. 1975. *A Chronicle of the Canadian West; North-West Mounted Police Report for 1875*. Calgary.

Hopkins, Donald R. 2002. *The Greatest Killer: Smallpox in History*. Chicago: University of Chicago Press.

Hornaday, William T. 1889. *The Extermination of the American Bison: With a Sketch of its Discovery and Life History*. Washington, DC: Government Printing Office.

Horrall, S.W. 1972. "Sir John A. Macdonald and the Mounted Police Force for the Northwest Territories," *Canadian Historical Review* 54, no. 2 (June).

——. 1974. "The March West." In Hugh A. Dempsey (ed.) *Men in Scarlet*. Calgary: Historical Society of Alberta/McClelland and Stewart West.

Howard, Joseph Kinsey. 1952. *Strange Empire: A Narrative of the Northwest*. New York: Morrow.

Huck, Barbara. 2000. *Exploring the Fur Trade Routes of North America*. Winnipeg: Heartland.

Hutton, Paul Andrew (ed.). 1962. *The Custer Reader*. Lincoln: University of Nebraska Press.

—— (ed.). 1987. *Soldiers West: Biographies from the Military Frontier*. Lincoln: University of Nebraska Press.

Ingles, Ernie B. and N. Merrill Distad (eds.). 2003. Peel's *Bibliography of the Canadian Prairies to 1953*. Toronto: University of Toronto Press.

Innis, Harold A. 1970. *The Fur Trade in Canada: An Introduction to Canadian Economic History*. Toronto: University of Toronto Press3.

Irwin, Leonard Bertram. 1968. *Pacific Railways and Nationalism in the Canadian-American Northwest, 1845–1873*. New York: Greenwood Press.

Isaac, Thomas. 1993. *Pre-1868 Legislation Concerning Indians*. Saskatoon: University of Saskatchewan, Native Law Centre.

Isenberg, Andrew C. 1992. "Towards a Policy of Destruction: Buffaloes, Law and the Market, 1802–83." *Great Plains Quarterly* 12, no. 4.

——. 2000. *The Destruction of the Bison: An Environmental History, 1750–1920*. Cambridge: Cambridge University Press.

Jahoda, Gloria. 1975. *The Trail of Tears*. New York: Wings Books.

Jenish, D'Arcy. 1999. *Indian Fall: The Last Great Days of the Plains Cree and the Blackfoot Confederacy*. Toronto: Viking.

——. 2003. *Epic Wanderer: David Thompson and the Mapping of the Canadian West*. Toronto: Doubleday Canada.

Jenness, Diamond. 1963. *Indians of Canada*. Ottawa: Queen's Printer.

Jobson, Valerie. 1985. "The Blackfoot and the Rationing System," *Alberta History* 33, no. 4.

Johnson, Dennis F. 2006. *York Boats of the Hudson's Bay Company*. Calgary: Fifth House.

Johnson, Virginia Weisel. 1962. *The Unregimented General*. Boston: Houghton Mifflin.

Johnston, Darlene. 1989. *The Taking of Indian Lands in Canada*. Saskatoon: University of Saskatchewan, Native Law Centre.

Josephy, Alvin M. 1968. *The Indian Heritage of America*. New York: Knopf.

——. 1971. *The Nez Perce Indians and the Opening of the Northwest*. Lincoln: University of Nebraska Press.

—— (ed.). 1993. *America in 1492*. New York: Vintage Books.

Joyner, Christopher C. 1974. "The Hegira of Sitting Bull to Canada: Diplomatic Realpolitik, 1876–1881," *Journal of the West* 13, no. 2 (April).

Karamanski, Theodore J. 1983. *Fur Trade and Exploration*. Norman: University of Oklahoma Press.

Keenan, Jerry. 2003. *The Great Sioux Uprising*. Cambridge, MA: Da Capo Press.

Kehoe, Thomas F. 1973. *The Gull Lake Site*. Milwaukee: Milwaukee Public Museum Publications.

Kelly, Carla (ed.). 2005. *On the Upper Missouri: The Journal of Randolph Friederich Kurz, 1851–1852*. Norman: University of Oklahoma Press.

Klaus, J.F. 1962. "Fort Livingstone," *Saskatchewan History* 15 (Autumn).

Koucky, Rudolph W. 1983. "The Buffalo Disaster of 1882," *North Dakota History* 50, no. 1 (Winter).

Krech, Shepard, III. 1999. *The Ecological Indian: Myth and History*. New York: Norton.

LaChance, Vernon. 1929. "The Mounted Police Detachment at Wood Mountain and its Activities from the Organization of the Force in 1873 until 1882," *Canadian Defence Quarterly* 6, no. 4: 493–500.

LaDow, Mary Beth. 1994. "The Medicine Line, Nations and Identity on the Montana-Saskatchewan Frontier, 1877–1920" (PhD dissertation, Brandeis University).

——. 2001. *The Medicine Line, Life and Death on a North American Borderland*. New York: Routledge.

———. 2001. "Sanctuary: Native Border Crossings and the North American West," *The American Review of Canadian Studies* 31 (Spring/Summer).

Langford, Nathaniel Pitt. 1912. *Vigilante Days and Ways*. New York: Grosset & Dunlap.

Larmour, Jean Bernice Drummond. 1969. "Edgar Dewdney, Commissioner of Indian Affairs and Lieutenant Governor of the North-West Territories, 1879–1888" (MA thesis, University of Saskatchewan, Regina Campus).

Laskin, David. 2004. *The Children's Blizzard*. New York: Harper Collins.

Laubin, Reginald and Gladys. 1977. *The Indian Tipi: Its History, Construction, and Use*. Norman: University of Oklahoma Press.

Laut, Agnes C. 1908. *The Conquest of the Great Northwest*. Toronto: Musson.

Laviolette, Gontran. 1944. *The Sioux Indians in Canada*. Regina: Marian Press.

———. 1991. *The Dakota Sioux in Canada*. Winnipeg: DLM Publications.

Lazarus, Edward. 1991. *Black Hills White Justice: The Sioux Nation Versus the United States, 1775 to the Present*. New York: Harper Collins.

Légaré, Edward A. 2004. *Sitting Bull and Jean-Louis Were Friends*. Self-published by the author.

Lott, Dale F. 2002. *American Bison: A Natural History*. Berkeley: University of California Press.

Looy, A.J. 1979. "Saskatchewan's First Indian Agent: M.G. Dickieson," *Saskatchewan History* 32, no. 3 (Autumn).

Loveridge, D.M. and Barry Potyandi. 1983. *From Wood Mountain to the Whitemud*. National Historic Parks and Sites Branch, Environment Canada.

Lussier, A.S. (ed.). 1979. *Louis Riel and the Métis*. Winnipeg: Pemmican Publications.

Lux, Maureen K. 2001. *Medicine That Walks: Disease, Medicine and Canadian Plains Native People, 1880–1940*. Toronto: University of Toronto Press.

Lytwyn, Victor P. 2002. *Muskekowuck Athinuwick (Original People of the Great Swampy Land)*. Winnipeg: University of Manitoba Press.

Macdonald, Henry Bayne. 1935. "The Killing of the Buffalo," *The Beaver* 3 (December).

MacEwan, Grant. 1973. *Sitting Bull: The Years in Canada*. Edmonton: Hurtig.

———. 1981. *Métis Makers of History*. Saskatoon: Western Producer Prairie Books.

MacGregor, James (Reverend). 1964. "Lord Lorne in Aberta," *Alberta Historical Review* 12, no. 2 (Spring).

MacGregor, James G. 1975. *Father Lacombe*. Edmonton: Hurtig.

———. 1978. *Senator Hardisty's Prairies, 1849–1889*. Saskatoon: Prairie Books.

———. 1981. *Vision of an Ordered Land*. Saskatoon: Prairie Books.

Machray, Robert. 1909. *Life of Robert Machray, D.D., LL.D., D.C.L., Archbishop of Rupert's Land, Primate of all Canada, Prelate of the Order of St. Michael and St. George*. Toronto: Macmillan Co. of Canada.

MacInnes, C.M. 1930. *In the Shadow of the Rockies*. London: Rivingtons.

MacKay, Douglas. 1966. *The Honourable Company: A History of the Hudson's Bay Company*. Toronto: McClelland and Stewart.

Mackenzie, Alexander. 1995. *Journal of the Voyage to the Pacific*. New York: Dover.

Maclean, John. 1927. *McDougall of Alberta: Life of Rev. John McDougall, D.D., Pathfinder of Empire and Prophet of the Plains*. Toronto: Ryerson Press.

MacLennan, Hugh. 1963. *Seven Rivers of Canada*. Toronto: Macmillan.

Macleod, Roderick Charles. 1971. "The North-West Mounted Police, 1873–1905." PhD dissertation, Duke University.

Macoun, John. 1882. *Manitoba and the Great Northwest*. Guelph, ON: World Publishing.

MacRae, Archibald Oswald. 1912. *History of the Province of Alberta*. Calgary: Western Canada History Co.

Mainville, Robert. 2001. *An Overview of Aboriginal Treaty Rights and Compensation for Their Breach*. Saskatoon: Purich Publishing.

Mandelbaum, David G. 1979. *The Plains Cree: An Ethnographic, Historical and Comparative Study*. Regina: Canadian Plains Research Center.

Mann, Charles C. 2002. "1491," *The Atlantic Monthly*.

Manning, Richard. 1995. *Grassland*. New York: Penguin.

Manzione, Joseph. 1991. *I am Looking to the North for My Life: Sitting Bull, 1876–1881*. Salt Lake City: University of Utah Press.

Marchildon, Greg and Sid Robinson. 2002. *Canoeing the Churchill*. Regina: Canadian Plains Research Center.

Martin, Chester. 1973. *Dominion Lands Policy*. Toronto: McClelland and Stewart.

Martin, Roderick G. 2005. "The North-West Mounted Police and Frontier Justice, 1874–1898" (PhD dissertation, University of Calgary).

McArthur, Alexander. 1882. *On the Causes of the Rising in the Red River Settlement, 1869–70*. Winnipeg: Manitoba Historical and Scientific Society.

McClintock, Walter. 1968. *The Old North Trail*. Lincoln: University of Nebraska Press.

McCrady, David Grant. 1992. "Beyond Boundaries: Aboriginal Peoples and the Prairie West, 1850–1885" (Master's thesis, University of Victoria).

——. 1998. "Living With Strangers" (PhD dissertation, University of Manitoba).

——. 2001. "History of the Canadian Plains Since 1870." In Raymond J. DeMallie (ed.) *Handbook of North American Indians*, Vol. 13. Washington: Smithsonian Institution.

——. 2006. *Living With Strangers*. Lincoln: University of Nebraska Press.

——. 2007. "Louis Riel and Sitting Bull's Sioux: Three Lost Letters." *Prairie Forum* 32, no. 2 (Fall).

McDougall, John. 1911. *In the Days of the Red River Rebellion*. Toronto: William Briggs.

McKercher, Robert B. and Bertram Wolfe. 1986. *Understanding Western Canada's Dominion Land Survey System*. Saskatoon: University of Saskatchewan.

McLaughlin, James. 1970. *My Friend the Indian*. Seattle: Superior Publishing Company.

McLean, Don. 1987. *Home from the Hill*. Regina: Gabriel Dumont Institute.

McManus, Sheila. 2005. *The Line Which Separates: Race, Gender and the Making of the Alberta-Montan Borderlands*. Edmonton: University of Alberta Press.

McMurtry, Larry. 1999. *Crazy Horse*. New York: Viking.

McNab, David. 1978. "The Colonial Office and the Prairies in the Mid-Nineteenth Century," *Prairie Forum* 3, no. 1.

McPherson, Arlean. 1967. *The Battlefords: A History*. Battleford and North Battleford: n.p.

Miles, Nelson A. 1896. *Personal Recollections and Observations of General Nelson A. Miles*. Chicago: Werner.

——. 1911. *Serving the Republic*. New York: Harper.

Milloy, John S. 1988. *The Plains Cree: Trade, Diplomacy and War, 1790 to 1870*. Winnipeg: University of Manitoba Press.

Morgan, E. 1973. "The North-West Mounted Police: Internal Problems and Public Criticism, 1874–1883," *Saskatchewan History* 26, no. 2 (Spring).

Morin, Jean-Pierre. 2003. "Empty Hills: Aboriginal Land Usage and the Cypress Hills Problem," *Saskatchewan History* 55, no. 1 (Spring).

Morris, Alexander. 1991 [1880]. *The Treaties of Canada with the Indians of Manitoba and the North-West Territories, including the negotiations on which they are based, and other information relating thereto.* Saskatoon: Fifth House Publishers.

Morse, Eric W. 1969. *Fur Trade Routes of Canada/Then and Now.* Ottawa: Queen's Printer.

Morton, Arthur S. and Chester Martin. 1938. *History of Prairie Settlement and "Dominion Lands" Policy.* Toronto: MacMillan.

Morton, W.L. 1957. *Manitoba: A History.* Toronto: University of Toronto Press.

——. 1961. *The Battle at the Grand Coteau, July 13 and 14, 1851.* Winnipeg: Papers of the Historical and Scientific Society of Manitoba, Series III, Number 16.

——. 1964. *The Critical Years: The Union of British North America, 1857–1873.* Toronto: McClelland and Stewart.

——. 1965. "The Geographical Circumstance of Confederation," *Canadian Geographic Journal* 70, no. 3 (March).

——. 1965. *Manitoba: The Birth of a Province,* Volume I. Winnipeg: Manitoba Record Society.

——. 1965. *The West and Confederation, 1857–1871.* N.p.: Canadian Historical Association.

——. 1970. "The Bias of Prairie Politics." In Donald Swainson (ed.), *Historical Essays on the Prairie Provinces.* Toronto: McCelland and Stewart.

Murphy, James. 1983. *Half Interest in a Silver Dollar: The Saga of Charles E. Conrad.* Missoula: Mountain Press Pub. Co.

Nerburn, Kent. 2005. *Chief Joseph and the Flight of the Nez Perce.* San Francisco: Harper.

Nestor, Robert J. 1997. "Hayter Reed, Severalty, and the Subdivision of Indian Reserves on the Canadian Prairies." MA thesis, University of Regina.

Newman, Peter C. 1998. *Empire of the Bay: The Company of Adventurers that Seized a Continent.* Toronto: Penguin Books.

Noel, Lynn E. (ed.). 1995. *Voyages: Canada's Heritage Rivers.* St. John's: Breakwater.

Nute, Grace Lee. 1987. *The Voyageur.* St. Paul: Minnesota Historical Society.

Ogilvie, William. 1974. "Field Notes of a Surveyor," *Alberta Historical Review* 22, no. 2 (Spring).

Oliver, E.H. 1915. *The Canadian North-West: Its early development and legislative records: minutes of the councils of the Red River Colony and the Northern Department of Rupert's Land,* vol. 2. Ottawa: Government Printing Bureau.

Ormsby, Margaret A. 1964. *British Columbia: A History.* Toronto: Macmillan.

Ostler, Jeffrey. 1999. "'They Regard Their Passing As Wakan': Interpreting Western Sioux Explanations for the Bison's Decline," *The Western Historical Quarterly* 30, no. 4 (Winter).

——. 2004. *The Plains Sioux and U.S. Colonialism from Lewis and Clark to Wounded Knee.* Cambridge: Cambridge University Press.

Overholser, Joel. 1987. *Fort Benton: World's Innermost Port.* Fort Benton, MT: River and Plains Society.

Owram, Doug. 1992. *Promise of Eden: The Canadian Expansionist Movement and the Idea of the West, 1856–1900.* Toronto: University of Toronto Press.

Palliser, John. 1969. *Solitary Rambles.* Edmonton: Hurtig.

Parkman, Francis. 1963. *La Salle and the Discovery of the Great West.* New York: New American Library.

Parsons, John E. 1963. *West on the 49th Parallel: Red River to the Rockies, 1872–1876.* New York: Morrow.

Pearce, William. N.d. "Unpublished manuscript" (Library and Archives Canada, F 5574, P4).

Pearson, Jeffrey V. 2005. "Tragedy at Red Cloud Agency; The Surrender, Confinement and Death of Crazy Horse," *Montana Magazine of Western History* 55, no. 2 (Summer).

Pettipas, Katherine. 1994. *Severing the Ties that Bind: Government Repression of Indigenous Religions*. Winnipeg: University of Manitoba Press.

Poirier, Thelma (ed.). 2000. *Wood Mountain Uplands*. Wood Mountain, SK: Wood Mountain Historical Society.

Poling, Jim, Sr. 2000. *The Canoe*. Toronto: Key Porter Books.

Pope, Joseph (Sir). N.d. *Memoirs of the Right Honourable John Alexander Macdonald, G.C.B., first Prime Minister of the Dominion of Canada*. Toronto: Musson .

Potyondi, Barry. 1995. *In Palliser's Triangle*. Saskatoon: Purich.

Preston, William. 1914. *The Life and Times of Lord Strathcona*. London: Eveleigh Nash.

Pringle, Heather. 1996. *In Search of Ancient North America: An Archaeological Journey to Forgotten Cultures*. New York: Wiley.

Purich, Donald. 1986. *Our Land*. Toronto: Lorimer.

Ray, Arthur J. 1974. *Indians in the Fur Trade: Their Role as Trappers, Hunters, and Middlemen in the Lands Southwest of Hudson Bay, 1660–1870*. Toronto: University of Toronto Press.

——. 1975. "Smallpox: The Epidemic of 1837–38," *The Beaver* (Autumn).

Ray, Arthur J., Jim Miller and Frank Tough. 2000. *Bounty and Benevolence: A History of Saskatchewan Treaties*. Montreal/Kingston: McGill-Queen's University Press.

Rees, Ronald. 1988. *New and Naked Land*. Saskatoon: Western Producer Prairie Books.

Rich, E.E. 1967. *The Fur Trade and the Northwest to 1857*. Toronto: McClelland and Stewart.

Richards, Mary Helen. 1974. "Cumberland House, Two Hundred Years of History." *Saskatchewan History* 27, no. 3 (Autumn).

Riddell, J.H. 1946. *Methodism in the Middle West*. Toronto: Ryerson Press.

Robertson, R.G. 2001. *Rotting Face: Smallpox and the American Indian*. Caldwell, ID: Caxton Press.

Robinson, Charles M., III. 1995. *A Good Year to Die: The Story of the Great Sioux War*. Norman: University of Oklahoma Press.

Robinson, H.M. 1972. *The Great Fur Land*. Toronto: Coles Canadiana Collection.

Roe, F.G. 1935. "The Red River Hunt." In *Transactions of the Royal Society of Canada*. Ottawa: Royal Society.

——. 1951. *The North American Buffalo: A Critical Study of the Species in its Wild State*. Toronto: University of Toronto Press.

——. 1955. *The Indian and the Horse*. Norman: University of Oklahoma Press.

Ronda, James P. 1990. *Astoria and Empire*. Lincoln: University of Nebraska Press.

Rondeau, Clovis (Reverend). 1970. *La Montagne de Bois, 1870–1920*. Winnipeg: Canadian Publishers Limited.

Ross, Alexander. 1972. *The Red River Settlement*. Edmonton: Hurtig.

Russell, R.C. 1971. *The Carlton Trail*. Saskatoon: Prairie Books.

Sandoz, Mari. 1954. *The Buffalo Hunters: The Story of the Hide Men*. New York: Hastings House.

Savage, Candace. 2005. "Back Home on the Range," *Canadian Geographic* 125, no. 1 (January/February).

Schilling, Rita. 1983. *Gabriel's Children*. Saskatoon: The Saskatoon Métis Society.

Schilz, Thomas F. 1984. "Brandy and Beaver Pelts: Assiniboine-European Trading Patterns, 1695–1805," *Saskatchewan History* 37, no. 3 (Autumn).

Sealey, D. Bruce and Antoine S. Lussier. 1975. *The Métis: Canada's Forgotten People*. Winnipeg: Manitoba Metis Federation Press.

Sharp, Paul F. 1973. *Whoop-Up Country: The Canadian-American West, 1865-1885*. Norman: University of Oklahoma Press.

Shewell, Hugh. 2004. *Enough to Keep Them Alive*. Toronto: University of Toronto Press.

Shillington, C. Howard. 1985. *Historic Land Trails of Saskatchewan*. Vancouver: Evvard Publications.

Silversides, Brock. 2005. *Fort de Prairies: The Story of Fort Edmonton*. Surrey, BC: Heritage House Publishing Company.

Slotkin, Richard. 1985. *The Fatal Environment*. New York: Atheneum.

Smits, David D. 1994. "The Frontier Army and the Destruction of the Buffalo, 1865–1883," *Western Historical Quarterly* 25 (Autumn): 313–88.

Snell, James G. 1979. "American Neutrality and the Red River Resistance, 1869–1870," *Prairie Forum* 4, no. 2.

Sprague, D.N. 1988. *Canada and the Métis, 1869–1885*. Waterloo, ON: Wilfrid Laurier University Press.

Sprague, D.N. and R.P. Frye. 1983. *The Genealogy of the First Méetis Nation*. Winnipeg: Pemmican Publications.

Spry, Irene M. (ed.). 1968. *The Papers of the Palliser Expedition 1857–1860*. Toronto: The Champlain Society.

———. 1975. "Early Visitors to the Canadian Prairies." In Brian W. Blouet and Merlin P. Lawson (eds.), *Images of the Plains: The Role of Human Nature in Settlement*. Lincoln: University of Nebraska Press.

———. 1976. "The Great Transformation: The Disappearance of the Commons in Western Canada." In Richard Allen (ed.), *Man and Nature on the Prairies*. Regina: Canadian Plains Research Center.

———. 1995. *The Palliser Expedition*. Calgary: Fifth House.

St. Germain, Jill. 2005. "'Feed or Fight': Rationing the Sioux and the Cree, 1868–1885," *Native Studies Review* 16, no. 1.

Stanley, George F.G. 1960. *The Birth of Western Canada: A History of the Riel Rebellions*. Toronto: University of Toronto Press.

———. 1963. *Louis Riel*. Toronto: Ryerson Press.

———. 1967. *Louis Riel: Patriot or Rebel?* N.p.: Canadian Historical Association.

———. 1967. "The 1870s," in J.M.S. Careless and R. Craig Brown (eds.), *The Canadians 1867–1967*. Toronto: Macmillan.

———. 1978. "Displaced Red Men: The Sioux in Canada," in *One Century Later, Western Canadian Reserve Indians Since Treaty 7*. Vancouver: University of British Columbia Press.

Stanley, George F.G. and Gilles Martel (eds.). 1985. *The Collected Writings of Louis Riel*. Edmonton: University of Alberta Press.

Starkey, H.M. 1938. "A Survey in Saskatchewan in 1883," *The Canadian Surveyor* 6, no. 5 (July).

Stearn, E. Wagner and Allen E. Stearn. 1945. *The Effect of Smallpox on the Destiny of the Amerindian*. Boston: Bruce Humphries Inc..

Steele, S.B. 2000. *Forty Years in Canada: Reminiscences of the Great North-West with Some Account of his Service in South Africa*. Toronto: Prospero Books.

Stegner, Wallace. 1962. *Wolf Willow: A History, A Story, and A Memory of the Last Plains Frontier*. New York: Viking Press.

———. 1992. *Beyond the Hundredth Meridian*. New York: Penguin.

Stevens, Isaac I. 1860. *Narrative and Final Report of Explorations For a Route For a Pacific Railroad Near 47th and 49th Parallels From St. Paul to Puget Sound, 1855*, Volume 12, Book 1. Washington, DC: United States Senate.

Stonechild, Blair and Bill Waiser. 1997. *Loyal till Death: Indians and the North-West Rebellion.* Calgary: Fifth House.

Sturtevant, William C. (ed.). 2001. Handbook of North American Indians. Washington, DC: Smithsonian Institution.

Taylor, John Leonard. 1975. "The Development of an Indian Policy for the Canadian North-West, 1869–79" (PhD dissertation, Queen's University, Kingston).

Terrell, John Upton. 1972. *Land Grab: The Truth About "The Winning of the West."* New York: The Dial Press.

Thomas, Lewis Herbert. 1956. *The Struggle For Responsible Government in the North-West Territories 1870–97.* Toronto: University of Toronto Press.

—— (ed.). 1975. *The Prairie West to 1905.* Toronto: Oxford University Press.

—— (ed.). 1976. *Essays on Western History.* Edmonton: University of Alberta Press.

Thompson, David. 1962. *David Thompson's Narrative, 1784–1812.* Toronto: Champlain Society.

Thomson, Don W. 1966. *Men and Meridians,* 2 Volumes. Ottawa: Queen's Printer.

Titley, Brian. 1999. *The Frontier World of Edgar Dewdney.* Vancouver: University of British Columbia Press.

Traill, Walter. 1970. *In Rupert's Land.* Toronto: McClelland and Stewart.

Trimble, Donald E. 1990. *The Geological Story of the Great Plains.* Medora, ND: Theodore Roosevelt Nature and History Association.

Trimble, Michael K. 1979. *An Ethnohistorical Interpretation of the Spread of Smallpox in the Northern Plains Utilizing Concepts Of Disease Ecology.* Columbia, MO: Department of Anthropology, University of Missouri-Columbia.

Turner, C. Frank. 1973. *Across The Medicine Line.* Toronto: McClelland and Stewart.

Turner, John Peter. 1950. *The North-West Mounted Police, 1873–1893,* Volumes 1 and 2. Ottawa: King's Printer.

——. N.d. "Surrender of Sitting Bull" (Saskatchewan Archives Board, SHS 205).

Utley, Robert M. 1973. *Frontier Regulars: The United States Army and the Indian, 1866–1890.* New York: Macmillan.

——. 1993. *The Lance and the Shield: The Life and Times of Sitting Bull.* New York: Ballantine.

——. 2004. *After Lewis and Clark: Mountain Men and the Paths to the Pacific.* Lincoln: University of Nebraska Press.

Vaughn, Robert. 1900. *Then and Now; or, Thirty-Six Years in the Rockies.* Minneapolis: Tribune Printing Company.

Venne, Sharon Helen. 1981. *Indian Acts and Amendments, 1868–1975.* Saskatoon: University of Saskatchewan, Native Law Centre.

Vestal, Stanley (Walter Stanley Campbell). 1945. *The Missouri.* New York: Farrar & Rinehart.

Viola, Herman J. 2003. *Trail to Wounded Knee; The Last Stand of the Plains Indians 1860–1890.* Washington, DC: National Geographic.

Wade, Arthur P. 1976. "The Military Command Structure: The Great Plains, 1853–1891," *Journal of the West* 15, no. 3: 5–22.

Walden, Keith. 1980. *The Great March of the Mounted Police in Popular Literature, 1873–1973.* N.p.: Canadian Historical Association.

Waiser, W.A. 1989. *The Field Naturalist: John Macoun, the Geological Survey and Natural Science.* Toronto: University of Toronto Press.

Waite, P.B. 1962. *The Life and Times of Confederation.* Toronto: University of Toronto Press.

—— (ed.). 1965. *Pre-Confederation,* Canadian Historical Documents Series, Volume 11. Scarborough, ON: Prentice-Hall.

Warkentin, John. *The Western Interior of Canada*. Toronto: McClelland and Stewart Limited.

Warren, William W. 1984. *History of the Ojibway People*. St. Paul: Minnesota Historical Society Press.

Webb, Walter Prescott. 1931. *The Great Plains*. Boston: Ginn and Company.

Weekes, Mary. 1994. *The Last Buffalo Hunter*. Calgary: Fifth House.

Willson, Beckles. 1915. *The Life of Lord Strathcona & Mount Royal*. London: Cassell and Company.

Wilson, James. 1998. *The Earth Shall Weep: A History of Native America*. New York: Grove Press.

Wood, W. Raymond and Thomas D. Thiessen. 1985. *Early Fur Trade on the Northern Plains*. Norman: University of Oklahoma Press.

Woodcock, George. 1975. *Gabriel Dumont: The Métis Chief and His Lost World*. Edmonton: Hurtig.

——. 1979. *The Canadians*. Toronto: Fitzhenry and Whiteside.

——. 1988. *A Social History of Canada*. Markham, ON: Penguin Books.

Wooster, Robert. 1988. *The Military and United States Indian Policy 1865–1903*. New Haven, CT: Yale University Press.

Wright, Ronald. 1992. *Stolen Continents*. Toronto: Penguin Books.

——. 2004. *A Short History of Progress*. Toronto: Anansi Press.

Zaslow, Morris. 1971. *The Opening of the Canadian North, 1870–1914*. Toronto: McClelland and Stewart.

1670: Hudson's Bay Company receives charter.

1673: Marquette and Jolliet discover the Missouri River.

1682: La Salle claims Louisiana Territory for France.

1684: York Factory established by Hudson's Bay Company.

1691: Henry Kelsey travels from York Factory and becomes the first European to visit the Canadian prairies.

1704: Two Canadian *coureurs de bois* are trading on the Missouri River.

1715: Fur trade opens "Voyageurs Road" connecting Lake Michigan and Mississippi River. **1738:** La Vérendrye reaches forks of Red and Assiniboine Rivers (later site of Fort Garry).

1743: Chevalier La Vérendrye plants plate near today's Pierre, South Dakota claiming Missouri River region for France.

1749: Chevalier La Vérendrye discovers the North Saskatchewan River.

1751: Fort La Jonquière established near today's Calgary.

1753: Fort St. Louis established at forks of North and South Saskatchewan Rivers.

1754: Fort Paskoyac established on Saskatchewan River near today's The Pas.

1754: Anthony Henday travels from York Factory to Blackfoot territory in today's Alberta.

1762: Louisiana Territory east of Mississippi River transferred to Britain, west of Mississippi and New Orleans transferred to Spain.

1763: In defeat at the end of the Seven Years's War, France surrenders its North American lands to Britain.

1764: Pierre Laclede founds St. Louis.

1765: First British traders from Montreal appear in the west.

1772: Matthew Cocking travels from Fort York to Blackfoot territory to investigate drop in furs coming to Hudson Bay.

1774: Hudson's Bay Company establishes Cumberland House.

1774: Britain enacts Quebec Act incorporating its portion of Louisiana and extends boundary of Province of Quebec to the Mississippi River.

1778: Peter Pond reaches the Athabaska country.

1779: North West Company is formed.

1779: Alexander Mackenzie journeys to the Arctic Ocean.

1780–82: Smallpox sweeps over the upper Missouri, the Saskatchewan and Columbia Rivers and Great Slave Lake region.

1783: Following American War of Independence, Britain cedes Louisiana east of the Mississippi to the United States. A boundary line between the remainder of British North America and the new United States is agreed upon as far as the North-West Angle of Lake of the Woods.

1787: Both the Hudson's Bay Company and the North West Company established trading posts on the Missouri River.

1793: Alexander Mackenzie travels overland to the Pacific Ocean, first across the continent.

1795: First Fort Edmonton built by Hudson's Bay Company.

1803: Napoleon sells Louisiana, including New Orleans, to the United States.

1804: Lewis and Clark expedition embarks up the Missouri River.

1806: Lewis and Clark return to St. Louis after successfully reaching the Pacific Ocean.

1806: Zebulon Pike reports existence of Great American Desert.

1808: North West Company builds trading posts in today's Montana.

1808: American Fur Company organized by John Jacob Astor.

1811: Lord Selkirk secures land grant from Hudson's Bay Company, first settlers arrive at the Forks of the Red and Assiniboine Rivers the next year.

1812: United States declares war on Britain, attacks Canada.

1814: North West Company surveyor David Thompson completes his map of the North West Territory.

1816: Battle of Seven Oaks between Red River Métis and Hudson's Bay Company personnel.

1818: Britain and the United States agree on the 49th Parallel as the border from Lake of the Woods to the Rocky Mountains.

1819: United States acquires Florida.

1820: Stephen Long confirms existence of Great American Desert.

1821: Hudson's Bay Company and North West Company merge after years of vicious competition. Name continues as Hudson's Bay Company.

1822: Fort Gibraltar at forks of Red and Assiniboine Rivers is renamed Fort Garry.

1822: David Thompson surveys border from Lake Superior to Lake of the Woods.

1828: American Fur Company builds Fort Union on Missouri River.

1837: The steamboat, *St. Peter*, carries smallpox to Fort Union. The disease rages through the Indian tribes of the Missouri and Saskatchewan River country.

1844: Trading begins between Red River and St. Paul, Minnesota.

1845: The United States acquires Texas.

1846: The United States acquires Oregon.

1846: Britain and United States agree that the 49th Parallel as boundary be extended across the Rocky Mountains to the Strait of Georgia.

1846: Red River Métis forward petition to London complaining of their treatment at the hands of the Hudson's Bay Company. It is presented to the Colonial Secretary by Alexander Isbister, a Métis born at Cumberland House.

1846–47: Jesuit priest Pierre de Smet overwinters at Fort Edmonton.

1847–48: John Palliser tours the Upper Missouri.

1848: The United States seizes a huge territory from Mexico.

1849: The Sayer Trial at Fort Garry. The Métis believe they have won the right to freely trade into the United States.

1851: Fort Laramie Treaty between United States and Plains Indians recognizes Sioux ownership of a great territory including the Black Hills.

1851: Battle of the Grand Coteau between Red River Métis and Sioux Indians.

1853: Governor Isaac Stevens heads expedition that travelled overland from St. Paul to Puget Sound.

1857: Parliamentary committee at Westminster reviews Hudson's Bay Company control of Rupert's Land. Alexander Isbister testifies and is critical of the Company's conduct.

1857–60: John Palliser heads expedition into Canadian West. He reports on a huge arid region unsuitable for settlement, the Palliser Triangle.

1857–58: H.Y. Hind explores the Canadian West. He identifies a "fertile belt" running from Red River along the North Saskatchewan to the Rocky Mountains.

1860–65: American Civil War.

1860: First steamboat reaches Fort Benton, Montana Territory. Fort Benton remains the head of navigation on the Missouri River.

1861: John Rae guides two British aristocrats into western plains as far as Old Wives Lakes which he renames Lake Johnson and Chaplin Lake after his charges.

1862: North Overland Expedition under Captain James Fisk journeys from St. Paul to Fort Benton and on to Helena and Walla Walla.

1862: Sioux Uprising in Minnesota. Hundreds of settlers are killed and 38 Sioux are executed in a mass hanging at Mankato. A number of Sioux escape into Canada.

1866: November 19. Colonies of Vancouver Island and British Columbia merge.

1867: March 30. The United States acquires Alaska.

1867: July 1. The British North America Act joins Upper Canada (Ontario), Lower Canada (Quebec), New Brunswick and Nova Scotia together as The Dominion of Canada. John A. Macdonald becomes first Prime Minister of Canada.

1868: Fort Laramie Treaty confirms Sioux ownership of Black Hills and United States undertakes to prevent encroachment by whites into the Hills.

1869: Canada agrees to acquire Rupert's Land and North-Western Territory from Britain in largest real estate deal in history.

1869: October 11. Louis Riel and a band of Métis stop a government of Canada survey near Fort Garry.

1869: October 31. Red River Métis stop William McDougall, the designated lieutenant governor of the new North West Territories, at Pembina and prevent him from crossing the border into Canada.

1869: November 2. Métis under Louis Riel seize Fort Garry.

1869: December. Louis Riel declares a provisional government at Red River.

1870: January 12. American flag is raised over Emmerling's Hotel at Red River. It came down on January 26.

1870: January 23. The Baker Massacre. United States Army attacks a sleeping village of peaceful Peigan Indians near the Canadian border. 173 men, women and children are killed.

1870: March 4. Thomas Scott is executed upon the order of Louis Riel.

1870: March 23. Delegation from Riel's provisional government leave Red River for Ottawa to negotiate terms of admission to confederation.

1870: April. Another smallpox epidemic attacks the Blackfoot on the western plains, moves north to the Saskatchewan River, and east.

1870: May. Ottawa agrees to provincial status for Manitoba, land grant for Métis, equality of French and English languages, and other demands.

1870: July 15. Rupert's Land and North-Western Territories are transferred to Canada. New province of Manitoba joins Confederation.

1870: August 24. Military expedition under Colonel G.J. Wolsley arrives at Fort Garry. Louis Riel flees.

1870: September. Adams Archibald, Lieutenant-Governor of the new North West Territories, arrives at Fort Garry.

1870: October. Lieutenant William F. Butler leaves Fort Garry on a reconnaissance mission into the western plains. He returns on February 20, 1871, after 119 days. Two years later Butler writes *The Great Lone Land*.

1870: October 25. The Battle at the Belly River between the Cree and the Blackfoot results in hundreds of casualties, mostly Cree.

1871: British Columbia enters Confederation, now the sixth province after Manitoba.

1871: The United States Congress concludes that it will no longer recognize Indian tribes as sovereign peoples. Future arrangements between Washington and the American Indians will be regarded as contracts, or agreements, only, not treaties.

1871: July. Survey parties commence laying out the Dominion Land Survey in the west.

1871: August 3. Treaty 1, the Stone Fort Treaty, is signed with the Saulteaux/Chippewa and Swampy Cree— 17,350 km^2 (6,700 mi^2) of today's southern Manitoba are surrendered to Ottawa.

1871: August 21. Treaty 2, The Manitoba Post Treaty, is signed with Saulteaux/Chippewa. Another 97,376 km^2 (37,600 mi^2) are surrendered.

1872: British, Canadian and American survey teams arrive and commence official survey of the 49th Parallel.

1872: Dominion Lands Act confirms the township survey system and sets forth regulations for free homesteads.

1873: May 23. Legislation to create the North-West Mounted Police receives royal assent.

1873: May. Boundary surveyors move west from Red River.

1873: June 1. Cypress Hills Massacre. A group of American wolfers attack and kill more than 20 Assiniboines.

1873: October. 150 man contingent of the NWMP travels to Fort Garry over the Dawson Route. Lieutenant Colonel George French is appointed first Commissioner of the Force.

1873: October 31. The last of the Boundary Survey crews return from the season's work after reaching 669 km (416 mi) west of Red River.

1873: November 5. Prime Minister Macdonald's government resigns in face of scandal involving the Canadian Pacific Railway. Alexander Mackenzie becomes Prime Minister.

1873–74: Métis at St. Laurent adopt a form of self-government.

1874: May 20. Boundary survey crews move west to pick up where they left off the previous fall

1874: July 8. NWMP leave Dufferin heading west to Fort Whoop-Up. Troops under Assistant Commissioner reach Whoop-Up on September 10. Fort Macleod is constructed.

1874: September 15. Treaty Number 4, The Qu'Appelle Treaty, is signed with Cree and Saulteaux at Fort Qu'Appelle. 193,200 km² (74,600 mi²), most of today's southern Saskatchewan, were surrendered.

1874: Lieutenant Colonel George A. Custer leads exploratory expedition into Black Hills, reports presence of gold.

1874: October 11. Boundary survey crews return to Dufferin their work completed after covering some 2,575 km (1,600 mi).

1875: September. Treaty 5, The Winnipeg Treaty, is signed. 258,980 km² (100,000 mi²) north of Treaties 2, 3 and 4 is surrendered.

1875: NWMP constructs Fort Walsh in Cypress Hills.

1875: November. American President Ulysses Grant secretly orders Army to discontinue protection of Black Hills.

1876: February. United States declares war against off-reservation Sioux

1876: June 25. Battle of Little Big Horn. Sioux defeat Army units under Custer.

1876: July. NWMP Commissioner French is dismissed. James Macleod appointed Commissioner.

1876: August–September. Treaty 6 signed at Fort Carlton and Fort Pitt.

1876: December. First Sioux refugees from the United States arrive at Wood Mountain.

1877: May. Crazy Horse surrenders to American Army.

1877: May. Nez Perce at war with American Army, commence long march towards sanctuary in Canada.

1877: May. Sitting Bull and followers cross border and seek sanctuary.

1877: August. United States president Hayes agrees to appoint Commission to meet with Sitting Bull.

1877: September. Treaty Number 7 signed with Blackfoot.

1877: September. Nez Perce stopped by U.S. Army at Bear's Paw Mountains, forty miles short of border.

1877: October 17. Presidential Commission meets with Sitting Bull at Fort Walsh.

1878: October. Sir John A. Macdonald re-elected Prime Minister.

1879: Macdonald appoints Edgar Dewdney as Indian Commissioner. Dewdney travels into West.

1879: Buffalo fail in Canada. Starvation strikes Plains Indians.

1880: Starving in Canada, Sioux begin returning to United States and surrendering.

1880: NWMP Commissioner Macleod resigns, succeeded by A.G. Irvine.

1881: Dewdney meets with Sitting Bull at Qu'Appelle and refuses provisions.

1881: July. Sitting Bull surrenders at Fort Buford.

1881: August–September. Governor General Lorne and party tours the West.

GARRETT WILSON is a Regina lawyer turned author. His first book, *Deny, Deny, Deny,* the best-selling account of the Colin Thatcher trial, was followed by *Diefenbaker for the Defence,* a biography of the legal career of the Saskatchewan lawyer who became Prime Minister. Then came *Guilty Addictions,* a mystery that delved deeply into the politics of Saskatchewan. *In the Temple of the Rain God,* Wilson's account of the life and times of his father, Charles Wilson, was published in 2012. The first edition of *Frontier Farewell,* published in 2007, was a winner of the Saskatchewan Book Award for Scholarly Writing.

ABOUT THE TYPE

The body of this book is set in Arno Pro. Named after the river that runs through Florence, the center of the Italian Renaissance, Arno draws on the warmth and readability of early humanist types of the 15th and 16th centuries. While inspired by the past, Arno is distinctly contemporary in both appearance and function. Designed by Robert Slimbach, Adobe principal designer, Arno is a meticulously crafted face in the tradition of early Venetian and Aldine book types. Embodying themes that Slimbach has explored in typefaces such as Minion and Brioso, Arno represents a distillation of his design ideals and a refinement of his craft.

The accents are set in Gill Sans. Designed by Eric Gill and released by the Monotype Corporation between 1928 and 1930, Gill Sans is based on the typeface Edward Johnston, the innovative British letterer and teacher, designed in 1916 for the signage of the London Underground. Gill's alphabet is more classical in proportion and contains his signature flared capital R and eyeglass lowercase g. With distinct roots in pen-written letters, Gill Sans is classified as a humanist sans serif, making it very legible and readable in text and display work.